W9-BVD-757

Management of Information Security

Fourth Edition

Michael E. Whitman, Ph.D., CISM, CISSP
Herbert J. Mattord, Ph.D., CISM, CISSP
Kennesaw State University

CENGAGE
Learning·

Australia · Brazil · Mexico · Singapore · United Kingdom · United States

CENGAGE
Learning®

Management of Information Security, Fourth Edition

Michael E. Whitman and Herbert J. Mattord

General Manager: Dawn Gerrain

Product Manager: Nick Lombardi

Senior Director, Development:
Marah Bellegarde

Product Development Manager:
Leigh Hefferon

Senior Content Developer:
Natalie Pashoukos

Developmental Editor: Kent Williams

Product Assistant: Torey Schantz

Brand Manager: Kristin McNary

Market Development Manager:
Gretchen Swann

Senior Production Director:
Wendy A. Troeger

Production Manager: Andrew Crouth

Content Project Manager: Allyson Bozeth

Art Director: GEX

Media Editor: Debbie Bordeaux

Cover Photo: ©iStockphoto.com/
polygraphus

© 2014, 2010 Cengage Learning

ALL RIGHTS RESERVED. No part of this work covered by the copyright herein may be reproduced, transmitted, stored or used in any form or by any means graphic, electronic, or mechanical, including but not limited to photocopying, recording, scanning, digitizing, taping, Web distribution, information networks, or information storage and retrieval systems, except as permitted under Section 107 or 108 of the 1976 United States Copyright Act, without the prior written permission of the publisher.

Some of the product names and company names used in this book have been used for identification purposes only and may be trademarks or registered trademarks of their respective manufacturers and sellers.

Microsoft and the Office logo are either registered trademarks or trademarks of Microsoft Corporation in the United States and/or other countries.

Any fictional data related to persons or companies or URLs used throughout this book is intended for instructional purposes only. At the time this book was printed, any such data was fictional and not belonging to any real persons or companies.

The programs in this book are for instructional purposes only. They have been tested with care, but are not guaranteed for any particular intent beyond educational purposes. The author and the publisher do not offer any warranties or representations, nor do they accept any liabilities with respect to the programs.

For product information and technology assistance, contact us at
Cengage Learning Customer & Sales Support, 1-800-354-9706

For permission to use material from this text or product,
submit all requests online at **www.cengage.com/permissions**
Further permissions questions can be emailed to
permissionrequest@cengage.com

Library of Congress Control Number: 2013945552

ISBN-13: 978-1-285-06229-7

ISBN-10: 1-285-06229-9

Cengage Learning
200 First Stamford Place, 4th Floor
Stamford, CT 06902
USA

Cengage Learning is a leading provider of customized learning solutions with office locations around the globe, including Singapore, the United Kingdom, Australia, Mexico, Brazil, and Japan. Locate your local office at **www.cengage.com/global**

Cengage Learning products are represented in Canada by Nelson Education, Ltd.

To learn more about Cengage Learning, visit **www.cengage.com**

Purchase any of our products at your local college store or at our preferred online store **www.cengagebrain.com**

Notice to the Reader

Publisher does not warrant or guarantee any of the products described herein or perform any independent analysis in connection with any of the product information contained herein. Publisher does not assume, and expressly disclaims, any obligation to obtain and include information other than that provided to it by the manufacturer. The reader is expressly warned to consider and adopt all safety precautions that might be indicated by the activities described herein and to avoid all potential hazards. By following the instructions contained herein, the reader willingly assumes all risks in connection with such instructions. The publisher makes no representations or warranties of any kind, including but not limited to, the warranties of fitness for particular purpose or merchantability, nor are any such representations implied with respect to the material set forth herein, and the publisher takes no responsibility with respect to such material. The publisher shall not be liable for any special, consequential, or exemplary damages resulting, in whole or part, from the readers' use of, or reliance upon, this material.

Printed in the United States of America
2 3 4 5 6 7 17 16 15 14

Brief Table of Contents

Table of Contents

Preface

As global networks continue to expand, the interconnections among them become ever more vital to the smooth operation of commerce, which depends on communication and computing systems. However, escalating attacks on information assets and the success of criminal attackers illustrate the weaknesses in current information technologies and the need for heightened information security.

To secure systems and networks, organizations must draw on the available pool of information security practitioners. These same organizations will in future count on the next generation of professionals to have the correct mix of skills and experiences to develop more secure computing environments. Students of technology must learn to recognize the threats and vulnerabilities present in existing systems. They must also learn how to design and implement secure systems that will address these threats in the future.

Why This Text Was Written

The purpose of this textbook is to fulfill the need for a quality academic textbook in the discipline of information security management. While there are dozens of quality publications on information security and assurance for the practitioner, there are few textbooks that provide the student with an in-depth study of information security management. Specifically, those in disciplines such as information systems, computer science, criminal justice, political science, and accounting information systems must understand the foundations of the management of information security and the development of managerial strategy for information security. The underlying tenet of this textbook is that information security in the modern organization is a management problem and not one that technology alone can answer; it is a problem that has important economic consequences and one for which management is accountable.

Approach

This book provides a management overview of information security and a thorough treatment of the administration of information security. It can be used to support course delivery for information security programs for information technology students, as well as for IT management and technology management curricula aimed at business or technical management students.

Certified Information Systems Security Professional, Certified Information Security Manager, and NIST Common Bodies of Knowledge—As the authors are Certified Information Systems Security Professionals (CISSP), and Certified Information Security Managers (CISM), these knowledge domains have had an influence on the design of this textbook. With the influence of the extensive library of information available from the Special Publications collection at the National Institute of Standards and Technologies (NIST, at *csrc.nist.gov*), the authors have also tapped into government and industry standards for information security management. Although this textbook is by no means a certification study guide, much of the Common Bodies of Knowledge, especially in the area of management of information security, have been integrated into the text.

Overview

Chapter 1—Introduction to the Management of Information Security

The opening chapter establishes the foundation for understanding the field of information security by explaining the importance of information technology and identifying who is responsible for protecting an organization's information assets. Students learn the definition and key characteristics of information security, as well as the differences between information security management and general management. This chapter also provides an overview of project management, a necessary skill in any IT/information security professional's portfolio.

Chapter 2—Planning for Security

This chapter explains the importance of planning and describes the principal components of organizational planning and information security system implementation planning.

Chapter 3—Planning for Contingencies

This chapter describes the need for contingency planning and explores the major components of contingency planning. It illustrates how to create a simple set of contingency plans using business impact analysis, and how to prepare and execute a test of contingency plans.

Chapter 4—Information Security Policy

This chapter defines information security policy and describes its central role in a successful information security program. Research has shown that there are three major types of information security policy; this chapter explains what goes into each type and demonstrates how to develop, implement, and maintain various types of information security policies.

Chapter 5—Developing the Security Program

Chapter 5 explores the various organizational approaches to information security and explains the functional components of the information security program. Students learn how to plan and staff an organization's information security department based on the size of the organization and other factors, as well as how to evaluate the internal and external factors that influence the activities and organization of an information security program. This chapter also identifies and describes the typical job titles and functions performed in the information security program and concludes with an exploration of the creation and management of a security education, training, and awareness program.

Chapter 6—Security Management Models

This chapter describes the components of the dominant information security management models, including U.S. government-sanctioned models, and discusses how to customize them for a specific organization's needs. Students learn how to implement the fundamental elements of key information security management practices. Models include NIST, ISO, and a host of specialized information security research models that help students understand confidentiality and integrity applications in modern systems.

Chapter 7—Security Management Practices

This chapter describes the fundamentals of and emerging trends in information security management practices and explains how these practices help organizations meet U.S. and international compliance standards. It also covers the certification and accreditation of U.S. federal IT systems.

Chapter 8—Risk Management: Identifying and Assessing Risk

This chapter defines risk management and its role in the organization, and demonstrates how to use risk management techniques to identify and prioritize risk factors for information assets. The risk management model presented here assesses risk based on the likelihood of adverse events and the effects on information assets when events occur. This chapter concludes with a brief discussion of how to document the results of the risk identification process.

Chapter 9—Risk Management: Controlling Risk

This chapter presents essential risk mitigation strategy options and opens the discussion on controlling risk. Students learn how to identify risk control classification categories, use existing conceptual frameworks to evaluate risk controls, and formulate a cost benefit analysis. They also learn how to maintain and perpetuate risk controls.

Chapter 10—Protection Mechanisms

This chapter introduces students to the world of technical risk controls by exploring access control approaches, including authentication, authorization, and biometric access controls as well as firewalls and the common approaches to firewall implementation. It also covers the technical control approaches for dial-up access, intrusion detection and prevention systems, and cryptography.

Chapter 11—Personnel and Security

This chapter expands upon the discussion of the skills and requirements for information security positions introduced in Chapter 5. It explores the various information security professional certifications and identifies which skills are encompassed by each. The second half of the chapter explores the integration of information security constraints—to control employee behavior and prevent misuse of information—into an organization's human resources processes.

Chapter 12—Law and Ethics

In this chapter, students learn about the legal environment and its relationship to information security. This chapter describes the major national and international laws that affect the practice of information security, as well as the role of culture in ethics as it applies to information security.

Appendix

The Appendix reproduces an essential security management self-assessment model from the NIST library. It also includes a questionnaire from the ISO 27002 body that could be used for organizational assessment. The Appendix provides additional detail on various risk management models, including OCTAVE and the OCTAVE variants, the Microsoft Risk Management Model, Factor Analysis of Information Risk (FAIR), ISO 27007, and NIST SP 800-30.

Features

Chapter Scenarios—Each chapter opens with a short story that follows the same fictional company as it encounters various information security issues. The final part of each chapter is a conclusion to the scenario and offers a few discussion questions to round out each scenario. These questions give the student and the instructor an opportunity to discuss the issues that underlie the content.

Viewpoints—An essay from an information security practitioner or academic is included in each chapter. These sections provide a range of commentary that illustrate interesting topics or share personal opinions, giving the student a wider view on the topics in the text.

Offline Boxes—These highlight interesting topics and detailed technical issues, allowing the student to delve more deeply into certain topics.

Hands-On Learning—At the end of each chapter, students will find a Chapter Summary and Review Questions as well as Exercises and Case Exercises, which give them the opportunity to examine the information security arena outside the classroom. Using the Exercises, students can research, analyze, and write to reinforce learning objectives and deepen their understanding of the text. The Case Exercises require that students use professional judgment, powers of observation, and elementary research to create solutions for simple information security scenarios.

New to This Edition

This fourth edition of *Management of Information Security* tightens its focus on the managerial aspects of information security, continues to expand the coverage of governance and compliance issues, and continues to reduce the coverage of foundational and technical components. While retaining enough foundational material to allow reinforcement of key concepts, the fourth edition has fewer technical examples, in-depth discussions, and Offline boxes. This edition also has additional coverage in key managerial areas: risk management, information security governance, access control models, and information security program assessment and metrics. Chapter 1 consolidates all the introductory and general IT managerial material.

In general, the entire text has been updated to reflect changes in the field, including revisions to sections on national and international laws and standards, such as the ISO 27000 series, among others. Throughout the text, the content has been updated, with newer and more relevant examples and discussions.

Instructor Resources

The following supplemental materials are available when this book is used in a classroom setting. All the supplements available with this book are provided to the instructor on the Instructor Companion Site at www.cengage.com. Instructors can access these resources through one single sign-on experience. If you do not already have a Cengage SSO account, click on "Click HERE to register" in the Faculty single sign-on box to get started right away.

- **Electronic Instructor's Manual**—The Instructor's Manual that accompanies this book includes additional material to assist in class preparation, including suggestions for classroom activities, discussion topics, and additional activities.

- **Solutions**—The instructor resources include solutions to all end-of-chapter material, including review questions and case projects.

- **ExamView®**—ExamView®, the ultimate tool for objective-based testing needs, is a powerful test generator that enables instructors to create paper, LAN, or Web-based tests from test banks designed specifically for their Cengage Learning text. Instructors can utilize the ultra-efficient Quick Test Wizard to create tests in less than five minutes by taking advantage of Cengage Learning's question banks, or customize their own exams from scratch.

- **PowerPoint Presentations**—This book comes with Microsoft PowerPoint slides for each chapter. These are included as a teaching aid for classroom presentation, to make available to students on the network for chapter review, or to be printed for classroom distribution. Instructors can add their own slides for additional topics they introduce to the class.

- **Figure files**—All figures and tables in the book are reproduced on the Instructor Companion Site. Similar to the PowerPoint presentations, they are included as a teaching aid for classroom presentation, to make available to students for review, or to be printed for classroom distribution.

Additional Resources

Lab Manual—Cengage Learning has produced a lab manual (*Hands-On Information Security Lab Manual, Fourth Edition*) written by the authors that can be used to provide technical hands-on exercises in conjunction with this book. Contact your Cengage Learning sales representative for more information.

Readings and Cases—Cengage Learning also produced two texts—*Readings and Cases in the Management of Information Security* (ISBN-13: 978-0-619-21627-6) and *Readings & Cases in Information Security: Law & Ethics* (ISBN-13: 978-1-435-44157-6)—by the authors, which make excellent companion texts. Contact your Cengage Learning sales representative for more information.

Curriculum Model for Programs of Study in Information Security and Assurance—In addition to the texts authored by this team, a curriculum model for programs of study in Information Security and Assurance is available from the Kennesaw State University Center for Information Security Education and Awareness (*http://infosec.kennesaw.edu*). This document provides details on designing and implementing security coursework and curricula in academic institutions, as well as guidance and lessons learned from the authors' perspective.

Author Team

Michael Whitman and Herbert Mattord have jointly developed this textbook to merge knowledge from the world of academic study with practical experience from the business world.

Michael Whitman, Ph.D., CISM, CISSP is a Professor of Information Security in the Information Systems Department, Coles College of Business at Kennesaw State University, Kennesaw, Georgia, where he is also the Director of the Coles Center for Information Security Education (*infosec.kennesaw.edu*). He and Herbert Mattord are the authors of *Principles of Information Security; Principles of Incident Response and Disaster Recovery; Readings and Cases in the Management of Information Security; Readings and Cases in Information Security: Law and Ethics; Guide to Firewall and VPNs; Guide to Network Security; Roadmap to the Management of Information Security* and *Hands-On Information Security Lab Manual*, all from Cengage Course Technology. Dr. Whitman is an active researcher in Information Security, Fair and Responsible Use Policies, Ethical Computing, and Information Systems Research Methods. He currently teaches graduate and undergraduate courses in Information Security. He has published articles in the top journals in his field, including *Information Systems Research*, the *Communications of the ACM*, *Information and Management*, the *Journal of International Business Studies*, and the *Journal of Computer Information Systems*. He is an active member of the Information Systems Security Association, the Association for Computing Machinery, ISACA, $(ISC)^2$, and the Association for Information Systems. Through his efforts and those of Dr. Mattord, his institution has been recognized by the Department of Homeland Security and the National Security Agency as a National Center of Academic Excellence in Information Assurance Education three times.

Herbert Mattord, Ph.D. CISM, CISSP completed 24 years of IT industry experience as an application developer, database administrator, project manager, and information security practitioner in 2002. He is currently an Assistant Professor of Information Security at Kennesaw State University, where he serves as the program coordinator for the Information Security and Assurance degree programs. He and Michael Whitman are the authors of *Principles of Information Security; Principles of Incident Response and Disaster Recovery; Readings and Cases in the Management of Information Security; Readings & Cases in Information Security: Law & Ethics; Guide to Network Security; and Hands-On Information Security Lab Manual*, all from Cengage Course Technology. During his career as an IT practitioner, Mattord has been an adjunct professor at Kennesaw State University; Southern Polytechnic State University in Marietta, Georgia; Austin Community College in Austin, Texas; and Texas State University, San Marcos. He currently teaches undergraduate courses in Information Security. He is also an active member of the Information Systems Security Association and Information Systems Audit and Control Association. He was formerly the Manager of Corporate Information Technology Security at Georgia-Pacific Corporation, where much of the practical knowledge found in this and his earlier textbooks was acquired.

Acknowledgments

The authors would like to thank their families for their support and understanding for the many hours dedicated to this project, hours taken, in many cases, from family activities. Special thanks to Carola Mattord, Ph.D., Professor of English at Kennesaw State University. Her reviews of early drafts and suggestions for keeping the writing focused on the students resulted in a more readable manuscript.

Reviewers

We are indebted to the following individuals for their respective contributions of perceptive feedback on the initial proposal, the project outline, and the chapter-by-chapter reviews of the text:

Wasim A. Al-Hamdani, Ph.D.
Professor of Cryptography and Information Security
Information Security Lab, Kentucky State University
Frankfort, KY

Michelle Ramim, Ph.D.
Instructor and IS consultant
Nova Southeastern University
Wayne Huizenga School of Business and Entrepreneurship
Fort Lauderdale, FL

James Rust, MSIS
Technical Services Engineer
Buford, GA

Dale Suggs, BBA, MA, MS
Instructor, Information Technology and Security
Campbell University
Buies Creek, NC

Paul Witman, Ph.D.
Associate Professor, IT Management
Director, Undergraduate Programs, School of Management
California Lutheran University
Thousand Oaks, CA

Special Thanks

The authors wish to thank the Editorial and Production teams at Cengage Learning. Their diligent and professional efforts greatly enhanced the final product:

Natalie Pashoukos, Senior Content Developer

Kent Williams, Developmental Editor

Nick Lombardi, Product Manager

Allyson Bozeth, Content Project Manager

In addition, several professional and commercial organizations and individuals have aided the development of this textbook by providing information and inspiration, and the authors wish to acknowledge their contribution:

Charles Cresson Wood

NetIQ Corporation

The Viewpoint authors:

Henry Bonin

Robert Lang

Karen Scarfone

David Lineman

Paul D. Witman & Scott Mackelprang

Mark Reardon

Martin Lee

George V. Hulme

Tim Callahan

Todd E. Tucker

Alison Gunnels

Lee Imrey

Our Commitment

The authors are committed to serving the needs of the adopters and readers. We would be pleased and honored to receive feedback on the textbook and its supporting materials. You can contact us through Cengage Learning at *mis@course.com*.

Foreword

By Charles Cresson Wood

Over the last 30+ years that I've worked in the information security field, I've had an opportunity to perform risk assessments for over 125 different organizations around the world. No matter how large the organization, no matter how well-respected it is in the public's eyes, and no matter how much high-tech gear it employs, in all cases I find that management doesn't take information security seriously enough.

In part, this is because information security is still a relatively new field and the long-run implications of doing it well or poorly are still being discovered (recent industrial espionage attacks originating in China provide a good example). In part, this lack of seriousness is because information security is a rapidly emerging multidisciplinary field and cross-domain creative thinking is in critically short supply. In part, this is also because top management often doesn't know much, and doesn't care to know much, about information systems technology. In part, this is additionally because top management has been making traditional tradeoff decisions, where information security loses when up against other recognized-as-important objectives such as lowered costs, greater user-friendliness, accelerated time to market with a new product, etc. If top management accurately understood the modern-day importance of information security, they would be spending much more money on it as well as giving it much more of their personal attention.

Times have changed dramatically, except top management in most cases hasn't yet appreciated how different things now are. For example, consider the case of Arthur Andersen, once one of the largest and most-highly-regarded public accounting firms in the world. Andersen did some auditing and consulting work for Enron, now a discredited and defunct energy trading concern. A U.S. Securities and Exchange Commission investigation into Enron's accounting practices caused certain Andersen employees to destroy documents that might have been relevant to the investigation. Aside from the fact that Andersen staff may have been involved in "cooking the books" along with Enron accounting staff, there was a major misunderstanding about the document destruction policy at Andersen. Certain staff believed they were doing the right thing when they destroyed thousands of pounds of Enron documents.

Of course, document destruction is an important part of the information security field. If these staff members had received much better training about this document destruction policy, Andersen might still be in existence. So, here we have a misunderstanding about and a lack of adequate training in information security, leading to the downfall of one the world's largest accounting firms. But in spite of this case and a host of other publicly revealed and very serious cases, top management at most organizations still believes that information security is a relatively unimportant issue, not worthy of considerable top management attention.

Additionally, please consider a recent poll conducted by Harris Interactive that indicated fully 79 percent of the American public believes that their personal information will be shared with other organizations without their permission. Apparently, Americans don't believe businesses and government agencies when they publish privacy policies. Apparently, Americans think these policies are just "window dressing" or something to please the auditors and regulators. What we have here is a major trust problem, where customers don't believe what businesses and government agencies say about the handling of private data. This is indicative of a serious failure on the part of these organizations; they have failed to convince customers that they will dutifully respect customer privacy rights.

An earlier study, performed by the same organization (then called Louis Harris Associates), indicated that the take-up or adoption rate for new electronic services, such as Internet merchant credit card sales, would double when adequate privacy safeguards were added. In other words, customers will be twice as likely to place an order online if they feel comfortable that their personal information will be adequately protected. Yet, top management so often doesn't allocate sufficient resources to information security—for instance by establishing a Chief Privacy Officer—and the net result is that sales suffer. Top management so often doesn't appreciate how doing a good job in the information security realm will lead to a variety of tangible business benefits, like increased sales and competitive advantage. If being able to double the level of sales isn't important to top management, what is?

So, information security very pressingly now needs to be recognized as a regular part of every modern organization. People need to have information security tasks expressly identified in their job descriptions, several departments need to have information security expressly stated in their mission statements, and outsourcing firms need to have information security expressly stated in their service-level agreements. Likewise, if it is used with employer-provided data, every worker's portable computer needs to be outfitted with a standard suite of software that includes a malware/spyware detection package, a hard drive encryption routine, a data wipe routine for use when the device is lost, and an automated software update program. End users also need to be well trained about information security. For instance, they need to know how to construct a fixed password that is difficult for others to guess but is, at the same time, easy for the user to remember. End users are now on the front line of the information security war. And a war is what it is because new, more complex, and more aggressive ways to compromise information systems security are being developed every day.

Information security cannot be something that is left to the technologists within the Information Technology Department. End users, for example, must deal with telephone callers who are seeking to get information through what is called social engineering. Also known as masquerading or spoofing, this technique involves leading users to believe that the caller is somebody other than who he really is. A caller could say he was from the IT Department, that he needed to have the user's user-ID and fixed password in order to correct a problem with the network. While it may sound unbelievable, unless users are told not to divulge such information, studies have shown that a large percentage of the user population will simply reveal their user-ID and password.

Everybody who comes into contact with sensitive, valuable, or critical information needs to know about information security. This means that the janitor needs to know how to dispose of confidential documents that may have been thrown away in the trash. This means that the temporary staff person who is answering the telephone at the front desk needs to know what information he or she can divulge to outsiders. This means that outsourcing firms must know how to respond to a hacker break-in so that losses are minimized, so that the subscribing organization's good reputation is maintained, and so that the subscribing firm's business activity can proceed without undue interruption.

In other words, information security must be approached with a team of individuals, all consistently using the same approaches to security, each with her own special part to play. In this context, I welcome the fourth edition of this textbook to train our future leaders. Every person working in modern businesses and/or government agencies will need to know a good deal about the management issues related to practical information security. If they cover information security at all, too many of the current college classes get bogged down in the technology. While the technology is interesting, it is an overview, a holistic perspective, that is needed so that these future leaders can understand the importance of and the ways to use information security. It is an overview like that provided by this textbook that can acquaint workers with the objectives of information security, and that will then assist them in making good judgment calls in the arena of information security.

Information security is multidisciplinary, multidepartmental, and increasingly multiorganizational in its scope. Future business leaders must appreciate how information security fits in with the other activities performed by the organizations where they will work.

The need for this information security knowledge gets more pressing every year. The U.S. Federal Bureau of Investigation teams up with the Computer Security Institute every year to do a survey about computer crime. In a recent year, some 50 percent of the respondents to this survey indicated that their organization doesn't have a policy informing them where they should report information security violations and incidents. If workers at an organization don't even know to whom, and when, they should report a violation or an incident, then there is no chance that top management will know what is really happening when it comes to information security. If top management doesn't know what's happening, then there will be no hope that they will be able to adequately manage the problem. In the interests of adequately managing this serious problem, this book helps by talking about best practices, which can help management figure out what's happening, and from there determine the best way to address the problems.

Charles Cresson Wood, MBA, MSE, CISA, CISSP, CISM
Independent Information Security Consultant
Mendocino, California

Introduction to the Management of Information Security

If this is the information superhighway, it's going through a lot of bad, bad neighborhoods.

DORIAN BERGER, 1997

One month into her new position at Random Widget Works, Inc. (RWW), Iris Majwabu left her office early one afternoon to attend a meeting of the local chapter of the Information Systems Security Association (ISSA). She had recently been promoted from her previous assignment at RWW as an information security risk manager to become the first chief information security officer (CISO) to be named at RWW.

This occasion marked Iris's first ISSA meeting. With a mountain of pressing matters on her cluttered desk, Iris wasn't certain of exactly why she was making it a priority to attend this meeting. She sighed. Since her early morning wake-up, she had spent many hours in business meetings, followed by long hours at her desk working toward defining her new position at the firm.

At the ISSA meeting, Iris saw Charley Moody, her supervisor from the company she used to work for, Sequential Label and Supply (SLS). Charley had been promoted to chief information officer (CIO) of SLS almost a year ago.

"Hi, Charley," she said.

"Hello, Iris," Charley said, shaking Iris's hand. "Congratulations on your promotion. How are things going in your new position?"

"So far," she replied, "things are going well—I think."

Charley noticed Iris's hesitancy. "You think?" he said. "Okay, tell me what's going on."

1

"Well, I'm struggling to get a consensus from the management team about the problems we have," Iris explained. "I'm told that information security is a priority, but everything is in disarray. Any ideas that are brought up, especially *my* ideas, are chopped to bits before they're even considered by management. There's no established policy covering our information security needs, and it seems that we have little hope of getting one approved. The information security budget covers my salary plus a little bit of funding that goes toward a position for one technician in the network department. The IT managers act like I'm a waste of their time, and they don't seem to take security issues as seriously as I do. It's like trying to drive a herd of cats!"

Charley thought for a moment and then said, "I've got some ideas that may help. We should talk more, but not now; the meeting is about to start. Here's my number—call me tomorrow and we'll arrange to get together for coffee."

LEARNING OBJECTIVES

Upon completion of this material, you should be able to:

- Describe the importance of the manager's role in securing an organization's use of information technology and explain who is responsible for protecting an organization's information assets

- List and discuss the key characteristics of information security

- Discuss the key characteristics of leadership and management

- Differentiate information security management from general business management

- Identify and describe basic project management practices and techniques

Introduction

In today's global markets, business operations are enabled by technology. From the boardroom to the mailroom, businesses make deals, ship goods, track client accounts, and inventory company assets, all through the implementation of systems based upon information technology (IT). IT enables the storage and transportation of information—often a company's most valuable resource—from one business unit to another. But what happens if the vehicle breaks down, even for a little while? Business deals fall through, shipments are lost, and company assets become more vulnerable to threats from both inside and outside the firm. In the past, the business manager's response to this possibility was to proclaim, "We have technology people to handle technology problems." This statement might have been valid in the days when technology was confined to the climate-controlled rooms of the data center and when information processing was centralized. In the last 20 years, however, technology has permeated every facet of the business environment. The business place is no longer static; it moves whenever employees travel from office to office, from city to city, or even from office to home. As businesses have become more fluid, "computer security" has evolved into "information security," which covers a broader range of issues, from the protection of data to the protection of human resources. Information security is no longer the sole responsibility of a small, dedicated group of professionals in the company. It is now the responsibility of all employees, especially managers.

Astute managers increasingly recognize the critical nature of information security as the vehicle by which the organization's information assets are secured. In response to this growing awareness, businesses are creating new positions to solve the newly perceived problems. The emergence of technical managers—like Iris in the opening scenario of this chapter—allows for the creation of professionally managed information security teams whose main objective is the protection of information assets.

Organizations must realize that information security funding and planning decisions involve more than just technical managers, such as information security managers or members of the information security team. Altogether, they should involve three distinct groups of decision makers, or **communities of interest:**

- Managers and professionals in the field of information security
- Managers and professionals in the field of IT
- Managers and professionals from the rest of the organization

These three groups should engage in constructive debate to reach consensus on an overall plan to protect the organization's information assets.

The communities of interest and the roles they fulfill include the following:

- The **information security community** protects the organization's information assets from the many threats they face.
- The **information technology community** supports the business objectives of the organization by supplying and supporting IT that is appropriate to the organization's needs.
- The **general business community** articulates and communicates organizational policy and objectives and allocates resources to the other groups.

Working together, these communities of interest make decisions about how to secure an organization's information assets most effectively. As the discussion between Iris and Charley in this chapter's opening scenario suggests, managing a successful information security program takes time, resources, and a lot of effort by all three communities within the organization. Each community of interest must understand that information security is about identifying, measuring, and mitigating (or at least documenting) the risk associated with operating information assets. It is up to the leadership of the various communities of interest to identify and support initiatives for controlling the risks faced by the organization's information assets. But to make sound business decisions concerning the security of information assets, managers must understand the concept of information security, the roles professionals play within that field, and the issues organizations face in a fluid, global business environment.

What Is Security?

In order to understand the varied aspects of information security, you must know the definitions of certain IT terms and concepts. This knowledge enables you to communicate effectively with the IT and information security communities.

In general, **security** is the quality or state of being secure—being free from danger. To be secure is to be protected from the risk of loss, damage, or unwanted modification, or other hazards. National security, for example, is a system of multilayered processes that protects the sovereignty of a state—its assets, resources, and people. Achieving an appropriate level of security for an organization also depends on the implementation of a multilayered system.

Security is often achieved by means of several strategies undertaken simultaneously or used in combination with one another. Many of those strategies will focus on specific areas of security, but they also have many elements in common. It is the role of management to ensure that each strategy is properly planned, organized, staffed, directed, and controlled.

Specialized areas of security include:

- **Physical security**—Protecting people, physical assets, and the workplace from various threats, including fire, unauthorized access, and natural disasters
- **Operations security**—Protecting the organization's ability to carry out its operational activities without interruption or compromise
- **Communications security**—Protecting the organization's communications media, technology, and content, and its ability to use these tools to achieve the organization's objectives
- **Network security**—Protecting the organization's data networking devices, connections, and contents as well as protecting the ability to use that network to accomplish the organization's data communication functions

The efforts in each of these areas contribute to the information security program as a whole. This textbook bases its definition of information security on the standards published by the Committee on National Security Systems (CNSS), formerly known as the National Security Telecommunications and Information Systems Security Committee (NSTISSC), chaired by the U.S. Secretary of Defense.

Information security (InfoSec) is the protection of information and its critical characteristics (confidentiality, integrity, and availability), including the systems and hardware that use, store, and transmit that information, through the application of policy, training and awareness programs, and technology. Figure 1-1 shows that InfoSec includes the broad areas of InfoSec management (the topic of this book), computer and data security, and network

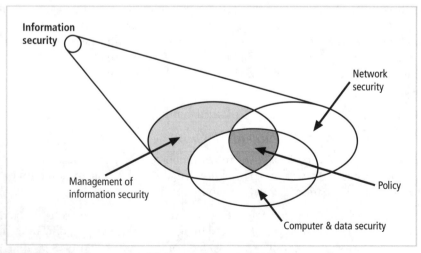

Figure 1-1 Components of information security

Copyright © 2014 Cengage Learning®.

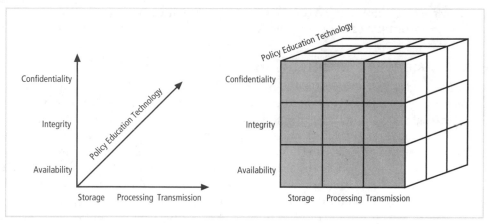

Figure 1-2 CNSS security model

Copyright © 2014 Cengage Learning®.

security; it also shows that policy is the space where these components overlap. (You will learn about policy in detail in Chapter 4.)

CNSS Security Model

The CNSS document *NSTISSI No. 4011 National Training Standard for Information Systems Security (InfoSec) Professionals*[1] presents a comprehensive model of InfoSec known as the McCumber Cube, which is named after its developer, John McCumber. Shown in Figure 1-2, which is an adaptation of the NSTISSI model, the McCumber Cube serves as the standard for understanding many aspects of InfoSec, shows the three dimensions that are central to the discussion of InfoSec: information characteristics, information location, and security control categories. If you extend the relationship among the three dimensions that are represented by the axes in the figure, you end up with a $3 \times 3 \times 3$ cube with 27 cells. Each cell represents an area of intersection among these three dimensions, which must be addressed to secure information. When using this model to design or review any InfoSec program, you must make sure that each of the 27 cells is properly addressed by each of the three communities of interest. For example, the cell representing the intersection of the technology, integrity, and storage criteria could include controls or safeguards addressing the use of technology to protect the integrity of information while in storage. Such a control might consist of a host intrusion detection system (HIDS), for example, which would alert the security administrators when a critical file was modified or deleted.

While the CNSS model covers the three dimensions of InfoSec, it omits any discussion of guidelines and policies that direct the implementation of controls, which are essential to an effective InfoSec program. Instead, the main purpose of the model is to identify gaps in the coverage of an InfoSec program.

Another weakness of this model emerges when it is viewed from a single perspective. For example, the HIDS control described earlier addresses only the needs and concerns of the InfoSec community, leaving out the needs and concerns of the broader IT and general business communities. In practice, thorough risk reduction requires the creation and dissemination of controls of all three types (policy, education, and technical) by all three communities. These controls can be implemented only through a process that includes consensus building and constructive conflict to reflect the balancing act that each organization faces as it designs and executes an InfoSec program. The rest of this book will elaborate on these issues.

Key Concepts of Information Security

To better understand the management of InfoSec, you must become familiar with the key characteristics of information that make it valuable to an organization. As expressed in the **C.I.A. triangle**, which has been the industry standard for computer security since the development of the mainframe, those characteristics are confidentiality, integrity, and availability. However, present-day needs have rendered these characteristics inadequate on their own to conceptualize InfoSec because they are limited in scope and cannot encompass today's constantly changing IT environment, which calls for a more robust model. The C.I.A. triangle, therefore, has been expanded into a more comprehensive list of critical characteristics and processes, including privacy, identification, authentication, authorization, and accountability. These characteristics are explained in more detail in the sections that follow.

Confidentiality Confidentiality is the characteristic of information whereby only those with sufficient privileges and a demonstrated need may access it. When unauthorized individuals or systems can view information, confidentiality is breached. To protect the confidentiality of information, a number of measures are used, including:

- Information classification
- Secure document (and data) storage
- Application of general security policies
- Education of information custodians and end users
- Cryptography (encryption)

Confidentiality is closely related to another key characteristic of information, privacy, which is discussed later in this chapter. The complex relationship between these two characteristics is examined in detail in later chapters. In an organization, confidentiality of information is especially important for personal information about employees, customers, or patients. People expect organizations to closely guard such information. Whether the organization is a government agency, a commercial enterprise, or a nonprofit charity, problems arise when organizations disclose confidential information. Disclosure can occur either deliberately or by mistake. For example, confidential information could be mistakenly e-mailed to someone outside the organization rather than the intended person inside the organization. Or perhaps an employee discards, rather than destroys, a document containing critical information. Or maybe a hacker successfully breaks into a Web-based organization's internal database and steals sensitive information about clients, such as names, addresses, or credit card information.

Integrity In general, **integrity** is the quality or state of being whole, complete, and uncorrupted. The integrity of information is threatened when it is exposed to corruption, damage, destruction, or other disruption of its authentic state. Corruption can occur while information is being entered, stored, or transmitted.

Many computer viruses and worms, for example, are designed to corrupt data. For this reason, the key method for detecting whether a virus or worm has caused an integrity failure to a file system is to look for changes in the file's state, as indicated by the file's size or, in a more advanced operating system, its hash value (discussed later in this section) or checksum (a computed value that remains fixed unless a file has been altered).

File corruption is not always the result of deliberate attacks. Faulty programming or even noise in the transmission channel or medium can cause data to lose its integrity. For example, a low-voltage state in a signal carrying a digital bit (a 1 or 0) can cause the receiving system to record the data incorrectly.

To compensate for internal and external threats to the integrity of information, systems employ a variety of error-control techniques, including the use of redundancy bits and check bits. During each transmission, algorithms, hash values, and error-correcting codes ensure the integrity of the information. Data that has not been verified in this manner is retransmitted or otherwise recovered. Because information is of little or no value or use if its integrity cannot be verified, information integrity is a cornerstone of InfoSec.

Availability
Availability of information occurs when users have access to it in a usable format, without interference or obstruction. (For the purposes of this definition, a user may be either a person or another computer system.) Availability does not imply that the information is accessible to any user; rather, it means it is accessible to authorized users.

To understand this concept more fully, consider the contents of a library—in particular, research libraries that require identification for access to the library as a whole or to certain collections. Library patrons must present the required identification before accessing the collection. Once they are granted access, patrons expect to be able to locate and access resources in the appropriate languages and formats.

Privacy
Information that is collected, used, and stored by an organization should be used only for the purposes stated by the data owner at the time it was collected. In this context, **privacy** does not mean freedom from observation (the meaning usually associated with the word); it means that the information will be used only in ways approved by the person who provided it. Many organizations collect, swap, and sell personal information as a commodity. Today, it is possible to collect and combine personal information from several different sources, which has resulted in databases containing data that could be used in ways the original data owner hasn't agreed to or even knows about. Many people have become aware of these practices and are looking to the government to protect their information's privacy.

Identification
An information system possesses the characteristic of **identification** when it is able to recognize individual users. Identification is the first step in gaining access to secured material, and it serves as the foundation for subsequent authentication and authorization. Identification and authentication are essential to establishing the level of access or authorization that an individual is granted. Identification is typically performed by means of a user name or other ID.

Authentication
Authentication is the process by which a control establishes whether a user (or system) has the identity it claims to have. Examples include the use of cryptographic certificates to establish Secure Sockets Layer (SSL) connections as well as the use of cryptographic hardware devices—for example, hardware tokens such as RSA's SecurID. Individual users may disclose a personal identification number (PIN) or a password to authenticate their identities to a computer system.

Authorization After the identity of a user is authenticated, a process called **authorization** defines what the user (whether a person or a computer) has been specifically and explicitly authorized by the proper authority to do, such as access, modify, or delete the contents of an information asset. An example of authorization is the activation and use of access control lists and authorization groups in a networking environment. Another example is a database authorization scheme to verify that the user of an application is authorized for specific functions, such as reading, writing, creating, and deleting.

Accountability Accountability of information occurs when a control provides assurance that every activity undertaken can be attributed to a named person or automated process. For example, audit logs that track user activity on an information system provide accountability.

What Is Management?

In its most basic form, **management** is the process of achieving objectives using a given set of resources. A manager is a member of the organization assigned to marshal and administer resources, coordinate the completion of tasks, and handle the many roles necessary to complete the desired objectives. Managers have many roles to play within organizations, including the following:

- **Informational role**—Collecting, processing, and using information that can affect the completion of the objective
- **Interpersonal role**—Interacting with superiors, subordinates, outside stakeholders, and other parties that influence or are influenced by the completion of the task
- **Decisional role**—Selecting from among alternative approaches and resolving conflicts, dilemmas, or challenges

Note that there are differences between leadership and management. A leader influences employees so that they are willing to accomplish objectives. He or she is expected to lead by example and demonstrate personal traits that instill a desire in others to follow. In other words, leadership provides purpose, direction, and motivation to those who follow.

By comparison, a manager administers the resources of the organization. He or she creates budgets, authorizes expenditures, and hires employees. This distinction between a leader and a manager is important because leaders do not always perform a managerial function, whereas nonmanagers are often assigned leadership roles. However, *effective* managers are also effective leaders.

Behavioral Types of Leaders

Among leaders, there are three basic behavioral types: autocratic, democratic, and laissez-faire. Autocratic leaders reserve all decision-making responsibility for themselves and are "do as I say" types of managers. Such leaders typically issue an order to accomplish a task and do not usually seek or accept alternative viewpoints. Democratic leaders work in the opposite way, typically seeking input from all interested parties, requesting ideas and suggestions, and then formulating positions that can be supported by a majority.

Each of these two diametrically opposed approaches has its strengths and weaknesses. The autocratic leader may be more efficient given that he or she is not constrained by the necessity to accommodate alternative viewpoints. The democratic leader may be less efficient because valuable time is spent in discussion and debate when planning for the task. On the other hand, the autocratic leader may be the less effective if his or her knowledge is less than sufficient for the task. And the democratic leader may be more effective when dealing with very complex topics and/or those in which subordinates have strongly held opinions.

The laissez-faire leader is also known as the "laid-back" leader. While both autocratic and democratic leaders tend to be action oriented, the laissez-faire leader often sits back and allows the process to develop as it goes, only making minimal decisions to avoid bringing the process to a complete halt.

Effective leaders function with a combination of these styles, shifting approaches as situations warrant. For example, depending on the circumstances, a leader may solicit input when the situation permits, make autocratic decisions when immediate action is required, and allow the operation to proceed if it is progressing in an efficient and effective manner.

Management Characteristics

The management of tasks requires certain basic skills. These skills are variously referred to as "management characteristics," "management functions," "management principles," or "management responsibilities." The two basic approaches to management are:

- *Traditional management theory*—This approach uses the core principles of planning, organizing, staffing, directing, and controlling (POSDC).
- *Popular management theory*—This approach uses the core principles of planning, organizing, leading, and controlling (POLC).

The traditional approach to management theory is often well covered in introductory business courses and will not be revisited here. Rather, we will focus on the POLC principles that managers employ when dealing with tasks. Figure 1-3 summarizes these principles and illustrates how they are conceptually related.

Planning The process of developing, creating, and implementing strategies for the accomplishment of objectives is called **planning**. Several different approaches to planning are examined more thoroughly in later chapters of this book. The three levels of planning are:

- *Strategic planning*—This occurs at the highest levels of the organization and for a long period of time, usually five or more years.
- *Tactical planning*—This focuses on production planning and integrates organizational resources at a level below the entire enterprise and for an intermediate duration (such as one to five years).
- *Operational planning*—This focuses on the day-to-day operations of local resources and occurs in the present or the short term.

Lack of planning can cause the kind of confusion and frustration among managers and staff that Iris describes in the opening scenario of this chapter.

The planning process begins with the creation of strategic plans for the entire organization. The resulting plan is then divided into planning elements relevant to each major business unit of the organization. These business units in turn create business plans that meet the requirements of the overall organizational strategy. The plans are communicated to mid-level

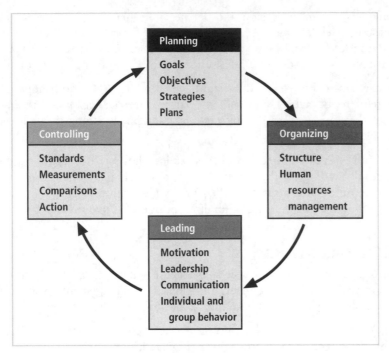

Figure 1-3 The planning–controlling link

Copyright © 2014 Cengage Learning®.

managers so that they can create tactical plans at their levels. Supervisors use the tactical plans to create operational plans that guide the day-to-day operations of the organization. To better understand its planning process, an organization must thoroughly define its goals and objectives. While the exact definition varies depending on context, the term **goal** refers to the end result of a planning process—for example, increasing market share by 2 percent. The term **objective** refers to an intermediate point that allows you to measure progress toward the goal—for example, a growth in sales for each quarter. If you accomplish all objectives in a timely manner, then you are likely to accomplish your goal.

The management of the planning function within an organization encompasses an entire field of study. It requires an understanding of how to plan and a thorough understanding of project management. Project management is discussed in detail later in this chapter.

Organizing The management function dedicated to the structuring of resources to support the accomplishment of objectives is called **organizing**. It includes the structuring of departments and their associated staffs, the storage of raw materials to facilitate manufacturing, and the collection of information to aid in the accomplishment of the task. Recent definitions of "organizing" include staffing, because organizing people so as to maximize their productivity is not substantially different from organizing time, money, or equipment.

Leading As noted earlier, **leadership** encourages the implementation of the planning and organizing functions. It includes supervising employee behavior, performance, attendance, and attitude while ensuring completion of the assigned tasks, goals, and objectives. Leadership generally addresses the direction and motivation of the human resource.

Controlling Monitoring progress toward completion and making necessary adjustments to achieve desired objectives require the exercise of **control**. In general, the control function ensures the validity of the organization's plan. The manager ensures that sufficient progress is made, that impediments to the completion of the task are resolved, and that no additional resources are required. Should the plan be found invalid in light of the operational reality of the organization, the manager takes corrective action.

The control function relies on the use of cybernetic control loops, often called "negative feedback." These involve performance measurements, comparisons, and corrective actions, as shown in Figure 1-4. Here, the cybernetic control process begins with a measurement of actual performance, which is then compared to the expected standard of performance as determined by the planning process. If the standard is being met, the process is allowed to continue toward completion. If an acceptable level of performance is not being attained, either the process is corrected to achieve satisfactory results or the expected level of performance is redefined.

Solving Problems

All managers encounter problems in the course of the organization's day-to-day operation. Whether a problem is low or high profile, the same basic process can be used to solve it.

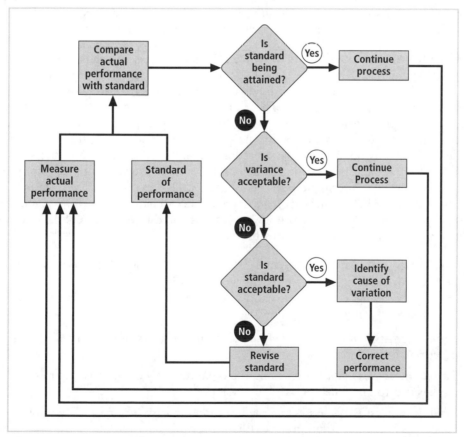

Figure 1-4 The control process

Copyright © 2014 Cengage Learning®.

Time pressures often constrain decision making when problems arise, however. The process of gathering and evaluating the necessary facts may be beyond available capabilities. Nevertheless, the methodology described in the following steps can be used as a basic blueprint for resolving many operational problems.

Step 1: Recognize and Define the Problem

The most frequent flaw in problem solving is failing to define the problem completely. Begin by clearly identifying exactly which problem needs to be solved: For example, if Iris receives complaints at RWW about the receipt of a large number of unsolicited commercial e-mails (also known as spam), she must first determine whether the complaints are valid. Are employees in fact receiving unsolicited spam, or have they signed up for notifications and mailing lists?

Step 2: Gather Facts and Make Assumptions

To understand the background and events that shape the problem, a manager can gather facts about the organizational, cultural, technological, and behavioral factors that are at the root of the issue. He or she can then make assumptions about the methods that are available to solve the problem. For example, by interviewing several employees, Iris might determine that they are receiving a large quantity of unsolicited e-mail. She might also determine that each of these employees has accessed approved vendor support sites, which require an e-mail sign-in process. In such a case, Iris would suspect that the problem of excessive e-mail is, in fact, the result of employees providing their company e-mail addresses, which are being improperly used by the site owners.

Step 3: Develop Possible Solutions

The next step is to begin formulating possible solutions. Managers can use several methods to generate ideas. One of these is brainstorming, a process in which a group of individuals air as many ideas as possible in a short time, without regard for their practicality. The group then reviews and filters the ideas to identify any feasible options. Problem solvers can also interview experts or perform research into solutions using the Web, magazines, journals, or books. In any case, the goal is to develop as many solutions as possible. In the preceding example, once Iris locates the source of the spam e-mails, she can speak with the e-mail server and firewall administrators and then turn to her Certified Information Systems Security Professional (CISSP) reading list. She might contact several of her friends from the local ISSA chapter as well as spend time surfing security-related Web sites. After a few hours, Iris could have dozens of pages of information that might be useful in solving this problem.

Step 4: Analyze and Compare Possible Solutions

Each proposed solution must be examined and ranked as to its likely success in solving the problem. This analysis may include reviewing economic, technological, behavioral, and operational feasibilities, which are described here:

- *Economic feasibility*—Comparing the costs and benefits of a possible solution with other possible solutions.
- *Technological feasibility*—Assessing the organization's ability to acquire the technology needed to implement a particular solution.
- *Behavioral feasibility*—Assessing the likelihood that subordinates will adopt and support a particular solution rather than resist it.
- *Operational feasibility*—Assessing the organization's ability to integrate a particular solution into its current business processes.

Using a feasibility analysis, you can compare various proposals. In the spam example, Iris might immediately eliminate any overly expensive solutions, throw out some technical solutions incompatible with RWW's systems, and narrow the field to three alternatives: (1) do nothing, accepting the spam as a cost of doing business, (2) have the e-mail administrator change the users' accounts, or (3) have the firewall administrator filter access to and traffic from the spam sites. Iris could then discuss these alternatives with all the involved administrators. Each solution is feasible, inexpensive, and does not negatively affect RWW's overall operations.

Step 5: Select, Implement, and Evaluate Once a solution is chosen and implemented, you must evaluate it to determine its effectiveness in solving the problem. It is important to monitor the chosen solution carefully so that if it proves ineffective it can be canceled or altered quickly. In Iris's case, she might decide to implement the firewall filters to reduce the spam, as most of it comes from a few common sources. She might also decide to require the affected employees to attend an e-mail security policy training program, where they can be reminded of the importance of controlling when and where they release company e-mail addresses. In addition, these employees might be required to submit periodic reports regarding the status of the e-mail problem.

Principles of Information Security Management

As part of the management team, the InfoSec management team operates like all other management units by using the common characteristics of leadership and management discussed earlier in this chapter. However, the InfoSec management team's goals and objectives differ from those of the IT and general management communities in that the InfoSec management team is focused on the secure operation of the organization. In fact, some of the InfoSec management team's goals and objectives may be contrary to or require resolution with the goals of the IT management team. The primary focus of the IT group is to ensure the effective and efficient processing of information, whereas the primary focus of the InfoSec group is to ensure the confidentiality, integrity, and availability of information. Security, by its very nature, will slow down the information flow into, through, and out of an organization as information is validated, verified, and assessed against security criteria. Because the CISO in charge of the security management team typically reports directly to the CIO, who is responsible for the IT function, issues and prioritization conflicts can arise unless upper-management intervenes. This issue, and possible resolutions, is discussed at length later in this text.

Because InfoSec management is in charge of a specialized program, certain aspects of its managerial responsibility are unique. These unique functions, which are known as "the six Ps" (planning, policy, programs, protection, people, and project management), are discussed throughout this book and briefly described in the following sections.

Planning

Planning in InfoSec management is an extension of the basic planning model discussed earlier in this chapter. Included in the InfoSec planning model are activities necessary to support the design, creation, and implementation of InfoSec strategies within the IT planning environment.

The business strategy is translated into the IT strategy. Both the business strategy and the IT strategy are then used to develop the InfoSec strategy. For example, the CIO uses the IT objectives gleaned from the business unit plans to create the organization's IT strategy.

The IT strategy then informs the planning efforts for each IT functional area. The IT strategy then provides critical information used for InfoSec planning, along with specifics from the strategies of other business units, as the CISO gets involved with the CIO or other executives to develop the strategy for the next lower level.

The CISO then works with the appropriate security managers to develop operational security plans. These security managers consult with security technicians to develop tactical security plans. Each of these plans is usually coordinated across the business and IT functions of the enterprise and placed into a master schedule for implementation. The overall goal is to create plans that support long-term achievement of the overall organizational strategy. If all goes as expected, the entire collection of tactical plans accomplishes the operational goals and the entire collection of operational goals accomplishes the subordinate strategic goals; this helps to meet the strategic goals and objectives of the organization as a whole.

Several types of InfoSec plans and planning functions exist to support normal and non-normal operations. These include incident response planning, business continuity planning, disaster recovery planning, policy planning, personnel planning, technology rollout planning, risk management planning, and security program planning. Each of these plans has unique goals and objectives, yet each benefits from the same methodical approach. These planning areas are discussed in detail in later chapters of this book.

Another basic planning consideration unique to InfoSec is the location of the InfoSec department within the organization structure. This topic is discussed in Chapter 5.

Policy

The set of organizational guidelines that dictates certain behavior within the organization is called "policy." In InfoSec, there are three general policy categories:

- *Enterprise information security policy (EISP)*—Developed within the context of the strategic IT plan, this sets the tone for the InfoSec department and the InfoSec climate across the organization. The CISO typically drafts the program policy, which is usually supported and signed by the CIO or the CEO.
- *Issue-specific security policies (ISSPs)*—These are sets of rules that define acceptable behavior within a specific technology, such as e-mail or Internet usage.
- *System-specific policies (SysSPs)*—Technical and/or managerial in nature, these control the configuration and/or use of a piece of equipment or technology. For example, an access control list (ACL) is a SysSP that defines the accesses permitted for the specified device.

Programs

InfoSec operations that are specifically managed as separate entities are called "programs." An example would be a security education training and awareness (SETA) program. SETA programs provide critical information to employees to maintain or improve their current levels of security knowledge. Other programs that may emerge include a physical security program, complete with fire protection, physical access, gates, guards, and so on. Some organization with specific regulations may have additional programs dedicated to client/customer privacy, awareness, and the like. Each organization will typically have one or more security programs that must be managed.

Protection

The protection function is executed via a set of risk management activities, including risk assessment and control, as well as protection mechanisms, technologies, and tools. Each of these mechanisms represents some aspect of the management of specific controls in the overall InfoSec plan.

People

People are the most critical link in the InfoSec program. This area encompasses security personnel and the security of personnel as well as aspects of the SETA program mentioned earlier.

Projects

Whether an InfoSec manager is asked to roll out a new security training program or select and implement a new firewall, it is important that the process be managed as a project. The final element for thoroughgoing InfoSec management is the application of a project management discipline to all elements of the InfoSec program. Project management involves identifying and controlling the resources applied to the project as well as measuring progress and adjusting the process as progress is made toward the goal. The next section explores project management in more detail.

Project Management

The final component of a security manager's skill set is the use of a project management approach. Whether the task is to roll out a new security training program or to select and implement a new firewall, it is important that the process be managed as a project. **Project management** involves identifying and controlling the resources applied to the project as well as measuring progress and adjusting the process as progress is made toward the goal.

The need for project management skills within InfoSec may not be evident at first. In fact, this very book emphasizes that InfoSec is a process, not a project. However, each element of an InfoSec program must be managed as a project, even if the overall program is perpetually ongoing.

How can InfoSec be both a process and a project? The answer is that it is, in fact, a continuous series or chain of projects, which comprise a process. As shown in Figure 1-5, each link in this chain of projects could be a specific project. Note that each project is to be guided by a security systems development life cycle (SecSDLC) methodology, as will be described in later chapters.

To be sure, some aspects of InfoSec are not project based; rather, they are managed processes. These managed processes include the monitoring of the external and internal environments during incident response, ongoing risk assessments of routine operations, and continuous vulnerability assessment and vulnerability repair. These activities are called operations and are ongoing.

Projects, on the other hand, are discrete sequences of activities with starting points and defined completion points. A project is different from a process in that it is a temporary activity that is used to create a specific product, service, or end result.[2] Although each individual InfoSec project has an end point, larger organizations never completely finish the InfoSec improvement process; they periodically review progress and realign planning to meet business and IT objectives. This realignment can lead to new goals and projects as well as to the modification, cancellation, or reprioritization of existing projects.

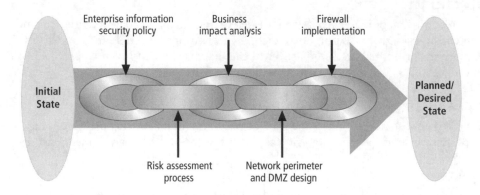

Figure 1-5 An information security program chain

Copyright © 2014 Cengage Learning®.

W. R. Duncan's *A Guide to the Project Management Body of Knowledge* (hereafter called "the PMBoK") defines **project management** as follows:

> *[Project management is] the application of knowledge, skills, tools, and techniques to project activities to meet project requirements. Project management is accomplished through the use of processes such as: initiating, planning, executing, controlling, and closing.*[3]

In other words, project management—which makes use of many of the approaches discussed earlier in this chapter—is focused on achieving the objectives of the project.

Unlike ongoing operations, project management involves the temporary assembling of a group to complete the project, after which its members are released and perhaps assigned to other projects. Projects are sometimes seen as opportunities for employees and managers to extend their skills toward earning promotions. In organizations that have operations groups and project teams, this can lead to a common pitfall: the "prima donna effect," in which certain groups are perceived as "better" or more skilled than others. An example of this is when workers in operations-support roles or software maintenance are seen as less dynamic or capable than their project-focused peers.

Although project management is focused on projects that have end points, this does not mean that these projects are one-time occurrences. Some projects are iterative and occur regularly. Budgeting processes, for example, are iterative projects. Each year, the budget committee meets, designs a proposed budget for the following year, and then presents it to the appropriate manager. The committee may not meet again until six or nine months later, when the next budget cycle begins. Another common practice is the creation of a sequence of projects, with periodic submission of grouped deliverables. Each project phase has a defined set of objectives and deliverables, and the authorization to progress to future phases is tied to the success of the preceding phase as well as to availability of funding or other critical resources.

Some organizational cultures have a long record of relying on project management and have put in place training programs and reward structures to develop a cadre of highly skilled project managers and a corresponding group of trained technical personnel. Other organizations implement each project from scratch and define the process as they go. Organizations that make project management skills a priority benefit in the following ways:

- Implementing a methodology—such as the SecSDLC—ensures that no steps are missed.

- Creating a detailed blueprint of project activities provides a common reference tool and makes all project team members more productive by shortening the learning curve when getting projects underway.

- Identifying specific responsibilities for all the involved personnel reduces ambiguity and also reduces confusion when individuals are assigned to new or different projects.

- Clearly defining project constraints (including time frame, budget) and minimum quality requirements increases the likelihood that the project will stay within them.

- Establishing performance measures and creating project milestones simplifies project monitoring.

- Identifying deviations in quality, time, or budget early on enables early correction of the problems.

Successful project management relies on careful and realistic project planning coupled with aggressive, proactive control. Project success may be defined differently in each organization, but in general a project is deemed a success when:

- It is completed on time or early.

- It is completed at or below its budgeted amount.

- It meets all specifications outlined in the approved project definition, and the deliverables are accepted by the end user and/or assigning entity.

To lead InfoSec projects, some organizations assign technically skilled IT or InfoSec experts; others assign experienced project and general managers. Some organizations use both approaches simultaneously. Regardless of the approach, the goal is the same: to have all elements of the InfoSec program completed with quality deliverables, on a timely basis, and within budget.

The job posting shown in Figure 1-6 shows the typical requirements for an InfoSec analyst. Note that this posting requires project management experience, as do many such positions.

Although project management and organizational skills are not included in every InfoSec analyst position description, many employers seek candidates who couple their InfoSec focus and skills with strong project management skills. Many consulting firms now offer InfoSec services in conjunction with, or in the context of, project management.

Applying Project Management to Security

To apply project management to InfoSec, you must first select an established project management methodology. InfoSec project managers often follow methodologies based on the PMBoK discussed earlier, a methodology promoted by the Project Management Institute. Although other

---

Information Security Analyst

Reporting to the Manager of Information Security Policy and Compliance, the Information Security Analyst is responsible for information security policy development and maintenance; design of security policy education, training, and awareness activities; monitoring compliance with organizational IT security policy and applicable law; and coordinating investigation and reporting of security incidents. Working with the Information Technology Systems (ITS) team, monitor, assess, and fine-tune the business continuity and disaster recovery program, perform network vulnerability assessments, application vulnerability assessments, and other risk assessment reviews as assigned.

Responsibilities:

- Monitor and advise on information security issues related to the systems and workflow to ensure the internal security controls are appropriate and operating as intended.
- Coordinate and execute IT security projects.
- Coordinate response to information security incidents.
- Develop and publish Information Security policies, procedures, standards and guidelines based on knowledge of best practices and compliance requirements.
- Conduct organization-wide data classification assessment and security audits and manage remediation plans.
- Collaborate with IT management, the legal department, safety and security, and law enforcement agencies to manage security vulnerabilities.
- Create, manage, and maintain user security awareness.
- Conduct ongoing security intelligence gathering so as to keep abreast of current security issues.
- Assist ITS in the preparation of documentation, including department policies and procedures, notifications, Web content, and ITS alerts
- Actively participate in at least some professional activities and professional societies
- Perform other related duties as assigned.

Requirements:

- BA or BS in Information Security and Assurance, Computer Science, Management Information Systems, or a related field. Advanced degree desirable.
- Five+ years of progressive experience in computing and information security, including experience with Internet technology and security issues.
- Experience should include security policy development, security education, network penetration testing, application vulnerability assessments, risk analysis and compliance testing.
- CISSP, GIAC, or other security certifications desired.
- Strong project management and organization skills are required.
- Knowledge of information security standards (ISO 17799/27002, etc.), rules and regulations related to information security and data confidentiality (FERPA, HIPAA, etc.) and desktop, server, application, database, network security principles for risk identification and analysis.
- Strong analytical and problem solving skills.
- Excellent communication (oral, written, presentation), interpersonal, and consultative skills.

This position requires some weekend and evening assignments as well as availability during off-hours for participation in scheduled and unscheduled activities.

Figure 1-6 Example of a position posting for an information security analyst

Copyright © 2014 Cengage Learning®.

project management approaches exist, the PMBoK is considered the industry best practice. The following sections examine the PMBoK in the context of InfoSec project management.

PMBoK Knowledge Areas

The PMBoK identifies the project management knowledge areas shown in Table 1-1. Each of these areas is discussed in the following sections.

Project Integration Management Project integration management includes the processes required to ensure that effective coordination occurs within and between the project's many components, including personnel. Most projects include a wide variety of elements: people, time, information, financial resources, internal coordination units (other

Knowledge area	Focus	Processes
Integration	Defining the pieces to be included and organizing and controlling the anticipated work	Developing the plan Executing the project plan Changing control
Scope	Defining what is included in the work to be done and what is to be excluded	Identifying included elements Articulating the boundaries of the project Verifying that the scope reflects management intent
Time	Managing the resource of elapsed time as well as time spent by resources	Defining work elements (work breakdown) Sequencing work elements Estimating resource effort time and elapsed time Preparing and using a schedule to control the project
Cost	Managing the financial resources committed to the project	Estimating financial cost of resources Developing the financial budget Using the financial budget to control costs
Quality	Assuring that the project meets initial or revised specifications	Measuring deliverables against specifications Controlling quality of deliverables
Human resource	Managing the use of workers effectively	Acquiring workers Allocating workers to tasks Supervising and controlling human resources Training and developing human resources
Communications	Assuring that all project participants communicate effectively	Developing a workable communications plan Implementing means to distribute project information Periodic reporting on worker performance and task completion Releasing workers to other assignments as tasks are completed
Risk	Minimizing impact of adverse occurrences	Identifying project risk factors Assessing the degree of risk to various project elements Preparing responses to anticipated adverse occurrences Responding to adverse events
Procurement	Acquiring resources (other than human resources) needed to complete project tasks	Planning for resource acquisition Preparing for competitive solicitation of high-value resources Supervising the solicitation (bidding) for high-value resources Managing contracts for suppliers Closing out contracts

Table 1-1   **Project management knowledge areas**

Copyright © 2014 Cengage Learning®.

departments), outside coordination units (regulatory agencies, standards organizations), computing resources, and physical resources (meeting rooms), to name a few.

Major elements of the project management effort that require integration include:

- Development of the initial project plan
- Monitoring of progress as the project plan is executed
- Control of the revisions to the project plan as well as control of the changes made to resource allocations as measured performance causes adjustments to the project plan

When integrating the disparate elements of a complex InfoSec project, complications are likely to arise. This will require resolving conflict and managing the impact of change.

Conflicts among Communities of Interest When business units do not perceive the need or purpose of an InfoSec project, they may not fully support it. When IT staff are not completely aligned with the objectives of the InfoSec project, or do not fully understand its impact or criticality, they may be less than fully supportive and may make less than a complete effort toward ensuring its success. The InfoSec community must educate and inform the other communities of interest so that InfoSec projects are afforded the same support as other IT and non-IT projects.

Resistance to New Technology InfoSec projects often introduce new technologies. Depending on an organization's appetite for risk, a project may execute technology-based controls that are new to the industry as well as to the organization. Sometimes, the disparate members of the communities of interest that are needed to make a project successful are not open to new or different technologies, and the project manager becomes engaged in debates about technology selections or is required to build consensus around technology choices. Project team members, as well as other workers in the organization, may require special training when new technologies are introduced. This increases the risk of human resource turnover because personnel trained in a new, high-demand skill are more likely to leave the organization for opportunities elsewhere. Proactive steps, such as retention bonuses or gain-sharing arrangements, may help mitigate this risk, but the project plan should include contingency standards for personnel turnover.

Project Scope Management
Project scope management ensures that the project plan includes only those activities that are necessary to complete it. One thing that undermines many projects once they are underway is scope creep. **Scope creep** occurs when the quantity or quality of project deliverables is expanded from the original project plan. Stopping scope creep can pose a challenge to many project managers, who seek to meet the objectives expressed to them by project sponsors. Experienced project managers, exposed to scope creep in the past, are prepared to ask for a corresponding expansion of project work time, project resources, or both.

Project scope management includes these processes:

- Scope planning
- Scope definition
- Scope verification

View Point
Okay, Go Ahead and Do It
By Henry Bonin, Former member of the Faculty, San Jose State University

Congratulations! You made a commitment to learn about the various components of InfoSec *management*. When done, you will be able to sew all the pieces together to make comprehensive InfoSec solutions actually happen. A comprehensive solution goes beyond the technology pieces and includes project management, writing supporting plans, developing policies and programs, performing risk assessments, identifying and controlling risks, and hiring the right people to work on the project. These are the skills you will learn in this book.

In the near future, you and your team will go through all the steps of planning and analyzing your idea for improving some technical element of your organization's InfoSec system, then present your proposal to the decision maker. Your boss will agree that this is the right thing to do, and he or she will give you the go-ahead. Will your response be "Yikes!" or "Cool!"?

There is no venture capitalist that invests solely in one technology. When an entrepreneur proposes a project, surely the technology is the focal point of the presentation. However, to receive funding, how this technology will be *managed* or steered to the marketplace is as important as the technology itself. Venture capitalists know that a failure in implementing critical *management* elements will have no less an impact on project success than a failure of the technology itself.

Projects have high failure rates, and the failure is usually traceable to not following an accepted methodology or to a lack of experience in various aspects of management. However, InfoSec projects introduce a third reason for possible failure: the incorrect assumption that they are just another IT project. They are not. This book will provide you with the skills to manage InfoSec at your firm.

In addition to these three processes that deal with project scope, those who wish to retain greater control of the planning process once the project is underway often include a change control for all requests that would expand project scope.

Project Time Management   Project time management entails ensuring that the project is finished by the identified completion date while meeting its objectives. Failure to meet deadlines is one of the most frequently cited failures in project management. Many completion deadlines are tied to external requirements, such as market demands, business alliances, or government regulations. Missing a deadline can sometimes make project completion moot.

The fact is that a given result (the deliverable of the project) requires a certain amount of time and resources (money, people, equipment, etc.) to accomplish. Trimming time or resources from these amounts requires reducing the quantity or quality of the deliverables. Many projects fail because of errors made in the planning phase. This occurs when management underestimates the necessary time and resources or overestimates the quantity and quality of project deliverables, given the available resources.

Project time management includes these processes:

- Activity definition
- Activity sequencing
- Activity duration estimating
- Schedule development
- Schedule control

Project Cost Management Project cost management includes the processes required to ensure that a project is completed within the resource constraints placed on it. Some projects are planned using only a financial budget from which all resources—personnel, equipment, supplies, and so forth—must be procured (see the section "Project Procurement Management" later in this chapter). Other projects have a variety of resources cobbled together with no real financial support, just whatever the managers can scrounge.

Project cost management includes these processes:

- Resource planning
- Cost estimating
- Cost budgeting
- Cost control

Project Quality Management Project quality management includes the processes required to ensure that the project adequately meets the project specifications. The common use of the word "quality" may seem vague—what is a quality product to one person may not be so to another. In fact, the definition of "quality" is quite clear. If the project deliverables meet the requirements specified in the project plan, the project has met its quality objective; if they do not, it has not met its quality objectives. Unfortunately, far too often, poorly planned projects do not provide clear descriptions of what the project is to deliver, whether it is a product, a service, or a revised process.

A good plan defines project deliverables in unambiguous terms against which actual results are easily compared. This enables the project team to determine at each step along the way whether all components are being developed to the original specifications. As noted earlier in the section on scope management, changes made along the way can threaten the overall success of the project. Any change to the definition of project deliverables must be codified, and then the other two areas of project planning—work time and resources—must be reconciled to the changes.

Project quality management includes these processes:

- Quality planning
- Quality assurance
- Quality control

Project Human Resource Management Project human resource management includes the processes necessary to ensure that the personnel assigned to a project are effectively employed. Staffing a project requires careful estimates of the number of worker hours required. Too few people working on a project almost guarantees it will not be completed on time. Too many people working on a project may be an inefficient use of resources and may cause the project to exceed its resource limits.

The management of human resources must address many complicating factors, including the following:

- Not all workers operate at the same level of efficiency; in fact, wide variance in the productivity of individuals is the norm. Project managers must accommodate the work style of each project resource while encouraging every worker to be as efficient as possible.

- Not all workers begin the project assignment with the same degree of skill. An astute project manager attempts to evaluate the skill level of some or all of the assigned resources to better match them to the needs of the project plan.

- Skill mixtures among actual project workers seldom match the needs of the project plan. Therefore, in some circumstances, workers may be asked to perform tasks for which they are not necessarily well suited, and those tasks take longer and/or cost more than planned.

- Some tasks may require skills that are not available from resources on hand. Therefore, the project manager may need to go outside normal channels for a key skill, which almost always results in delays and higher costs.

Managing human resources in InfoSec projects has additional complexities, including the following:

- Extended clearances may be required. Since some InfoSec projects involve working in sensitive areas of the organization, project managers may have restrictions placed on which resources can be used (e.g., only those with the requisite clearances). While this is not yet a common restriction in most commercial organizations, it does affect organizations in the financial sector (banking and brokerage) as well as in many government agencies.

- Often, InfoSec projects deploy technology controls that are new to the organization, and in such cases there is not a pool of skilled resources in that area from which to draw. This can occur in any project that faces a skill shortage but is more likely to occur in an InfoSec project than in a routine development project.

Project human resource management includes these processes:

- Organizational planning
- Staff acquisition
- Team development

Project Communications Management Project communications management includes the processes necessary to convey to all involved parties the details of activities associated with the project. This includes the creation, distribution, classification, storage, and ultimate destruction of documents, messages, and other associated project information.

Overcoming resistance to change may be more of a challenge in InfoSec projects than in traditional development projects. In some cases, users and IT partners may be uncertain about the reasons for the project and may be wary of its effect on their work lives. In extreme cases, a project may face hostility from the future users of the system. The only way to counter this resistance is to initiate education, training, and awareness programs. The project manager, usually working in conjunction with the SETA program within the InfoSec department, should communicate the need for the project as early as possible, and should answer any questions about the effect on users of the deployment of the project deliverables.

Project communications management includes these processes:

- Communications planning
- Information distribution
- Performance reporting
- Administrative closure

Project Risk Management

Project risk management includes the processes necessary to assess, mitigate, manage, and reduce the impact of adverse occurrences on the project. Project risk management is very similar to normal security risk management, except the scope and scale are usually much smaller because the area to be protected is the individual project and not the entire organization. In many cases, simply identifying and rating the threats facing the project and assessing the probability of the occurrence of these threats is sufficient. The usual purpose of this component is to identify large risks and to plan the mitigation of adverse events should the risks manifest themselves.

InfoSec projects do face different risks from those faced by other types of projects, as noted in the preceding sections. Those projects that face higher-than-normal risks should allow for appropriate planning and perhaps allow for preemptive action to mitigate these risks.

Project risk management includes these processes:

- Risk identification
- Risk quantification
- Risk response development
- Risk response control

Project Procurement Management

Project procurement management includes the processes necessary to acquire needed resources to complete the project. Depending on the common practices of the organization, project managers may simply requisition human resources, hardware, software, or supplies from the organization's stocks. Or they may have to specify the required resources, request and evaluate bids, and then negotiate contracts for them.

InfoSec projects may have more complex procurement needs than other types of projects because they are more likely than other projects to need different software or hardware products and/or differently skilled human resources than other common types of IT projects.

Project procurement management includes these processes:

- Procurement planning
- Solicitation planning
- Solicitation

- Source selection
- Contract administration
- Contract closeout

Project Management Tools

Many tools are available to support the management of the diverse resources usually found in complex projects. Some of these tools are modeling approaches, such as the program evaluation and review technique or critical path method, and others involve the use of software. Most project managers combine software tools that implement one or more of the dominant modeling approaches. A few of the more common models are discussed here.

Most project managers who deal with project plans that are nontrivial in scope use tools to facilitate scheduling and execution of the project. A project manager usually determines that certain tasks cannot be performed until prerequisite tasks are complete. It is almost always important to determine in what order tasks must be performed. It is equally important to determine what tasks must not be delayed to avoid holding up the entire project.

Using complex project management tools may result in a complication called **projectitis**—a common pitfall of IT and InfoSec projects. Projectitis occurs when the project manager spends more time documenting project tasks, collecting performance measurements, recording project task information, and updating project completion forecasts than accomplishing meaningful project work. The development of an overly elegant, microscopically detailed plan before gaining consensus for the work and related coordinated activities that it requires may be a precursor to projectitis. However, the proper use of project tools can help project managers organize and coordinate project activities and can enhance communication among the project team. Each professional project manager will strive to find the proper balance between the detailed planning and recordkeeping and focusing on the actual work that has to be done to achieve the project's objectives.

The following sections discuss some of the more commonly used project management tools.

Work Breakdown Structure

A project plan can be created using a very simple planning tool called a **work breakdown structure** (WBS), such as the one shown in Table 1-2. The WBS can be prepared with a simple desktop PC spreadsheet program as well as with more complex project management software tools.

Using a WBS, the project plan is first broken down into a few major tasks. Each of these major tasks is placed on the WBS task list. The minimum attributes that should be identified for each task are:

- The work to be accomplished (activities and deliverables)
- Estimated amount of effort required for completion, in hours or workdays
- The common or specialty skills needed to perform the task
- Task interdependencies

Task	Effort (hours)	Skill	Dependencies
1. Contact field office and confirm network assumptions	2	Network architect	
2. Purchase standard firewall hardware	4	Network architect and purchasing group	1
3. Configure firewall	8	Network architect	2
4. Package and ship firewall to field office	2	Intern	3
5. Work with local technical resource to install and test firewall	6	Network architect	4
6. Complete network vulnerability assessment	12	Network architect and penetration test team	5
7. Get remote office sign-off and update network drawings and documentation	8	Network architect	6

Table 1-2 **Example of an early-draft work breakdown structure**

Copyright © 2014 Cengage Learning®.

As the project plan develops, attributes can be added, including:

- Estimated capital expenses for the task
- Estimated noncapital expenses for the task
- Task assignment according to specific skills
- Start and end dates, once tasks have been sequenced and dates projected

Each major task on the WBS is then further divided into either smaller tasks or specific action steps. For simplicity, the WBS example discussed later in this chapter divides each task only into action steps. In an actual project plan, tasks are often more complex; you may need to subdivide major tasks before action steps can be determined and assigned. Although there are few hard-and-fast rules as to the appropriate level of detail, generally a task or subtask becomes an action step when it can be completed by one individual or skill set and when it results in a single deliverable.

Task-Sequencing Approaches

In a large and complex project, sequencing tasks and subtasks can be truly daunting. Once a project reaches even a relatively modest size, say a few dozen tasks, there can be almost innumerable possibilities for task assignment and scheduling. Fortunately, a number of approaches are available to assist the project manager in this sequencing effort.

Network Scheduling One method for sequencing tasks and subtasks in a project plan is known as "network scheduling." The word "network" in this context does not refer in any way to computer networks; rather, it refers to the web of possible pathways to project completion from the beginning task to the ending task. For example, activity A must occur before activity B, which in turn must occur before activity C; a network diagram illustrating this network dependency is shown in Figure 1-7.

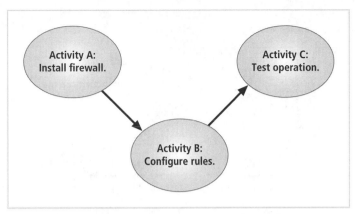

Figure 1-7 Example of a simple network dependency

Copyright © 2014 Cengage Learning®.

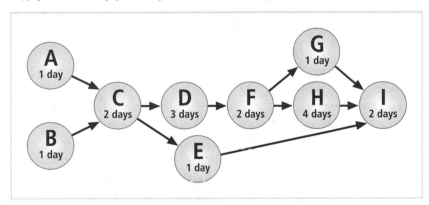

Figure 1-8 Example of a complex network dependency

Copyright © 2014 Cengage Learning®.

While this illustration is very simple, the method of depiction gains value as the number of tasks and subtasks increases and information is added about the effort and type of resources necessary to complete each activity. If multiple activities can be completed concurrently, this can be shown in the diagram. If a single activity has two or more prerequisites or is the common prerequisite for two or more activities, this can also be depicted, as shown in Figure 1-8.

The most popular networking dependency diagramming technique is the **Program Evaluation and Review Technique (PERT)**. PERT was originally developed in the late 1950s to meet the needs of the rapidly expanding engineering projects associated with government acquisitions such as weapons systems. At the same time, a similar technique, called the **Critical Path Method (CPM)**, was being developed in the industry. The PERT diagram, an example of which is shown in Figure 1-9, depicts a number of events followed by key activities and their durations. It is possible to take a very complex operation and diagram it in PERT if you can answer three key questions about each activity:

- How long will this activity take?
- What activity occurs immediately before this activity can take place?
- What activity occurs immediately after this activity?

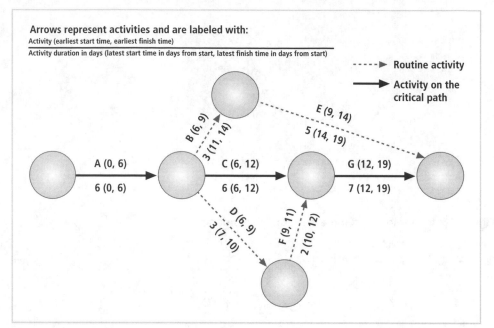

Figure 1-9 Example of a PERT

Copyright © 2014 Cengage Learning®.

By identifying the path through the various activities, you can determine the critical path. The **critical path** is the sequence of events or activities that requires the longest duration to complete and that therefore cannot be delayed without delaying the entire project. The difference in time between the critical path and any other path is called **slack time**. All tasks not on the critical path have slack time, and thus can be delayed or postponed, within the limits of their slack time, without delaying the entire project. In Figure 1-9, the critical path is the sequence of events ACG, shown by the heavier arrows. A project can have more than one critical path, if two or more paths have the same total time requirement. In the example shown in Figure 1-9, the noncritical path ADFG has one day of slack time. This path can incur a delay of up to one day without adversely affecting the overall completion of the project.

The advantages of using the PERT method include:

- Planning large projects is made easier by facilitating the identification of pre- and postactivities.

- Planning to determine the probability of meeting requirements (i.e., timely delivery through calculation of critical paths) is allowed.

- The impact of changes on the system is anticipated. Should a delay in one area occur, how does it affect the overall project schedule?

- Information is presented in a straightforward format that both technical and nontechnical managers can understand and refer to in planning discussions.

- No formal training is required. After a brief explanation, most people understand it thoroughly.

The disadvantages of using the PERT method include:

- Diagrams can become awkward and cumbersome, especially in very large projects.
- Diagrams can become expensive to develop and maintain, due to the complexities of some project development processes.
- It can be difficult to place an accurate "time to complete" on some tasks, especially in the initial construction of a project; inaccurate estimates invalidate any close critical path calculations.

CPM is similar to the PERT method. It relies on a scheduling process designed to identify the sequence of tasks that make up the shortest elapsed time to complete the project. Other tasks may then be scheduled in ways that do not lengthen the total time of the project.

Gantt Chart Another popular project management tool is the Gantt chart, named for Henry Gantt, who developed this method in the early 1900s. Like network diagrams, Gantt charts are simple to read and understand and thus easy to present to management. These simple bar charts are even easier to design and implement than the PERT diagrams and yield much of the same information.

The Gantt chart lists activities on the vertical axis of a bar chart and provides a simple time line on the horizontal axis. A bar represents each activity, with its starting and ending points coinciding with the appropriate points on the time line. The length of the bar thus represents the duration of that particular phase. Activities that overlap can be performed concurrently. Those that do not must be performed sequentially. A vertical reference line can be used to evaluate the current date. Some implementations of the Gantt chart use a fill method to show the percentage completion of particular activities. As shown in Figure 1-10, the Gantt chart can provide a wealth of information in a simple format. Activity A has been completed; activity B is ahead of schedule; activity C is behind schedule. Milestones can be added to individual activities and are usually represented by a numbered triangle just above the bar. These

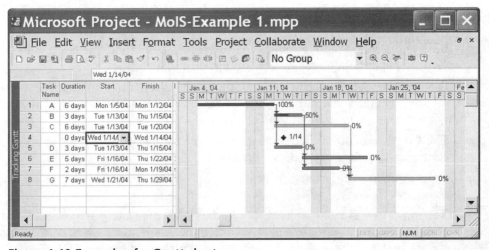

Figure 1-10 Example of a Gantt chart

Source: Microsoft Project.

milestones might include the completion of a key report or a component that requires outside interventions. Whatever the case, this method of tracking has proven so simple to use, yet so effective, that it is frequently the preferred method for tracking project progress.

Automated Project Tools

Microsoft Project is a commonly used project management tool. While it is not the only automated project management tool (there are quite a few) and is not universally perceived as the best (i.e., a matter of heated opinion among project managers), it is generally acknowledged to be the most widely used. If you are considering using an automated project management tool, keep the following in mind:

- A software program cannot take the place of a skilled and experienced project manager who understands how to define tasks, allocate scarce resources, and manage the resources that are assigned. While an automated tool can be powerful in the hands of someone who knows how to use it, it can temporarily disguise the shortcomings of an unprepared project manager.

- A software tool can get in the way of the work. A project manager who spends more than a small amount of time using a tool to record progress and forecast options is on the way to projectitis. When project workers must use unfamiliar procedures to report progress in minute detail, they may become less productive. When status meetings turn into lengthy slideshows detailing each aspect of progress, experienced project managers will wonder why team members are not working on their assigned tasks.

- Choose a tool that you can use effectively. Project managers are better served using a tool they know than an overly complex tool they cannot use to good effect. Multimillion-dollar projects have been brought in on time and under budget using nothing more than a simple spreadsheet and lots of hard work. On the other hand, a project manager using state-of-the-art tools can trim weeks from a schedule and save thousands of dollars while meeting every deliverable requirement.

Chapter Summary

- Because businesses and technology have become more fluid, the concept of computer security has been replaced by the concept of InfoSec.

- From an InfoSec perspective, organizations often have three communities of interest: InfoSec managers and professionals, IT managers and professionals, and nontechnical managers and professionals.

- The C.I.A. triangle is based on three desirable characteristics of information: confidentiality, integrity, and availability.

- In its simplest form, management is the process of achieving objectives by using resources.

- The important distinction between a leader and a manager is that a leader influences employees so that they are willing to accomplish objectives, whereas a manager creates budgets, authorizes expenditures, and hires employees.

- The traditional approach to management theory uses the core principles of planning, organizing, staffing, directing, and controlling (POSDC). Another approach to management theory categorizes the principles of management into planning, organizing, leading, and controlling (POLC).

■ The process that develops, creates, and implements strategies for the accomplishment of objectives is called "planning." There are three levels of planning: strategic, tactical, and operational.

■ InfoSec management operates like all other management units, but the goals and objectives of the InfoSec management team are different in that they focus on the secure operation of the organization.

■ Project management is the application of knowledge, skills, tools, and techniques to project activities to meet project requirements. Project management is accomplished through the use of processes that include initiation, planning, execution, controlling, and closing.

■ The creation of a project plan can be accomplished using a very simple planning tool, such as the work breakdown structure (WBS).

■ A set of methods that can be used to sequence the tasks and subtasks in a project plan is known as "network scheduling." Popular techniques include the Program Evaluation and Review Technique (PERT), the Critical Path Method (CPM), and the Gantt chart.

■ Automated project management tools can assist experienced project managers in the complexities of managing a large project but may get in the way when used by novice project managers or when used on simple projects.

Review Questions

1. List and describe the three communities of interest that engage in an organization's efforts to solve InfoSec problems. Give two or three examples of who might be in each community.

2. What is information security? What essential protections must be in place to protect information systems from danger?

3. What is the importance of the C.I.A. triangle? Define each of its components.

4. Describe the CNSS security model. What are its three dimensions?

5. What is the definition of "privacy" as it relates to InfoSec? How is this definition different from the everyday definition? Why is this difference significant?

6. Define the InfoSec processes of identification, authentication, authorization, and accountability.

7. What is management and what is a manager? What roles do managers play as they execute their responsibilities?

8. How are leadership and management similar? How are they different?

9. What are the characteristics of management based on the method described in the text as the "popular approach" to management? Define each characteristic.

10. What are the three types of general planning? Define each.

11. List and describe the five steps of the general problem-solving process.

12. Define "project management." Why is project management of particular interest in the field of InfoSec?

13. Why are project management skills important to the InfoSec professional?

14. How can security be both a project and a process?

15. What are the nine areas that make up the component processes of project management?

16. What are the three planning parameters that can be adjusted when a project is not being executed according to plan?

17. Name and very briefly describe some of the manual and automated tools that can be used to help manage projects.

18. What is a work breakdown structure (WBS) and why is it important?

19. List and describe the various approaches to task sequencing.

20. How do PERT/CPM methods help to manage a project?

Exercises

1. Assume that a security model is needed for the protection of information used in the class you are taking—say, the information found in your course's learning management system (if your class uses one). Use the CNSS model to identify each of the 27 cells needed for complete information protection. Write a brief statement on how you would address the components represented in each of the 27 cells.

2. Consider the information stored in your personal computer. Do you, at this moment, have information stored in your computer that is critical to your personal life? If that information became compromised or lost, what effect would it have on you?

3. Draft a work breakdown structure for the task of implementing and using a PC-based virus detection program (one that is not centrally managed). Don't forget to include tasks to remove or quarantine any malware it finds.

4. Your instructor has been provided with an Instructor Resources Kit that includes several MS Project files. If you have access to MS Project and can access the file 978-1285062297_12_01.mpp, you can perform this exercise.

Closing Case

Charley and Iris met for a working lunch.

"First thing you need to do," Charley told Iris when they met, "is gain some consensus from your higher management to fund a new position for a security analyst. Then fill it by finding someone who knows the security skills but is primarily skilled in project management. Or find a strong security analyst and send them off for PM training."

"Why so?" Iris asked.

"A good project manager can help the entire team learn how to manage all the security projects to keep you from getting overwhelmed with deadlines and deliverables," Charley said, smiling. "A good PM can make your operations proactive rather than reactive."

"That sounds good," Iris replied. "What else do I need to know?"

Discussion

1. Based on your reading of the chapter and what you now know about the issues, list at least three other things Charley could recommend to Iris.

2. What do you think is the most important piece of advice Charley gave Iris? Why?

Ethical Decision Making

Assume that Charlie then tells Iris, "I have a friend that runs a placement service and can find you exactly the right person for this position. Once you have the job posted, you can have them help you fill it. If they find you a great candidate and the placement is made, I will split the finder's fee with you."

Iris knows that her company may pay as much as half a year's salary for the placement services needed for such a hire. Charlie's friend is likely to pay him a pretty substantial finder's fee if Iris awards the placement contract to them and someone gets placed. If she can get a quality employee and a little extra money on the side, everyone wins. But Iris is not comfortable with such an arrangement. And she's pretty sure it's against company policy.

If this comes to pass, is Charlie doing anything illegal? Is Iris? What's ethically wrong with Charlie's proposal?

Endnotes

1. "NSTISSI No. 4011: National Training Standard for Information Systems Security (InfoSec) Professionals." *National Security Telecommunications and Information Systems Security*, June 20, 1994. Accessed December 12, 2012 @ *www.cnss.gov /Assets/pdf/nstissi_4011.pdf*.

2. Duncan, W. R. *A Guide to the Project Management Body of Knowledge*, 3rd edition. 1996, Project Management Institute. 3.

3. Duncan, W. R. *A Guide to the Project Management Body of Knowledge*, 3rd edition. 1996, Project Management Institute. 6.

4. Ibid.

5. Henry Bonin is a former faculty member in the MIS Department of San Jose State University's School of Business. He can be reached at *h_bonin@yahoo.com*.

Planning for Security

*You got to be careful if you don't know where you're going,
because you might not get there.*

YOGI BERRA

Iris was a little uneasy. While this wasn't her first meeting with Mike Edwards, the chief information officer (CIO), it was her first planning meeting. Around the table, the other information technology (IT) department heads were chatting, drinking their coffee. Iris stared at her notepad, where she had carefully written "Strategic Planning Meeting" and nothing else.

Mike entered the room, followed by his assistants. Stan, his lead executive assistant, was loaded down with stacks of copied documents, which he and the other assistants began handing out. Iris took her copy and scanned the title: Random Widget Works, Inc. (RWW), Strategic Planning Document, Information Technology Division, FY 2014–2018.

"As you know, it's annual planning time again," Mike began. "You just got your copies of the multiyear IT strategic plan. Last month, you each received your numbered copy of the company strategic plan." Iris remembered the half-inch-thick document she had carefully read and then locked in her filing cabinet.

Mike continued: "I'm going to go through the IT vision and mission statements, and then review the details of how the IT plan will allow us to meet the objectives articulated in the strategic plan. In 30 days, you'll submit your draft plans to me for review. Don't hesitate to come by to discuss any issues or questions."

Later that day, Iris dropped by Mike's office to discuss her planning responsibilities. This duty was not something he had briefed her about yet.

"I'm sorry, Iris," Mike said. "I meant to spend some time outlining your role as security manager. I'm afraid I can't do it this week; maybe we can start next week by reviewing some key points I want you to make sure are in your plan. In the meantime, I suggest you ask the other business section chiefs for copies of their strategic plans and look for areas that don't overlap with IT's."

The next day, Iris had lunch with her mentor, Charley Moody.

After they ordered, Iris said, "We just started on our strategic planning project and I'm developing a security strategic plan. You know, I've never worked up one of these from scratch before. Got any good advice on what to look for?"

"Sure," Charley responded. "Actually, I have something for you in my car that might help."

After they finished lunch, the pair went out to the parking lot. Inside Charley's trunk were two cardboard boxes marked "BOOKS." He opened one and rummaged around for a few seconds. "Here," he said, handing Iris a textbook.

She read the title out loud: "*Strategic Planning*."

"This one is from a planning seminar I did a while back," Charley explained. "I have a later edition, but there really isn't much difference between the two. I was cleaning out some of my redundant books. I was going to donate these to the library book sale. It's yours if you want it. It might help with your planning project."

Charley closed the trunk and said, "Read over the first few chapters—that'll give you the basics. Then sit down with your planning documents from corporate management and from IT. For each goal stated by the CEO and CIO, think about what your department needs to do to meet it. Write up how you think the company as a whole, and your team in particular, can satisfy that objective. Then go back and describe the resources you'll need to make it happen."

"That's it?" Iris asked.

Charley shook his head. "There's more to it than that, but this will get you started. Once you've got that done, I can share some of what I know about how to frame your plans and format them for use in the planning process."

LEARNING OBJECTIVES
Upon completion of this material, you should be able to:

- Identify the roles in organizations that are active in the planning process
- Explain the principal components of information security (InfoSec) system implementation planning in the organizational planning scheme
- Differentiate between strategic organization InfoSec planning and specialized contingency planning (CP)
- List and explain the unique considerations and relationships that exist among the types of specialized CP—incident response, disaster recovery, and business continuity planning (BCP)

Introduction

Chapter 1 discussed InfoSec management within the context of general management, covering many of the elements of general and project management as they apply to InfoSec. The broader subject of planning encompasses general organizational planning as well as the specific processes involved with planning for InfoSec. This subject is divided into two chapters (see Figure 2-1). This chapter covers organizational planning—specifically, the process of planning for InfoSec. And Chapter 3 covers a very important topic in InfoSec planning—contingency planning—in greater detail.

It is difficult to overstate how essential planning is to business and organizational management. In a setting where there are continual constraints on resources, both human and financial, good planning enables an organization to make the most out of the materials at hand. While a chief information security officer (CISO)—also called a "chief security officer" (CSO), "director of InfoSec," or "vice president for InfoSec"—and other InfoSec managers can generate an urgent response to an immediate threat, they are well advised to utilize a portion of their routinely allocated resources toward the long-term viability of the InfoSec program. However, some organizations spend too much time, money, and human effort on planning with too little return to justify their investment. Each organization must balance the benefits of the chosen degree of planning effort against the costs of the effort.

The Role of Planning

Planning usually involves many interrelated groups and organizational processes. The groups involved in planning represent the three communities of interest discussed in Chapter 1; they may be internal or external to the organization and can include employees, management,

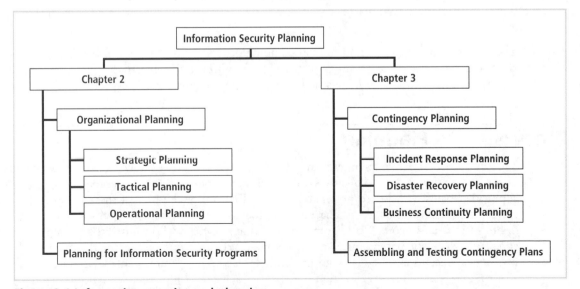

Figure 2-1 Information security and planning

Copyright © 2014 Cengage Learning®.

stockholders, and other outside stakeholders. Among the other factors that affect planning are the physical environment, the political and legal environment, the competitive environment, and the technological environment. For the purposes of this text, the term **stakeholder** is used to describe those entities, whether people or organizations, that have a "stake" or vested interest in a particular aspect of the planning or operation of the organization. In this case, the area of concern is the information assets in use in a particular organization. This is distinctly different from the term "stockholder," which describes someone who is an owner of the organization via ownership of the organization's common or preferred stock shares. Stakeholders are typically asked for input whenever strategic decisions affecting their "stake" are planned.

When planning, members of the InfoSec community of interest use the same processes and methodologies that the general management and IT management communities of interest use. Because the InfoSec community of interest seeks to influence the entire organization, an effective InfoSec planner should know how the organizational planning process works so that participation in this process can yield measurable results. Before you can explore the positioning of InfoSec within an organization's planning processes, however, you must first understand the concept of organizational planning.

Planning is the dominant means of managing resources in modern organizations. It entails the enumeration of a sequence of actions intended to achieve specific goals during a defined period of time, and then controlling the implementation of these steps. Planning provides direction for the organization's future. Without specific and detailed planning, organizational units would attempt to meet objectives independently, with each unit being guided by its own initiatives and ideas. Such an uncoordinated effort would not only fail to meet objectives, it will result in an inefficient use of resources. Organizational planning, when conducted by the various segments of the organization, provides a uniform script that increases efficiency and reduces waste and duplication of effort by each organizational unit within the individual communities of interest.

Organizational planning should make use of a top-down process in which the organization's leadership chooses the direction and initiatives that the entire organization should pursue. Initially, the organizational plan contains few specific detailed objectives; instead, it outlines general objectives.

The primary goal of the organizational planning process is the creation of detailed plans—that is, systematic directions for how to meet the organization's objectives. This task is accomplished with a process that begins with the general and ends with the specific.

Precursors to Planning

To implement effective planning, an organization's leaders usually begin from previously developed positions that explicitly state the organization's ethical, entrepreneurial, and philosophical perspectives. In recent years, the critical nature of the first of these perspectives—the ethical perspective—has come sharply into focus. Widely publicized ethical lapses at such organizations as Enron, WorldCom, Fannie Mae, IBM, and HP illustrate the importance of solid and well-articulated ethical underpinnings. While ethical failures of this magnitude are, one hopes, exceptional, industry groups and regulators have implemented standards and regulations that assess an organization's ability to achieve compliance with legal requirements and industry-recommended practices. When an organization's stated positions do not match the demonstrated ethical, entrepreneurial, and philosophical approaches of its management teams, the developmental plan—which is guided by the organization's values, vision, mission, and strategy—becomes unmanageable.

Values Statement

One of the first positions that management must articulate is the values statement. The trust and confidence of stakeholders and the public are important factors for any organization. By establishing a formal set of organizational principles and qualities in a values statement, as well as benchmarks for measuring behavior against these published values, an organization makes its conduct and performance standards clear to its employees and the public. The quality management movement of the 1980s and 1990s amply illustrated that organizations with strong values can earn greater loyalty from customers and employees.

Microsoft has a formal employee mission and values statement published on its Web site, as shown in Figure 2-2.

Integrity, honesty, passion, and respectfulness are significant parts of Microsoft's corporate philosophy. RWW's values statement might take the following form:

> *Random Widget Works values commitment, honesty, integrity, and social responsibility among its employees and is committed to providing its services in harmony with its corporate, social, legal, and natural environments.*

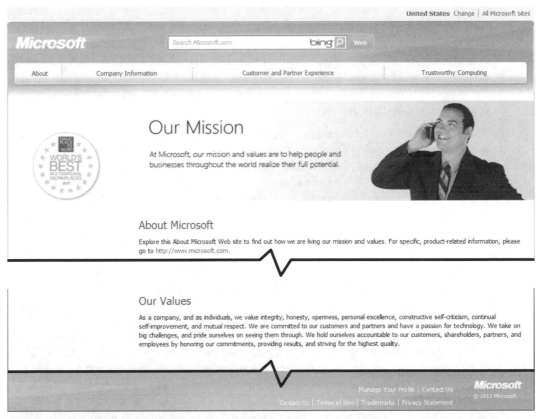

Figure 2-2 Microsoft's mission and values statement

Source: Microsoft.

Vision Statement

The second underpinning of organizational planning is the vision statement. The vision statement expresses what the organization wants to become. Vision statements should therefore be ambitious; after all, they are meant to express the aspirations of the organization and to serve as a means for visualizing its future. In other words, the vision statement is the best-case scenario for the organization's future. Many organizations mix or combine the vision statement and the mission statement. RWW's vision statement might take the following form:

> *Random Widget Works will be the preferred manufacturer of choice for every business's widget equipment needs, with an RWW widget in every gizmo in use.*

This is a very bold, ambitious vision statement. It may not seem very realistic, but vision statements are not meant to express the probable, only the possible. The vision statement is a concise statement of where the organization wants to go.

Mission Statement

The mission statement explicitly declares the business of the organization and its intended areas of operations. It is, in a sense, the organization's identity card. RWW's mission statement might take the following form:

> *Random Widget Works designs and manufactures quality widgets and associated equipment and supplies for use in modern business environments.*

Not the 12-page sleeping pill you expected? A mission statement should be concise, should reflect both internal and external operations, and should be robust enough to remain valid for a period of four to six years. Simply put, the mission statement must explain *what* the organization does and for *whom.*

Many organizations encourage or require each division or major department—including the InfoSec department—to generate its own mission statement. These mission statements can be as concise as the example provided, expressing a strong commitment to the confidentiality, integrity, and availability of information, or they can provide a more detailed description of the InfoSec department's function, as shown in the following example. This mission statement appears in *Information Security Roles and Responsibilities Made Easy*, by Charles Cresson Wood.

> *The Information Security Department is charged with identifying, assessing, and appropriately managing risks to Company X's information and information systems. It evaluates the options for dealing with these risks, and works with departments throughout Company X to decide upon and then implement controls that appropriately and proactively respond to these same risks. The Department is also responsible for developing requirements that apply to the entire organization as well as external information systems in which Company X participates (for example, extranets) [these requirements include policies, standards, and procedures]. The focal point for all matters related to information security, this Department is ultimately responsible for all endeavors within Company X that seek to avoid, prevent, detect, correct, or recover from threats to information or information systems.*[1]

According to Wood, these threats include:

- Unauthorized access to information
- Unauthorized use of information
- Unauthorized disclosure of information
- Unauthorized diversion of information
- Unauthorized modification of information
- Unauthorized destruction of information
- Unauthorized duplication of information
- Unavailability of information[2]

The mission statement is the follow-up to the vision statement. If the vision statement states where the organization wants to go, the mission statement describes how it wants to get there. Taken together, the mission, vision, and values statements provide the philosophical foundation for planning and guide the creation of the strategic plan.

Strategic Planning

Strategic planning lays out the long-term direction to be taken by the organization. It guides organizational efforts and focuses resources toward specific, clearly defined goals in the midst of an ever-changing environment.

As you learned in Chapter 1, a clearly directed strategy flows from top to bottom, and a systematic approach is required to translate it into a program that can inform and lead all members of the organization. As shown in the sample hierarchical chart in Figure 2-3, strategic plans formed at the highest levels of the organization are translated into more specific strategic plans for intermediate layers of management. These plans are then converted into tactical

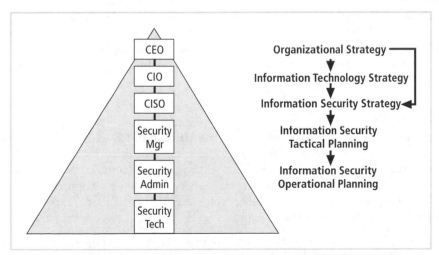

Figure 2-3 Top-down strategic planning

Copyright © 2014 Cengage Learning®.

planning for supervisory managers and eventually provide direction for the operational plans undertaken by the nonmanagement members of the organization. This multilayered approach encompasses two key objectives: general strategy and overall strategic planning. First, general strategy is translated into specific strategy; second, overall strategic planning is translated into lower-level tactical and operational planning. Each of these steps is discussed next.

Creating a Strategic Plan

After an organization develops a general strategy, it must create an overall strategic plan by extending that general strategy into specific strategic plans for major divisions. Each level of each division translates those objectives into more specific objectives for the level below. For example, a CEO might develop the following general statement of strategy:

Providing the highest quality health care service in the industry.

To execute this broad strategy and turn the general statement into action, the executive team (sometimes called the C-level of the organization, as in CEO, COO, CFO, CIO, and so on) must first define individual responsibilities. For example, the CIO might respond to the CEO's statement with this more specific statement:

Providing high-level health care information service in support of the highest quality health care service in the industry.

The chief operations officer (COO) might derive a different strategic goal that focuses more on his or her specific responsibilities:

Providing the highest quality medical services.

The CISO might interpret the CIO's and COO's goals as follows:

Ensuring that quality health care information services are provided securely and in compliance with all local, state, and federal information processing, information security, and privacy statutes, including HIPAA.

The conversion of goals from the strategic level to the next lower level is perhaps more art than science. It relies on the executive's ability to know and understand the strategic goals of the entire organization, to know and appreciate the strategic and tactical abilities of each unit within the organization, and to negotiate with peers, superiors, and subordinates. This mix of skills helps to achieve the proper balance in articulating goals that fall within performance capabilities.

Planning Levels

Once the organization's overall strategic plan is translated into strategic goals for each major division or operation, the next step is to translate these strategies into tasks with specific, measurable, achievable, and time-bound objectives. Strategic planning then begins a transformation from general, sweeping statements toward more specific and applied objectives. Strategic plans are used to create tactical plans, which are in turn used to develop operational plans. Figure 2-4 illustrates the various planning levels discussed in this section.

Tactical planning has a more short-term focus than strategic planning—usually one to three years. It breaks down each applicable strategic goal into a series of incremental objectives. Each objective should be specific and ideally will have a delivery date within a year.

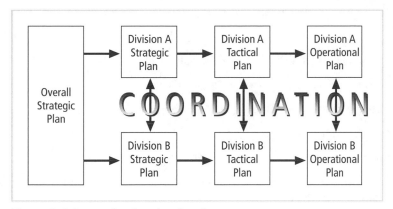

Figure 2-4 Strategic planning levels

Copyright © 2014 Cengage Learning®.

Budgeting, resource allocation, and personnel are critical components of the tactical plan. Although these components may be discussed in general terms at the strategic planning level, they are crucial at the tactical level because they must be in place before the tactical plan can be translated into the operational plan. Tactical plans often include project plans and resource acquisition planning documents (such as product specifications), project budgets, project reviews, and monthly and annual reports.

Because tactical plans are often created for specific projects, some organizations call this process project planning or intermediate planning. The CISO and the security managers use the tactical plan to organize, prioritize, and acquire resources necessary for the major projects and to provide support for the overall strategic plan.

Managers and employees use operational plans, which are derived from the tactical plans, to organize the ongoing, day-to-day performance of tasks. An operational plan includes clearly identified coordination activities that span department boundaries, communications requirements, weekly meetings, summaries, progress reports, and associated tasks. These plans are carefully designed to reflect the organizational structure, with each subunit, department, or project team conducting its own operational planning and reporting components. Frequent communication and feedback from the teams to the project managers and/or team leaders and then up to the various management levels will make the planning process as a whole more manageable and successful.

For example, operational planning within InfoSec may encompass such objectives as the selection, configuration, and deployment of a firewall, or the design and implementation of a security education, training, and awareness (SETA) program. Each of these tasks needs effective tactical planning that covers its entire development life cycle.

Planning and the CISO

The first priority of the CISO and the InfoSec management team should be the structure of a strategic plan. While each organization may have its own format for the design and distribution of a strategic plan, the fundamental elements of planning are the same for all types of enterprises. There are a number of excellent text, trade, and reference books on strategic planning, and the serious InfoSec manager is encouraged to explore this topic.

Here are the basic components of a typical strategic plan:

    I. Executive Summary

   II. Mission Statement and Vision Statement

  III. Organizational Profile and History

  IV. Strategic Issues and Core Values

   V. Program Goals and Objectives

  VI. Management/Operations Goals and Objectives

 VII. Appendices (optional) [strengths, weaknesses, opportunities, and threats (SWOT) analyses, surveys, budgets, etc.][3]

You have already learned about some of these components. Those areas not previously discussed are very straightforward, such as the organizational profile/history, and the appendices. They originate in studies conducted by the organization or highlight information about the environment in which the organization operates. The appendices may help the organization identify new directions or eliminate directions that are less profitable than anticipated. InfoSec planners can consult studies such as the CSI surveys, the "Threats to Information Security" studies described in detail later in this chapter, and internal risk assessments to help identify trends of interest or relevance to the organization. These documents are key resources that can identify areas that should be addressed by the InfoSec strategic plan.

Brian Ward, a principal with Affinity Consulting, offers the following tips for planning:

1. Articulate a comprehensive and meaningful vision statement that communicates what the organization strives to accomplish. It should attract those persons of a like mind to join in the effort to achieve that goal.

2. Endeavor to bring a sense of logical analysis of the objectives and what has been accomplished. Many organizations use a model known as the "balanced scorecard" to track outcomes against intentions to measure effects against prior actions.

3. Work from an overarching plan that has been developed with the input from key stakeholders.

4. Strive for transparency in the planning process so that inevitable changes to plans are explained to stakeholders.

5. Work to make planning a process that engages all involved to work toward the common objectives.

6. Stick with the process over time since results may not always be achieved as quickly as intended.

7. Develop consistent and repeatable methods of planning that are adopted as part of the organization's culture.

8. Explain what is being done so that stakeholders perceive the intentions of the process.

9. Use processes that fit the organization's culture.

10. Make the process as engaging as possible so that participants are not overwhelmed and feel put upon by the required actions.[4]

Information Security Governance

Strategic planning and corporate responsibility is best accomplished using an approach many call **governance, risk management, and compliance (GRC)**. GRC seeks to integrate these three, previously separate responsibilities into one holistic approach that can provide sound executive-level strategic planning and management of the InfoSec function. Governance is covered in the following section; risk management is covered in Chapters 8 and 9; compliance to regulations is covered in Chapter 12. The subjects themselves are neither new nor unique to InfoSec; however, the recognition of the need to integrate the three at the executive level is becoming increasingly important to practitioners in the field.

The governance of InfoSec is a strategic planning responsibility whose importance has grown in recent years. Many consider good InfoSec practices and sound InfoSec governance a component of U.S. homeland security. Unfortunately, InfoSec is all too often regarded as a technical issue when it is, in fact, a management issue. In order to secure information assets, an organization's management must integrate InfoSec practices into the fabric of the organization, expanding corporate governance policies and controls to encompass the objectives of the InfoSec process.

InfoSec objectives must be addressed at the highest levels of an organization's management team in order to be effective and offer a sustainable approach. When security programs are designed and managed as a technical specialty in the IT department, they are less likely to be effective. A broader view of InfoSec encompasses all of an organization's information assets, including the knowledge being managed by those IT assets. These valuable commodities must be protected regardless of how the information is processed, stored, or transmitted, and with a thorough understanding of the risks to, and the benefits of, the information assets.

According to the Information Technology Governance Institute (ITGI), InfoSec governance includes all the accountabilities and methods undertaken by the board of directors and executive management to provide strategic direction, establishment of objectives, measurement of progress toward those objectives, verification that risk management practices are appropriate, and validation that the organization's assets are used properly.[5]

According to the ITGI, boards of directors should supervise strategic InfoSec objectives by:

- Inculcating a culture that recognizes the criticality of information and InfoSec to the organization
- Verifying that management's investment in InfoSec is properly aligned with organizational strategies and the organization's risk environment
- Assuring that a comprehensive InfoSec program is developed and implemented
- Demanding reports from the various layers of management on the InfoSec program's effectiveness and adequacy[6]

Desired Outcomes

InfoSec governance consists of the leadership, organizational structures, and processes that safeguard information. Critical to the success of these structures and processes is effective communication among all parties, which requires constructive relationships, a common language, and shared commitment to addressing the issues.

Done properly, this should result in five basic outcomes of InfoSec governance:

- Strategic alignment of InfoSec with business strategy to support organizational objectives
- Risk management by executing appropriate measures to manage and mitigate threats to information resources
- Resource management by utilizing InfoSec knowledge and infrastructure efficiently and effectively
- Performance measurement by measuring, monitoring, and reporting InfoSec governance metrics to ensure that organizational objectives are achieved
- Value delivery by optimizing InfoSec investments in support of organizational objectives

The National Association of Corporate Directors (NACD), the leading membership organization for boards and directors in the United States, recognizes the importance of InfoSec. It recommends four essential practices for boards of directors:

1. *Place InfoSec on the board's agenda.*
2. *Identify InfoSec leaders, hold them accountable, and ensure support for them.*
3. *Ensure the effectiveness of the corporation's InfoSec policy through review and approval.*
4. *Assign InfoSec to a key committee and ensure adequate support for that committee.*[7]

Benefits of Information Security Governance

InfoSec governance, if properly implemented, can yield significant benefits, including:

- An increase in share value for organizations
- Increased predictability and reduced uncertainty of business operations by lowering information-security-related risks to definable and acceptable levels
- Protection from the increasing potential for civil or legal liability as a result of information inaccuracy or the absence of due care
- Optimization of the allocation of limited security resources
- Assurance of effective InfoSec policy and policy compliance
- A firm foundation for efficient and effective risk management, process improvement, and rapid incident response
- A level of assurance that critical decisions are not based on faulty information
- Accountability for safeguarding information during critical business activities, such as mergers and acquisitions, business process recovery, and regulatory response.[8]

When developing an InfoSec governance program, the designers should ensure that the program includes:

- An InfoSec risk management methodology
- A comprehensive security strategy explicitly linked with business and IT objectives
- An effective security organizational structure
- A security strategy that talks about the value of information being protected and delivered
- Security policies that address each aspect of strategy, control, and regulation
- A complete set of security standards for each policy to ensure that procedures and guidelines comply with policy

- Institutionalized monitoring processes to ensure compliance and provide feedback on effectiveness and mitigation of risk
- A process to ensure continued evaluation and updating of security policies, standards, procedures, and risks

Implementing Information Security Governance

How can an organization implement effective security governance? According to the Corporate Governance Task Force (CGTF), the organization should engage in a core set of activities suited to their needs:

- Conduct an annual InfoSec evaluation, the results of which the CEO should review with staff and then report to the board of directors
- Conduct periodic risk assessments of information assets as part of a risk management program
- Implement policies and procedures based on risk assessments to secure information assets
- Establish a security management structure to assign explicit individual roles, responsibilities, authority, and accountability
- Develop plans and initiate actions to provide adequate InfoSec for networks, facilities, systems, and information
- Treat InfoSec as an integral part of the system life cycle
- Provide InfoSec awareness, training, and education to personnel
- Conduct periodic testing and evaluation of the effectiveness of InfoSec policies and procedures
- Create and execute a plan for remedial action to address any InfoSec deficiencies
- Develop and implement incident response procedures
- Establish plans, procedures, and tests to provide continuity of operations
- Use security best practices guidance, such as the ISO 27000 series, to measure InfoSec performance[9]

The CGTF recommends following a governance framework such as the initiating, diagnosing, establishing, acting, and learning (IDEAL) model, which is named for its stages, as shown in Figure 2-5. The IDEAL model is shown in more detail in Figure 2-6.

This framework, discussed in detail in the document "Information Security Governance: A Call to Action," defines the responsibilities of the board of directors/trustees, the senior organizational executive (i.e., CEO), executive team members, senior managers, and all employees and users. The source document can be found at *www.cyber.st.dhs.gov/docs/Information% 20Security%20Governance-%20A%20Call%20to%20Action%20(2004).pdf*. Figure 2-7 shows the various responsibilities of these functional roles. The document also outlines the requirements for an InfoSec program, discussed in additional detail in Chapter 6 of this text, and provides recommendations for organizational unit reporting and program evaluation.

Security Convergence

The convergence of security-related governance in organizations has been observed since the broad deployment of information systems began in the 1970s and 1980s. The trade press has discussed the issues surrounding this merging of management accountability in the areas of

I	**Initiating**	Lay the groundwork for a successful improvement effort.
D	**Diagnosing**	Determine where you are relative to where you want to be.
E	**Establishing**	Plan the specifics of how you will reach your destination.
A	**Acting**	Do the work according to the plan.
L	**Learning**	Learn from the experience and improve your ability to adopt new improvements in the future.

Figure 2-5 General governance framework

Source: Software Engineering Institute. This publication incorporates portions of "IDEALISM: A User's Guide for Software Process Improvement" by Bob McFeeley, Copyright 1996 Carnegie Mellon University, with special permission from its Software Engineering Institute. Any material of Carnegie Mellon University and/or its Software Engineering Institute contained herein is furnished on an "as-is" basis. Carnegie Mellon University makes no warranties of any kind, either expressed or implied, as to any matter, including, but not limited to, warranty of fitness for purpose or merchant ability, exclusivity, or results obtained from use of the material. Carnegie Mellon University does not make any warranty of any kind with respect to freedom from patent, trademark, or copyright infringement. This publication has not been reviewed nor is it endorsed by Carnegie Mellon University or its Software Engineering Institute. IDEAL^{SM} is a service mark of Carnegie Mellon University.

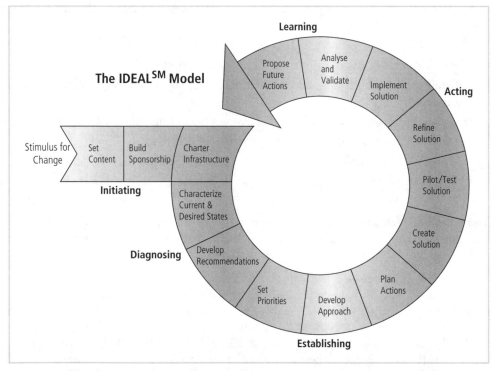

Figure 2-6 The IDEAL model governance framework

Source: Software Engineering Institute. This publication incorporates portions of "IDEALISM: A User's Guide for Software Process Improvement" by Bob McFeeley, Copyright 1996 Carnegie Mellon University, with special permission from its Software Engineering Institute. Any material of Carnegie Mellon University and/or its Software Engineering Institute contained herein is furnished on an "as-is" basis. Carnegie Mellon University makes no warranties of any kind, either expressed or implied, as to any matter, including, but not limited to, warranty of fitness for purpose or merchant ability, exclusivity, or results obtained from use of the material. Carnegie Mellon University does not make any warranty of any kind with respect to freedom from patent, trademark, or copyright infringement. This publication has not been reviewed nor is it endorsed by Carnegie Mellon University or its Software Engineering Institute. IDEAL^{SM} is a service mark of Carnegie Mellon University.

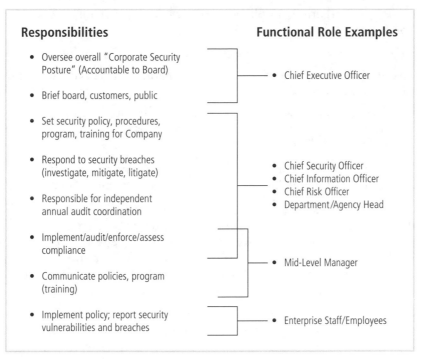

Responsibilities

- Oversee overall "Corporate Security Posture" (Accountable to Board)

- Brief board, customers, public

- Set security policy, procedures, program, training for Company

- Respond to security breaches (investigate, mitigate, litigate)

- Responsible for independent annual audit coordination

- Implement/audit/enforce/assess compliance

- Communicate policies, program (training)

- Implement policy; report security vulnerabilities and breaches

Functional Role Examples

- Chief Executive Officer

- Chief Security Officer
- Chief Information Officer
- Chief Risk Officer
- Department/Agency Head

- Mid-Level Manager

- Enterprise Staff/Employees

Figure 2-7 Information security governance responsibilities

Source: Software Engineering Institute. This publication incorporates portions of "IDEALISM: A User's Guide for Software Process Improvement" by Bob McFeeley, Copyright 1996 Carnegie Mellon University, with special permission from its Software Engineering Institute. Any material of Carnegie Mellon University and/or its Software Engineering Institute contained herein is furnished on an "as-is" basis. Carnegie Mellon University makes no warranties of any kind, either expressed or implied, as to any matter, including, but not limited to, warranty of fitness for purpose or merchant ability, exclusivity, or results obtained from use of the material. Carnegie Mellon University does not make any warranty of any kind with respect to freedom from patent, trademark, or copyright infringement. This publication has not been reviewed nor is it endorsed by Carnegie Mellon University or its Software Engineering Institute. IDEAL℠ is a service mark of Carnegie Mellon University.

corporate (physical) security, corporate risk management, computer security, network security, and InfoSec as such trends waxed and waned over the years. More formal discussion has also occurred, such as a 2005 report titled "Convergence of Enterprise Security Organizations," which the consulting firm Booz Allen Hamilton issued in conjunction with the professional organizations ASIS, ISACA, and ISSA.[10] The report looked at industry practices in the areas of security convergence at U.S.-based global organizations with annual revenues from $1 to $100 billion. And it identified key drivers toward more convergence, including how organizations seek to reduce costs and gain improved results as they reduce their reliance on physical assets and make increased use of logical assets. This is occurring as organizations face increasing compliance and regulatory requirements as well as ongoing pressures to reduce costs. The report concluded that while convergence is a driving force, the real value remains in aligning security functions (whether converged or diverged) with the business mission.

A 2007 report prepared by the consulting firm Deloitte, which was commissioned by the Alliance for Enterprise Security Risk Management, further explored the topic of convergence and identified enterprise risk management (ERM) as a value-adding approach that can gain superior alignment of security functions with the business mission while offering opportunities to lower costs.[11] While that report limits its perspective to the two traditional facets of ERM control elements (i.e., IT security and physical security), it does identify the key approaches organizations are using to achieve unified ERM, including:

- Combining physical security and InfoSec under one leader as one business function
- Using separate business functions (each with a separate budget and autonomy) that report to a common senior executive
- Using a risk council approach to provide a collaborative approach to risk management where representatives from across the organization work collectively to set policy about assuming risk to the organization

The Deloitte report proposes the risk council approach as the preferred mechanism and goes on to explore what makes effective ERM and how risk councils can be used to best effect.

In 2007, the Open Compliance and Ethics Group commissioned a report to explore some of the complexities of GRC and how these key functions might best be executed.[12] The key finding of this report is that GRC functions (including those defined as part of ERM) are often fragmented and often not integrated to the degree needed for streamlined operations. The report also identified the benefits of increased levels of ERM along with integration and convergence of governance and compliance business functions.

The current accepted industry practices are toward achieving a synthesis of these approaches to reap the benefits of ERM. This could mean the degree to which an organization integrates managerial command and control over the multiple risk control facilities within that organization in order to address the business mission requirements to manage risk and conform to compliance objectives.

Today, most organizations of appreciable size have moved toward the maximum degree of convergence suitable for their form of governance while working within the limits of geographic and organizational dispersion. We can therefore assume that there is a natural inclination toward more security convergence.

Planning for Information Security Implementation

The CIO and CISO play important roles in translating overall strategic planning into tactical and operational InfoSec plans. Depending on the InfoSec function's placement within the organizational chart (discussed in detail in Chapter 5), the objectives of the CIO and the CISO may differ. Most commonly, the CISO reports directly to the CIO. In that case, the CIO charges the CISO and other IT department heads with creating and adopting plans that are consistent with and supportive of the entire organizational strategy. The CIO must also ensure that the various IT functional areas in the organization provide broad support for the plan and that no areas are omitted or ignored.

The CISO plays a more active role in the development of the planning details than the CIO does. Consider the following job description for the InfoSec department manager from Charles Cresson Wood's *Information Security Roles and Responsibilities Made Easy*:

- *Creates a strategic InfoSec plan with a vision for the future of InfoSec at Company X (utilizing evolving InfoSec technology, this vision meets a variety of objectives such as management's fiduciary and legal responsibilities, customer expectations for secure modern business practices, and the competitive requirements of the marketplace)*

View Point
The Role of the Chief Security Officer
By Robert Lang, Assistant Vice President for Strategic Security and Safety at Kennesaw State University

The evolution of the role of the CSO should instead be called a "revolution" of the role of the CSO since that role has seen great change in recent years, to the betterment of all concerned. In prior years, the CSO position was usually dedicated to InfoSec, focusing mainly on the ever-present disaster recovery issue, which every company using IT faces. In that role, the CSO's primary concern was to maintain a continuity of operations for the IT department. However, some CSOs also focused on physical security (personnel as well as the physical plant and critical infrastructure), leading them to an interest in the IT needed to maintain those operations.

The main weakness in putting one person in charge of both the IT infrastructure and the physical security of people and buildings is the inherent tendency to point fingers when incidents occur. If controls to mitigate loss fail or the plans to optimize incident response come up short, the situation usually devolves into name-calling and accusations of professional malfeasance toward the other half of the security program.

Many people use the term "convergence" to describe the effort to merge the IT protection role and the physical asset protection and personnel safety role. This trend has progressed rapidly in recent years. This is particularly noticeable in the convergence of the technical means of control used by each side merging into common systems. For example, video surveillance using security cameras and central monitoring stations is often implemented over the common networking infrastructure from the IT department. As physical security programs using security guards and even sworn officers seek to optimize costs, they rely on advanced and integrated IT systems. This convergence is resisted by some, with claims of specialized expertise or incompatible objectives. However, the trend toward security convergence continues.

By accepting the emerging reality that a CSO is no longer limited to being the chief *physical* security officer, the door is now open to enable more organizations to navigate their way to a security convergence that is the right way for them to organize their efforts. Done properly, this will result in a seamless program that embraces the concept that all organization members—employee or contractor, security guard or secretary, salesman or manager—are responsible for what happens within the facility.

Best practices in business, government, and nonprofit organizations alike require a collective responsibility for InfoSec, incident response, disaster recovery, and business

(Continued)

continuity. Most organizations resisting the convergence of these practices focus on one at the expense of the others. Eventually, the imperative to converge will become obvious. In the meantime, organizations that seek to "put on a show" of physical security, with security officers stationed at the front door, but that don't try to integrate their physical and InfoSec are essentially waiting for the next crisis or incident to forced them to account for their lack of preparation.

In each organization, the CSO's new role awaits the emergence of a manager who has the power to invoke change, who looks at the broad view of the organization, and who is motivated to institutionalize control programs to limit the risk from the broad spectrum of security concerns. This new vision for converged security goes well beyond guards, badges, and sign-in procedures. It seeks to integrate the best of physical security and asset protection with InfoSec processes. Thus, it spans disaster recovery, password protection, identity management, and all of the solutions that are deployed to manage operational risk from the myriad threats all organizations face. The best organizations achieve an integrated ERM program in which business continuity is not just a program or a check box on an audit report, but an organizational culture making all processes in the organization seamlessly resilient and recoverable.

The CSO's new role is that of an agent of change. Without easing up on the roles they've been playing in physical security and safety, CSOs must integrate those aspects that come from information protection. Finding the change agent needed to make this a reality is challenging. That person must have skills and understanding that embrace physical security and InfoSec while also having a deep understanding of the threat environment. Creating an ERM and business continuity culture will require definition or redefinition of the many processes and procedures already in place, but with an understanding that no real change can occur until all the people in the organization know what to do, how to do it, and are comfortable with reacting swiftly and diligently during any untoward event.

Does this new CSO have to be equipped with all the detailed expertise and all the experience to perform each and every aspect of the job? In a perfect world, probably. In this world, the knowledge and experience may not need to be as deep or as detailed. The more important ability is a vision that transcends the arbitrary division of security responsibilities that are keeping an organization from being able to plan, react, and recover from *any* untoward event. This person must do all that while maintaining a security posture that, though unobtrusive, maintains an effective degree of security and safety presence at all times.

The CSO's role is undergoing significant change. Every new threat that emerges, each new risk that is identified, and every new technology that emerges will continue to change the role. A better tile for this role might therefore be "chief resilience officer," since the quest for resilience is a key element of every successful organization and the key characteristic of the new CSO.

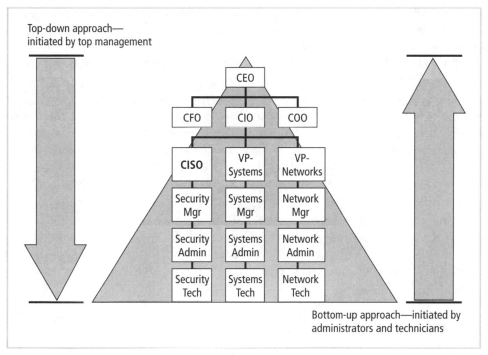

Top-down approach—
initiated by top management

Bottom-up approach—initiated by
administrators and technicians

Figure 2-8 Approaches to security implementation

Copyright © 2014 Cengage Learning®.

- *Understands the fundamental business activities performed by Company X and, based on this understanding, suggests appropriate InfoSec solutions that uniquely protect these activities*
- *Develops action plans, schedules, budgets, status reports, and other management communications intended to improve the status of InfoSec at Company X[13]*

Once the organization's overall strategic plan has been translated into IT and InfoSec departmental objectives by the CIO, and then further translated into tactical and operational plans by the CISO, the implementation of InfoSec can begin.

Implementation of InfoSec can be accomplished in two ways: bottom-up or top-down. These two basic approaches are illustrated in Figure 2-8.

The **bottom-up approach** might begin as a grass-roots effort in which systems administrators attempt to improve the security of their systems. The key advantage of this approach is that it utilizes the technical expertise of the individual administrators who work with the information systems on a daily basis. System and network administrators possess in-depth knowledge that can greatly enhance the state of InfoSec in the organization. These professionals know and understand many of the threats to their systems and the mechanisms needed to protect them successfully. Unfortunately, this approach seldom works, as it lacks a number of critical features, such as coordinated planning from upper management, coordination between departments, and the provision of sufficient resources.

The **top-down approach**, in contrast, features strong upper-management support, a dedicated champion, usually assured funding, a clear planning and implementation process, and the ability to influence organizational culture. High-level managers provide resources; give direction; issue policies, procedures, and processes; dictate the goals and expected outcomes of the project; and determine who is accountable for each of the required actions. The most successful top-down approach also incorporates a formal development strategy referred to as the systems development life cycle (SDLC).

For any top-down approach to succeed, high-level management must buy into the effort and provide its full support to all departments. Such an initiative must have a **champion**—ideally, an executive with sufficient influence to move the project forward, ensure that it is properly managed, and push for its acceptance throughout the organization. Typically, the champion of a far-reaching InfoSec program is the CIO or another senior executive such as the vice president of information technology (VP-IT). Without this high-level support, many mid-level administrators fail to dedicate enough resources to the project or dismiss it as a low priority.

Involvement and support of end users is also critical to the success of this type of effort. Because the process and outcome of the initiative most directly affect these individuals, they must be included in the InfoSec planning process. Key end users should be assigned to design teams, known as **joint application design (JAD)—teams**. A successful JAD must be able to survive employee turnover; it should not be vulnerable to changes in personnel. For this reason, the processes and procedures must be documented and integrated into organizational culture. They must be adopted and promoted by the organization's management. These attributes are seldom found in projects that begin as bottom-up initiatives. In order for the JAD approach to be successful, the following key steps are recommended:

1. Identify project objectives and limitations.
2. Identify critical success factors.
3. Define project deliverables.
4. Define the schedule of workshop activities.
5. Select the participants.
6. Prepare the workshop material.
7. Organize workshop activities and exercises.
8. Prepare, inform, and educate the workshop participants.
9. Coordinate workshop logistics.[14]

The success of InfoSec plans can be enhanced by using the processes of system analysis and design, a discipline that is an integral part of most academic curricula in the field of IT. The following sections offer a brief overview of this topic but do not replace a more detailed study of the discipline.

Introduction to the Security Systems Development Life Cycle

In general, an SDLC is a methodology for the design and implementation of an information system in an organization. A **methodology** is a formal approach to solving a problem based on a structured sequence of procedures. Using a methodology ensures a rigorous process and increases the likelihood of achieving the desired final objective. Organizations often reuse a successful methodology as they gain experience with it. This tried-and-true approach is combined with sound project management practices to develop key project milestones, allocate resources, select personnel, and perform the tasks needed to accomplish a project's objectives.

Sometimes, the SDLC is used to develop custom applications or deploy a purchased solution. A variation of this methodology, used to create a comprehensive security posture, is called the security systems development life cycle (SecSDLC).

System projects may be initiated in response to specific conditions or combinations of conditions. The impetus to begin an SDLC-based project may be **event-driven**—that is, a response to some event in the business community, inside the organization, or within the ranks of employees, customers, or other stakeholders. Alternatively, it could be **plan-driven**—that is, the result of a carefully developed planning strategy. Either way, once an organization recognizes the need for a project, the use of a methodology can ensure that development proceeds in an orderly, comprehensive fashion. At the end of each phase, a **structured review** or reality check takes place, during which the team and its management-level reviewers decide whether the project should be continued, discontinued, outsourced, or postponed until additional expertise or organizational knowledge is acquired.

The following sections illustrate an approach to the SecSDLC that uses a traditional waterfall model SDLC. The term "waterfall model" indicates that the work products of each phase fall into the next phase to serve as its starting point. While the SecSDLC may differ from the traditional SDLC in several specific activities, the overall methodology is the same. The SecSDLC process involves the identification of specific threats and the risks that they represent as well as the subsequent design and implementation of specific controls to counter those threats and manage the risk. The process turns InfoSec into a coherent program rather than a series of responses to individual threats and attacks. Figure 2-9 shows the phases in the SecSDLC.

While there are a number of other models besides the waterfall model, the intent is to use the waterfall as an illustrative method of understanding the base requirements. The current recommended practice is to use a methodology that has a specific set of stages, which also requires periodic review of previous efforts, and can, as needed, revert or redirect to a previous stage if progress is currently unsatisfactory. The waterfall model is not intended as the definitive approach, nor is it represented as the only approach. Organizations may prefer other models, like the Spiral, agile development, or rapid application development. Here, however, the waterfall approach will serve as a basis for discussion.

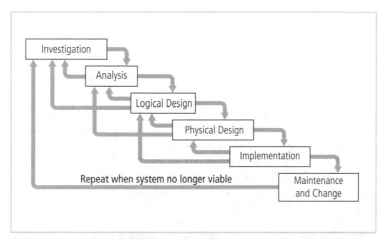

Figure 2-9 SDLC Waterfall methodology

Copyright © 2014 Cengage Learning®.

Investigation in the SecSDLC The investigation phase of the SecSDLC begins with a directive from upper management specifying the process, outcomes, and goals of the project as well as its budget and other constraints. Frequently, this phase begins with the affirmation or creation of security policies on which the security program of the organization is or will be founded. Teams of managers, employees, and consultants are assembled to investigate problems, define their scope, specify goals and objectives, and identify any additional constraints not covered in the enterprise security policy. (A more detailed treatment of InfoSec policy is presented in Chapter 4.) Finally, an organizational feasibility analysis determines whether the organization has the resources and commitment to conduct a successful security analysis and design.

Unfortunately, many InfoSec projects are initiated in response to a significant security breach within an organization. While these circumstances may not be the ideal conditions under which to begin work on an organization's InfoSec posture, the SecSDLC team should emphasize that improvement is now under way.

Analysis in the SecSDLC In the analysis phase, the team studies the documents from the investigation phase. The development team that was assembled during the investigation phase conducts a preliminary analysis of existing security policies or programs along with documented current threats and associated controls. This phase also includes an analysis of relevant legal issues that could affect the design of the security solution. Increasingly, privacy laws are a major consideration when making decisions about information systems that manage personal information. Recently, many state legislatures have made certain computer-related activities that were once unregulated illegal, so a detailed understanding of these issues is vital.

The risk management task also begins in this stage. Risk management is the process of identifying, assessing, and evaluating the levels of risk an organization faces—specifically, the threats to the organization's security and to the information stored and processed by the organization. In this context, it is helpful to ponder the words of the famous Chinese general Sun Tzu:

> If you know the enemy and know yourself, you need not fear the result of a hundred battles. If you know yourself but not the enemy, for every victory gained you will also suffer a defeat. If you know neither the enemy nor yourself, you will succumb in every battle.[15]

The analysis process begins by getting to know your adversary. In InfoSec, the adversary is the entire set of threats and attacks that your systems face as they provide services to your organization and its customers.

To better understand the analysis phase of the SecSDLC, you should know something about the kinds of threats facing organizations in the modern, connected world of IT. In this context, a **threat** is an object, person, or other entity that represents a constant danger to an asset. While each enterprise's categorization of threats will vary, threats are relatively well researched and consequently fairly well understood. To better understand the numerous threats facing an organization, a scheme has been developed to group threats by their respective activities. This model consists of 12 general categories that represent real and present dangers to an organization's information and systems. Table 2-1 lists and briefly describes these 12 categories, which are discussed in the following sections.

Compromises to Intellectual Property The owner of intellectual property has the right to control proprietary ideas as well as their tangible or virtual representations. Information

Threat	Description/Example
Compromises to intellectual property	Software piracy or other copyright infringement
Deviations in quality of service from service providers	Fluctuations in power, data, and other services
Espionage or trespass	Unauthorized access and/or data collection
Forces of nature	Fire, flood, earthquake, lightning, etc.
Human error or failure	Accidents, employee mistakes, failure to follow policy
Information extortion	Blackmail threat of information disclosure
Sabotage or vandalism	Damage to or destruction of systems or information
Software attacks	Malware: viruses, worms, macros, denial-of-services, or script injections
Technical hardware failures or errors	Hardware equipment failure
Technical software failures or errors	Bugs, code problems, loopholes, back doors
Technological obsolescence	Antiquated or outdated technologies
Theft	Illegal confiscation of equipment or information

Table 2-1   Threats to information security[16]

Copyright © 2014 Cengage Learning®.

about an organization's intellectual property can be of great interest to its competitors and can be accidentally or deliberately disseminated to those outside the organization.

Deviations in Quality of Service by Service Providers Sometimes, a product or service is not delivered as expected. The organization's information system depends on the successful operation of many interdependent support systems, including power grids, telecommunications networks, parts suppliers, service vendors, and even the janitorial staff and garbage haulers.

The threat of irregularities from power utilities is common. When they occur they can lead to several types of power fluctuations:

- A voltage-level spike (a momentary increase)
- A surge (a prolonged increase)
- A momentary low voltage or sag
- A more prolonged drop in voltage, called a brownout
- A complete loss of power for a moment, called a fault
- A more lengthy loss, known as a blackout

Espionage or Trespass This category encompasses a broad array of electronic and human activities that can breach the confidentiality of information. When an unauthorized individual gains access to information that an organization is trying to protect, that access is categorized as a deliberate act of espionage or trespass.

Forces of Nature   Forces of nature (known as "force majeure") or acts of God pose some of the most dangerous threats imaginable because they can occur with very little warning. These include fire, flood, earthquake, and lightning, as well as volcanic eruption and insect infestation.

Human Error or Failure   When people use information systems, mistakes sometimes happen. Inexperience, improper training, the making of incorrect assumptions, and other circumstances can cause these problems. People also fail to follow policy, whether through ignorance or intentionally. Such failures can also threaten an organization's information assets.

Information Extortion   Information extortion occurs when an attacker or formerly trusted insider steals information from a computer system and then demands compensation for its return or for an agreement to not disclose the information. This practice is common in credit card number theft.

Sabotage or Vandalism   Individuals or groups may attempt to sabotage the operations of a computer system or business, or they may perform acts of vandalism, either to destroy an asset or damage the organization's image. These threats range from petty vandalism by employees to Web page defacement by outside persons or groups.

Software Attacks   Deliberate software attacks occur when an individual or group designs software—often called malicious code or software, or malware—to attack a vulnerable system. Some of the more common types of malicious code are viruses, worms, Trojan horses, logic bombs, and back doors.

Technical Hardware Failures or Errors   Technical hardware failures or errors occur when a manufacturer distributes equipment containing a known or unknown flaw. These defects can cause the system to perform outside of expected parameters, resulting in unreliable service or lack of availability.

Technical Software Failures or Errors   Technical software failures or errors occur when a developer distributes software with known or unknown hidden faults. These faults may range from bugs to untested failure conditions.

Technological Obsolescence   When the infrastructure becomes antiquated or outdated, it leads to unreliable and untrustworthy systems that may be difficult to maintain without extensive investment of resources.

Theft   Theft is the illegal taking of another's property, whether physical, electronic, or intellectual.

The preceding list of threats may be manifested as attacks against the assets of the organization. An **attack** is an act or event that exploits a vulnerability. A **vulnerability** is an identified weakness of a controlled information asset and is the result of absent or inadequate controls. An attack is accomplished by a **threat agent**—the specific instance of a threat—that damages or steals an organization's information or physical assets. An **exploit** is a technique or mechanism used to compromise an information asset. A technical attack may use an exploit to compromise a controlled system, whereas a nontechnical attack may result from natural events or less sophisticated approaches. Here are some types of technical attacks:

- *Back door*—A feature left behind by system designers or maintenance staff or installed by malicious code to allow quick access at a later time, bypassing access controls

- *Brute force*—The application of computing and network resources to try every possible combination of values in order to compromise a control, read encrypted data, or crack a password

- *Buffer overflow*—An application error that occurs when more data is sent to a buffer than it can handle, often performed intentionally to force a system to interpret data as system commands or to overwhelm a system's ability to process input

- *Denial-of-service (DoS) and distributed denial-of-service (DDoS)*—The transmission of a large number of connection or information requests to a target, thereby blocking other, legitimate traffic; called a DDoS when multiple systems are organized into a simultaneous attack

- *Dictionary*—An attempt to narrow the field of possible password values by selecting specific accounts as targets and/or using a list of common values (the dictionary) with which to guess, rather than simply trying random combinations

- *DNS cache poisoning*—The replacement of legitimate information in a DNS server with a Web site or other Internet location the attacker wants the user to view; also known as a "redirect attack"

- *Hoax*—False report of a threat or attack, resulting in a waste of time and resources

- *Mail bombing*—The routing of large quantities of e-mail to the target in an effort to overwhelm the system

- *Malicious code*—The execution of viruses, worms, Trojan horses, and active Web scripts with the intent to destroy, steal, or deny access to information assets

- *Man-in-the-middle*—The commandeering of a network connection session so that an attacker can read and perhaps modify the data transferred in that connection; one approach to this end is also known as a "TCP hijacking attack"

- *Password crack*—An attempt to reverse-calculate or guess a password; includes dictionary attacks, brute force attacks, and man-in-the-middle attacks

- *Phishing*—A specialized social engineering attack in which the attacker uses an e-mail or forged Web site to attempt to extract personal information from a user

- *Sniffer*—A program or device that can monitor and intercept data traveling over a network; a legal tool when used by the network owners to regulate traffic, an illegal tool when used as part of an attack

- *Social engineering*—The use of social skills to convince people to reveal access credentials or other valuable information

- *Spam*—Unsolicited commercial e-mail, the electronic equivalent of junk mail; often used as a denial of service effort, an element of a compromise that introduces a malware attack, or an effort to waste organizational resources

- *Spear phishing*—A targeted social engineering attack in which the attacker crafts an individualized letter or e-mail to attempt to extract personal information from an unsuspecting user

- *Spoofing*—A technique used to gain unauthorized access to computers, whereby the intruder sends network-level messages to a computer with an IP address indicating that the message is coming from a trusted host

- *Timing*—An attack that enables an attacker to extract secrets maintained in a security system by observing the time it takes the system to respond to various queries

The last step in "knowing the enemy" is to find some method of prioritizing the risk posed by each category of threat and its related methods of attack. This can be done by adopting threat levels from an existing study of threats or by creating your own categorization of threats for your environment, based on scenario analyses.

The next task in the analysis phase is to assess the relative risk for each of the information assets via a process called risk assessment or risk analysis, both of which are components of risk management. **Risk management** is the part of the SecSDLC analysis phase that identifies vulnerabilities in an organization's information system and takes carefully reasoned steps to assure the confidentiality, integrity, and availability of all components in the organization's information system. Risk management is covered in detail in Chapter 9.

Risk assessment assigns a comparative risk rating or score to each specific information asset. While this number does not mean anything in absolute terms, it is useful in gauging the relative risk introduced by each vulnerable information asset and allows you to make comparative ratings later in the risk control process. Risk assessment is covered in detail in Chapter 8.

Design in the SecSDLC   The SecSDLC design phase consists of two distinct phases: the logical design and the physical design. In the logical design phase, team members create and develop the blueprint for security, and they examine and implement key policies that influence later decisions. At this stage, critical contingency plans for incident response are developed. Next, a feasibility analysis determines whether the project should continue in-house or should be outsourced.

In the physical design phase, team members evaluate the technology needed to support the security blueprint, generate alternative solutions, and agree on a final design. The security blueprint may be revisited to keep it synchronized with the changes needed when the physical design is completed. Criteria for determining the definition of successful solutions are also prepared during this phase, as are designs for physically securing the technological solutions. At the end of this phase, a feasibility study should determine the readiness of the organization for the proposed project, and then the champion and users should be presented with the design. At that point, the interested parties have a chance to approve (or not approve) the project before implementation begins.

During the logical and physical design phases, a security manager may seek to use established security models to guide the design process. Security models provide frameworks for ensuring that all areas of security are addressed; organizations can adapt or adopt a framework to meet their own InfoSec needs. A number of InfoSec frameworks have been published; several are discussed in detail in Chapters 5 and 6 and in the appendix.

One of the design elements (or, in some projects, redesign elements) of the InfoSec program is the organization's InfoSec policy. The meaning of the term "security policy" differs depending on the context in which it is used. Governmental agencies, for example, discuss security policy in terms of national security and interaction with foreign states. In another context, a security policy can be part of a credit card agency's method of processing credit card numbers. In general, a security policy consists of a set of rules that protects an organization's assets. An information security policy provides rules for the protection of the information assets of an organization. As stated in Chapter 1, the task of the InfoSec program is to protect the confidentiality, integrity, and availability of information and information systems, whether in transit, storage, or processing. This task is accomplished by the application of policy, education and training programs, and technology. Management must define three types of security policies, as specified in the National Institute of Standards and Technology's (NIST's) "Special Publication 800-100": general or enterprise InfoSec policy (EISP), issue-specific security policies (ISSPs), and systems-specific security policies (SysSPs). Each of these is covered in detail in Chapter 4.

Another integral part of the InfoSec program is the SETA program, discussed in detail in Chapter 5. Part of the CISO's responsibilities, the SETA program is a control measure designed to reduce accidental security breaches by employees. As mentioned earlier, employee errors represent one of the top threats to information assets; for this reason, it is well worth expending resources to develop programs to combat this problem. SETA programs are designed to supplement the general InfoSec education and training programs that are already in place. Good practice dictates that the SDLC include user training during the implementation phase. Employee training should be managed to ensure that all employees are trained properly.

The design phase continues with the formulation of the controls and safeguards used to protect information from attacks by threats. The terms **control** and **safeguard** are often used interchangeably. There are three categories of controls: managerial controls, operational controls, and technical controls.

Managerial controls cover security processes that are designed by the strategic planners and executed by the security administration of the organization. They set the direction and scope of the security process and provide detailed instructions for its conduct. Managerial controls address the design and implementation of the security planning process and security program management. They also address risk management and security controls reviews (discussed in detail in Chapters 8 and 9). Management controls further describe the necessity and scope of legal compliance and the maintenance of the entire security life cycle.

Operational controls deal with the operational functionality of security in the organization. They cover detailed/tactical management functions and lower-level planning, such as disaster recovery and incident response planning (IRP). In addition, these controls address personnel security, physical security, and the protection of production inputs and outputs. Operational controls also provide structure to the development of education, training, and awareness programs for users, administrators, and management. Finally, they address hardware and software systems maintenance and the integrity of data.

Technical controls address technical approaches used to implement security in the organization. Operational controls address specific operational issues, such as control development and integration into business functions, while technical controls must be selected, acquired (made or bought), and integrated into the organization's IT structure. Technical controls include logical access controls, such as those used for identification, authentication, authorization, and accountability.

Another element of the design phase is the creation of essential preparedness documents. Managers in the IT and InfoSec communities engage in strategic planning to assure the continuous availability of the organization's information systems. In addition, managers of the organization must be ready to respond when an attack occurs. The various plans for handling attacks, disasters, or other types of incidents include business continuity plans, disaster recovery plans (DRPs), and incident response plans (IR plans). These are often known collectively as contingency plans. In large, complex organizations, each of these named plans may represent separate but related planning functions, differing in scope, applicability, and design. In a small organization, the security administrator (or systems administrator) may have one simple plan, which consists of a straightforward set of media backup and recovery strategies and a few service agreements from the company's service providers. The sad reality is that many organizations have a level of response planning that is woefully deficient.

Incident response, disaster recovery, and BCP are all components of CP. CP is the overall planning conducted by the organization to prepare for, react to, and recover from events that threaten the security of information assets in the organization, and to provide for the subsequent restoration to normal business operations. Organizations need to develop DRPs, IR plans, and business continuity plans as subsets of the overall CP. IRP is the planning process associated with the identification, classification, response, and recovery from an incident. DRP is the planning process associated with the preparation for and recovery from a disaster, whether natural or human-made. BCP is the planning process associated with ensuring that critical business functions continue if a catastrophic incident or disaster occurs. These critical building blocks of response planning are presented in Chapter 3.

The design phase next addresses physical security, which requires the design, implementation, and maintenance of countermeasures to protect the physical resources of an organization. Physical resources include people, hardware, and the supporting system elements and resources associated with the management of information in all its states—transmission, storage, and processing. Many technology-based controls can be circumvented if an attacker gains physical access to the devices being controlled. For example, when employees fail to secure a server console, the operating system running on that computer becomes vulnerable to attack. Some computer systems are constructed in such a way that it is easy to steal the hard drive and the information it contains. As a result, physical security should receive as much attention as logical security in the security development life cycle. For further discussions on the dimension of physical security, consult one of the many fine text, trade, or reference books on the subject.

Implementation in the SecSDLC The SecSDLC implementation phase is similar to the corresponding phase of the traditional SDLC. Security solutions are acquired (made or bought), tested, implemented, and retested. Personnel issues are evaluated and specific training and education programs are conducted. Finally, the entire tested package is presented to upper management for final approval.

The InfoSec systems software or application systems selection process is not appreciably different from that for general IT needs. Vendors should be provided with detailed specifications, and they should in turn provide detailed information about products and costs. As in IT system implementation, it is essential to establish clear specifications and rigorous test plans to assure a high-quality implementation.

Perhaps the most important element of the implementation phase is the management of the project plan. Project management is a process that underlies all phases of the SecSDLC. The execution of the project plan proceeds in three steps:

1. Planning the project
2. Supervising the tasks and action steps within the project plan
3. Wrapping up the project plan

The project plan can be developed in any number of ways. Each organization must determine its own project management methodology for IT and InfoSec projects. Whenever possible, InfoSec projects should follow the organizational practices of project management. For organizations that have not established clearly defined project management practices, the following pages supply general guidelines on recommended practices. Project management and its relationship to InfoSec were described in detail in Chapter 1.

InfoSec is a field with a vast array of technical and nontechnical requirements. For this reason, the project team should include individuals who are experienced in one or more requirements of both the technical and nontechnical areas. Many of the same skills needed to manage and implement security are needed to design it. Members of the development team fill the following roles:

- *Champion*—A senior executive who promotes the project and ensures its support, both financially and administratively, at the highest levels of the organization
- *Team leader*—A project manager (perhaps a departmental line manager or staff unit manager) who understands project management, personnel management, and InfoSec technical requirements
- *Security policy developers*—Individuals who understand the organizational culture, existing policies, and requirements for developing and implementing successful policies
- *Risk assessment specialists*—Individuals who understand financial risk assessment techniques, the value of organizational assets, and the security methods to be used
- *Security professionals*—Dedicated, trained, and well-educated specialists in all aspects of InfoSec from both technical and nontechnical standpoints
- *Systems administrators*—Individuals with the primary responsibility for administering the systems that house the information used by the organization
- *End users*—The individuals whom the new system will most directly affect; ideally, a disparate group of users from various departments and levels, and with varying

degrees of technical knowledge, to assist the team in applying realistic controls in ways that do not disrupt the essential business activities they seek to safeguard

Just as each potential employee and each potential employer looks for the best fit during the hiring process, so each organization should thoroughly examine its options when staffing the InfoSec function. When implementing InfoSec in an organization, many human resource issues must be addressed. First, the entire organization must decide how to position and name the security function within the organization. Second, the InfoSec community of interest must plan for the proper staffing (or adjustments to the staffing plan) for the InfoSec function. Third, the IT community of interest must understand how InfoSec affects every role in the IT function and adjust job descriptions and documented practices accordingly. Finally, the general management community of interest must work with the InfoSec professionals to integrate solid InfoSec concepts into the personnel management practices of the organization as a whole.

It takes a wide range of professionals to support a diverse InfoSec program. Because a good security plan is initiated from the top down, senior management is the key component and vital force driving the successful implementation of an InfoSec program. To develop and execute specific security policies and procedures, additional administrative support is required. Finally, technical expertise is necessary to implement the details of the security operation.

Here are more precise descriptions of the various roles involved in InfoSec:

- **Chief information officer (CIO)**—Senior technology officer responsible for aligning the strategic efforts of the organization and integrating them into action plans for the information systems or data-processing division of the organization
- **Chief security officer (CSO)**—This job title may be used in lieu of "CISO"; however, when it is used to refer to a role that is superior to the CISO, this is the individual responsible for the protection of all physical and information resources within the organization
- **Chief information security officer (CISO)**—The individual responsible for the assessment, management, and implementation of information-protection activities in the organization
- **Security managers**—The individuals accountable for ensuring the day-to-day operation of the InfoSec program, accomplishing the objectives identified by the CISO and resolving issues identified by technicians
- **Security technicians**—Technically qualified individuals who are tasked with configuring firewalls and intrusion detection systems (commonly referred to as IDSs), implementing security software, diagnosing and troubleshooting problems, and coordinating with systems and network administrators to ensure that security technology is properly implemented
- **Data owners**—Individuals who control (and are therefore responsible for) the security and use of a particular set of information. Data owners may rely on custodians for the practical aspects of protecting their information, specifying which users are authorized to access it, but they are ultimately responsible for it
- **Data custodians**—Individuals who work directly with data owners and are responsible for the storage, maintenance, and protection of the information
- **Data users**—Systems users who work with the information to perform their daily jobs supporting the mission of the organization, everyone in the organization being responsible for the security of data (and thus playing an InfoSec role)

All these roles are presented in greater depth in Chapter 11.

Many organizations seek employees or contractors who have professional certifications so that they can more easily identify these individuals' proficiency. A thorough discussion of InfoSec industry certification approaches and programs is also provided in Chapter 11.

Maintenance in the SecSDLC The maintenance and change phase, though last, is perhaps the most important, given the flexibility and persistence of many of the threats facing the modern organization. Today's InfoSec systems need constant monitoring, testing, modifying, updating, and repairing. Traditional applications systems that are developed within the framework of the SDLC are not designed to anticipate a vicious attack that requires some degree of application reconstruction as a normal course of operation. In security, the battle for stable, reliable systems is a defensive one. As new threats emerge and old threats evolve, the InfoSec profile of an organization requires constant adaptation to prevent threats from successfully penetrating sensitive data.

Once the InfoSec program is implemented, it must be operated, properly managed, and kept up-to-date by means of established procedures. If the program is not adjusting adequately to the changes in the internal or external environment, it may be necessary to begin the cycle

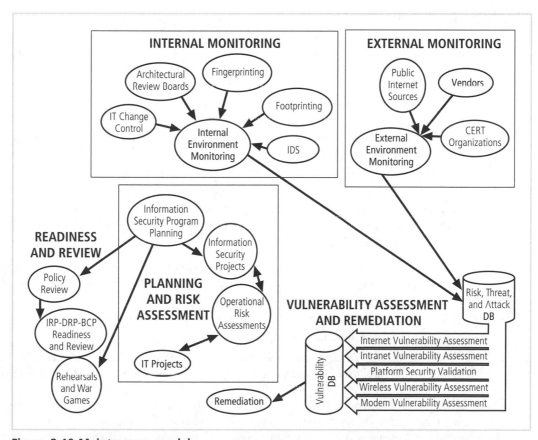

Figure 2-10 Maintenance model

Copyright © 2014 Cengage Learning®.

again. The CISO determines whether the InfoSec group can adapt adequately and maintain the InfoSec profile of the organization, or whether the macroscopic process of the SecSDLC must start anew to redevelop a fundamentally different InfoSec profile. It is less expensive and more effective when an InfoSec program is able to deal with change. Even when an InfoSec program is adapting and growing, those processes of maintenance and change mirror the overall process of the SecSDLC, differing only in scope. As deficiencies are found and vulnerabilities pinpointed, projects to maintain, extend, or enhance the program follow the SecSDLC steps. Therefore, for maintenance, the steps include investigation, analysis, design, and implementation.

Whereas a systems management model is designed to manage and operate systems, a maintenance model is intended to complement a systems management model and focus those ongoing maintenance efforts that are needed to keep systems useable and secure. Figure 2-10 presents one recommended approach for dealing with InfoSec. The model consists of five subject areas or domains, as described in the following sections.

External Monitoring   The objective of external monitoring within the maintenance model shown in Figure 2-10 is to provide early awareness of new and emerging threats, threat agents, vulnerabilities, and attacks, thereby enabling the creation of an effective and timely defense.

Internal Monitoring   The primary objective of internal monitoring is to maintain an informed awareness of the state of all the organization's networks, information systems, and InfoSec defenses. This status must be communicated and documented, especially the status of the parts of information systems that are connected to the external network.

Planning and Risk Assessment   The primary objective of planning and risk assessment is to keep a wary eye on the entire InfoSec program. This is achieved in part by identifying and planning ongoing InfoSec activities that further reduce risk. Also, the risk assessment group identifies and documents risks introduced by both IT projects and InfoSec projects. Furthermore, it identifies and documents risks that may be latent in the present environment.

Vulnerability Assessment and Remediation   The primary objective of vulnerability assessment and remediation is the identification of specific, documented vulnerabilities and their timely remediation. This is accomplished by:

- Using documented vulnerability assessment procedures to safely collect intelligence about networks (internal and public-facing), platforms (servers, desktops, and process control), dial-in modems, and wireless network systems
- Documenting background information and providing tested remediation procedures for the reported vulnerabilities
- Tracking, communicating, and reporting to management the itemized facts about the discovered vulnerabilities and the success or failure of the organization to remediate them

Vulnerability assessment involves the physical and logical assessment of the vulnerabilities present in both InfoSec and related nonsecurity systems. This analysis is most often accomplished with penetration testing. In **penetration testing**, security personnel simulate or perform specific and controlled attacks to compromise or disrupt their own systems by exploiting documented vulnerabilities. This kind of testing is commonly performed on network connections from outside the organization, as security personnel attempt to exploit vulnerabilities in the organization's system from the attacker's standpoint. Penetration testing is often conducted by consultants or outsourced contractors, who are commonly referred to as **white-hat hackers, ethical hackers, tiger teams,** or **red teams.** What they are called is less important than what they do, which is critical. InfoSec administrators who have not looked at their systems through the eyes of an attacker are failing to maintain readiness. The best procedures and tools to use in penetration testing and other vulnerability assessments are the procedures and tools of the hacker community. Fortunately, many intrusion detection systems spot the signatures of these tools and can alert InfoSec management to their use.

Readiness and Review The primary objectives of readiness and review are to keep the InfoSec program functioning as designed and, it is hoped, continuously improve it over time.

Chapter Summary

- Planning is central to the management of any organization and is based on the preparation, application, and control of a sequence of action steps to achieve specific goals.

- To develop and implement effective planning, documents representing the philosophical, ethical, and entrepreneurial perspectives of the company are first created—namely, the values, vision, mission, and strategy of the organization. Strategic planning lays out the long-term direction to be taken by the organization and guides organizational efforts.

- Security can begin either as a grass-roots effort (a bottom-up approach) or with plans formulated by senior management (a top-down approach). InfoSec governance is the process of creating and maintaining the organizational structures that manage the InfoSec function within an enterprise. It has five key objectives: strategic alignment of InfoSec and business objectives; use of risk management practices to guide InfoSec decision making; implementation of rational resource management practices for InfoSec programs; measurement of performance of InfoSec functions; and delivering value to the organization.

- The systems development life cycle (SDLC) is a methodology for the design and implementation of an information system in an organization. A methodology is a formal approach to solving a problem based on a structured sequence of procedures. Using a methodology ensures a rigorous process and increases the likelihood of achieving the desired final objective. The process of phased system development described by the traditional SDLC can be adapted to support the specialized implementation of a security project by using the security systems development life cycle (SecSDLC). The fundamental process is the identification of specific threats and the risks that they represent to the organization, followed by the design and implementation of specific controls to counter those threats and assist in the management of the risks.

- The investigation phase of the SecSDLC begins with a directive from upper management dictating the process, outcomes, and goals of the project, as well as its budget and other constraints. In the analysis phase, the team examines existing security policies or programs, along with documented current threats and associated controls. This phase also includes an analysis of relevant legal issues that could affect the design of the security solution. Risk management begins in this stage as well. Risk management is the process of identifying, assessing, and evaluating the levels of risk facing the organization—specifically, threats to the organization's security and to the information stored and processed by the organization. Analysis begins with knowing your enemy. In InfoSec, the enemy consists of threats and attacks that your systems face.

■ The design phase includes two distinct phases: the logical design and the physical design. In the logical design phase, blueprints for security are created, and key policies that influence later decisions are examined and implemented. In the physical design phase, the security technology needed to support these blueprints is evaluated, alternative solutions are generated, and a final design is determined.

■ The maintenance and change phase, though last, is perhaps most important, given the flexibility and persistence of many of the threats facing the modern organization. Once the InfoSec program is implemented, it must be operated and properly managed through the establishment of procedures. Additional procedures are needed to keep the organization safe as change occurs.

Review Questions

1. What is planning? How does an organization determine if planning is necessary?

2. What are the three common levels of planning?

3. Who are stakeholders? Why is it important to consider their views when planning?

4. What is a values statement? What is a vision statement? What is a mission statement? Why are they important? What do they contain?

5. What is strategy?

6. What is InfoSec governance?

7. What should a board of directors recommend as an organization's InfoSec objectives?

8. What are the five basic outcomes that should be achieved through InfoSec governance?

9. Describe top-down strategic planning. How does it differ from bottom-up strategic planning? Which is usually more effective in implementing security in a large, diverse organization?

10. How does the SecSDLC differ from the more general SDLC?

11. What is the primary objective of the SecSDLC? What are its major steps, and what are the major objectives of each step?

12. What is a threat in the context of InfoSec? What are the 12 categories of threats presented in this chapter?

13. What is the difference between a threat and an attack?

14. How can a vulnerability be converted into an attack?

15. What name is given to an attack that makes use of viruses and worms? What name is given to an attack that does not actually cause damage other than wasted time and resources?

16. What questions might be asked to help identify and classify information assets? Which is the most important question to ask?

17. What name is given to the process of assigning a comparative risk rating to each specific information asset? What are the uses of such a rating?

18. What term is used to describe the provision of rules intended to protect the information assets of an organization?

19. What term is used to describe the control measure that reduces security incidents among members of the organization by familiarizing them with relevant policies and practices in an ongoing manner?

20. What are the three categories of InfoSec controls? How is each used to reduce risk for the organization?

Exercises

1. Using a Web search engine, find an article from a reputable source, published within the past six months, that reports on the risk coming from inside the organization compared to the risk coming from outside the organization. If the article notes that this relative risk is changing, how is it changing and to what is the change attributed?

2. Using a Web search engine, find five examples of values, vision, and mission statements as well as public declarations of organizational strategy. Do these examples express concern for the security of corporate information?

3. Search your institution's (or another organization's) published documents, including its Web pages. Locate its values, vision, and/or mission statement, as well as strategic goals. Identify any references to InfoSec. Also look for any planning documents related to InfoSec.

4. Using a Web browser, go to *http://gocsi.com*. Search for the link offering a free copy of the latest CSI study. Summarize the key points and bring your summary to class to discuss with your fellow students.

5. Visit your library's newspaper archives and search for recent articles on the subject of threats to InfoSec in your locality. How many examples of threats to InfoSec in the last week can you find?

Closing Case

Mike and Iris met to discuss the strategic plan that would be presented at the upcoming company-wide strategic planning workshop. Mike had given Iris the IT Division's list of strategic goals. She had already seen RWW's most recent set of corporate strategic goals.

"Mike, I see that you have kept a one-to-one alignment of your goals to the company goals," Iris said. "Do you think it's necessary for InfoSec's goals to have the same arrangement?"

"I've found that by keeping the alignment in place, it helps those higher up to stay focused on what IT will be doing to help them execute their important priorities," Mike replied. "But you'll notice that there are in fact a lot of differences."

Mike then pointed to a section of the plan. "Notice here that corporate goal number three is an overall reduction in operating costs as a percentage of revenue," Mike explained. "I have the IT plan element in support still as goal number three, but it now has four parts listed within it. Each of those is a specific IT-related goal to reduce costs.

"Now look at corporate goal one, which really just says we need to increase revenue," Mike continued. "Since RWW doesn't really have any profit centers in the IT parts of the company, I just wrote a short section on how we will assist the revenue-producing parts of the company in doing more of that. Even though the IT goal isn't really very concrete, taking it out may be confusing if someone is trying to identify alignment."

Iris nodded.

"So alignment is about making sure that what the lower-level business unit can do supports the higher-level unit's objectives," she said.

"Exactly right," Mike said, also nodding.

"So do you want the InfoSec goals to be subordinate to the corporate goals or just subordinate to the IT goals?" Iris asked.

"Well, I think either approach will come to about the same thing," Mike responded. "But for this cycle, you can work from the draft IT planning goals in this version so long as you keep up the alignment in the numbering. Since you are new at this, that might make it go a little faster."

Discussion

1. Few InfoSec business units can generate revenue. Do you think Iris should word her plans to be in support of IT efforts to support revenue-generating business units, or should she adopt Mike's goal and also seek to support the profit centers of the company directly? Why is the second choice better for Iris and the InfoSec unit?

2. What options will Iris have if she finds an IT strategic objective that she thinks would reduce the security of RWW's information assets?

Ethical Decision Making

Suppose Iris discovers an element of the IT strategic plan stating that IT will reduce costs by implementing a specific new technology. Suppose also that Iris knows that technology has not been shown to reduce costs even though it does improve the quality of IT services. Should Iris challenge Mike on this issue, or should she leave that subject alone? Is she ethically obligated to raise this issue with higher management?

Endnotes

1. Wood, Charles Cresson. *Information Security Roles and Responsibilities Made Easy*, Version 3. Houston, TX: Information Shield, Inc., 2012. 137.

2. Ibid.

3. Allison, Michael, and Jude Kaye. *Strategic Planning for Nonprofit Organizations*, 2nd ed. Hoboken, NJ: John Wiley & Sons, 2005.

4. Ward, Brian. "Planning as Doing: Accelerating the Business Planning Process." *Managerwise.com*. Accessed February 5, 2013 @ *www.managerwise.com/article .phtml?id=329*.

5. *Information Security Governance: A Call to Action*, 2nd edition. Rolling Meadows, IL: IT Governance Institute, 2006.

6. Ibid.

7. Ibid.

8. Ibid.

9. Corporate Governance Task Force. "Information Security Governance: A Call to Action." *National Cyber Security Partnership*, 2004.

10. Booz Allen Hamilton. "Convergence of Enterprise Security Organizations," 2005. Accessed February 5, 2013 @ *www.asisonline.org/newsroom/alliance.pdf*.

11. Deloitte and Touche. "The Convergence of Physical and Information Security in the Context of Enterprise Risk Management." *Alliance for Enterprise Security Risk Management (AESRM)*, 2007.

12. "Findings from the OCEG GRC Strategy Study: How We Develop, Manage, and Evaluate GRC Efforts." *OECG, Deloitte and Touche, SAP, Cisco*, 2007. Accessed February 7, 2013 @ *www.oceg.org/view/20056*.

13. Wood, Charles Cresson. *Information Security Roles and Responsibilities Made Easy*, Version 3. Houston, TX: Information Shield, Inc., 2012. 174.

14. Jennerich, Bill. "Joint Application Design: Business Requirements Analysis for Successful Re-engineering." Accessed August 24, 2012 @ *www.bee.net/bluebird/jaddoc.htm*.

15. Sun Tzu. *The Art of War*. Trans. by Samuel B. Griffith. Oxford: Oxford University Press, 1988.

16. Whitman, Michael, and Herbert Mattord. "Threats to Information Security Revisited." *Journal of Information Systems Security* 8(1), 2012.

## chapter 3

Planning for Contingencies

Anything that can go wrong will go wrong.

MURPHY'S LAW

A week after the strategic planning meeting, Iris was just finishing a draft of the information security strategic plan. Satisfied with her progress thus far, she opened her calendar and began reviewing her schedule, hoping to find a good day and time to meet with Mike to discuss contingency planning. During their last luncheon, her friend Charley had warned Iris not to wait too long before addressing the issue again. She knew he had a point. It simply was not a good idea to put off discussing such an important project until the end of the month, as Mike had suggested during last week's strategic planning meeting. Having a plan in place in case of an emergency just made good business sense, even if it was not perceived as a high priority by many of her management peers.

Suddenly, the building's fire alarm went off. Heart pumping, Iris left her office. With or without a contingency plan, it was her responsibility to assess this situation as quickly and as safely as possible. Was this an incident? A disaster? Or was it simply a false alarm? As she quickly moved down the line of cubicles, Iris called for everyone who had not yet left the floor to leave by way of the nearest exit. Then she rushed to the floor's fire control panel, which was located in the elevator lobby. A blinking light showed that one heat-sensitive sprinkler head had been activated. Iris waited a moment to see whether any other blinking lights came on. None did, but the existing light stayed on. It seemed that she was dealing with an incident, and not a disaster.

Iris headed down the hall to the place shown on the fire panel where the sprinkler had been triggered. She turned the corner and saw Harry and Joel from the accounting department in the break room, which was right next to their offices. Harry was inspecting what had once been the coffeepot, while Joel held a fire extinguisher. Both were wet and irritated. The room was filled with smoke and smelled of scorched coffee. To Iris's relief, there was no fire.

"Is everyone all right?" she asked.

"Yeah," Harry replied, "but our offices are a mess. There's water everywhere."

Joel shook his head in disgust. "What a time for this to happen. We were just finishing the quarterly reports, too."

"Never mind that," Iris said. "The important thing is that you're both okay. Do you guys need to make a trip home so you can get changed?"

Before they could answer, Mike Edwards ran over to join them.

"What happened?" he asked.

Iris shrugged. "It's a minor incident, Mike, everything's under control. The fire department will be here any minute."

"Incident? Incident?" Joel said in dismay as he pointed at his desk, where steam rose from his soaked CPU and a pile of drenched reports littered the floor. "This isn't an incident. This is a disaster!"

LEARNING OBJECTIVES

Upon completion of this material, you should be able to:

- Discuss the need for contingency planning
- Describe the major components of contingency planning
- Develop a simple set of contingency plans, using business impact analysis
- Discuss how the organization would prepare and execute a test of contingency plans
- Explain the unified contingency plan approach

Introduction

Chapter 2 introduced the topic of planning and provided some specifics about planning for the organization in general and for the information security (InfoSec) program in particular. This chapter focuses on planning for unexpected adverse events, when the use of technology is disrupted and business operations can come to a standstill. Because technology drives business, planning for an unexpected adverse event usually involves managers from among general business management as well as the information technology (IT) and the InfoSec communities of interest. They collectively analyze and assess the entire technological infrastructure of the organization using the mission statement and current organizational objectives to drive their planning activities. But, for a plan to gain the support of all members of the organization, it must also be sanctioned and actively supported by the general business community of interest.

The need to have a plan in place that systematically addresses how to identify, contain, and resolve an unexpected adverse event was identified in the earliest days of IT. Professional practice in the area of contingency planning continues to evolve, as reflected in "Special Publication 800-34 Rev. 1, Contingency Planning Guide for Federal Information Systems," issued by the National Institute of Standards and Technology (NIST). NIST is a nonregulatory federal agency within the U.S. Department of Commerce that serves to enhance innovation and competitiveness in the United States by acting as a clearinghouse for standards related to technology.[1] The Computer Security Division of NIST facilitates sharing of information about practices that can be used to secure information systems.[2] NIST advises the following:

> *Because information system resources are essential to an organization's success, it is critical that identified services provided by these systems are able to operate effectively without excessive interruption. Contingency planning supports this requirement by establishing thorough plans, procedures, and technical measures that can enable a system to be recovered as quickly and effectively as possible following a service disruption.*[3]

Some organizations—particularly federal agencies for national security reasons—are charged by law or other mandate to have such plans and procedures in place at all times.

Organizations of every size and purpose should also prepare for the unexpected. In general, an organization's ability to weather losses caused by an unexpected event depends on proper planning and execution of such a plan; without a workable plan, an unexpected event can cause severe damage to an organization's information resources and assets from which it may never recover. The Hartford insurance company estimates that, on average, over 40 percent of businesses that don't have a disaster plan go out of business after a major loss like a fire, a break-in, or a storm.[4]

In 1991, as an example, two key executives of the Bruno's Supermarket chain, Angelo and Lee Bruno, were killed in a plane crash, and the company's steady growth from its founding during the Great Depression seems to have reversed course at that point. In fact, it declared bankruptcy in 2000. Although the brand still has a presence in a few southern markets, the business as it operated before the incident no longer exists. The development of a plan for handling unexpected events should be a high priority for all managers. That plan should take into account the possibility that key members of the organization will not be available to assist in the recovery process.

Fundamentals of Contingency Planning

The overall process of preparing for unexpected adverse events is called **contingency planning (CP)**. During CP, the IT and InfoSec communities of interest position their respective organizational units to prepare for, detect, react to, and recover from events that threaten the security of information resources and assets, including human, information, and capital. The main goal of CP is to restore normal modes of operation with minimal cost and disruption to normal business activities after an unexpected adverse event—in other words, to make sure things get back to the way they were within a reasonable period of time. Ideally, CP should ensure the continuous availability of information systems to the organization even in the face of the unexpected.

CP consists of four major components:

- Business impact analysis (BIA)
- Incident response plan (IR plan)
- Disaster recovery plan (DR plan)
- Business continuity plan (BC plan)

The BIA, a preparatory activity common to both CP and risk management, is covered in Chapters 8 and 9. It helps the organization determine which business functions and information systems are the most critical to the success of the organization. The IR plan focuses on the immediate response to an incident. Any unexpected adverse event is treated as an incident, unless and until a response team deems it to be a disaster. Then the DR plan, which focuses on restoring operations at the primary site, is invoked. If operations at the primary site cannot be quickly restored—for example, when the damage is major or will affect the organization's functioning over the long term—the BC plan occurs concurrently with the DR plan, enabling the business to continue at an alternate site, until the organization is able to resume operations at its primary site or select a new primary location.

Depending on the organization's size and business philosophy, IT and InfoSec managers can either (1) create and develop these four CP components as one unified plan or (2) create the four separately in conjunction with a set of interlocking procedures that enable continuity. Typically, larger, more complex organizations create and develop the CP components separately, as the functions of each component differ in scope, applicability, and design. Smaller organizations tend to adopt a one-plan method, consisting of a straightforward set of recovery strategies.

Ideally, the chief information officer (CIO), systems administrators, the chief information security officer (CISO), and key IT and business managers should be actively involved during the creation and development of all CP components, as well as during the distribution of responsibilities among the three communities of interest. The elements required to begin the CP process are: a planning methodology; a policy environment to enable the planning process; an understanding of the causes and effects of core precursor activities, known as the BIA; and access to financial and other resources, as articulated and outlined by the planning budget. Each of these is explained in the sections that follow. Once formed, the **contingency planning management team (CPMT)** begins developing a CP document, for which NIST recommends using the following steps:

1. *Develop the CP policy statement. A formal policy provides the authority and guidance necessary to develop an effective contingency plan.*

2. *Conduct the BIA. The BIA helps identify and prioritize information systems and components critical to supporting the organization's mission/business processes. A template for developing the BIA is provided to assist the user.*

3. *Identify preventive controls. Measures taken to reduce the effects of system disruptions can increase system availability and reduce contingency life cycle costs.*

4. *Create contingency strategies. Thorough recovery strategies ensure that the system may be recovered quickly and effectively following a disruption.*

5. *Develop a contingency plan. The contingency plan should contain detailed guidance and procedures for restoring damaged organizational facilities unique to the each business unit's impact level and recovery requirements.*

6. *Ensure plan testing, training, and exercises. Testing validates recovery capabilities, whereas training prepares recovery personnel for plan activation and exercising the plan identifies planning gaps; combined, the activities improve plan effectiveness and overall organization preparedness.*

7. *Ensure plan maintenance. The plan should be a living document that is updated regularly to remain current with system enhancements and organizational changes.*[5]

Source: NIST

Effective CP begins with effective policy. Before the CPMT can fully develop the planning document, the team must receive guidance from executive management, as described earlier, through formal CP policy. This policy defines the scope of the CP operations and establishes managerial intent in regard to timetables for response to incidents, recovery from disasters, and reestablishment of operations for continuity. It also stipulates responsibility for the development and operations of the CPMT in general and may also provide specifics on the constituencies of all CP-related teams. It is recommended that the CP policy contain, at a minimum, the following sections:

- An introductory statement of philosophical perspective by senior management as to the importance of CP to the strategic, long-term operations of the organizations

- A statement of the scope and purpose of the CP operations, stipulating the requirement to cover all critical business functions and activities

- A call for periodic (e.g., yearly) risk assessment and BIA by the CPMT, to include identification and prioritization of critical business functions (while the need for such studies is well understood by the CPMT, the formal inclusion in policy reinforces that need to the rest of the organization)

- A description of the major components of the CP to be designed by the CPMT, as described earlier

- A call for, and guidance in, the selection of recovery options and BC strategies

- A requirement to test the various plans on a regular basis (e.g., semiannually, annually, or more often as needed)

- Identification of key regulations and standards that impact CP planning and a brief overview of their relevance

- Identification of key individuals responsible for CP operations, such as establishment of the chief operations officer (COO) as CPMT lead, the CISO as IR team lead, the manager of business operations as DR team lead, the manager of information systems and services as BC team lead, and legal counsel as crisis management team lead

- An appeal to the individual members of the organizations, asking for their support and reinforcing their importance as part of the overall CP process

- Additional administrative information, including the original date of the document, revision dates, and a schedule for periodic review and maintenance

A number of individuals and teams are involved in CP and contingency operations:

- *CPMT*—This team collects information about the organization and about the threats it faces, conducts the BIA, and then coordinates the development of contingency plans for incident response, disaster recovery, and business continuity. The CPMT often consists of a coordinating executive and representatives from major business units and the managers responsible for each of the other three teams. It should include the following personnel:

  - *Champion*—As with any strategic function, the CP project must have a high-level manager to support, promote, and endorse the findings of the project. This champion could be the COO or (ideally) the CEO/president.

  - *Project manager*—A champion provides the strategic vision and the linkage to the power structure of the organization but does not manage the project. A project manager—possibly a mid-level operations manager or even the CISO—leads the project, putting in place a sound project planning process, guiding the development of a complete and useful project, and prudently managing resources.

  - *Team members*—The team members should be the managers or their representatives from the various communities of interest: business, IT, and InfoSec. Business managers supply details of their activities and insight into those functions critical to running the business. IT managers supply information about the at-risk systems used in the development of the BIA and the IR, DR, and BC plans. InfoSec managers oversee the security planning and provide information on threats, vulnerabilities, attacks, and recovery requirements. A representative from the legal affairs or corporate counsel's office helps keep all planning steps within legal and contractual boundaries. A member of the corporate communications department makes sure the crisis management and communications plan elements are consistent with the needs of that group.

- **Incident response team**—This team manages and executes the IR plan by detecting, evaluating, and responding to incidents.

- **Disaster recovery team**—This team manages and executes the DR plan by detecting, evaluating, and responding to disasters and by reestablishing operations at the primary business site.

- **Business continuity team**—This team manages and executes the BC plan by setting up and starting off-site operations in the event of an incident or disaster.

As indicated earlier, in larger organizations these teams are distinct entities, with non-overlapping memberships, although the latter three teams have representatives on the CPMT. In smaller organizations, the four teams may include overlapping groups of people.

As illustrated in the opening scenario of this chapter, many organizations' contingency plans are woefully inadequate. CP often fails to receive the high priority necessary for the efficient and timely recovery of business operations during and after an unexpected event. The fact that many organizations do not place an adequate premium on CP does not mean that it is unimportant, however. Here is how NIST's Computer Security Resource Center (CSRC) describes the need for this type of planning:

> *These procedures (contingency plans, business interruption plans, and continuity of operations plans) should be coordinated with the backup, contingency, and*

recovery plans of any general support systems, including networks used by the application. The contingency plans should ensure that interfacing systems are identified and contingency/disaster planning coordinated.[6]

As you learn more about CP, you may notice that it shares certain characteristics with risk management and the SecSDLC methodology. Many IT and InfoSec managers are already familiar with these processes; they can readily adapt their existing knowledge to the CP process.

Components of Contingency Planning

As noted earlier, CP includes four major components: the BIA and the IR, DR, and BC plans. Whether an organization adopts the one-plan method or the multiple-plan method with interlocking procedures, each of these CP components must be addressed and developed in its entirety. The following sections describe each component in detail, including when and how each should be used. They also explain how to determine which plan is best suited for the identification, containment, and resolution of any given unexpected event. Figure 3-1 depicts the major project modules performed during CP efforts. Figure 3-2 shows the overall stages of a 12-step CP process, based on NIST's seven steps, which were presented earlier.

Business Impact Analysis

The **business impact analysis (BIA)** is the first phase of the CP process. A crucial component of the initial planning stages, it serves as an investigation and assessment of the impact that various adverse events can have on the organization.

One of the fundamental differences between a BIA and the risk management processes discussed in Chapters 8 and 9 is that risk management focuses on identifying the threats, vulnerabilities, and attacks to determine which controls can protect the information. The BIA assumes that these controls have been bypassed, have failed, or have otherwise proved ineffective, that the attack succeeded, and that the adversity that was being defended against has come to fruition. By assuming the worst has happened, then assessing how that adversity will

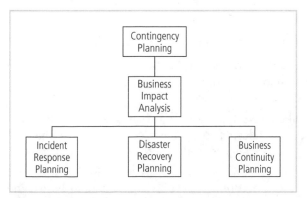

Figure 3-1 Contingency planning hierarchies

Copyright © 2014 Cengage Learning®.

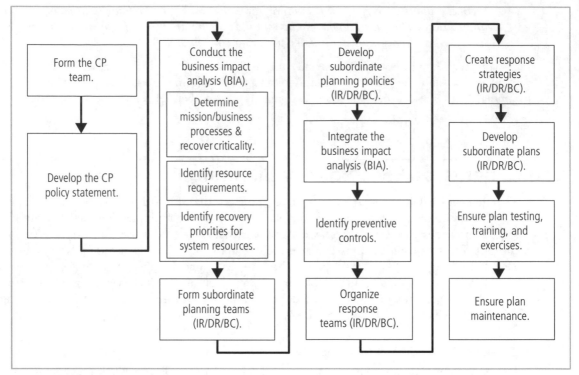

Figure 3-2 Contingency planning life cycle

Copyright © 2014 Cengage Learning®.

impact the organization, insight is gained regarding how the organization must respond to the adverse event, minimize the damage, recover from the effects, and return to normal operations.

The BIA begins with the prioritized list of threats and vulnerabilities identified in the risk management process discussed in Chapter 1 and enhances the list by adding the information needed to respond to the adversity. Obviously, the organization's security team does everything in its power to stop these attacks, but as you have seen, some attacks, such as natural disasters, deviations from service providers, acts of human failure or error, and deliberate acts of sabotage and vandalism, may be unstoppable.

When undertaking the BIA, the organization should consider the following:

1. *Scope*—The parts of the organization to be included in the BIA should be carefully considered to determine which business units to cover, which systems to include, and the nature of the risk being evaluated.

2. *Plan*—The needed data will likely be voluminous and complex, so work from a careful plan to assure the proper data is collected to enable a comprehensive analysis. Getting the correct information to address the needs of decision makers is important.

3. *Balance*—Some information may be objective in nature, while other information may be only available as subjective or anecdotal references. Facts should be weighted properly against opinions; however, sometimes the knowledge and experience of key personnel can be invaluable.

4. *Know the objective*—Identify what the key decision makers require for making choices in advance. Structure the BIA to bring the information they need to them organized to facilitate consideration of those choices.

5. *Follow-up*—Communicate periodically to insure process owners and decision makers will support the process and the end result of the BIA.[7]

According to NIST's "SP 800-34, Rev. 1," the CPMT conducts the BIA in three stages, as shown in Figure 3-2 and described in the sections that follow[8]:

1. Determine mission/business processes and recovery criticality.

2. Identify resource requirements.

3. Identify recovery priorities for system resources.

Determine Mission/Business Processes and Recovery Criticality

The first major BIA task is the analysis and prioritization of business processes within the organization, based on their relationship to the organization's mission. Each business department, unit, or division must be independently evaluated to determine how important its functions are to the organization as a whole. For example, recovery operations would probably focus on the IT Department and network operation before turning to the Personnel Department's hiring activities. Likewise, recovering a manufacturing company's assembly line is more urgent than recovering its maintenance tracking system. This is not to say that personnel functions and assembly line maintenance are not important to the business, but unless the organization's main revenue-producing operations can be restored quickly, other functions are irrelevant.

Note that throughout this section, the term "mission/business process" is used frequently, as some agencies that adopt this methodology aren't businesses and thus don't have business processes per se. Don't let the term confuse you. Whenever you see the term, it's essentially describing a **business process**—a task performed by an organization or organizational subunit in support of the overall organization's mission. NIST prefers this term, although the term "business process" is just as accurate.

It is important to collect critical information about each business unit before beginning the process of prioritizing the business units. The important thing to remember is to avoid "turf wars" and instead focus on the selection of those business functions that must be sustained in order to continue business operations. While one manager or executive might feel that his or her function is the most critical to the organization, that particular function might prove to be less critical in the event of a major incident or disaster. It is the role of senior management to arbitrate these inevitable conflicts about priority; after all, senior management has the perspective to make these types of trade-off decisions.

A weighted analysis table (sometimes called a "weighted factor analysis") can be useful in resolving the issue of what business function is the most critical. The CPMT can use this tool by first identifying the characteristics of each business function that matter most to the organization. The team should then allocate relative weights to each of these categories. Each of the characteristics (called a "criterion" in this type of analysis) is assessed on its influence toward overall importance in the decision-making process. Once the characteristics to be used as criteria have been identified and weighted (usually as columns in a worksheet), the various business functions are listed (usually as rows on the same worksheet). Each business function (row) is assessed a score for each of the criteria (column). Once this activity has been accomplished, the weights can be multiplied against the scores in each of the criteria, and then the rows are summed to obtain the overall scored value of the function to the organization. In the process just described, the higher the value computed for a given business function, the more important that function is to the organization.

One useful tool in identifying and collecting information about business functions for the analysis just described is the BIA questionnaire, discussed later in this chapter. The BIA questionnaire can be used to allow functional managers to directly enter information about their functions, the impacts the functions have on the business and other functions, and the dependencies that exist for the functions from specific resources and outside service providers.

NIST Business Process and Recovery Criticality NIST's "SP 800-34, Revision 1" recommends that organizations use categories like low impact, moderate impact, or high impact for the security objectives of confidentiality, integrity, and availability (NIST's Risk Management Framework [RMF] Step 1). Note that large quantities of information are assembled and a data collection process is essential if all meaningful and useful information collected in the BIA process is to be made available for use in the overall CP development process.

When organizations consider recovery criticality, key recovery measures are usually described in terms of how much of the asset they must recover within a specified time frame. The terms most commonly used to describe this value are:

- Maximum Tolerable Downtime
- Recovery time objective
- Recovery point objective

NIST defines **maximum tolerable downtime (MTD)** as "the total amount of time the system owner/authorizing official is willing to accept for a mission/business process outage or disruption and includes all impact considerations." Failing to determine MTD, NIST goes on to say, "could leave contingency planners with imprecise direction on (1) selection of an appropriate recovery method, and (2) the depth of detail that will be required when developing recovery procedures, including their scope and content."[9]

The **recovery time objective (RTO)**, according to NIST, is "the maximum amount of time that a system resource can remain unavailable before there is an unacceptable impact on other system resources, supported mission/business processes, and the MTD." Determining the information system resource's RTO, NIST adds, "is important for selecting appropriate technologies that are best suited for meeting the MTD."[10] As for reducing RTO, that requires mechanisms to shorten the start-up time or provisions to make data available online at a failover site.

The **recovery point objective (RPO)**, according to NIST, is "the point in time, prior to a disruption or system outage, to which mission/business process data can be recovered (given the most recent backup copy of the data) after an outage." Unlike RTO, NIST adds, "RPO is not considered as part of MTD. Rather, it is a factor of how much data loss the mission/business process can tolerate during the recovery process."[11] Reducing RPO requires mechanisms to increase the synchronicity of data replication between production systems and the backup implementations for those systems.

Some organizations have further refined the RTO concept by adding an element called **work recovery time (WRT)** as the amount of effort (expressed as elapsed time) that is necessary to

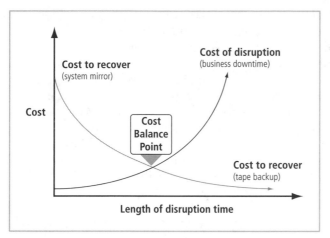

Figure 3-3 Cost balancing

Copyright © 2014 Cengage Learning®.

get the business function operational AFTER the technology element is recovered (as identi-fied with RTO). WRT typically involves the addition of nontechnical tasks required for the organization to make the particular information asset usable for its intended business func-tion again. The WRT can be added to the RTO to determine the realistic amount of elapsed time before a business function is back in useful service. Because of the critical need to recover business functionality, the total time needed to place the business function back in service must be shorter than the MTD. Planners should determine the optimal point to recover the information system to in order to meet BIA-mandated recovery needs while bal-ancing the cost of system inoperability against the cost of the resources required for restor-ing systems. This must be done in the context of the BIA-identified critical business processes and can be shown with a simple chart, such as the one in Figure 3-3.

The longer an interruption to system availability remains, the more impact and cost it will have for the organization and its operations. When plans require a short RTO, the solutions that will be required are usually more expensive to design and use. For example, if a system must be recovered immediately it will have an RTO of 0. These types of solutions will require fully redundant alternative processing sites and will therefore have much higher costs. On the other hand, a longer RTO would allow a less expensive recovery system. Plotting the cost bal-ance points will show an optimal point between disruption and recovery costs. The intersect-ing point, labeled the cost balance point in Figure 3-3, will be different for every organization and system, based on the financial constraints and operating requirements.[12]

Information Asset Prioritization As the CPMT conducts the BIA, it will be asses-sing priorities and relative values on mission/business processes. To do so, it needs to under-stand the information assets used by those processes. The presence of high-value information assets may influence the valuation of a particular business process. Normally, this task would be performed as part of the risk-assessment function within the risk management pro-cess. The organization should identify, classify, and prioritize its information assets, placing classification labels on each collection or repository of information in order to better under-stand its value and to prioritize its protection. If the organization has not performed this task, the BIA process is the appropriate time to do so.

Identify Resource Requirements Once the organization has created a prioritized list of its mission/business processes, it needs to determine what resources would be required in order to recover those processes and the assets associated with them. Some processes are resource intensive—like IT functions. Supporting customer data, production data, and other organizational information requires extensive quantities of information processing, storage, and transmission (through networking). Other business-production–oriented processes require complex or expensive components to operate. For each process (and information asset) identified in the previous BIA stage, the organization should identify and describe the relevant resources needed to provide or support that process. A simplified method for organizing this information is to put it into a resource/component table like the example shown in Table 3-1. Note in the table how one business process will typically have multiple components, each of which must be enumerated separately.

Identify System Resource Recovery Priorities The last stage of the BIA is prioritizing the resources associated with the mission/business processes, which provides a better understanding of what must be recovered first, even within the most critical processes. With the information from previous steps in hand, the organization can create additional weighted

Mission/Business Process	Required Resource Components	Additional Resource Details	Description and Estimated Costs
Provide customer support (help desk)	Trouble ticket and resolution application	Application server w/ LINUX OS, Apache server, and SQL database	Each helpdesk technician requires access to the organization's trouble ticked and resolution software application, hosted on a dedicated server. See current cost recovery statement for valuation.
Provide customer support (help desk)	Help desk network segment	25 Cat5e network drops, gigabit network hub	The helpdesk applications are networked and require a network segment to access. See current cost recovery statement for valuation.
Provide customer support (help desk)	Help desk access terminals	1 Laptop/PC per technician, with Web-browsing software	The helpdesk applications require a Web interface on a laptop/PC to access. See current cost recovery statement for valuation.
Provide customer billing	Customized accounts receivable application	Application server with Linux OS, Apache server, and SQL database	Accounts Receivable requires access to its customized AR software and customer database to process customer billing. See current cost recovery statement for valuation.

Table 3-1   Example resource/components table

Copyright © 2014 Cengage Learning®.

tables of the resources needed to support the individual processes. By assigning values to each resource, the organization will have a custom-designed "to-do" list available once the recovery phase commences. Whether it is an IR- or DR-scaled recovery or the implementation of critical processes in an alternate site during business continuity, these lists will prove invaluable to those who are tasked to establish (or reestablish) critical processes quickly.

In addition to the weighted tables described earlier, a simple valuation and classification scale, such as Primary/Secondary/Tertiary, or Critical/Very Important/Important/Routine can be used to provide a quicker method of valuating the supporting resources. What is most important is to not get so bogged down in the process so as to lose sight of the objective (the old "can't see the forest for the trees" problem). Teams that spend too much time developing and completing weighted tables may find a simple classification scheme more suited for their task. However, in a complex process with a large number of resources, a more sophisticated valuation method like the weighted tables may be more appropriate. One of the jobs of the CPMT, while preparing to conduct the BIA, is to determine what method of valuating processes and their supporting resources should be used.

Contingency Planning Policies

Prior to the development of each of the types of CP documents outlined in this chapter, the CP team should work to develop the policy environment that will enable the BIA process and should provide specific policy guidance toward authorizing the creation of each of the planning components (IR, DR, and BC). These policies provide guidance on the structure of the subordinate teams and the philosophy of the organization, and they assist in the structuring of the plan.

Each of the CP documents will include a policy similar in structure to all other policies used by the organization. Just as the enterprise InfoSec policy defines the InfoSec roles and responsibilities for the entire enterprise, each of the CP documents is based on a specific policy that defines the related roles and responsibilities for that element of the overall CP environment within the organization.

Incident Response

The **incident response plan (IR plan)** is a detailed set of processes and procedures that anticipate, detect, and mitigate the effects of an unexpected event that might compromise information resources and assets. **Incident response planning (IRP)** is therefore the preparation for such an event. In CP, an unexpected event is called an incident. An incident occurs when an attack (natural or human-made) affects information resources and/or assets, causing actual damage or other disruptions. **Incident response (IR)**, then, is a set of procedures that commences when an incident is detected. IR must be carefully planned and coordinated because organizations heavily depend on the quick and efficient containment and resolution of incidents. The IR plan is usually activated when an incident causes minimal damage—according to criteria set in advance by the organization—with little or no disruption to business operations.

Getting Started   An early task for the CPMT is to form a **computer security incident response team (CSIRT)**. Key members of the CSIRT become the IR planning committee and begin work by developing policy to define the operations of the team, to articulate the organizational response to various types of incidents, and to advise end users on how to contribute to the effective response of the organization (rather than contributing to the problem at hand). You will learn more about the CSIRT's roles and composition later in this section.

Incident Response Policy An important early step for the CSIRT is to develop an IR policy. NIST's "Special Publication 800-61, Rev. 2: The Computer Security Incident Handling Guide" identifies the following key components of a typical IR policy:

- *Statement of management commitment*
- *Purpose and objectives of the policy*
- *Scope of the policy (to whom and what it applies and under what circumstances)*
- *Definition of InfoSec incidents and related terms*
- *Organizational structure and definition of roles, responsibilities, and levels of authority; should include the authority of the incident response team to confiscate or disconnect equipment and to monitor suspicious activity, and the requirements for reporting certain types of incidents, the requirements and guidelines for external communications and information sharing (e.g., what can be shared with whom, when, and over what channels), and the handoff and escalation points in the incident management process*
- *Prioritization or severity ratings of incidents*
- *Performance measures (discussed in Chapter 6)*
- *Reporting and contact forms*[13]

IR policy, like all policies, must gain the full support of top management and be clearly understood by all affected parties. It is especially important to gain the support of those communities of interest that will be required to alter business practices or make changes to their IT infrastructures. For example, if the CSIRT determines that the only way to stop a massive denial-of-service attack is to sever the organization's connection to the Internet, it should have a signed document locked in an appropriate filing cabinet preauthorizing such action. This ensures that the CSIRT is performing authorized actions, and protects both the CSIRT members and the organization from misunderstanding and potential liability.

Planning to Respond The scenario at the beginning of this chapter depicts an incident and not a disaster, despite Joel's declaration otherwise. By now, it should be clear why a technology manager, like Iris, must become involved in assessing the damage to two drenched accounting offices and the break room. Because the incident at RWW was determined by Iris to have caused minimal damage, a corresponding IR plan would have been activated if RWW had a properly developed IR plan. If the fire had spread beyond the break room, triggered the sprinkler systems throughout the building, and caused employee injuries, then an IR plan (even if RWW had one) would not have been adequate to deal with the situation. Instead, it would be necessary to initiate the DR plan and the BC plan, both of which are discussed later in this chapter. When one of the threats that were identified in Chapter 2 is made manifest in an actual adverse event, the adverse event is classified as an InfoSec incident, but only if it has all of the following characteristics:

- It is directed against information assets.
- It has a realistic chance of success.
- It threatens the confidentiality, integrity, or availability of information resources and assets.

The prevention of threats and attacks has been intentionally omitted from this discussion because guarding against such possibilities is primarily the responsibility of the InfoSec department, which works with the rest of the organization to implement sound policy, effective risk controls, and ongoing training and awareness programs. It is important to understand that IR is a *reactive* measure, not a *preventive* one.

The responsibility for creating an organization's IR plan usually falls to the CISO or an IT manager with security responsibilities. With the aid of other managers and systems administrators on the CP team, the CISO should select members from each community of interest to form an independent IR team, which executes the IR plan. The roles and responsibilities of the members of the IR team should be clearly documented and communicated throughout the organization. The IR plan also includes an alert roster, which lists certain critical agencies to be contacted during the course of an incident.

Using the multistep CP process discussed in the previous section as a model, the CP team can create the IR plan. During this planning process, the IR procedures take shape. For every incident scenario, the CP team creates three sets of incident-handling procedures:

1. *During the incident*—The planners develop and document the procedures that must be performed during the incident. These procedures are grouped and assigned to individuals. Systems administrators' tasks differ from managerial tasks, so members of the planning committee must draft a set of function-specific procedures.

2. *After the incident*—Once the procedures for handling an incident are drafted, the planners develop and document the procedures that must be performed immediately after the incident has ceased. Again, separate functional areas may develop different procedures.

3. *Before the incident*—The planners draft a third set of procedures, those tasks that must be performed to prepare for the incident. These procedures include details of the data-backup schedules, disaster recovery preparation, training schedules, testing plans, copies of service agreements, and BC plans, if any. At this level, the BC plan could consist of just additional material on a service bureau that stores data off-site via electronic vaulting, with an agreement to provide office space and lease equipment as needed.

Figure 3-4 presents an example of pages from the IR plan that support each of these phases. Once these sets of procedures are clearly documented, the IR portion of the IR plan is assembled and the critical information outlined in these planning sections is recorded.

Planning for an incident and the responses to it requires a detailed understanding of the information systems and the threats they face. The BIA provides the data used to develop the IR plan. The IRP team seeks to develop a series of predefined responses that will guide the team and InfoSec staff through the IR steps. Predefining incident responses enables the organization to react to a detected incident quickly and effectively, without confusion or wasted time and effort.

The execution of the IR plan typically falls to the CSIRT. As noted previously, the CSIRT is a subset of the IR team and is composed of technical and managerial IT and InfoSec professionals prepared to diagnose and respond to an incident. In some organizations, the CSIRT may simply be a loose or informal association of IT and InfoSec staffers who would be called up if an attack was detected on the organization's information assets. In other, more formal implementations, the CSIRT is a set of policies, procedures, technologies,

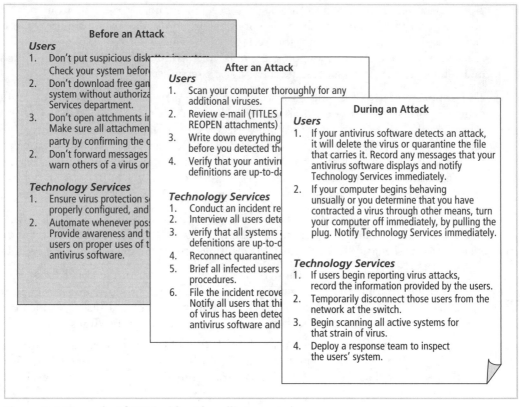

Before an Attack

Users
1. Don't put suspicious disk___ in ___. Check your system befor___
2. Don't download free gan___ system without authoriza___ Services department.
3. Don't open attchments i___ Make sure all attachmen___ party by confirming the ___
2. Don't forward messages ___ warn others of a virus or ___

Technology Services
1. Ensure virus protection s___ properly configured, and ___
2. Automate whenever pos___ Provide awareness and t___ users on proper uses of t___ antivirus software.

After an Attack

Users
1. Scan your computer thoroughly for any additional viruses.
2. Review e-mail (TITLES ___ REOPEN attachments) ___
3. Write down everything ___ before you detected th___
4. Verify that your antivir___ definitions are up-to-d___

Technology Services
1. Conduct an incident re___
2. Interview all users dete___
3. verify that all systems ___ defenitions are up-to-d___
4. Reconnect quarantined ___
5. Brief all infected users ___ procedures.
6. File the incident recove___ Notify all users that thi___ of virus has been dete___ antivirus software and ___

During an Attack

Users
1. If your antivirus software detects an attack, it will delete the virus or quarantine the file that carries it. Record any messages that your antivirus software displays and notify Technology Services immediately.
2. If your computer begins behaving unsually or you determine that you have contracted a virus through other means, turn your computer off immediately, by pulling the plug. Notify Technology Services immediately.

Technology Services
1. If users begin reporting virus attacks, record the information provided by the users.
2. Temporarily disconnect those users from the network at the switch.
3. Begin scanning all active systems for that strain of virus.
4. Deploy a response team to inspect the users' system.

Figure 3-4 Example of IRP incident-handling procedures

Copyright © 2014 Cengage Learning®.

people, and data put in place to prevent, detect, react to, and recover from an incident that could potentially damage the organization's information. At some level, every member of an organization is a member of the CSIRT, since every action they take can cause or avert an incident.

The CSIRT should be available for contact by anyone who discovers or suspects that an incident involving the organization has occurred. One or more team members, depending on the magnitude of the incident and availability of personnel, then handles the incident. The incident handlers analyze the incident data, determine the impact of the incident, and act appropriately to limit the damage to the organization and restore normal services. Although the CSIRT may have only a few members, the team's success depends on the participation and cooperation of individuals throughout the organization.

The CSIRT consists of professionals who are capable of handling the information systems and functional areas affected by an incident. For example, imagine a firefighting team responding to an emergency call. Rather than responding to the fire as individuals, every member of the team has a specific role to perform, so that the team acts as a unified body that assesses the situation, determines the appropriate response, and coordinates the response. Similarly, each member of the IR team must know his or her specific role, work in concert with other team members, and execute the objectives of the IR plan.

Detecting Incidents The challenge for every IR team is determining whether an event is the product of routine systems use or an actual incident. **Incident classification** is the process of examining a possible incident, or **incident candidate**, and determining whether it constitutes an actual incident. Classifying an incident is the responsibility of the IR team. Initial reports from end users, intrusion detection systems, host- and network-based virus detection software, and systems administrators are all ways to track and detect incident candidates. Careful training in the reporting of an incident candidate allows end users, help desk staff, and all security personnel to relay vital information to the IR team. Once an actual incident is properly identified, members of the IR team can effectively execute the corresponding procedures from the IR plan.

A number of occurrences signal the presence of an incident candidate. Unfortunately, these same events can result from an overloaded network, computer, or server, and some are similar to the normal operation of these information assets. Other incident candidates mimic the actions of a misbehaving computing system, software package, or other less serious threat. To help make the detection of actual incidents more reliable, D. L. Pipkin has identified three categories of incident indicators: possible, probable, and definite.[14]

Possible Indicators The following types of incident candidates are considered possible indicators of actual incidents:

- *Presence of unfamiliar files*—Users might discover unfamiliar files in their home directories or on their office computers. Administrators might also find unexplained files that do not seem to be in a logical location or owned by an authorized user.

- *Presence or execution of unknown programs or processes*—Users or administrators might detect unfamiliar programs running, or processes executing, on office machines or network servers.

- *Unusual consumption of computing resources*—An example of this would be a sudden spike or fall in consumption of memory or hard disk space. Many computer operating systems, including Windows, Linux, and UNIX variants, allow users and administrators to monitor CPU and memory consumption. Most computers also have the ability to monitor hard drive space. In addition, servers maintain logs of file creation and storage.

- *Unusual system crashes*—Computer systems can crash. Older operating systems running newer programs are notorious for locking up or spontaneously rebooting whenever the operating system is unable to execute a requested process or service. You are probably familiar with systems error messages such as "Unrecoverable Application Error," "General Protection Fault," and the infamous Windows "Blue Screen of Death." However, if a computer system seems to be crashing, hanging, rebooting, or freezing more frequently than usual, the cause could be an incident candidate.

Probable Indicators The following types of incident candidates are considered probable indicators of actual incidents:

- *Activities at unexpected times*—If traffic levels on the organization's network exceed the measured baseline values, an incident candidate is probably present. If this activity surge occurs when few members of the organization are at work, this probability becomes much higher. Similarly, if systems are accessing drives, such as floppy and

CD-ROM drives, when the end user is not using them, an incident may also be occurring.

- *Presence of new accounts*—Periodic review of user accounts can reveal an account (or accounts) that the administrator does not remember creating or that is not logged in the administrator's journal. Even one unlogged new account is an incident candidate. An unlogged new account with root or other special privileges has an even higher probability of being an actual incident.

- *Reported attacks*—If users of the system report a suspected attack, there is a high probability that an attack has occurred, which constitutes an incident. The technical sophistication of the person making the report should be considered.

- *Notification from IDPS*—If the organization has installed and correctly configured a host or network-based Intrusion Detection and Prevention System (IDPS), then notification from the IDPS indicates that an incident might be in progress. However, IDPSs are difficult to configure optimally, and even when they are, they tend to issue many false positives or false alarms. The administrator must then determine whether the notification is real or the result of a routine operation by a user or other administrator.

Definite Indicators   The following five types of incident candidates are definite indicators of an actual incident. That is, they clearly signal that an incident is in progress or has occurred. In these cases, the corresponding IR must be activated immediately.

1. *Use of dormant accounts*—Many network servers maintain default accounts, and there often exist accounts from former employees, employees on a leave of absence or sabbatical without remote access privileges, or dummy accounts set up to support system testing. If any of these accounts begins accessing system resources, querying servers, or engaging in other activities, an incident is certain to have occurred.

2. *Changes to logs*—Smart systems administrators back up system logs as well as system data. As part of a routine incident scan, systems administrators can compare these logs to the online versions to determine whether they have been modified. If they have and the systems administrator cannot determine explicitly that an authorized individual modified them, an incident has occurred.

3. *Presence of hacker tools*—Network administrators sometimes use system vulnerability and network evaluation tools to scan internal computers and networks to determine what a hacker can see. These tools are also used to support research into attack profiles. All too often, however, they are used by employees, contractors, or outsiders with local network access to hack into systems. To combat this problem, many organizations explicitly prohibit the use of these tools without written permission from the CISO, making any unauthorized installation a policy violation. Most organizations that engage in penetration-testing operations require that all tools in this category be confined to specific systems, and that they not be used on the general network unless active penetration testing is under way. Finding hacker tools, or even legal security tools, in places they shouldn't be is an indicator an incident has occurred.

4. *Notifications by partner or peer*—If a business partner or another connected organization reports an attack from your computing systems, then an incident has occurred.

5. *Notification by hacker*—Some hackers enjoy taunting their victims. If an organization's Web pages are defaced, it is an incident. If an organization receives an extortion request for money in exchange for its customers' credit card files, an incident is in progress.

Occurrences of Actual Incidents When the following actual incidents are confirmed, the corresponding IR must be immediately activated:

- *Loss of availability*—Information or information systems become unavailable.
- *Loss of integrity*—Users report corrupt data files, garbage where data should be, or data that just looks wrong.
- *Loss of confidentiality*—There is a notification of a sensitive information leak, or information that was thought to be protected has been disclosed.
- *Violation of policy*—There is a violation of organizational policies addressing information or InfoSec.
- *Violation of law or regulation*—The law has been broken and the organization's information assets are involved.

Responding to Incidents Once an actual incident has been confirmed and properly classified, the IR plan moves from the detection phase to the reaction phase.

The steps in IR are designed to stop the incident, mitigate its effects, and provide information for the recovery from the incident. In the IR phase, a number of action steps taken by the CSIRT and others must occur quickly and may take place concurrently. An effective IR plan prioritizes and documents these steps to allow for efficient reference in the midst of an incident. These steps include notification of key personnel, assignment of tasks, and documentation of the incident.

Notification of Key Personnel As soon as the CSIRT determines that an incident is in progress, the right people must be notified in the right order. Most response organizations, such as firefighters or the military, maintain an alert roster for all emergencies. An **alert roster** is a document containing contact information on the individuals to be notified in the event of an actual incident.

There are two ways to activate an alert roster: sequentially and hierarchically. A sequential roster requires that a contact person call each and every person on the roster. A hierarchical roster requires that the first person call designated people on the roster, who in turn call designated other people, and so on. Each approach has both advantages and disadvantages. The hierarchical system is quicker because more people are calling at the same time, but the message can become distorted as it is passed from person to person. The sequential system is more accurate but slower because a single contact person provides each responder with the message.

The **alert message** is a scripted description of the incident and consists of just enough information so that each responder, CSIRT or otherwise, knows what portion of the IR plan to implement without impeding the notification process. It is important to recognize that not everyone is on the alert roster—only those individuals who must respond to a specific actual incident. As with any part of the IR plan, the alert roster must be regularly maintained, tested, and rehearsed if it is to remain effective.

During this phase, other key personnel not on the alert roster, such as general management, must be notified of the incident as well. This notification should occur only after the incident has been confirmed but before media or other external sources learn of it. Among those likely to be included in the notification process are members of the legal, communications, and human resources departments. In addition, some incidents are disclosed to the employees in general, as a lesson in security, and some are not, as a measure of security. Furthermore, other organizations may need to be notified if it is determined that the incident is not confined to internal information resources, or if the incident is part of a larger-scale assault. For example, during the distributed denial-of-service attack on multiple high-visibility Web-based vendors in late 1999, many of the target organizations reached out for help. In general, the IR planners should determine in advance whom to notify and when, and should offer guidance about additional notification steps to take as needed.

Documenting an Incident As soon as an incident has been confirmed and the notification process is under way, the team should begin to document it. The documentation should record the who, what, when, where, why, and how of each action taken while the incident is occurring. This documentation serves as a case study after the fact to determine whether the right actions were taken and if they were effective. It also proves, should it become necessary, that the organization did everything possible to prevent the spread of the incident. Legally, the standards of due care may offer some protection to the organization should an incident adversely affect individuals inside and outside the organization, or other organizations that use the target organization's systems. Incident documentation can also be used as a simulation in future training sessions on future versions of the IR plan.

Incident Containment Strategies One of the most critical components of IR is stopping the incident or containing its scope or impact. Incident containment strategies vary depending on the incident and on the amount of damage caused. Before an incident can be stopped or contained, however, the affected areas must be identified. Now is not the time to conduct a detailed analysis of the affected areas; those tasks are typically performed after the fact, in the forensics process. Instead, simple identification of what information and systems are involved determines the containment actions to be taken. Incident containment strategies focus on two tasks: stopping the incident and recovering control of the affected systems.

The CSIRT can stop the incident and attempt to recover control by means of several strategies. If the incident originates outside the organization, the simplest and most straightforward approach is to disconnect the affected communication circuits. Of course, if the organization's lifeblood runs through that circuit, this step may be too drastic; if the incident does not threaten critical functional areas, it may be more feasible to monitor the incident and contain it another way. One approach used by some organizations is to apply filtering rules dynamically to limit certain types of network access. For example, if a threat agent is attacking a network by exploiting a vulnerability in the Simple Network Management Protocol (SNMP), then applying a blocking filter for the commonly used IP ports for that vulnerability will stop the attack without compromising other services on the network. Depending on the nature of the attack and the organization's technical capabilities, ad hoc controls can sometimes gain valuable time to devise a more permanent control strategy. Other containment strategies include the following:

- Disabling compromised user accounts
- Reconfiguring a firewall to block the problem traffic

- Temporarily disabling the compromised process or service
- Taking down the conduit application or server—for example, the e-mail server
- Stopping all computers and network devices

Obviously, the final strategy is used only when all system control has been lost and the only hope is to preserve the data stored on the computers so that operations can resume normally once the incident is resolved. The CSIRT, following the procedures outlined in the IR plan, determines the length of the interruption.

Consider the chapter-opening scenario again. What if, instead of a fire, the event had been a malware attack? And what if the key incident response personnel had been on sick leave, on vacation, or otherwise not there? Think how many people in your class or office are not there on a regular basis. Many businesses involve travel, with employees going off-site to meetings, seminars, training, vacations, or other diverse requirements. In considering these possibilities, the importance of preparedness becomes clear. Everyone should know how to handle an incident, not just the CISO and systems administrators.

Incident Escalation An incident may increase in scope or severity to the point that the IR plan cannot adequately handle it. An important part of knowing how to handle an incident is knowing at what point to escalate the incident to a disaster, or to transfer the incident to an outside authority such as law enforcement or another public response unit. Each organization will have to determine, during the BIA, the point at which an incident is deemed a disaster. These criteria must be included in the IR plan. The organization must also document when to involve outside responders, as discussed in other sections. Escalation is one of those things that, once done, cannot be undone, so it is important to know when and where it should be used.

Recovering from Incidents Once the incident has been contained and system control has been regained, incident recovery can begin. As in the incident response phase, the first task is to inform the appropriate human resources. Almost simultaneously, the CSIRT must assess the full extent of the damage so as to determine what must be done to restore the systems. Each individual involved should begin recovery operations based on the appropriate incident recovery section of the IR plan.

The immediate determination of the scope of the breach of confidentiality, integrity, and availability of information and information assets is called incident damage assessment. Incident damage assessment can take days or weeks, depending on the extent of the damage. The damage can range from minor (a curious hacker snooping around) to severe (hundreds of computer systems infected by malware). System logs, intrusion detection logs, configuration logs, and other documents, as well as the documentation from the incident response, provide information on the type, scope, and extent of damage. Using this information, the CSIRT assesses the current state of the information and systems and compares it to a known state. Individuals who document the damage from actual incidents must be trained to collect and preserve evidence, in case the incident is part of a crime or results in a civil action.

Once the extent of the damage has been determined, the recovery process begins. According to noted security consultant and author Donald Pipkin, this process involves the following steps[15]:

- Identify the vulnerabilities that allowed the incident to occur and spread. Resolve them.
- Address the safeguards that failed to stop or limit the incident or were missing from the system in the first place. Install, replace, or upgrade them.

- Evaluate monitoring capabilities (if present). Improve detection and reporting methods or install new monitoring capabilities.

- Restore the data from backups. The IR team must understand the backup strategy used by the organization, restore the data contained in backups, and then use the appropriate recovery processes from incremental backups or database journals to recreate any data that was created or modified since the last backup.

- Restore the services and processes in use. Compromised services and processes must be examined, cleaned, and then restored. If services or processes were interrupted in the course of regaining control of the systems, they need to be brought back online.

- Continuously monitor the system. If an incident happened once, it could easily happen again. Hackers frequently boast of their exploits in chat rooms and dare their peers to match their efforts. If word gets out, others may be tempted to try the same or different attacks on your systems. It is therefore important to maintain vigilance during the entire IR process.

- Restore the confidence of the members of the organization's communities of interest. Management, following the recommendation from the CSIRT, may want to issue a short memorandum outlining the incident and assuring all that the incident was handled and the damage was controlled. If the incident was minor, say so. If the incident was major or severely damaged systems or data, reassure users that they can expect operations to return to normal as soon as possible. The objective of this communication is to prevent panic or confusion from causing additional disruption to the operations of the organization.

Before returning to its routine duties, the CSIRT must conduct an **after-action review (AAR).** The AAR is a detailed examination of the events that occurred, from first detection to final recovery. All key players review their notes and verify that the IR documentation is accurate and precise. All team members review their actions during the incident and identify areas where the IR plan worked, did not work, or should improve. This exercise allows the team to update the IR plan. The AAR can serve as a training case for future staff. It also brings the CSIRT's actions to a close.

Law Enforcement Involvement

When an incident violates civil or criminal law, it is the organization's responsibility to notify the proper authorities. Selecting the appropriate law enforcement agency depends on the type of crime committed. The Federal Bureau of Investigation (FBI), for example, handles computer crimes that cross state lines and investigates terrorism and cyberterrorism, which can include attacks against businesses and other organizations. The U.S. Secret Service examines crimes involving U.S. currency, counterfeiting, credit cards, and identity theft. The U.S. Treasury Department has a bank fraud investigation unit, and the Securities and Exchange Commission has investigation and fraud control units as well. However, the heavy case loads of these agencies means that they typically prioritize those incidents that affect the national critical infrastructure or that have significant economic impact. The FBI Web site, for example, states that it has "built a whole new set of technological and investigative capabilities and partnerships—so we're as comfortable chasing outlaws in cyberspace as we are down back alleys and across continents." It then describes some of these capabilities and partnerships:

- *A "Cyber Division" at FBI Headquarters to address cybercrime in a coordinated and cohesive manner*

- *Specially trained "cyber squads" at FBI headquarters and in each of our 56 field offices, staffed with agents and analysts who protect against investigate*

View Point
The Causes of Incidents and Disasters

Karen Scarfone, Principal Consultant, Scarfone Cybersecurity

The term *incident* has somewhat different meanings in the contexts of incident response and disaster recovery. People in the incident response community generally think of an "incident" as being caused by a malicious attack and a "disaster" as being caused by natural causes (fire, flood, earthquake, etc.) Meanwhile, people in the disaster recovery community tend to use the term *incident* in a cause-free manner, with the cause of the incident or disaster generally being irrelevant and the difference between "incident" and "disaster" being solely based on the scope of the impact of the event, with an incident being a milder event and a disaster a more serious event.

The result of this is that people who are deeply embedded in the incident response community often think of incident response as being largely unrelated to disaster recovery, because they think of a disaster as being caused by a natural disaster, not an attack. Incident responders also often think of operational problems, such as major service failures, as not being incidents nor disasters. Meanwhile, people who are deeply embedded in the disaster recovery community see incident response and disaster recovery as being much more similar and covering a much more comprehensive range of problems.

So where does the truth lie? Well, it depends on the organization. Some organizations take a more integrated approach to business continuity and have their incident response, disaster recovery, and other business continuity components closely integrated with one another so that they work together fairly seamlessly. Other organizations treat these business continuity components as more discrete elements and focus on making each element strong rather than establishing strong commonalities and linkages among the components. There are pluses and minuses to each of these approaches.

Personally, I find that the most important thing is to avoid turf wars between the business continuity component teams. There is nothing more frustrating than delaying the response to an incident or disaster because people disagree on its cause. The security folks say it's an operational problem, the operational folks say it's a disaster, and the disaster folks say it's a security incident. So, like a hot potato, the event gets passed from team to team while people argue about its cause. In reality, for some problems, the cause is not immediately apparent.

What's really important to any organization is that each adverse event, regardless of the cause, be assessed and prioritized as quickly as possible. That means that teams need to be willing to step up and address adverse events whether or not the event is clearly their responsibility. The impact of the incident is generally the same, no matter what the cause is. If later information shows that there's a particular cause that better fits a different team, the handling of the event can be transferred to the other team. Teams should be prepared to transfer events to other teams and to receive transferred events from other teams at any time.

computer intrusions, theft of intellectual property and personal information, child pornography and exploitation, and online fraud

- *New "Cyber Action Teams" that travel around the world on a moment's notice to assist in computer intrusion cases and that gather vital intelligence that helps us identify the cybercrimes that are most dangerous to our national security and to our economy*

- *Our 93 "Computer Crimes Task Forces" nationwide that combine state-of-the-art technology and the resources of our federal, state, and local counterparts*

- *A growing partnership with other federal agencies, including the Department of Defense, the Department of Homeland Security, and others—which share similar concerns and resolve in combating cyber crime*[16]

Each state, county, and city in the United States has its own law enforcement agencies. These agencies enforce all local and state laws, and they handle suspects and security at crime scenes for state and federal cases. Local law enforcement agencies rarely have computer crimes task forces, but the investigative (detective) units are quite capable of processing crime scenes and handling most common criminal violations (such as physical theft or trespassing as well as damage to property), including the apprehension and processing of suspects in computer-related crimes.

Involving law enforcement agencies has both advantages and disadvantages. Such agencies are usually much better equipped to process evidence than a business. Unless the security forces in the organization have been trained in processing evidence and computer forensics, they may do more harm than good when attempting to extract information that can lead to the legal conviction of a suspected criminal. Law enforcement agencies are also prepared to handle the warrants and subpoenas necessary when documenting a case. They are adept at obtaining statements from witnesses, affidavits, and other required documents. For all these reasons, law enforcement personnel can be a security administrator's greatest allies in prosecuting a computer crime. It is therefore important to become familiar with the appropriate local and state agencies before you have to make a call announcing a suspected crime. Most state and federal agencies sponsor awareness programs, provide guest speakers at conferences, and offer programs such as the FBI's InfraGard program (*www.infragard.net*), currently assigned to the Department of Homeland Security's Cyber Division. These agents clearly understand the challenges facing security administrators.

The disadvantages of law enforcement involvement include possible loss of control over the chain of events following an incident, including the collection of information and evidence and the prosecution of suspects. An organization that simply wants to reprimand or dismiss an employee should not involve a law enforcement agency in the resolution of an incident. Additionally, the organization may not hear about the case for weeks or even months due to heavy caseloads or resource shortages. A very real issue for commercial organizations when involving law enforcement agencies is the taking of equipment vital to the organization's business as evidence. Assets can be removed, stored, and preserved to prepare the criminal case. Despite these difficulties, if the organization detects a criminal act, it has the legal obligation to notify the appropriate law enforcement officials. Failure to do so can subject the organization and its officers to prosecution as accessories to the crimes or for impeding the course of an investigation. It is up to the security administrator to ask questions of law enforcement agencies to determine when each agency should be involved, and specifically which crimes will be addressed by each agency.

The "CSI Computer Crime and Security Survey, 2010/2011" relates how organizations have responded to intrusions:

- 62.3 percent—Patched any vulnerable software
- 49.3 percent—Patched or remediated other vulnerable hardware or infrastructure
- 48.6 percent—Installed additional computer security software
- 44.2 percent—Conducted an internal forensic investigation
- 42.0 percent—Provided additional security awareness training to their end users
- 40.6 percent—Changed their organization's security policies
- 32.6 percent—Changed or replaced software or systems
- 27.5 percent—Reported the intrusion(s) to a law enforcement agency
- 26.8 percent—Installed additional computer security hardware
- 26.1 percent—Reported intrusion(s) to their legal counsel
- 25.4 percent—Did not report the intrusion(s) to anyone outside the organization
- 23.9 percent—Attempted to identify perpetrator using their own resources
- 18.1 percent—Reported the intrusion(s) to individuals whose personal data was breached
- 15.9 percent—Provided new security services to users/customers
- 14.5 percent—Reported the intrusion(s) to business partners or contractors
- 13.8 percent—Contracted a third-party forensic investigator
- 3.6 percent—Reported the intrusion(s) to public media[17]

What is shocking is how few organizations notify individuals that their personal data has been breached. Should it ever be exposed to the public, those organizations could find themselves confronted with criminal charges or corporate negligence suits. Laws like the Sarbanes-Oxley Act of 2002 specifically implement personal ethical liability requirements for organizational management. Failure to report loss of personal data can run directly afoul of these laws.

Disaster Recovery

The next vital part of CP is disaster recovery planning. The IT community of interest, under the leadership of the CIO, is often made responsible for disaster recovery planning, including aspects that are not necessarily technology based.

Disaster recovery planning (DRP) entails the preparation for and recovery from a disaster, whether natural or human-made. In some cases, actual incidents detected by the IR team may escalate to the level of disaster, and the IR plan may no longer be able to handle the effective and efficient recovery from the loss. For example, if a malicious program evades containment actions and infects and disables many or most of an organization's systems and its ability to function, the **disaster recovery plan (DR plan)** is activated. Sometimes, events are by their nature immediately classified as disasters, such as an extensive fire, flood, damaging storm, or earthquake.

As you learned earlier in this chapter, the CP team creates the DR plan. In general, a disaster has occurred when either of two criteria is met: (1) The organization is unable to contain or control the impact of an incident or (2) the level of damage or destruction from an incident is so severe that the organization cannot quickly recover from it. The distinction between an incident and a disaster may be subtle. The CP team must document in the DR plan whether an event is classified as an incident or a disaster. This determination is critical because it determines which plan is activated. The key role of a DR plan is defining how to reestablish operations at the location where the organization is usually located.

You learned earlier in this chapter about the CP planning process recommended by NIST, which uses seven steps. In the broader context of organizational CP, these steps form the overall CP process. These steps are adapted and applied here within the narrower context of the DRP process, resulting in an eight-step DR process.

1. *Organize the DR team*—The initial assignments to the DR team, including the team lead, will most likely be performed by the CPMT; however, additional personnel may need to be assigned to the team as the specifics of the DR policy and plan are developed, and their individual roles and responsibilities defined and assigned.

2. *Develop the DR planning policy statement*—A formal department or agency policy provides the authority and guidance necessary to develop an effective contingency plan.

3. *Review the BIA*—The BIA was prepared to help identify and prioritize critical information and its host systems. A review of what was discovered is an important step in the process.

4. *Identify preventive controls*—Measures taken to reduce the effects of business and system disruptions can increase information availability and reduce contingency life cycle costs.

5. *Create DR strategies*—Thorough recovery strategies ensure that the system can be recovered quickly and effectively following a disruption.

6. *Develop the DR plan document*—The plan should contain detailed guidance and procedures for restoring a damaged system.

7. *Ensure DR Plan testing, training, and exercises*—Testing the plan identifies planning gaps, whereas training prepares recovery personnel for plan activation; both activities improve plan effectiveness and overall agency preparedness.

8. *Ensure DR Plan maintenance*—The plan should be a living document that is updated regularly to remain current with system enhancements.

Disaster Recovery Policy As noted in step 2, the DR team, led by the manager designated as the DR team leader, begins with the development of the DR policy soon after the team is formed. The policy presents an overview of the organization's philosophy on the conduct of DR operations and serves as the guide for the development of the DR plan. The DR policy itself may have been created by the organization's CP team and handed down to the DR team leader. Alternatively, the DR team may be assigned the role of developing the DR policy. In either case, the DR policy contains the following key elements:

- *Purpose*—The purpose of the DR program is to provide direction and guidance for all DR operations. In addition, the program provides for the development and support of the DR plan. In everyday practice, those responsible for the program must also work to emphasize the importance of creating and maintaining effective DR functions. As with any major enterprise-wide policy effort, it is important for the DR program to begin with a clear statement of executive vision.

- *Scope*—This section of the policy identifies the organizational units and groups of employees to which the policy applies. This clarification is important if the organization is geographically dispersed or is creating different policies for different organizational units.

- *Roles and responsibilities*—This section of the policy identifies the roles and responsibilities of the key players in the DR operation. It can include a delineation of the responsibilities of executive management down to individual employees. Some sections of the DR policy may be duplicated from the organization's overall CP policy. In smaller organizations, this redundancy can be eliminated, as many of the functions are performed by the same group.

- *Resource requirements*—An organization can allocate specific resources to the development of DR plans here. While this may include directives for individuals, it can be separated from the previous section for emphasis and clarity.

- *Training requirements*—This section defines and highlights the training requirements for the units within the organization and the various categories of employees.

- *Exercise and testing schedules*—This section stipulates the testing intervals of the DR plan as well as the type of testing and the individuals involved.

- *Plan maintenance schedule*—This section states the required review and update intervals of the plan, and identifies who is involved in the review. It is not necessary for the entire DR team to be involved, but the review can be combined with a periodic test of the DR plan as long as the resulting discussion includes areas for improving the plan.

- *Special considerations*—This includes such things as information storage and maintenance.

Disaster Classification

A DR plan can classify disasters in a number of ways. The most common method is to separate natural disasters, such as those described in Table 3-2, from human-made disasters. Acts of terrorism, including cyber-terrorism or hacktivism, acts of war, and acts of man that may begin as incidents and escalate into disasters are all examples of human-made disasters.

Another way of classifying disasters is by speed of development. **Rapid-onset disasters** occur suddenly, with little warning, taking the lives of people and destroying the means of production. Rapid-onset disasters may be caused by earthquakes, floods, storm winds, tornadoes, or mud flows. **Slow-onset disasters** occur over time and gradually degrade the capacity of an organization to withstand their effects. Hazards causing these disaster conditions typically include droughts, famines, environmental degradation, desertification, deforestation, and pest infestation.

Planning to Recover

To plan for disaster, the CPMT engages in scenario development and impact analysis, along the way categorizing the level of threat that each potential disaster poses. When generating a DR scenario, start with the most important asset: people. Do you have the human resources with the appropriate organizational knowledge to restore business operations? Organizations must cross-train their employees to ensure that operations and a sense of normalcy can be restored. In addition, the DR plan must be tested regularly so that the DR team can lead the recovery effort quickly and efficiently. Key elements that the CPMT must build into the DR plan include the following:

1. *Clear delegation of roles and responsibilities*—Everyone assigned to the DR team should be aware of his or her duties during a disaster. Some team members may be responsible for coordinating with local services, such as fire, police, and medical personnel. Some may be responsible for the evacuation of company personnel, if required. Others may be assigned to simply pack up and leave.

Natural Disaster	Effects and Mitigation
Fire	Damages the building housing the computing equipment that constitutes all or part of the information system. Also encompasses smoke damage from the fire and water damage from sprinkler systems or firefighters. Can usually be mitigated with fire casualty insurance or business interruption insurance.
Flood	Can cause direct damage to all or part of the information system or to the building that houses all or part of the information system. May also disrupt operations by interrupting access to the buildings that house all or part of the information system. Can sometimes be mitigated with flood insurance or business interruption insurance.
Earthquake	Can cause direct damage to all or part of the information system or, more often, to the building that houses it. May also disrupt operations by interrupting access to the buildings that house all or part of the information system. Can sometimes be mitigated with specific casualty insurance or business interruption insurance but is usually a specific and separate policy.
Lightning	Can directly damage all or part of the information system or its power distribution components. Can also cause fires or other damage to the building that houses all or part of the information system. May also disrupt operations by interrupting access to the buildings that house all or part of the information system as well as the routine delivery of electrical power. Can usually be mitigated with multipurpose casualty insurance or business interruption insurance.
Landslide or mudslide	Can damage all or part of the information system or, more likely, the building that houses it. May also disrupt operations by interrupting access to the buildings that house all or part of the information system as well as the routine delivery of electrical power. Can sometimes be mitigated with casualty insurance or business interruption insurance.
Tornado or severe windstorm	Can directly damage all or part of the information system or, more likely, the building that houses it. May also disrupt operations by interrupting access to the buildings that house all or part of the information system as well as the routine delivery of electrical power. Can sometimes be mitigated with casualty insurance or business interruption insurance.
Hurricane or typhoon	Can directly damage all or part of the information system or, more likely, the building that houses it. Organizations located in coastal or low-lying areas may experience flooding. May also disrupt operations by interrupting access to the buildings that house all or part of the information system as well as the routine delivery of electrical power. Can sometimes be mitigated with casualty insurance or business interruption insurance.
Tsunami	Can directly damage all or part of the information system or, more likely, the building that houses it. Organizations located in coastal areas may experience tsunamis. May also cause disruption to operations by interrupting access or electrical power to the buildings that house all or part of the information system. Can sometimes be mitigated with casualty insurance or business interruption insurance.
Electrostatic discharge (ESD)	Can be costly or dangerous when it ignites flammable mixtures and damages costly electronic components. Static electricity can draw dust into clean-room environments or cause products to stick together. The cost of servicing ESD-damaged electronic devices and interruptions can range from a few cents to millions of dollars for critical systems. Loss of production time in information processing due to the effects of ESD is significant. While not usually viewed as a threat, ESD can disrupt information systems and is not usually an insurable loss unless covered by business interruption insurance. ESD can be mitigated with special static discharge equipment and by managing HVAC temperature and humidity levels.
Dust contamination	Can shorten the life of information systems or cause unplanned downtime. Can usually be mitigated with an effective HVAC filtration system and quality housekeeping.

Table 3-2   Natural disasters and their effects on information systems

Copyright © 2014 Cengage Learning®.

2. *Execution of the alert roster and notification of key personnel*—These notifications may extend outside the organization to include the fire, police, or medical services mentioned earlier, as well as insurance agencies, disaster teams such as those of the Red Cross, and management teams.

3. *Clear establishment of priorities*—During a disaster response, the first priority is always the preservation of human life. Data and systems protection is subordinate when the disaster threatens the lives, health, or welfare of the employees or members of the community. Only after all employees and neighbors have been safeguarded can the DR team attend to protecting other organizational assets.

4. *Procedures for documentation of the disaster*—Just as in an incident response, the disaster must be carefully recorded from the onset. This documentation is used later to determine how and why the disaster occurred.

5. *Action steps to mitigate the impact of the disaster on the operations of the organization*—The DR plan should specify the responsibilities of each DR team member, such as the evacuation of physical assets or making sure that all systems are securely shut down to prevent further loss of data.

6. *Alternative implementations for the various systems components, should primary versions be unavailable*—These components include stand-by equipment, either purchased, leased, or under contract with a DR service agency. Developing systems with excess capacity, fault tolerance, autorecovery, and fail-safe features facilitates a quick recovery. Something as simple as using Dynamic Host Control Protocol (DHCP) to assign network addresses instead of using static addresses can allow systems to regain connectivity quickly and easily without technical support. Networks should support dynamic reconfiguration; restoration of network connectivity should be planned. Data recovery requires effective backup strategies as well as flexible hardware configurations. System management should be a top priority. All solutions should be tightly integrated and developed in a strategic plan to provide continuity. Piecemeal construction can result in a disaster after the disaster, as incompatible systems are unexpectedly thrust together.

There are a number of options with which an organization can protect its information and assist in getting operations up and running quickly, including the following:

- *Traditional data backups*—The organization can use a combination of on-site and off-site tape-drive or hard-drive backup methods, in a variety of rotation schemes; because the backup point is some time in the past, recent data is potentially lost. Most common data backup schemes involve random array of independent disks (RAID) or disk-to-disk-to-tape methods.

- *Electronic vaulting*—The organization can employ bulk batch-transfer of data to an off-site facility; transfer is usually conducted via leased lines or secure Internet connections. The receiving server archives the data as it is received. Some DR companies specialize in **electronic vaulting** services.

- *Remote journaling*—The organization can transfer live transactions to an off-site facility; **remote journaling** differs from electronic vaulting in two ways: (1) Only transactions are transferred, not archived data; and (2) the transfer takes place online and in much closer to real time. While electronic vaulting is akin to a traditional backup, with a dump of data to the off-site storage, remote journaling involves online activities on a systems level, much like server fault tolerance, where data is written to two locations simultaneously.

- *Database shadowing*—The organization can store duplicate online transaction data, along with duplicate databases, at the remote site on a redundant server; **database shadowing** combines electronic vaulting with remote journaling by writing multiple copies of the database simultaneously to two separate locations.

Industry recommendations for data backups include the "3-2-1 rule," which encourages maintaining three copies of important data (the original and two backup copies) on at least two different media (like hard drives and tape backups), with at least one copy stored off-site.

As part of DR plan readiness, each employee should have two types of emergency information card in his or her possession at all times. The first lists personal emergency information—the person to notify in case of an emergency (next of kin), medical conditions, and a form of identification. The second contains a set of instructions on what to do in the event of an emergency. This snapshot of the DR plan should contain a contact number or hotline for calling the organization during an emergency, emergency services numbers (fire, police, medical), evacuation and assembly locations (e.g., storm shelters), the name and number of the DR coordinator, and any other needed information.

Responding to the Disaster When a disaster strikes, actual events can at times overwhelm even the best of DR plans. To be prepared, the CPMT should incorporate a degree of flexibility into the plan. If the physical facilities are intact, the DR team should begin the restoration of systems and data to work toward full operational capability. If the organization's facilities are destroyed, alternative actions must be taken until new facilities can be acquired. When a disaster threatens the viability of an organization at the primary site, the DR process becomes a business continuity process, which is described next.

Simple Disaster Recovery Plan Figure 3-5 shows an example of what may be found in a simple DR plan. The plan has nine major sections, each of which is outlined below. Many organizations—particularly ones with multiple locations and hundreds of employees—would find this plan too simple. Nevertheless, the basic structure provides a solid starting point for any organization.

1. *Name of agency*—The first section identifies the department, division, or institution to which this particular plan applies. This identification is especially important in organizations that are large enough to require more than one plan.

2. *Date of completion or update of the plan and the date of the most recent test.*

3. *Agency staff to be called in the event of a disaster*—This roster should be kept current; it will not help the organization to have a list of employees who are no longer with the company. This section should also identify key support personnel, such as building maintenance supervisors, physical security directors, legal counsel, and the starting points on the alert roster. A copy of the alert roster (also known as the telephone tree) should be attached.

4. *Emergency services to be called (if needed) in event of a disaster*—While dialing 911 will certainly bring police, fire, and ambulance services, the organization may have equally pressing needs for emergency teams from the gas, electric, and water companies. This section should also list electricians, plumbers, locksmiths, and software and hardware vendors.

EXAMPLE DISASTER RECOVERY PLAN

1. Company_____

2. Date of completion or update of the plan_____

3. Staff to be called in the event of a disaster:

   Disaster Recovery Team:

   Name: Numbers: Position:

   _____

   _____

   _____

   _____

   _____

   _____

   _____

   _____

   _____

   _____

   _____

   _____

   _____

   _____

   Building Maintenance_____

   Building Security_____

   Legal Advisor_____

   Note below who is to call whom upon the discovery of a disaster (Telephone Tree):

4. Emergency services to be called (if needed) in event of a disaster:

   Service: Contact Person: Number:

   Ambulance_____

   Carpenters_____

   Data Processing Backup_____

   Electrician_____

   Emergency Management Coordinator_____

   Exterminator_____

   Fire Department_____

Figure 3-5 Example disaster recovery plan

Food Services_____

Locksmith_____

Plumber_____

Police_____

Security Personnel (extra)_____

Software Vendor_____

Temporary Personnel_____

Utility Companies:

    Electric_____

    Gas_____

    Water_____

Others:

5. Locations of in-house emergency equipment and supplies (attach map or floor plan with locations marked):

Batteries_____

Badges (employee identification)_____

Camera/Film_____

Cut-off Switches and Valves:

    Electric_____

    Gas_____

    Water_____

Sprinkler System (if separate)_____

Extension Cords (heavy-duty)_____

Fire Extinguishers_____

Flashlights_____

Ladders_____

Mops/Sponges/Buckets/Brooms_____

Nylon Monofilament_____

Packing Tape/String/Scissors_____

Paper Towels (white)_____

Plastic Trash Bags_____

Figure 3-5 Example disaster recovery plan (continued)

Rubber Gloves_____

Transistor Radio (battery powered)_____

6. Sources of off-site equipment and supplies (if maintained on-site, note location):

Item: Contact/Company: Number:

Cellular Phone_____

Dehumidifiers_____

Drying Space_____

Dust Masks_____

Fans_____

Fork Lift_____

Freezer/Wax Paper_____

Freezer Space/Refrigeration Truck_____

Fungicides_____

Generator (portable)_____

Hard Hats_____

Pallets_____

Plastic Milk Crates_____

Pumps (submersion)_____

Rubber Boots_____

Safety Glasses_____

Trash Can (all sizes)_____

Vacuum/Freeze Drying Facilities_____

Waterproof Clothing_____

Wet Dry Vacuum_____

7. Salvage Priority List:

Attach a copy of the records retention schedule identifying all vital/essential records series. The location and record medium of the preservation duplicate for each vital records series should be noted.

It is also very helpful if other records series are reviewed to determine their priority for salvage should a disaster occur. The following questions can be helpful in determining priorities:

1. Can the records be replaced? At what cost?
2. Would the cost of replacement be less or more than restoration of the records?

Figure 3-5 Example disaster recovery plan (continued)

3. How important are the records to the agency?
4. Are the records duplicated elsewhere?

To simplify this process, priorities may be assigned as follows:

1. Salvage at all costs.
   (example, records that are historically valuable or non-vital records that are important to agency Operations and very difficult to recreate)

2. Salvage if time and resources permit.
   (example, records that are less important to the agency or somewhat easier to recreate)

3. Dispose of as part of general cleanup.
   (example, records mat do not need to be salvaged because they are convenience copies and the record copy is at another location)

8. Disaster Recovery Procedures:

   Attach a list of specific procedures to be followed in the event of a disaster in you agency, including responsibilities of in-house recovery team members.

9. Follow-up Assessment:

   A written report, including photographs, should be prepared after recovery and attached to a copy of the disaster plan. The report should note the effectiveness of the plan, and should include an evaluation of the sources of supplies and equipment, and of any off-site facilities used.

Figure 3-5 Example disaster recovery plan (continued)

Copyright © 2014 Cengage Learning®.

5. *Locations of in-house emergency equipment and supplies*—This section should include maps and floor plans with directions to all critical in-house emergency materials, including shut-off switches and valves for gas, electric, and water. Directions to key supplies, including first aid kits, fire extinguishers, flashlights, batteries, and a stash of office supplies, should also be provided. It is a good idea to place a disaster pack on every floor in an unlocked closet or readily accessible location. These items should be inventoried and updated as needed.

6. *Sources of off-site equipment and supplies*—These items include contact sources for mobile phones, dehumidifiers, industrial equipment (such as forklifts and portable generators), and other safety and recovery components.

7. *Salvage priority list*—While the IT director may have just enough time to grab the last on-site backup before darting out the door in the event of a fire, additional materials can most likely be salvaged if recovery efforts permit. In this event, recovery teams should know what has priority. This list should specify whether to recover hard copies or if the effort should be directed toward saving equipment. Similarly, it specifies whether the organization should focus on archival records or recent documents. The plan should include the locations and priorities of all items of value to the organization. When determining priorities, ask questions such as: Are these records archived elsewhere (i.e., off-site), or is this the only copy? Can these records be reproduced if lost,

and if so, at what cost? Is the cost of replacement more or less than the cost of the value of the materials? It may be useful to create a simple rating scheme for materials. Data classification labels can be adapted to include DR information. For example, some records may be labeled "Salvage at all costs," "Salvage if time and resources permit," or "Do not salvage."

8. *Agency disaster recovery procedures*—This very important section outlines the specific assignments given to key personnel, including the DR team, to be performed in the event of a disaster. If these duties differ by type of disaster, it may be useful to create multiple scenarios, each listing the duties and responsibilities of the parties involved. It is equally important to make sure that all personnel identified in this section have a copy of the DR plan stored where they can easily access it, and that they are familiar with their responsibilities.

9. *Follow-up assessment*—The final section details what is to be accomplished after disaster strikes—specifically, what documentation is required for recovery efforts, including mandatory insurance reports, required photographs, and the AAR format.

Business Continuity

Business continuity planning (BCP) ensures that critical business functions can continue if a disaster occurs. Unlike the DR plan, which is usually managed by the IT community of interest, the **BC plan** is most properly managed by the CEO or COO of an organization. It is activated and executed concurrently with the DR plan when the disaster is major or long term and requires fuller and more complex restoration of information and IT resources. If a disaster renders the current business location unusable, there must be a plan to allow the business to continue to function. While the BC plan reestablishes critical business functions at an alternate site, the DR plan team focuses on the reestablishment of the technical infrastructure and business operations at the primary site. Not every business needs such a plan or such facilities. Some small companies or fiscally sound organizations may be able to simply cease operations until the primary facilities are restored. Manufacturing and retail organizations, however, depend on continued operations for revenue. Thus, these entities must have a BC plan in place so as to relocate operations quickly with minimal loss of revenue.

BC is an element of CP, and it is best accomplished using a repeatable process or methodology. NIST's "Special Publication 800-34, Rev. 1: Contingency Planning Guide for Federal Information Systems"[18] includes guidance for planning for incidents, disasters, and situations calling for BC. The approach used in that document has been adapted for BC use here.

The first step in all contingency efforts is the development of policy; the next step is planning. In some organizations, these are considered concurrent operations where development of policy is a function of planning, while in others policy comes before planning and is a separate process. In this text, the BC policy is developed prior to the BC plan; and both are developed as part of BC planning. The same seven-step approach that NIST recommends for CP can be adapted to an eight-step model that can be used to develop and maintain a viable BC program. Those steps are as follows:

1. *Form the BC Team*—As was done with the DR planning process, the initial assignments to the BC team, including the team lead, will most likely be performed by the CPMT; however, additional personnel may need to be assigned to the team as the specifics of the BC policy and plan are developed, and their individual roles and responsibilities will have to be defined and assigned.

2. *Develop the BC planning policy statement*—A formal organizational policy provides the authority and guidance necessary to develop an effective continuity plan. As with any enterprise-wide policy process, it is important to begin with the executive vision.

3. *Review the BIA*—Information contained within the BIA can help identify and prioritize critical organizational functions and systems for the purposes of business continuity, making it easier to understand what functions and systems will need to be reestablished elsewhere in the event of a disaster.

4. *Identify preventive controls*—Little is done here exclusively for BC. Most of the steps taken in the CP and DRP processes will provide the necessary foundation for BCP.

5. *Create relocation strategies*—Thorough relocation strategies ensure that critical business functions will be reestablished quickly and effectively at an alternate location, following a disruption.

6. *Develop the BC plan*—The BC plan should contain detailed guidance and procedures for implementing the BC strategies at the predetermined locations in accordance with management's guidance.

7. *Ensure BC plan testing, training, and exercises*—Testing the plan identifies planning gaps, whereas training prepares recovery personnel for plan activation; both activities improve plan effectiveness and overall agency preparedness.

8. *Ensure BC plan maintenance*—The plan should be a living document that is updated regularly to remain current with system enhancements.

Business Continuity Policy BCP begins with the development of the BC policy, which reflects the organization's philosophy on the conduct of BC operations and serves as the guiding document for the development of BCP. The BC team leader might receive the BC policy from the CP team or might guide the BC team in developing one. The BC policy contains the following key sections:

- *Purpose*—What is the purpose of the BC program? To provide the necessary planning and coordination to facilitate the relocation of critical business functions should a disaster prohibit continued operations at the primary site.

- *Scope*—This section identifies the organizational units and groups of employees to which the policy applies. This is especially useful in organizations that are geographically dispersed or that are creating different policies for different organizational units.

- *Roles and responsibilities*—This section identifies the roles and responsibilities of key players in the BC operation, from executive management down to individual employees. In some cases, sections may be duplicated from the organization's overall CP policy. In smaller organizations, this redundancy can be eliminated because many of the functions are performed by the same group of individuals.

- *Resource requirements*—Organizations can allocate specific resources to the development of BC plans. Although this may include directives for individuals, it can be separated from the roles and responsibilities section for emphasis and clarity.

- *Training requirements*—This section specifies the training requirements for the various employee groups.

- *Exercise and testing schedules*—This section stipulates the frequency of BC plan testing and can include both the type of exercise or testing and the individuals involved.

- *Plan maintenance schedule*—This section specifies the procedures and frequency of BC plan reviews and identifies the personnel who will be involved in the review. It is not necessary for the entire BC team to be involved; the review can be combined with a periodic test of the BC (as in a talk-through) as long as the resulting discussion includes areas for improvement of the plan.

- *Special considerations*—In extreme situations, the DR and BC plans overlap, as described earlier. Thus, this section provides an overview of the information storage and retrieval plans of the organization. While the specifics do not have to be elaborated in this document, at a minimum the plan should identify where more detailed documentation is kept, which individuals are responsible, and any other information needed to implement the strategy.

You may have noticed that this structure is virtually identical to that of the disaster recovery policy and plans. The processes are generally the same, with minor differences in implementation.

The identification of critical business functions and the resources to support them is the cornerstone of the BC plan. When a disaster strikes, these functions are the first to be reestablished at the alternate site. The CP team needs to appoint a group of individuals to evaluate and compare the various alternatives and to recommend which strategy should be selected and implemented. The strategy selected usually involves an off-site facility, which should be inspected, configured, secured, and tested on a periodic basis. The selection should be reviewed periodically to determine whether a better alternative has emerged or whether the organization needs a different solution.

Many organizations with operations in New York City had their BC efforts (or lack thereof) tested critically on September 11, 2001. Similarly, organizations located in the Gulf Coast region of the United States had their BC plan effectiveness tested during the aftermath of Hurricane Katrina in 2005.

Continuity Strategies The CPMT can choose from several strategies in its CP and BC planning. The determining factor is usually cost. In general, there are three types of usage strategies in which the organization has the right to the exclusive use of a facility and access is not shared with other organizations:

- **Hot site**—A hot site is a fully configured computer facility, with all services, communications links, and physical plant operations. It duplicates computing resources, peripherals, phone systems, applications, and workstations. Essentially, this duplicate facility needs only the latest data backups and the personnel to function. If the organization uses one of the data services listed in the following sections, a hot site can be fully functional within minutes. Not surprisingly, it is the most expensive alternative. Other disadvantages include the need to provide maintenance for all the systems and equipment at the hot site, as well as physical and information security. However, if the organization requires a 24/7 capability for near real-time recovery, the hot site is the optimal strategy.

- **Warm site**—A warm site provides many of the same services and options as the hot site, but typically software applications are not included or are not installed and configured. A warm site frequently includes computing equipment and peripherals with servers but not client workstations. Overall, it offers many of the advantages of a hot site at a lower cost. The disadvantage is that several hours—perhaps days—are required to make a warm site fully functional.

- **Cold site**—A cold site provides only rudimentary services and facilities. No computer hardware or peripherals are provided. All communications services must be installed after the site is occupied. A cold site is an empty room with standard heating, air conditioning, and electrical service. Everything else is an added-cost option. Despite these disadvantages, a cold site may be better than nothing. Its primary advantage is its low cost. The most useful feature of this approach is that it ensures that an organization has floor space should a widespread disaster strike, but some organizations are prepared to struggle to lease new space rather than pay maintenance fees on a cold site.

Likewise, there are three strategies in which an organization can gain shared use of a facility when needed for contingency options:

- **Timeshare**—A timeshare operates like one of the three sites described above but is leased in conjunction with a business partner or sister organization. It allows the organization to provide a DR/BC option while reducing its overall costs. The primary disadvantage is the possibility that more than one time-share participant will need the facility simultaneously. Other disadvantages include the need to stock the facility with the equipment and data from all organizations involved, the complexity of negotiating the timeshare with the sharing organizations, and the possibility that one or more parties might exit the agreement or sublease their options. Operating under a timeshare is much like agreeing to co-lease an apartment with a group of friends. One can only hope that the organizations remain on amicable terms, as they all could potentially gain physical access to each other's data.

- **Service bureau**—A service bureau is a service agency that provides a service for a fee. In the case of DR/BC planning, this service is the provision of physical facilities in the event of a disaster. Such agencies also frequently provide off-site data storage for a fee. Contracts with service bureaus can specify exactly what the organization needs under what circumstances. A service agreement usually guarantees space when needed; the service bureau must acquire additional space in the event of a widespread disaster. In this sense, it resembles the rental car provision in a car insurance policy. The disadvantage is that service contracts must be renegotiated periodically and rates can change. It can also be quite expensive.

- **Mutual agreement**—A mutual agreement is a contract between two organizations in which each party agrees to assist the other in the event of a disaster. It stipulates that each organization is obligated to provide the necessary facilities, resources, and services until the receiving organization is able to recover from the disaster. This arrangement can be a lot like moving in with relatives or friends—it does not take long for an organization to wear out its welcome. Many organizations balk at the idea of having to fund (even in the short term) duplicate services and resources. Still, mutual agreements between divisions of the same parent company, between subordinate and senior organizations, or between business partners may be a cost-effective solution when both parties to the agreement have a mutual interest in the other's continued operations and both have similar capabilities and capacities.

In addition to these basic strategies, there are specialized alternatives, such as a **rolling mobile site**, configured in the payload area of a tractor/trailer, or externally stored resources, such as a rental storage area containing duplicate or older equipment. These alternatives are similar to the Prepositioning of Material Configured to Unit Sets (POM-CUS) sites of the Cold War era, in which caches of materials to be used in the event of an emergency or war were stored outside normal work areas. An organization might arrange with a prefabricated building contractor for immediate, temporary facilities (mobile offices) on site in the event of a disaster.

Timing and Sequence of CP Elements As indicated earlier, the IR plan focuses on immediate response, but if the incident escalates into a disaster, the IR plan may give way to the DR plan and BC plan, as illustrated in Figure 3-6. The DR plan typically focuses on restoring systems after disasters occur and is therefore closely associated with the BC plan. The BC plan occurs concurrently with the DR plan when the damage is major or long term, requiring more than simple restoration of information and information resources, as illustrated in Figure 3-7.

Some experts argue that the three planning components (IR, DR, and BC) of CP are so closely linked that they are indistinguishable. Actually, each has a distinct place, role, and planning requirement. Furthermore, each component comes into play at a specific time in the life of an incident. Figure 3-8 illustrates this sequence and shows the overlap that may occur. How the plans interact and the ways in which they are brought into action are discussed in the following sections.

Crisis Management

Another process that many organizations plan for separately is **crisis management (CM)**—that is, the action steps affecting the people inside and outside the organization that are taken during and after a disaster. While some organizations include crisis management as a subset of the DR plan, the protection of human life and the organization's image is such a high priority that it may deserve its own committee, policy, and plan. The DR

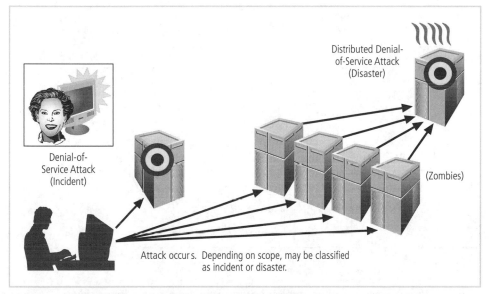

Figure 3-6 Incident response and disaster recovery

Copyright © 2014 Cengage Learning®.

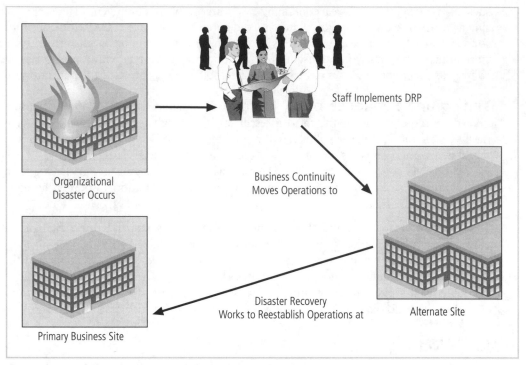

Figure 3-7 Disaster recovery and business continuity planning

Copyright © 2014 Cengage Learning®.

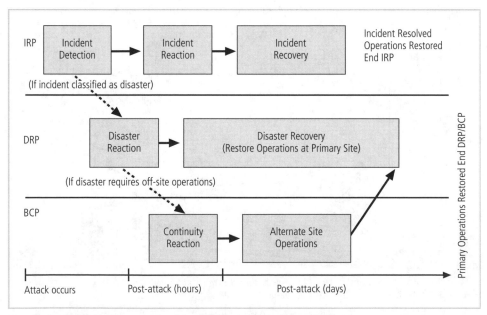

Figure 3-8 Contingency planning implementation timeline

Copyright © 2014 Cengage Learning®.

team works closely with the crisis management team to assure complete and timely communication during a disaster. According to Gartner Research, the crisis management team is responsible for managing the event from an enterprise perspective and performs the following roles:

- Supporting personnel and their loved ones during the crisis
- Keeping the public informed about the event and the actions being taken to ensure the recovery of personnel and the enterprise
- Communicating with major customers, suppliers, partners, regulatory agencies, industry organizations, the media, and other interested parties[19]

The **crisis management team** (**CMT**) should establish a base of operations or command center near the site of the disaster as soon as possible. The CMT should include individuals from all functional areas of the organization in order to facilitate communications and cooperation. The CMT is charged with two primary responsibilities:

1. *Verifying personnel status*—Everyone must be accounted for, including individuals who are on vacations, leaves of absence, and business trips.

2. *Activating the alert roster*—Alert rosters and general personnel phone lists are used to notify individuals whose assistance may be needed or to simply tell employees not to report to work until the disaster is over.

The CMT should plan an approach for releasing information in the event of a disaster and should perhaps even have boilerplate scripts prepared for press releases. Advice from Lanny Davis, former counselor to President Bill Clinton, is relevant here. When beset by damaging events, heed the subtitle to Davis's memoir: *Tell it Early, Tell It All, Tell It Yourself.*[20]

Business Resumption

Because the DR and BC plans are closely related, most organizations prepare the two at the same time and may even combine them into a single planning document called the **business resumption plan** (**BR plan**). Such a comprehensive plan must be able to support the reestablishment of operations at two different locations—one immediately at an alternate site and one eventually back at the primary site. Therefore, although a single planning team can develop the BR plan, execution of the plan requires separate execution teams.

The planning process for the BR plan should be tied to, but distinct from, the IR plan. As noted earlier in the chapter, an incident may escalate into a disaster when it grows dramatically in scope and intensity. It is important that the three planning development processes be so tightly integrated that the reaction teams can easily make the transition from incident response to disaster recovery and BCP.

One useful resource is the BC Plan template provided by the Federal Agency Security Practices section of NIST's CSRC (*http://csrc.nist.gov/groups/SMA/fasp/areas.html*). Although it is labeled as a contingency plan, this Web page provides a template BR plan in the form of a joint DR/BC plan, complete with instructions designed for Department of Justice (DOJ)–related agencies. The instructions specifically describe the approach taken for the template, allowing easy conversion to suit many public and private organizations. Table 3-3 provides the table of contents for this document.

Contents	
1.	Executive Summary
2.	Introduction 2.1 Purpose 2.2 Scope 2.3 Plan Information

3.	Contingency Plan Overview
	3.1 Applicable Provisions and Directives
	3.2 Objectives
	3.3 Organization
	3.4 Contingency Phases
	    3.4.1 Response Phase
	    3.4.2 Resumption Phase
	    3.4.3 Recovery Phase
	    3.4.4 Restoration Phase
	3.5 Assumptions
	3.6 Critical Success Factors and Issues
	3.7 Mission-Critical Systems/Applications/Services
	3.8 Threats
	    3.8.1 Probable Threats

4.	System Description 4.1 Physical Environment 4.2 Technical Environment

5.	Plan
	5.1 Plan Management
	    5.1.1 Contingency Planning Workgroups
	    5.1.2 Contingency Plan Coordinator
	    5.1.3 System Contingency Coordinators
	    5.1.4 Incident Notification
	    5.1.5 Internal Personnel Notification
	    5.1.6 External Contact Notification
	    5.1.7 Media Releases
	    5.1.8 Alternate Site(s)
	5.2 Teams
	    5.2.1 Damage Assessment Team
	    5.2.2 Operations Team
	    5.2.3 Communications Team
	    5.2.4 Data Entry and Control Team
	    5.2.5 Off-Site Storage Team
	    5.2.6 Administrative Management Team
	    5.2.7 Procurement Team
	    5.2.8 Configuration Management Team
	    5.2.9 Facilities Team
	    5.2.10 System Software Team
	    5.2.11 Internal Audit Team
	    5.2.12 User Assistance Team
	5.3 Data Communications
	5.4 Backups
	    5.4.1 Vital Records/Documentation

Table 3-3 Contingency plan template

Contents	
	5.5 Office Equipment, Furniture, and Supplies
	5.6 Recommended Testing Procedures
6.	Recommended Strategies
	6.1 Critical Issues
	6.1.1 Power
	6.1.2 Diversification of Connectivity
	6.1.3 Offsite Backup Storage
7.	Terms and Definitions
8.	Appendices
Appendix A	Contingency Plan Contact Information
Appendix B	Emergency Procedures
Appendix C	Team Staffing and Tasking
Appendix D	Alternate Site Procedures
Appendix E	Documentation List
Appendix F	Software Inventory
Appendix G	Hardware Inventory
Appendix H	Communications Requirements
Appendix I	Vendor Contact Lists
Appendix J	External Support Agreements
Appendix K	Data Center/Computer Room Emergency Procedures and Requirements
Appendix L	Plan Maintenance Procedures
Appendix M	Contingency Log

Table 3-3   Contingency plan template (continued)

Copyright © 2014 Cengage Learning®.

Testing Contingency Plans

Very few plans are executable as initially written; instead, they must be tested to identify vulnerabilities, faults, and inefficient processes. Once problems are identified during the testing process, improvements can be made, and the resulting plan can be relied on in times of need. Five strategies can be used to test contingency plans:

- **Desk check**—The simplest kind of validation involves distributing copies of the appropriate plans to all individuals who will be assigned roles during an actual incident or disaster. Each of these individuals performs a desk check by reviewing the plan and creating a list of correct and incorrect components. While not a true test, this strategy is a good way to review the perceived feasibility and effectiveness of the plan.

- **Structured walk-through**—In a structured walk-through, all involved individuals walk through the steps they would take during an actual incident or disaster. This exercise can consist of an on-site walk-through, in which everyone discusses their actions at each particular location and juncture, or it may be more of a **talk-through** or **chalk talk**, in which all involved individuals sit around a conference table and discuss, in turn, their responsibilities as the incident unfolds.

- **Simulation**—In a simulation, each person works individually, rather than in a group setting, to simulate the performance of each task. The simulation stops short of performing the actual physical tasks required, such as installing the backup data or disconnecting a communications circuit. The major difference between a walk-through and a simulation is that individuals work on their own tasks and are responsible for identifying the faults in their own procedures.

- **Parallel testing**—In parallel testing, individuals act as if an actual incident or disaster occurred and begin performing their required tasks and executing the necessary procedures, without interfering with the normal operations of the business. Great care must be taken to ensure that these procedures do not halt the operations of the business functions, thereby creating an actual incident.

- **Full interruption**—In full-interruption testing, the individuals follow each and every IR/DR/BC procedure, including the interruption of service, restoration of data from backups, and notification of appropriate individuals. This exercise is often performed after normal business hours in organizations that cannot afford to disrupt or simulate the disruption of business functions. Although full-interruption testing is the most rigorous testing strategy, it is unfortunately too risky for most businesses.

At a minimum, organizations should conduct periodic walk-throughs (or chalk talks) of each of the CP component plans. Failure to update these plans as the business and its information resources change can erode the team's ability to respond to an incident, or possibly cause greater damage than the incident itself. If this sounds like a major training effort, note what the author Richard Marcinko, a former Navy SEAL, has to say about motivating a team:[21]

- The more you sweat to train, the less you bleed in combat.
- Training and preparation can hurt.
- Lead from the front, not the rear.
- You don't have to like it; you just have to do it.
- Keep it simple.
- Never assume.
- You are paid for results, not methods.

One often-neglected aspect of training is cross-training. In a real incident or disaster, the people assigned to particular roles are often not available. In some cases, alternate people must perform the duties of personnel who have been incapacitated by the disastrous event that triggered the activation of the plan. The testing process should train people to take over in the event that a team leader or integral member of the execution team is unavailable.

Final Thoughts

As in all organizational efforts, iteration results in improvement. A critical component of the NIST-based methodologies presented in this chapter is continuous process improvement (CPI). Each time the organization rehearses its plans, it should learn from the process, improve the plans, and then rehearse again. Each time an incident or disaster occurs, the organization should review what went right and what went wrong. The actual results should be so thoroughly analyzed that any changes to the plans that could have resulted in an improved outcome will be implemented into a revised set of plans. Through ongoing evaluation and improvement, the organization continues to move forward and continually improves upon the process so that it can strive for an even better outcome.

Chapter Summary

- Planning for unexpected events is usually the responsibility of managers from both the information technology and the information security communities of interest.

- For a plan to be seen as valid by all members of the organization, it must be sanctioned and actively supported by the general business community of interest.

- Some organizations are required by law or other mandate to have CP procedures in place at all times, but all business organizations should prepare for the unexpected.

- Contingency planning (CP) is the process by which the information technology and information security communities of interest position their organizations to prepare for, detect, react to, and recover from events that threaten the security of information resources and assets, both human and artificial.

- CP is made up of four major components: the data collection and documentation process known as the business impact analysis (BIA), the incident response (IR) plan, the disaster recovery (DR) plan, and the business continuity (BC) plan.

- Organizations can either create and develop the three planning elements of the CP process (the IR, BC, and DR plans) as one unified plan, or they can create the three elements separately in conjunction with a set of interlocking procedures that enable continuity.

- To ensure continuity during the creation of the CP components, a seven-step CP process is used:

  1. Develop the contingency planning policy statement.
  2. Conduct the BIA.
  3. Identify preventive controls.
  4. Create contingency strategies.
  5. Develop a contingency plan.
  6. Ensure plan testing, training, and exercises.
  7. Ensure plan maintenance.

- Four teams of individuals are involved in contingency planning and contingency operations: the CP team, the IR team, the DR team, and the BC team. The IR team ensures the CSIRT is formed.

- The IR plan is a detailed set of processes and procedures that plan for, detect, and resolve the effects of an unexpected event on information resources and assets.

- For every scenario identified, the CP team creates three sets of procedures—for before, during, and after the incident—to detect, contain, and resolve the incident.

- Incident classification is the process by which the IR team examines an incident candidate and determines whether it constitutes an actual incident.

- Three categories of incident indicators are used: possible, probable, and definite.

- When any one of the following happens, an actual incident is in progress: loss of availability of information, loss of integrity of information, loss of confidentiality of information, violation of policy, or violation of law.

- DR planning encompasses preparation for handling and recovering from a disaster, whether natural or human made.

- The DR plan must include crisis management, the action steps taken during and after a disaster.

- BC planning ensures that critical business functions continue if a catastrophic incident or disaster occurs. BC plans can include provisions for hot sites, warm sites, cold sites, timeshares, service bureaus, and mutual agreements.

- Because the DR and BC plans are closely related, most organizations prepare the two at the same time and may combine them into a single planning document called the business resumption (BR) plan.

- All plans must be tested to identify vulnerabilities, faults, and inefficient processes. Five testing strategies can be used to test contingency plans: desk check, structured walkthrough, simulation, parallel testing, and full-interruption.

Review Questions

1. What is the name for the broad process of planning for the unexpected? What are its primary components?

2. Which two communities of interest are usually associated with contingency planning? Which community must give authority to ensure broad support for the plans?

3. According to some reports, what percentage of businesses that do not have a disaster plan go out of business after a major loss?

4. List the seven-step CP process recommended by NIST.

5. List and describe the teams that perform the planning and execution of the CP plans and processes. What is the primary role of each?

6. Define the term "incident" as used in the context of IRP. How is it related to the concept of incident response?

7. List and describe the criteria used to determine whether an actual incident is occurring.

8. List and describe the sets of procedures used to detect, contain, and resolve an incident.

9. List and describe the IR planning steps.

10. List and describe the actions that should be taken during an incident response.

3

11. What is an alert roster? What is an alert message? Describe the two ways they can be used.

12. List and describe several containment strategies given in the text. On which tasks do they focus?

13. What is an incident damage assessment? What is it used for?

14. What criteria should be used when considering whether or not to involve law enforcement agencies during an incident?

15. What is a disaster recovery plan, and why is it important to the organization?

16. List and describe two rapid-onset disasters. List and describe one slow-onset disaster.

17. What is a business continuity plan, and why is it important?

18. What is a business impact analysis, and what is it used for?

19. Why should continuity plans be tested and rehearsed?

20. Which types of organizations might use a unified continuity plan? Which types of organizations might use the various contingency planning components as separate plans? Why?

Exercises

1. Using a Web search engine, search for the terms "disaster recovery" and "business continuity." How many responses do you get for each term? Note how many companies do not distinguish between the two.

2. Go to *http://csrc.nist.gov*. Under "Publications," select **Special Publications**, then locate **SP 800-34, Contingency Planning Guide for Information Technology Systems, June 2002.** Download and review this document. Summarize the key points for an in-class discussion.

3. Using a Web search engine, visit one of the popular disaster recovery/business continuity sites, such as *www.disasterrecoveryworld.com/*, *www.drj.com/*, *www.drie.org/*, *www.drii.org*, or *csrc.nist.gov*. Search for the terms "hot site," "warm site," and "cold site." Do the provided descriptions match those of this chapter? Why or why not?

4. Using the format provided in the text, design an incident response plan for your home computer. Include actions to be taken if each of the following events occur:
   - Virus attack
   - Power failure
   - Fire
   - Burst water pipe
   - ISP failure

   What other scenarios do you think are important to plan for?

5. Look for information on incident response on your institution's Web site. Does your institution have a published plan? Identify the areas in an academic institution's contingency planning that might differ from those of a for-profit institution.

Closing Case

Iris tried not to smile. "Of course, it isn't technically a disaster," she explained, "but I understand what you mean. How much information is lost?"

Joel looked at her in dismay. "Lost? All of it! We had just saved the report and sent it to the department print server!"

"Where did you save it," Iris asked. "To your local drive or to the department share?"

Joel tried to remember. "I think it was to the G: drive," he said. "Why?"

"Well, the G: drive is on a machine at the end of the hall, which wasn't affected by this incident," Iris replied. "It's probably fine. And if you did save it to your local drive, there's a high probability we can get it anyway, one way or another. I doubt the water damaged the hard drive itself."

Iris paused for a moment, then continued: "We were lucky this time," she said. "No one was hurt, and if the fire had spread to the next room, where there are more valuable assets, things would have been much worse."

Discussion

1. Extrapolate on the case. At what point could this incident have been declared a disaster?

2. What would Iris have done differently if this adverse event had been much worse and had been declared a disaster?

3. Identify the procedures that Joel could have taken to minimize the potential loss in this incident. What would he need to do differently in the event of a disaster, if anything?

Ethical Decision Making

Imagine that the fire in the break room was caused by Joel, who accidentally started it while taking an unauthorized cigarette break in the break room, then dropping a still-lit cigarette in the trash bin. In that case, would Joel have been responsible for the damage caused to the break room and adjoining office? What if no one knew who the smoker had been? Would it then be unethical for Joel to deny that it was his cigarette if Iris asked him about it?

Endnotes

1. "NIST General Information." *National Institute of Standards and Technology.* Accessed February 11, 2013 @ *www.nist.gov/public_affairs/general_information.cfm.*

2. "Computer Security Division Mission Statement." *NIST Computer Security Division.* Accessed February 11, 2013 @ *http://csrc.nist.gov/mission/index.html.*

3. Swanson, M., P. Bowen, A. Phillips, D. Gallup, and D. Lynes. "Special Publication 800-34 Rev. 1: Contingency Planning Guide for Federal Information Systems." National Institute of Standards and Technology. Accessed February 17, 2013 @ *http://csrc.nist.gov/publications/nistpubs/800-34-rev1/sp800-34-rev1_errata-Nov11-2010.pdf.*

4. "Disaster Recovery Tips." *The Hartford.* Accessed February 13, 2013 @ *www.thehartford.com/business/disaster-recovery-guide.*

5. Swanson, M., P. Bowen, A. Phillips, D. Gallup, and D. Lynes. "Special Publication 800-34 Rev. 1: Contingency Planning Guide for Federal Information Systems." National Institute of Standards and Technology. Accessed February 17, 2013 @ *http:// csrc.nist.gov/publications/nistpubs/800-34-rev1/sp800-34-rev1_errata-Nov11-2010.pdf*.

6. Swanson, M., J. Hash, and P. Bowen. "Special Publication 800-18 Rev 1: Guide for Developing Security Plans for Information Systems." (February 2006). National Institute of Standards and Technology (February 2006, p. 31). Accessed December 13, 2012 @ *csrc.nist.gov/publications/nistpubs/800-18-Rev1/sp800-18-Rev1-final.pdf*.

7. Zawada, B., and L. Evans. "Creating a More Rigorous BIA," CPM Group, November/ December 2002. Accessed May 12, 2005 @ *www.contingencyplanning.com/archives /2002/novdec/4.aspx*.

8. Swanson, M., P. Bowen, A. Phillips, D. Gallup, and D. Lynes. "Special Publication 800-34 Rev. 1: Contingency Planning Guide for Federal Information Systems." National Institute of Standards and Technology. Accessed February 17, 2013 @ *http:// csrc.nist.gov/publications/nistpubs/800-34-rev1/sp800-34-rev1_errata-Nov11-2010.pdf*.

9. Ibid.

10. Ibid.

11. Ibid.

12. Ibid.

13. Cichonski, P., T. Millar, T. Grance, and K. Scarfone. "Special Publication 800-61, Rev. 2: Computer Security Incident Handling Guide." National Institute of Standards and Technology (August 2012). Accessed February 17, 2103 @ *http://csrc.nist.gov/publications /nistpubs/800-61rev2/SP800-61rev2.pdf*.

14. Pipkin, Donald. *Information Security: Protecting the Global Enterprise*. Upper Saddle River, NJ: Prentice Hall PTR, 2000: 256.

15. Pipkin, Donald. *Information Security: Protecting the Global Enterprise*. Upper Saddle River, NJ: Prentice Hall PTR, 2000: 285.

16. Federal Bureau of Investigation. "Computer Intrusions." *FBI.gov*. Accessed August 27, 2012 @ *www.fbi.gov/about-us/investigate/cyber/computer-intrusions*.

17. "CSI Computer Crime and Security Survey, 2010/2011." *Computer Security Institute*. Accessed February 17, 2013 @ *http://reports.informationweek.com/abstract/21/7377 /Security/research-2010-2011-csi-survey.html*.

18. Swanson, M., P. Bowen, A. Phillips, D. Gallup, and D. Lynes. "Special Publication 800-34 Rev. 1: Contingency Planning Guide for Federal Information Systems." National Institute of Standards and Technology. Accessed August 27, 2012 @ *http:// csrc.nist.gov/publications/nistpubs/800-34-rev1/sp800-34-rev1_errata-Nov11-2010.pdf*.

19. Witty, Roberta. "What is Crisis Management?" *Gartner Online*, September 19, 2001. Accessed February 17, 2013 @ *http://www.gartner.com/id=340971*.

20. Davis, Lanny. *Truth to Tell: Tell It Early, Tell It All, Tell It Yourself: Notes from My White House Education*. New York: Free Press, May 1999.

21. Marcinko, Richard, and Weisman, John. *Designation Gold*. New York: Pocket Books, 1998.

## chapter 4

Information Security Policy

Each problem that I solved became a rule which served afterwards to solve other problems.

RENÉ DESCARTES

Iris was returning from lunch when she ran into Susan Weinstein, one of Random Widget Works, Inc.'s (RWW's) senior account executives, who was accompanied by a man Iris didn't know. Susan introduced him as Bob Watson, a prospective client. As they were chatting, Iris noticed Bob's distracted demeanor and Susan's forced smile and formal manner.

We didn't get the account, Iris realized.

A few minutes later, she saw why the meeting between the RWW's account executive and the prospective client did not go well. In the cubicle across the hall from Susan's office, two programmers were having lunch. Tim had his feet propped up on the desk. In one hand was a half-eaten hamburger; in the other, he held several playing cards. John had made himself comfortable by taking off his shoes. Next to his elbow was an open cup of coffee, which he had placed in the open tray of the PC's CD-ROM drive.

Iris went into her office and pulled the company's policy manual off the shelf. She was familiar with most of RWW's policies, but for the actions she had in mind, she needed specifics. But RWW's policy and procedure manual did not contain policies about alerting employees to meetings with prospective clients, or eating and drinking in the workplace, or even specifics about practices that supported data protection and other information security objectives.

Before Iris left that evening, she typed up her notes and scheduled an early morning meeting with her boss, Mike Edwards. As she left for home, she thought, "Tim and John playing cards and eating in their office may have cost us a new account. I'll suggest to Mike that it's time for us to reconvene the policy review committee."

LEARNING OBJECTIVES

Upon completion of this material, you should be able to:

- Define information security policy and understand its central role in a successful information security program

- Describe the three major types of information security policy and discuss the major components of each

- Discuss the process of developing, implementing, and maintaining various types of information security policies

Introduction

In this chapter, you will learn about information security (InfoSec) policy: what it is, how to write it, how to implement it, and how to maintain it. The success of any InfoSec program lies in policy development. In 1989, the National Institute of Standards and Technology (NIST) addressed this point in "Special Publication (SP) 500-169, Executive Guide to the Protection of Information Resources":

> *The success of an information resources protection program depends on the policy generated, and on the attitude of management toward securing information on automated systems. You, the policy maker, set the tone and the emphasis on how important a role information security will have within your agency. Your primary responsibility is to set the information resource security policy for the organization with the objectives of reduced risk, compliance with laws and regulations and assurance of operational continuity, information integrity, and confidentiality.*[1]

Policy is the essential foundation of an effective InfoSec program. As stated by consultant Charles Cresson Wood in his book *Information Security Policies Made Easy*:

> *The centrality of information security policies to virtually everything that happens in the information security field is increasingly evident. For example, system administrators cannot securely install a firewall unless they have received a set of clear information security policies. These policies will stipulate the type of transmission services that should be permitted, how to authenticate the identities of users, and how to log security-relevant events. An effective information security training and awareness effort cannot be initiated without writing information security policies because policies provide the essential content that can be utilized in training and awareness material.*[2]

Why Policy?

A quality InfoSec program begins and ends with policy. **Information security policies** are written instructions, provided by management, to inform employees and others in the workplace of the proper behavior regarding the use of information and information assets. This policy is designed to provide structure in the workplace and explain the will of the organization's management in controlling the behavior of its employees with regard to the appropriate and secure use of its information and information resources. Policy is designed to create a productive and effective work environment, free from unnecessary distractions and inappropriate actions. Properly developed and implemented policies enable the InfoSec program to function almost seamlessly within the workplace. Although InfoSec policies are considered the least expensive means of control, they are often the most difficult to implement. Policy controls cost only the time and effort that the management team spends to create, approve, and communicate them, and the time and effort that employees spend integrating the policies into their daily activities. Even when the management team hires an outside consultant to assist in the development of policy, the costs are minimal compared to the other forms of control, especially technical controls.

Some basic rules must be followed when shaping a policy:

- Policy should never conflict with law.
- Policy must be able to stand up in court if challenged.
- Policy must be properly supported and administered.

Consider some of the facts that were revealed during the Enron scandal in 2001. The management team at Enron Energy Corporation was found to have lied about the organization's financial records, specifically about reported profits. The management team was also accused of a host of dubious business practices, including concealing financial losses and debts. The depth and breadth of the fraud was so great that tens of thousands of investors lost significant amounts of money and at least one executive committed suicide rather than face criminal charges. One of the company's accounting firms, Arthur Andersen, contributed to the problem by shredding literally tons of financial documents. Andersen's auditors and information technology (IT) consultants claimed that this shredding of working papers was Andersen's established policy. The former chief auditor from Andersen was fired after an internal probe revealed that the company shredded these documents and deleted e-mail messages related to Enron with the intent to conceal facts from investigators. He pleaded guilty to obstruction of justice, which carries a maximum sentence of 10 years in prison. Although the Supreme Court overturned the conviction and the charges were subsequently dropped, the lesson remains valid: An organization must conform to its own policy, and that policy must be consistently applied.

Following a policy that conflicts with law is a criminal act. In the Enron/Andersen scandal, managers, employees, and others affiliated with Enron and Andersen could have claimed they were simply following policy. And since the policy as written did not violate any laws, they might have been able to use that as a defense, but they would need to have been consistently following that policy prior to the incidents in question. Andersen's document-retention policy originally stated that staff must keep working papers for six years before destroying them. On the other hand, client-related files, such as correspondence or other records, were to be kept only "until not useful." Managers and individual partners keeping such material in client folders or other files were supposed to "purge" the documents, according to the policy. But in cases of threatened litigation, the policy dictated that Andersen staff not destroy "related information." However, a subsequent change to the documentation-retention policy at Andersen was interpreted as a mandate to shred all but the most essential working papers as soon as possible unless destruction was precluded by an order for legal discovery. The shredding began right after Andersen management found out that Enron was to be investigated for fraudulent business practices, which pointed toward an intent to cover the firm's tracks and those of its business partners. The shredding policy was a problem because it was not consistently applied—members of the Andersen organization assigned to the Enron project could not demonstrate that they followed the policy routinely, only when it enabled them to shred incriminating documents.

Policy may be difficult to implement. According to Bergeron and Bérubé, the following guidelines can help in the formulation of IT policy as well as InfoSec policy.

- All policies must contribute to the success of the organization.
- Management must ensure the adequate sharing of responsibility for proper use of information systems.
- End users of information systems should be involved in the steps of policy formulation.[3]

Policy must be tailored to the specific needs of the organization. It makes little sense to have policies that are not well aligned with the organization. Those organizations that handle extremely sensitive information should not have relaxed or InfoSec policies. Likewise, organizations with little need for strong security measures would be poorly served with a stringent policy environment. While it is an admirable goal for policies to be complete and comprehensive, the existence of too many policies, or policies that are too complex, can cause confusion and possibly demoralize employees.

One implementation model that emphasizes the role of policy in an InfoSec program is the bull's-eye model. Because it provides a proven mechanism for prioritizing complex changes, the bull's-eye model has become widely accepted among InfoSec professionals. In this model, issues are addressed by moving from the general to the specific, always starting with policy. That is, the focus is on systemic solutions instead of individual problems. Figure 4-1 illustrates the four layers of the bull's-eye model, which are as follows:

1. *Policies*—This is the outer layer in the bull's-eye diagram, reflecting that it is the initial viewpoint that most users have for interacting with InfoSec. It is available from the published documents that express the will of management and seeks to guide user behavior.
2. *Networks*—This is the environment where threats from public networks meet the organization's networking infrastructure. In the past, most InfoSec efforts focused on networks. Until recently, in fact, InfoSec was often thought to be synonymous with network security.
3. *Systems*—These are the collections of hardware and software being used as servers or desktop computers as well as those systems used for process control and manufacturing systems.
4. *Applications*—These are the application systems, ranging from packaged applications, such as office automation and e-mail programs, to high-end enterprise resource planning (ERP) packages to custom application software or process control applications developed by the organization.

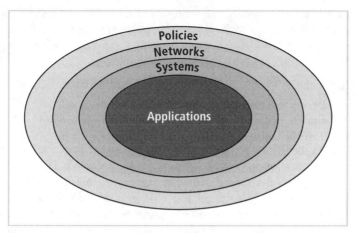

Figure 4-1 Bull's-eye model

Copyright © 2014 Cengage Learning®.

Whether via the use of the bull's-eye model or any other methodology, until sound and usable IT and InfoSec policy is developed, communicated, and enforced, no additional resources should be spent on controls.

In *Information Security Policies Made Easy*, Wood summarizes the need for policy as follows:

> [P]olicies are important reference documents for internal audits and for the resolution of legal disputes about management's due diligence, [and] policy documents can act as a clear statement of management's intent.[4]

However, policy isn't just a management tool to meet legal requirements. It's necessary to protect the organization and the jobs of its employees. Consider this scenario: An employee behaves inappropriately in the workplace, perhaps by viewing unsuitable Web pages or reading another employee's e-mail. Another employee is aggrieved by this behavior and sues the company. The company does not have policy that prohibits the behavior, so any direct action against the offending employee risks further litigation. The lawsuit is settled in the disgruntled employee's favor, and the resulting judgment awarding large financial damages puts the organization into bankruptcy. Once the organization goes out of business, the rest of the employees lose their jobs—all because the company did not have effective policies in place that would have enabled it to terminate the misbehaving employee.

Policy, Standards, and Practices

Policy is generally defined as a plan or course of action, as of a government, political party, or business, intended to influence and determine decisions, actions, and other matters. Policy represents a formal statement of the organization's managerial philosophy—in the case of our focus, the organization's InfoSec philosophy. The communities of interest described in previous chapters use policy to express their views regarding the security environment of the organization. This policy then becomes the basis for planning, management, and maintenance of the InfoSec profile. Once policies are designed, created, approved, and implemented, the technologies and procedures that are necessary to accomplish them can be designed, developed, and implemented. In other words, policies comprise a set of rules that dictate acceptable and unacceptable behavior within an organization. Policies direct how issues should be addressed and technologies should be used. Policies should not specify the proper operation of equipment or software—this information should be placed in other documentation called "standards," "procedures," "practices," and "guidelines."

Policies must also specify the penalties for unacceptable behavior and define an appeals process. For example, an organization that prohibits the viewing of inappropriate Web sites at the workplace must implement a set of standards that clarifies and defines exactly what it means by "inappropriate," and what the organization will do to stop the behavior. A **standard** is a more detailed statement of what must be done to comply with policy. In the implementation of an inappropriate-use policy, the organization might create a standard that all inappropriate content will be blocked and then list the material that is considered inappropriate. Later in the process, technical controls and their associated procedures might block network access to pornographic Web sites. **Practices, procedures,** and **guidelines** explain how employees are to comply with -policy. Figure 4-2 illustrates the relationship among policies, standards, and practices/procedures/guidelines.

To produce a complete InfoSec policy, management must define three types of InfoSec policies. These are based on NIST's "Special Publication 800-14," which outlines what is required of senior manager when writing policy. (This document, which is discussed in greater detail later in this chapter, is recommended for professionals involved in creating policy; it can be found at *csrc.nist.gov/publications/nistpubs/800-14/800-14.pdf*.) The three types of policy are as follows:

- Enterprise information security policy (EISP)
- Issue-specific security policies (ISSP)
- System-specific security policies (SysSP)

Each of these policy types is found in most organizations. The usual procedure is to first create the EISP—the highest level of policy. After that, general security policy needs are met by developing ISSP and SysSP policies. The three types of policy are described in detail in the following sections.

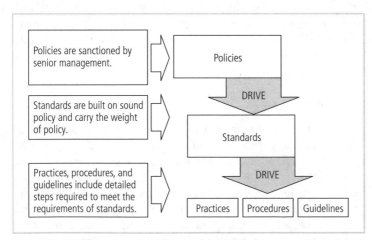

Figure 4-2 Policies, standards, and practices

Copyright © 2014 Cengage Learning®.

Enterprise Information Security Policy

An **enterprise information security policy (EISP)**—also known as a "security program policy," "general security policy," "IT security policy," "high-level InfoSec policy," or simply "InfoSec policy"—sets the strategic direction, scope, and tone for all of an organization's security efforts. It assigns responsibilities for the various areas of InfoSec, including maintenance of InfoSec policies and the practices and responsibilities of end users. In particular, the EISP guides the development, implementation, and management requirements of the InfoSec program, which must be met by InfoSec management, IT development, IT operations, and other specific security functions.

The EISP must directly support the organization's vision and mission statements. It must also be defensible if legal challenges arise. It is an executive-level document, drafted by the chief information security officer (CISO) in consultation with the chief information officer (CIO) and other executives. Usually 2–10 pages long, it shapes the security philosophy in the IT environment. The EISP does not typically require frequent or routine modification unless the strategic direction of the organization changes.

Integrating an Organization's Mission and Objectives into the EISP

The EISP plays a number of vital roles, not the least of which is to state the importance of InfoSec to the organization's mission and objectives. As demonstrated in the organizational and InfoSec planning processes discussed in Chapter 2, InfoSec strategic planning derives from other organizational strategic policies, such as the IT strategic policy and key business unit strategic policies, which are in turn derived from the organization's strategic planning. Unless the EISP directly reflects this association, the policy will likely become confusing and counterproductive.

How can the EISP be crafted to reflect the organization's mission and objectives? Suppose that an academic institution's mission statement promotes academic freedom, independent research, and the relatively unrestricted pursuit of knowledge. This institution's EISP should reflect great tolerance in the use of organizational technology, a commitment to protecting the intellectual property of the faculty, and a degree of tolerance for study that delves into what could be described as specialized or sensitive areas. The EISP should not contradict the organizational mission statement. For example, if the academic institution's mission statement supports the unrestricted pursuit of knowledge, then the EISP should not restrict access to legal but potentially objectionable Web sites or specify penalties for such access. Such a policy would directly contradict the academic institution's mission statement. However, it would be prudent for that institution to have policies that govern such access and ensure that such access does not interfere or create a hostile work environment for other employees. For example, the institution could require that an employee, while accessing potentially objectionable material, take steps to ensure that others are not exposed to the material.

EISP Elements

Although the specifics of EISPs vary from organization to organization, EISP documents should include the following elements:

- An overview of the corporate philosophy on security
- Information on the structure of the InfoSec organization and individuals who fulfill the InfoSec role

Component	Description
Purpose	Answers the question "What is this policy for?" Provides a framework that helps the reader understand the intent of the document. Can include text such as the following, which is taken from Washington University at St. Louis: "This document will: • Identify the elements of a good security policy • Explain the need for information security • Specify the various categories of information security • Identify the information security responsibilities and roles • Identify appropriate levels of security through standards and guidelines This document establishes an overarching security policy and direction for our company. Individual departments are expected to establish standards, guidelines, and operating procedures that adhere to and reference this policy while addressing their specific and individual needs."[5]
Elements	Defines the whole topic of information security within the organization as well as its critical components. For example, the policy may state: "Protecting the confidentiality, integrity, and availability of information while in processing, transmission, and storage, through the use of policy, education and training, and technology" and then identify where and how the elements are used. This section can also lay out security definitions or philosophies to clarify the policy.
Need	Justifies the need for the organization to have a program for information security. This is done by providing information on the importance of InfoSec in the organization and the obligation (legal and ethical) to protect critical information, whether regarding customers, employees, or markets.
Roles and responsibilities	Defines the staffing structure designed to support InfoSec within the organization. It will likely describe the placement of the governance elements for InfoSec as well as the categories of individuals with responsibility for InfoSec (IT department, management, users) and their InfoSec responsibilities, including maintenance of this document.
Reference to other policies, standards, and guidelines	Lists other standards that influence and are influenced by this policy document, perhaps including relevant laws (federal and state) and other policies.

Table 4-1   Components of the EISP

Copyright © 2014 Cengage Learning®

• Fully articulated responsibilities for security that are shared by all members of the organization (employees, contractors, consultants, partners, and visitors)
• Fully articulated responsibilities for security that are unique to each role within the organization

The components of an effective EISP are shown in Table 4-1

Example EISP Components

In *Information Security Policies Made Easy*, Wood includes a sample high-level InfoSec policy. Table 4-2 shows some of the specific components of this model, which, when integrated into the framework described in Table 4-1, provide detailed guidance for the creation of

1. Protection of Information	
Policy:	Information must be protected in a manner commensurate with its sensitivity, value, and criticality.
Commentary:	This policy applies regardless of the media on which information is stored, the locations where the information is stored, the systems technology used to process the information, or the people who handle the information. This policy encourages examining the ways information flows through an organization. The policy also points to the scope of Information Security management's work throughout, and often even outside, an organization.
Audience:	Technical staff
2. Use of Information	
Policy:	Company X information must be used only for the business purposes expressly authorized by management.
Commentary:	This policy states that all nonapproved uses of Company X information are prohibited.
Audience:	All
3. Information Handling, Access, and Usage	
Policy:	Information is a vital asset and all accesses to, uses of, and processing of Company X information must be consistent with policies and standards.
Commentary:	This policy sets the context for a number of other information security policies. Such a statement is frequently incorporated into the first set of policies and summary material oriented toward users and members of the top management team. It is necessary for these people to appreciate how information has become a critical factor of production in business. This policy motivates the need for information security measures and to create a new understanding of the importance of information systems in organizations.
Audience:	All
4. Data and Program Damage Disclaimers	
Policy:	Company X disclaims any responsibility for loss or damage to data or software that results from its efforts to protect the confidentiality, integrity, and viability of the information handled by computers and communications systems.
Commentary:	This policy notifies users that they cannot hold Company X liable for damages associated with management's attempts to secure its system.
Audience:	End users
5. Legal Conflicts	
Policy:	Company X information security policies were drafted to meet or exceed the protections found in existing laws and regulations, and any Company X information security policy believed to be in conflict with existing laws or regulations must be promptly reported to Information Security management.
Commentary:	This policy creates a context for the requirements specified in an information security policy document. Sound policies go beyond laws and regulations, or at least ensure that an organization will meet the requirements specified by laws and regulations. This policy acknowledges support for laws and regulations, and expresses an intention to stay in compliance with existing laws and regulations. The policy is suitable for both internal information security policies and those made available to the public.
Audience:	End users

Table 4-2   Sample EISP document components

6. Exceptions to Policies	
Policy:	Exceptions to information security policies exist in rare instances where a risk assessment examining the implications of being out of compliance has been performed, where a standard risk acceptance form has been prepared by the data owner or management, and where this form has been approved by both Information Security management and Internal Audit management.
Commentary:	Management will be called upon to approve certain exceptions to policies. This policy clarifies that exceptions will be granted only after a risk acceptance form has been completed, signed, and approved. The form should include a statement where the data owner or management takes responsibility for any losses occurring from the out-of-compliance situation. The existence of such a form provides an escape value that can be used to address those situations where users insist on being out of compliance with policies. It is desirable to make all out-of-compliance situations both known and documented. This means that if there were to be a loss that occurred as a result of the situation, management could demonstrate to a judge or jury that it was aware of the situation, examined the risks, and decided to waive the relevant policy or standard.
Audience:	Management
7. Policy Nonenforcement	
Policy:	Management's nonenforcement of any policy requirement does not constitute its consent.
Commentary:	This policy notifies policy statement readers that they should not expect out-of-compliance conditions to be continued only because management has not yet enforced the policy. This policy eliminates any claim that local management may state that an out-of-compliance condition should remain as it is because the condition has been in existence for a considerable period of time.
Audience:	End users
8. Violation of Law	
Policy:	Company X management must seriously consider prosecution for all known violations of the law.
Commentary:	This policy encourages the prosecution of abusive and criminal acts. While a decision to prosecute will be contingent on the specifics of the case, management should not dismiss prosecution without review. This policy may be important in terms of communicating to those would-be perpetrators of abusive or criminal acts. Many computer crimes are not prosecuted and perpetrators often know this, expecting victim organizations to terminate them and suppress the entire affair.
Audience:	Management
9. Revocation of Access Privileges	
Policy:	Company X reserves the right to revoke a user's IT privileges at any time.
Commentary:	This policy notifies users that they jeopardize their status as authorized users if they engage in activities that interfere with the normal and proper operation of Company X information systems, that adversely affect the ability of others to use these information systems, or that are harmful or offensive to others. For example, crashing the system could be expected to be harmful to other users, and would subject the perpetrator to disciplinary action including privilege revocation. The policy attempts to broadly describe an ethic for computing. Rather than specifying all of the adverse things that people could do, such as crashing a system, this policy is discreet and at a high level. This policy may give management latitude when it comes to deciding about privilege revocation.
Audience:	End users

Table 4-2 Sample EISP document components (continued)

10. Industry-Specific Information Security Standards	
Policy:	Company X information systems must employ industry-specific information security standards.
Commentary:	This policy requires systems designers and other technical staff to employ industry-standard controls. For example, in banking, encryption systems should use industry-specific systems for key management. Other industry-specific controls are relevant to the medical services industry, the aerospace and defense community, and other industry groups.
Audience:	Technical staff

11. Use of Information Security Policies and Procedures	
Policy:	All Company X information security documentation, including, but not limited to, policies, standards, and procedures, must be classified as "Internal Use Only," unless expressly created for external business processes or partners.
Commentary:	This policy prevents workers from disclosing to outsiders the specifics of how Company X secures its information and systems. These details may be used to compromise Company X information and systems.
Audience:	All

12. Security Controls Enforceability	
Policy:	All information systems security controls must be enforceable prior to being adopted as a part of standard operating procedure.
Commentary:	Controls that are not enforced have a tendency to become useless. For example, if management has a policy about clean desks by locking up all sensitive materials after work, and it is not enforced, then employees quickly learn to ignore the policy. This policy is intended to require management to review the enforcement of controls, an issue that may not occur before adopting a control. A definition of the word "enforceable" may be advisable in some instances. For a control to be enforceable, it must be possible for management to clearly determine whether staff is in compliance with the control, and whether the control is effectively doing its intended job. The policy is purposefully vague about what constitutes standard operating procedure. This permits the policy to apply to a wide variety of circumstances, regardless of whether the control is documented, specific to a certain department, or used in an experimental way. In some instances, this policy may require the control designers to add a monitoring mechanism that reports on the status of the control. For example, encryption boxes from some vendors have lights that indicate that they are working as they should.
Audience:	Management and technical staff

Table 4-2   Sample EISP document components (continued)

Note: Table 4-2 lists some components that could be worked into an EISP, and is not intended to represent a stand-alone EISP framework.

Source: From Information Security Roles and Responsibilities Made Easy, Version 3, Copyright 2005–2012 by Information Shield, Inc., used with permission.

an organization-specific EISP. In his EISP version, Wood also provides justification for each policy statement and the target audience, information that would not typically be included in the policy document itself. Note: Table 4-2 lists some components that could be worked into an EISP and is not intended to represent a stand-alone EISP framework.

The formulation of the EISP establishes the overall InfoSec environment. As noted earlier, any number of specific issues may require policy guidance beyond what can be offered in the EISP. The next level of policy document, the issue-specific policy, delivers this needed specificity.

Issue-Specific Security Policy

A sound **issue-specific security policy (ISSP)** provides detailed, targeted guidance to instruct all members of the organization in the use of a resource, such as a process or a technology employed by the organization. The ISSP should begin by introducing the organization's fundamental resource-use philosophy. It should assure members of the organization that its purpose is not to establish a foundation for administrative enforcement or legal prosecution but rather to provide a common understanding of the purposes for which an employee can and cannot use the resource. Once this understanding is established, employees are free to use the resource without seeking approval for each type of use. This type of policy serves to protect both the employee and the organization from inefficiency and ambiguity. The ISSP can sometimes become a confusing policy document. Its structure allows for more detailed elements than those found in higher-level policy documents like the EISP. While it is true that an ISSP may have some elements of a procedure included, its intent is to act as a readily accessible standard for compliance with the more broadly defined policies established in the EISP. You will later learn that the system-specific policy document is even more procedural in some cases.

An effective ISSP accomplishes the following:

- It articulates the organization's expectations about how its technology-based system should be used.

- It documents how the technology-based system is controlled and identifies the processes and authorities that provide this control.

- It indemnifies the organization against liability for an employee's inappropriate or illegal use of the system.

An effective ISSP is a binding agreement between parties (the organization and its members) and shows that the organization has made a good faith effort to ensure that its technology will not be used in an inappropriate manner. Every organization's ISSP has three characteristics:

- It addresses specific technology-based resources.

- It requires frequent updates.

- It contains an issue statement explaining the organization's position on a particular issue.[6]

What are the areas for which an ISSP may be used? The following are typical in that their use would require an ISSP in most organizations. Note that this list is designed to be exemplary, not comprehensive:

- Use of e-mail, instant messaging (IM), and other electronic communications applications

- Use of the Internet and the World Wide Web on company and personal time

- Malware protection requirements (such as anti-malware software implementation)

- Installation and use of nonorganizationally issued software or hardware

- Prohibitions against hacking or testing the organization's security controls or attempting to modify or escalate access control privileges

- Home use of company-owned computer equipment or removal of organizational equipment from organizational property
- Use of personal equipment on company networks
- Use of telecommunications technologies (fax, phone, mobile phone)
- Use of photocopying and scanning equipment

While many other issue-specific policies in the organization, such as those described in the opening scenario, may fall outside the responsibility of InfoSec, representatives of the InfoSec unit can serve on policy committees and advise other departments in the creation and management of their policies.

Components of the ISSP

Table 4-3 lists typical ISSP components. Each of these components is, in turn, discussed in the sections that follow. The specific situation of the particular organization dictates the exact wording of the security procedures as well as issues not covered within these general guidelines.

Statement of Purpose The ISSP should begin with a clear statement of purpose that outlines the scope and applicability of the policy. It should address the following questions: What purpose does this policy serve? Who is responsible and accountable for policy implementation? What technologies and issues does the policy document address?

Authorized Uses This section of the policy statement explains who can use the technology governed by the policy and for what purposes. Recall that an organization's information systems are the exclusive property of the organization, and users have no particular rights of use. Each technology and process is provided for business operations. This section defines "fair and responsible use" of equipment and other organizational assets, and it addresses key legal issues, such as protection of personal information and privacy. The policy makes any use for any purpose not explicitly identified a misuse of equipment. When it is management's intention to allow some selective, extraorganizational uses, such as using company systems and networks for personal e-mail, such use must be specifically allowed for, and defined, in the policy.

Prohibited Uses While the previous section specifies what the issue or technology can be used for, this section outlines what it cannot be used for. Unless a particular use is clearly prohibited, the organization cannot penalize employees for it. For example, the following actions might be prohibited: personal use; disruptive use or misuse; criminal use; use of offensive or harassing materials; and infringement of copyrighted, licensed, or other intellectual property.

In some organizations, that which is not permitted is prohibited; in others, that which is not prohibited is permitted. In either case, be sure to state clearly the assumptions and then spell out the exceptions. The organization's stance will make a difference in how the topic of usage is addressed. Some organizations use the approach given in this example list, which explicitly states what is allowed and prohibited. Other organizations might want to be less explicit and combine the Authorized and Prohibited Uses sections into a single section titled Appropriate Uses.

1	Statement of Purpose
	a. Scope and Applicability
	b. Definition of Technology Addressed
	c. Responsibilities
2	Authorized Uses
	a. User Access
	b. Fair and Responsible Use
	c. Protection of Privacy
3	Prohibited Uses
	a. Disruptive Use or Misuse
	b. Criminal Use
	c. Offensive or Harassing Materials
	d. Copyrighted, Licensed, or Other Intellectual Property
	e. Other Restrictions
4	Systems Management
	a. Management of Stored Materials
	b. Employer Monitoring
	c. Virus Protection
	d. Physical Security
	e. Encryption
5	Violations of Policy
	a. Procedures for Reporting Violations
	b. Penalties for Violations
6	Policy Review and Modification
	a. Scheduled Review of Policy
	b. Procedures for Modification
7	Limitations of Liability
	a. Statements of Liability
	b. Other Disclaimers

Table 4-3   Components of a typical ISSP

Copyright © 2014 Cengage Learning®.

Systems Management This section focuses on the users' relationships to systems management. A company may want to issue specific rules regarding the use of e-mail and electronic documents, and storage of those documents, as well as guidelines about authorized employer monitoring and the physical and electronic security of e-mail and other electronic documents. The Systems Management section should specify users' and systems administrators' responsibilities, so that all parties know what they are accountable for.

Violations of Policy This section specifies the penalties and repercussions of violating the usage and systems management policies. Penalties should be laid out for each violation. This section should also provide instructions on how to report observed or suspected violations, either openly or anonymously, because some employees may fear that powerful individuals in the organization could retaliate against someone who reports violations. Anonymous submissions are often the only way to convince individual users to report the unauthorized activities of other, more influential employees.

Policy Review and Modification Every policy should contain procedures and a timetable for periodic review. This section should outline a specific methodology for the review and modification of the ISSP, so as to ensure that users always have guidelines that reflect the organization's current technologies and needs.

Limitations of Liability The final section offers a general statement of liability or a set of disclaimers. If an individual employee is caught conducting illegal activities with organizational equipment or assets, management does not want the organization to be held liable. In other words, if employees violate a company policy or any law using company technologies, the company will not protect them and the company is not liable for their actions, assuming that the violation is not known or sanctioned by management.

Implementing the ISSP

A number of approaches for creating and managing ISSPs are possible. Three of the most common are:

- Create a number of independent ISSP documents, each tailored to a specific issue.
- Create a single comprehensive ISSP document that covers all issues.
- Create a modular ISSP document that unifies policy creation and administration while maintaining each specific issue's requirements.

Table 4-4 describes the advantages and disadvantages of each approach.

The recommended approach is the modular policy, as it results in a document that relies on sections (modules), each with a standard template for structure and appearance, in which certain aspects are standardized while others—including much of the content—are customized for each issue. The end result is several independent ISSP documents, all derived from a common template and physically well managed and easy to use. This approach offers a balance between ease of policy development and effectiveness for policy management. The policies generated via this approach are individual modules, each created and updated by the individuals who are responsible for a specific issue. These individuals report to a central policy administration group that incorporates these specific issues into an overall policy.

Approach	Advantages	Disadvantages
Individual policy	• Clear assignment to a responsible department • Written by those with superior subject matter expertise for technology-specific systems	• Typically yields a scattershot result that fails to cover all of the necessary issues • Can suffer from poor policy dissemination, enforcement, and review
Comprehensive policy	• Well controlled by centrally managed procedures, assuring complete topic coverage • Often provides better formal procedures than when policies are individually formulated • Usually identifies processes for dissemination, enforcement, and review	• May overgeneralize the issues and skip over vulnerabilities • May be written by those with less complete subject matter expertise
Modular policy	• Often considered an optimal balance between the individual ISSP and the comprehensive ISSP approaches • Well controlled by centrally managed procedures, assuring complete topic coverage • Clear assignment to a responsible department • Written by those with superior subject matter expertise for technology-specific systems	• May be more expensive than other alternatives • Implementation can be difficult to manage

Table 4-4 ISSP Document organization approaches

Copyright © 2014 Cengage Learning®.

System-Specific Security Policy

While an EISP is a high-level policy and an ISSP is a policy document that may contain procedural elements, both are formalized as written documents readily identifiable as policy. The **system-specific security policies (SysSPs)** sometimes have a different look and may, in fact, seem like procedures to some readers. SysSPs often function as standards or procedures to be used when configuring or maintaining systems—for example, to configure and operate a network firewall. Such a document could include: a statement of managerial intent; guidance to network engineers on selecting, configuring, and operating firewalls; and an access control list that defines levels of access for each authorized user. Note that the policy framework ensures that the creation and use of an ISSP or SysSP is enabled by the EISP policy position on those topic areas.

SysSPs can be separated into two general groups, managerial guidance and technical specifications, or they may combine these two types of SysSP content into a single unified SysSP document, as described earlier.

Managerial Guidance SysSPs

A managerial guidance SysSP document is created by management to guide the implementation and configuration of technology as well as to address the behavior of people in the organization in ways that support the security of information. For example, while the specific configuration of a firewall belongs in the technical specifications SysSP, the process of

View Point
Information Security Policies: The Contract with Employees, Customers, and Partners
By David Lineman, President, Information Shield

InfoSec policies used to be a group of arcane documents that most people didn't read or understand. InfoSec was for the technical folks. So policies often stayed locked in paper binders or virtual binders on the corporate intranet.

But the world has changed. Today, written InfoSec policies are a key way to communicate your InfoSec program with the outside world.

One of the growing trends in risk management is the requirement to validate the security risk of vendors. A single vendor with a laptop full of customer information can cost the organization millions of dollars. In many industries, including financial services and health care, regulations require organizations to validate the InfoSec programs of their vendors. And in every case, examples of written policies are a key piece of evidence.

InfoSec policies can have three primary audiences. First, policies are used to inform employees and contractors on the proper and secure use of information. Second, policies are used to communicate the InfoSec posture of the organization to senior management, including the board of directors. Finally, InfoSec policies are used to communicate with customers and business partners.

While I use the term "contract" loosely as a way to formalize an agreement between parties, policies are increasingly considered real contracts when security ends up in court. For example, organizations that suffer a data breach must often produce written policies to document that they were making best-efforts to protect customer information. In cases where employees have been terminated for violating InfoSec policies, the written policy is a key piece of evidence supporting the organization. Outdated or nonexistent policies send a message that the organization was lax in both intent and enforcement. Customers view privacy policies as a contract for handing their personal information. Groups of customers have been known to sue an organization for having a misleading privacy policy.

If your organization still considers InfoSec policies as unimportant or not relevant to modern business, you might think again. Today, you must have written policies to document your compliance posture to concerned parties. In the not-too-distant future, it will be impossible to earn business without them. Sooner or later, someone with a gavel or a purchase order will come knocking on your door, asking to see your written security policies.

constructing and implementing the firewall must follow guidelines established by management. Why? In the absence of this guidance, a firewall administrator may configure the firewall as he or she sees fit, which may or may not coincide with the organization's intent. For example, suppose the new firewall administrator for Boom! Technologies, a Department of

Defense contractor for explosives development, implements a new firewall using a set of rules identical to those used on the firewall that was used at his or her previous employer, Open Idea University. These rules, ideal for an institution that promotes the free and open flow of knowledge but not sufficiently stringent for the defense contractor, would allow a hacker to steal the blueprints for the company's newest secret weapon.

Firewalls are not the only area that may require SysSPs. Any technology that affects the confidentiality, integrity, or availability of information must be assessed to evaluate the trade-off between improved security and restrictions.

SysSPs can be developed at the same time as ISSPs, or they can be prepared in advance of their related ISSPs. Before management can craft a policy informing users what they can do with the technology and how they may do it, it might be necessary for systems administrators to configure and operate the system. Some organizations may prefer to develop ISSPs and SysSPs in tandem, so that operational procedures and user guidelines are created simultaneously.

Technical Specification SysSPs

While a manager may work with a systems administrator to create managerial policy, as described in the previous section, the systems administrator may in turn need to create a different type of policy to implement the managerial policy. For example, an ISSP may require that user passwords be changed quarterly; a systems administrator can implement a technical control within a specific application to enforce this policy. The screenshots in Figure 4-3 illustrate network operating systems configured to implement a password-change requirement. There are two general methods of implementing such technical controls: access control lists and configuration rules.

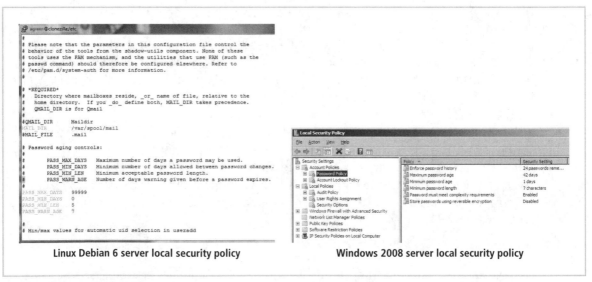

| Linux Debian 6 server local security policy | Windows 2008 server local security policy |

Figure 4-3 Password SysSP

Source: Redhat Enterprise Linux.

Access Control Lists Access control lists (ACLs) include the user access lists, matrices, and capability tables that govern the rights and privileges of users. ACLs can control access to file storage systems, object brokers, or other network communications devices. A capability table specifies which subjects and objects that users or groups can access; in some systems, capability tables are called "user profiles" or "user policies." These specifications frequently take the form of complex matrices in which assets are listed along the column headers while users are listed along the row headers. The resulting matrix would then contain ACLs in columns for a particular device or asset, while a row would represent the capability table for a particular user.

Most modern server operating systems translate ACLs into configuration sets that administrators can use to control access to their systems. The level of detail and specificity (often called granularity) may vary from system to system, but in general ACLs enable administrators to restrict access according to user, computer, time, duration, or even a particular file. This range gives a great deal of control to the administrator. In general, ACLs regulate the following aspects of access:

- *Who* can use the system
- *What* authorized users can access
- *When* authorized users can access the system
- *Where* authorized users can access the system from
- *How* authorized users can access the system

Restricting who can use the system requires no explanation. To restrict what users can access—for example, which printers, files, communications, and applications—administrators assign user privileges (also known as permissions), such as the following:

- Read
- Write
- Execute
- Delete

This list is not exhaustive, but it contains some key ACL privilege types. Figures 4-4 and 4-5 show how the ACL security model has been implemented by Linux and Microsoft operating systems, respectively. Note that in the Linux example the ls command shows a simple list of the files in the current directory, and the subsequent ls -l command shows the files in the current directory along with all the other general information about each file. The example shows the same file (named Desktop). The first character, d, informs us that this is a directory file (i.e., a file that contains more files). Then the string rwxr-xr-x provides the permissions for file access placed onto this directory by its owner. This permission is actually three sets of three characters. The first set, rwx, reveals the directory owner's permissions, the second shows the group permissions for groups that the accessing user may belong to. The final set provides the permissions for all other users. Each of these three clusters provides the read, write, and execute permissions for the file or directory. The characters themselves are codes in which 'r'=read, 'w'=write, 'x'=execute, and '–'=no permission. So, in this case, the owner can read, write, and execute the contents of the directory. All other users can read and execute, but they cannot write to the directory.

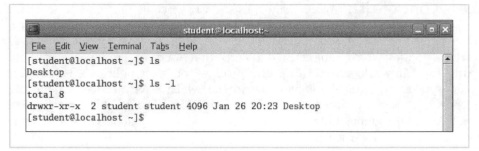

Figure 4-4 Linux ACL

Source: Linux.

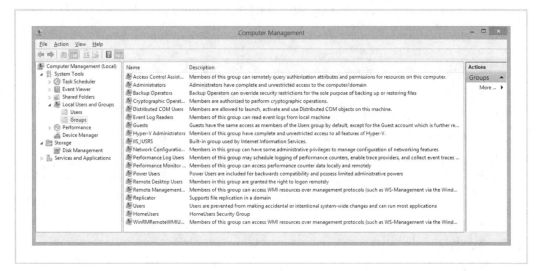

Figure 4-5 Windows ACL

Source: Windows.

Configuration Rules Configuration rules are instructional codes that guide the execution of the system when information is passing through it. Rule-based policies are more specific to the operation of a system than ACLs are, and they may or may not deal with users directly. Many security systems require specific configuration scripts that dictate which actions to perform on each set of information they process. Examples include firewalls, intrusion detection and prevention systems (IDPSs), and proxy servers. Figures 4-6 and 4-7 show how this security model has been implemented by Check Point in a firewall rule set and by Tripwire in an IDPS rule set, respectively.

Combination SysSPs Many organizations create a single document that combines elements of the management guidance SysSP and the technical specifications SysSP. While this document can be somewhat confusing to the users of the policies, it is very practical to have the guidance from both perspectives in a single place. Such a document should carefully articulate the required actions for each procedure described.

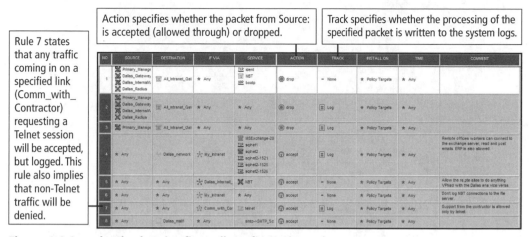

Action specifies whether the packet from Source: is accepted (allowed through) or dropped.

Track specifies whether the processing of the specified packet is written to the system logs.

Rule 7 states that any traffic coming in on a specified link (Comm_with_ Contractor) requesting a Telnet session will be accepted, but logged. This rule also implies that non-Telnet traffic will be denied.

Figure 4-6 Sample Check Point firewall configuration rules

Source: Check Point.

Guidelines for Effective Policy

How policy is developed and implemented can help or hinder its usefulness to the organization. In general, policy is only enforceable if it is properly designed, developed, and implemented using a process that assures repeatable results. One effective approach has six stages: development, dissemination (distribution), review (reading), comprehension (understanding), compliance (agreement), and uniform enforcement. Thus, for policies to be effective, they must be properly:

1. Developed using industry-accepted practices
2. Distributed using all appropriate methods
3. Read by all employees
4. Understood by all employees
5. Formally agreed to by act or affirmation
6. Uniformly applied and enforced

We will examine each of these stages in the sections that follow. But before beginning an explanation about developing policy, the student should realize that almost every organization has a set of existing policies, standards, procedures, and/or practices. This installed base of guidance may not always have been prepared using an approach that delivers consistent or even usable results. Most of the situations you will find yourself in are actually going to involve more of *policy maintenance* than policy development. When maintaining policy, all of the complexity of the policy process described here may not be needed. But when the policy maintenance project gets sufficiently large and complex, it might best be considered as *policy redevelopment*, and then most of the process described here can come into use.

Developing Information Security Policy

It is often useful to view policy development as a two-part project. In the first part of the project, policy is designed and developed (or, in the case of an outdated policy, redesigned

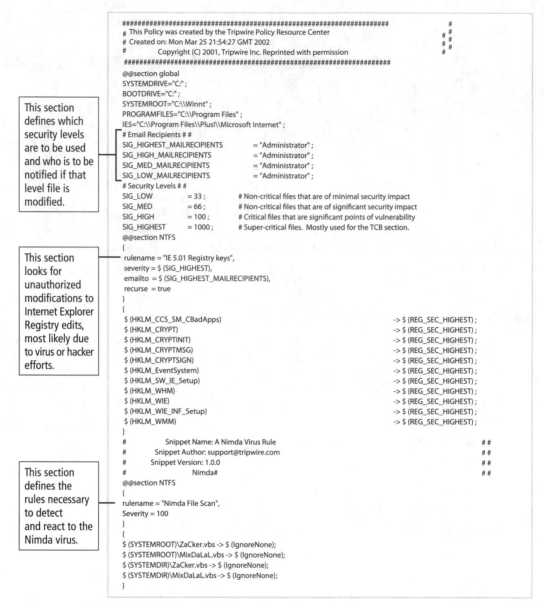

```
####################################################################     #
# This Policy was created by the Tripwire Policy Resource Center       # #
# Created on: Mon Mar 25 21:54:27 GMT 2002                             # #
#            Copyright (C) 2001, Tripwire Inc. Reprinted with permission    #
####################################################################     #
@@section global
SYSTEMDRIVE="C:" ;
BOOTDRIVE="C:" ;
SYSTEMROOT="C:\\Winnt" ;
PROGRAMFILES="C:\\Program Files" ;
IE5="C:\\Program Files\\Plus!\\Microsoft Internet" ;
# Email Recipients # #
SIG_HIGHEST_MAILRECIPIENTS        = "Administrator" ;
SIG_HIGH_MAILRECIPIENTS           = "Administrator" ;
SIG_MED_MAILRECIPIENTS            = "Administrator" ;
SIG_LOW_MAILRECIPIENTS            = "Administrator" ;
# Security Levels # #
SIG_LOW        = 33 ;        # Non-critical files that are of minimal security impact
SIG_MED        = 66 ;        # Non-critical files that are of significant security impact
SIG_HIGH       = 100 ;       # Critical files that are significant points of vulnerability
SIG_HIGHEST    = 1000 ;      # Super-critical files.  Mostly used for the TCB section.
@@section NTFS
{
rulename = "IE 5.01 Registry keys",
severity = $ (SIG_HIGHEST),
emailto  = $ (SIG_HIGHEST_MAILRECIPIENTS),
recurse  = true
}
{
$ (HKLM_CCS_SM_CBadApps)                              -> $ (REG_SEC_HIGHEST) ;
$ (HKLM_CRYPT)                                        -> $ (REG_SEC_HIGHEST) ;
$ (HKLM_CRYPTINIT)                                    -> $ (REG_SEC_HIGHEST) ;
$ (HKLM_CRYPTMSG)                                     -> $ (REG_SEC_HIGHEST) ;
$ (HKLM_CRYPTSIGN)                                    -> $ (REG_SEC_HIGHEST) ;
$ (HKLM_EventSystem)                                  -> $ (REG_SEC_HIGHEST) ;
$ (HKLM_SW_IE_Setup)                                  -> $ (REG_SEC_HIGHEST) ;
$ (HKLM_WHM)                                          -> $ (REG_SEC_HIGHEST) ;
$ (HKLM_WIE)                                          -> $ (REG_SEC_HIGHEST) ;
$ (HKLM_WIE_INF_Setup)                                -> $ (REG_SEC_HIGHEST) ;
$ (HKLM_WMM)                                          -> $ (REG_SEC_HIGHEST) ;
}
#           Snippet Name: A Nimda Virus Rule                          # #
#           Snippet Author: support@tripwire.com                      # #
#           Snippet Version: 1.0.0                                    # #
#                     Nimda#                                          # #
@@section NTFS
{
rulename = "Nimda File Scan",
Severity = 100
}
{
$ (SYSTEMROOT)\ZaCker.vbs -> $ (IgnoreNone);
$ (SYSTEMROOT)\MixDaLaL.vbs -> $ (IgnoreNone);
$ (SYSTEMDIR)\ZaCker.vbs -> $ (IgnoreNone);
$ (SYSTEMDIR)\MixDaLaL.vbs -> $ (IgnoreNone);
}
```

This section defines which security levels are to be used and who is to be notified if that level file is modified.

This section looks for unauthorized modifications to Internet Explorer Registry edits, most likely due to virus or hacker efforts.

This section defines the rules necessary to detect and react to the Nimda virus.

Figure 4-7 Sample Tripwire IDPS configuration rules

Source: Tripwire.

and rewritten), and in the second part, management processes are established to perpetuate the policy within the organization. The former is an exercise in project management, whereas the latter requires adherence to good business practices.

Like any major project, a policy development or redevelopment project should be well planned, properly funded, and aggressively managed to ensure that it is completed on time and within budget. One way to accomplish this goal is to use a systems development life cycle (SDLC). You are already familiar with the security systems development life cycle (SecSDLC), from

Chapter 2. The following discussion expands the use of the SecSDLC model by discussing the tasks that could be included in each phase of the SecSDLC during a policy development project. You will have learned about InfoSec-focused project management in Chapter 1.

Investigation Phase During the investigation phase the policy development team should attain the following:

- Support from senior management, because any project without it has a reduced chance of success. Only with the support of top management will a specific policy receive the attention it deserves from the intermediate-level managers who must implement it and from the users who must comply with it.

- Support and active involvement of IT management, specifically the CIO. Only with the CIO's active support will technology-area managers be motivated to participate in policy development and support the implementation efforts to deploy it once created.

- Clear articulation of goals. Without a detailed and succinct expression of the goals and objectives of the policy, broken into distinct expectations, the policy will lack the structure it needs to obtain full implementation.

- Participation of the correct individuals from the communities of interest affected by the recommended policies. Assembling the right team, by ensuring the participation of the proper representatives from the groups that will be affected by the new policies, is very important. The team must include representatives from the legal department, the human resources department, and end users of the various IT systems covered by the policies, as well as a project champion with sufficient stature and prestige to accomplish the goals of the project, and a capable project manager to see the project through to completion.

- A detailed outline of the scope of the policy development project and sound estimates for the cost and scheduling of the project.

Analysis Phase The analysis phase should produce the following:

- A new or recent risk assessment or IT audit documenting the current InfoSec needs of the organization. This risk assessment should include any loss history, as well as past lawsuits, grievances, or other records of negative outcomes from InfoSec areas.

- The gathering of key reference materials—including any existing policies. Sometimes policy documents that affect InfoSec will be housed in the human resources department as well as the accounting, finance, legal, or corporate security departments.

According to Wood's *Information Policies Made Easy*:

> *To identify the policy areas needing further attention, copies of all other relevant and current organizational policy documents should be collected. Relevant policies include application systems development policies, computer operations policies, computer equipment acquisition policies, human resources policies, information systems quality control policies, and physical security policies. If they are obtainable, policies from other organizations in the same industry can also provide useful background information. If the organization is a subsidiary or affiliate of another organization, then the parent organization's policies should be obtained and used as reference material. If the organization is a participant in*

an extranet, an electronic data interchange, value added network, a multi-organizational Internet commerce arrangement, or any other multi-organizational networks, the policies of these networks should be obtained and reviewed. The security policies of various information systems related service providers, such as an Internet service provider, or a data center outsourcing firm, should also be obtained.

Some who are facing significant time or resource constraints will be tempted to skip the above-mentioned data-gathering processes. Whenever data gathering is significantly abbreviated, the likelihood that management will reject the resulting document increases. It is through this data-gathering process that management's view of information security can be identified, the policies that already exist, the policies that need to be added or changed, how management enforces policies, the unique vulnerabilities that the organization faces, and other essential background information. If serious consideration has not been given to this background information, it is unlikely that a newly written information security policy will be responsive to the true needs of the organization.[7]

Design Phase During the design phase, the team must create a plan to distribute and verify the distribution of the policies. Members of the organization must explicitly acknowledge that they have received and read the policy. Otherwise, an employee can claim never to have seen a policy, and unless the manager can produce strong evidence to the contrary, any enforcement action, such as dismissal for inappropriate use of the Web, can be overturned and punitive damages might be awarded to the former employee. The simplest way to document acknowledgment of a written policy is to attach a cover sheet that states "I have received, read, understood, and agreed to this policy." The employee's signature and date provide a paper trail of his or her receipt of the policy.

Some situations preclude a formal documentation process. Take, for instance, student use of campus computer labs. Most universities have stringent policies on what students can and cannot do in a computer lab. These policies are usually posted on the Web, in the student handbook, in course catalogs, and in a number of other locations, including bulletin boards in the labs. For the policies to be enforceable, however, some mechanism must be established that records the student's acknowledgment of the policy. This is frequently accomplished with a banner screen that displays a brief statement warning the user that the policy is in place and that use of the system constitutes acceptance of the policy. The user must then click an OK button or press a key to get past the screen. However, this method can be ineffective if the acknowledgment screen does not require any unusual action to move past it; such a screen is often called a "blow-by screen," as users can "blow by" the screen without even seeing it.

In the past, companies used banners or pop-up windows to display end-user license agreements (EULAs). An EULA, which is usually presented on a screen to the user during software installation, spells out fair and responsible use of the software being installed. At one time, EULAs were typically presented on blow-by screens, with an instruction like "Press any key to accept," so that users could install the software by simply hitting the Enter key without explicitly reviewing and acknowledging the restrictions on software use, thus potentially negating the software company's legal claim. Today, most EULA screens require that the user click a specific button, press a function key, or type words to agree to the terms of

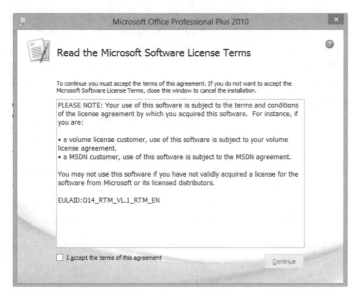

Figure 4-8 End-user license agreement

Source: Microsoft.

the EULA. Some even require the user to scroll down to the bottom of the EULA before the "I accept" button is activated. Similar methods are used on network and computer logins to reinforce acknowledgement of the system use policy. Figure 4-8 provides an example of a EULA screen that requires specific user input.

The design should also include specifications for any automated tool used for the creation and management of policy documents, as well as revisions to feasibility analysis reports based on improved costs and benefits as the design is clarified.

Implementation Phase In the implementation phase, the policy development team actually writes the policies. This can be a challenging process, but you do not have to come up with a good policy document from scratch. A number of resources are at your disposal, including:

- *The Web*—You can search for other, similar policies. The point here is not to advocate wholesale copying of these policies but to encourage you to look for ideas on what should be contained in your policy. For example, dozens of policies available on the Web describe fair and responsible use of various technologies. What you may not find, however, are policies that relate to sensitive internal documents or processes.

- *Government sites*—Sites such as *csrc.nist.gov* and *csrc.nist.gov/groups/SMA/fasp/index. html* contain numerous sample policies and policy support documents, including "SP 800-100, Information Security Handbook: A Guide for Managers." While these policies are typically directed toward or applicable to federal government Web sites, you may be able to adapt some sections to meet your organization's needs.

- *Professional literature*—Several authors have published books on the subject. Of particular note is Charles Cresson Wood's *Information Security Policies Made Easy* series, which not only provides more than 1,000 pages of policies, but also makes those policies available in electronic format, complete with permission to use them in internal documents. Exercise caution when using such resources, however; it is extremely easy to take large sections of policy and end up with a massive document that is neither publishable nor enforceable.

- *Peer networks*—Other InfoSec professionals have to write similar policies and implement similar plans. Attend meetings like those offered by the Information Systems Security Association (*www.issa.org*) or the Information Systems Auditing and Control Association (*www.isaca.org*) and ask your peers.

- *Professional consultants*—Policy is one area of InfoSec that can certainly be developed in-house. However, if you simply cannot find the time to develop your own policy, then hiring an outside consultant may be your best option. Keep in mind that no consultant can know your organization as thoroughly as you do, and the consultant may simply design generic policies that you can then adapt to your specific need.

During the implementation phase, the policy development team ensures that the policy is prepared correctly, distributed, read, understood, and agreed to by those to whom it applies, and that those individuals' understanding and acceptance of the policy are documented as described in later sections of this chapter.

Maintenance Phase During the maintenance phase, the policy development team monitors, maintains, and modifies the policy as needed to ensure that it remains effective as a tool to meet changing threats. The policy should have a built-in mechanism through which users can report problems, preferably anonymously.

Policy Distribution

While it might seem straightforward, actually getting the policy document into the hands of employees can require a substantial investment by the organization in order to be effective. The most common alternatives are hard copy distribution and electronic distribution. Hard copies involve either directly distributing a copy to the employee or posting the policy in a publicly available location. Posting a policy on a bulletin board or other public area may be insufficient unless another policy requires the employees to read the bulletin board on a specified schedule (daily, weekly, etc.). Distribution by internal or external mail may still not guarantee that the individual receives the document. Unless the organization can prove that the policy actually reached the end users, it cannot be enforced. Unlike in civil or criminal law, ignorance of policy, where policy is inadequately distributed, is considered an acceptable excuse. Distribution of classified policies—those containing confidential internal information—requires additional levels of controls, in the labeling of the document, in the dissemination of new policy, and in the collection and destruction of older versions to assure the confidentiality of the information contained within the policy documents themselves.

Another common method of dissemination is by electronic means: e-mail, newsletter, intranet, or document management systems. Perhaps the easiest way is to post current and archived versions of policies on a secure intranet in HTML or PDF (Adobe) form. The organization must still enable a mechanism to prove distribution, such as an auditing log tracking when users access the documents. As an alternative delivery mechanism, e-mail has advantages and disadvantages. While it is easy to send a document to an employee and even track when the employee opens the e-mail, it becomes cumbersome for employees to review inapplicable policies, and the document can quickly fill the e-mail application's storage capacity. Perhaps the best method is electronic policy distribution software, which is described in the section on automated tools. Electronic policy management software not only assists in the distribution of policy documents, it supports the development and assessment of comprehension.[8]

Policy Reading

Barriers to employees' reading policies can arise from literacy or language issues. A surprisingly large percentage of the workforce is considered functionally illiterate. A 2003 survey conducted by the National Assessment of Adult Literacy (NAAL), a federal agency that works in concert with the U.S. Department of Education, found that 14 percent of American adults scored at a "below basic" level in prose literacy.[9] Many jobs do not require literacy skills—for example, custodial staff, groundskeepers, or production line workers. Because such workers can still pose risks to InfoSec, they must be made familiar with the policy even if it must be read to them. Visually impaired employees also require additional assistance, either through audio or large-type versions of the document.

Of the 11 million adults identified as illiterate in the NAAL survey, 7 million could not answer simple test questions due to pure reading deficiencies, and 4 million could not take the test because of language barriers.[10] The number of non-English speaking residents in the United States continues to climb. However, language challenges are not restricted to those organizations with locations in the United States. Multinational organizations also must deal with the challenges of gauging reading levels of foreign citizens. Simple translations of policy documents, while a minimum requirement, necessitate careful monitoring. Translation issues have long created challenges for organizations. For example, a translation error in 1989 resulted in the Nike Corporation running an advertisement showing a Samburu tribesman speaking in his native language, ostensibly echoing the company slogan. What he really said was, "I don't want these. Give me big shoes."[11]

Policy Comprehension

A quote attributed to Confucius states: "Tell me and I forget; show me and I remember; let me do and I understand." In the policy arena, this means that simply making certain that a copy of the policy gets to employees in a form they can review may not ensure that they truly understand what the policy requires of them. Bloom, Mesia, and Krathwohl define comprehension as "the ability to grasp the meaning of material. [It] may be shown ... to go one step beyond the simple remembering of material, and represent the lowest level of understanding."[12]

To be certain that employees understand the policy, the document must be written at a reasonable reading level, with minimal technical jargon and management terminology. The readability statistics supplied by most productivity suite applications—such as Microsoft Word—can help determine the current reading level of a policy. Figure 4-9 shows the readability statistics rendered by Microsoft Word for a sample of text taken from this chapter.

The next step is to use some form of assessment to gauge how well employees understand the policy's underlying issues. Quizzes and other forms of examination can be employed to assess quantitatively which employees understand the policy by earning a minimum score (e.g., 70 percent), and which employees require additional training and awareness efforts before the policy can be enforced. Quizzes can be distributed in either hard copy or electronic formats. The electronic policy management systems mentioned earlier can assist the assessment of employee performance on policy comprehension.[13]

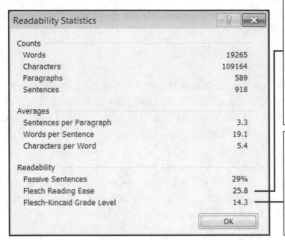

The Flesch Reading Ease test evaluates the writing on a scale of 1–100. The higher the score, the easier it is to understand the writing.
In this case, the text that had been selected for this assessment was scored at 25.8 and included writing that is too complex for most policies but would be appropriate for a college text.
For most corporate documents, a score of 60 to 70 is preferred.

The Flesch-Kincaid Grade Level test evaluates writing on a U.S. grade-school level.
While a 14th-grade level may be appropriate for this textbook, it is too high for organizational policy intended for a broad audience.
For most corporate documents, a score of 7.0 to 8.0 is preferred.

Figure 4-9 Readability statistics

Source: Microsoft.

Policy Compliance

Policy compliance means the employee must agree to the policy. According to Whitman in *Security Policy: From Design to Maintenance*:

> *Policies must be agreed to by act or affirmation. Agreement by act occurs when the employee performs an action, which requires them to acknowledge understanding of the policy, prior to use of a technology or organizational resource. Network banners, end-user license agreements, and posted warnings can serve to meet this burden of proof. However, these in and of themselves may not be sufficient. Only through direct collection of a signature or the equivalent digital alternative can the organization prove that it has obtained an agreement to comply with policy, which also demonstrates that the previous conditions have been met.*[14]

What if an employee refuses explicitly to agree to comply with policy? Can the organization deny access to information that the individual needs to do his or her job? While this situation has not yet been adjudicated in the legal system, it seems clear that failure to agree to a policy is tantamount to refusing to work and thus may be grounds for termination. Organizations can avoid this dilemma by incorporating policy confirmation statements into employment contracts, annual evaluations, or other documents necessary for the individual's continued employment.

Policy Enforcement

The final component of the design and implementation of effective policies is uniform and impartial enforcement. As in law enforcement, policy enforcement must be able to withstand external scrutiny. Because this scrutiny may occur during legal proceedings—for example, in a civil suit contending wrongful termination—organizations must establish high standards of due care with regard to policy management. For instance, if policy mandates that all employees wear identification badges in a clearly visible location and select members of management decide they are not required to follow this policy, any actions taken against other employees will not withstand legal challenges. If an employee is punished, censured, or dismissed as a result of a refusal to follow policy and is subsequently able to demonstrate that the policies are not uniformly applied or enforced, the organization may find itself facing punitive as well as compensatory damages.

One forward-thinking organization found a way to enlist employees in the enforcement of policy. After the organization had just published a new ID badge policy, the manager responsible for the policy was seen without his ID. One of his employees chided him in jest, saying, "You must be a visitor here, since you don't have an ID. Can I help you?" The manager smiled and promptly produced his ID, along with a $20 bill, which he presented to the employee as a reward for vigilant policy enforcement. Soon, the entire staff was routinely challenging anyone without a badge.[15]

Automated Tools   The need for effective policy management has led to the emergence of a class of software tools that supports policy development, implementation, and maintenance. At the forefront of these tools is the VigilEnt Policy Center (VPC), a centralized policy approval and implementation system from NetIQ (*www.informationshield.com/vpcmain. html*). VPC allows policy developers to create policy, manage the approval process with multiple individuals or groups, and distribute approved policy throughout their organizations. VPC assesses readers' understanding of the policy and electronically records reader acknowledgments. Use of VPC reduces or eliminates the need to distribute hard copies of documents that might go unread and to manage multiple policy receipt acknowledgment forms. Tools like VPC keep policies confidential, behind password-protected intranets, and generate periodic reports indicating which employees have and have not read and acknowledged the policies. Figure 4-10 illustrates the VPC architecture.

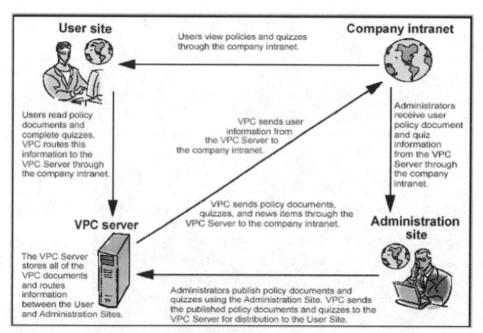

Figure 4-10 VigilEnt Policy Center (VPC) architecture

Copyright © 2014 Cengage Learning®.

When policies are created and distributed in hard copy form, it is often not clear where a policy originated and which manager approved it, unless the organization enforces a process to include such notations in the policy document. However, with tools such as VPC, the primary manager responsible for the policy has his or her name prominently displayed on the policy, along with the date of approval. This identification can make managers reluctant to implement policies using automated software tools, because it can associate a particular manager with new restrictions or rules. This hesitancy is a difficult hurdle to overcome but can be addressed by evaluating managerial job performance on achieved objectives—in this case, an effective policy process—rather than on the basis that an unobserved failure is a success.

The Information Securities Policy Made Easy Approach

The following section, which is adapted from Wood's *Information Security Policies Made Easy* and is used with his permission, discusses another approach to policy development.

Checklist of Steps in the Policy Development Process

This checklist is intended to provide a quick overview of the major steps associated with the development, refinement, and approval of an internal information security policy document. [...] Many of the following steps can be pursued simultaneously or in an order different than the following:

1. Perform a risk assessment or information technology audit to determine your organization's unique information security needs. These needs must be addressed in a policy document.

2. Clarify what the word "policy" means within your organization so that you are not preparing a "standard," "procedure," or some other related material.

3. Ensure that roles and responsibilities related to information security are clarified, including responsibility for issuing and maintaining policies.

4. Convince management that it is advisable to have documented information security policies.

5. Identify the top management staff that will be approving the final information security document and all influential reviewers.

6. Collect and read all existing internal information security awareness material and make a list of the included bottom-line messages.

7. Conduct a brief internal survey to gather ideas that stakeholders believe should be included in a new or updated information security policy.

8. Examine other policies issued by your organization, such as those from Human Resources management, to identify prevailing format, style, tone, length, and cross-references. The goal is to produce information that conforms to previous efforts.

9. Identify the audience to receive information security policy materials and determine whether [each person will] get a separate document or a separate page on an intranet site.

10. Determine the extent to which the audience is literate, computer knowledgeable, and receptive to security messages. This includes understanding the corporate culture surrounding information security.

11. Decide whether some other awareness efforts must take place before information security policies are issued. For example, one effort might show that information itself has become a critical factor of production.

12. Using ideas from the risk assessment, prepare a list of absolutely essential policy messages that must be communicated. Consult the policy statements as well as the sample policies found in this book.

13. If there is more than one audience, match the audiences with the bottom-line messages to be communicated through a coverage matrix. [...]

14. Determine how the policy material will be disseminated, noting the constraints and implications of each medium of communication. An intranet site is recommended. [...]

15. Review the compliance checking process, disciplinary process, and enforcement process to ensure that they all can work smoothly with the new policy document.

16. Determine whether the number of messages is too large to be handled all at one time, and if so, identify different categories of material that will be issued at different times.

17. Have an outline of topics to be included in the first document reviewed by several stakeholders. An information security management committee is the ideal review board.

18. Based on comments from the stakeholders, revise the initial outline and prepare a first draft. [...]

19. Have the first draft document reviewed by the stakeholders for initial reactions, presentation suggestions, and implementation ideas.

20. Revise the draft in response to comments from stakeholders. Expect this step to [be repeated] several times.

21. Request top management approval on the policy. Changes may be necessary, in which case this step may [be repeated] several times.

22. Prepare extracts of the policy document for selected purposes—for example, for a form signed by users receiving new or renewed user IDs and passwords.

23. Develop an awareness plan that uses the policy document as a source of ideas and requirements.

24. Create a working papers memo indicating the disposition of all comments received from reviewers, even if no changes were made.

25. Write a memo about the project, what you learned, and what needs to be fixed so that the next version of the policy document can be prepared more efficiently, better received by the readers, and more responsive to the unique circumstances facing your organization.

26. Prepare a list of next steps that will be required to implement the requirements specified in the policy document. [These steps] can include the development of an information security architecture, manual procedures documents, and technical information security standards, and acquisition of new products, hiring new technical staff, and other matters.

> ### Next Steps
> There are many paths available after an information security policy has been approved. [...]
> There will typically be many other projects that are initiated as a result of preparing an information
> security policy document. For example, a policy preparation effort may have illuminated the fact
> that an existing information security requirement is obsolete. [...][16]

SP 800-18 Rev. 1: Guide for Developing Security Plans for Federal Information Systems

NIST's "Special Publication 800-18, Rev. 1" reinforces a business-process–centered approach to policy management. Although this document is targeted at U.S. federal agencies, it puts forward a very practical approach to InfoSec planning that many other organizations may be able to use. Because policies are living documents that constantly change and grow, organizations cannot simply create such an important set of documents and then shelve them. Instead, these documents must be properly disseminated (distributed, read, understood, and agreed to) and managed. Good management practices for policy development and maintenance make for a more resilient organization. For example, all policies, including security policies, undergo tremendous stress when corporate mergers and divestitures occur. In these situations, changes happen quickly, and employees suffer uncertainty and are faced with many distractions; these stresses can reveal weaknesses in the management of security policies. When two companies come together as one but still have separate policies, it can be very difficult to implement security controls. Likewise, when one company with unified policies splits in two, the policy needs of both spin-offs change and must be accommodated.

To keep policies current and viable, an individual must be responsible for scheduling reviews, defining review practices and procedures, and ensuring that policy and revision dates are present.

Policy Administrator Just as information systems and InfoSec projects must have a champion and a manager, so must policies. The policy champion position combined with the manager position is called the policy administrator. Typically, this person is a mid-level staff member who is responsible for the creation, revision, distribution, and storage of the policy. The policy administrator does not necessarily have to be technically oriented. While practicing InfoSec professionals require extensive technical knowledge, policy management and policy administration require only a moderate technical background. The policy administrator solicits input both from the technically adept InfoSec experts and from the business-focused managers in each community of interest. In turn, he or she notifies all affected members of the organization when the policy is modified.

It is rather disheartening when a policy that requires hundreds of staff hours of development time is inserted into a three-ring binder and then placed on a manager's bookcase to gather dust. A good policy administrator can prevent this by making sure that the policy document and all subsequent revisions to it are appropriately distributed. The policy administrator must be clearly identified on the policy document as the primary contact for providing additional information or suggesting revisions to the policy.

Review Schedule In a changing environment, policies can retain their effectiveness only if they are periodically reviewed for currency and accuracy, and modified to keep them current. As stated in Chapter 3, to ensure due diligence, an organization must demonstrate that it is continually attempting to meet the requirements of the market in which it operates. This applies to both public (government, academic, and nonprofit) and private (commercial and for-profit) organizations. For this reason, any policy document should contain a properly organized schedule of reviews. Generally, a policy should be reviewed at least annually. The policy administrator should solicit input from representatives of all affected parties, management and staff, and then use this input to modify the document accordingly.

Review Procedures and Practices To facilitate policy reviews, the policy administrator should implement a mechanism by which individuals can easily make recommendations for revisions to the policies and other related documentation. Recommendation methods could include e-mail, office mail, or an anonymous drop box. If the policy is controversial, the policy administrator may feel that anonymous submission of information is the best way to determine the suitability of the policy as perceived by employees. Many employees feel intimidated by management and will hesitate to voice honest opinions about a policy in a more open forum.

Once the policy has come up for review, all comments should be examined and management-approved changes should be implemented. Additional review methods could involve including representative users in the revision process and allowing for direct comment on the revision of the policy. In reality, most policies are drafted by a single responsible individual and are then reviewed, or "signed into law," by a higher-level manager. This method should not preclude the collection and review of employee input, however.

Policy and Revision Date In some organizations, policies are drafted and published without a date, leaving users of the policy unaware of its age or status. This practice can create problems, including legal ones, if employees are complying with an out-of-date policy. Such problems are particularly common in an environment where there is high turnover. Ideally, the policy document should include its date of origin, along with the dates, if any, of revisions. Some policies may need a "sunset clause," particularly if they govern information use for a short-term association with second-party businesses or agencies. The inclusion of such an expiration date prevents a temporary policy from becoming a permanent mistake.

A Final Note On Policy

As mentioned earlier, while policies can help organizations avoid litigation, their first and foremost function is to inform employees of what is and is not acceptable behavior in the organization. Policy development is meant to improve employee productivity and prevent potentially embarrassing situations. In a worst-case scenario, an employee could be fired for failure to comply with a policy. If the organization cannot verify that the policy was not properly implemented, as mentioned earlier in the chapter, the employee could sue the organization for wrongful termination. Lawsuits cost money, and the organization could be so financially devastated that it has to go out of business. Other employees will then lose their livelihoods, and no one wins.

In reality, most employees inherently want to do what is right. If properly educated on what is acceptable and what is not, they will choose to follow the rules for acceptable behavior. Most people prefer systems that provide fair treatment. If they know the penalties for failure to comply, no outrage will arise when someone is caught misbehaving and the penalties are applied. Knowing what is prohibited, what the penalties are, and how penalties will be enforced is a preventive measure that should free employees to focus on the business at hand.

Chapter Summary

- A quality InfoSec program begins and ends with policy.

- Policy drives the performance of personnel in ways that enhance the InfoSec of an organization's information assets.

- Developing proper guidelines for an InfoSec program is a management problem, not a technical one. The technical aspect of an InfoSec program is merely one part of the entire program and should be dealt with only after management has created relevant policies.

- Although InfoSec policies are the least expensive means of control, they are often the most difficult to implement. Policy controls cost only the time and effort that the management team spends to create, approve, and communicate them, and that employees spend to integrate the policies into their daily activities.

- The InfoSec policy must satisfy several criteria:
  - Policy should never conflict with law.
  - Policy must stand up in court, when it is challenged.
  - Policy must be properly supported and administered.

- Guidelines for the formulation of InfoSec policy are as follows:
  - Policy generators must recognize that all policies contribute to the success of the organization.
  - Management must ensure the adequate sharing of responsibility.
  - End users should be involved in the policy development process.

- A policy is a statement of the organization's position that is intended to influence and determine decisions and actions and that is used to control the actions of people and the development of procedures.

- A policy may be viewed as a set of rules that dictates acceptable and unacceptable behavior within an organization.

- Policies must contain information on what is required and what is prohibited, on the penalties for violating policy, and on the appeals process.

- For a policy to be effective, it must be properly written, distributed, read, understood, agreed to, and uniformly applied to those for whom it is intended.

- Management must define three types of InfoSec policies:
  - Enterprise information security program policy, which sets the strategic direction, scope, and tone for all security efforts; and must be based on and support the organization's vision and mission statements
  - Issue-specific information security policies, which provide guidance to all members of an organization regarding the use of IT
  - System-specific information security policies, which guide the management and technical specifications of particular technologies and systems

Review Questions

1. What is information security policy? Why it is critical to the success of the InfoSec program?

2. Of the controls or countermeasures used to control InfoSec risk, which is viewed as the least expensive? What are the primary costs of this type of control?

3. List and describe the three challenges in shaping policy.

4. List and describe the three guidelines for sound policy, as stated by Bergeron and Bérubé.

5. Describe the bull's-eye model. What does it say about policy in the InfoSec program?

6. In what way are policies different from standards?

7. In what way are policies different from procedures?

8. For a policy to have any effect, what must happen after it is approved by management? What are some ways to accomplish this?

9. Is policy considered static or dynamic? Which factors might determine this status?

10. List and describe the three types of InfoSec policy as described by NIST SP 800-14.

11. What is the purpose of an EISP?

12. What is the purpose of an ISSP?

13. What is the purpose of a SysSP?

14. To what degree should the organization's values, mission, and objectives be integrated into the policy documents?

15. List and describe four elements that should be present in the EISP.

16. List and describe three functions that the ISSP serves in the organization.

17. What should be the first component of an ISSP when it is presented? Why? What should be the second major component? Why?

18. List and describe three common ways in which ISSP documents are created and/or managed.

19. List and describe the two general groups of material included in most SysSP documents.

20. List and describe the three approaches to policy development presented in this chapter. In your opinion, which is best suited for use by a smaller organization and why? If the target organization were very much larger, which approach would be more suitable and why?

Exercises

1. Using the Internet, go to the International Information Systems Security Certifications Consortium (ISC)² Web site (*www.isc2.org*) and look for the InfoSec common body of knowledge (CBK). When you review the list of 10 areas in the CBK, is policy listed? Why do you think this is so?

2. Search your institution's intranet or Web sites for its security policies. Do you find an enterprise security policy? What issue-specific security policies can you locate? Are all

of these policies issued or coordinated by the same individual or office, or are they scattered throughout the institution?

3. Using the framework presented in this chapter, evaluate the comprehensiveness of each policy you located in Exercise 2. Which areas are missing?

4. Using the framework presented in this chapter, draft a sample issue-specific security policy for an organization. At the beginning of your document, describe the organization for which you are creating the policy and then complete the policy using the framework.

5. Search for sample security policies on the Web. Identify five EISP and five ISSP sample policies and bring them to class. Compare these with the framework presented in this chapter and comment on the policies' comprehensiveness.

Closing Case

Prior to the first meeting of the RWW Enterprise Policy Review Committee, Mike asked Iris to meet him in his office.

"You've convinced me that IT and InfoSec policy are tightly integrated," Mike said, motioning for Iris to sit down. "And you've convinced me that InfoSec policy is critical to this enterprise. Since we are each members of the Enterprise Policy Review Committee, I think we may want to coordinate our efforts when we bring issues up in that group. You agree?"

Iris, who knew how important policy was to her program's success, smiled.

"Sure, no problem" she said. "I see it the same way you do, I think."

"Good," Mike said. "We'll work together to make sure the EISP you've drafted is integrated with the other top-level enterprise policies. What we need to watch out for now is all the cross-references between the top-level policies and the second-tier and third-tier policies. The entire problem of internal consistency between supporting policies is a problem, especially with getting the HR department policies to integrate fully."

Iris nodded while Mike continued.

"I want you to take the current HR policy document binder and make a wish list of possible changes," he said. "You should focus on making sure we get the right references in place. If you can send me the change plan by the end of the weekend, I will have time to review it."

Discussion

1. If the Enterprise Policy Review Committee is not open to the approach that Mike and Iris want to use for structuring InfoSec policies into three tiers, how should Mike and Iris proceed?

2. Should the CISO (Iris) be assessing HR policies? Why or why not?

Ethical Decision Making

Suppose that Iris sends Mike her detailed plan for an EISP along with a draft of a fully revised Enterprise IT Policy, with all of the necessary changes in the supporting polices. Suppose further that, during the Enterprise Policy Review Committee meeting, Charlie submits the revised EITP exactly as Iris has revised it but does not include any reference to the work that Iris did. In fact, Charlie presents the enhanced EITP as his own work. Has Charlie broken any laws in representing Iris' policy work as his own? Has Charlie committed an ethical lapse in doing so, or is he just being inconsiderate?

Endnotes

1. Helsing, C., M. Swanson, and M. Todd. "Special Publication 500-169: Executive Guide to the Protection of Information Resources." October 1989. *National Institute of Science and Technology.* Accessed December 14, 2012 @ *http://csrc.nist .gov/publications/PubsSPArch.html.*

2. Wood, Charles Cresson. *Information Security Policies Made Easy*, 12th ed. Information Shield, Inc., 2012: 1.

3. Bergeron, F., and C. Bérubé. "End Users Talk Computer Policy." *Journal of Systems Management*, December 1990, 41(12), 14–17.

4. Wood, Charles Cresson. *Information Security Policies Made Easy*, 12th ed. Information Shield, Inc., 2012: 1.

5. "Information Security Policy." *Washington University in St. Louis.* Accessed September 4, 2012 @ *www.wustl.edu/policies/infosecurity.html.*

6. Ibid.

7. Wood, Charles Cresson. *Information Security Policies Made Easy*, 12th ed. Information Shield, Inc., 2012: 9.

8. Whitman, Michael E. "Security Policy: From Design to Maintenance." *Information Security Policies and Strategies—An Advances in MIS Monograph.* Goodman, S., D. Straub, and V. Zwass (eds). Armonk NY: M. E. Sharp, Inc.

9. "National Assessment of Adult Literacy: 2003 Survey Results." *Institute of Education Sciences.* Accessed December 21, 2012 @ *http://nces.ed.gov/NAAL/index.asp?file =KeyFindings/Demographics/Overall.asp&PageId=16#2.*

10. Ibid.

11. Ricks, David A. *Blunders in International Business.* Cambridge, MA: Blackwell, 1993: 40.

12. Bloom, Benjamin S., Bertram B. Mesia, and David R. Krathwohl. *Taxonomy of Educational Objectives.* New York: David McKay, 1964.

13. Whitman, Michael E. "Security Policy: From Design to Maintenance." *Information Security Policies and Strategies—An Advances in MIS Monograph.* Goodman, S., D. Straub, and V. Zwass (eds). Armonk NY: M. E. Sharp, Inc.

14. Ibid.

15. Ibid.

16. Wood, Charles Cresson. *Information Security Policies Made Easy*, 12th ed. Information Shield, Inc., 2012.

## chapter 5

Developing the Security Program

We trained hard ... but every time we formed up teams we would be reorganized. I was to learn that we meet any new situation by reorganizing. And a wonderful method it can be for creating the illusion of progress while producing confusion, inefficiency, and demoralization.

PETRONIUS ARBITER, ROMAN WRITER AND SATIRIST, 210 B.C.

Iris was looking over the freshly printed first issue of Random Widget Works, Inc.'s (RWW's) information security newsletter, *The Paladin*, when Mike Edwards walked into her office.

"What's new, Iris?" he asked.

"See for yourself!" Iris replied with a grin, handing Mike her latest completed project.

"Very nice," he commented. "How close are you to publication?"

"We've just put it on the intranet, and we're going to run off a few dozen hard copies for our office. That's your copy."

"Thanks!" Mike said while scanning the cover article. "What is this disclosure situation all about?"

Mike was referring to the recent state law that mandated very specific definitions and penalties for computer-related crimes such as computer trespassing and theft of computer information. What had caught his attention was the clause providing penalties for the disclosure of some types of personal data, such as Social Security numbers and account passwords. The penalties ranged from $500 to $5000 per incident and even included up to a year in jail.

"We need to talk about this issue at the senior staff meeting," Mike said. "We should get the other departments involved to make sure we don't have any problems complying with this law."

Iris nodded and said, "Maybe someone from corporate legal should be there, too."

"Good idea," Mike said while looking at the newsletter's listing of information security training sessions.

"Where did you get the training staff?" he asked Iris.

"I've been meaning to talk to you about that," she said. "I'll teach the classes until my security manager, Tom, can take over. But we should ask the corporate training office about getting some of their staff up to speed on our topics."

"Sounds good," Mike said. "I'll get with Jerry tomorrow after the staff meeting."

LEARNING OBJECTIVES

Upon completion of this material, you should be able to:

- Explain the organizational approaches to information security

- List and describe the functional components of an information security program

- Discuss how to plan and staff an organization's information security program based on its size

- Describe the internal and external factors that influence the activities and organization of an information security program

- List and describe the typical job titles and functions performed in the information security program

- Discuss the components of a security education, training, and awareness program and explain how organizations create and manage these programs

Introduction

Some organizations use the term "security program" to describe the entire set of personnel, plans, policies, and initiatives related to information security. Others use the term "information security" to refer to the broader context of corporate or physical security plus those areas usually associated with computer, network, or data security. The term **information security program** is used in this book to describe the structure and organization of the effort that strives to contain the risks to the information assets of the organization.

There's an old joke about management that goes something like this:

A new executive reports for work and is shown to his desk. On the top of his desk is a letter from his predecessor and three sealed envelopes numbered from one to three. The letter congratulates him on his new position, the former executive regretting he was unable to stick around and help with the transition. However, the outgoing executive notes he has provided the incoming executive with three pieces of advice, should he run into problems. Each of these nuggets is stored in one of the three numbered envelopes and is to be opened in order and only when advice is truly needed. The new executive scoffs at the idea that he would ever need any help at all and tosses the still-sealed envelopes in the desk drawer.

Months go by and the new executive finds himself in a position where he just doesn't know how to handle a problem. He recalls the three envelopes. Frustrated and desperate, he opens the first envelope. Inside, the note states "Blame everything on me." The new executive calls in his subordinates. He declares that all of the problems facing the organization are due to his predecessor and that the executive's division will now turn in a new direction. This buys him some time.

A few months later, the next insurmountable problem emerges. The executive finally brings himself to open the second envelope. The message inside reads "Reorganize everything." The executive promptly calls a meeting of his subordinates and declares that the current situation is a result of poor organization and that in order to resolve it they must restructure the entire division. It's a very busy time and everyone is occupied with the rigors of reorganization for months and months. Eventually, however, the next problem presents itself to the executive. Confidently, the executive reaches for the third envelope. The message this time: "Fill out three new envelopes."

Sometimes, the problems faced by executives must be answered head-on, without looking to place the blame on others or the organizational structure.

Organizing for Security

Among the variables that determine how a given organization chooses to structure its information security (InfoSec) program are organizational culture, size, security personnel budget, and security capital budget. The first and most influential of these variables is the organizational culture. If upper management and staff believe that InfoSec is a waste of time and resources, the InfoSec program will remain small and poorly supported. Efforts made by the InfoSec staff will be viewed as contrary to the mission of the organization and detrimental to the organization's productivity. Conversely, where there is a strong, positive view of InfoSec, the InfoSec program is likely to be larger and well supported, both financially and otherwise. There is a need for an alignment between the InfoSec program in place and the culture of the organization. When these are not well aligned, conflicts may result in the program being less effective.

An organization's size and available resources directly affect the size and structure of its InfoSec program. Organizations with complex IT infrastructures and sophisticated system users are likely to require more InfoSec support. In fact, large, complex organizations may have entire divisions dedicated to InfoSec, including a chief information security officer (CISO), multiple security managers, multiple administrators, and many technicians. Such divisions might have specialized staff focusing on specific areas—for example, policy, planning, firewalls, and intrusion detection and prevention systems (IDPSs). In general, the larger the organization is, the larger its InfoSec program will be. By contrast, smaller organizations may have a single security administrator, or they may assign the InfoSec responsibilities to a systems or network administrator or manager.

Offline
Organizational Culture

What is organizational culture? Simply put, it is the way the values of the management and employees of an organization are turned into everyday activities and recurring practices. Also known as "corporate culture," organizational culture may be reflected in the *values statement* of the organization; however, in many organizations, it is represented by the collective consciousness that the organization manifests when interacting with its stakeholders and other constituents. An organization's culture is reflected in how management deals with employees and outsiders such as suppliers and customers. Those individuals who have worked for multiple organizations often report a distinct difference in organizational cultures beyond the conduct of business functions and processes. Organizational culture is as much about attitude and perspective as it is about skills and capabilities. In most cases, organizational culture is undocumented and learned through observation and interaction with others.

BusinessDictionary.com explains that organizational culture manifests itself in "(1) how the organization conducts its business, treats its employees, customers, and the wider community, (2) the extent to which autonomy and freedom is allowed in decision making, developing new ideas, and personal expression, (3) how power and information flow through the organizational hierarchy, and (4) the employees' commitment to collective objectives."[1]

A strong and positive organizational culture often supports employees in having effective interactions with one another, with management, and with business partners and customers. A weak or negative organizational culture can impede an organization's ability to function, perhaps to the level of making an organization dysfunctional. Improving destructive or dysfunctional organizational culture is an extreme challenge.

Another variable is the personnel budget for the InfoSec program. The size of the InfoSec budget typically corresponds to the size of the organization. Although no standard exists for the size of the InfoSec budget and/or the number of security personnel an organization has, industry averages are available. These vary widely and may be expressed in terms of InfoSec budget per unit of revenue, InfoSec staff per number of total employees, or InfoSec budget per unit of IT budget. Determining the industry average in any given case may be a challenge, but the reality is that regardless of the industry average, it is the management of the particular organization that has the most influence over this variable, for better or worse. In general, security programs are understaffed for the tasks they have been assigned. Top security managers must constantly struggle to create policy and policy plans, manage personnel issues, plan training, and keep the administrative and support staff focused on their assigned responsibilities and tasks.

According to Andrew Briney and Frank Prince, authors of the journal article "Does Size Matter?" which is referenced in the adjoining offline box:

> *As organizations get larger in size, their security departments are not keeping up with the demands of increasingly complex organizational infrastructures. Security spending per user and per machine declines exponentially as organizations grow, leaving most handcuffed when it comes to implementing effective security procedures.*[2]

Office politics, the economy, and budget forecasts are just some of the factors that cause upper management to juggle with staffing levels. In today's environment, the InfoSec programs in most organizations do not yet receive the support they need to function properly. That situation may change, however, because the current political climate and the many reported events regarding InfoSec breaches are rapidly forcing organizational cultures to view InfoSec as a critical function.

Another important variable is the portion of the capital and expense budget for physical resources that is dedicated to InfoSec. This budget includes allocation of offices, computer labs, and testing facilities as well as the general InfoSec expense budget. Because the InfoSec staff handle confidential information regarding security plans, policies, structures, designs, and a host of other items, it is prudent to provide this group with its own secured physical resources, including office space.

Although the size of an organization influences the makeup of its InfoSec program, certain basic functions should occur in every organization, and thus these functions should be included in any budget allocation. Table 5-1 outlines the suggested functions for a successful InfoSec program. These functions are not necessarily performed within the InfoSec department, but they must be performed somewhere within the organization.

Security in Large Organizations

Organizations that have more than 1000 devices and require security management are likely to be staffed and funded at a level that enables them to accomplish most of the functions identified in Table 5-1. Large organizations often create an internal entity to deal with the specific InfoSec challenges they face. Not surprisingly, the security functions and organizational approaches implemented by larger organizations are as diverse as the organizations themselves. InfoSec departments in such organizations tend to form and reform internal groups to meet long-term challenges even as they handle day-to-day security operations. Thus, functions are likely to be split into groups in larger organizations; in contrast, smaller organizations typically create fewer groups, perhaps only having one general group representing the whole department.

One recommended approach is to separate the functions into four areas:

1. Functions performed by nontechnology business units outside the IT area of management control, such as:
   - Legal
   - Training
2. Functions performed by IT groups outside the InfoSec area of management control, such as:
   - Systems security administration
   - Network security administration
   - Centralized authentication

Offline
Does Size Matter?

While many IT professionals may think they would be better off in the big IT departments of nationally renowned organizations, they may in fact be better off at a smaller organization. Big organizations have large staffs, full-time and part-time security professionals, and more problems than the typical smaller organization. Here, we define small, medium, large, and very large organizations, and describe the problems inherent in each and how they are staffed to deal with them.

- The small organization has 10–100 computers. Most small organizations have a simple, centralized IT organizational model and spend disproportionately more on security, averaging almost 20 percent of the total IT budget. The typical security staff in this organization is usually only one person (the lone ranger!), if in fact there is a full-time security professional. Much more frequently, InfoSec is an additional duty of one of the IT staffers. However, financially, the small organizations, including ones with the smallest budgets, spend more per user than medium- and large-sized organizations.[3]

- The medium-sized organization has 100–1000 computers and has a smaller budget (averaging about 11 percent of the total IT budget), about the same security staff, and a larger need for InfoSec than the small organization. The medium-sized organization's security people must rely on help from IT staff to carry out security plans and practices. "Their ability to set policy, handle incidents in a regular manner, and effectively allocate resources are, overall, worse than any other group. Considering their size, the number of incidents they recognize is skyrocketing."[4]

- The large organization has 1000–10,000 computers. Organizations of this size have generally integrated planning and policy into the organizational culture; "eight in 10 organizations say at least some of their security decisions are guided by them."[5] Unfortunately, the large organization tends to spend substantially less on security (an average of only about 5 percent of the total IT budget), creating issues across the organization, especially in the "people" areas.

- The very large organization has more than 10,000 computers and large InfoSec budgets, which grow faster than IT budgets. However, in these multimillion-dollar security budgets, the average amount per user is still less than in any other type of organization. "Where small organizations spend more than $5000 per user on security, very large organizations spend about one-eighteenth of that, roughly $300 per user," or approximately 6 percent of the total IT budget. The very large organization does a better job in the policy and resource management areas.[6]

Function	Description	Comments
Risk assessment	Identifies and evaluates the risk present in IT initiatives and/or systems	This function includes identifying the sources of risk and may include offering advice on controls that can reduce risk.
Risk management	Implements or oversees use of controls to reduce risk	This function is often paired with risk assessment.
Systems testing	Evaluates patches used to close software vulnerabilities and acceptance testing of new systems to assure compliance with policy and effectiveness	This function is usually part of the incident response and/or risk management functions.
Policy	Maintains and promotes InfoSec policy across the organization	This function must be coordinated with organization-wide policy processes.
Legal assessment	Maintains awareness of planned and actual laws and their impact, and coordinates with outside legal counsel and law enforcement agencies	This function is almost always external to the InfoSec and IT departments.
Incident response	Handles the initial response to potential incidents, manages escalation of actual incidents, and coordinates the earliest responses to incidents and disasters	Often spanning other functions and drawn from multiple departments. It should include middle management to manage escalation processes.
Planning	Researches, creates, maintains, and promotes InfoSec plans; often takes a project management approach to planning as contrasted with strategic planning for the whole organization	This function must coordinate with organization-wide policy processes.
Measurement	Uses existing control systems (and perhaps specialized data collection systems) to measure all aspects of the InfoSec environment	Managers rely on timely and accurate statistics relied on to make informed decisions.
Compliance	Verifies that system and network administrators repair identified vulnerabilities promptly and correctly	This function poses problems for good customer service because it is difficult to be customer focused and enforce compliance at the same time.
Centralized authentication	Manages the granting and revocation of network and system credentials for all members of the organization	This function is often delegated to the help desk or staffed in conjunction (and colocated) with the help desk function.
Systems security administration	Administers the configuration of computer systems, which are often organized into groups by the operating system they run	Many organizations may have originally assigned some security functions to these groups outside of the InfoSec function. This can be a source of conflict when organizations update their InfoSec programs.
Training	Trains general staff in InfoSec topics, IT staff in specialized technical controls, and internal InfoSec staff in specialized areas of InfoSec, including both technical and managerial topics	Some or all of this function may be carried out in conjunction with the corporate training department.

Table 5-1 Functions needed to implement the InfoSec program

Function	Description	Comments
Network security administration	Administers configuration of computer networks; often organized into groups by logical network area (i.e., WAN, LAN, DMZ) or geographic location	Many organizations may have originally assigned some security functions to these groups outside of the InfoSec function, which may require close coordination or reassignment.
Vulnerability assessment (VA)	Locates exposure within information assets so these vulnerabilities can be repaired before weaknesses are exploited	VA is sometimes performed by a penetration testing team or ethical hacking unit. This function is often outsourced to specialists hired as consultants that test system controls to find weak spots. They are sometimes known as "red teams" or "tiger teams."

Table 5-1   **Functions needed to implement the InfoSec program (continued)**

Copyright © 2014 Cengage Learning®.

3. Functions performed within the InfoSec department as a customer service to the organization and its external partners, such as:

- Risk assessment
- Systems testing
- Incident response
- Planning
- Measurement
- Vulnerability assessment

4. Functions performed within the InfoSec department as a compliance enforcement obligation, such as:

- Policy
- Compliance/audit
- Risk management

It remains the CISO's responsibility to see that InfoSec functions are adequately performed somewhere within the organization. As indicated in Figures 5-1 and 5-2, respectively, large and very large organizations typically have dedicated staffs—sometimes large ones—to support the security program. The deployment of full-time security personnel depends on a number of factors, including sensitivity of the information to be protected, industry regulations (as in the financial and health care industries), and general profitability. The more resources the company can dedicate to its personnel budget, the more likely it is to maintain a large InfoSec staff. As shown in Figure 5-1, a typical large organization has an average of one to two full-time administrators, three to four full-time administrators/technicians, and as many as 16 part-time staff members who have InfoSec duties in addition to their duties in other areas. For example, a systems administrator of a Windows 2012 server may be responsible for maintaining both the server and the security applications running on it. The very large organization, as illustrated in Figure 5-2, may have more than 20 full-time security personnel and 40 or more individuals with part-time responsibilities.

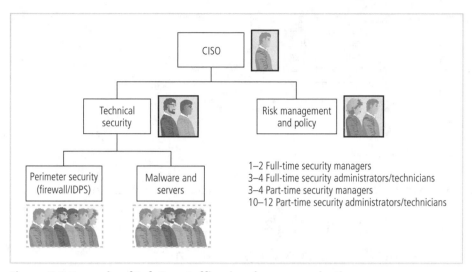

Figure 5-1 Example of InfoSec staffing in a large organization

Copyright © 2014 Cengage Learning®.

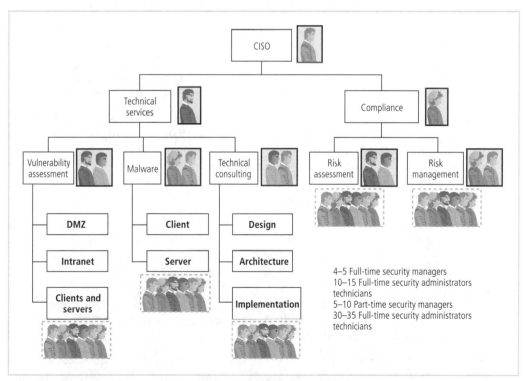

Figure 5-2 Example of InfoSec staffing in a very large organization

Copyright © 2014 Cengage Learning®.

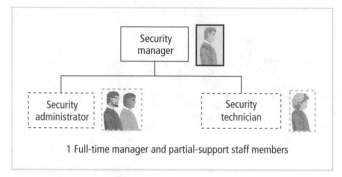

Figure 5-3 Example of InfoSec staffing in a medium-sized organization

Copyright © 2014 Cengage Learning®.

Security in Medium-Sized Organizations

Medium-sized organizations have between 100 and 1000 machines requiring security management. These organizations may still be large enough to implement the multi-tiered approach to security described earlier for large organizations, though perhaps with fewer dedicated groups and more functions assigned to each group. In a medium-sized organization, more of the functional areas from Table 5-1 are assigned to other departments within IT but outside the InfoSec department. Also, the central authentication function often gets handed off to systems administration personnel within the IT department.

Medium-sized organizations tend to ignore some of the functions from Table 5-1—in particular, when the InfoSec department cannot staff a certain function and the IT or another department is not encouraged or required to perform that function in its stead. In these cases, the CISO must improve the collaboration among these groups and must provide leadership in advocating decisions that stretch the capabilities of the organization.

As illustrated in Figure 5-3, the full-time and part-time staff of a medium-sized organization is dramatically smaller than that of its larger counterparts. This organization may only have one full-time security person, with perhaps three individuals with part-time InfoSec responsibilities.

Security in Small Organizations

Smaller organizations—those with fewer than 100 systems to supervise—face particular challenges. In a small organization, InfoSec often becomes the responsibility of a jack-of-all-trades, a single security administrator with perhaps one or two assistants for managing the technical components. It is not uncommon in smaller organizations to have the systems or network administrators play these many roles. Such organizations frequently have little in the way of formal policy, planning, or security measures, and they usually outsource their Web presence or e-commerce operations. As a result, the security administrator most often deals with desktop management, virus protection, and local area network security issues.

Because resources are often limited in smaller organizations, the security administrator frequently turns to freeware or open source software to lower the costs of assessing and implementing security. As you will learn in Chapter 10, these tools can be quite effective in both providing access to otherwise unavailable utilities and lowering the total cost of security.

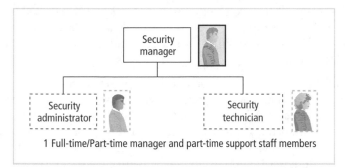

Figure 5-4 Example of InfoSec staffing in a smaller organization

Copyright © 2014 Cengage Learning®.

In small organizations, security training and awareness is most commonly conducted on a one-on-one basis, with the security administrator providing advice to users as needed. Any published policies are likely to be issue-specific—for example, on Web and Internet use and fair and responsible use of office equipment. Formal planning, when it happens, is usually part of the IT planning conducted by the chief information officer (CIO).

Some observers feel that small organizations, to their advantage, avoid some threats precisely because of their small size. The thinking is that hacktivists, hackers, and other threat agents may be less likely to go after smaller companies, opting instead to attack larger, more prestigious targets. Although this questionable strategy has not been proven, it is not wise to gamble the future of the organization on its staying unnoticed. As the saying goes, "There is no security in obscurity."

Threats from insiders are also less likely in an environment where every employee knows every other employee. In general, the less anonymity an employee has, the less likely he or she feels able to get away with abuse or misuse of company assets. The lack of resources available to the smaller organization's security administrators is somewhat offset by the lower risk of becoming a target. Figure 5-4 shows the limited staffing found in smaller organizations, which typically have either one individual who has full-time duties in InfoSec or, more likely, one individual who manages or conducts InfoSec duties in addition to those of other functional areas, most likely IT. This individual may have partial supervision of one or two assistants.

Placing Information Security within an Organization

In large organizations, the InfoSec department is often located within an IT division headed by the CISO, who reports directly to the CIO. Such a structure implies that the goals and objectives of the CISO and CIO are closely aligned. In reality, this is not always the case. By its very nature, an InfoSec program, operating as a department within an IT division, may sometimes find itself at odds with the goals and objectives of the broader IT division as a whole. On the one hand, the CIO, as the executive in charge of the organization's technology, manages the efficiency in processing and accessing the organization's information. Anything that limits access or slows information processing directly contradicts the CIO's mission. On the other hand, the CISO functions more like an internal auditor, with the InfoSec department examining existing systems to discover InfoSec faults and flaws in technology, software, and employees' activities and processes. At times, these activities may disrupt the processing and accessing of the organization's information. Because the goals and objectives of the CIO and the CISO may come in conflict, it is not difficult to understand the current movement to separate InfoSec from the IT division.

The vision of separate IT and InfoSec functions is shared by many executives. A survey conducted by Meta Group found that while only 3 percent of the consulting firm's clients positioned the InfoSec department outside IT, the clients viewed this positioning as what a forward-thinking organization should do. An article titled "Where the Chief Security Officer Belongs," which appeared in *InformationWeek*, states this more succinctly: "The people who do and the people who watch shouldn't report to a common manager."[7]

The challenge is to design a reporting structure for the InfoSec program that balances the competing needs of the communities of interest. In many cases, the unit that executes the InfoSec program is shoehorned into the organizational chart in a way that reflects its marginal status, and it may be shuffled from place to place within the organization with little attention paid to how such organizational moves hinder its effectiveness. Organizations searching for a rational compromise will attempt to find a place for the InfoSec program that allows it to balance policy enforcement with education, training, awareness, and customer service needs. This approach can help make InfoSec part of the organizational culture.

There are many ways to position the InfoSec program within an organization. In his book *Information Security Roles and Responsibilities Made Easy*, Charles Cresson Wood compiled many of the best practices on InfoSec program positioning from many industry groups. His chapter covering this topic, titled "Reporting Relationships," has been condensed here with the author's permission.

This [area] covers the generally accepted and frequently encountered reporting relationships for an Information Security Department. The pros and cons of twelve options are explored and six reporting relationships are recommended. Because there are many places in the organizational hierarchy where an Information Security Department could be situated, you should review the list of pros and cons for each option, thinking about what is most important in your organization. [...] You should then summarize these considerations in a memo, and after this memo is prepared, you will most likely be leaning in the direction of one of these reporting relationships. At that point in time, a clear and well-justified proposal for an Information Security Department reporting relationship can be formulated.

[...] In these successful organizational structures, the Department reports high up in the management hierarchy. Reporting directly to top management is advisable for the Information Security Department Manager [or CISO] because it fosters objectivity and the ability to perceive what's truly in the best interest of the organization as a whole, rather than what's in the best interest of a particular department (such as the Information Technology Department). A highly placed executive in charge of information security will also be more readily able to gain management's attention, and this in turn will increase the likelihood that the Information Security Department will obtain the necessary budget and staffing resources. An Information Security Department that reports high up on the management ladder will also be more readily able to force compliance with certain requirements, such as a standard specifying consistent implementation of certain encryption technology.

In an increasing number of progressive organizations, being located high on the management ladder means that the Information Security Department Manager is a Senior Vice President who reports directly to the Chief Executive Officer (CEO). This is, for example, the organizational structure now found at a well-known credit card company. Those organizations which are less dependent on highly-visible and absolutely impeccable information security will typically have the Information Security Department Manager reporting further down on the organizational ladder.

Nonetheless, in the latter organizations, having an Information Security Department Manager who reports directly to the CEO may be appropriate for a short while until major improvements in the information security area have been made. This temporary reporting structure clearly communicates that information security is important and worthy of top management's attention. Such a direct reporting relationship with the CEO may then appropriately exist for a year or two after a major security related incident, in order to emphasize the importance of the function, to both insiders and outsiders.

[...] If you are establishing an information security function for the first time, or if a major reorganization is under way, you should seriously think about which middle managers would best serve as the conduit for messages sent to the CEO. Other desirable attributes are:

- Openness to new ideas
- Clout with top management
- Respect in the eyes of a wide variety of employees
- Comfort and familiarity with basic information systems concepts
- Willingness to take a stand for those things that are genuinely in the long-term best interest of the organization
- Comfort and familiarity with basic information systems concepts
- An overall understanding of the future trajectory of information technology, and an appreciation for how important information security will soon become

The ideal middle level manager, to whom you may wish to have the Information Security Department Manager report, should report directly to the CEO, or as high-up on the organizational hierarchy as possible. This middle level manager's organizational unit will also need a credible day-to-day relationship with, or a strategic tie-in with, the information security function. For example, a Risk and Insurance Management Department would have such a tie-in, but an Assembly Line Operations Department most often would not. The candidates are many, but some common choices are: the Executive Vice President Administrative Services, the Legal Department Manager (Chief Legal Officer), and the Chief Information Officer (CIO). [...]

This [section] makes reference to six [figures that illustrate] Options 1 through 6. These six reporting relationships are explored in that sequence. After that, six other options, which are not as frequently encountered, are discussed. The six [figures] are illustrative of real-world organizations and are not in any way meant to be hypothetical or normative. Throughout [...] the author has attempted to be descriptive rather than to propose a new paradigm, and in that respect, because these options are based on real-world experience, you can be assured that any one of these six initial options could be effective within your organization. The [figures] are also meant to convey an indication of good practice on which you can rely. [...]

Option 1: Information Technology

In [Figure 5-5], you will note that in this organizational structure the Information Security Department reports to the Information Technology Department. [...] Here the Information Security Department Manager reports directly to the Chief Information Officer (CIO), or the Vice President of Information Systems. In this option, you will find the most common organizational structure. Various statistical studies show that about 33 percent of organizations worldwide use this reporting relationship. This option is desirable because the manager to whom the Information Security Department Manager reports generally has clout with top management, and understands (in broad and general terms) the information systems technological issues. This option is also advantageous because it involves only one manager between the Information Security Department Manager and the Chief Executive Officer (CEO)—generally the CIO. The option is additionally attractive because the Information Security Department staff, on a day-to-day basis, must spend a good deal of time with the Information Technology Department staff. In that respect, this option is convenient [...].

Nonetheless, in spite of these advantages, this option is flawed because it includes an inherent conflict of interest. When confronted with resource allocation decisions, or when required to make tradeoffs, the CIO is likely to discriminate against the information security function. In these cases, other objectives such as cost minimization, enhanced user friendliness, or rapid time-to-market with a new product or service, will likely take precedence over information security. [...] As long as information security is seen as just another technological specialty, it will be treated as a routine technical matter, like data administration and other information

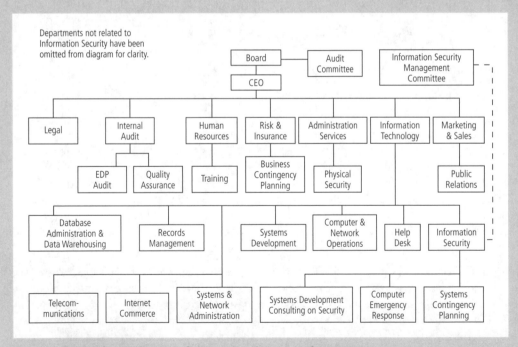

Figure 5-5 Wood's Option 1: InfoSec reporting to IT department

Source: From *Information Security Roles and Responsibilities Made Easy*, Version 3, Copyright 2005–2012 by Information Shield, Inc., used with permission.

technology sub-specialties. Although being part of the Information Technology Department is common, it is not as desirable as several of the other options listed below, and for that reason is not recommended.

Note that [Figure 5-5] does not have information security reporting to a Computer Operations Manager, the Management Information Systems Manager, the Information Resources Manager, or some other manager who in turn reports to the CIO or the Vice President of Information Systems. [...] Having an additional level of management also increases the likelihood that messages sent from the Information Security Department to the CEO will be corrupted in transit (the "whisper down the lane" problem). Other reasons not to pursue this organizational structure are covered [below in "Other Options."]

In [Figure 5-5], you should note that the Information Security Department Manager also has a dotted-line reporting relationship with the Information Security Management Committee. Although they are highly recommended, both this dotted-line relationship and the Committee can be omitted for smaller organizations. A Committee of this nature is a good idea because it provides a sounding board, a management direction-setting body, and a communication path with the rest of the organization. A drawback of using a committee like this is that it may take longer to get management approval for certain initiatives, but the approval that is obtained is likely to be more lasting and more widely distributed throughout the organization.

Option 2: Security

Another popular option, which again is not necessarily recommended, involves the Information Security Department reporting to the Security Department. In this case, the information security function is perceived to be primarily protective in nature, and therefore comparable to the Physical Security Department as well as the Personnel Security and Safety Department. Where this organizational design prevails, you may occasionally find the Information Security Department is instead referred to as the Information Protection Department. Shown in [Figure 5-6], this approach is desirable because it facilitates communication with others who have both a security perspective and related security responsibilities. This may help with incident investigations as well as reaching practical solutions to problems like laptop computer theft (which involves a combination of physical and information security). This option is also desirable because it brings a longer-term preventive viewpoint to information security activities, which in turn is likely to lower overall information security costs.

Nonetheless, there are some problems with this structure. Although the information security and physical security functions may at first seem to be philosophically aligned, there is a significant cultural difference between the two. For example, information security staff see themselves as high-tech workers, while physical security staff see themselves as participants in the criminal justice system. These cultural differences may cause some information security specialists to feel that it's not appropriate to be managed by a specialist in physical security, which will most often be the background of the Security Department Manager. This option is moreover undesirable because, at most firms, the budget for physical security has not increased much over the last few years, but the budget for information security has rapidly escalated; by combining these two departments under the Security Department umbrella, top management may underestimate the resources that the information security function will need. Option 2 is furthermore undesirable because the Security Department Manager will often lack an appreciation of information systems

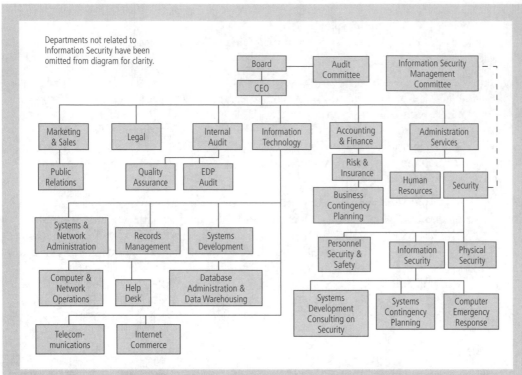

Figure 5-6 Wood's Option 2: InfoSec reporting to broadly defined security department

Source: From *Information Security Roles and Responsibilities Made Easy*, Version 3, Copyright 2005–2012 by Information Shield, Inc., used with permission.

technology, and so may be a poor communicator with top management. This option is further-more ill advised because it involves two middle managers in the communication path between the Information Security Department Manager and the CEO. To make it still less appealing, this option is likely to indirectly communicate that the Information Security Department is a new type of police; this perspective will make it more difficult for the Information Security Department to establish consultative relationships with other departments. On balance, this organizational structure is acceptable, but not as desirable as some of the other diagrams described.

Option 3: Administrative Services

Another way to do things, which is a significant improvement over both Options 1 and 2, is shown in [Figure 5-7]. Here the Information Security Department reports to the Administrative Services Department (which may also be called Administrative Support). In this case, the Information Security Department Manager reports to the Administrative Services Department Manager or the Vice President of Administration. This approach assumes that the Information Security Department is advisory in nature (also called a staff function), and performs services for workers throughout the organization, much like the Human Resources Department. This option is desirable because there is only one middle manager between the Information Security Department Manager and the CEO. The approach is also advisable because it acknowledges that information and information systems are found everywhere throughout the organization,

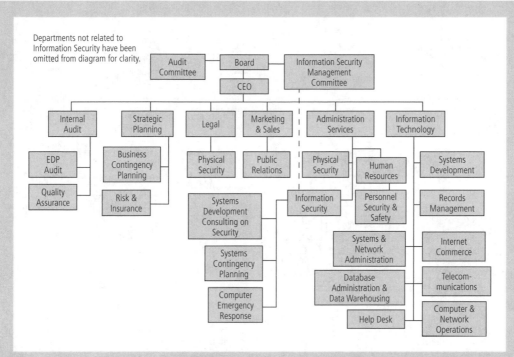

Figure 5-7 Wood's Option 3: InfoSec reporting to administrative services department

Source: From *Information Security Roles and Responsibilities Made Easy*, Version 3, Copyright 2005–2012 by Information Shield, Inc., used with permission.

and that workers throughout the organization are expected to work with the Information Security Department. This option is also attractive because it supports efforts to secure information no matter what form it takes (on paper, verbal, etc.), rather than viewing the information security function as strictly a computer- and network-oriented activity.

In many cases, depending on who fills the Administrative Services Vice President position, this option suffers because the Vice President doesn't know much about information systems technology, and this in turn may hamper his or her efforts to communicate with the CEO about information security. This option may also be ill advised for those organizations that could severely suffer, or even go out of business, if major information security problems were encountered. An Internet merchant (a "dot-com" firm) fits this billing. For these firms, this option doesn't give information security the prominence it deserves, nor does it give it the strategic and long-term focus that information security requires. Thus, with this option, the Information Security Department may be subject to more cost-cutting pressure from top management than it would with Option 4 or 5. On balance, though, for organizations that are not highly information intensive, such as a chain of restaurants, this is a desirable and recommended option.

Option 4: Insurance and Risk Management

[Figure 5-8] shows how the Information Security Department can report to the Insurance and Risk Management Department. With this approach, the Information Security Department

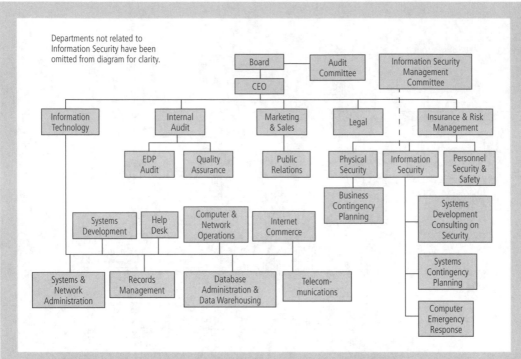

Departments not related to Information Security have been omitted from diagram for clarity.

Figure 5-8 Wood's Option 4: InfoSec reporting to insurance and risk management department

Source: From *Information Security Roles and Responsibilities Made Easy*, Version 3, Copyright 2005–2012 by Information Shield, Inc., used with permission.

Manager would typically report to the Chief Risk Manager (CRM) or the Vice President of Risk and Insurance Management. This option is desirable because it fosters what is often called an integrated risk management perspective. With this viewpoint, a centralized perspective prioritizes and compares all risks across the organization. The application of this idea typically involves assessing the extent of potential losses and the likelihood of losses across all functional departments, including Information Security, Physical Security, Legal, Internal Audit, Customer Relations, Accounting and Finance, etc. The intention is to see the big picture and be able to allocate resources to those departments and risk management efforts that most need these resources. You are strongly urged to foster the integrated risk management viewpoint, even if the current or proposed organizational structure doesn't reflect it, because information security will often be shown to be a serious and largely unaddressed problem area deserving greater organizational resources and greater management attention. Beyond integrated risk management, this option is desirable because it involves only one middle manager between the Information Security Department Manager and the CEO.

The CRM is also likely to be prevention oriented, adopt a longer-term viewpoint, and is able to engage the CEO in intelligent discussions about risk acceptance (doing nothing), risk mitigation (adding controls), and risk transfer (buying insurance). A CRM is also likely to be comfortable thinking about the future and generating scenarios reflecting a number of different possibilities, including information security scenarios such as a denial-of-service (DoS) attack. The CRM, however, is often not familiar with information systems technology, and so may need some special coaching or extra background research from the Information Security Department Manager to make important points with the CEO. Another problem with this approach is that its focus is strategic, and the operational and administrative aspects of information security (such as changing privileges when people change jobs) may not get the attention that they deserve from the CRM. Nonetheless, on balance this is a desirable option and is recommended for organizations that are information intensive, such as banks, stock brokerages, telephone companies, and research institutes.

Option 5: Strategy and Planning

In [Figure 5-9], you will find still another possible organizational structure found in the real world. Here the Information Security Department reports to the Strategy and Planning Department. In this case, the Information Security Department Manager reports directly to the Vice President of Strategy and Planning. This option views the information security function as critical to the success of the organization. This option would be appropriate for an Internet merchant (a "dot-com" enterprise) or a credit card company, both of which are critically dependent on the success of the information security function. This option is desirable because it involves only one middle manager between the Information Security Department Manager and the CEO. It is thus just one step down from the option mentioned at the beginning of this chapter, where the Senior Vice President of Information Security reports directly to the CEO.

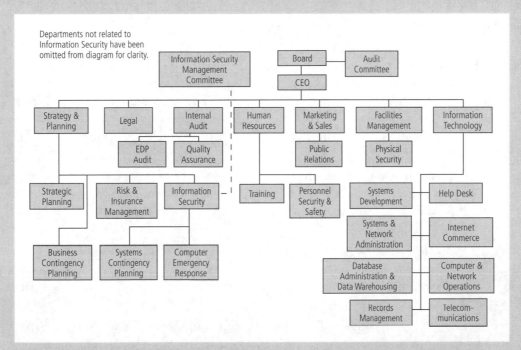

Figure 5-9 Wood's Option 5: InfoSec reporting to strategy and planning department

Source: From *Information Security Roles and Responsibilities Made Easy*, Version 3, Copyright 2005–2012 by Information Shield, Inc., used with permission.

Option 5 is desirable because it underscores the need for documented information security requirements (policies, standards, procedures, etc.) that apply to the entire organization. Like Options 3 and 4, this reporting structure also acknowledges the multidepartmental and multidisciplinary nature of information security tasks such as risk analysis and incident investigations. This option is also advisable because the Information Security Department works with others that share a scenario-oriented view of the world (they often ask "what if ..." questions). Another desirable aspect of this approach is that it implicitly communicates that information security is very importantly a management and people issue, not just a technological issue.

This same advantage can be a disadvantage if workers in the Information Technology Department consider the staff in the Information Security Department to be management oriented, and out of touch when it comes to the technology (of course, the work of the Information Security Department can clearly communicate that this is a misperception).

One problem with this approach is that the focus is strategic, and the operational and administrative aspects of information security (such as changing privileges when people change jobs) may not get the attention that they deserve from the Vice President of Strategy and Planning. On balance, though, this is an advisable reporting relationship for the information security function, and should be something that the Information Department Manager is considering for the long run even if he or she is not proposing it today.

Other Options

Other options for positioning the security department include:

- In the Legal Department: This option emphasizes copyrights, patents, trademarks, and related intellectual property protection mechanisms, as well as compliance with laws, regulations, and ethical standards (like privacy). An advantage to this reporting structure is that members of the Legal Department are comfortable with, and spend a lot of time developing, documentation such as policies and procedures; documentation showing that the organization is in compliance with the information security standard of due care is increasingly important.

- In the Internal Auditing Department, reporting directly to the IAD manager: because Internal Audit is charged with reviewing the work done by other units, including the Information Security Department, this reporting structure would yield a conflict of interest.

- Under the Help Desk: This option is not advised. The Help Desk is a lower-level technical group that does not get much top management attention or respect; nor does it command many resources, a scarcity that might be carried over into the Information Security Department.

- Under the Accounting and Finance Department, via the Information Technology Department: This option is undesirable because the Information Security Department would be buried deep in the organizational hierarchy, and would therefore not get the resources and top management attention that it needs. Also, the needs of the Information Security Department could be lost within, and overshadowed by, the needs of the Accounting and Finance Department.

- Under the Human Resources Department: Both groups develop policies that must be followed by workers throughout the organization. However, this is generally considered an ill-advised organizational position for the Information Security Department because the Human Resources Department manager often knows very little about information systems and is therefore most often not a credible conduit for communications to top management.

- Reporting to the Facilities Management Department (sometimes called Buildings and Grounds). With this organizational structure, the Information Security Department is seen by top management as an asset protection function, much like the Physical Security Department.

- The operations approach: The Information Security Department manager reports to the Chief Operating Officer (COO). This approach assumes that information security is a line management responsibility and a topic that all department managers must consider in their day-to-day activities.

Summary of Reporting Relationships

The Information Security Department at many organizations has been an unwelcome stepchild, handed back and forth between various groups, none of which felt as though they were its proper home. [...]

Smaller organizations will want to have a part-time Information Security Coordinator or Information Security Manager. [...] Small to medium-sized organizations will often require at least one full-time person, and medium-sized to large organizations will often require several full-time information security staff. [...] Since so few people are involved, in smaller organizations, the formal designation of a separate department will be considered to be unwarranted. But for all other organizations, no matter where the information security function happens to report, it is desirable to designate a separate department that has been formally recognized by top management. [...][8]

Source: From *Information Security Roles and Responsibilities Made Easy*, Version 3, Copyright 2005–2012 by Information Shield, Inc., used with permission.

Components of the Security Program

The InfoSec needs of any organization are unique to the culture, size, and budget of that organization. Determining the level at which the InfoSec program operates depends on the organization's strategic plan, and in particular on the plan's vision and mission statements. The CIO and CISO should use these two documents to formulate the mission statement for the InfoSec program. In *Information Security Roles and Responsibilities Made Easy*, Wood provides the following guidance regarding the formulation of mission statements:

> *A mission statement is a brief statement of objectives that describes what top management expects from the involved organizational unit. Although a broad-brush overview of activities is often helpful in a mission statement, specifics about these activities should instead appear in [associated] job description[s]. A mission statement should deal with a whole department or similar multi-person organizational unit, and should not talk about the objectives for a specific job title. [...] Likewise, a mission statement should not use any technical language, acronyms, or other jargon that will not be immediately understood by nontechnical workers or top management.*[9]

Two documents from the National Institute of Standards and Technology (NIST) also provide guidance for developing an InfoSec program. "SP 800-14, Generally Accepted Principles and Practices for Securing Information Technology Systems" includes this self-description in its Introduction:

> *[This] document gives a foundation that organizations can reference when conducting multi-organizational business as well as internal business. Management, internal auditors, users, system developers, and security practitioners can use the guideline to gain an understanding of the basic security requirements most IT systems should contain. The foundation begins with generally accepted system security principles and continues with common practices that are used in securing IT systems.*[10]

Another informative NIST publication is "SP 800-12, An Introduction to Computer Security: The NIST Handbook." This manual "provides a broad overview of many of the core topics included in computer [and information] security to help readers understand their computer security needs and develop a sound approach to the selection of appropriate security controls."[11]

The "NIST Handbook" covers many topics, including the following:

- Elements of computer security
- Roles and responsibilities
- Common threats
- Common InfoSec controls
- Risk management
- Security program management
- Contingency planning

Table 5-2 summarizes the essential program elements presented in these two NIST publications. There are many other NIST documents that provide additional details (and updated discussions) of these topics. These documents can be found at *http://csrc.nist.gov/publications /PubsSPs.html*.

There is much overlap between the elements of Table 5-2 and the earlier list of functions of an InfoSec program given in Table 5-1. Both resources could be used when reviewing the components of any specific InfoSec program.

Primary Element	Components
Policy	Program policy, issue-specific policy, system-specific policy
Program management	Central security program, system-level program
Risk management	Risk assessment, risk mitigation, uncertainty analysis
Life cycle planning	Security plan, initiation phase, development/acquisition phase, implementation phase, operation/maintenance phase
Personnel/user issues	Staffing, user administration
Preparing for contingencies and disasters	Business plan, identify resources, develop scenarios, develop strategies, test and revise plan
Computer security incident handling	Incident detection, reaction, recovery, and follow-up
Awareness and training	SETA plans, awareness projects, and policy and procedure training
Security considerations in computer support and operations	Help desk integration, defending against social engineering, and improving system administration
Physical and environmental security	Guards, gates, locks and keys, and alarms
Identification and authentication	Identification, authentication, passwords, advanced authentication
Logical access control	Access criteria, access control mechanisms
Audit trails	System logs, log review processes, and log consolidation and management
Cryptography	TKI, VPN, key management, and key recovery

Table 5-2   Elements of a security program

Source: NIST.

View Point
Building your Security Program from Inside and Outside
Paul D. Witman, Ph.D., California Lutheran University School of Management
by Scott Mackelprang, M.S., CSO, Asurion

Like shoes, security programs need to fit their owners and they need to conform to the objectives and activities of their owner. Just as a ballerina cannot be effective while wearing lumberjack boots and a lumberjack can't be effective while wearing a banker's shoes, your security program needs to fit your company and conform to the business activities of your company. Good security programs are composed of similar functional elements and employ similar commercial security tools, but in order to be

(Continued)

effective they need to be shaped to reflect important characteristics of the company they are intended to protect.

It's the security leader's job to determine which of the company's characteristics should be used to design an optimal security program. A company's size, its products and services, its regulatory obligations, and the funding for its security function are important considerations in the decision.

Many organizations operate their security programs in-house, while others choose to outsource parts of that program to third parties. This may be due to the organization's size (not enough people to put sufficient specialization and expertise to bear on security) or to core competencies (third parties may bring sufficient unique expertise to be worth the cost).

Some industries have security requirements defined at least in part by government regulations—banking, health care, and education come to mind, with their multiple acronyms, such as FFIEC, HIPAA, FERPA, and SOX. Other industries impose regulations on themselves—for example, the credit card processing requirements from the Payment Card Industry Security Standards Council.

If a company develops software to offer highly sensitive services like online banking or health care over the Internet, its security program must include a focus on secure software development processes, tools, and training. Brick and mortar businesses without similar online offerings will lack such a focus.

Thinking about your organization's capabilities and its risk tolerance will contribute to the insourcing/outsourcing discussion. Insourcing provides greater control; outsourcing often provides access to more specialized resources and skills that may be otherwise unavailable. In addition, the security program needs to address not only the explicit outsourcing of security activities but the security functions performed by all of the organization's suppliers.

Good security programs have a number of common elements. They lay out the security function's mission and scope of responsibilities. They make clear how the security program supports the company's strategic objectives. They describe the resources, tools, and processes that will be used to accomplish security objectives. They openly acknowledge the importance of balancing costs of the program with the benefits of managing security risk. They clearly describe the governance functions that ensure consistency of results over time and seek to provide recurring measures of the program's success to senior stakeholders.

Finally, core to every security program is an overarching ethical obligation to act in the best interests of the company's stakeholders, to protect their information and systems, and to manage the company's risks. The security leader must consider all options for fulfilling the objectives of the security program. The purpose must be to ensure the viability and ongoing operations of the organization and the value chain of which they are a part.

Information Security Roles and Titles

A study of InfoSec positions by Schwartz, Erwin, Weafer, and Briney found that they can be classified into three types: those that define, those that build, and those that administer. Here is how the study describes these types:

> *Definers provide the policies, guidelines, and standards. [...] They're the people who do the consulting and the risk assessment, who develop the product and technical architectures. These are senior people with a lot of broad knowledge, but often not a lot of depth. Then you have the builders. They're the real techies, who create and install security solutions. [...] Finally, you have the people who operate and administrate the security tools, the security monitoring function, and the people who continuously improve the processes. [...] What I find is we often try to use the same people for all of these roles. We use builders all the time. [...] If you break your InfoSec professionals into these three groups, you can recruit them more efficiently, with the policy people being the more senior people, the builders being more technical, and the operating people being those you can train to do a specific task.*[12]

A typical organization has a number of individuals with InfoSec responsibilities. While the titles used may be different from one organization to the next, most of the job functions fit into one of the following categories:

- CISO or CSO
- Security managers
- Security administrators and analysts
- Security technicians
- Security staffers and watchstanders
- Security consultants
- Security officers and investigators
- Help desk personnel

Each of these positions is discussed briefly here and more fully in Chapter 11.

Chief Information Security Officer

The CISO (or, in some cases, the CSO) is primarily responsible for the assessment, management, and implementation of the program that secures the organization's information. One difference is that the CSO (chief security officer) may often have one or more physical security staff members, whereas the CISO will likely not.

In *Information Security Roles and Responsibilities Made Easy*, Charles Cresson Wood wrote the following:

> *The appointment of a CISO ... does seem to nevertheless be a trend. This was evident because the more mature information security functions included a CISO, while the less mature functions marginally did not. The average age of the information security function for who said "no" to this question was 4.58 years, while the average age for those who said "yes" was 6.57. This trend is consistent with*

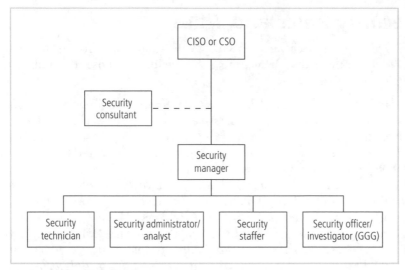

Figure 5-10 InfoSec roles

Copyright © 2014 Cengage Learning®.

prior surveys. For example, www.infosecurity-magazine.com *published an article by Avtar Sehmbi in July 2010, describing survey results from Deloitte, which indicated that fully 85 percent of large organizations worldwide had named a CISO.*[13]

The senior executive responsible for security may also be called the director of security, senior security manager, or by some similar title. The CISO usually reports directly to the CIO, although in larger organizations one or more layers of management may separate the two officers. Figure 5-10 shows the CISO as the most senior InfoSec role.

Convergence and the Rise of the True CSO Most organizations use the title "Chief Security Officer" to describe the CISO. However, depending on the maturity of the organization, there will be differences in approach with regard to security and processes. The more mature (and often the larger organizations) will use the CSO title to identify a role that is responsible for the convergence of the physical and IT risks into one complete program to control all those risks. Some, however, will simply call the senior executive for physical security the CSO and define a role for the CSO that is not integrated into a holistic risk management program. As was discussed in more detail in Chapter 2, convergence of the physical and digital security roles is a widely reported trend in larger organizations around the world.

Security Managers

Security managers are accountable for the day-to-day operations of the InfoSec program. They accomplish objectives identified by the CISO, to whom they report (as shown in Figure 5-10), and they resolve issues identified by technicians, administrators, analysts, or staffers whom they supervise. Managing security requires an understanding of technology but not necessarily technical mastery—configuration, operation, fault resolution, and so on. Some team leaders or project managers within the InfoSec community may be responsible for management-like functions, such as scheduling, setting priorities, or administering any number of procedural tasks, but they are not necessarily held accountable for making a particular technology function. Accountability for the actions of others is the hallmark of a true manager and is the criterion that distinguishes actual managers from those whose job titles merely include the word "manager."

Security Administrators and Analysts

The security administrator is a hybrid of a security technician (see the following section) and a security manager (described in the previous section). Such individuals have both technical knowledge and managerial skill. They are frequently called on to manage the day-to-day operations of security technology as well as to assist in the development and conduct of training programs, policy, and the like.

The security analyst is a specialized security administrator. In traditional IT, the security administrator corresponds to a systems administrator or database administrator, and the security analyst corresponds to a systems analyst. The systems analyst, in addition to performing security administration duties, must analyze and design security solutions within a specific domain (firewall, IDS, antivirus program). Systems analysts must be able to identify users' needs and understand the technological complexities and capabilities of the security systems they design.

Security Technicians

Security technicians are the technically qualified individuals who configure firewalls and IDPSs, implement security software, diagnose and troubleshoot problems, and coordinate with systems and network administrators to ensure that security technology is properly implemented. A security technician is usually an entry-level position. Some technical skills are required, however, which can make this job challenging for those who are new to the field, given that it is difficult to get the job without experience and yet experience comes with the job.

Just as in networking, security technicians tend to specialize in one major security technology group (firewalls, IDPSs, servers, routers, or software) and further specialize in one particular software or hardware package within that group, such as Checkpoint firewalls, Nokia firewalls, or Tripwire IDPS. These technologies are sufficiently complex to warrant a high level of specialization. Security technicians who want to move up in the corporate hierarchy must expand their technical knowledge horizontally, gaining an understanding of the general organizational issues of InfoSec as well as all technical areas.

Security Staffers and Watchstanders

"Security staffer" is a catchall title that applies to individuals who perform routine watchstanding or administrative activities. The term "watchstander" includes the people who watch intrusion consoles, monitor e-mail accounts, and perform other routine administrative or contingent yet critical roles that support the mission of the InfoSec department. The role of the watchstander continues to evolve as security operations centers become more common in larger organizations. Watchstanders are often entry-level InfoSec professionals responsible for monitoring some aspect of the organization's security posture, whether technical (as in the case of an IDPS watchstander) or managerial. They assist with the research and development of security policy, plans, or risk management efforts. In this position, new InfoSec professionals have the opportunity to learn more about the organization's InfoSec program before becoming critical components of its administration.

Security Consultants

The InfoSec consultant is typically an independent expert in some aspect of InfoSec (disaster recovery, business continuity planning, security architecture, policy development, or strategic planning). He or she is usually brought in when the organization makes the decision to outsource one or more aspects of its security program. While it is usually preferable to involve a formal security services company, qualified individual consultants are available for hire.

Security Officers and Investigators

Occasionally, the physical security and InfoSec programs are blended into a single, converged functional unit. When that occurs, several roles are added to the pure IT security program, including physical security officers and investigators. Sometimes referred to as the guards, gates, and guns (GGG) aspect of security, these roles are often closely related to law enforcement and may rely on employing persons trained in law enforcement and/or criminal justice. Physical security professionals comprise a vital component of InfoSec, since, as has been referenced in prior chapters, physical access trumps logical security in most settings.

Help Desk Personnel

An important part of the InfoSec team is the help desk, which enhances the security team's ability to identify potential problems. When a user calls the help desk with a complaint about his or her computer, the network, or an Internet connection, the user's problem may turn out to be related to a bigger problem, such as a hacker, a DoS attack, or a virus.

Because help desk technicians perform a specialized role in InfoSec, they need specialized training. These staff members must be prepared to identify and diagnose both traditional technical problems and threats to InfoSec. Their ability to do so may cut precious hours off of an incident response.

Implementing Security Education, Training, and Awareness Programs

Once the InfoSec program's place in the organization is established, planning for **security education, training, and awareness (SETA)** programs begins. The SETA program is the responsibility of the CISO and is designed to reduce the incidence of accidental security breaches by members of the organization, including employees, contractors, consultants, vendors, and business partners who come into contact with its information assets. As mentioned in Chapter 2, acts of "human error or failure" (known generally as "errors") are among the top threats to information assets.

SETA programs offer three major benefits:

- They can improve employee behavior.
- They can inform members of the organization about where to report violations of policy.
- They enable the organization to hold employees accountable for their actions.

Employee accountability is necessary to ensure that the acts of an individual do not threaten the long-term viability of the entire organization. When employees recognize that the organization protects itself by enforcing accountability, they will be less likely to view these programs as punitive. In fact, when an organization does not enforce accountability, it increases the risk of incurring a substantial loss that might cause it to fail, costing the entire workforce their jobs.

SETA programs enhance general education and training programs by focusing on InfoSec. For example, if an organization finds that many employees are using e-mail attachments in an unsafe manner, then e-mail users must be trained or retrained. As a matter of good practice, all systems development life cycles (SDLCs) include user training during both the implementation and maintenance phases. InfoSec projects are no different; they require initial training programs as systems are deployed and occasional retraining as needs arise.

A SETA program consists of three elements: security education, security training, and security awareness. An organization may not be able or willing to undertake the development of all these components in-house and may therefore outsource them to local educational institutions. The purpose of SETA is to enhance security in three ways:

- By building in-depth knowledge, as needed, to design, implement, or operate security programs for organizations and systems

- By developing skills and knowledge so that computer users can perform their jobs while using IT systems more securely

- By improving awareness of the need to protect system resources[14]

Table 5-3 shows some of the features of SETA within the organization, how they are delivered, and how outcomes are assessed.

Security Education

Some organizations may have employees within the InfoSec department who are not prepared by their background or experience for the InfoSec roles they are supposed to perform. When tactical circumstances allow and/or strategic imperatives dictate, these employees may be encouraged to use a formal education method. Resources that describe InfoSec training programs include the NIST training and education site at *http://csrc.nist.gov/groups/SMA/ate/index.html*, the Virginia Alliance for Secure Computing and Networking (VA SCAN) at *www.vascan.org/resources/index.html*, and the National Security Agency (NSA)–identified Centers of Academic Excellence in Information Assurance Education (CAEIAE) at *www.nsa.gov/ia/academic_outreach/nat_cae/index.shtml*. Local resources might also provide information and services in educational areas. For example, Kennesaw State University's Center for Information Security Education and Awareness (*http://infosec.kennesaw.edu*) provides information on information security educational opportunities and initiatives in the KSU community. The Center also serves to increase the level of information security awareness in the KSU community. InfoSec training programs must address the following issues:

- The InfoSec educational components required of all InfoSec professionals

- The general educational requirements that all IT professionals must have

A number of colleges and universities provide formal coursework in InfoSec. Unfortunately, a recent review found that the majority of InfoSec or computer security degrees (bachelor's or master's) are, in reality, computer science or information systems degrees that include a few courses in InfoSec. While some programs do offer depth and breadth in InfoSec education,

	Awareness	Training	Education
Attribute	Seeks to teach members of the organization *what* security is and what the employee should do in some situations.	Seeks to train members of the organization *how* they should react and respond when threats are encountered in specified situations.	Seeks to educate members of the organization as to *why* the organization has prepared in the way that it has and why the organization reacts in the ways that it does.
Level	Offers basic *information* about threats and responses.	Offers more detailed *knowledge* about detecting threats and teaches skills needed for effective reaction.	Offers the background and depth of knowledge to gain *insight* into how processes are developed and enables ongoing improvement.
Objective	Members of the organization can *recognize* threats and formulate simple responses.	Members of the organization can mount effective responses using learned *skills*.	Members of the organization can engage in active defense and use *understanding* of the organizations objectives to make continuous improvement.
Teaching methods	• Media videos • Newsletters • Posters • Informal training	• Formal training • Workshops • Hands-on practice	• Theoretical instruction • Discussions/seminars • Background reading
Assessment	True/False or Multiple Choice (identify learning)	Problem solving (apply learning)	Essay (interpret learning)
Impact timeframe	Short-term	Intermediate	Long-term

Table 5-3   **Framework of security education, training, and awareness**

Source: NIST SP 800-12.

prospective students must carefully examine the curriculum before enrolling. Students planning for careers in InfoSec should review the number of courses offered as well as the content of those courses.

The general IT educational curriculum needs to prepare students to work in a setting that values a secure and ethical computing environment. As noted by Irvin, Chin, and Frincke in their article "Integrating Security into the Curriculum":

> *An educational system that cultivates an appropriate knowledge of computer security will increase the likelihood that the next generation of IT workers will have the background needed to design and develop systems that are engineered to be reliable and secure.*[15]

The need for improved InfoSec education is so great that in May 1998 President Clinton issued Presidential Decision Directive 63, Policy on Critical Infrastructure Protection. Among other requirements, the directive mandated that the NSA establish outreach programs like the CAEIAE. The CAEIAE program's stated goal is "to reduce vulnerabilities in our National Information Infrastructure by promoting higher education in information assurance, and producing a growing number of professionals with IA expertise."[16] These initiatives are intended to increase not only the number of InfoSec professionals but also the InfoSec awareness of all technologists.

Developing Information Security Curricula Hybrid IT/InfoSec programs have emerged to fill the gap created by the lack of formal guidance from established curricula bodies. Established organizations that have developed and promoted standardized curricula, such as the Association for Computing Machinery (ACM), the Institute of Electrical and Electronics Engineers (IEEE), and the Accreditation Board for Engineering and Technology (ABET), do not have formal InfoSec curricula models. For two-year institutions, however, the National Science Foundation (NSF) and the American Association of Community Colleges sponsored a workshop in 2002 that drafted recommendations for a report entitled "The Role of Community Colleges in Cybersecurity Education." This report serves as a starting point for community colleges developing curricula in the field. A similar effort is currently underway for four-year institutions.

Any institution designing a formal curriculum in InfoSec must carefully link expected learning outcomes from the planned curriculum to the courses' learning objectives, which establishes the body of knowledge to be taught. This knowledge map defined by the links between the program learning objectives and the course learning objectives helps potential students assess InfoSec programs and identifies the skills and knowledge clusters obtained by the program's graduates. Graduate-level programs are more complex and possibly more managerial in nature, depending on the program. At the undergraduate level, program planners examine the areas that graduates are expected to work in and then define the required skills and knowledge.

Creating a knowledge map can be difficult because many academics are unaware of the numerous subdisciplines within the field of InfoSec, each of which may have different knowledge requirements. For example, a student wanting a managerial focus needs to be educated in policy, planning, personnel administration, and other relevant topics, and thus would want to take courses like the ones for which this textbook is written. In contrast, a student whose interests are more technical would want courses in specific hardware areas such as Windows network security, firewalls and IDPSs, or remote access and authentication.

Because many institutions have no frame of reference for the skills and knowledge that are required for a particular job area, they frequently refer to the certifications offered in that field. Certification is discussed in Chapter 11. A managerial program would examine certifications like the Certified Information Systems Security Professional (CISSP), Certified Information Security Manager (CISM), or Global Information Assurance Certification (GIAC) or Global Information Security Officer (GISO); a technical program would examine the specific GIAC or Security+ certifications. A balanced program takes the best of both programs and maps the knowledge areas from each specialty area backward to specific courses.

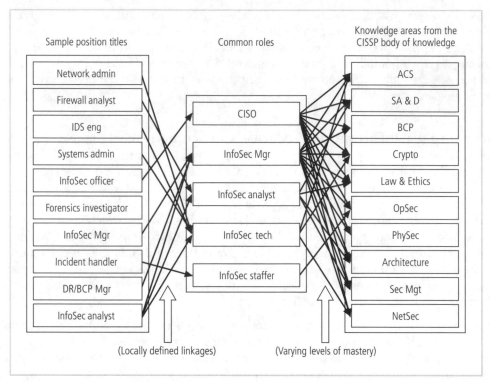

Figure 5-11 InfoSec knowledge map

Copyright © 2014 Cengage Learning®.

Figure 5-11 shows the complex process of mapping InfoSec positions to the roles they perform and the corresponding core knowledge requirements of those roles. These roles (defined earlier) must then be carefully mapped to the required knowledge domains. For example, a CISO may need to have a working understanding of all knowledge areas, while a firewall administrator may need true expertise in only one or two areas. The depth of knowledge is indicated by a level of mastery based on an established taxonomy of learning objectives or a simple scale such as "understanding < accomplishment < proficiency < mastery."

Once the knowledge areas are identified, common knowledge areas are aggregated into teaching domains, from which individual courses can be created. Courses should be designed so that the student can obtain the required knowledge and skills upon completion of the program. For example, in a program for firewall administrators, an introductory class (to supply understanding) might be followed by a technical security class (to supply accomplishment), which might be followed by a firewall administration class (to supply proficiency and mastery).

The final step is to identify the prerequisite knowledge for each class. Figure 5-12 provides examples of increasingly more technical classes, with their knowledge areas and prerequisite requirements.

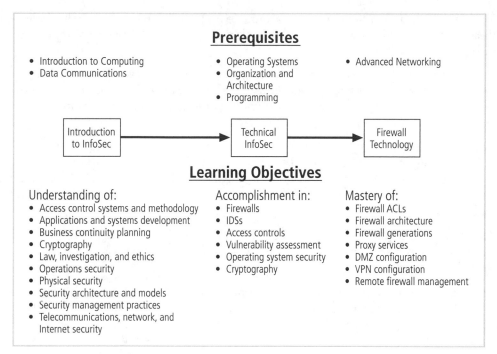

Figure 5-12 Technical course progression

Copyright © 2014 Cengage Learning®.

Security Training

Security training involves providing members of the organization with detailed information and hands-on instruction to enable them to perform their duties securely. Management of InfoSec can develop customized in-house training or outsource all or part of the training program. Alternatively, organizations can subsidize or underwrite industry training conferences and programs offered through professional agencies such as SANS (*www.sans.org*), (ISC)² (*www.isc2.org*), ISSA (*www.issa.org*), and CSI (*www.gocsi.com*). Many of these programs are too technical for the average employee, but they may be ideal for the continuing education requirements of InfoSec professionals.

A number of resources can help organizations put together SETA programs. The Computer Security Resource Center at NIST, for example, provides several very useful documents free of charge in its special publications area (*http://csrc.nist.gov*).

Among the most useful of these documents for InfoSec practitioners and those developing training programs is "NIST SP 800-16, Rev. 1: Information Technology Security Training Requirements." With extensive appendices, this document emphasizes training criteria and standards rather than specific curricula or content. The training criteria are established according to trainees' role(s) within their organizations and are measured by their on-the-job performance. This emphasis on roles and results, rather than on fixed content, gives the training requirements flexibility, adaptability, and longevity.[17]

This approach makes the document a durable and useful guide. Although it was originally directed toward federal agencies and organizations, its overall approach applies to all types of organizations:

> *Federal agencies and organizations cannot protect the integrity, confidentiality, and availability of information in today's highly networked systems environment without ensuring that each person involved understands their roles and responsibilities and is adequately trained to perform them.*[18]

The Computer Security Act of 1987 requires federal agencies to provide mandatory periodic training in computer security awareness and accepted computer practices to all employees involved with the management, use, or operation of the agencies' computer systems. Specific federal requirements for computer security training are contained in other federal documents.[19]

The more closely the training is designed to match specific needs, the more effective it is. Training includes teaching users not only what they should or should not do but also how they should do it.

There are two methods for customizing training for users. The first is by functional background: general user, managerial user, and technical user. The second is by skill level: novice, intermediate, and advanced. Because traditional training models are accustomed to using skill level as course customization criteria, the more detailed discussion that follows focuses on the development of training by functional area.

Training for General Users One method of ensuring that policies are read and understood by general users is to provide training on those policies. This strategy allows users to ask questions and receive specific guidance, and it allows the organization to collect the required letters of compliance. These general users also require training on the technical details of how to do their jobs securely, including good security practices, password management, specialized access controls, and violation reporting.

A convenient time to conduct this type of training is during employee orientation. At this critical time, employees are educated on a wide variety of organizational policies and on the expectations that the organization has for its employees. Because employees should have no preconceived notions or established methods of behavior at that point, they are more likely to be receptive to this instruction. This openness is balanced against their lack of familiarity with the systems and/or their jobs, so any particular issues that they might have questions about will not have arisen yet.

Training for Managerial Users Management may have the same training requirements as the general user, but managers typically expect a more personal form of training, characterized by smaller groups and more interaction and discussion. In fact, managers often resist organized training of any kind. This is an area in which a champion can exert influence. Support at the executive level can convince managers to attend training events, which in turn reinforces the entire training program.

Training for Technical Users Technical training for IT staff, security staff, and technically competent general users is more detailed than general user or managerial training, and it may therefore require the use of consultants or outside training organizations. There are three methods for selecting or developing advanced technical training:

- By job category—for example, technical users versus managers
- By job function—for example, accounting versus marketing versus operations
- By technology product—for example, e-mail client, database

Training Techniques

Good training techniques are as essential to successful training as thorough knowledge of the subject area. As explained by Charles Trepper in his article "Training Developers More Efficiently":

> *Using the wrong method can actually hinder the transfer of knowledge and lead to unnecessary expense and frustrated, poorly trained employees. Good training programs, regardless of delivery method, take advantage of the latest learning technologies and best practices. Recent developments include less use of centralized public courses and more on-site training. Training is often needed for one or a few individuals, not necessarily for a large group. Waiting until there is a large enough group for a class can cost companies lost productivity. Other best practices include the increased use of short, task-oriented modules and training sessions, available during the normal work week, that are immediate and consistent. Newer concepts in training also provide students with the training they need when they need it—a practice often called just-in-time training.*[20]

Delivery Methods Selection of the training delivery method is not always based on the best outcome for the trainee. Often, other factors—most usually budget, scheduling, and needs of the organization—come first. Table 5-4 lists the most common delivery methods.

Selecting the Training Staff To provide employee training, an organization can use a local training program, a continuing education department, or another external training agency. Alternatively, it can hire a professional trainer, a consultant, or someone from an accredited institution to conduct on-site training. It can also organize and conduct training in-house using its own employees. This last option should not be undertaken without careful consideration. Effective training requires a special set of skills and abilities. Teaching a class of five or more peers (or subordinates) is very different than offering friendly advice to coworkers.

Implementing Training While each organization develops its own strategy based on the techniques discussed previously, the following seven-step methodology generally applies:

Step 1: Identify program scope, goals, and objectives.
Step 2: Identify training staff.
Step 3: Identify target audiences.
Step 4: Motivate management and employees.
Step 5: Administer the program.
Step 6: Maintain the program.
Step 7: Evaluate the program.

This methodology and the material that follows are drawn from the NIST publication "SP 800-12: An Introduction to Computer Security: The NIST Handbook."[21]

Method	Advantages	Disadvantages
One-on-one: A dedicated trainer works with each trainee on the areas specified.	• Informal • Personal • Customized to the needs of the trainee • Can be scheduled to fit the needs of the trainee	• Resource intensive, to the point of being inefficient
Formal class: A single trainer works with multiple trainees in a formal setting.	• Formal training plan, efficient • Trainees able to learn from each other • Interaction possible with trainer • Usually considered cost-effective	• Relatively inflexible • May not be sufficiently responsive to the needs of all trainees • Difficult to schedule, especially if more than one session is needed
Computer-based training (CBT): Prepackaged software that provides training at the trainees workstation.	• Flexible, no special scheduling requirements • Self-paced, can go as fast or as slow as the trainee needs • Can be very cost-effective	• Software can be very expensive. • Content may not be customized to the needs of the organization
Distance learning/Web seminars: Trainees receive a seminar presentation at their computers. Some models allow teleconferencing for voice feedback; others have text questions and feedback.	• Can be live or can be archived and viewed at the trainee's convenience • Can be low- or no-cost	• If archived, can be very inflexible, with no mechanism for trainee feedback • If live, can be difficult to schedule
User support group: Support from a community of users is commonly facilitated by a particular vendor as a mechanism to augment the support for products or software.	• Allows users to learn from each other • Usually conducted in an informal social setting	• Does not use a formal training model • Centered on a specific topic or product
On-the-job training: Trainees learn the specifics of their jobs while working, using the software, hardware, and procedures they will continue to use.	• Very applied to the task at hand • Inexpensive	• A sink-or-swim approach • Can result in substandard work performance until trainee gets up to speed
Self-study (noncomputerized): Trainees study materials on their own, usually when not actively performing their jobs.	• Lowest cost to the organization • Places materials in the hands of the trainee • Trainees can select the material they need to focus on the most • Self-paced	• Shifts responsibility for training onto the trainee, with little formal support

Table 5-4   **Training delivery methods**

Copyright © 2014 Cengage Learning®.

Identify Program Scope, Goals, and Objectives

The scope of the security training program should encompass all personnel who interact with computer systems. Because users need training that relates directly to their use of particular systems, an organization-wide training program may need to be supplemented by more specific programs targeted at specific groups. Generally, the goal of a security training program is to sustain an appropriate level of protection for computer resources by increasing employee awareness of, and ability to fulfill, computer security responsibilities. More specific goals may need to be established as well. Objectives should be defined to meet the organization's specific goals.

Identify Training Staff

Whether the trainer is an in-house expert or a hired professional, the organization should carefully match the capabilities of the training to the needs of the class. It is also vital that the trainer know how to communicate information and ideas effectively.

Identify Target Audiences

A security training program that distinguishes between groups of people, presents only the information needed by the particular audience, and omits irrelevant information yields the best results. In larger organizations, some individuals will fit into more than one group. In smaller organizations, it may not be necessary to draw distinctions between groups.

For training, employees can be divided into groups in the following ways:

- By *level of awareness*—Dividing individuals into groups according to level of awareness may require research to determine how well employees follow computer security procedures or understand how computer security fits into their jobs.

- By *general job task or function*—Individuals may be grouped as data providers, data processors, or data users.

- By *specific job category*—Many organizations assign individuals to job categories. As each job category generally has different job responsibilities, training for each will necessarily be different. Examples of job categories are general management, technology management, applications development, and security.

- By *level of computer knowledge*—Computer experts may find a program containing highly technical information more valuable than one covering management issues in computer security. Conversely, a computer novice would benefit more from a training program that presents fundamentals.

- By *types of technology or systems used*—Security techniques used for each off-the-shelf product or application system usually vary. The users of major applications normally require training specific to that application.

Motivate Management and Employees

To successfully implement an awareness and training program, it is important to gain the support of both management and employees. For this reason, SETA program designers should consider incorporating motivational techniques. Motivational techniques should demonstrate to management and employees how participation in the security training program benefits the organization. To motivate managers, for example, make them aware of the potential for losses and the role of training in computer security. Employees must understand how computer security benefits them and the organization.

Administer the Program

There are several important things to consider when administering a security training program:

- *Visibility*—The visibility of a security training program plays a key role in its success. Efforts to achieve a highly prominent place in the organization should begin during the early stages of security training program development.

- *Methods*—The methods used in the security training program should be consistent with the material presented and should be tailored to the specific audience's needs. Some training and awareness methods and techniques were listed earlier in the "Training Techniques" section.

- *Topics*—Topics should be selected based on the audience's requirements.

- *Materials*—In general, higher-quality training materials are more favorably received but are more expensive. To reduce costs, you can obtain training materials from other organizations. Modifying existing materials is usually cheaper than developing them from scratch.

- *Presentation*—Presentation issues to consider include the frequency of training (e.g., annually or as needed), the length of presentations (e.g., 20 minutes for general presentations, one hour for updates, or one week for an off-site class), and the style of presentation (e.g., formal, informal, computer-based, humorous).

Maintain the Program

Efforts should be made to keep abreast of changes in computer technology and security requirements. A training program that meets an organization's needs today may become ineffective if the organization begins using a new application or changes its environment, such as by connecting to the Internet. Likewise, an awareness program can become obsolete if laws, organizational policies, or common usage practices change. For example, if an awareness program uses examples from Thunderbird (a popular e-mail client program) to train employees about a new e-mail usage policy even though the organization actually uses the e-mail client Outlook, employees may discount the security training program and, by association, the importance of computer security.

Evaluate the Program

Organizations can evaluate their training programs by ascertaining how much information is retained, to what extent computer security procedures are being followed, and the attitudes toward computer security. The results of such an evaluation should help identify and correct problems. Some popular evaluation methods (which can be used in conjunction with one another) are:

- Using trainee evaluations as feedback
- Observing how well employees follow recommended security procedures after being trained
- Testing employees on material after it has been covered in training
- Monitoring the number and kind of computer security incidents reported before and after the training program is implemented

5

Security Awareness

One of the least frequently implemented but most effective security methods is the security awareness program. As noted in NIST SP 800-12:

> *Security awareness programs: (1) set the stage for training by changing organizational attitudes to realize the importance of security and the adverse consequences of its failure; and (2) remind users of the procedures to be followed.*[22]

A security awareness program keeps InfoSec at the forefront of users' minds on a daily basis. Awareness serves to instill a sense of responsibility and purpose in employees who handle and manage information, and it leads employees to care more about their work environment. When developing an awareness program, be sure to do the following:

- Focus on people both as part of the problem and as part of the solution.
- Refrain from using technical jargon; speak the language the users understand.
- Use every available venue to access all users.
- Define at least one key learning objective, state it clearly, and provide sufficient detail and coverage to reinforce the learning of it.
- Keep things light; refrain from "preaching" to users.
- Do not overload users with too much detail or too great a volume of information.
- Help users understand their roles in InfoSec and how a breach in that security can affect their jobs.
- Take advantage of in-house communications media to deliver messages.
- Make the awareness program formal; plan and document all actions.
- Provide good information early, rather than perfect information late.

Advice for Information Security Awareness Training Programs
The following are observations about SETA training practices:

- Information security is about people and only incidentally related to technology.
- If you want others to understand, learn how to speak a language they can understand.
- If they don't understand what they are being told, they will not be able to learn it.

- Make your points so that you can identify them clearly and so can they.

- Keep a sense of humor with your students at all times.

- First tell students what you plan to tell them, then tell it to them, then remind them what you told them.

- Unambiguously tell students how the behavior you request will affect them as well as how failure to conform to that behavior will affect them.

- Ride the tame horses—that is, continue to train with information about problems and solutions for those issues that have already been resolved, to keep them fresh in peoples' minds.

- Formalize your training methodology until it is a repeatable process.

- Always be timely, even if it means slipping schedules to include urgent information.

Susan Hansche, in an article titled "Designing a Security Awareness Program," has this to say about security awareness programs:

> [They should be] supported and led by example from management, simple and straightforward, a continuous effort. They should repeat important messages to ensure they get delivered. They should be entertaining, holding the users' interest and humorous where appropriate in order to make slogans easy to remember. They should tell employees what the dangers are (threats) and how they can help protect the information vital to their jobs.[23]

Hansche continues by noting that an awareness program should focus on topics that the employees can relate to, including:

> … threats to physical assets and stored information, threats to open network environments, [and] federal and state laws [the employees'] are required to follow, including copyright violations or privacy act information. It can also include specific organization or department policies and information on how to identify and protect sensitive or classified information, as well as how to store, label, and transport information. This awareness information should also address who [the employees] should report security incidents to, whether real or suspect.[24]

Employee Behavior and Awareness Security awareness and security training are designed to modify any employee behavior that endangers the security of the organization's information. By teaching employees how to properly handle information, use applications, and operate within the organization, the risk of accidental compromise, damage, or destruction of information is minimized. Making employees aware of threats to InfoSec, the potential damage that can result from these threats, and the ways that these threats can occur increases the probability that the employees will take such threats seriously. By making employees aware of policy, the penalties for failure to comply with policy, and the mechanism by which policy violations are discovered, the probability that an employee will try to get away with intentional misuse and abuse of information is reduced. As noted in Chapter 2, penalties for policy violations are effective only when (1) employees fear the penalty, (2) employees believe they may be caught, and (3) employees believe that, if caught, they will be penalized.

Security training and awareness activities can be undermined if management does not set a good example. Failure of management—especially upper management—to follow organizational policy is quickly mirrored by the actions and activities of all employees. For example, suppose

RWW has a policy that all employees, at all times, must wear identification badges that can be easily seen. If, over time, employees observe that senior executives do not wear badges, then soon no one will wear a badge, and attempts to penalize employees for this failure will be compromised. Policy breaches by upper management are always perceived as a lack of support for the policy. For that reason, management must always lead by example.

Employee Accountability Effective training and awareness programs make employees accountable for their actions. The legal principle *ignorantia legis neminem excusat* (ignorance of the law excuses no one) applies in a criminal courtroom, but ignorance does excuse employees who are fighting policy violation penalties in labor disputes, administrative law hearings, or civil court cases. As you learned in Chapter 4, comprehensive and properly disseminated policies enable organizations to require employee compliance. Dissemination and enforcement of policy become easier when training and awareness programs are in place.

Demonstrating **due care** and due diligence—warning employees that misconduct, abuse, and misuse of information resources will not be tolerated and that the organization will not defend employees who engage in this behavior—can help indemnify the institution against lawsuits. Lawyers tend to seek compensation from employers, which have more assets than employees, and thus attempt to prove that the alleged conduct was not clearly prohibited by organizational policy, thereby making the organization liable for it.

Awareness Techniques The NIST publication "SP 800-12: An Introduction to Computer Security: The NIST Handbook" describes the essentials of developing effective awareness techniques as follows:

> Awareness can take on different forms for particular audiences. Appropriate awareness for management officials might stress management's pivotal role in establishing organizational attitudes toward security. Appropriate awareness for other groups, such as system programmers or information analysts, should address the need for security as it relates to their job. In today's systems environment, almost everyone in an organization may have access to system resources and therefore may have the potential to cause harm.
>
> A security awareness program can use many methods to deliver its message, many of them listed in the following section. Awareness is often incorporated into basic security training and can use any method that can change employees' attitudes. Effective security awareness programs need to be designed with the recognition that people tend to practice a tuning out process (also known as acclimation). For example, after a while, a security poster, no matter how well designed, will be ignored; it will, in effect, simply blend into the environment. For this reason, awareness techniques should be creative and frequently changed.[25]

Developing Security Awareness Components Many security awareness components are available at low cost, or virtually no cost, except for the time and energy of the developer. Others can be very expensive if purchased externally. Security awareness components include the following:

- Videos
- Posters and banners

- Lectures and conferences
- Computer-based training
- Newsletters
- Brochures and flyers
- Trinkets (coffee cups, pens, pencils, T-shirts)
- Bulletin boards

Several of these options are discussed in detail in the following sections.

Security Newsletter A security newsletter is the most cost-effective method of disseminating security information and news to employees. Newsletters can be disseminated via hard copy, e-mail, or intranet. Newsworthy topics can include new threats to the organization's information assets, the schedule for upcoming security classes, and the addition of new security personnel. The goal is to keep InfoSec uppermost in users' minds and to stimulate them to care about it.

Consider the newsletter example shown in Figure 5-13. Its components are the cover page, the back cover, and the interior.

The cover should include a nameplate—a banner at the top of the page highlighting the newsletter's title. The title itself should evoke an image of security, such as *The Guardian*,

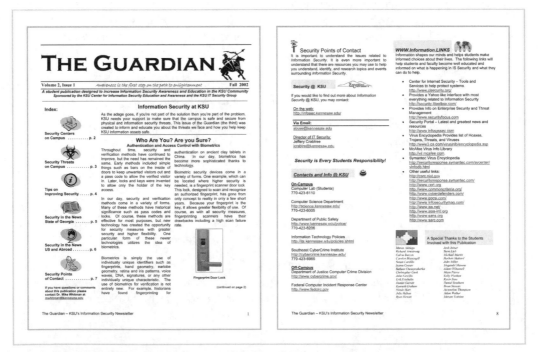

Figure 5-13 SETA awareness components: newsletters

Copyright © 2014 Cengage Learning®.

The Sentinel, The Protector, or *A Higher Plane*. Graphics should be used, but sparingly. Clipart works well, as do company logos or designs. The cover should also contain standard literary denotations such as volume, issue, date, and so on to allow for archiving, which provides proof of due care and due diligence in the event the process is audited. In addition, a simple index or table of contents should appear on the cover. While each issue's content will be distinct, in most cases the layout is standardized. Developing a template containing just the frame, page numbers, and a common back cover simplifies the creation of newsletters.

The back cover is most often used to provide contact information for InfoSec personnel, the help desk, physical security (law enforcement), and other quick reference items. It might also include editorial and author information.

The newsletter should contain articles of interest gleaned from InfoSec publications along with local publications, summaries of policies, security-related activities, and the like. It might also include these items:

- Summaries of key policies (one per issue, to avoid overloading the reader)
- Summaries of key news articles (one or two each at the national, state, and local levels)
- A calendar of security events, including training sessions, presentations, and other activities
- Announcements relevant to InfoSec, such as planned installations, upgrades, or deployment of new technologies or policies
- How-to articles, such as:
  - How to make sure virus definitions are current
  - How to report an incident
  - How to properly classify, label, and store information
  - How to determine whether e-mail is dangerous
  - How to secure the office before leaving (clean-desk policies)
  - How to avoid tailgaters, those who follow other people through controlled entry gates or doors closely to avoid presenting credentials of their own

The form in which the newsletter is published will vary according to organizational needs. Hard copies, especially in color, may be inordinately expensive, even if the institution owns its own reproduction equipment. Larger organizations may prefer to distribute color Portable Document Format (PDF) copies or even HTML documents via e-mail or intranet. Some companies may choose to create an HTML Web site and e-mail links to users rather than distribute hard copy or send attachments.

Security Poster A security poster series—which can be displayed in common areas, especially where technology is used—is a simple and inexpensive way to keep security on people's minds. The examples shown in Figure 5-14, along with eight others, were developed in one long afternoon, with the bulk of the time spent looking for the right clipart. Professionally developed graphic posters can be quite expensive, so in-house development may be the best solution (but don't simply copy someone else's work), especially if the organization has the ability to print on poster-sized paper. If not, most copy shops can enlarge letter-sized copies to poster size.

Figure 5-14 SETA awareness components: posters

Copyright © 2014 Cengage Learning®.

Several keys to a good poster series are:

- Varying the content and keeping posters updated
- Keeping them simple but visually interesting
- Making the message clear
- Providing information on reporting violations

A variation on the poster series is the screen saver slideshow. Many modern operating systems allow you to create a rotating slideshow, which you can configure as a screen saver.

Trinket Program This option is one of the most expensive security awareness programs. Trinkets may not cost much on a per-unit basis, but they can be expensive to distribute throughout an organization. Trinkets are everyday items with specialized security messages printed on them, as shown in Figure 5-15.

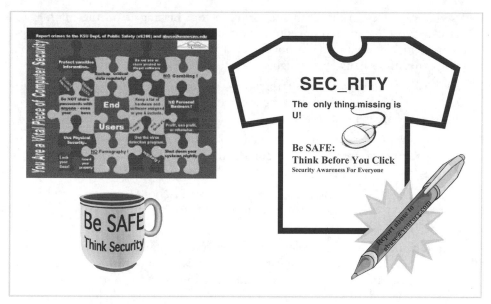

Figure 5-15 SETA awareness components: trinkets

Copyright © 2014 Cengage Learning®.

Several types of trinkets are commonly used:

- Pens and pencils
- Mouse pads
- Coffee mugs
- Plastic cups
- Hats
- T-shirts

Trinket programs can get people's attention at first, but the messages they impart will eventually be lost unless reinforced by other means.

Information Security Awareness Web Site Organizations can establish Web pages or sites dedicated to promoting InfoSec awareness, like Kennesaw State University's InfoSec Web site at *infosec.kennesaw.edu.* As with other SETA awareness methods, the challenge lies in updating the messages frequently enough to keep them fresh. When new information is posted, employees can be informed via e-mail. The latest and archived newsletters can reside on the Web site, along with press releases, awards, and recognitions.

Here are some tips from Scott Plous on creating and maintaining an educational Web site[26]:

1. *See what's already out there*—You do not have to reinvent the wheel. Look at what other organizations have done with their InfoSec awareness Web sites. Determine ownership, as you do not want to infringe on another organization's intellectual property. It is one thing to adopt a good idea; it is another thing to present it as your own. Where necessary, give credit where credit is due. A good rule of thumb is to look at a large number of sites, then design your site from memory using the best things you have seen.

2. *Plan ahead*—Design the Web site offline before placing it on the Internet or intranet. Standardize file-naming conventions, file and image locations, and other development components, so that you do not have to recode links or pages because you changed your convention halfway through.

3. *Keep page loading time to a minimum*—Avoid large images and complex/long pages. Design for the lowest common denominator. Use .jpg graphics wherever possible, as opposed to larger file formats.

4. *Appearance matters*—Create a themed look and feel for the pages, using templates and visually attractive formats. Keep quick links on the side, on the bottom, or in floating palettes.

5. *Seek feedback*—Ask others to review your work, and accept the best suggestions for improvement. Use statistical measurements to determine which parts of the Web site are used most frequently.

6. *Assume nothing and check everything*—Verify your standards by using other computers to view the documents. Try out the Web site with multiple browsers, platforms, and systems. Each may claim to use a standardized interpreter, but their idiosyncrasies may yield unexpected results.

7. *Spend time promoting your site*—Let everyone at the company know it is there. Send notifications when new content is posted. Posting information on a Web site can reduce e-mail traffic.

One final recommendation is to place your Web site on the intranet. You can then include phone numbers and information not generally released to the public, such as notices of breaches and violations, as well as company policies and procedures for handling problems.

Security Awareness Conference/Presentations Another means of renewing the InfoSec message is to have a guest speaker or even a mini-conference dedicated to the topic—perhaps in association with International Computer Security Day! Never heard of it? That's not surprising. Even though it's been around since 1988, International Computer Security Day (November 30) is an underpromoted event. (For more information, see the Association for Computer Security Day at *www.computersecurityday.org*.) If this date does not suit your organization's calendar, you can always choose the semi-annual National Cyber Security Days—October 31 and April 4. These dates are aligned with the changes to daylight savings time directives and are used to raise awareness in the United States on cybersecurity topics and practices since 2002.

Guest speakers at this event could discuss vital industry-specific InfoSec issues. The drawbacks: Speakers seldom speak for free, and few organizations are willing to suspend work for such an event, even a half-day conference.

Chapter Summary

- The term "InfoSec program" is used to describe the structure and organization of the effort that contains risks to the information assets of an organization.

- In the largest organizations, specific InfoSec functions are likely to be performed by specialized groups of staff members; in smaller organizations, these functions may be carried out by all members of the department.

- InfoSec functions should be separated into four areas:
    - Functions performed by nontechnical areas of the organization outside the IT area of management control
    - Functions performed by IT groups outside the InfoSec area of management control
    - Functions performed within the InfoSec department as a customer service to the organization and its external partners
    - Functions performed within the InfoSec department as a compliance enforcement obligation
- Implementation of full-time security personnel will vary depending on the organizational size:
    - A typical large organization will have on average one to two full-time managers, three to four full-time technicians/administrators, and as many as 16 part-time staff members.
    - A very large organization may have more than 20 full-time security personnel and 40 or more individuals with part-time responsibilities.
    - A medium-sized organization may have only one full-time security person and as many as three individuals with part-time responsibilities.
    - Smaller organizations may have either one individual with full-time duties in InfoSec or one individual who is a part-time manager.
- InfoSec positions can be classified into one of three areas: those that define, those that build, and those that administer.
- The SETA program is the responsibility of the CISO and is designed to reduce the incidence of accidental security breaches.
- SETA programs improve employee behavior and enable the organization to hold employees accountable for their actions.
- Training is most effective when it is designed for a specific category of users. Training includes teaching users not only what they should or should not do but also how they should do it.
- There are two methods for customizing training for users: by functional background and by level of skill. Training delivery methods include one-on-one, formal classes, computer-based training, distance learning/Web seminars, user support groups, on-the-job training, and self-study (noncomputerized).
- A security awareness program can deliver its message via videotapes, newsletters, posters, bulletin boards, flyers, demonstrations, briefings, short reminder notices at log-on, talks, or lectures.

Review Questions

1. What is an InfoSec program?
2. What functions constitute a complete InfoSec program?

3. What organizational variables can influence the size and composition of an InfoSec program's staff?

4. What is the typical size of the security staff in a small organization? A medium-sized organization? A large organization? A very large organization?

5. Where should an InfoSec unit be placed within an organization? Where shouldn't it be placed?

6. Into what four areas should the InfoSec functions be divided?

7. What are the roles that an InfoSec professional can assume?

8. What are the three areas of a SETA program?

9. What can influence the effectiveness of a training program?

10. What are some of the various ways to implement an awareness program?

11. Which two NIST documents largely determine the shape of an InfoSec program? Which other documents can assist in this effort?

12. What are the elements of a security program, according to NIST SP 800-14?

13. InfoSec positions can be classified into what three areas? Describe each briefly.

14. Describe the two overriding benefits of education, training, and awareness.

15. What is the purpose of a SETA program?

16. Which of the SETA program's three elements—education, training, and awareness—is the organization best prepared to provide itself? Which should it consider outsourcing?

17. How does training differ from education? Which of the two is offered to a larger audience with regard to InfoSec?

18. What are the various delivery methods for training programs?

19. List the steps in a seven-step methodology for implementing training.

20. When developing an awareness program, what priorities should you keep in mind?

Exercises

1. Search the term "security awareness" on the Internet. Choose two or three sites that offer materials and services and describe what they offer.

2. Choose one of the Web sites you found in Exercise 1 that you think might work for a security awareness program at your institution. Write a short essay about how you would go about getting that awareness material or service into place on your campus.

3. Using a Web browser or local newspaper, search for advertisements for training and education in security- and technology-related areas. What are the costs of the advertised security-specific training? Network certification? General computer training?

4. Design five security posters on various aspects of InfoSec using a graphics presentation program and clipart. Bring the posters to class and discuss the methods you used to develop your materials.

5. Examine your institution's Web site and identify full- and part-time InfoSec jobs. Create an organizational chart showing the reporting structures for these individuals.

Closing Case

"Thanks, that was very helpful," Mike Edwards said to the attorney from the corporate legal office, who'd just given a presentation on the newly enacted state computer crime and privacy law. "So, when does this law take effect, and how should we comply?"

The attorney gave a full analysis of RWW's responsibilities, laying out in concrete terms what the law required of them. Mike then turned to his staff of department managers and said, "It's important that we comply with the new law. First, however, we need to determine how much it will cost us to comply with the privacy requirement. I need from each of you a budget impact analysis that encompasses the effort needed to meet this mandate."

Discussion

1. What elements will each department manager have to consider to complete Mike's assignment?

2. How is a changing U.S. state privacy law likely to affect an organization like RWW? What other laws affect privacy in the workplace?

Ethical Decision Making

Assume the costs for compliance with the law are far higher than the budget that is available in the current year. Is Mike ethically required to comply with all aspects of the law? If Mike is not ethically bound to comply with the law, where does this ethical responsibility lie within the organization?

Endnotes

1. *www.businessdictionary.com/definition/organizational-culture.html#ixzz25fO3oqwS*

2. Briney, Andrew, and Frank Prince. "Does Size Matter?" *Information Security*, September 2002, 36–54.

3. Ibid.

4. Ibid.

5. Ibid.

6. Ibid.

7. Hayes, M. "Where the Chief Security Officer Belongs." *InformationWeek*, February 25, 2002. Accessed February 16, 2013 @ *www.informationweek.com/story/showArticle.jhtml? articleID=6500913*.

8. Wood, Charles Cresson. *Information Security Roles and Responsibilities Made Easy, Version 3*. Houston: Information Shield, Inc., 2012: 95–105.

9. Ibid., 45.

10. "Special Publication 800-14: Generally Accepted Principles and Practices for Securing Information Technology Systems." *National Institute of Standards and Technology (NIST)*. Accessed February 17, 2013 @ *csrc.nist.gov/publications/nistpubs/800-14/800-14.pdf*.

11. "Special Publication 800-12: An Introduction to Computer Security: The NIST Handbook." *National Institute of Standards and Technology (NIST)*. Accessed February 17, 2013 @ *csrc.nist.gov/publications/nistpubs/800-12/handbook.pdf*.

12. Schwartz, Eddie, Dan Erwin, Vincent Weafer, and Andy Briney. "Roundtable: InfoSec Staffing Help Wanted!" *Information Security Magazine Online*, April 2001. Accessed November 22, 2006 @ *www.infosecuritymag.com/articles/april01/features_roundtables .html*.

13. Wood, Charles Cresson. *Information Security Roles and Responsibilities Made Easy, Version 3*. Houston: Information Shield, Inc., 2012: 530.

14. "Special Publication 800-12: An Introduction to Computer Security: The NIST Handbook." *National Institute of Standards and Technology (NIST)*. Accessed February 17, 2013 @ *csrc.nist.gov/publications/nistpubs/800-12/handbook.pdf*.

15. Irvine, C, S.-K. Chin, and D. Frincke. "Integrating Security into the Curriculum." *Computer*, December 1998, 31(12), 25–30.

16. "National InfoSec Education and Training Program (NIETP)." *Centers of Academic Excellence in Information Assurance Education*. Accessed November 22, 2006 @ *www.nsa.gov/ia/academic_outreach/nat_cae/index.shtml*.

17. "Special Publication 800-16, Rev.1 (Draft): (DRAFT) Information Security Training Requirements: A Role- and Performance-Based Model." *National Institute of Standards and Technology*. Accessed February 17, 2013 @ *csrc.nist.gov/publications/drafts/800-16-rev1/Draft-SP800-16-Rev1.pdf*.

18. Ibid.

19. "CIRCULAR NO. A-130 Revised." *Office of Management and Budget*. Accessed February 17, 2013 @ *www.whitehouse.gov/omb/circulars/a130/a130trans4.html*.

20. Trepper, Charles. "Training Developers More Efficiently." *InformationWeek Online*. Accessed November 22, 2006 @ *www.informationweek.com/738/38addev.htm*.

21. "Special Publication 800-12: An Introduction to Computer Security: The NIST Handbook." *National Institute of Technology and Standards*. Accessed February 17, 2013 @ *csrc.nist.gov/publications/nistpubs/800-12*.

22. Ibid.

23. Hansche, Susan. "Designing a Security Awareness Program: Part I." *Information Systems Security*, January/February 2001, 9(6), 14–23.

24. Ibid.

25. "Special Publication 800-12: An Introduction to Computer Security: The NIST Handbook." *National Institute of Technology and Standards*. Accessed February 17, 2013 @ *csrc.nist.gov/publications/nistpubs/800-12*.

26. Plous, S. "Tips on Creating and Maintaining an Educational Web Site." *Teaching of Psychology*, 2000, 27, 63–70.

## chapter 6

Security Management Models

Security can only be achieved through constant change, through discarding old ideas that have outlived their usefulness and adapting others to current facts.

WILLIAM O. DOUGLAS, U.S. SUPREME COURT JUSTICE (1898–1980)

Iris looked at the mound of documents on her desk. Each one was neatly labeled with its own acronym and number: NIST, ISO, Special Publication, and RFC. Her head was swimming. She had not imagined that it would be quite so difficult to choose a security management model for her review of Random Widget Works, Inc.'s (RWW) ongoing security program. She wanted an independent framework that would allow her to perform a thorough analysis of RWW's program. Iris had known that networking with her colleagues was important. But this set of references was a concrete example of the benefits of staying professionally engaged.

She was almost finished skimming the stack when she found what she was looking for: a document that contained a self-assessment checklist with page after page of specific items important in the management of information security (InfoSec). In fact, there were 17 *categories* of control elements to be considered. Iris found the full document on the Web and downloaded it. After making some changes, she created copies for the managers who worked for her and then scheduled a meeting.

At the meeting, the risk assessment and policy manager seemed surprised. "Gee, Iris," he said, "when did you have time to design this checklist?"

"I didn't," Iris replied. "I was lucky enough to find one that was close enough for us. I just changed a few items to make it specific to our needs."

Iris then quickly outlined her plan. Using the checklist, each manager would indicate the progress that RWW had made in that area—specifically, whether policy had been created and, if so, whether it had been integrated into the company culture. Iris explained how to use the forms and noted when she expected the assessment to be complete.

"What happens once we're done?" one manager asked.

"That's when the real work begins," Iris said. "We'll establish priorities for improving the areas that need revision and sustaining the areas that are satisfactory. Then we'll determine whether we have the resources to accomplish that work; if not, I'll go to the CIO and request more resources."

LEARNING OBJECTIVES

Upon completion of this material, you should be able to:

- Describe the dominant InfoSec blueprints, frameworks, and InfoSec management models, including U.S. government–sanctioned models

- Explain why access control is an essential element of InfoSec management

- Recommend an InfoSec management model and explain how it can be customized to meet the needs of a particular organization

- Describe the fundamental elements of key InfoSec management practices

- Discuss emerging trends in the certification and accreditation of U.S. federal information technology (IT) systems

Introduction

InfoSec models are standards that are used for reference or comparison and often serve as the stepping-off point for emulation and adoption. One way to select a methodology is to adapt or adopt an existing security management model or set of practices. A number of published InfoSec models and frameworks exist, such as those from government organizations presented later in this chapter. Because each InfoSec environment is unique, you may need to modify or adapt portions of several frameworks; what works well for one organization may not precisely fit another.

In this chapter, you will learn about the various security management models, including access control models, security architecture models, and security management models.

Blueprints, Frameworks, and Security Models

The communities of interest accountable for the security of an organization's information assets must design a working security plan and then implement a management model to execute and maintain that plan. This effort may begin with the creation or validation of a security framework, followed by the development of an InfoSec blueprint that describes existing controls and identifies other necessary security controls. The terms "framework" and "blueprint" are closely related. A **framework** is the outline of the more thorough **blueprint**, which sets out the model to be followed in the creation of the design, selection, and initial and ongoing implementation of all subsequent security controls, including InfoSec policies, security education and training programs, and technological controls.

To generate a security blueprint, most organizations draw on established security models and practices. **A security model** is a generic blueprint offered by a service organization. Some of these models are proprietary and are only available for a significant fee; others are relatively inexpensive, such as International Organization for Standardization (ISO) standards; and some are free. Free models are available from the National Institute of Standards and Technology (NIST) and a variety of other sources. The model you choose must be flexible, scalable, robust, and sufficiently detailed.

Another way to create a blueprint is to look at the paths taken by other organizations. In this kind of benchmarking, you follow the recommended practices or industry standards. Benchmarking is the comparison of two related measurements—for example, comparing how many hours of unscheduled downtime your company had last year with the average hours of unscheduled downtime in all the companies in your industry. Is your performance better or worse than that average? Benchmarking can provide details on how controls are working or which new controls should be considered, but it does not provide implementation details that explain how controls should be put into action.

Access Control Models

Access controls regulate the admission of users into trusted areas of the organization—both logical access to information systems and physical access to the organization's facilities. Access control is maintained by means of a collection of policies, programs to carry out those policies, and technologies that enforce policies. You will learn the specifics of physical access controls and technology-based access controls later in this book. The general application of access control comprises four processes: obtaining the identity of the entity requesting access to a logical or physical area (identification); confirming the identity of the entity seeking access to a logical or physical area (authentication); determining which actions an authenticated entity can perform in that physical or logical area (authorization); and finally, documenting the activities of the authorized individual and systems (accountability).

Access control enables organizations to restrict access to information, information assets, and other tangible assets to those with a bona fide business need. Access control is built on several key principles, including the following:

- **Least privilege**—This is the principle by which members of the organization can access the minimum amount of information for the minimum amount of time necessary to perform their required duties. Least privilege presumes a need-to-know and also implies restricted access to the level required for assigned duties. For example, if a task requires only the reading of data, the user is given read-only access, which does not allow the creation, updating, or deletion of data.

- **Need-to-know**—This principle limits a user's access to the specific information required to perform the currently assigned task, and not merely to the category of data required for a general work function. For example, a manager who needs to change a specific employee's pay rate is granted access to read and update that data but is restricted from accessing pay data for other employees. This principle is most frequently associated with data classification.

- **Separation of duties**—This principle requires that significant tasks be split up in such a way that more than one individual is responsible for their completion. For example, in accounts payable situations, one person may set up a vendor, another may request payment to the vendor, and a third person may authorize the payment. Separation of duties, which you will learn more about in Chapter 11, reduces the chance of an individual violating InfoSec policy and breaching the confidentiality, integrity, and availability of the information.

Categories of Access Control

A number of approaches are used to categorize access control methodologies. One approach depicts the controls by their inherent characteristics and classifies each control as one of the following:

- *Deterrent*—Discourages or deters an incipient incident
- *Preventative*—Helps an organization avoid an incident
- *Detective*—Detects or identifies an incident or threat when it occurs
- *Corrective*—Remedies a circumstance or mitigates damage done during an incident
- *Recovery*—Restores operating conditions back to normal
- *Compensating*—Resolves shortcomings[1]

A second approach, described in the NIST Special Publication Series (*http://csrc.nist.gov/publications/PubsSPs.html*), categorizes controls based on their operational impact on the organization:

- *Management*—Controls that cover security processes that are designed by strategic planners, integrated into the organization's management practices, and routinely used by security administrators to design, implement, and monitor other control systems
- *Operational (or administrative)*—Controls that deal with the operational functions of security that have been integrated into the repeatable processes of the organization
- *Technical*—Controls that support the tactical portion of a security program and that have been implemented as reactive mechanisms to deal with the immediate needs of the organization as it responds to the realities of the technical environment

Table 6-1 shows examples of controls categorized by their characteristics as well as by the operational impact.[2]

A third approach describes the degree of authority under which the controls are applied. They can be mandatory, nondiscretionary, or discretionary. Each of these categories of controls regulates access to a particular type or collection of information, as explained in the following sections.

Mandatory Access Controls A **mandatory access control-** (**MAC-**) is, as the name indicates, required and is structured and coordinated within a data classification scheme that rates each collection of information as well as each user. These ratings are often referred to as sensitivity or classification levels. When MACs are implemented, users and data owners have limited control over access to information resources.

Data Classification Model Corporate and military organizations use a variety of classification schemes. As you might expect, the U.S. military classification scheme relies on a more complex categorization system than the schemes of most corporations. The military

	Deterrent	**Preventative**	**Detective**	**Corrective**	**Recovery**	**Compensating**
Management	Policies	Registration procedures	Periodic violation report reviews	Employee or account termination	Disaster recovery plan	Separation of duties, job rotation
Operational	Warning signs	Gates, fences, and guards	Sentries, CCTVs	Fire suppression systems	Disaster recovery procedures	Defense in depth
Technical	Warning banners	Login systems, Kerberos	Log monitors and IDPSs	Forensics procedures	Data backups	Key logging and keystroke monitoring

Table 6-1   Categories of access control

Copyright © 2014 Cengage Learning®.

is perhaps the best-known user of data classification schemes. It has invested heavily in Info-Sec, operations security (OpSec), and communications security (ComSec). In fact, many developments in data communications and InfoSec are the result of Department of Defense (DoD) and military-sponsored research and development.

For most information, the U.S. military uses a five-level classification scheme, the top levels of which are defined in Executive Order 12958. Here are the classifications along with descriptions from the document:

- *Unclassified data*—Generally free for distribution to the public; poses no threat to U.S. national interests.

- *Sensitive but unclassified (SBU) data*—"Any information of which the loss, misuse, or unauthorized access to, or modification of, might adversely affect U.S. national interests, the conduct of DoD programs, or the privacy of DoD personnel."[3] Common designations include "For Official Use Only," "Not for Public Release," and "For Internal Use Only."

- *Confidential data*—"Any information or material the unauthorized disclosure of which reasonably could be expected to cause damage to the national security. Examples of damage include the compromise of information that indicates strength of ground, air, and naval forces in the United States and overseas areas; disclosure of technical information used for training, maintenance, and inspection of classified munitions of war; and revelation of performance characteristics, test data, design, and production data on munitions of war."[4]

- *Secret data*—"Any information or material the unauthorized disclosure of which reasonably could be expected to cause serious damage to the national security. Examples of serious damage include disruption of foreign relations significantly affecting the national security; significant impairment of a program or policy directly related to the national security; revelation of significant military plans or intelligence operations; compromise of significant military plans or intelligence operations; and compromise of significant scientific or technological developments relating to national security."[5]

- *Top secret data*—"Any information or material the unauthorized disclosure of which reasonably could be expected to cause exceptionally grave damage to the national security. Examples of exceptionally grave damage include armed hostilities against the United States or its allies; disruption of foreign relations vitally affecting the national security; the compromise of vital national defense plans or complex cryptologic and communications intelligence systems; the revelation of sensitive intelligence operations; and the disclosure of scientific or technological developments vital to national security."[6] This classification comes with the general expectation of "cradle to grave" protection, meaning that individuals entrusted with top secret information are expected to honor the classification of the information for life, even after they are no longer employed in the role that originally allowed them to access the information.

In addition, federal agencies such as the FBI and CIA use specialty classification schemes, such as "Need-to-Know" and "Named Projects." Obviously, Need-to-Know authorization allows access to information by individuals who need the information to perform their work. The use of such specialty classification schemes is also commonly referred to as **compartmentalization**. Compartmentalization is the restriction of information, such as a secret military operation or corporate research project, to the very fewest people possible— those with a need to know—to prevent compromise or disclosure to unauthorized individuals. Named Projects are clearance levels based on a scheme similar to Need-to-Know. When an operation, project, or set of classified data is created, the project is assigned a code name. Next, a list of authorized individuals is created and assigned to either the Need-to-Know or the Named Projects category.

Most organizations do not need the detailed level of classification used by military or federal agencies. Nevertheless, they may find it necessary to classify data to provide protection. A general data classification scheme might have three categories: confidential, internal, and external. Data owners must classify the information assets for which they are responsible, reviewing these classifications to ensure that the data are still classified correctly and the appropriate access controls are in place. Many commercial organizations have procedures that call for this review to be done at least annually.

With a simple scheme like the following, an organization can protect its sensitive information, such as marketing or research data, personnel data, customer data, and general internal communications:

- *Public*—For general public dissemination, such as an advertisement or press release
- *For official use only*—Not for public release but not particularly sensitive, such as internal communications
- *Sensitive*—Important information that, if compromised, could embarrass the organization or cause loss of market share
- *Classified*—Essential and confidential information, disclosure of which could severely damage the well-being of the organization

Security Clearances Another data classification scheme is the personnel **security clearance** structure, in which each user of an information asset is assigned an authorization level that identifies the level of information classification he or she can access. This is usually accomplished by assigning each employee to a named role, such as data entry clerk, development programmer, InfoSec analyst, or even chief information officer (CIO). Most organizations have developed a set of roles and corresponding security clearances so that individuals are assigned authorization levels correlating with the classifications of the information assets.

Beyond a simple reliance on the security clearance is the incorporation of the need-to-know principle, based on the requirement that people are not allowed to view data simply because it falls within their level of clearance; they must also have a business-related need to know. This extra requirement ensures that the confidentiality of information is properly maintained.

Managing Classified Information Assets Managing an information asset includes all aspects of its life cycle—from specification to design, acquisition, implementation, use, storage, distribution, backup, recovery, retirement, and destruction. An information asset, such as a report, that has a classification designation other than unclassified or public must be clearly marked as such. The U.S. government, for example, uses color-coordinated cover sheets to protect classified information from the casual observer, as shown in Figure 6-1. Every classified document should also contain the appropriate security

Figure 6-1 Military data classification cover sheets

Copyright © 2014 Cengage Learning®.

designation at the top and bottom of each page. Classified documents must be accessible only to authorized individuals, which usually requires locking file cabinets, safes, or other such protective devices for hard copies and systems. When someone carries a classified report, it should be concealed, kept in a locked briefcase or portfolio, and in compliance with appropriate policies (requirements for double-sealed envelopes, tamper-proof seals, etc.). Operational controls need to take into account these classification systems and their associated control mechanisms, which, despite their simplicity, can have significant impact. In April 2009, a British military operation was compromised when a press photographer photographed a secret document that was not properly covered.[7]

Among the many controls that managers can use to maintain the confidentiality of classified documents is a risk management control known as the "clean desk policy." This policy usually meets with resistance because it requires each employee to secure all information in its appropriate storage container at the end of every business day.

When copies of classified information are no longer valuable or too many copies exist, care should be taken to destroy them properly, usually after double signature verification. Documents should be destroyed by means of shredding, burning, or transfer to a service offering authorized document destruction. Policy should ensure that no classified information is inappropriately disposed of in trash or recycling areas. Otherwise, people who engage in **dumpster diving**, the retrieval of information from refuse or recycling bins, may compromise the security of the organization's information assets. If dumpster bins are located on public property, such as a public street or alley, individuals may not be violating the law to search through these receptacles. However, if the bin is located on private property, individuals may be charged with trespassing, although prosecution is unlikely. In its 1998 decision *California v. Greenwood*, the Supreme Court ruled that there is no expectation of privacy for items thrown away in trash or refuse containers.[8]

Lattice-based access control, a variation on this form of access control, assigns users a matrix of authorizations for particular areas of access. The level of authorization may vary depending on the classification authorizations that individuals possess for each group of information assets or resources. The lattice structure contains subjects and objects, and the boundaries associated with each subject/object pair are clearly demarcated. Lattice-based access control then specifies the level of access each subject has to each object, if any. With this type of control, the column of attributes associated with a particular object (such as a printer) is referred to as an access control list (ACL). The row of attributes associated with a particular subject (such as a user) is referred to as a **capabilities table**.

Nondiscretionary Controls

Nondiscretionary controls are determined by a central authority in the organization and can be based on roles—called "role-based controls" (RBAC)—or on a specified set of tasks—called "task-based controls." Task-based controls can, in turn, be based on lists maintained on subjects or objects. **Role-based controls** are tied to the role that a particular user performs in an organization, whereas **task-based controls** are tied to a particular assignment or responsibility.

The role-based and task-based controls make it easier to maintain controls and restrictions, especially if the person performing the role or task changes often. Instead of constantly assigning and revoking the privileges of people who come and go, the administrator simply assigns the associated access rights to the role or task. The person assigned to that role or task automatically receives the corresponding access. The administrator can easily remove people's associations with roles and tasks, thereby revoking their access.

Discretionary Access Controls Discretionary access controls (DACs) are implemented at the discretion or option of the data user. The ability to share resources in a peer-to-peer configuration allows users to control and possibly provide access to information or resources at their disposal. Users can allow general, unrestricted access, or they can allow specific individuals or sets of individuals to access these resources. For example, suppose a user has a hard drive containing information to be shared with office coworkers. This user can allow specific individuals to access this drive by listing their names in the share control function. Most personal computer operating systems are designed based on the DAC model.

One discretionary model is rule-based access controls, in which access is granted based on a set of rules specified by the central authority. This is a DAC model because the individual user is the one who creates the rules. Role-based models, described in the previous section, can also be implemented under DAC if an individual system owner wants to create the rules for other users of that system or its data.

Other Forms of Access Control Access control is an area that is developing rapidly in both its principles and technologies. Other models of access control include the following:

- *Content-dependent access controls*—As the name suggests, access to a specific set of information may be dependent on its content. For example, the marketing department needs access to marketing data, the accounting department needs access to accounting data, and so forth.

- *Constrained user interfaces*—Some systems are designed specifically to restrict what information an individual user can access. The most common example is the bank automated teller machine (ATM), which restricts authorized users to simple account queries, transfers, deposits, and withdrawals.

- *Temporal (time-based) isolation*—In some cases, access to information is limited by a time-of-day constraint. A physical example is a time-release safe, found in most convenience and fast-food establishments. The safe can only be opened during a specific time frame, even by an authorized user (e.g., the store manager).

One area of discussion among practitioners is whether access controls should be centralized or decentralized. A collection of users with access to the same data typically has a centralized access control authority, even under a DAC model. The level of centralization appropriate to a given situation varies by organization and the type of information protected. The less critical the protected information, the more controls tend to be decentralized. When critical information assets are being protected, the use of a highly centralized access control toolset is indicated. These specialized tools, including RADIUS and Kerberos, are described in more detail in a later chapter.

Security Architecture Models

Security architecture models illustrate InfoSec implementations and can help organizations quickly make improvements through adaptation. Formal models do not usually find their way directly into useable implementations; instead, they form the basic approach that an implementation uses. These formal models are discussed here so that the reader can become familiar with them and see how they are used in various security architectures. When a specific implementation is put into place, noting that it is based on a formal model may lend credibility, improve its reliability, and lead to improved results. Some models are implemented into computer hardware and software, some are implemented as policies and practices, and some are implemented in both. Some models focus on the confidentiality of information, while others focus on the integrity of the information as it is being processed.

The first models discussed here—specifically, the Trusted Computing Base, the Information Technology System Evaluation Criteria, and The Common Criteria—are used as evaluation models and are also used to demonstrate the evolution of trusted system assessment. The later models—Bell-LaPadula, Biba, and so forth—are used as demonstrations of models implemented in some computer security systems to ensure that the confidentiality, integrity, and availability of information is protected.

Trusted Computing Base

The **Trusted Computer System Evaluation Criteria** (TCSEC) is an older DoD standard that defines the criteria for assessing the access controls in a computer system. This standard is part of a larger series of standards collectively referred to as the "Rainbow Series" because of the color-coding used to uniquely identify each document. TCSEC is also known as the "Orange Book" and is considered the cornerstone of the series. As described later in this chapter, this series was replaced in 2005 with a set of standards known as the "Common Criteria," but InfoSec professionals should be familiar with the terminology and concepts of this legacy approach. TCSEC defines a **trusted computing base** (TCB) as the combination of all hardware, firmware, and software responsible for enforcing the security policy. In this context, "security policy" refers to the rules of configuration for a system rather than a managerial guidance document. TCB is only as effective as its internal control mechanisms and the administration of the systems being configured. TCB is made up of the hardware and software that has been implemented to provide security for a particular information system. This usually includes the operating system kernel and a specified set of security utilities, such as the user login subsystem.

The term "trusted" can be misleading—in this context, it means that a component is part of TCB's security system, not that is necessarily trustworthy. The frequent discovery of flaws and the delivery of patches by software vendors to remedy security vulnerabilities attest to the relative level of trust you can place in current generations of software.

Within TCB is a conceptual object known as the **reference monitor**, which is the piece of the system that manages access controls—in other words, it mediates all access to objects by subjects. Systems administrators must be able to audit or periodically review the reference monitor to ensure it is functioning effectively, without unauthorized modification.

One of the biggest challenges in TCB is the existence of **covert channels**. Covert channels are unauthorized or unintended methods of communications hidden inside a computer system. For example, some researchers discovered that the indicator lights blinking on the face of some network routers were flashing in synch with the content of the data bits being transmitted, thus unintentionally displaying the contents of the data. TCSEC defines two kinds of covert channels:

- **Storage channels**, which communicate by modifying a stored object—for example, in steganography, which is described in Chapter 10.

- **Timing channels**, which transmit information by managing the relative timing of events—for example, in a system that places a long pause between packets to signify a 1 and a short pause between packets to signify a 0.

Products evaluated under TCSEC are assigned one of the following levels of protection:

- *D: Minimal protection*—A default evaluation when a product fails to meet any of the other requirements.
- *C: Discretionary protection*
  - *C1: Discretionary Security Protection*—Product includes DAC with standard identification and authentication functions, among other requirements.
  - *C2: Controlled Access Protection*—Product includes improved DAC with accountability and auditability, among other requirements.
- *B: Mandatory protection*
  - *B1: Labeled Security Protection*—Product includes MAC over some subjects and objects, among other requirements.
  - *B2: Structured Protection*—Product includes MAC and DAC over all subjects and objects, among other requirements.
  - *B3: Security Domains*—The highest mandatory protection level; meets reference monitory requirements and clear auditability of security events, with automated intrusion detection functions, among other requirements.
- *A: Verified protection*
  - *A1: Verified Design*—B3 level certification plus formalized design and verification techniques, among other requirements.
  - *Beyond A1*—Highest possible protection level; reserved only for systems that demonstrate self-protection and completeness of the reference monitor, with formal top-level specifications and a verified TCB down to the source code level, among other requirements.[9]

Information Technology System Evaluation Criteria

The **Information Technology System Evaluation Criteria (ITSEC)**, an international set of criteria for evaluating computer systems, is very similar to TCSEC. Under ITSEC, Targets of Evaluation (ToE) are compared to detailed security function specifications, resulting in an assessment of systems functionality and comprehensive penetration testing. Like TCSEC, ITSEC was, for the most part, functionally replaced by the Common Criteria (described in the following section). The ITSEC rates products on a scale of E1 (lowest level) to E6 (highest level), in much the same way that TCSEC and the Common Criteria do, with E1 roughly equivalent to EAL2 evaluation of the Common Criteria, and E6 roughly equivalent to EAL7.

The Common Criteria

The **Common Criteria for Information Technology Security Evaluation** (often called "Common Criteria" or "CC") is an international standard (ISO/IEC 15408) for computer security certification. It is widely considered the successor to both TCSEC and ITSEC in that it reconciles some of the differences between the various other standards. Most governments have discontinued their use of the other standards. CC is a combined effort of contributors from Australia,

New Zealand, Canada, France, Germany, Japan, the Netherlands, Spain, the United Kingdom, and the United States. In the United States, the National Security Agency (NSA) and the NIST were the primary contributors. CC and its companion, the Common Methodology for Information Technology Security Evaluation (CEM), are the technical basis for an international agreement, the Common Criteria Recognition Agreement (CCRA), which ensures that products can be evaluated to determine their particular security properties. CC seeks the widest possible mutual recognition of secure IT products.[10] The CC process assures that the specification, implementation, and evaluation of computer security products are performed in a rigorous and standard manner.[11]

CC terminology includes:

- *Target of Evaluation (ToE)*—The system being evaluated
- *Protection Profile (PP)*—User-generated specification for security requirements
- *Security Target (ST)*—Document describing the ToE's security properties
- *Security Functional Requirements (SFRs)*—Catalog of a product's security functions
- *Evaluation Assurance Levels (EAL)*—The rating or grading of a ToE after evaluation

EAL is typically rated on the following scale:

- *EAL1: Functionally Tested*—Confidence in operation against nonserious threats
- *EAL2: Structurally Tested*—More confidence required but comparable with good business practices
- *EAL 3: Methodically Tested and Checked*—Moderate level of security assurance
- *EAL4: Methodically Designed, Tested, and Reviewed*—Rigorous level of security assurance but still economically feasible without specialized development
- *EAL5: Semiformally Designed and Tested*—Certification requires specialized development above standard commercial products
- *EAL6: Semiformally Verified Design and Tested*—Specifically designed security ToE
- *EAL7: Formally Verified Design and Tested*—Developed for extremely high-risk situations or for high-value systems.[12]

Bell-LaPadula Confidentiality Model

The **Bell-LaPadula (BLP) confidentiality model** is a "state machine reference model"—in other words, a model of an automated system that is able to manipulate its state or status over time. BLP ensures the confidentiality of the modeled system by using MACs, data classification, and security clearances. The intent of any state machine model is to devise a conceptual approach wherein the system being modeled can always be in a known secure condition; in other words, this kind of model is provably secure. A system that serves as a reference monitor compares the level of classification of the data with the clearance of the entity requesting access; it allows access only if the clearance is equal to or higher than the classification. BLP security rules prevent information from being moved from a level of higher security to a level of lower security. Access modes can be one of two types: simple security and the * (star) property.

Simple security (also called the "read property") prohibits a subject of lower clearance from reading an object of higher clearance but allows a subject with a higher clearance level to read an object at a lower level (read down).

The * property (the "write property"), on the other hand, prohibits a high-level subject from sending messages to a lower-level object. In short, subjects can read down and objects can write or append up. BLP uses access permission matrices and a security lattice for access control.[13]

This model can be explained by imagining a fictional interaction between General Bell, whose thoughts and actions are classified at the highest possible level, and Private LaPadula, who has the lowest security clearance in the military. It is prohibited for Private LaPadula to read anything written by General Bell and for General Bell to write in any document that Private LaPadula could read. In short, the principle is "no read up, no write down."

Biba Integrity Model

The **Biba integrity model** is similar to BLP. It is based on the premise that higher levels of integrity are more worthy of trust than lower ones. The intent is to provide access controls to ensure that objects or subjects cannot have less integrity as a result of read/write operations. The Biba model assigns integrity levels to subjects and objects using two properties: the simple integrity (read) property and the integrity * property (write).

The simple integrity property permits a subject to have read access to an object only if the security level of the subject is either lower or equal to the level of the object. The integrity * property permits a subject to have write access to an object only if the security level of the subject is equal to or higher than that of the object.

The Biba model ensures that no information from a subject can be passed on to an object in a higher security level. This prevents contaminating data of higher integrity with data of lower integrity.[14]

This model can be illustrated by imagining fictional interactions among some priests, a monk named Biba, and some parishioners of the Middle Ages. Priests are considered holier (i.e., to have greater integrity) than monks, who are holier (i.e., have greater integrity) than parishioners. A priest cannot read (or offer) Masses or prayers written by Biba the Monk, who in turn cannot read items written by his parishioners. This is to prevent the lower integrity of the lower level from corrupting the holiness of the upper level. On the other hand, higher-level entities could share their writings with the lower levels without compromising the integrity of the information. This illustrates the "no write up, no read down" principle behind the Biba model.

Clark-Wilson Integrity Model

The Clark-Wilson integrity model, which is built upon principles of change control rather than integrity levels, was designed for the commercial environment. The change control principles upon which it operates are:

- No changes by unauthorized subjects
- No unauthorized changes by authorized subjects
- The maintenance of internal and external consistency

Internal consistency means that the system does what it is expected to do every time, without exception. External consistency means that the data in the system is consistent with similar data in the outside world.

This model establishes a system of subject-program-object relationships such that the subject has no direct access to the object. Instead, the subject is required to access the object using a well-formed transaction via a validated program. The intent is to provide an environment where security can be proven through the use of separated activities, each of which is provably secure. The following controls are part of the Clark-Wilson model:

- Subject authentication and identification
- Access to objects by means of well-formed transactions
- Execution by subjects on a restricted set of programs

The elements of the Clark-Wilson model are:

- *Constrained data item (CDI)*—Data item with protected integrity
- *Unconstrained data item*—Data not controlled by Clark-Wilson; nonvalidated input or any output
- *Integrity verification procedure (IVP)*—Procedure that scans data and confirms its integrity
- *Transformation procedure (TP)*—Procedure that only allows changes to a constrained data item

All subjects and objects are labeled with TPs. The TPs operate as the intermediate layer between subjects and objects. Each data item has a set of access operations that can be performed on it. Each subject is assigned a set of access operations that it can perform. The system then compares these two parameters and either permits or denies access by the subject to the object.[15]

Graham-Denning Access Control Model

The Graham-Denning access control model has three parts: a set of objects, a set of subjects, and a set of rights. The subjects are composed of two things: a process and a domain. The domain is the set of constraints controlling how subjects may access objects. The set of rights governs how subjects may manipulate the passive objects. This model describes eight primitive protection rights, called commands, that subjects can execute to have an effect on other subjects or objects. Note that these are similar to the rights a user can assign to an entity in modern operating systems.[16]

The eight primitive protection rights are:

1. Create object
2. Create subject
3. Delete object
4. Delete subject
5. Read access right
6. Grant access right
7. Delete access right
8. Transfer access right

Harrison-Ruzzo-Ullman Model

The Harrison-Ruzzo-Ullman (HRU) model defines a method to allow changes to access rights and the addition and removal of subjects and objects, a process that the BLP model does not. Since systems change over time, their protective states need to change. HRU is built on an access control matrix and includes a set of generic rights and a specific set of commands. These include:

- Create subject/create object
- Enter right X into
- Delete right X from
- Destroy subject/destroy object

By implementing this set of rights and commands and restricting the commands to a single operation each, it is possible to determine if and when a specific subject can obtain a particular right to an object.[17]

Brewer-Nash Model (Chinese Wall)

The Brewer-Nash model, commonly known as a "Chinese Wall," is designed to prevent a conflict of interest between two parties. Imagine that a law firm represents two individuals who are involved in a car accident. One sues the other, and the firm has to represent both. To prevent a conflict of interest, the individual attorneys should not be able to access the private information of these two litigants. The Brewer-Nash model requires users to select one of two conflicting sets of data, after which they cannot access the conflicting data.[18]

Security Management Models

It sometimes seems that there are as many security management models as there are consultants who offer them. Organizations may seek management models to use within their InfoSec processes, and among the most accessible places to find a quality security management model are U.S. federal agencies and international standard-setting organizations.

Some of the documents discussed in detail in the following sections are proprietary. Organizations wanting to adopt proprietary models must purchase the right to do so. Alternatively, some public domain sources for security management models offer free documentation. In the forefront of this category are those documents provided by NIST's Computer Security Resource Center (*http:// csrc.nist.gov*). This Web resource houses many publications, including some containing various security management models and practices. Earlier chapters of this book made reference to some of these publications. Other organizations provide freely accessible documentation for review to various professional groups. Other open source and proprietary sources are described in the rest of this chapter.

The ISO 27000 Series

One of the most widely referenced InfoSec management models is the Information Technology— Code of Practice for Information Security Management, which was originally published as British Standard BS7799. In 2000, the Code of Practice was adopted as an international standard framework for InfoSec by the International Organization for Standardization (ISO) and the International Electrotechnical Commission (IEC) as ISO/IEC 17799. The document was revised in 2005 (becoming ISO 17799:2005), and in 2007 it was renamed ISO 27002 to align it with the document ISO 27001 (discussed later in this chapter). While the details of

- Structure
- Risk Assessment and Treatment
- Security Policy
- Organization of Information Security
- Asset Management
- Human Resource Security
- Physical and Environmental Security
- Communications and Operations
- Access Control
- Information Systems Acquisition, Development, and Maintenance
- Information Security Incident Management
- Business Continuity Management
- Compliance

Table 6-2   Sections of the ISO/IEC 27002[19]

Source: 27000.org.

ISO/IEC 27002 are only available to those who purchase the standard, its structure and general organization are well known. For a summary description, see Table 6-2. For more details on ISO/IEC sections, see *www.praxiom.com/iso-17799-intro.htm*.

The original purpose of ISO/IEC 17799 was to offer guidance for the management of InfoSec to individuals responsible for their organization's security programs. According to 27000.org, the standard was "intended to provide a common basis for developing organizational security standards and effective security management practice and to provide confidence in inter-organizational dealings."[20] ISO 27002, the successor to 17799, continues that focus. Where ISO/IEC 27002 is focused on a broad overview of the various areas of security, providing information on 127 controls over 10 areas, ISO/IEC 27001 provides information on how to implement ISO/IEC 27002 and how to set up an information security management system (ISMS). The overall methodology for this process and its major steps are presented in Figure 6-2.

In the United Kingdom, correct implementation of these standards (both volumes), as determined by a BS7799 certified evaluator, allows organizations to obtain ISMS certification and accreditation. When the standard first came out, several countries (including the United States, Germany, and Japan) refused to adopt it, claiming that it had several fundamental problems, including:

- The global InfoSec community had not defined any justification for the code of practice as identified in the ISO/IEC 17799.
- ISO/IEC 17799 lacked (according to NIST) "the necessary measurement precision of a technical standard."[21]
- There was no reason to believe that ISO/IEC 17799 was more useful than any other approach.
- ISO/IEC 17799 was not as complete as other frameworks.
- ISO/IEC 17799 was hurriedly prepared, given the tremendous impact its adoption could have on industry InfoSec controls.[22]

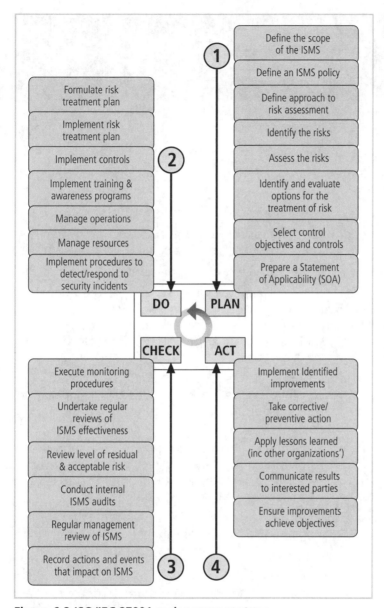

Figure 6-2 ISO/IEC 27001 major process steps

Copyright © 2014 Cengage Learning®.

The ISO/IEC 27000 series of standards forms an increasingly important framework for the management of InfoSec. It is rapidly becoming increasingly significant to U.S. organizations, especially those that are large to very large in size, are obligated to follow certain industry standards that leverage the ISO/IEC 27000 series of standards, and/or operate in the European Union (or are otherwise obliged to meet its terms).

One way to determine how closely an organization is complying with ISO 27002 is to use the SANS SCORE (Security Consensus Operational Readiness Evaluation) Audit Checklist,

Technical Details
ISO/IEC 27002 (17799:2005) Sections

The SANS Audit Checklist provides some insight into the 11 sections of 17799:

1. *Security Policy*—Focuses mainly on InfoSec policy

2. *Organization of Information Security*—For both the internal organization and external parties

3. *Asset Management*—Includes responsibility for assets and information classification

4. *Human Resources Security*—Ranges from controls prior to employment and during employment to termination or change of employment

5. *Physical and Environmental Security*—Includes secure areas and equipment security

6. *Communications and Operations Management*—Incorporates operational procedures and responsibilities, third-party service delivery management, system planning and acceptance, protection against malicious and mobile code, backup, network security management, media handling, exchange of information, electronic commerce services, and monitoring

7. *Access Control*—Focuses on business requirement for access control, user access management, user responsibilities, network access control, operating system access control, application and information access control, and mobile computing and teleworking

8. *Information Systems Acquisition, Development and Maintenance*—Includes security requirements of information systems, correct processing in applications, cryptographic controls, security of system files, security in development and support processes, and technical vulnerability management

9. *Information Security Incident Management*—Addresses reporting InfoSec events and weaknesses and management of InfoSec incidents and improvements

10. *Business Continuity Management*—InfoSec aspects of business continuity management

11. *Compliance*—Includes compliance with legal requirements, compliance with security policies and standards, and technical compliance and information systems audit considerations[23]

which is based on 17799:2005. This checklist can be downloaded for free from *www.sans .org/score/ISO_17799checklist2.php*. (See the Technical Details box for an overview of the sections of ISO/IEC 17799/ISO 27002.) Even though the standard's number changed, the content has not been substantially modified since the original 17799 was published.

While the improvements to the ISO/IEC 27000 series make it an even more relevant InfoSec management framework, it is difficult to predict how it will affect small- and medium-sized

U.S. organizations. Perhaps only organizations with European Union customer bases will be required to adopt it; however, there are some indications that this standard may have broader uses in other U.S. organizations.

"ISO/IEC 27001:2005: The InfoSec Management System" provides implementation details using a Plan-Do-Check-Act cycle, as was described in Figure 6-2.

Although ISO/IEC 27001 provides some implementation information, it simply specifies what must be done—not how to do it. As noted by Gamma Secure Systems, "The standard has an appendix that gives guidance on the use of the standard, in particular to expand on the Plan-Do-Check-Act concept. It is important to realize that there will be many Plan-Do-Check-Act cycles within a single ISMS all operating asynchronously at different speeds."[24]

As stated earlier, ISO/IEC 27001's primary purpose is to enable organizations that adopt it to obtain certification, and thus the standard makes a better assessment tool than an implementation framework.

In 2007, the ISO announced plans for the numbering of current and impending standards related to InfoSec issues and topics. It is expected that over the next few years, the standards shown in Table 6-3 will be published in the areas shown.

NIST Security Models

Other approaches to structuring InfoSec management are found in the many documents available from NIST's Computer Security Resource Center. These documents, which are among the references cited by the U.S. government as reasons not to adopt ISO/IEC 17799 standards, enjoy two notable advantages over many other sources of security information: (1) They are publicly available at no charge, and (2) they have been available for some time and thus have been broadly reviewed by government and industry professionals. You can use the NIST SP documents listed earlier, along with the discussion provided in this book, to help design a custom security framework for your organization's InfoSec program.

NIST Special Publication 800-12 "SP 800-12: Computer Security Handbook" is an excellent reference and guide for routine management of InfoSec. It provides little guidance, however, on the design and implementation of new security systems; use it as a supplement to gain a deeper understanding of the background and terminology of security. The following excerpt gives an idea of the kind of information found in SP 800-12:

> SP 800-12 draws upon the OECD's Guidelines for the Security of Information Systems, which was endorsed by the United States. It provides for:
>
> * Accountability—The responsibilities and accountability of owners, providers, and users of information systems and other parties [...] should be explicit.
>
> * Awareness—Owners, providers, users, and other parties should readily be able, consistent with maintaining security, to gain appropriate knowledge of and be informed about the existence and general extent of measures [...] for the security of information systems.
>
> * Ethics—The information systems and the security of information systems should be provided and used in such a manner that the rights and legitimate interests of others are respected.

ISO 27000 Series Standard	Year/Status	Title or Topic	Comment
27000	2009	Series Overview and Terminology	Defines terminology and vocabulary for the standard series
27001	2005	Information Security Management System Specification	Drawn from BS 7799:2
27002	2007	Code of Practice for Information Security Management	Renamed from ISO/IEC 17799, drawn from BS 7799:1
27003	2010	Information Security Management Systems Implementation Guidelines	Provides guidance in implementing an ISMS
27004	2009	Information Security Measurements and Metrics	Designed to assist in measuring, reporting, and improving ISMSs
27005	2008/2011	ISMS Risk Management	ISO 27005:2011 is the updated version
27006	2007	Requirements for Bodies Providing Audit and Certification of an ISMS	Largely intended to support the accreditation of certification bodies, providing ISMS certification
27007	Planned	Guidelines for ISMS Auditing	Focuses on management systems
27008	Planned	Guidelines for ISMS Auditing	Focuses on security controls
27010	2012	Infosec Management For Inter-Sector And Inter-Organizational Communications	Focuses on security during information exchanges between organizations and entities
27011	2008	Information Security Guidelines for the Telecommunications Industry	Focuses on InfoSec management within telecom organizations, based on ISO 27002
27014	Planned	Information Security Governance Framework	
27015	Planned	Information Security Management Guidelines for the Finance and Insurance Sectors	
27032	Planned	Guideline for Cybersecurity	
27034	Planned	Guideline for Application Security	

Table 6-3 ISO 27000 series current and planned standards[25]

Source: 27000.org.

- *Multidisciplinary—Measures, practices, and procedures for the security of information systems should address all relevant considerations and viewpoints. [...]*

- *Proportionality—Security levels, costs, measures, practices, and procedures should be appropriate and proportionate to the value and degree of reliance on the information systems, and to the severity, probability, and extent of potential harm. [...]*

- *Integration—Measures, practices, and procedures for the security of information systems should be coordinated and integrated with each other and other measures, practices, and procedures of the organization so as to create a coherent system of security.*

- *Timeliness—Public and private parties, at both national and international levels, should act in a timely, coordinated manner to prevent and to respond to breaches of security of information systems.*

- *Reassessment—The security of information systems should be reassessed periodically, as information systems and the requirements for their security vary over time.*

- *Democracy—The security of information systems should be compatible with the legitimate use and flow of data and information in a democratic society.*[26]

SP 800-12 also lays out NIST's philosophy on security management by identifying 17 controls organized into the three categories discussed earlier:

- Management controls
- Operational controls
- Technical controls

The 17 specific areas of control were adapted into control "families" by the newer NIST SP 800-53, discussed later in this chapter.

NIST Special Publication 800-14 "SP 800-14: Generally Accepted Principles and Practices for Securing Information Technology Systems" describes recommended practices and provides information on commonly accepted InfoSec principles that can direct the security team in the development of a security blueprint. It also describes the philosophical principles that the security team should integrate into the entire InfoSec process, expanding on the components of SP 800-12.

The more significant points made in NIST SP 800-14 are as follows:

- *Security supports the mission of the organization*—The implementation of InfoSec is not independent of the organization's mission. On the contrary, it is driven by it. An InfoSec system that is not grounded in the organization's mission, vision, and culture is guaranteed to fail. The InfoSec program must support and further the organization's mission, which means that it must include elements of the mission in each of its policies, procedures, and training programs.

- *Security is an integral element of sound management*—Effective management includes planning, organizing, leading, and controlling activities. Security supports the planning function when InfoSec policies provide input into the organization initiatives, and it supports the controlling function when security controls enforce both managerial and security policies.

- *Security should be cost-effective*—The costs of InfoSec should be considered part of the cost of doing business, much like the cost of the computers, networks, and voice communications systems. None of these systems generates any profit, and they may not lead to competitive advantages. As discussed in Chapter 5, however, InfoSec should justify its own costs. Security measures whose costs outweigh their benefits must be rationalized based on other business reasons (such as legal requirements).

- *Systems owners have security responsibilities outside their own organizations*—Whenever systems store and use information from customers, patients, clients, partners, or others, the security of such data becomes a serious responsibility for the owners of the systems. Also, the owners have the general duty to protect information assets on behalf of all stakeholders of the organization. These stakeholders may include shareholders in publicly held organizations, and the government and taxpayers in the case of public agencies and institutions.

- *Security responsibilities and accountability should be made explicit*—Policy documents should clearly identify the security responsibilities of users, administrators, and managers. To be legally binding, such documents must be disseminated, read, understood, and agreed to. As discussed in Chapter 4, ignorance of the law is no excuse, but ignorance of policy can be. Any relevant legislation must also become part of the security program.

- *Security requires a comprehensive and integrated approach*—As emphasized throughout this book, security is everyone's responsibility. Throughout each stage of the SecSDLC, the three communities of interest—IT management and professionals, InfoSec management and professionals, and the nontechnical general business managers and professionals of the broader organization—should participate in all aspects of the InfoSec program.

- *Security should be periodically reassessed*—InfoSec that is implemented and then ignored lacks due diligence and is considered negligent. Security is an ongoing process. To remain effective in the face of a constantly shifting set of threats and a constantly changing user base, the security process must be periodically repeated. Continuous analyses of threats, assets, and controls must be conducted and new blueprints developed.

- *Security is constrained by societal factors*—Many factors influence the implementation and maintenance of security. Legal demands, shareholder requirements, and even business practices affect the implementation of security controls and safeguards. While security professionals prefer to isolate information assets from the Internet—the major source of threats to those assets—the business requirements of the organization may preclude this control measure.

Table 6-4 presents the NIST SP 800-14 principles for securing information technology systems. This table serves as a checklist for the blueprint process, and it provides a method to ensure that all key elements are present in the design of an InfoSec program and that the planning efforts produce a blueprint for effective security architecture.

NIST Special Publication 800-18 Rev. 1 "NIST SP 800-18 Rev. 1: Guide for Developing Security Plans for Federal Information Systems" provides detailed methods for assessing, designing, and implementing controls and plans for applications of various sizes.

Principle 1	Establish a sound security policy as the "foundation" for the design
Principle 2	Treat security as an integral part of the overall system design
Principle 3	Clearly delineate the physical and logical security boundaries governed by associated security policies
Principle 4	Reduce risk to an acceptable level
Principle 5	Assume that external systems are insecure
Principle 6	Identify potential trade-offs between reducing risk and increased costs and decreases in other aspects of operational effectiveness
Principle 7	Implement layered security (ensure no single point of vulnerability)
Principle 8	Implement tailored system security measures to meet organizational security goals
Principle 9	Strive for simplicity
Principle 10	Design and operate an IT system to limit vulnerability and to be resilient in response
Principle 11	Minimize the system elements to be trusted
Principle 12	Implement security through a combination of measures distributed physically and logically
Principle 13	Provide assurance that the system is, and continues to be, resilient in the face of expected threats
Principle 14	Limit or contain vulnerabilities
Principle 15	Formulate security measures to address multiple overlapping information domains
Principle 16	Isolate public access systems from mission-critical resources (e.g., data, processes)
Principle 17	Use boundary mechanisms to separate computing systems and network infrastructures
Principle 18	Where possible, base security on open standards for portability and interoperability
Principle 19	Use a common language in developing security requirements
Principle 20	Design and implement audit mechanisms to detect unauthorized use and to support incident investigations
Principle 21	Design security to allow for regular adoption of new technologies, including a secure and logical technology upgrade process
Principle 22	Authenticate users and processes to ensure appropriate access control decisions both within and across domains
Principle 23	Use unique identities to ensure accountability
Principle 24	Implement least privilege (process of granting the lowest level of access consistent with accomplishing the assigned role)
Principle 25	Do not implement unnecessary security mechanisms

Table 6-4   **NIST SP 800-14 principles for securing information technology systems**

Principle 26	Protect information while being processed, in transit, and in storage
Principle 27	Strive for operational ease of use
Principle 28	Develop and exercise contingency or disaster recovery procedures to ensure appropriate availability
Principle 29	Consider custom products to achieve adequate security
Principle 30	Ensure proper security in the shutdown or disposal of a system
Principle 31	Protect against all likely classes of "attacks"
Principle 32	Identify and prevent common errors and vulnerabilities
Principle 33	Ensure that developers are trained in how to develop secure software

Table 6-4   NIST SP 800-14 principles for securing information technology systems (continued)

Source: NIST SP 800-14.

It serves as a guide for the security planning activities described later and for the overall InfoSec planning process. In addition, this document includes templates for major application security plans. As with any publication of this scope and magnitude, SP 800-18 must be customized to fit the particular needs of the organization.

NIST Special Publication 800-30, Rev. 1

"NIST SP 800-30, Rev. 1: Guide for Conducting Risk Assessments" provides a foundation for the development of an effective risk management program, containing both the definitions and the practical guidance necessary for assessing and mitigating risks identified within IT systems. The ultimate goal is to help organizations better manage IT-related mission risks.[27] It is organized into three chapters that explain the overall risk management process as well as preparing for, conducting, and communicating a risk assessment. The original document, SP 800-30, was functionally replaced by "SP 800-53, Rev. 3: Guide for Assessing the Security Controls in Federal Information Systems and Organizations," which was described earlier. The document was substantially revised, and SP 800-30 (Revision 1) became a process document for the subtask of conducting risk assessment. The original SP 800-30 document can still be found in the archives area of *http://csrc.nist.gov*.

NIST Special Publications 800-53 Rev. 3 and 800-53A Rev. 1

"NIST SP 800-53A, Rev. 1: Guide for Assessing the Security Controls in Federal Information Systems and Organizations: Building Effective Security Assessment Plans" is the functional successor to "SP 800-26: Security Self-Assessment Guide for Information Technology Systems." A companion guide to "SP 800-53, Revision 3: Recommended Security Controls for Federal Information Systems," it provides a systems developmental life cycle (SDLC) approach to security assessment of information systems.[28]

As shown in Figure 6-3, NIST has a comprehensive security control assessment program that guides organizations through the preparation for, assessment of, and remediation of critical security controls.

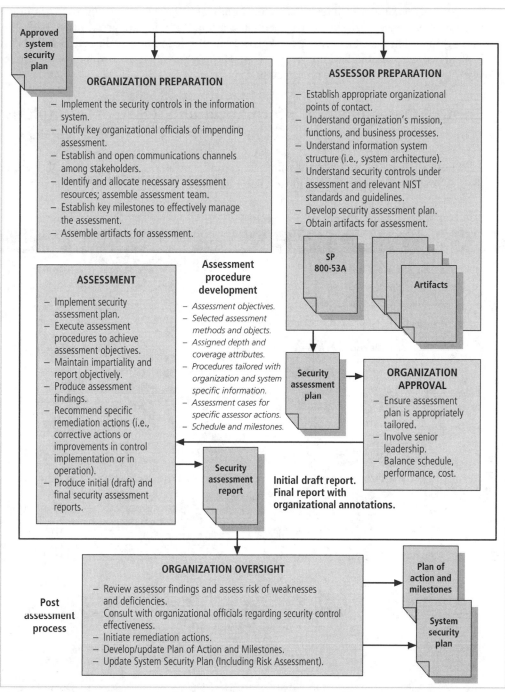

Approved system security plan

ORGANIZATION PREPARATION

- Implement the security controls in the information system.
- Notify key organizational officials of impending assessment.
- Establish and open communications channels among stakeholders.
- Identify and allocate necessary assessment resources; assemble assessment team.
- Establish key milestones to effectively manage the assessment.
- Assemble artifacts for assessment.

ASSESSOR PREPARATION

- Establish appropriate organizational points of contact.
- Understand organization's mission, functions, and business processes.
- Understand information system structure (i.e., system architecture).
- Understand security controls under assessment and relevant NIST standards and guidelines.
- Develop security assessment plan.
- Obtain artifacts for assessment.

SP 800-53A

Artifacts

ASSESSMENT

- Implement security assessment plan.
- Execute assessment procedures to achieve assessment objectives.
- Maintain impartiality and report objectively.
- Produce assessment findings.
- Recommend specific remediation actions (i.e., corrective actions or improvements in control implementation or in operation).
- Produce initial (draft) and final security assessment reports.

Assessment procedure development

- *Assessment objectives.*
- *Selected assessment methods and objects.*
- *Assigned depth and coverage attributes.*
- *Procedures tailored with organization and system specific information.*
- *Assessment cases for specific assessor actions.*
- *Schedule and milestones.*

Security assessment plan

ORGANIZATION APPROVAL

- Ensure assessment plan is appropriately tailored.
- Involve senior leadership.
- Balance schedule, performance, cost.

Security assessment report

Initial draft report. Final report with organizational annotations.

Post assessment process

ORGANIZATION OVERSIGHT

- Review assessor findings and assess risk of weaknesses and deficiencies.
  Consult with organizational officials regarding security control effectiveness.
- Initiate remediation actions.
- Develop/update Plan of Action and Milestones.
- Update System Security Plan (Including Risk Assessment).

Plan of action and milestones

System security plan

Figure 6-3 NIST security control assessment process overview[29]

Source: NIST.

6

The controls recommended by NIST in this family of SPs are organized into 17 "families" of controls, as mentioned earlier. These 17 families, along with a managerial family called "Program Management" are used to structure the protection of information and as part of the NIST security control assessment methodology. The controls are classified according to the three-category system used by NIST and are presented in Table 6-5.

Control Objectives for Information and Related Technology

"Control Objectives for Information and Related Technology" (COBIT) provides advice about the implementation of sound controls and control objectives for InfoSec. This document can be used not only as a planning tool for InfoSec but also as a control model. COBIT was created by the Information Systems Audit and Control Association (ISACA) and the IT Governance Institute

Identifier	Family	Class
AC	Access Control	Technical
AT	Awareness and Training	Operational
AU	Audit and Accountability	Technical
CA	Security Assessment and Authorization	Management
CM	Configuration Management	Operational
CP	Contingency Planning	Operational
IA	Identification and Authentication	Technical
IR	Incident Response	Operational
MA	Maintenance	Operational
MP	Media Protection	Operational
PE	Physical and Environmental Protection	Operational
PL	Planning	Management
PS	Personnel Security	Operational
RA	Risk Assessment	Management
SA	System and Services Acquisition	Management
SC	System and Communications Protection	Technical
SI	System and Information Integrity	Operational
PM	Program Management	Management

Table 6-5   NIST security control classes, families, and identifiers[30]

Source: NIST 800-53.

(ITGI) in 1992. Documentation on COBIT was first published in 1996 and was updated in 1998, 2000, 2003, and 2005, with COBIT 5 being released in 2012. According to ISACA:

COBIT 5 is the only business framework for the governance and management of enterprise IT. This evolutionary version incorporates the latest thinking in enterprise governance and management techniques, and provides globally accepted principles, practices, analytical tools and models to help increase the trust in, and value from, information systems. COBIT 5 builds and expands on COBIT 4.1 by integrating other major frameworks, standards and resources, including ISACA's Val IT and Risk IT, Information Technology Infrastructure Library (ITIL®) and related standards from the International Organization for Standardization (ISO).[31]

In the move to COBIT 5, ISACA replaces its previous 34 high-level objectives that covered 215 control objectives with an approach based on five principles and seven enablers. COBIT 5 provides five principles focused on the governance and management of IT in an organization:

- *Principle 1: Meeting Stakeholder Needs*
- *Principle 2: Covering the Enterprise End-to- End*
- *Principle 3: Applying a Single, Integrated Framework*
- *Principle 4: Enabling a Holistic Approach*
- *Principle 5: Separating Governance From Management*[32]

The COBIT 5 framework also incorporates a series of "enablers" to support the principles:

- *Principles, policies and frameworks are the vehicle to translate the desired behavior into practical guidance for day-to-day management.*
- *Processes describe an organized set of practices and activities to achieve certain objectives and produce a set of outputs in support of achieving overall IT-related goals.*
- *Organizational structures are the key decision-making entities in an enterprise.*
- *Culture, ethics and behavior of individuals and of the enterprise are very often underestimated as a success factor in governance and management activities.*
- *Information is required for keeping the organization running and well governed, but at the operational level, information is very often the key product of the enterprise itself.*
- *Services, infrastructure and applications include the infrastructure, technology and applications that provide the enterprise with information technology processing and services.*[33]

The principles and enablers are dependent on the organization's employees' skills and abilities. The primary enabler, "principles, policies, and frameworks," is depicted as guiding and affecting the others.

Although COBIT was designed to be an IT governance structure, it provides a framework to support InfoSec requirements and assessment needs. Organizations that incorporate COBIT assessments into their IT governance are better prepared for general InfoSec risk management operations.

Committee of Sponsoring Organizations

Another control-based model is that of the Committee of Sponsoring Organizations (COSO) of the Treadway Commission, a private-sector initiative formed in 1985. Its major objective is to identify the factors that cause fraudulent financial reporting and to make recommendations to reduce its incidence. COSO has established a common definition of internal controls, standards, and criteria against which companies and organizations can assess their control systems.[34] COSO helps organizations comply with critical regulations like the Sarbanes-Oxley Act of 2002.

COSO Definitions and Key Concepts According to COSO:

[I]nternal control is a process, effected by an entity's board of directors, management and other personnel, designed to provide reasonable assurance regarding the achievement of objectives in the following categories:

- *Effectiveness and efficiency of operations*
- *Reliability of financial reporting*
- *Compliance with applicable laws and regulations*[35]

COSO describes its key concepts as follows:

Internal control is a process. It is a means to an end, not an end in itself. Internal control is affected by people. It's not merely policy manuals and forms, but people at every level of an organization. Internal control can be expected to provide only reasonable assurance, not absolute assurance, to an entity's management and board. Internal control is geared to the achievement of objectives in one or more separate but overlapping categories.[36]

COSO Framework The COSO framework is built on five interrelated components. Again, while COSO is designed to serve as a framework that can describe and analyze internal control systems, some of those internal control systems are on IT systems that incorporate InfoSec controls. COSO's five components are:

- *Control environment*—This is the foundation of all internal control components. The environmental factors include integrity, ethical values, management's operating style, delegation of authority systems, and the processes for managing and developing people in the organization.

- *Risk assessment*—Risk assessment assists in the identification and examination of valid risks to the defined objectives of the organizations. It can also include assessment of risks to information assets.

- *Control activities*—This includes those policies and procedures that support management directives. These activities occur throughout the organization and include approvals, authorizations, verifications, reconciliations, reviews of operating performance, security of assets, and segregation of duties.

- *Information and communication*—This encompasses the delivery of reports—regulatory, financial, and otherwise. Effective communication should also include those made to third parties and other stakeholders.

- *Monitoring*—Continuous or discrete activities to ensure internal control systems are functioning as expected; internal control deficiencies detected during these monitoring activities should be reported upstream, and corrective actions should be taken to ensure continuous improvement of the system.[37]

Information Technology Infrastructure Library

The Information Technology Infrastructure Library (ITIL) is a collection of methods and practices for managing the development and operation of IT infrastructures. It has been produced as a series of books, each of which covers an IT management topic. The names "ITIL" and "IT Infrastructure Library" are registered trademarks of the United Kingdom's Office of Government Commerce (OGC). Since ITIL includes a detailed description of many significant IT-related practices, it can be tailored to many IT organizations.

Information Security Governance Framework

The Information Security Governance Framework is a managerial model provided by an industry working group, National Cyber Security Partnership (*www.cyberpartnership.org*), and is the result of developmental efforts by the National Cyber Security Summit Task Force.[38] The framework provides guidance in the development and implementation of an organizational InfoSec governance structure and recommends the responsibilities that various members should have toward an organization, including the following:

- *Board of directors/trustees*—Provide strategic oversight regarding InfoSec
- *Senior executives*—Provide oversight of a comprehensive InfoSec program for the entire organization
- *Executive team members who report to a senior executive*—Oversee the organization's security policies and practices
- *Senior managers*—Provide InfoSec for the information and information systems that support the operations and assets under their control
- *All employees and users*—Maintain security of information and information systems accessible to them

The framework specifies that each independent organizational unit should develop, document, and implement an InfoSec program consistent with the guidance of accepted security practices such as ISO/IEC 17799 (now 27001). This program should provide security for the information and information systems that support the operations and assets of the organizational unit, including those provided or managed by another organizational unit, contractor, or other source. The document also recommends that each organization establish clear, effective, and periodic reporting regarding its InfoSec program from each organizational unit and that each unit perform a regular evaluation to validate the effectiveness of its InfoSec program.[39]

View Point
Selecting the Appropriate Framework for an Organization
By Mark Reardon, State Chief Information Security Officer, Georgia Technology Authority

To acquire a strong commitment from an organization's leadership, InfoSec must be integrated with the organization's governance structure. In state government, the information technology (IT) governance function has the goal of assuring that IT investments generate value for the sponsoring agency while mitigating the risks associated with those IT investments. Therefore, in most state agencies, InfoSec is viewed as part of the IT organization, and the security management program must be well integrated with IT governance.

In a federated state government such as Georgia's, IT governance is a distributed set of functions that occur in over 100 agencies, departments, etc. that make up that government. Each has an IT function focused on supporting the agency's overall mission. The InfoSec functions must operate within the IT organization supporting that agency's mission, protecting its information assets while also guiding the agency's compliance with the various laws, regulations, policies, and standards that apply.

This implies that the agency must properly fund its IT program and its companion InfoSec program to carry out the agency's mission. It also requires that the InfoSec program be aligned with and support the agency's mission by becoming an enabler of the agency's overall strategy. InfoSec does not exist in a vacuum.

The state also has another level of governance represented by elected officials. These officials, who operate in the legislative branch and in the office of the governor, have a vested interest in understanding the state's InfoSec posture as it is reflected in the state agencies. They must be aware of the issues requiring remediation. For this reason, it is best to have a uniform security model for all agencies to follow, including a suite of standardized measurements and reporting. The funding decisions will be made by officials who do not necessarily fully understand the complexity of InfoSec.

A second set of considerations is created by the various organizations that provide oversight. What are the requirements from a security audit and reporting perspective? Much of the information used by any state is federally regulated. Education records, tax records, social security information, health care records, and criminal justice information all have unique, overlapping, and even conflicting requirements. There is also state-level oversight from the various State Auditor functions and, in some cases, Inspector Generals to ensure proper protection of state information assets.

The agencies of state government must create compliance reports and use the terminology of these various oversight organizations, and this in turn drives the agencies' compliance efforts. The state's InfoSec model must support these compliance requirements or the state's model will be at cross purposes with agency InfoSec

(Continued)

efforts. Forcing agencies to support multiple models will waste scarce resources and create duplication of effort. Past experience has shown that a state's selection of the wrong model has caused agencies to disengage from the state's program and attempt to function independently.

Fortunately, the federal government has been standardizing its security efforts on the (Federal Information Security Management Act) FISMA risk management framework (RMF) for all information systems that use federally regulated information. Even defense and national intelligence systems that are exempt from FISMA may optionally follow it. Many federal oversight organizations have mapped their older security requirements to the FISMA RMF. For example, most of HIPAA's security requirements are mapped to the FISMA controls for moderate impact systems, as seen in "NIST Special Publication 800-66: An Introductory Resource Guide for Implementing the Health Insurance Portability and Accountability Act (HIPAA) Security Rule." There is a similar mapping in the IRS's document "IRS 1075."

InfoSec is an ever-changing threat landscape and state-level InfoSec leaders need to adapt to the situation at hand while maintaining a vision of the future. Most of our InfoSec risk management models are based on unknown enemies with unknown goals. They are blueprints or plans for protection. In the words of Colin Powell, "No battle plan survives contact with the enemy." Therefore, the model must allow for adaptation as situations change. FISMA is such an adaptive model. It focuses on creating and understanding the risks inherent in the operation of each system, and it provides the different layers of the governance structure with information for ongoing governance decisions. FISMA itself can be adapted to work with various governance models by determining where these touch points exist and ensuring that the appropriate information is available to drive appropriate decisions.

Due to these considerations (and more), Georgia models its security program after the central security program and multiple, system-level InfoSec programs described in "NIST Special Publication 800-12: An Introduction to Computer Security: The NIST Handbook." In addition, we have adopted the FISMA RMF with some slight modifications for use by all agencies. Those deviations are mostly due to Georgia's unique governance structure. As our InfoSec efforts mature, and as our adversaries' capabilities do likewise, we reserve the right to adapt our model to the situation at hand.

Chapter Summary

- A framework is the outline of a more thorough blueprint, used in the creation of the InfoSec environment. A security model is a generic blueprint offered by a service organization.

- Access controls regulate the admission of users into trusted areas of the organization. Access control comprises four elements: identity, authentication, authorization, and accountability.

- Access control is built on the principles of least privilege, need-to-know, and separation of duties.

- Approaches to access control include preventative, deterrent, detective, corrective, recovery, and compensating. Access controls may be classified as management, operational (or administrative), or technical.

- Mandatory access controls (MACs) are those controls required by the system that operate within a data classification and personnel clearance scheme.

- Nondiscretionary controls are determined by a central authority in the organization and can be based on roles or on a specified set of tasks. Discretionary access controls (DACs) are implemented at the discretion or option of the data user.

- Security architecture models illustrate InfoSec implementations and can help organizations make quick improvements through adaptation. The most common models are the Trusted Computer System Evaluation Criteria (TCSEC) that includes the Bell-LaPadula (BLP) confidentiality model, the Biba integrity model, the Clark-Wilson integrity model, the Graham-Denning access control model, the Harrison-Ruzzo-Ullman (HRU) model for access rights, and the Brewer-Nash model.

- One of the most widely referenced security models is "ISO/IEC 27001: 2005 Information Technology—Code of Practice for InfoSec Management," which is designed to give recommendations for InfoSec management. Other approaches to structuring InfoSec management are found in the many documents available from NIST's Computer Security Resource Center.

- "Control Objectives for Information and Related Technology" (COBIT) provides advice about the implementation of sound controls and control objectives for InfoSec; the Committee of Sponsoring Organizations (COSO) of the Treadway Commission has established a common definition of internal controls, standards, and criteria against which companies and organizations can assess their control systems; and the Information Technology Infrastructure Library (ITIL) is a collection of methods and practices useful for managing the development and operation of information technology infrastructures.

- The Information Security Governance Framework is a managerial model provided by an industry working group that provides guidance in the development and implementation of an organizational InfoSec governance structure.

Review Questions

1. What is an InfoSec framework?

2. What is an InfoSec blueprint?

3. What is a security model?

4. How might an InfoSec professional use a security model?

5. What is access control?

6. What are the essential processes of access control?

7. What are the key principles on which access control is founded?

8. Identify at least two approaches used to categorize access control methodologies. List the types of controls found in each.

9. What is a mandatory access control?

10. What is a data classification model? How is data classification different from a clearance level?

11. Which international InfoSec standards have evolved from the BS 7799 model? What do they include?

12. What is an alternative model to the BS 7799 model (and its successors)? What does it include?

13. What are the documents in the ISO/IEC 27000 series?

14. What is COBIT? Who is its sponsor? What does it accomplish?

15. What are the two primary advantages of NIST security models?

16. What is the common name for NIST SP 800-12? What is the document's purpose? What resources does it provide?

17. What is the common name for NIST SP 800-14? What is the document's purpose? What resources does it provide?

18. What are the common names for NIST SP 800-53 and NIST SP 800-53A? What is the purpose of each document? What resources do they provide?

19. What is the common name for NIST SP 800-30? What is the document's purpose? What resources does it provide?

20. What is COSO, and why is it important?

Exercises

1. Visit the U.S. Postal Service Web site at *http://about.usps.com/handbooks/as805.pdf*. Review the contents page of this extensive manual. Compare this program to the NIST documents outlined in this chapter. Which areas are similar to those covered in the NIST documents? Which areas are different?

2. Compare the ISO/IEC 27001 outline with the NIST documents discussed in this chapter. Which areas, if any, are missing from the NIST documents? Identify the strengths and weaknesses of the NIST programs compared to the ISO standard.

3. Search the Internet for the term "security best practices." Compare your findings to the recommended practices outlined in the NIST documents.

4. Search the Internet for the term "data classification model." Identify two such models and then compare and contrast the categories those models use for the various levels of classification.

5. Search the Internet for the term "Treadway Commission." What was the Treadway Commission, and what is its major legacy in the field of InfoSec?

Closing Case

Iris sighed as she completed her initial review of her staff's checklist results. She pulled out a notepad and began outlining the projects she foresaw, based on the shortcomings identified via the checklist. She had decided to use the NIST approach for her security management planning and was fortunate to have found a useful model for an InfoSec review of her program.

Discussion

1. Based on your understanding of the chapter, from which NIST Special Publication did Iris draw her initial checklist?

2. Will the use of the NIST SP that Iris has identified to create a "To Do" list create a customized and repeatable InfoSec program for the company? What else is needed to make a security management model into a working security program?

Ethical Decision Making

Iris had gathered her planning team and announced the choice for the model on which they would base their approach, and now one of the more senior people was asking her why she had not chosen the ISO/IEC 27000 series as a model.

"Since the 27000 series is mostly complete these days, why wouldn't we use that?" he asked.

"Well, I looked at the details of that approach," Iris said, "and I decided that the expense of purchasing a copy of the standard for our use was not worth the few extra benefits it would provide us."

"But why do we have to pay a license fee?" the senior analyst asked. "I have a copy of the standard that I got from a friend of mine. It's a PDF file and we can use it right away."

Iris sighed, then paused.

"It's a copyright-protected document," she finally said.

Discussion

3. What did Iris mean by her final remark?

4. If the company intended to develop its own plan based on an unlicensed but copyrighted document, and if detection and prosecution for having violated the copyright was unlikely, would it still be unethical to take that approach?

Endnotes

1. Tiller, J. S. "Access Control." *Official (ISC)² Guide to the CISSP CBK*. Tipton, H. and K. Henry (eds). Boca Raton, FL: Auerbach Publishers, 2007.

2. Ibid.

3. "Controlled Unclassified Information: Appendix C to DOD 5200.1-R InfoSec Program." Accessed April 9, 2013 @ *www.fas.org/irp/doddir/dod/5200-1r/appendix_c.htm*.

4. Deputy Assistant Secretary of Defense (Administration). "InfoSec Supplement to DoD 5200.1-R." Accessed April 10, 2013 @ *www.scribd.com/doc/84154447/DoD-InfoSec -Vol-4-Controlled-Unclassified-Info*.

5. Ibid.

6. Ibid.

7. Evans, Michael, and Russell Jenkins. "Major MI5 Operation Against al-Qaeda Endangered by Security Breach." *The Times*, April 9, 2009. Accessed April 10, 2013 @ *http://www.thetimes.co.uk/tto/news/uk/crime/article1875995.ece*.

8. "California v. Greenwood, 486 U.S. 35." Supreme Court of the United States. 1988 Accessed April 10, 2013 @ *http://caselaw.lp.findlaw.com/scripts/getcase.pl?court=us&vol=486&invol=35*.

9. "Department Of Defense Trusted Computer System Evaluation Criteria." Accessed April 10, 2013 @ *http://csrc.nist.gov/publications/history/dod85.pdf*.

10. "The Common Criteria." *Common Criteria*. Accessed April 10, 2013 @ *www.commoncriteriaportal.org*.

11. Ibid.

12. Ibid.

13. Lipiczky, W. "Security Architecture and Design." *Official (ISC)^2 Guide to the CISSP CBK*. Tipton, H. and K. Henry (eds). Boca Raton, FL: Auerbach Publishers, 2007.

14. Ibid.

15. Ibid.

16. Ibid.

17. Ibid.

18. Ibid.

19. "Introduction to ISO 27002 (ISO 27002)." Accessed April 10, 2013 @ *www.27000.org/iso-27002.htm*.

20. Ibid.

21. "International Standard ISO/IEC 17799:2000 Code of Practice for Information Security Management." November 2002. *International Standards Organization*. Accessed April 10, 2013 @ *csrc.nist.gov/publications/secpubs/otherpubs/reviso-faq-110502.pdf*.

22. Ibid.

23. Thiagarajan, Val. "SANS Audit Check List—InfoSec Management—BSISO/ IEC 17799:2005." *SANS*. Accessed April 10, 2013 @ *www.sans.org/score/ISO_17799checklist2.php*.

24. "ISO/IEC 27001 and 27002." *Gamma Secure Systems Limited*. Accessed April 10, 2013 @ *www.gammassl.co.uk/27001/works.php*.

25. "ISO 27000 Standards." Accessed April 10, 2013 @ *www.27000.org*.

26. "NIST SP 800-12: An Introduction to Computer Security." October 1995. *National Institute of Standards and Technology*. Accessed April 12, 2013 @ *http://csrc.nist.gov/publications/nistpubs/800-12*.

27. "NIST SP 800-30: Risk Management Guide for Information Technology Systems." January 2002. *National Institute of Standards and Technology*. Accessed April 12, 2013 @ *http://csrc.nist.gov/publications/nistpubs/800-30/sp800-30.pdf*.

28. "NIST SP 800-53A: Guide for Assessing the Security Controls in Federal Information Systems: Building Effective Security Assessment Plans." Accessed April 10, 2013 @ *http://csrc.nist.gov/publications/nistpubs/800-53A-rev1/sp800-53A-rev1-final.pdf*.

29. Ibid.

30. "NIST SP 800-53, Rev. 3: Recommended Security Controls for Federal Information Systems and Organizations." *National Institute of Standards and Technology.* Accessed April 10, 2013 @ *http://csrc.nist.gov/publications/nistpubs/800-53-Rev3/sp800-53-rev3-final _updated-errata_05-01-2010.pdf.*

31. "COBIT 5: A Business Framework for the Governance and Management of Enterprise IT." *ISACA.* Accessed April 10, 2013 @ *www.isaca.org/COBIT/Pages/default.aspx.*

32. Ibid.

33. Ibid.

34. "Committee of Sponsoring Organizations of the Treadway Commission." Accessed April 10, 2013 @ *http://www.coso.org/guidance.htm.*

35. "Guidance on Internal Control." COSO. Accessed April 10, 2013 @ *www.coso.org/ IC.htm.*

36. Ibid.

37. "Committee of Sponsoring Organizations of the Treadway Commission." Accessed April 10, 2013 @ *http://www.coso.org/guidance.htm.*

38. "Information Security Governance: A Call to Action." April, 2004. *Corporate Governance Task Force.* Accessed April 10, 2013 @ *www.criminal-justice-careers.com/sites /default/files/resources/InfoSecGov4_04.pdf.*

39. Ibid.

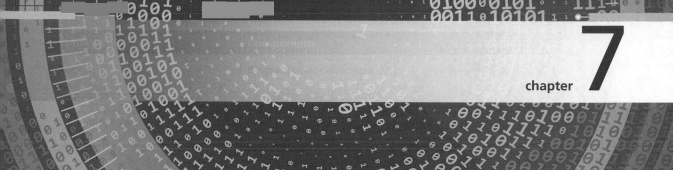

## chapter 7

Security Management Practices

In theory there is no difference between theory and practice, but in practice there is.

ATTRIBUTED TO MULTIPLE SOURCES, INCLUDING YOGI BERRA AND JAN L. A.
VAN DE SNEPSCHEUT

"Come in," Iris said to Maria Rodriguez, one of the managers in the Information Security Department. "Have a seat, please."

As Iris closed her office door, Maria sat down at a small table by the window.

"Maria," Iris said, "we've been working together since I joined RWW. I've been very happy with your work as the manager of the policy compliance team. You and your team have done a good job helping our business-unit partners fix vulnerabilities across the company. I know how much collaboration and teamwork goes into that process. Now I'm ready to offer you another opportunity in a different part of the security group. Are you ready for some new challenges?"

"Yes, I think I am," Maria said.

"Good," Iris said. "Who do you think is the best choice to groom for your replacement?"

Maria thought for a moment. "I think Linda would be the best candidate for that role," she finally said.

Iris nodded. She had come to the same conclusion after seeing the last succession planning report Linda had prepared.

"Great," Iris said. "After I check with her, you can start her transition to policy compliance team leader while we get you started as the project manager for our ISO 27000 compliance effort."

"Well, I don't have any experience with ISO 27000," Maria said, "but I'm willing to learn."

Iris smiled. "Maria, you have a great track record as a technician and as a manager here at RWW," she said. "Plus, you've got the right attitude for this new role. I'm here to help you, and we can spend some of your training budget to see that you get the right skills. I'd like you to take next week to work out the transition of your team lead role, and we'll arrange for you to spend the following week in an ISO 27000 compliance class."

Maria thought about it for a second, and then said, "I'm ready."

LEARNING OBJECTIVES

Upon completion of this material, you should be able to:

- List the elements of key information security management practices
- Describe the key components of a security metrics program
- Identify suitable strategies for the implementation of a security metrics program
- Discuss emerging trends in the certification and accreditation (C&A) of information technology (IT) systems

Introduction

Organizations strive to deliver the most value with a given level of investment—this is called the "value proposition." The development and use of sound and repeatable information security (InfoSec) management practices brings organizations closer to meeting this objective. Executives and supervisory groups want assurance that organizations are working toward the value proposition and measuring the quality of management practices, either by comparing their programs to those of other organizations or by measuring compliance according to established standards. This chapter explores various methods of program comparison, including using benchmarks, baselines, and compliance measurement as a means of verifying that processes can be certified and accredited as meeting required or recognized levels of maturity.

Benchmarking

As you learned in Chapter 6, to generate a security blueprint, organizations usually draw from established security models and practices. Another way to create such a blueprint is to look at the paths taken by organizations similar to the one whose plan you are developing. Using this method, which is called **benchmarking**, you either follow the recommended or existing practices of a similar organization or you follow industry-developed standards. Because each organization is unique, you may need to modify or adapt portions of several recognized practices, since what works well for one organization may not precisely fit another. Benchmarking can help to determine which controls should be considered, but it cannot determine how those controls should be implemented in your organization.

In InfoSec, two categories of benchmarks are used: standards of due care and due diligence as well as recommended practices. Recommended practices are also known as "best security practices," the very best of which are nominally referred to as the "gold standard."

Standards of Due Care/Due Diligence

For legal reasons, certain organizations may be compelled to adopt a stipulated minimum level of security. Organizations that do so to establish a future legal defense may need to verify that they have done what any prudent organization would do in similar circumstances. This is known as a **standard of due care** or simply **due care**. Implementing controls at this minimum standard—and maintaining them—demonstrates that an organization has performed due diligence. Although some argue that the two terms are interchangeable, the term **due diligence** (as in a **standard of due diligence**) encompasses a requirement that the implemented standards continue to provide the required level of protection. Failure to establish and maintain standards of due care and due diligence can expose an organization to legal liability if it can be shown that the organization was negligent in its application or lack of application of information protection. This is especially important in organizations that maintain customer or client information, including medical, legal, or other personal data.

The InfoSec environment that an organization must maintain is often large and complex. It may therefore be impossible to implement recommended practices in all categories at once. It may also be financially impossible for some organizations to provide security levels on a par with those maintained by organizations that can spend more money on InfoSec. InfoSec practices are often viewed relatively; as noted by F. M. Avolio, "Good security now is better than perfect security never."[1]

Some organizations might want to implement the best, most technologically advanced controls available but for financial, personnel, or other reasons cannot do so. Ultimately, it is counterproductive to establish costly, state-of-the-art security in one area, only to leave other areas exposed. Instead, organizations must make sure that they have met a reasonable level of security in all areas and that they have adequately protected all information assets before making efforts to improve individual areas to meet the highest standards.

Recommended Security Practices

Security efforts that seek to provide a superior level of performance in the protection of information are called **recommended business practices**, whereas security efforts that are considered among the best in the industry are termed **best security practices (BSPs)**, although the terms are sometimes used interchangeably. These practices balance the need for information access with the need for adequate protection while demonstrating fiscal responsibility. Of course, companies with best practices may not have practices that are the best in every area; they may establish an extremely high-quality or successful security effort in only one area. Yet, well managed security programs recognize the requirement that minimum quality standards are needed for the protection of *all* information assets.

The federal government maintains a Web site that allows government agencies to share their recommended security practices with other agencies and the general public. This site, found at *csrc.nist.gov/groups/SMA/fasp/index.html*, was begun as part of the Federal Agency Security Project (FASP), which was established by the Federal Chief Information Officer (CIO) Council. The Federal BSPs pilot effort sought to identify, evaluate, and disseminate recommended practices for computer information protection and security across the U.S. federal information systems landscape. The FASP site contains examples of many agencies' policies, procedures, and practices as well as the CIO pilot BSPs and a frequently asked questions (FAQ) section.[2]

While few commercial equivalents exist at this time, many of the BSPs found on the FASP Web site can be applied to InfoSec practices in both the public and private sectors. These BSPs are organized into the areas shown in Table 7-1, which also lists BSP examples that can be found on the Web site.

Area	Description	Examples
Audit Trail	A record of system activity by system or application processes and by user activity	• Sample Generic Policy • High-Level Procedures for Audit Trails
Authorize Processing (C&A)	A method of assurance of the security of the system	• Certification and Accreditation Documentation Performance Work Summary • Sample Generic Policy and High-Level Procedures for Certification/Accreditation • C&A of Core Financial System for USAID • How to Accredit Information Systems for Operation
Contingency Planning	Strategies for keeping an organization's critical functions operating in the event of disruptions, whether large or small	• Contingency Planning Template • Contingency Planning Template Instructions • Sample Generic Policy and High-Level Procedures for Contingency Plans • Continuity of Operations from the U.S. Treasury
Data Integrity	Controls used to protect data from accidental or malicious alteration or destruction and to provide assurance to the user that the information meets expectations about its quality and integrity	• How to Protect Against Viruses Using Attachment Blocking • Sample Generic Policy and High-Level Procedures for Data Integrity/Validation
Documentation	Descriptions of the hardware, software, policies, standards, procedures, and approvals related to the system document and formalized description of the system's security controls	• Sample Generic Policy and High-Level Procedures for System Documentation
Hardware and System Software Maintenance	Controls used to monitor the installation of, and updates to, hardware and software to ensure that the system functions as expected and that a historical record is maintained of changes	• Configuration Management Plan • Interim Policy Document on Configuration Management • Sample Generic Policy and High-Level Procedures for Hardware and Application Software Security

Table 7-1   Federal agency best security practices

Area	Description	Examples
Identification and Authentication	Technical measures that prevent unauthorized people (or unauthorized processes) from entering an IT system	• Creating Strong Passwords • Password Cracking Information • Password Management Standard • Sample Generic Policy and High-Level Procedures for Passwords and Access Forms
Incident Response Capability	The capacity to provide help to users when a security incident occurs in a system	• Computer Incident Response Team Desk Reference • Identification and Authentication on Agency Systems • Computer Virus Incident Report Form • Agency Computer Incident Response Guide • Sample Generic Policy and High-Level Procedures for Incident Response • Developing an Agency Incident Response Process
Life Cycle	IT system life cycles contain five basic phases: initiation, development and/or acquisition, implementation, operation, and disposal	• Sample Generic Policy and High-Level Procedures for Life Cycle Security • Integrating Security into Systems Development Life Cycle
Logical Access Controls	System-based mechanisms used to designate who or what is to have access to a specific system resource and the type of transactions and functions that are permitted	• Decision Paper on Use of Screen Warning Banner • Sample Warning Banner from the National Labor Relations Board
Network Security	Secure communication capability that allows one user or system to connect to another user or system	• E-Mail Spam Policy • Network Perimeter Security Policy • Securing POP Mail on Windows Clients • How to Deploy Firewalls • Configuration of Technical Safeguards • Network Security Management Policy • How to Secure a Domain Name Server (DNS)
Personnel Security	Human users, designers, implementers, and managers—how they interact with computers and the access and authorities they need to do their jobs	• Policy on Limited Personnel Use of Government Office Equipment • E-mail Policy • Internet Use Policy • Limited Personnel Use of Government Equipment • Nondisclosure Form • Guidelines for Evaluating Information on Public Web Sites • Receipt of Proprietary Information

Table 7-1   Federal agency best security practices (continued)

Area	Description	Examples
		• Sample Generic Policy and High-Level Procedures for Personnel Security • Investigative Requirements for Contractor Employees
Physical and Environment Protection	Measures taken to protect systems, buildings, and related supporting infrastructures against threats associated with their physical environment	• Securing Portable Electronic Media Agency • Sample Generic Policy and High-Level Procedures for Facility Protection
Production, Input/Output Controls	Covers topics ranging from user help desks to procedures for storing, handling, and destroying media	• Disk Sanitization Procedures • Sample Generic Policy and High-Level Procedures for Marking, Handling, Processing, Storage, and Disposal of Data
Policy and Procedures	Formally documented security policies and procedures	• Internet Security Policy • Telecommuting and Mobile Computer Security Policy • Sample of Agency Large Service Application (LSA) Information Technology (IT) Security Program Policy • Security Handbook and Standard Operating Procedures for the GSA
Program Management	Overall scope of the program (i.e., policies, security program plans, and guidance)	• IT Security Cost Estimation Guide from the Department of Education • A Summary Guide: Public Law, Executive Orders, and Policy Documents • Position Description for Computer System Security Officer

Table 7-1 Federal agency best security practices (continued)

Source: Federal Agency Security Practices, NIST.

Selecting Recommended Practices

Industries that are regulated by laws and standards and are subject to government or industry oversight are *required* to meet the regulatory or industry guidelines in their security practices. For other organizations, government and industry guidelines can serve as excellent sources of information about what is required to control InfoSec risks. These standards of performance can inform the selection of recommended practices.

When choosing from among recommended practices for your organization, consider the following questions:

- Does your organization resemble the target organization of the recommended practice? A recommended practice is only relevant if your organization is similar to the organization from which it comes.

- Are you in a similar industry as the target of the recommended practice? A strategy that works well in the manufacturing sector might have little relevance to a nonprofit organization or a retailing enterprise.

- Do you face similar challenges as the target of the recommended practice? If your organization lacks a functioning InfoSec program, a recommended practice that assumes such a program is in place is not likely to be applicable.

- Is your organizational structure similar to the target of the recommended practice? A recommended practice proposed for an organization with a highly converged risk management infrastructure is not appropriate for an organization that performs its risk management practice using loosely federated units.

- Can your organization expend resources at the level required by the recommended practice? A recommended practice that demands funding beyond what your organization can afford is of limited value.

- Is your threat environment similar to the one assumed by the recommended practice? Recommended practices that are years or even months old may not answer the current threat environment. Consider how many of the recommended practices for Internet connectivity over the past five years have become obsolete.

There are many resources available from public and private organizations that promote sound recommended security practices. The use of National Institute of Standards and Technology (NIST) practices has been referenced multiple times in this textbook. Another excellent source of information on recommended practices is the Web site operated by Carnegie Mellon University's Computer Emergency Response Team Coordination Center (CERT/CC). For example, the publication titled "Which Best Practices Are Best for Me?" can be found at *www.cert.org/archive/pdf/secureit_bestpractices.pdf*. This report presents various security improvement practices that could be useful. Similarly, most vendors, such as Microsoft, Oracle, and Cisco, publish recommended practices in security on their Web sites.

Investing a few hours in Web research will reveal dozens of other sources that may align with your specific circumstances. However, finding information on security design is the easy part; sorting through all the information can require a substantial investment in time and human resources. The goal is to obtain a methodology for creating a framework that meets your situation, which in turn leads to a blueprint that sets out the specifics on a security system that contains all the necessary components—policy, education and training programs, and technical control.

Limitations to Benchmarking and Recommended Practices

The biggest barrier to benchmarking in InfoSec is the fact that many organizations do not share results with other organizations. A successful attack is often perceived as an organizational failure and is kept secret, if possible. Sometimes, these events (especially the details) may have negative consequences for the organization in the marketplace or among various stakeholders. As a result, the entire industry suffers because valuable lessons are not recorded, disseminated, and evaluated. Today, however, an increasing number of security administrators are joining professional associations and societies, such as the Information Systems Security Association (ISSA) or ISACA (previously known as the Information Systems Audit and Control Association, but known by its acronym only), and they are sharing their stories and the lessons they've learned. Some industry groups sponsor information-sharing opportunities where peers can share experiences without some of the negative consequences that come from public dissemination. Other groups publish, in security journals, versions of the attacks on their organizations and information while leaving out the identifying details.

Another barrier to benchmarking is that no two organizations are identical. Organizations that offer products or services in the same market may differ dramatically in size, composition, management philosophy, organizational culture, technological infrastructure, and planned expenditures for security. What organizations seek most are lessons that can help them strategically, rather than information about specific technologies they should adopt. If security were a technical problem, then implementing the technology that has succeeded elsewhere would solve the problem regardless of industry or organizational composition. Because it is a managerial and personnel problem, however, the number and types of variables that affect the security of the organization are likely to differ radically between any two organizations.

A third problem with benchmarking is that recommended practices are a moving target. Knowing what happened a few years ago, which is typical in benchmarking, does not necessarily tell you what to do next. While it is true that, in security, those who do not prepare for the attacks of the past will see them again, it is also true that preparing for past threats does not protect you from what lies ahead. Security programs must keep abreast of new threats as well as the methods, techniques, policies, guidelines, educational and training approaches, and, yes, technologies to combat them.

Baselining

A practice related to benchmarking is baselining measured against a prior assessment or an internal goal. A **baseline** is an assessment of the performance of some action or process. That performance measurement (sometimes called a performance measure) can then be used to compare the current performance against a prior observed value or an intended value for that action or process. An example of a performance measurement incorporating a baseline might be the number of external attacks per week that an organization experiences. It may be that an organization establishes an *initial baseline* by counting the instances of that activity over time to derive an average observed weekly value. This value serves as a reference for future measurements. Later, the organization could compare the observed number of attacks per week against the initial baseline to see if the number is increasing or decreasing and what effect (if any) their security efforts are having on that measure.

Thus, **baselining** is the process of measuring against an established *internal* value or standard. In InfoSec, baseline measurements of security activities and events are used to provide a comparison of the organization's current security performance against prior performance and/or the level of performance that has been set as a goal. The information gathered for an organization's initial risk assessment often can become a baseline for future comparisons to track improvements in performance. The value of baselines is realized in organizations that implement thoughtful process measurement practices. The next major section of this chapter discusses in more detail the measurement of ongoing practices in InfoSec management.

Support for Benchmarks and Baselines

Baselining and researching benchmarks found in recommended practices provide less design and implementation detail for a security program than does the use of a complete methodology. Nevertheless, by baselining and seeking to use benchmarks from recommended practices, you can piece together the desired outcome of the security process, then work backward to achieve an effective design of a methodology. NIST offers a number of publications specifically written to support baselining activities:

- "SP 800-27, Rev. A: Engineering Principles for Information Technology Security (A Baseline for Achieving Security)," June 2004.
- "SP 800-53, Rev. 4: Security and Privacy Controls for Federal Information Systems and Organizations (Draft)," February 2012. (Revision 3 is still available via the Computer Security Resource Center [CSRC] Web site.)
- "SP 800-53A, Rev 1: Guide for Assessing the Security Controls in Federal Information Systems and Organizations: Building Effective Security Assessment Plans," June 2010.

These documents are available at *csrc.nist.gov* under the Special Publications link.

Another widely referenced source for recommended practices is CERT (*www.cert.org*), which promotes a series of security modules. CERT's Web site provides links to security practices and implementations that organizations can use to develop a security methodology. Another source of recommended practices is professional societies. The Technology Managers Forum (*www.techforum.com*) bestows annual recommended practice awards in a number of areas, including InfoSec. The Information Security Forum's (*www.securityforum.org*) annual publication, "Standard of Good Practice for Information Security," outlines InfoSec recommended practices and is exclusively available to its members.

Many organizations sponsor seminars and classes on recommended practices for implementing security. For example, the Information Systems Audit and Control Association (*www.isaca.org*) hosts such seminars on a regular basis. Similarly, the International Association of Professional Security Consultants (*www.iapsc.org*) has a listing of recommended practices. You can also review Web portals for posted security recommended practices. Several free portals dedicated to security maintain collections of practices, such as SearchSecurity.com and NIST's Computer Security Resources Center.

The Gartner Group has published 12 questions that can be used as a self-assessment for recommended security practices. The questions are organized into three categories—people, processes, and technology—that loosely map to the managerial, operational, and technical areas of the NIST methodology:

People

1. Do you perform background checks on all employees with access to sensitive data, areas, or access points?
2. Would the typical employee recognize a security issue?
3. Would the typical employee choose to report it?
4. Would the typical employee know how to report it to the right people?

Processes

5. Are enterprise security policies updated on at least an annual basis, employees educated on changes, and policies consistently enforced?
6. Does your enterprise follow a patch/update management and evaluation process to prioritize and mediate new security vulnerabilities?

7. Are the user accounts of former employees immediately removed on termination?

8. Are security group representatives involved in all stages of the project life cycle for new projects?

Technology

9. Is every possible network route to the Internet protected by a properly configured firewall?

10. Is sensitive data on laptops and remote systems secured with functional encryption practices?

11. Are your information assets and the systems they use regularly assessed for security exposures using a vulnerability analysis methodology?

12. Are systems and networks regularly reviewed for malicious software and telltales from prior attacks?[3]

The Payment Card Industry Security Standards Council has published Data Security Standards (PCI DSS) that are considered recommended or best practices for organizations using payment cards (MasterCard, Visa, American Express, Discover, etc.). While adhered to by organizations that require the certification to process those cards, the list also serves as a generic set of recommended practices for any organization.

Build and Maintain a Secure Network:

- *Requirement 1: Install and maintain a firewall configuration to protect cardholder data.*
- *Requirement 2: Do not use vendor-supplied defaults for system passwords and other security parameters.*

Protect Cardholder Data:

- *Requirement 3: Protect stored cardholder data.*
- *Requirement 4: Encrypt transmission of cardholder data across open, public networks.*

Maintain a Vulnerability Management Program:

- *Requirement 5: Use and regularly update antivirus software.*
- *Requirement 6: Develop and maintain secure systems and applications.*

Implement Strong Access Control Measures:

- *Requirement 7: Restrict access to cardholder data to business need-to-know.*
- *Requirement 8: Assign a unique ID to each person with computer access.*
- *Requirement 9: Restrict physical access to cardholder data.*

Regularly Monitor and Test Networks:

- *Requirement 10: Track and monitor all access to network resources and cardholder data.*
- *Requirement 11: Regularly test security systems and processes.*

Maintain an InfoSec Policy:

- *Requirement 12: Maintain a policy that addresses InfoSec.*[4]

While the standards are published through the PCI Security Standards Council, they are enforced through the individual card vendors. In order to be qualified to collect payment for a particular card, the organization should coordinate closely with a particular merchant bank or card processing center to determine what specific requirements are mandated for that particular card. In most cases, if the organization is simply using a card-swipe device at a point-of-sale terminal, the requirements are minimal, as these devices typically are provided by a credit-card processing service and only communicate with that center for approval and with the point-of-sale terminal to provide an approval code.

Performance Measurement in InfoSec Management

Executives often ask the chief information security officer (CISO) questions like "What will this security control cost?" or "Is it working?" or the even more ominous "Why is this control system not working?" As noted by CISO and author Gerald Kovacich, "This last question often comes right after a successful … attack."[5] While CISOs sometimes claim that the costs and benefits and performance of InfoSec are almost impossible to measure, in fact they are measurable; doing so requires the design and ongoing use of an InfoSec performance management program based on effective performance metrics.

InfoSec Performance Management

InfoSec performance management is the process of designing, implementing, and managing the use of the collected data elements (called measurements or metrics) to determine the effectiveness of the overall security program. **Performance measurements** are the data points or the trends computed from such measurements that may indicate the effectiveness of security countermeasures or controls—technical and managerial—as implemented in the organization. Some countermeasures, as you've learned, are technical, while others are managerial. Both types require some method of assessing the results of their use. Those control approaches that are not effective should be modified or replaced, while those that are effective should be supported and continued. Measurement supports managerial decision making, increasing accountability, and improving the effectiveness of the InfoSec function. Also, by enabling the collection, analysis, and reporting of critical performance data, they help organizations align InfoSec performance and objectives with the organization's overall mission.[6]

Organizations use three types of measurements:

- Those that determine the effectiveness of the execution of InfoSec policy, most commonly issue-specific security policies
- Those that determine the effectiveness and/or efficiency of the delivery of InfoSec services, whether they be managerial services, such as security training, or technical services, such as the installation of antivirus software
- Those that assess the impact of an incident or other security event on the organization or its mission[7]

Performance measurements are increasingly required in today's regulated InfoSec environment. It is no longer sufficient to simply assert effective InfoSec; an organization must document that it is taking effective steps to control risk in order to document due diligence. According to NIST's "SP 800-55 Rev. 1: Performance Measurement Guide for Information

Security," the following factors must be considered during development and implementation of an InfoSec performance management program:

- Measurements must yield quantifiable information (percentages, averages, and numbers).
- Data that supports the measurements needs to be readily obtainable.
- Only repeatable InfoSec processes should be considered for measurement.
- Measurements must be useful for tracking performance and directing resources.[8]

Also according to "SP 800-55, Rev. 1," four factors are critical to the success of an InfoSec performance program:

- *Strong upper-level management support*—This is critical not only for the success of the program but for the program's implementation.
- *Practical InfoSec policies and procedures*—These should specify the InfoSec management structure, identify key responsibilities, and lay the foundation to reliably measure progress and compliance.
- *Quantifiable performance measurements*—These should be designed to capture and provide meaningful performance data. Based on InfoSec performance goals and objectives, the performance measurements should be easily obtainable and feasible to implement.
- *Results-oriented measurement analysis*—These should be used to apply lessons learned, improve effectiveness of existing security controls, and plan for the implementation of future security controls to meet new InfoSec requirements as they occur.[9]

Information Security Metrics

When an organization applies statistical and quantitative forms of mathematical analysis to the data points collected in order to measure the activities and outcomes of the InfoSec program, it is using InfoSec metrics. InfoSec metrics enable organizations to measure the level of effort required to meet the stated objectives of the InfoSec program. In some organizations, the terms "metrics" and "measurements" are used interchangeably. In others, the term **metrics** is used for more granular, detailed measurements, whereas the term "performance measurement" is used for aggregate, higher-level results. Metrics traditionally described any statistical analysis technique on performance; the term "measurement" is growing more popular because it is a more generalized concept. This text treats the two terms as interchangeable.

Managing the use of InfoSec performance measurements or metrics requires commitment from the InfoSec management team. This effort will consume resources, including people's time, hardware cycles, and perhaps an investment in specialty software. The results of the effort must be periodically and consistently reviewed to make sure they remain relevant and useful. Before beginning the process of designing, collecting, and using measurements, the CISO should be prepared to answer the following questions posed by Gerald Kovacich in *The Information Systems Security Officer's Guide*[10]:

- Why should these measurements be collected?
- What specific measurements will be collected?
- How will these measurements be collected?

- When will these measurements be collected?
- Who will collect these measurements?
- Where (at what point in the function's process) will these measurements be collected?

Building the Performance Measurement Program

Even with strong management support, an InfoSec performance measurement program, as part of a security performance management program, must be able to demonstrate value to the organization. The CISO, who is a key participant in the InfoSec measurement program development, must assist in building the case for the program.

The benefits of using InfoSec performance measurements, according to "SP 800-55, Rev. 1," include "increasing accountability for InfoSec performance; improving effectiveness of Info-Sec activities; demonstrating compliance with laws, rules, and regulations; and providing quantifiable inputs for resource allocation decisions."[11]

One of the most popular of the many references that support the development of process improvement and performance measurement is from the publication *CMMI Distilled*, which is available from the CMMI Institute at Carnegie Mellon (*http://cmmiinstitute.com*).

> *The Capability Maturity Model Integrated (CMMI) is [...] designed specifically to integrate an organization's process improvement activities across disciplines. [CMMI Distilled: A Practical Introduction to Integrated Process Improvement] provides a concise introduction to the CMMI product suite, highlighting the benefits of integrated process improvement, explaining key features of the new, integrated approach to process improvement, and suggesting how to choose appropriate CMMI models and model representations for your organization.*[12]

Another popular approach, the one upon which this chapter is based, is that of NIST's "SP 800-55, Rev. 1: Performance Measurement Guide for InfoSec." The InfoSec measurement development process recommended by NIST is shown in Figure 7-1. It is divided into two major activities:

1. Identification and definition of the current InfoSec program
2. Development and selection of specific measurements to gauge the implementation, effectiveness, efficiency, and impact of the security controls

Phase 1 of the performance measurement development process identifies relevant stakeholders and their interests in InfoSec measurement. The primary stakeholders are those with key InfoSec responsibilities or data ownership. Secondary stakeholders, such as training and human resources personnel, may not be primarily responsible for InfoSec but have relevant tasks in some aspect of their jobs.

Phase 2 of the performance measurement development process is to identify and document the InfoSec performance goals and objectives that would guide security control implementation for the InfoSec program of a specific information system.

Phase 3 focuses on organization-specific InfoSec practices. Details of how security controls should be implemented are usually specified in organization-specific policies and procedures that define a baseline of InfoSec practices for the information system.

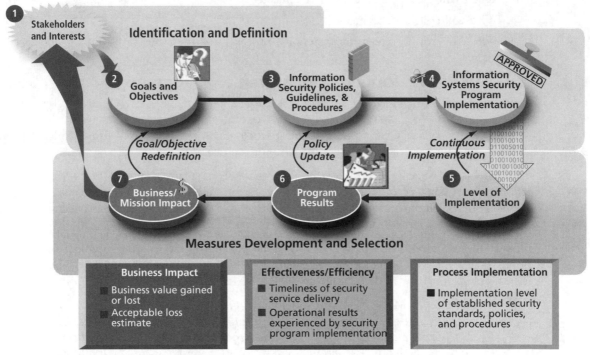

Figure 7-1 Information security performance measurement development process

Source: © Cengage Learning 2014. (Based on "NIST SP 800-55, Rev. 1: Performance Management for Information Security")

In Phase 4, any existing measurements and data repositories that can be used to derive measurement data are reviewed. Following the review, applicable information is extracted and used to identify appropriate implementation evidence to support measurement development and data collection.

Phases 5, 6, and 7 involve developing measurements that track process implementation, efficiency/effectiveness, and mission impact.[13]

Specifying InfoSec Measurements

One of the critical tasks in the measurement process is to assess and quantify what will be measured. While InfoSec planning and organizing activities may only require time estimates, you must obtain more detailed measurements when assessing the effort spent to complete production and project tasks. This usually means some form of time reporting system, either a paper-based or automated time accounting mechanism.

Measurements collected from production statistics depend greatly on the number of systems and the number of users of those systems. As the number of systems changes and/or the number of users of those systems changes, the effort to maintain the same level of service will vary. Some organizations simply track these two values to measure the service being delivered. Other organizations need more detailed measurement, perhaps including the number of new users added, number of access control changes, number of users removed or deauthorized, number of access control violations, number of awareness briefings, number of systems by type, number of incidents by category (such as virus or worm outbreaks), number of malicious code instances blocked by filter, or many, many other possible measurements.

Collecting measurements about project activities may be even more challenging. Unless the organization is satisfied with a simple tally of who spent how many hours doing what tasks (which is more project management than performance measurement), it needs some mechanism to link the outcome of each project, in terms of loss control or risk reduction, to the resources consumed. This is a nontrivial process, and most organizations rely on narrative explanation rather than measurement-driven calculations to justify project expenditures.

Collecting InfoSec Measurements

The prospect of collecting performance measurements is daunting to some organizations. At large organizations, merely counting up the number of computing systems in a production state may be a time-consuming project. Some thought must go into the processes used for data collection and record keeping. Once the question of what to measure is answered, the how, when, where, and who questions of metrics collection must be addressed. Designing the collection process requires thoughtful consideration of the intent of the measurement along with a thorough knowledge of how production services are delivered.

Measurements Development Approach
One of the priorities in building an InfoSec process measurement program is determining whether these measurements will be macro- or micro-focus. Macro-focus measurements examine the performance of the overall security program. Micro-focus measurements examine the performance of an individual control or group of controls within the InfoSec program. Some organizations may want to conduct a limited assessment using both macro- and micro-focus measurements.

What is important is that the measurements are specifically tied to individual InfoSec goals and objectives.[14] Implementing InfoSec process measurement just for the sake of collecting data wastes valuable resources. Therefore, it is imperative that the process measurement program be driven by specific needs in the organization and not by the whims of any one manager.

Measurement Prioritization and Selection
Because organizations seem to better manage what they measure, it is important to ensure that individual metrics are prioritized in the same manner as the processes that they measure. This can be achieved with a simple low-, medium-, or high-priority ranking system or a weighted scale approach, which would involve assigning values to each measurement based on its importance in the context of the overall InfoSec program and in the overall risk-mitigation goals and criticality of the systems.[15] While there are literally hundreds of measurements that could be used, only those associated with appropriate-level priority activities should be incorporated. After all, the personnel resources needed to develop, implement, collect, analyze, and report the data are most likely limited, and other activities will inevitably compete for the use of those resources.

Establishing Performance Targets
Performance targets make it possible to define success in the security program. For example, a goal of 100 percent employee InfoSec training as an objective for the training program validates the continued collection of training measurements. A periodic report indicating the current status of employee training represents progress toward the goal. Many InfoSec performance measurements targets are represented by a 100 percent target goal. Other types of performance measurements, such as

those used to determine the relative effectiveness or efficiency or impact of InfoSec on the organization's goals, tend to be more subjective and will require management to assess the purpose and value of such measurements. For example, the increase in *relative* or perceived security of the organization's information after the installation of a firewall requires a completely different perspective than that required from assessing personnel training performance through empirical measurement of attendance at training sessions or the evaluation of posttraining quiz scores.[16]

This example highlights one of the fundamental challenges in InfoSec performance measurement, namely defining *effective security*. When is InfoSec effective? Researchers who study InfoSec success continue to grapple with this question. There is little agreement about how to define a successful program; some argue that simply avoiding losses is the best measurement, while others argue that any valid measure must be provable. The avoidance of losses may be attributed to luck or other nonprogram factors. This dilemma remains unresolved.

Measurements Development Template NIST recommends the documentation of performance measurements in a standardized format to ensure the repeatability of the measurement development, customization, collection, and reporting activities. One way to accomplish this would be to develop a custom template that an organization could use to document performance measurements that are to be used. Instructions for the development and format of such a template are provided in Table 7-2.

An example of how one measurement might be documented using this template is provided in Table 7-3.

Field	Data
Measurement ID	State the unique identifier used for measure tracking and sorting. The unique identifier can be from an organization-specific naming convention or can directly reference another source. It should be meaningful to the source and/or use of the measurement.
Goal	Statement of strategic goal and/or InfoSec goal. For system-level security control measures, the goal would guide security control implementation for that information system. For program-level measures, both strategic goals and InfoSec goals can be included. For example, InfoSec goals can be derived from enterprise-level goals in support the organization's mission. These goals are usually articulated in strategic and performance plans. When possible, include both the enterprise-level goal and the specific InfoSec goal extracted from agency documentation, or identify an InfoSec program goal that would contribute to the account was that of the selected strategic goal.
Measurement	Statement of measurement. Identify precisely the numeric element to be measured. Start with one of percentage, number, frequency, average, or a similar term. If applicable, list the NIST SP 800-53 security control(s) being measured. Any related security controls providing supporting data should be identified. If the measures are applicable to a specific FIPS 199 impact level (high, moderate, or low), provide that means of evaluation.
Measurement type	Statement of whether the measure is implementation, effectiveness/efficiency, or impact.

Table 7-2   Performance measurements template and instructions

Field	Data
Formula	Calculation to be performed that results in a numeric expression of a measure. The information gathered through listing implementation evidence serves as an input into the formula for calculating the measure.
Target	Threshold for a satisfactory rating for the measure, such as milestone completion or a statistical measure. Target can be expressed in percentages, time, dollars, or other appropriate units of measure. Target may be tied to a required completion timeframe. Select final and interim target to enable tracking of progress toward stated goal.
Implementation evidence	Implementation evidence is used to compute the measure, validate that the activity is performed, and identify probable causes of unsatisfactory results for a specific measure. 1. For manual data collection, identified questions and data elements that would provide the data inputs necessary to calculate the measure's formula, qualify the measure for acceptance, and validate provided information. 2. For each question or query, status security control number from "NIST SP 800-53" that provides information, if applicable 3. If the measure is applicable to a specific FIPS 199 impact level, questions should state the impact level. 4. For automated data collection, identify data elements that would be required for the formula, qualify the measure for acceptance, and validate the information provided.
Frequency	Indication of how often the data is collected and analyzed, and how often the data is reported. State the frequency of data collection based on a rate of change in a particular security control that is being evaluated. State the frequency of data reporting based on external reporting requirements and internal customer preferences.
Responsible parties	Indicate the following key stakeholders: • Information owner: Identify organizational component, an individual who owns required pieces of information. • Information collector: Identify the organizational component and individual responsible for collecting the data. (Note: If possible, information collector should be a different individual or even a representative of a different organizational unit than the information owner, to avoid the possibility of conflict of interest and ensure separation of duties. Smaller organizations will need to determine whether it is feasible to separate these two responsibilities.) • Information customer: Identify the organizational component and individual who will receive the data.
Data source	Location of the data to be used in calculating the measure. Include databases, tracking tools, organizations, or specific roles within organizations that can provide required information.
Reporting format	Indication of how the measure will be reported, such as pie charts, line charts, bar graphs, or other format. State the type of format or provide a sample.

Table 7-2   **Performance measurements template and instructions (continued)**

Source: NIST SP 800-55, Rev. 1.

Field	Example Data
Measurement ID	Security training coverage
Goal	Strategic goal: Ensure a high-quality workforce supported by modern and secure infrastructure and operational capabilities. InfoSec goal: Ensure that organization personnel are adequately trained to carry out their assigned InfoSec-related duties and responsibilities.
Measurement	The percentage of InfoSec personnel who have received security training.
Measure type	Implementation
Formula	Number of InfoSec personnel who have completed security training within the past year divided by the total number of InfoSec personnel, then multiplied by 100
Target	100 percent

Implementation evidence	1. Are significant security responsibilities defined with qualifications criteria and documented in policy? Yes/No
	2. Are records kept regarding which employees have significant security responsibilities? Yes/No
	3. How many employees in your department have significant security responsibilities?
	4. Are training records maintained? Yes/No
	5. How many of those with significant security responsibilities have received the required training?
	6. If all personnel have not received training, document all reasons that apply:
	  a. Insufficient funding
	  b. Insufficient time
	  c. Courses unavailable
	  d. Employee not registered
	  e. Other (specify)

Frequency	Collected as training is delivered Reported annually
Responsible parties	Information owner: training division Information collector: training division Information customer: CIO
Data source	Training and awareness tracking records
Reporting format	Pie chart illustrating the percentage of security personnel who have received training versus those who have not received training. If performance is below target, pie chart illustrating causes of performance falling short of targets.

Table 7-3 **Performance measurement example**

Copyright © 2014 Cengage Learning®.

Candidate Measurements A number of example candidate measurements are provided in Table 7-4. Additional details on these measurements, including how they are calculated and used, are provided in "NIST SP 800-55, Rev 1."

Implementing InfoSec Performance Measurement

Once developed, InfoSec performance measurements must be implemented and integrated into ongoing InfoSec management operations. For the most part, it is insufficient

Percentage of the organization's information systems budget devoted to InfoSec
Percentage of high vulnerabilities mitigated within organizationally defined time periods after discovery
Percentage space of remote access points used to gain unauthorized access
Percentage of information systems personnel who have received security training
Average frequency of audit records review and analysis for inappropriate activity
Percentage of new systems that have completed C&A prior to their implementation
Percentage of approved and implemented configuration changes identified in the latest automated baseline configuration
Percentage of information systems that have conducted annual contingency plan testing
Percentage of users with access to shared accounts
Percentage of incidents reported within required time frame per applicable incident category
Percentage of system components that undergo maintenance in accordance with formal maintenance schedules
Percentage of media that passes sanitization procedures testing
Percentage of physical security incidents allowing unauthorized entry into facilities containing information assets
Percentage of employees who are authorized access to information systems only after they sign an acknowledgment that they have read and understood the appropriate policies
Percentage of individuals screened before being granted access to organizational information and information systems
Percentage of vulnerabilities remediated within organizationally specified time frames
Percentage of system and service acquisition contracts that include security requirements and/or specifications
Percentage of mobile computers and devices that perform all cryptographic operations using organizationally specified cryptographic modules operating in approved modes of operations
Percentage of operating system vulnerabilities for which patches have been applied or that have been otherwise mitigated

Table 7-4 Examples of possible security performance measurements

Source: NIST SP 800-55, Rev. 1.

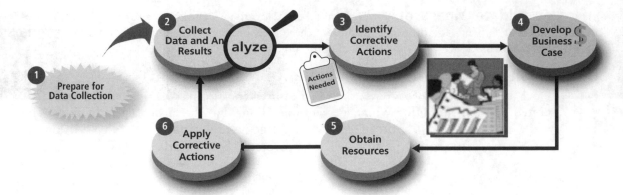

Figure 7-2 Information security measurement program implementation process

Source: © Cengage Learning 2014. (Based on "NIST SP 800-55, Rev. 1: Performance Management for Information Security")

to simply collect these measurements once (although some activities only require the collection of data for one particular purpose, such as C&A, described later in this chapter). Performance measurement is an ongoing, continuous improvement operation. The collection of all measurement data should be part of standard operating procedures across the organization.

The process for performance measurement implementation recommended in NIST SP 800-55, Rev. 1 involves six subordinate tasks, as is shown in Figure 7-2:

- *Phase 1*—Prepare for data collection; identify, define, develop, and select InfoSec measures.

- *Phase 2*—Collect data and analyze results; collect, aggregate, and consolidate metric data collection and compare measurements with targets (gap analysis).

- *Phase 3*—Identify corrective actions; develop a plan to serve as the roadmap for closing the gap identified in Phase 2. This includes determining the range of corrective actions, prioritizing corrective actions based on overall risk-mitigation goals, and selecting the most appropriate corrective actions.

- *Phase 4*—Develop the business case.

- *Phase 5*—Obtain resources; address the budgeting cycle for acquiring resources needed to implement remediation actions identified in Phase 3.

- *Phase 6*—Apply corrective actions; close the gap by implementing the recommended corrective actions in the security program or in the security controls.

Reporting InfoSec Performance Measurements

In most cases, simply listing the measurements collected does not adequately convey their meaning. For example, a line chart showing the number of malicious code attacks occurring per day may communicate a basic fact, but unless the reporting mechanism can provide the context—for example, the number of new malicious code variants on the Internet in that time period—the measurement will not serve its intended purpose. In addition, you must

View Point
Measuring Success
By Martin Lee, Security Practitioner

Metrics tell the security professional how effective the organization's protections are and if the situation is getting better or worse. These metrics should seek to cover measurement of the threats that the organization faces and the effectiveness of the mitigation strategies. Used judiciously, metrics illustrate the state of security to specialists and non-specialists alike.

Too much data may confuse the situation; also, metrics that are difficult or onerous to collect can lead to security staff members devoting their time to gathering data rather than trying to understand the situation.

The adage "Not everything that can be counted counts, not everything that counts can be counted" ought to be remembered. Professionals should determine the figures that best illustrate how the organization is attaining its security policy goals. However, many of these metrics can only be measured in an ideal environment or with more resources than are available. If a metric cannot be easily measured, proxy metrics can be found for the ideal measure. These figures are indirectly related to the ideal measure but are far easier to measure. A good example is the staff's knowledge and awareness of security. Ideally, this can be measured through an annual comprehensive exam on all aspects of security that is given to all staff members. However, a 10-question quiz taken by a small random selection of staff may give data that is just as informative and much easier to collect.

We can learn much from the methods by which metrics are collected in other domains. In many safety-critical environments, statistics relating to "near misses"—events where major incidents were only narrowly averted—must be collected and reported. These can be taken as evidence of both the effectiveness of mitigations in averting a disaster and as evidence of a failing in the overall mitigation regime since the threat was only neutralized at the last line of defense. Patterns of near misses illustrate where further measures of protection should be deployed. Additionally, calculating the potential financial consequences if the threat had not been caught in time can provide powerful justification for security budgets.

Analyzing metrics by business unit identifies the departments that require attention to remedy security weaknesses. For instance, a metric that demonstrates that the entire organization meets the policy requirements for keeping systems patched may, on closer examination, show that most business units exceed policy requirements but a few do not meet the required standard. Devoting resources to resolve these local problems can be an effective means of improving the levels of protection in the organization.

The collection of metrics should not be seen as an end in itself but as a means by which security professionals identify weaknesses in protection and demonstrate the level of attainment of security goals.

make decisions about how to present correlated metrics—whether to use pie, line, bar, scatter, or bar charts, and which colors denote which kinds of results.

The CISO must also consider to whom the results of the performance measurement program should be disseminated and how they should be delivered. Many times, the CISO presents these types of reports in meetings with key executive peers. It is seldom advisable to broadcast complex and nuanced metrics-based reports to large groups unless the key points are well established and embedded in a more complete context, such as a newsletter or press release.

Trends in Certification and Accreditation

In security management, **accreditation** is the authorization of an IT system to process, store, or transmit information. Accreditation is issued by a management official and serves as a means of assuring that systems are of adequate quality. It also challenges managers and technical staff to find the best methods to assure security, given technical constraints, operational constraints, and mission requirements. **Certification** is a comprehensive assessment of both technical and nontechnical protection strategies for a particular system, as specified by a particular set of requirements. Thus, while systems may be certified as meeting a specific set of criteria—like the PCI DSS—they must be accredited (or approved by an appropriate authority) before being allowed to process a specific set of information (such as classified documents) at an acceptable level of risk.[17]

Organizations pursue accreditation or certification to gain a competitive advantage or to provide assurance or confidence to their customers. Prior to 2009, federal information systems required C&A as specified in the U.S. Federal Office of Management and Budget (OMB) Circular A-130 and the Computer Security Act of 1987. Accreditation, whether done by a federal agency or a private business, demonstrates that management has defined an acceptable risk level and that provided resources bring risks to that level.

In 2009, the U.S. government, through NIST, changed the fundamental approach to the C&A of federal information systems, bringing the government into alignment with industry. The focus moved from formal C&A activities to a risk-management life cycle approach. With the publication of "NIST SP 800-37, Rev. 1: Guide for Applying the Risk Management Framework to Federal Information Systems: A Security Life Cycle Approach," the approach shifted to a process of risk management-based assessment and authorization, much of which was driven by the Federal Information Security Management Act of 2002 (FISMA). This change was then reflected in "NIST SP 800-53, Rev. 4: Security and Privacy Controls for Federal Information Systems and Organizations," currently in draft form.

NIST SP 800-37 Rev. 1: Guide for Applying the Risk Management Framework to Federal Information Systems: A Security Life Cycle Approach

With the publication of "NIST SP 800-37, Rev. 1," a common approach to a Risk Management Framework (RMF) for InfoSec practice became the standard for the U.S. government. According to this document:

> *NIST, in partnership with the Department of Defense (DoD), the Office of the Director of National Intelligence (ODNI), and the Committee on National*

Security Systems (CNSS), has developed a common InfoSec framework for the federal government and its contractors. The intent of this common framework is to improve InfoSec, strengthen risk management processes, and encourage reciprocity among federal agencies. This publication, developed by the Joint Task Force Transformation Initiative Working Group, transforms the traditional Certification and Accreditation (C&A) process into the six-step Risk Management Framework (RMF). The revised process emphasizes:

(i)   *building InfoSec capabilities into federal information systems through the application of state-of-the-practice management, operational, and technical security controls;*

(ii) *maintaining awareness of the security state of information systems on an ongoing basis though enhanced monitoring processes; and*

(iii) *providing essential information to senior leaders to facilitate decisions regarding the acceptance of risk to organizational operations and assets, individuals, other organizations, and the Nation arising from the operation and use of information systems.*

The RMF has the following characteristics:

- *Promotes the concept of near real-time risk management and ongoing information system authorization through the implementation of robust continuous monitoring processes*

- *Encourages the use of automation to provide senior leaders the necessary information to make cost-effective, risk-based decisions with regard to the organizational information systems supporting their core missions and business functions*

- *Integrates InfoSec into the enterprise architecture and system development life cycle Provides emphasis on the selection, implementation, assessment, and monitoring of security controls, and the authorization of information systems*

- *Links risk management processes at the information system level to risk management processes at the organization level through a risk executive (function)*

- *Establishes responsibility and accountability for security controls deployed within organizational information systems and inherited by those systems (i.e., common controls)*

The risk management process described in this publication changes the traditional focus of C&A as a static, procedural activity to a more dynamic approach that provides the capability to more effectively manage information system-related security risks in highly diverse environments of complex and sophisticated cyber threats, ever-increasing system vulnerabilities, and rapidly changing missions.[18]

NIST follows a three-tiered approach to risk management. Most organizations work from the top down, focusing first on aspects affecting the entire organization, such as governance (tier 1). Then, after the more strategic issues are addressed, they move toward more tactical issues around business processes (tier 2). The most detailed aspects are addressed in tier 3, dealing with information systems. This relationship is shown in Figure 7-3.

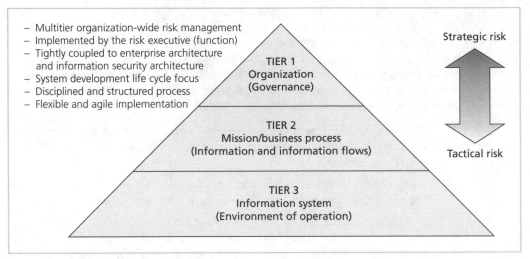

- Multitier organization-wide risk management
- Implemented by the risk executive (function)
- Tightly coupled to enterprise architecture and information security architecture
- System development life cycle focus
- Disciplined and structured process
- Flexible and agile implementation

TIER 1
Organization
(Governance)

TIER 2
Mission/business process
(Information and information flows)

TIER 3
Information system
(Environment of operation)

Strategic risk

Tactical risk

Figure 7-3 Tiered risk management approach

Source: © Cengage Learning 2014. (Based on "NIST SP 800-37, Rev. 1: Guide for Security Authorization of Federal Information Systems: A Security Life Cycle Approach")

The RMF, which is shown in Figure 7-4, applies this multi-tiered approach to a six-step process. According to "NIST SP 800-37, Rev. 1":

> The RMF operates primarily at Tier 3 in the risk management hierarchy but can also have interactions at Tiers 1 and 2 (e.g., providing feedback from ongoing authorization decisions to the risk executive [function], dissemination of updated threat, and risk information to authorizing officials and information system owners). The RMF steps include:
>
> 1) Categorize *the information system and the information processed, stored, and transmitted by that system based on an impact analysis.*
>
> 2) Select *an initial set of baseline security controls for the information system based on the security categorization; tailoring and supplementing the security control baseline as needed based on an organizational assessment of risk and local conditions.*
>
> 3) Implement *the security controls and describe how the controls are employed within the information system and its environment of operation.*
>
> 4) Assess *the security controls using appropriate assessment procedures to determine the extent to which the controls are implemented correctly, operating as intended, and producing the desired outcome with respect to meeting the security requirements for the system.*
>
> 5) Authorize *information system operation based on a determination of the risk to organizational operations and assets, individuals, other organizations, and the Nation resulting from the operation of the information system and the decision that this risk is acceptable.*
>
> 6) Monitor *the security controls in the information system on an ongoing basis including assessing control effectiveness, documenting changes to the*

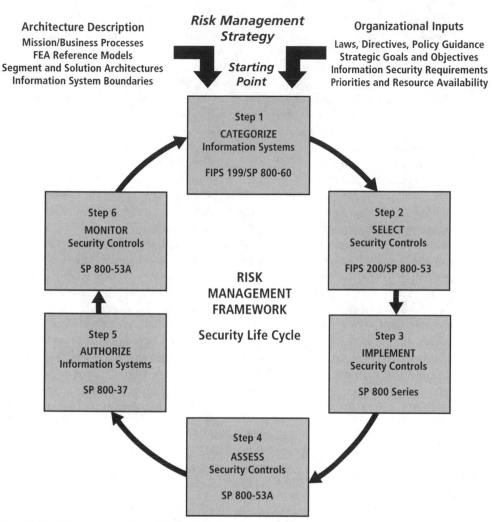

Figure 7-4 Risk management framework

Source: © Cengage Learning 2014. (Based on content from "NIST SP 800-53, Rev. 1: Risk Management Framework")

> *system or its environment of operation, conducting security impact analyses of the associated changes, and reporting the security state of the system to designated organizational officials.*[19]

While the tasks that make up all the elements of the RMF are discussed in later chapters, Step 4 (Assess) and Step 5 (Authorize) have replaced the C&A approach previously used for federal information systems.

Step 4: Assess The process of assessing the security of an information system involves the development of a plan to assess the security controls in place. According to "NIST SP 800-37, Rev.1":

> *The security assessment plan provides the objectives for the security control assessment, a detailed roadmap of how to conduct such an assessment, and*

assessment procedures. The assessment plan reflects the type of assessment the organization is conducting (e.g., developmental testing and evaluation, independent verification and validation, assessments supporting security authorizations or reauthorizations, audits, continuous monitoring, assessments subsequent to remediation actions). Conducting security control assessments in parallel with the development/acquisition and implementation phases of the life cycle permits the identification of weaknesses and deficiencies early and provides the most cost-effective method for initiating corrective actions. Issues found during these assessments can be referred to authorizing officials for early resolution, as appropriate. The results of security control assessments carried out during system development and implementation can also be used (consistent with reuse criteria) during the security authorization process to avoid system fielding delays or costly repetition of assessments. The security assessment plan is reviewed and approved by appropriate organizational officials to ensure that the plan is consistent with the security objectives of the organization, employs state-of-the-art practice tools, techniques, procedures, and automation to support the concept of continuous monitoring and near real-time risk management, and is cost-effective with regard to the resources allocated for the assessment. The purpose of the security assessment plan approval is two-fold: (1) to establish the appropriate expectations for the security control assessment; and (2) to bound the level of effort for the security control assessment. An approved security assessment plan helps to ensure that an appropriate level of resources is applied toward determining security control effectiveness. When security controls are provided to an organization by an external provider (e.g., through contracts, interagency agreements, lines of business arrangements, licensing agreements, and/or supply chain arrangements), the organization obtains a security assessment plan from the provider.[20]

Step 5: Authorize The process of "authorizing" an information system to process a predefined set of information fundamentally replaces the concept of C&A. Once a system has been authorized, it is deemed ready to process information, based on the assessment of its controls and safeguards, provided of course that those controls and safeguards are maintained, reviewed, and improved as needed. The authorization process as explained by "NIST SP 800-37, Rev.1" involves four tasks:

1. Prepare the plan of action and milestones based on the findings and recommendations of the security assessment report excluding any remediation actions taken.

   The plan of action and milestones, prepared for the authorizing official by the information system owner or the common control provider, is one of three key documents in the security authorization package and describes the specific tasks that are planned: (i) to correct any weaknesses or deficiencies in the security controls noted during the assessment; and (ii) to address the residual vulnerabilities in the information system. The plan of action and milestones identifies: (i) the tasks to be accomplished with a recommendation for completion either before or after information system implementation; (ii) the resources required to accomplish the tasks; (iii) any milestones in meeting the tasks; and (iv) the scheduled completion dates for the milestones.[21]

2. Assemble the security authorization package and submit the package to the authorizing official for adjudication.

The security authorization package contains: (i) the security plan; (ii) the security assessment report; and (iii) the plan of action and milestones. The information in these key documents is used by authorizing officials to make risk-based authorization decisions. For information systems inheriting common controls for specific security capabilities, the security authorization package for the common controls or a reference to such documentation is also included in the authorization package.[22]

3. Determine the risk to organizational operations (including mission, functions, image, or reputation), organizational assets, individuals, other organizations, or the Nation.

The authorizing official or designated representative, in collaboration with the senior InfoSec officer, assesses the information provided by the information system owner or common control provider regarding the current security state of the system or the common controls inherited by the system and the recommendations for addressing any residual risks. Risk assessments (either formal or informal) are employed at the discretion of the organization to provide needed information on threats, vulnerabilities, and potential impacts as well as the analyses for the risk mitigation recommendations....[23]

4. Determine if the risk to organizational operations, organizational assets, individuals, other organizations, or the Nation is acceptable.

The explicit acceptance of risk is the responsibility of the authorizing official and cannot be delegated to other officials within the organization. The authorizing official considers many factors when deciding if the risk to organizational operations (including mission, function, image, or reputation), organizational assets, individuals, other organizations, and the Nation, is acceptable. Balancing security considerations with mission and operational needs is paramount to achieving an acceptable authorization decision. The authorizing official issues an authorization decision for the information system and the common controls inherited by the system after reviewing all of the relevant information and, where appropriate, consulting with other organizational officials, including the organization's risk executive (function). Security authorization decisions are based on the content of the security authorization package and, where appropriate, any inputs received from key organizational officials, including the risk executive (function)...

The authorization decision document conveys the final security authorization decision from the authorizing official to the information system owner or common control provider, and other organizational officials, as appropriate. The authorization decision document contains the following information: (i) authorization decision; (ii) terms and conditions for the authorization; and (iii) authorization termination date.[24]

Thus, the issuance of an authorization decision document with a favorable review *authorized to operate* has become the standard means of *Certifying & Accrediting* modern federal information systems. This move to a formal RMF approach brings a much more manageable and sustainable process to those systems impacted by this approach and allows those responsible for managing those systems the ability to integrate a life cycle approach to C&A and overall better security to all information. The former process of C&A had the tendency to result in a frantic short-term preparation in expectation of the C&A process, which was relaxed immediately after the C&A process was complete. The RMF approach results in an ongoing, continuous-improvement approach, which offers better long-term security.

Accreditation and certification are not permanent. Just as standards of due diligence and due care require an ongoing maintenance effort, most accreditation and certification processes require reaccreditation or recertification every few years (typically every three to five years). Approaches such as the RMF are designed to follow a continuous-improvement method, ensuring that the organization does not ramp up for a C&A cycle, then relax in the years following, potentially resulting in lapses in security, only to ramp up again prior to the next C&A cycle.

Chapter Summary

- Benchmarking is a process of following the recommended or existing practices of a similar organization or industry-developed standards. Two categories of benchmarks are used: standards of due care/due diligence and recommended practices.

- Organizations may be compelled to adopt a stipulated minimum level of security (that which any prudent organization would do), which is known as a standard of due care. Implementing controls at this minimum standard is deemed due diligence.

- Security efforts that seek to provide a superior level of performance in the protection of information are called recommended business practices or best practices. Security efforts that are among the best in the industry are termed best security practices.

- A practice related to benchmarking is baselining—a level of performance against which changes can be usefully compared. Baselining can provide the foundation for internal benchmarking.

- InfoSec performance management is the process of designing, implementing, and managing the use of the collected data elements called "measurements" to determine the effectiveness of the overall security program.

- There are three types of InfoSec performance measures: those that determine the effectiveness of the execution of InfoSec policy, those that determine the effectiveness and/or efficiency of the delivery of InfoSec services, and those that assess the impact of an incident or other security event on the organization or its mission.

- One of the critical tasks in the measurement process is to assess and quantify what will be measured and how it is measured.

- In security management, accreditation is the authorization of an IT system to process, store, or transmit information.

- Certification is the evaluation of the technical and nontechnical security controls of an IT system to establish the extent to which a particular design and implementation meets a set of specified security requirements. In recent years, the C&A approach has been replaced in federal information systems by a Risk Management Framework, which follows a cyclic six-step approach: Categorize, Select, Implement, Assess, Authorize, and Monitor.

Review Questions

1. What is benchmarking?

2. What is the standard of due care? How does it relate to due diligence?

3. What is a recommended security practice? What is a good source for finding such recommended practices?

4. When selecting recommended practices, what criteria should you use?

5. When choosing recommended practices, what limitations should you keep in mind?

6. What is baselining? How does it differ from benchmarking?

7. What are the NIST-recommended documents that support the process of baselining?

8. What is a performance measurement in the context of InfoSec management?

9. What types of measures are used for InfoSec management measurement programs?

10. According to Gerald Kovacich, what are the critical questions to be kept in mind when developing a measurements program?

11. What factors are critical to the success of an InfoSec performance program?

12. What is a performance target, and how is it used in establishing a measurement program?

13. List and describe the fields found in a properly and fully defined performance measurement.

14. Describe the recommended process for the development of InfoSec measurement program implementation.

15. Why is a simple list of measurement data usually insufficient when reporting InfoSec measurements?

16. What is the Capability Maturity Model Integrated (CMMI), and which organization is responsible for its development?

17. What is systems accreditation?

18. What is systems certification?

19. What industry standard requires system certification? How is this certification enforced?

20. What is the new Risk Management Framework initiative? How is it superior to the previous approach for the certification and accreditation of federal IT systems?

Exercises

1. Search the Web for the term "security best practices." Compare your findings to the recommended practices outlined in the NIST documents.

2. Visit the NIST federal agency security practices Web site at *csrc.nist.gov/groups/SMA /fasp/index.html*. Review some of the listed FASPs and identify five drawbacks to adopting the recommended practices for a typical business.

3. Visit the Web sites of the major technology organizations listed in this chapter (Microsoft, Oracle, and Cisco), plus two more that you choose on your own. Search the Web sites for best security practices. What do you find?

4. Download and review "NIST SP 800-55 Rev. 1: Performance Measurement Guide for Information Security." Using this document, identify five measures you would be interested in finding the results from based on your home computing systems and/or network.

5. Using the template provided in Table 7-2, develop documentation for one of the performance measurements you selected in Exercise 4.

Closing Case

Maria sighed as she considered her new assignment. It had seemed like a great idea when Iris offered her the role, but now she wondered if she could get her arms around the complex process of getting RWW certified as an ISO 27000-compliant organization. After reviewing the outline of the training class she would soon attend, she pulled out a notepad and began outlining the RWW compliance project. She hoped she could find a useful set of documents to prepare her for this project.

Discussion

1. Which documents should Maria read before her class?

2. Based on what you know about ISO 27000 program certification, what are the major steps of the process Maria will have to oversee?

Ethical Decision Making

Maria was troubled by her recommendation of Linda to supervise the policy compliance team. As she considered the nature of the job and some of the personal issues that Linda faced, she wondered if she should go back to Iris and revise her recommendation.

Linda was a single mother with three children; she also had a history of substance abuse, although she was in recovery. Maria found her to be good at her work and felt she had made remarkable progress during the time Maria had supervised her. But Linda had a higher than average number of sick days due to her busy home life. And although Maria had no concrete evidence that Linda was struggling with her recovery, there were some indications that everything was not as it should be.

1. Should Linda's history of past improprieties lead Maria to withdraw her support and replace her without giving detailed reasons to Iris?

2. Should Maria's ethical responsibility to the company lead her to give a full report of her concerns to Iris?

3. Should Maria's ethical responsibility to Linda lead her to keep these concerns to herself and allow the recommendation to stand?

Endnotes

1. Avolio, Frederick. "Best Practices in Network Security." *Network Computing*, March 20, 2000.

2. "Federal Agency Security Practices (FASP)." *National Institute of Standards and Technology*. Accessed February 24, 2013 @ *csrc.nist.gov/groups/SMA/fasp/index.html*.

3. Gartner Group. *Enterprise Security Diagnostic: Best Practices*. Accessed May 1, 2003 @ *www.gartnerinfo.com/sec_diagnostic*.

4. PCI Security Standards Council. "PCI DSS Quick Reference Guide: Understanding the Payment Card Industry Data Security Standard, Version 2.0." Accessed January 17, 2013 @ *www.pcisecuritystandards.org/documents/PCI%20SSC%20Quick%20Reference %20Guide.pdf*.

5. Kovacich, Gerald L. *The Information Systems Security Officer's Guide*, 2nd ed. Elsevier Science, 2003: 196.

6. Chew, E., M. Swanson, K. Stine, N. Bartol, A. Brown, and W. Robinson. "Special Publication 800-55, Rev. 1: Performance Measurement Guide for Information Security." *National Institute of Standards and Technology*, July 2008. Accessed February 24, 2013 @ *csrc.nist.gov/publications/nistpubs/800-55-Rev1/SP800-55-rev1.pdf*.

7. Ibid.

8. Ibid.

9. Ibid.

10. Kovacich, Gerald L. *The Information Systems Security Officer's Guide*, 2nd ed. Elsevier Science, 2003: 196.

11. Chew, E., M. Swanson, K. Stine, N. Bartol, A. Brown, and W. Robinson. "Special Publication 800-55, Rev. 1: Performance Measurement Guide for Information Security." *National Institute of Standards and Technology*, July 2008. Accessed February 24, 2013 @ *csrc.nist.gov/publications/nistpubs/800-55-Rev1/SP800-55-rev1.pdf*.

12. Ahern, D., A. Clouse, and R. Turner. "CMMI Distilled: A Practical Introduction to Integrated Process Improvement." Accessed April 9, 2013 @ *http://cmmiinstitute.com /resource/cmmi-distilled-a-practical-introduction-to-integrated-process-improvement/*.

13. Chew, E., M. Swanson, K. Stine, N. Bartol, A. Brown, and W. Robinson. "Special Publication 800-55, Rev. 1: Performance Measurement Guide for Information Security." *National Institute of Standards and Technology*, July 2008. Accessed February 24, 2013 @ *csrc.nist.gov/publications/nistpubs/800-55-Rev1/SP800-55-rev1.pdf*.

14. Ibid.

15. Ibid.

16. Ibid.

17. Ross, R., and Swanson, M. "SP 800-37: Guidelines for the Security Certification and Accreditation of Federal Information Technology Systems." *National Institute of Standards and Technology*, October 2002.

18. "SP 800-37 Revision 1: Guide for Applying the Risk Revision 1 Management Framework to Federal Information Systems—A Security Life Cycle Approach." *National Institute of Standards and Technology*, February 2010. Accessed April 9, 2013 @ *csrc.nist.gov/publications/nistpubs/800-37-rev1/sp800-37-rev1-final.pdf*.

19. Ibid.

20. Ibid.

21. Ibid.

22. Ibid.

23. Ibid.

24. Ibid.

## chapter 8

Risk Management: Identifying and Assessing Risk

Once we know our weaknesses, they cease to do us any harm.
G. C. (GEOG CHRISTOPH) LICHTENBERG (1742–1799),
GERMAN PHYSICIST AND PHILOSOPHER

Iris Majwabu and Mike Edwards sat side by side on the short flight to the nearby city where the Random Widget Works, Inc. (RWW) board of directors audit committee was meeting that afternoon. The two had been invited to present RWW's information technology (IT) risk management program to the committee. The board's concerns stemmed from a recent briefing by the National Association of Corporate Directors, which focused on trends affecting the potential liability of board members in the areas of InfoSec in general and risk management in particular.

After the plane leveled off, Mike pulled out his copy of the presentation he planned to give that afternoon. He and Iris had been working on it for the past two weeks, and each knew the slides by heart. Iris was along to assist with the question-and-answer period that would follow Mike's presentation.

"They're not going to be happy campers when you're done," Iris said.

"No, they're not," Mike said. "The CEO is worried about how they'll respond and about what might come up at the full board meeting next month. I'm afraid the disconnect between IT and Internal Audit may have some unexpected consequences."

Iris considered what she knew about the weaknesses of the Internal Audit Department's approach to the company's non-IT assets. Where Mike and Iris had built a sound, fact-based approach to estimating and controlling IT risk, some of the other company divisions used less empirical methods.

"I think we should come out of this okay," Iris told Mike. "After all, the main concern of the audit committee members is the new perception of their liability for IT security and the impact that IT risk has on the issues surrounding privacy. We have a solid risk management plan in place that's working well, in my opinion."

Mike looked up from his notes and said, "It's not us I'm worried about. I'm afraid we may create some discomfort and unwanted attention for our peers after the board sees the wide variety of risk management approaches used in other divisions."

LEARNING OBJECTIVES

Upon completion of this material, you should be able to:

- Define risk management and its role in the organization
- Describe risk management techniques to identify and prioritize risk factors for information assets
- Explain how risk is assessed based on the likelihood of adverse events and the effects on information assets when events occur
- Discuss the use of the results of the risk identification process

Introduction

Information security (InfoSec) in an organization exists primarily to manage IT risk. Managing risk is one of the key responsibilities of every manager within an organization. In any well-developed risk management program, two formal processes are at work. The first, risk identification and assessment, is discussed in this chapter; the second, risk control, is the subject of the next chapter.

Each manager in the organization should focus on reducing risk. This is often done within the context of one of the three communities of interest, as follows:

- General management must structure the IT and InfoSec functions in ways that will result in the successful defense of the organization's information assets, including data, hardware, software, procedures, and people.
- IT management must serve the IT needs of the broader organization and at the same time exploit the special skills and insights of the InfoSec community.
- InfoSec management must lead the way with skill, professionalism, and flexibility as it works with the other communities of interest to balance the constant trade-offs between InfoSec utility and security.

Risk Management

If you know the enemy and know yourself, you need not fear the result of a hundred battles. If you know yourself but not the enemy, for every victory gained you will also suffer a defeat. If you know neither the enemy nor yourself, you will succumb in every battle.[1]

Chinese general Sun Tzu's observation, made more than 2,400 years ago, continues to have direct relevance to the philosophy of InfoSec today. InfoSec strategy and tactics are in many ways similar to those employed in conventional warfare. InfoSec managers and technicians are the defenders of information. They constantly face a myriad of threats to the organization's information assets. A layered defense is the foundation of any InfoSec program. So, as Sun Tzu recommends, to reduce risk, an organization must (1) know itself and (2) know its enemy. This means that managers from all three communities of interest must locate the weaknesses of their organization's operations; understand how the organization's information is processed, stored, and transmitted; and identify what resources are available. Only then can they develop a strategic plan of defense.

Knowing Yourself

When operating any kind of organization, a certain amount of risk is always involved. Risk is inherent in hiring, marketing products, and even in making decisions about where to place the building that houses the organization. Risk finds its way into the daily operations of every organization, and if it is not properly managed, it can cause operational failures and even lead to complete collapse.

For an organization to manage risk properly, managers should understand how information is processed, stored, and transmitted. Knowing yourself in this context requires knowing which information assets are valuable to the organization, identifying, categorizing, and classifying those assets, and understanding how they are currently being protected. Armed with this knowledge, the organization can then initiate an in-depth risk management program. Note that the mere existence of a risk management program is not sufficient. Frequently, risk management mechanisms are implemented but not maintained or kept current. Risk management is a process, which means the safeguards and controls that are devised and implemented are not "install-and-forget" devices (see Chapter 9).

Knowing the Enemy

Once an organization becomes aware of its weaknesses, managers can take up Sun Tzu's second dictum: Know the enemy. This means identifying, examining, and understanding the threats facing the organization's information assets. Managers must be fully prepared to identify those threats that pose risks to the organization and the security of its information assets. **Risk management** is the process of discovering and assessing the risks to an organization's operations and determining how those risks can be controlled or mitigated. **Risk analysis** is the identification and assessment of levels of risk in the organization; it is a major component of risk management.

Accountability for Risk Management

All of the communities of interest bear responsibility for the management of risks. The management of the organization is accountable for the risk management program that is used. Of the three communities of interest directly linked to managing the risks to information assets, each has a particular strategic role to play:

- *InfoSec*—Because members of the InfoSec community best understand the threats and attacks that introduce risk, they often take a leadership role in addressing risk.

- *IT*—This group must help to build secure systems and ensure their safe operation. For example, IT builds and operates information systems that are mindful of operational risks and have proper controls implemented to reduce risk.

- *Management and users*—When properly trained and kept aware of the threats faced by the organization, this group plays a part in the early detection and response process. Members of this community also ensure that sufficient resources (money and personnel) are allocated to the InfoSec and IT groups to meet the security needs of the organization. For example, business managers must ensure that supporting records for orders remain intact in case of data entry error or transaction corruption. Users must be made aware of threats to data and systems and must be educated on practices that minimize those threats.

The three communities of interest must work together to address every level of risk, ranging from full-scale disasters (whether natural or human-made) to the smallest mistake made by an employee. To do so, they must be actively involved in the following activities:

- Evaluating the risk controls

- Determining which control options are cost effective

- Acquiring or installing the appropriate controls

- Overseeing processes to ensure that the controls remain effective

- Identifying risks, which includes:

  - Creating an inventory of information assets

  - Classifying and organizing those assets meaningfully

  - Assigning a value to each information asset

  - Identifying threats to the cataloged assets

  - Pinpointing vulnerable assets by tying specific threats to specific assets

- Assessing risks, which includes:

  - Determining the likelihood that vulnerable systems will be attacked by specific threats

  - Assessing the relative risk facing the organization's information assets, so that risk management and control activities can focus on assets that require the most urgent and immediate attention

  - Calculating the risks to which assets are exposed in their current setting

  - Looking in a general way at controls that might come into play for identified vulnerabilities and ways to control the risks that the assets face

  - Documenting and reporting the findings of risk identification and assessment

- Summarizing the findings, which involves stating the conclusions of the analysis stage of risk assessment in preparation for moving into the stage of controlling risk by exploring methods to mitigate risk

Figure 8-1 outlines the steps in the risk identification and assessment process.

Risk Identification

Risk identification begins with the process of self-examination. At this stage, managers *identify* the organization's information assets, *classify* and *categorize* them into useful groups, and

Plan and Organize Process	
Create System Component Categories	
Develop Inventory of Assets	
Identify Threats	
Specify Vulnerable Assets	
Assign Value or Impact Rating to Assets	
Assess Likelihood for Vulnerabilities	
Calculate Relative Risk Factor for Assets	
Preliminary Review of Possible Controls	
Document Findings	

Figure 8-1 Risk identification and assessment process

Copyright © 2014 Cengage Learning®.

prioritize them by their overall importance. This can be a daunting task, but it must be done to identify weaknesses and the threats they present.

Creating an Inventory of Information Assets

The risk identification process begins with the identification of information assets, including people, procedures, data, software, hardware, and networking elements. This step should be done

IT System Components	Risk Management Components	Example Risk Management Components
People	Internal personnel External personnel	Trusted employees Other staff members People we trust outside our organization Strangers
Procedures	Procedures	IT and business standard procedures IT and business sensitive procedures
Data	Data/information	Transmission Processing Storage
Software	Software	Applications Operating systems Security components
Hardware	Hardware	Systems and peripherals Security devices
Networking	Networking	Local Area Network components Intranet components Internet or extranet components Cloud-based components

Table 8-1 **Organizational assets used in systems**

Copyright © 2014 Cengage Learning®.

without prejudging the value of each asset; values will be assigned later in the process. Table 8-1 shows a model outline of the identified assets subcategorized into risk management components.

The risk management components presented in Table 8-1 are organized as follows:

- The people asset is divided into internal personnel (employees) and external personnel (nonemployees). Insiders are further divided into those employees who hold trusted roles and therefore have correspondingly greater authority and accountability and those regular staff members who do not have any special privileges. Outsiders consist of other users who have access to the organization's information assets, some trusted and some untrusted.

- Procedures are assets because they are used to create value for the organization. They are divided into (1) IT and business standard procedures and (2) IT and business sensitive procedures. Sensitive procedures have the potential to enable an attack or to otherwise introduce risk to the organization. For example, the procedures used by a telecommunications company to activate new circuits pose special risks because they reveal aspects of the inner workings of a critical process, which can be subverted by outsiders for the purpose of obtaining unbilled, illicit services.

- The data asset includes information in all states: transmission, processing, and storage. This is an expanded use of the term "data," which is usually associated with databases, not the full range of information used by modern organizations.

- Software is divided into applications, operating systems, and security components. Software that provides security controls may fall into the operating systems or applications category but is differentiated by the fact that it is part of the InfoSec control environment and must therefore be protected more thoroughly than other systems components.

- Hardware is divided into (1) the usual systems devices and their peripherals and (2) the devices that are part of InfoSec control systems. The latter must be protected more thoroughly than the former.

- Networking components include networking devices (such as firewalls, routers, and switches) and the systems software within them, which is often the focal point of attacks, with successful attacks continuing against systems connected to the networks. Of course, most of today's computer systems include networking elements. You will have to determine whether a device is primarily a computer or primarily a networking device. A server computer that is used exclusively as a proxy server or bastion host may be classified as a networking component, while an identical server configured as a database server may be classified as hardware. For this reason, networking devices should be considered separately rather than combined with general hardware and software components.

In some corporate models, this list may be simplified into three groups: People, Processes and Technology, often referred to as "PPT." Whichever model is used, an organization, in the development of its risk assessment methods, should ensure that all of its information resources are properly identified, assessed, and managed for risk.

Identifying Hardware, Software, and Network Assets

Many organizations use purchased asset inventory systems to keep track of their hardware, network, and perhaps their software components. Numerous packages are available in the market today, and it is up to the chief information security officer (CISO) or chief information officer (CIO) to determine which package best serves the needs of the organization. Organizations that do not use an automated inventory system must create an equivalent manual process.

Whether automated or manual, the inventory process requires a certain amount of planning. Most importantly, you must determine which attributes of each of these information assets should be tracked. That determination will depend on the needs of the organization and its risk management efforts as well as the preferences and needs of the InfoSec and IT communities. When deciding which attributes to track for each information asset, consider the following list of potential attributes:

- *Name*—This is a list of all the names commonly used for the device or program. Some organizations may have several names for the same product, and each of them should be cross-referenced in the inventory. This redundancy accommodates the usage across the organization and makes it accessible for everyone. No matter how many names you track or how you select a name, always provide a definition of the asset in question. Adopt naming standards that do not convey critical information to potential system attackers. For instance, a server named CASH1 or HQ_FINANCE may entice attackers.

- *Asset tag*—This is used to facilitate the tracking of assets. Asset tags are unique numbers assigned to assets during the acquisition process.

- *Internet Protocol (IP) address*—This attribute is useful for network devices and servers but rarely applies to software. You can, however, use a relational database and track software instances on specific servers or networking devices. Many larger organizations use the Dynamic Host Configuration Protocol (DHCP) within TCP/IP, which reassigns IP numbers to devices as needed, making the use of IP numbers as part of the asset-identification process very difficult.

- *Media Access Control (MAC) address*—As per the TCP/IP standard, all network-interface hardware devices have a unique number called the MAC address (also called an "electronic serial number" or a "hardware address"). The network operating system uses this number to identify specific network devices. The client's network software uses it to recognize traffic that it needs to process. In most settings, MAC addresses can be a useful way to track connectivity, but they can be spoofed by some hardware/software combinations. Note that some devices may have multiple network interfaces, each with its own MAC address, and others may have configurable MAC addresses, making MAC addresses even less useful as a unique identifier. Given the possibility of MAC address spoofing, the use of MAC addresses as a reliable identifier has been discontinued in many organizations.

- *Asset type*—This attribute describes the function of each asset. For hardware assets, a list of possible asset types that includes servers, desktops, networking devices, and test equipment should be developed. For software assets, a list that includes operating systems, custom applications by type (accounting, human resources, or payroll, to name a few), and packaged applications and/or specialty applications (such as firewall programs) should be developed. The degree of specificity is determined by the needs of the organization. Asset types can be recorded at two or more levels of specificity by first recording one attribute that classifies the asset at a high level and then adding attributes for more detail. For example, one server might be listed as follows:

DeviceClass = S (server)

DeviceOS = Win2008 (Windows 2008)

DeviceCapacity = AS (Advanced Server)

- *Serial number*—This is a number that uniquely identifies a specific device. Some software vendors also assign a software serial number to each instance of the program licensed by the organization.

- *Manufacturer name*—This attribute can be useful for analyzing threat outbreaks when specific manufacturers announce specific vulnerabilities.

- *Manufacturer's model or part number*—This number that identifies exactly what the asset is can be very useful in the later analysis of vulnerabilities because some threats apply only to specific models of certain devices and/or software components.

- *Software version, update revision, or FCO number*—This attribute includes information about software and firmware versions and, for hardware devices, the current field change order number. A **field change order** (FCO) occurs when a manufacturer performs an upgrade to a hardware component at the customer's premises. Tracking this information is particularly important when inventorying networking devices that function mainly through the software running on them. For example, a firewall device may have three version numbers associated with it: a Basic Input/Output System (BIOS) firmware version, the running operating system version, and the firewall appliance application software version. Each organization will have to determine which of those version numbers will be tracked, or if they would like to track all three.

- *Physical location*—This attribute does not apply to software elements. Nevertheless, some organizations may have license terms that indicate where software can be used. This may include systems leased at remote locations (so-called "co-lo equipment"), often described as being "in the cloud."

- *Logical location*—This attribute specifies where an asset can be found on the organization's network. The logical location is most applicable to networking devices and indicates the logical network segment (including "virtual local area networks" or VLANs) that houses the device.

- *Controlling entity*—This refers to the organizational unit that controls the asset. In some organizations, a remote location's onsite staff could be placed in control of network devices; in other organizations, a central corporate group might control all the network devices. The inventory should determine which group controls each asset because the controlling group will want a voice in determining how much risk that device can tolerate and how much expense can be sustained to add controls.

Identifying People, Procedures, and Data Assets Human resources, documentation, and data information assets are not as readily identified and documented as hardware and software. Responsibility for identifying, describing, and evaluating these information assets should be assigned to managers who possess the necessary knowledge, experience, and judgment. As these assets are identified, they should be recorded via a reliable data-handling process like the one used for hardware and software.

The record-keeping system should be flexible, allowing you to link assets to attributes based on the nature of the information asset being tracked. Basic attributes for various classes of assets include:

People

- Position name/number/ID—Avoid names; use position titles, roles, or functions.
- Supervisor name/number/ID—Avoid names; use position titles, roles, or functions.

- Security clearance level
- Special skills

Procedures

- Description
- Intended purpose
- Software/hardware/networking elements to which the procedure is tied
- Location where procedure documents are stored for reference
- Location where it is stored for update purposes

Data

- Classification
- Owner/creator/manager
- Size of data structure
- Data structure used (e.g., sequential or relational)
- Online or offline
- Location
- Backup procedures

Consider carefully what should be tracked for specific assets. Often, larger organizations find that that they can effectively track only a few valuable facts about the most critical information assets. For instance, a company may track only IP address, server name, and device type for its mission-critical servers. The organization might forgo additional attribute tracking on all devices and completely omit the tracking of desktop or laptop systems.

Classifying and Categorizing Assets

Once the initial inventory is assembled, you must determine whether its asset categories are meaningful to the organization's risk management program. Such a review may cause managers to further subdivide the categories presented in Table 8-1 or create new categories that better meet the needs of the risk management program. For example, if the category "Internet components" is deemed too general, it could be further divided into subcategories of servers, networking devices (routers, hubs, switches), protection devices (firewalls, proxies), and cabling.

The inventory should also reflect the sensitivity and security priority assigned to each information asset. A classification scheme should be developed (or reviewed, if already in place) that categorizes these information assets based on their sensitivity and security needs. Consider the following classification scheme for an information asset: *confidential*, *internal*, and *public*. Each of these classification categories designates the level of protection needed for a particular information asset. Some asset types, such as personnel, may require an alternative classification scheme that identifies the InfoSec processes used by the asset type. For example, based on need-to-know and right-to-update, an employee might be given a certain level of security clearance, which identifies the level of information that individual is authorized to use.

Classification categories must be comprehensive and mutually exclusive. "Comprehensive" means that all inventoried assets fit into a category; "mutually exclusive" means that each asset is found in only one category. For example, an organization may have a public key infrastructure certificate authority, which is a software application that provides crypto-graphic key management services. Using a purely technical standard, a manager could cate-gorize the application in the asset list of Table 8-1 as software, a general grouping with no special classification priority. Because the certificate authority must be carefully protected as part of the InfoSec infrastructure, it should be categorized into a higher priority classification, such as *software/security component/cryptography*, and it should be verified that no overlap-ping category exists, such as *software/security component/PKI*.

Assessing Values for Information Assets

As each information asset is identified, categorized, and classified, a relative value must be assigned to it. Relative values are comparative judgments intended to ensure that the most valuable informa-tion assets are given the highest priority when managing risk. It may be impossible to know in advance—in absolute economic terms—what losses will be incurred if an asset is compromised; however, a relative assessment helps to ensure that the higher value assets are protected first.

As each information asset is assigned to its proper category, posing the following basic ques-tions can help you develop the weighting criteria to be used for information asset valuation or impact evaluation. It may be useful to refer to the information collected in the business impact analysis (BIA) process (covered in Chapter 3) to help you assess a value for an asset.

- *Which information asset is the most critical to the success of the organization?* When determining the relative importance of each information asset, refer to the organization's mission statement or statement of objectives. From this source, determine which assets are essential for meeting the organization's objectives, which assets support the objec-tives, and which are merely adjuncts. For example, a manufacturing company that makes aircraft engines may decide that the process control systems that control the machine tools on the assembly line are the first order of importance. Although shipping and receiving data entry consoles are important to those functions, they may be less critical if alternatives are available or can be easily arranged. Another example is an online organi-zation such as Amazon.com. The Web servers that advertise the company's products and receive its orders 24 hours a day are essential, whereas the desktop systems used by the customer service department to answer customer e-mails are less critical.

- *Which information asset generates the most revenue?* The relative value of an infor-mation asset depends on how much revenue it generates—or, in the case of a nonprofit organization, how critical it is to service delivery. Some organizations have different systems in place for each line of business or service they offer. Which of these assets plays the biggest role in generating revenue or delivering services?

- *Which information asset generates the highest profitability?* Managers should evaluate how much profit depends on a particular asset. For instance, at Amazon.com, some servers support the book sales operations, others support the auction process, and still others support the customer book review database. Which of these servers contributes the most to profitability? Although important, the review database server does not directly generate profits. Note the distinction between revenues and profits: Some sys-tems on which revenues depend operate on thin or nonexistent margins and do not generate profits. In nonprofit organizations, you can determine what percentage of the agency's clientele receives services from the information asset being evaluated.

- *Which information asset is the most expensive to replace?* Sometimes an information asset acquires special value because it is unique. If an enterprise still uses a Model-129 keypunch machine to create special punch-card entries for a critical batch run, for example, that machine may be worth more than its cost, because spare parts or service providers may no longer be available. Another example is a specialty device with a long delivery time frame because of manufacturing or transportation requirements. Organizations must control the risk of loss or damage to such unique assets—for example, by buying and storing a backup device. Any device stored as such must, of course, be periodically updated and tested.

- *Which information asset is the most expensive to protect?* Some assets are by their nature difficult to protect, and formulating a complete answer to this question may not be possible until the risk identification phase is complete, because the costs of controls cannot be computed until the controls are identified. However, you can still make a preliminary assessment of the relative difficulty of establishing controls for each asset.

- *Which information asset's loss or compromise would be the most embarrassing or cause the greatest liability?* Almost every organization is aware of its image in the local, national, and international spheres. Loss or exposure of some assets would prove especially embarrassing. Microsoft's image, for example, was tarnished when an employee's computer system became a victim of the QAZ Trojan horse and, as a result, the latest version of Microsoft Office was stolen.[2]

You can use a worksheet, such as the one shown in Figure 8-2, to collect the answers to the preceding list of questions for later analysis.

System Name: SLS E-Commerce		
Date Evaluated: February 2008		
Evaluated By: D. Jones		
Information assets	**Data classification**	**Impact to profitability**
Information Transmitted:		
EDI Document Set 1 — Logistics BOL to outsourcer (outbound)	Confidential	High
EDI Document Set 2 — Supplier orders (outbound)	Confidential	High
EDI Document Set 2 — Supplier fulfillment advice (inbound)	Confidential	Medium
Customer order via SSL (inbound)	Confidential	Critical
Customer service Request via e-maill (inbound)	Private	Medium
DMZ Assets:		
Edge Router	Public	Critical
Web server #1—home page and core site	Public	Critical
Web server #2—Application server	Private	Critical
Notes: BOL: Bill of Lading DMZ: Demilitarized Zone EDI: Electronic Data Interchange SSL: Secure Sockets Layer		

Figure 8-2 Sample asset classification scheme

Copyright © 2014 Cengage Learning®.

You may also need to identify and add other institution-specific questions to the evaluation process.

 Throughout this chapter, numbers are assigned to example assets to illustrate the concepts being discussed. This highlights one of the challenging issues in risk management. While other industries use actuarially derived sources to make estimates, InfoSec risk management lacks such data. Many organizations use a variety of estimating methods to assess values. Some in the industry question the use of "guesstimated" values in calculations with other estimated values, claiming this degree of uncertainty undermines the entire risk management endeavor. Research in this field is ongoing, and you are encouraged to study those sections of Chapter 9 where alternative, qualitative risk management techniques are discussed.

Listing Assets in Order of Importance

The final step in the risk identification process is to list the assets in order of importance. This goal can be achieved by using a weighted factor analysis worksheet similar to the one shown in Table 8-2. In this process, each information asset is assigned a score for each critical factor. Table 8-2 uses values from 0.1 to 1.0. Your organization may choose to use another weighting system, such as 1 to 10 or 1 to 100. Each criterion has an assigned weight showing its relative importance in the organization.

Information Asset	Criterion 1: Impact on Revenue	Criterion 2: Impact on Profitability	Criterion 3: Impact on Public Image	Weighted Score
Criterion weight (1–100); must total 100	30	40	30	
EDI Document Set 1—Logistics bill of lading to outsourcer (outbound)	0.8	0.9	0.5	75
EDI Document Set 2—Supplier orders (outbound)	0.8	0.9	0.6	78
EDI Document Set 2—Supplier fulfillment advice (inbound)	0.4	0.5	0.3	41
Customer order via SSL (inbound)	1	1	1	100
Customer service request via e-mail (inbound)	0.4	0.4	0.9	55

Table 8-2   Example of a weighted factor analysis worksheet

Note: EDI = Electronic Data Interchange; SSL = Secure Sockets Layer

Copyright © 2014 Cengage Learning®.

A quick review of Table 8-2 shows that the Customer order via Secure Sockets Layer (SSL) (inbound) data flow is the most important asset on this worksheet, and that the EDI Document Set 2—Supplier fulfillment advice (inbound) is the least critical asset.

Threat Identification

As mentioned at the beginning of this chapter, the ultimate goal of risk identification is to assess the circumstances and setting of each information asset to reveal any vulnerabilities. Armed with a properly classified inventory, you can assess potential weaknesses in each information asset—a process known as **threat identification**.

Any organization typically faces a wide variety of threats. If you assume that every threat can and will attack every information asset, then the project scope becomes too complex. To make the process less unwieldy, each step in the threat identification and vulnerability identification processes is managed separately and then coordinated at the end. At every step, the manager is called on to exercise good judgment and draw on experience to make the process function smoothly.

Identify and Prioritize Threats and Threat Agents
Chapter 2 identified 12 categories of threats to InfoSec, which are listed alphabetically in Table 8-3. Each of these threats presents a unique challenge to InfoSec and must be handled with specific controls that directly address the particular threat and the threat agent's attack strategy. Before

Threat	Examples
Compromises to intellectual property	Software piracy or other copyright infringement
Deviations in quality of service from service providers	Fluctuations in power, data, and other services
Espionage or trespass	Unauthorized access and/or data collection
Forces of nature	Fire, flood, earthquake, lightning, etc.
Human error or failure	Accidents, employee mistakes, failure to follow policy
Information extortion	Blackmail threat of information disclosure
Sabotage or vandalism	Damage to or destruction of systems or information
Software attacks	Malware: viruses, worms, macros, denial-of-services, or script injections
Technical hardware failures or errors	Hardware equipment failure
Technical software failures or errors	Bugs, code problems, loopholes, backdoors
Technological obsolescence	Antiquated or outdated technologies
Theft	Illegal confiscation of equipment or information

Table 8-3   Threats to InfoSec

Copyright © 2014 Cengage Learning®.

threats can be assessed in the risk identification process, however, each threat must be further examined to determine its potential to affect the targeted information asset. In general, this process is referred to as threat assessment.

Posing the following questions can help you understand the various threats and their potential effects on an information asset:

- *Which threats present a danger to this organization's information assets in its current environment?* Not all threats endanger every organization, of course. Examine each of the categories in Table 8-3 and eliminate any that do not apply to your organization. It is unlikely for an organization to eliminate an entire category of threats, but doing so speeds up the threat assessment process. The Offline box titled "Threats to Information Security" describes the threats that some CIOs of major companies identified for their organizations. Although the box directly addresses only InfoSec, note that a weighted ranking of threats should be compiled for any information asset that is at risk. Once you have determined which threats apply to your organization, identify particular examples of threats within each category, eliminating those that are not relevant. For example, a company with offices on the 23rd floor of a high-rise building in Denver, Colorado, might not be subject to flooding unless they had critical infrastructure resources on a lower floor. Similarly, a firm with an office in Oklahoma City, Oklahoma, might not be concerned with landslides.

- *Which threats represent the gravest danger to the organization's information assets?* The amount of danger posed by a threat is sometimes difficult to assess. It may be tied to the probability that the threat will attack the organization, or it may reflect the amount of damage that the threat could create or the frequency with which the attack may occur. During this preliminary assessment phase, the analysis is limited to examining the existing level of preparedness and improving the strategy of InfoSec. The results should give a quick overview of the components involved.

As you will discover in Chapter 9, you can use both quantitative and qualitative measures to rank values. Since information in this case is preliminary, the organization may want to rank threats subjectively in order of danger. Alternatively, it may simply rate each of the threats on a scale of 1 to 5, with "1" designating an insignificant threat and "5" designating a highly significant threat.

Frequency of Attacks Remarkably, the number of detected attacks is steadily decreasing; after a peak in 2000, fewer organizations have reported unauthorized use of their computer systems (i.e., hacking) every year. Meanwhile, the number of organizations reporting malware attacks has dramatically increased. Unfortunately, the number of organizations willing to report the number or costs of successful attacks is also decreasing. The fact is, almost every company has experienced an attack. Whether that attack was successful depends on the company's security efforts; whether the perpetrators were caught or the organization was willing to report the attack is another matter entirely.

- *How much would it cost to recover from a successful attack?* One of the calculations that guides corporate spending on controls is the cost of recovery operations if an attack occurs and is successful. At this preliminary phase, it is not necessary to conduct a detailed assessment of the costs associated with recovering from a particular attack.

Offline
Threats to Information Security: Survey of Industry

What are the threats to InfoSec according to top computing executives?

Table 8-4 presents data collected in a study published in the Journal of Information Systems Security (JISSec) and based on a previous study published in the Communications of the ACM (CACM) that asked that very question. Based on the categories of threats presented earlier, more than 1,000 top computing executives were asked to rate each threat category on a scale ranging from "not significant" to "very significant." The results were converted to a five-point scale, where "5" represented "very significant," and are shown under the heading "Rate" in the following table. The executives were also asked to identify the top five threats to their organizations. Their responses were weighted, with five points assigned to a first-place vote and one point assigned to a fifth-place vote. The sum of weights is presented under the

2012 JISSec Ranking	Categories of Threats	Rate	Rank	Combined	2003 CACM Rank
1	Espionage or trespass	3.54	462	16.35	4
2	Software attacks	4.00	306	12.24	1
3	Human error or failure	4.30	222	9.55	3
4	Theft	3.61	162	5.85	7
5	Compromises to intellectual property	3.59	162	5.82	9
6	Sabotage or vandalism	3.11	111	3.45	5
7	Technical software failures or errors	3.17	105	3.33	2
8	Technical hardware failures or errors	2.88	87	2.51	6
9	Forces of nature	2.76	81	2.24	8
10	Deviations in quality of service from service providers	2.88	72	2.07	10
11	Technological obsolescence	2.66	57	1.52	11
12	Information extortion	2.68	18	0.48	12

Table 8-4   Weighted ranks of threats to InfoSec[3,4]

Source: Journal of Information Systems Security and Communications of the ACM.   *(Continued)*

heading "Rank" in the table. The two ratings were then calculated into a combined score by multiplying the two ratings and then dividing by 100. The final column shows the same threat as ranked in the 2003 CACM study.

Another popular study that examines the threats to InfoSec is the annual survey of computer users conducted by the Computer Security Institute. Table 8-5 shows biannual results since 2000.

Type of Attack or Misuse	2010/11	2008	2006	2004	2002	2000
Malware infection (revised after 2008)	67%	50%	65%	78%	85%	85%
Being fraudulently represented as sender of phishing message	39%	31%	(new category)			
Laptop/mobile hardware theft/loss	34%	42%	47%	49%	55%	60%
Bots/zombies in organization	29%	20%	(new category)			
Insider abuse of Internet access or e-mail	25%	44%	42%	59%	78%	79%
Denial-of-service	17%	21%	25%	39%	40%	27%
Unauthorized access or privilege escalation by insider	13%	15%	(revised category)			
Password sniffing	11%	9%	(new category)			
System penetration by outsider	11%		(revised category)			
Exploit of client Web browser	10%		(new category)			
Attack/Misuse categories with less than 10% responses (listed in decreasing order): Financial fraud						
Web site defacement						
Exploit of wireless network						
Other exploit of public-facing Web site						
Theft of or unauthorized access to PII or PHI due to all other causes						
Instant Messaging misuse						
Theft of or unauthorized access to IP due to all other causes						
Exploit of user's social network profile						
Theft of or unauthorized access to IP due to mobile device theft/loss						
Theft of or unauthorized access to PII or PHI due to mobile device theft/loss						
Exploit of DNS server						
Extortion or blackmail associated with threat of attack or release of stolen data						

Table 8-5   CSI survey results for types of attack or misuse (2000–2011)[5]

Source: CSI surveys 2000 to 2010/11 (www.gocsi.com)

Instead, organizations often create a subjective ranking or listing of the threats based on recovery costs. Alternatively, an organization can assign a rating for each threat on a scale of 1 to 5, with "1" representing "not expensive at all" and "5" representing "extremely expensive." If the information is available, a raw value (such as $5,000, $10,000, or $2 million) can be assigned. In other words, the goal at this phase is to provide a rough assessment of the cost to recover operations should the attack interrupt normal business operations.

- *Which threats would require the greatest expenditure to prevent?* Another factor that affects the danger posed by a particular threat is the amount it would cost to protect against that threat. Some threats have a nominal cost to protect against (e.g., malicious code), while others are very expensive, as in protections from forces of nature. Here again the manager ranks, rates, or attempts to quantify the level of danger associated with protecting against a particular threat by using the same techniques outlined earlier for calculating recovery costs. (See the Offline box on what issues executives are focusing their efforts on, financially.)

This list of questions may not cover everything that affects risk identification. An organization's specific guidelines or policies should influence the process and will inevitably require that some additional questions be answered.

Methods of Assessing Threats

A 2012 survey of computing executives also asked the following question: "In your organization's risk management efforts, what basis do you use to assess threats? (Select all that apply.)" The percentages of respondents who selected each option are shown in Table 8-6.

Vulnerability Assessment Once you have identified the information assets of the organization and documented some threat assessment criteria, you can begin to review

Answer Options	Response Percentage
Probability of occurrence	85.4%
Reputation loss if successful	77.1%
Financial loss if successful	72.9%
Cost to protect against	64.6%
Cost to recover from successful attack	64.6%
Frequency of attack	52.1%
Competitive advantage loss if successful	35.4%
None of these	6.3%

Table 8-6   Basis of threat assessment

Copyright © 2014 Cengage Learning®.

Offline
Expenditures for Threats to Information Security

Table 8-7 presents data from a JISSec study discussed earlier asked computing executives to list the priorities their organizations used in determining the expenditures devoted to InfoSec. Each executive responded by identifying his or her top five expenditures. A value of "5" was assigned to the highest expenditure, a value of "1" for the lowest. These ratings were used to create a rank order of the expenses. The results are presented in the following table, which compares the 2012 study with its 2003 CACM counterpart.

Threat (Based on Money and Effort Spent to Defend Against or React to It)	2012 Rating Average	2012 Ranking	2003 CACM Ranking
Espionage or trespass	4.07	1	6
Software attacks	3.94	2	1
Theft	3.18	3	7
Quality-of-service deviations by service providers	3.10	4	5
Forces of nature	3.06	5	10
Sabotage or vandalism	3.00	6	8
Technological obsolescence	2.99	7	9
Technical software failures or errors	2.71	8	3
Technical hardware failures or errors	2.64	9	4
Compromises to intellectual property	2.55	10	11
Human error or failure	2.25	11	2
Information extortion	2.00	12	12

Table 8-7   Weighted ranking of top threat-driven expenditures

Copyright © 2014 Cengage Learning®.

every information asset for each threat. This review leads to the creation of a list of vulnerabilities that remain potential risks to the organization. What are vulnerabilities? They are specific avenues that threat agents can exploit to attack an information asset. In other words, they are chinks in the asset's armor—a flaw or weakness in an information asset, security procedure, design, or control that can be exploited accidentally or on purpose to breach security. For example, Table 8-8 analyzes the threats to, and possible vulnerabilities of, a DMZ router.

A list like the one in Table 8-8 must be created for each information asset to document its vulnerability to each possible or likely attack. This list is usually long and shows all the vulnerabilities of the information asset. Some threats manifest themselves in multiple ways, yielding multiple vulnerabilities for that asset–threat pair. Of necessity, the process of listing vulnerabilities is somewhat subjective and is based on the experience and knowledge of the people who create the list. Therefore, the process works best when groups of people with diverse backgrounds work together in a series of brainstorming sessions. For instance, the

Threat	Possible Vulnerabilities
Compromises to intellectual property	Router has little intrinsic value, but other assets protected by this device could be attacked if it is compromised.
Espionage or trespass	Router has little intrinsic value, but other assets protected by this device could be attacked if it is compromised.
Forces of nature	All information assets in the organization are subject to forces of nature unless suitable controls are provided.
Human error or failure	Employees or contractors may cause an outage if configuration errors are made.
Information extortion	Router has little intrinsic value, but other assets protected by this device could be attacked if it is compromised.
Quality-of-service deviations from service providers	Unless suitable electrical power conditioning is provided, failure is probable over time.
Sabotage or vandalism	IP is vulnerable to denial-of-service attacks. Device may be subject to defacement or cache poisoning.
Software attacks	IP is vulnerable to denial-of-service attacks. Outsider IP fingerprinting activities can reveal sensitive information unless suitable controls are implemented.
Technical hardware failures or errors	Hardware could fail and cause an outage. Power system failures are always possible.
Technical software failures or errors	Vendor-supplied routing software could fail and cause an outage.
Technological obsolescence	If it is not reviewed and periodically updated, a device may fall too far behind its vendor support model to be kept in service.
Theft	Router has little intrinsic value, but other assets protected by this device could be attacked if it is compromised.

Table 8-8   Vulnerability assessment of a DMZ router

Copyright © 2014 Cengage Learning®.

team that reviews the vulnerabilities for networking equipment should include networking specialists, the systems management team that operates the network, InfoSec risk specialists, and even technically proficient users of the system.

The TVA Worksheet

At the end of the risk identification process, an organization should have a prioritized list of assets and their vulnerabilities. This list serves as the starting point (with its supporting documentation from the identification process) for the next step in the risk management process: risk assessment. Another list prioritizes threats facing the organization based on the weighted table discussed earlier. These two lists can be combined into a Threats-Vulnerabilities-Assets (TVA) worksheet, in preparation for the addition of vulnerability and control information during risk assessment. Along one axis lies the prioritized set of assets. Table 8-9 shows the placement of assets along the horizontal axis, with the most important asset at the left. The prioritized list of threats is placed along the vertical axis, with the most important or most dangerous threat listed at the top. The resulting grid provides a convenient method of examining the "exposure" of assets, allowing a simple

	Asset 1	Asset 2	....	....	....	....	....	....	....	....	....	Asset n
Threat 1												
Threat 2												
....												
....												
....												
....												
....												
....												
....												
....												
....												
Threat n												
Priority of Controls	1		2		3		4		5		6	
These bands of controls should be continued through all asset–threat pairs.												

Table 8-9   **Sample TVA spreadsheet**

Copyright © 2014 Cengage Learning®.

vulnerability assessment. We now have a starting point for our risk assessment, along with the other documents and forms.

As you begin the risk assessment process, create a list of the TVA "triples" to facilitate your examination of the severity of the vulnerabilities. For example, between Threat 1 and Asset 1 there may or may not be a vulnerability. After all, not all threats pose risks to all assets. If a pharmaceutical company's most important asset is its research and development database and that database resides on a stand-alone network (i.e., one that is not connected to the Internet), then there may be no vulnerability to external hackers. If the intersection of T1 and A1 has no vulnerability, then the risk assessment team simply crosses out that box. It is much more likely, however, that one or more vulnerabilities exist between the two, and as these vulnerabilities are identified, they are categorized as follows:

T1V1A1—Vulnerability 1 that exists between Threat 1 and Asset 1

T1V2A1—Vulnerability 2 that exists between Threat 1 and Asset 1

T2V1A1—Vulnerability 1 that exists between Threat 2 and Asset 1...

and so on.

In the risk assessment phase, discussed in the next section, not only are the vulnerabilities examined, the assessment team analyzes any existing controls that protect the asset from the threat or mitigate the losses that may occur. Cataloging and categorizing these controls is the next step in the TVA spreadsheet.

8

View Point
Getting at Risk

By George V. Hulme, an independent business and technology journalist who has covered information security for more than 15 years for such publications as InformationWeek and Information Security Magazine

The risks that organizations face have never been higher. More systems are interconnected today than ever before, and there is only one constant to those systems: change. Aside from hackers, disgruntled employees, and corporate spies, a growing number of laws and regulations (such as Sarbanes-Oxley, Gramm-Leach-Bliley, and the Health Information Portability and Accountability Act) have forever changed the role of the InfoSec professional as the gatekeeper of information and the manager of risk.

The role of the security professional is to help the organization manage risks poised against the confidentiality, integrity, and availability of its information assets. And the foundation of all InfoSec programs begins and forever lives with the process of risk assessment. Risk isn't static. Rather, risk is fluid and evolves over time. A risk assessment conducted on the first day of the month can be quite different than the same assessment conducted several weeks later. The levels of risks for particular information systems can change as quickly as IT systems change. And geopolitical events such as war,

(Continued)

economics, new employee hires, layoffs, and the steady introduction of new technologies all work to change the amount of risk faced by an organization.

The first task in risk assessment is to identify, assess, classify, and then decide on the value of digital assets and systems. Many believe that the most difficult aspect of risk assessment is uncovering the myriad system and configuration vulnerabilities that place systems at risk, but that's not so; an abundance of tools are available that can help automate that task. It's really deciding, organization-wide, the value of information and intellectual property that poses one of the most daunting challenges for the security professional.

How much is the research and development data worth? How much will it cost the organization if it loses access to the accounting or customer relationship management systems for a day? Without knowing the value of information and the systems that ensure its flow, it's impossible to make reasonable decisions about how much can reasonably be spent protecting that information. It makes little sense to spend $200,000 annually to protect information that wouldn't cost an organization more than $25,000 if exposed or lost. In a perfect world, with unlimited budgets and resources in hand, everything could be protected all of the time. But we don't live in a perfect world, and tough decisions need to be made. That means bringing together management, legal, human resources, physical security, and other groups in the organization. In assessing risk, you must decide what needs to be protected and how much that information is worth. Only then can reasonable decisions be made as to how to mitigate risk by implementing defensive measures and sound policy.

During the risk assessment process, vulnerabilities to systems will inevitably be uncovered. The challenge here is to determine which ones pose the greatest threats to protected assets. It's a challenge that security professionals face every day. Does a low-risk vulnerability (something unlikely to be exploited) on a system holding highly valuable corporate information need to be remediated more quickly than a high-risk vulnerability (one that is easily and likely to be exploited) on a system holding information of little value? Maybe. It all depends. And each situation is different.

Risk can never be entirely eliminated; it can only be managed to levels that an organization can tolerate. The best way to keep risk low is to remain eternally vigilant by following a four-step process: (1) identify new assets, vulnerabilities, and threats; (2) assess and classify assets, vulnerabilities, and threats; (3) remediate and defend; and (4) return to Step 1.

Risk Assessment

Assessing the relative risk for each vulnerability is accomplished via a process called **risk assessment**. Risk assessment assigns a risk rating or score to each specific vulnerability. While this number does not mean anything in absolute terms, it enables you to gauge the relative risk associated with each vulnerable information asset, and it facilitates the creation of comparative ratings later in the risk control process.

Introduction to Risk Assessment

Estimating risk is not an exact science. Some practitioners use calculated values for risk estimation, whereas others rely on broader methods of estimation. Figure 8-3 shows the factors, some of which are estimates, that go into the risk-rating estimate for each of the vulnerabilities.

The goal is to develop a repeatable method to evaluate the *relative* risk of each of the vulnerabilities that have been identified and added to the list. Chapter 9 describes how to determine more precise costs that may be experienced from vulnerabilities that lead to losses as well as projected expenses for the controls that reduce the risks. For now, you can use the simpler risk model shown in Figure 8-3 to evaluate the risk for each information asset. The next section describes the factors used to calculate the relative risk for each vulnerability.

Likelihood

Likelihood is the overall rating—a numerical value on a defined scale—of the probability that a specific vulnerability will be exploited. In "Special Publication 800-30," NIST recommends that vulnerabilities be assigned a likelihood rating between 0.1 (low) and 1.0 (high). For example, the likelihood of an employee or system being struck by a meteorite while indoors would be rated 0.1, while the likelihood of receiving at least one e-mail containing a virus or worm in the next year would be rated 1.0. You could also choose to use a number between 1 and 100, but not 0, since vulnerabilities with a 0 likelihood should have already been removed from the asset/vulnerability list. Whatever rating system you employ for assigning likelihood, use professionalism, experience, and judgment to determine the rating—and use it consistently. Whenever possible, use external references for likelihood values, after reviewing and adjusting them for your specific circumstances. For many asset/vulnerability combinations, existing sources have already determined their likelihood. For example:

- The likelihood of a fire has been estimated actuarially for each type of structure.
- The likelihood that a given e-mail will contain a virus or worm has been researched.
- The number of network attacks can be forecast depending on how many network addresses the organization has been assigned.

Risk is
The **likelihood** of the occurrence of a vulnerability
Multiplied by
The **value** of the information asset
Minus
The percentage of risk mitigated by **current controls**
Plus
The **uncertainty** of current knowledge of the vulnerability

---

Figure 8-3 Risk assessment estimate factors

Copyright © 2014 Cengage Learning®.

Assessing Potential Loss

Using the information documented during the risk identification process, you can assign weighted scores based on the value of each information asset. The actual number used will vary according to the needs of the organization. Some groups use a scale of 1–100, with "100" reserved for those information assets the loss of which would stop company operations within a few minutes. Other recommended scales, including the one in "NIST SP 800-30," use assigned weights in broad categories, with all-important assets having a value of 100, low-criticality assets having a value of 1, and all other assets having a medium value of 50. Still other scales employ weights from 1 to 10, or assigned values of 1, 3, and 5 to represent low-, medium-, and high-valued assets, respectively. Alternatively, you can create unique weighted values customized to your organization's specific needs. To be effective, the values must be assigned by asking the questions included in the section titled "Identify and Prioritize Threats and Threat Agents." These questions are restated here for easy reference:

- Which threats present a danger to this organization's assets in its current environment?
- Which threats represent the gravest danger to the organization's information assets?
- How much would it cost to recover from a successful attack?
- Which threats would require the greatest expenditure to prevent?

After reconsidering these questions, use the background information from the risk identification process and add to that information by posing yet another question:

- Which of the aforementioned questions is the most important to the protection of information from threats within this organization?

The answer to this question determines the priorities used in the assessment of vulnerabilities. Which is the most important to the organization—the cost to recover from a threat attack or the cost to protect against a threat attack? More generally, which of the threats has the highest probability of leading to a successful attack? Recall that the purpose of risk assessment is to look at the threats an organization faces in its current state. Once these questions are answered, move to the next step in the process: examining how current controls can reduce the risk faced by specific vulnerabilities.

Percentage of Risk Mitigated by Current Controls

If a vulnerability is fully managed by an existing control, it can be set aside. If it is partially controlled, estimate what percentage of the vulnerability has been controlled.

Uncertainty

It is not possible to know everything about every vulnerability, such as how likely an attack against an asset is, or how great an impact a successful attack would have on the organization. The degree to which a current control can reduce risk is also subject to estimation error. A factor that accounts for uncertainty must always be added to the equations; it consists of an estimate made by the manager using good judgment and experience.

Risk Determination

For the purpose of relative risk assessment, risk *equals* likelihood of vulnerability occurrence *times* value (or impact) *minus* percentage risk already controlled *plus* an element of uncertainty. To see how this equation works, consider the following scenario:

- Information asset A has a value score of 50 and one vulnerability: Vulnerability 1 has a likelihood of 1.0 with no current controls. You estimate that assumptions and data are 90 percent accurate.

- Information asset B has a value score of 100 and two vulnerabilities: Vulnerability 2 has a likelihood of 0.5 with a current control that addresses 50 percent of its risk; vulnerability 3 has a likelihood of 0.1 with no current controls. You estimate that assumptions and data are 80 percent accurate.

The resulting ranked list of risk ratings for the three vulnerabilities just described, using the equation *(value times likelihood) minus risk mitigated plus uncertainty*, is as follows:

- Asset A: Vulnerability 1 rated as $55 = (50 - 1.0) - 0\% + 10\%$ where

  $55 = (50 - 1.0) - ((50 - 1.0) - 0.0) + ((50 - 1.0) - 0.1)$

  $55 = 50 - 0 + 5$

- Asset B: Vulnerability 2 rated as $35 = (100 \times 0.5) - 50\% + 20\%$ where

  $35 = (100 - 0.5) - ((100 - 0.5) - 0.5) + ((100 - 0.5) - 0.2)$

  $35 = 50 - 25 + 10$

- Asset B: Vulnerability 3 rated as $12 = (100 - 0.1) - 0\% + 20\%$ where

  $12 = (100 - 0.1) - ((100 - 0.1) - 0.0) + ((100 - 0.1) - 0.2)$

  $12 = 10 - 0 + 2$

Likelihood and Consequences

Another approach to calculating risk based on likelihood is the likelihood and consequences rating from the Australian and New Zealand Risk Management Standard 4360,[6] which uses qualitative methods to determine risk based on a threat's probability of occurrence and expected results of a successful attack. **Qualitative risk assessment**, which is examined elsewhere in this chapter, consists of using categories instead of specific values to determine risk.

As shown in Table 8-10, consequences (i.e., impact assessment) are evaluated on five levels ranging from insignificant (level 1) to catastrophic (level 5). It is up to the organization to evaluate its threats and assign the appropriate consequence level.

Level	Descriptor	Example of Description
1	Insignificant	No injuries, low financial loss
2	Minor	First aid treatment, onsite release immediately contained, medium financial loss
3	Moderate	Medical treatment required, onsite release contained with outside assistance, high financial loss
4	Major	Extensive injuries, loss of production capability, offsite release with no detrimental effects, major financial loss
5	Catastrophic	Death, toxic release offsite with detrimental effect, huge financial loss

Table 8-10   **Consequence levels for organizational threats[7]**

Copyright © 2014 Cengage Learning®.

Level	Descriptor	Explanation
A	Almost certain	Is expected to occur in most circumstances
B	Likely	Will probably occur in most circumstances
C	Possible	Might occur at some time
D	Unlikely	Could occur at some time
E	Rare	May occur only in exceptional circumstances

Table 8-11 Likelihood levels for organizational threats[8]

Copyright © 2014 Cengage Learning®.

Table 8-11 shows the qualitative likelihood assessment levels ranging from A (almost certain) to E (rare). Again, the organization must determine the likelihood or probability of an attack from each specific threat category.

When the two are combined, the organization should be able to determine which threats represent the greatest danger to the organization's information assets, as shown in Table 8-10. The resulting rankings can then be inserted into the TVA tables for use in risk assessment.

Table 8-12 identifies the potential consequences at various risk levels. If the organization has a tie in two or more threats in the same resulting category (such as Extreme Risk), then a 5A would be ranked higher than a 5B or a 4A, and so on. Replacing the A through E categories

Risk Level	Consequences				
Likelihood	Insignificant 1	Minor 2	Moderate 3	Major 4	Catastrophic 5
A (almost certain)	H	H	E	E	E
B (likely)	M	H	H	E	E
C (possible)	L	M	H	E	E
D (unlikely)	L	L	M	H	E
E (rare)	L	L	M	H	H

Table 8-12 Qualitative risk assessment matrix

Note: E = Extreme risk: Immediate action required

H = High risk: Senior management attention required

M = Moderate risk: Management responsibility must be specified

L = Low risk: Management by routine procedures required

Source: Risk management plan templates and forms from www.treasury.act.gov.au/actia/Risk.htm

with a 5 (almost certain) to 1 (rare) would allow a simple multiplication for prioritization. For example, 3 (moderate) times 4 (likely) equals 12, versus 4 (major) times 4 (likely), which equals 16.

Identify Possible Controls

For each threat and its associated vulnerabilities that have residual risk, the organization should create a preliminary list of control ideas. The purpose of this list, which begins with the identification of extant controls, is to identify areas of residual risk that may nor may not need to be reduced. **Residual risk** is the risk that remains even after the existing control has been applied. "Controls," "safeguards," and "countermeasures" are all terms used to describe security mechanisms, policies, and procedures. These mechanisms, policies, and procedures counter attacks, reduce risk, resolve vulnerabilities, and otherwise improve the general state of security within an organization.

Three general categories of controls exist: policies, programs, and technical controls. You learned about policies in Chapter 4. **Programs** are activities performed within the organization to improve security; they include security education, training, and awareness programs. Technical controls—also known as "security technologies"—are the technical implementations of the policies defined by the organization. These controls, whether in place or planned, should be added to the TVA worksheet as they are identified.

Access Controls

Access controls specifically address the admission of users into a trusted area of the organization. These areas can include information systems, physically restricted areas such as computer rooms, and even the organization in its entirety. Access controls usually consist of a combination of policies, programs, and technologies.

A number of approaches to, and categories of, access controls exist. They can be mandatory, nondiscretionary, or discretionary. Each category of controls regulates access to a particular type or collection of information, as explained in Chapter 6.

Documenting the Results of Risk Assessment

The goal of the risk management process so far has been to identify information assets and their vulnerabilities and to rank them according to the need for protection. In preparing this list, a wealth of factual information about the assets and the threats they face is collected. Also, information about the controls that are already in place is collected. The final summarized document is the ranked vulnerability risk worksheet, as shown in Table 8-9. This document is an extension of the TVA spreadsheet discussed earlier, showing only the assets and relevant vulnerabilities. A review of this worksheet reveals similarities to the weighted factor analysis worksheet depicted in Table 8-2. Table 8-13 illustrates the use of a weighted spreadsheet to calculate risk vulnerability for a number of information assets. The columns in the worksheet shown in Table 8-13 are used as follows:

- *Asset*—List each vulnerable asset.

- *Asset impact*—Show the results for this asset from the weighted factor analysis worksheet. (In our example, this value is a number from 1 to 100.)

Asset	Asset Impact	Vulnerability	Vulnerability Likelihood	Risk-Rating Factor
Customer service request via e-mail (inbound)	55	E-mail disruption due to hardware failure	0.2	11
Customer service request via e-mail (inbound)	55	E-mail disruption due to software failure	0.2	11
Customer order via SSL (inbound)	100	Lost orders due to Web server hardware failure	0.1	10
Customer order via SSL (inbound)	100	Lost orders due to Web server or ISP service failure	0.1	10
Customer service request via e-mail (inbound)	55	E-mail disruption due to SMTP mail relay attack	0.1	5.5
Customer service request via e-mail (inbound)	55	E-mail disruption due to ISP service failure	0.1	5.5
Customer service request via e-mail (inbound)	55	E-mail disruption due to power failure	0.1	5.5
Customer order via SSL (inbound)	100	Lost orders due to Webserver denial-of-service attack	0.025	2.5
Customer order via SSL (inbound)	100	Lost orders due to Web server software failure	0.1	1
Customer order via SSL (inbound)	100	Lost orders due to Web server buffer overrun attack	0.1	1

Table 8-13 Ranked vulnerability risk worksheet

Copyright © 2014 Cengage Learning®.

- *Vulnerability*—List each uncontrolled vulnerability.
- *Vulnerability likelihood*—State the likelihood of the realization of the vulnerability by a threat agent as indicated in the vulnerability analysis step. (In our example, the potential values range from 0.1 to 1.0.)
- *Risk-rating factor*—Enter the figure calculated by multiplying the asset impact and its likelihood. (In our example, the calculation yields a number ranging from 0.1 to 100.)

Looking at Table 8-13, you may be surprised that the most pressing risk requires making the mail server or servers more robust. Even though the impact rating of the information asset represented by the customer service e-mail is only 55, the relatively high likelihood of a hardware failure makes it the most pressing problem.

Deliverable	Purpose
Information asset classification worksheet	Assembles information about information assets and their impact on or value to the organization
Weighted criteria analysis worksheet	Assigns a ranked value or impact weight to each information asset
TVA worksheet	Combines the output from the information asset identification and prioritization with the threat identification and prioritization and identifies potential vulnerabilities in the "triples"; also incorporates extant and planned controls
Ranked vulnerability risk worksheet	Assigns a risk-rating ranked value to each uncontrolled asset-vulnerability pair

Table 8-14   Risk identification and assessment deliverables

Copyright © 2014 Cengage Learning®.

8

Now that the risk identification process is complete, what should the documentation package look like? In other words, what are the deliverables from this stage of the risk management project? The risk identification process should designate what function the reports serve, who is responsible for preparing them, and who reviews them. The ranked vulnerability risk worksheet is the initial working document for the next step in the risk management process: assessing and controlling risk. Table 8-14 shows an example list of the worksheets that should have been prepared by an information asset risk management team up to this point.

In the last stage of the risk analysis (identification and assessment) process, you use the TVA worksheet, along with the other worksheets you have created, to develop a prioritized list of tasks. Obviously, the presence of uncontrolled vulnerabilities in high-ranking assets is the first priority for the implementation of new controls as part of the risk management process discussed in the next chapter. Before any additional controls are added, though, an organization must determine the levels of risk it is willing to accept, based on a cost-benefit analysis, which is the subject of Chapter 9.

Chapter Summary

- Risk management examines and documents an organization's information assets.

- Management is responsible for identifying and controlling the risks that an organization encounters. In the modern organization, the InfoSec group often plays a leadership role in risk management.

- A key component of a risk management strategy is the identification, classification, and prioritization of the organization's information assets.

- Assessment is the identification of assets, including all the elements of an organization's system: people, procedures, data, software, hardware, and networking elements.

- The human resources, documentation, and data information assets of an organization are not as easily identified and documented as tangible assets, such as hardware and software. These more elusive assets should be identified and described using knowledge, experience, and judgment.

- You can use the answers to the following questions to develop weighting criteria for information assets:

  - Which information asset is the most critical to the success of the organization?

  - Which information asset generates the most revenue?

  - Which information asset generates the highest profitability?

  - Which information asset is the most expensive to replace?

  - Which information asset is the most expensive to protect?

  - Which information asset's loss or compromise would be the most embarrassing or cause the greatest liability?

  - What questions should be added to cover the needs of the specific organization and its environment?

- After identifying and performing a preliminary classification of information assets, the threats facing an organization should be examined. There are 12 general categories of threats to InfoSec.

- Each threat must be examined during a threat assessment process that addresses the following questions: Which of these threats exist in this organization's environment? Which are the most dangerous to the organization's information? Which require the greatest expenditure for recovery? Which require the greatest expenditure for protection?

- Each information asset is evaluated for each threat it faces; the resulting information is used to create a list of the vulnerabilities that pose risks to the organization. This process results in an information asset and vulnerability list, which serves as the starting point for risk assessment.

- A Threats-Vulnerabilities-Assets (TVA) worksheet lists the assets in priority order along one axis, and the threats in priority order along the other axis. The resulting grid provides a convenient method of examining the "exposure" of assets, allowing a simple vulnerability assessment.

- The goal of risk assessment is the assignment of a risk rating or score that represents the relative risk for a specific vulnerability of a specific information asset.

- If any specific vulnerability is completely managed by an existing control, it no longer needs to be considered for additional controls.

- Controls, safeguards, and countermeasures should be identified for each threat and its associated vulnerabilities.

- In general, three categories of controls exist: policies, programs, and technologies.

- Access controls can be classified as mandatory, discretionary, or nondiscretionary.

- The risk identification process should designate what function the resulting reports serve, who is responsible for preparing them, and who reviews them. The TVA worksheet and the ranked vulnerability risk worksheet are the initial working documents for the next step in the risk management process: assessing and controlling risk.

Review Questions

1. What is risk management?

2. List and describe the key areas of concern for risk management.

3. Why is identification of risks, through a listing of assets and their vulnerabilities, so important to the risk management process?

4. According to Sun Tzu, what two things must be achieved to secure information assets successfully?

5. Who is responsible for risk management in an organization?

6. Which community of interest usually takes the lead in information asset risk management?

7. Which community of interest usually provides the resources used when undertaking information asset risk management?

8. In risk management strategies, why must periodic reviews be a part of the process?

9. Why do networking components need more examination from an InfoSec perspective than from a systems development perspective?

10. What value would an automated asset inventory system have for the risk identification process?

11. Which information attributes are seldom or never applied to software elements?

12. Which information attribute is often of great value for networking equipment when Dynamic Host Configuration Protocol (DHCP) is not used?

13. When you document procedures, why is it useful to know where the electronic versions are stored?

14. Which is more important to the information asset classification scheme, that it be comprehensive or that it be mutually exclusive?

15. What is the difference between an asset's ability to generate revenue and its ability to generate profit?

16. How many categories should a data classification scheme include? Why?

17. How many threat categories are listed in this chapter? Which is noted as being the most frequently encountered, and why?

18. What are vulnerabilities?

19. Describe the TVA worksheet. What is it used for?

20. Examine the simplest risk formula presented in this chapter. What are its primary elements?

Exercises

1. If an organization has three information assets to evaluate for risk management purposes, as shown in the accompanying data, which vulnerability should be evaluated for additional controls first? Which vulnerability should be evaluated last?

Data for Exercise 1:

- Switch L47 connects a network to the Internet. It has two vulnerabilities: (1) susceptibility to hardware failure, with a likelihood of 0.2, and (2) susceptibility to an SNMP buffer overflow attack, with a likelihood of 0.1. This switch has an impact rating of 90 and has no current controls in place. There is a 75 percent certainty of the assumptions and data.

- Server WebSrv6 hosts a company Web site and performs e-commerce transactions. It has Web server software that is vulnerable to attack via invalid Unicode values. The likelihood of such an attack is estimated at 0.1. The server has been assigned an impact value of 100, and a control has been implemented that reduces the impact of the vulnerability by 75 percent. There is an 80 percent certainty of the assumptions and data.

- Operators use the MGMT45 control console to monitor operations in the server room. It has no passwords and is susceptible to unlogged misuse by the operators. Estimates show the likelihood of misuse is 0.1. There are no controls in place on this asset, which has an impact rating of 5. There is a 90 percent certainty of the assumptions and data.

2. Using the Web, search for at least three tools to automate risk assessment. Collect information on automated risk assessment tools. What do they cost? What features do they provide? What are the advantages and disadvantages of each one?

3. Using the list of threats to InfoSec presented in this chapter, identify and describe three instances of each that were not mentioned in the chapter.

4. Using the data classification scheme presented in this chapter, identify and classify the information contained in your personal computer or personal digital assistant. Based on the potential for misuse or embarrassment, what information is confidential, sensitive but unclassified, or suitable for public release?

5. Using the asset valuation method presented in this chapter, conduct a preliminary risk assessment on the information contained in your home. Answer each of the valuation questions listed in the section of this chapter titled "Identify and Prioritize Threats and Threat Agents." What would it cost if you lost all your data?

6. Using the Internet, locate the National Association of Corporate Directors' Web site. Describe its function and purpose. What does this association say about board member liability for InfoSec issues?

Closing Case

Mike and Iris were flying home from the meeting. The audit committee's reaction had not been what they expected.

"I'm glad they understood the situation," Mike said. "I'd like you to start revising our risk management documentation to make it a little more general. It sounds like the board will want to take our approach company-wide soon."

Iris nodded and pulled out her notepad to make a to-do list.

Discussion

1. What will Iris have on her to-do list?

2. What resources can Iris call on to assist her?

Ethical Decision Making

Suppose that after they returned to the office, Mike was called to a private meeting with a senior executive from another division of the firm. During the discussion, Mike felt he was being subtly threatened with nonspecific but obviously devastating consequences to his career prospects at RWW as well as long-term damage to his professional reputation if he did not back off on his efforts to improve company-wide risk management at RWW. The other executive was adamant that the costs of improving the risk management process would hurt the firm without gaining any real improvement.

Was this executive simply expressing her disagreement with Mike's approach, or has some ethical line been crossed? Should Mike take any overt actions based on this conversation or inform others about the perceived threats? What could Mike do that would not embarrass the other executive and still offer him some protection in this situation?

8

Endnotes

1. Tzu, Sun. *The Art of War.* Translation by Samuel B. Griffith. Oxford, UK: Oxford University Press, 1988.

2. Quaglieri, Ernest. "The Hacking of Microsoft." *SANS Institute.* Accessed March 10, 2013 @ *www.giac.org/paper/gsec/488/hacking-microsoft/101184.*

3. Whitman, Michael, and Herb Mattord. "Threats to Information Security Revisited." *Journal of Information Systems Security*, 2012, 8(1).

4. Whitman, Michael. "Enemy at the Gates: Threats to Information Security." *Communications of the ACM*, August, 2003, 46(8).

5. This table is compiled from data published by the Computer Security Institute and the FBI over the years.

6. "AS/NZS 4360:1999: Risk Management." Accessed March 10, 2013 @ *www.schleupen .de/content/schleupen/schleupen013223/A.4.1.4_Australia_and_New_Zealand_Methodology _AS_NZ%25204360_1999.pdf.*

7. "Introduction to Territory Wide Risk Management: Risk Management Templates." *Australian Capital Territory Insurance Authority.* Accessed April 10, 2013 @ *www .treasury.act.gov.au/actia/RiskManagementTemplate.docx.*

8. Ibid.

## chapter 9

Risk Management: Controlling Risk

Weakness is a better teacher than strength. Weakness must learn to understand the obstacles that strength brushes aside.

MASON COOLEY, U.S. APHORIST (1927–2002)

Iris went into the manager's lounge to get a soda. As she was leaving, she saw Jane Harris—the accounting supervisor at Random Widget Works, Inc. (RWW)—at a table, poring over a spreadsheet that Iris recognized.

"Hi, Jane," Iris said. "Can I join you?"

"Sure, Iris," Jane said. "Perhaps you can help me with this form Mike wants us to fill out."

Jane was working on the asset valuation worksheet that Iris had designed to be completed by all RWW managers. The worksheet listed all of the information assets in Jane's department. Mike Edwards had asked each manager to provide three values for each item: its cost, its replacement value, and its ranked criticality to the company's mission, with the most important item being ranked number one. Mike hoped that Iris and the rest of the risk management team could use the data to build a consensus about the relative importance of various assets.

"What's the problem?" Iris asked.

"I understand these first two columns. But how am I supposed to decide what's the most important?"

"Well," Iris began, "with your accounting background, you could base your answers on some of the data you collect about each of these information assets. For this quarter, what's more important to senior management—revenue or profitability?"

"Profitability is almost always more important," Jane replied. "We have some projects that generate lots of revenue but operate at a loss."

"Well, there you go," Iris said. "Why not calculate the profitability margin for each listed item and use that to rate and rank them?"

"Oh, okay Iris. Thanks for the idea," Jane said. She then started making notes on her copy of the form.

LEARNING OBJECTIVES

Upon completion of this material, you should be able to:

- Recognize the strategy options used to control risk and be prepared to select from them when given background information

- Evaluate risk controls and formulate a cost-benefit analysis (CBA) using existing conceptual frameworks

- Explain how to maintain and perpetuate risk controls

- Describe popular approaches used in the industry to manage risk

Introduction

In the early days of information technology (IT), corporations used IT systems mainly to gain advantages over their competition. Managers discovered that establishing a competitive business model, method, or technique allowed an organization to provide a product or service that was superior in some decisive way, thus creating a competitive advantage. But this is seldom true today. The current IT industry has evolved from this earlier model to one in which almost all competitors operate using similar levels of automation. Because IT is now readily available, almost all organizations are willing to make the investment to react quickly to changes in the market. In today's highly competitive environment, managers realize that investing in IT systems at a level that merely maintains the status quo is no longer sufficient to gain a competitive advantage. In fact, even the implementation of new technologies does not necessarily enable an organization to gain or maintain a competitive lead. Instead, the concept of **competitive disadvantage**—the state of falling behind the competition—has emerged as a critical factor. Effective IT-enabled organizations now quickly absorb emerging technologies, not to gain or maintain the traditional competitive advantage but to avoid the possibility of losing market share when faltering systems make it impossible to maintain the current standard of service.

To keep up with the competition, organizations must design and create a safe environment in which business processes and procedures can function and evolve effectively. This environment must maintain confidentiality and privacy and assure the integrity and availability of organizational data. These objectives are met via the application of the principles of risk management.

This chapter builds on the concepts developed in Chapter 8, which focused on the identification of risk and the assessment of the relative impact from all identified vulnerabilities. That effort produced a list of documented vulnerabilities, ranked by criticality of impact. In this chapter, you will learn how to use such a list to assess options, estimate costs, weigh the relative merits of options, and gauge the benefits of various control approaches.

Controlling risk begins with an understanding of what risk mitigation strategies are and how to formulate them. The chosen strategy may include applying controls to some or all of the assets and vulnerabilities found in the ranked vulnerability worksheet prepared in Chapter 8. This chapter explores a variety of control approaches and then discusses how such approaches can be categorized. It also explains the critical concepts of CBA and residual risk, and it describes control strategy assessment and maintenance.

Risk Control Strategies

When an organization's general management team determines that risks from information security (InfoSec) threats are creating a competitive disadvantage, it empowers the IT and InfoSec communities of interest to control those risks. Once the project team for InfoSec development has created the ranked vulnerability worksheet (see Chapter 8), the team must choose one of five basic strategies to control the risks that arise from these vulnerabilities:

- *Defense*—Applying safeguards that eliminate or reduce the remaining uncontrolled risk
- *Transferal*—Shifting risks to other areas or to outside entities
- *Mitigation*—Reducing the impact to information assets should an attacker successfully exploit a vulnerability
- *Acceptance*—Understanding the consequences of choosing to leave a risk uncontrolled and then properly acknowledging the risk that remains without an attempt at control
- *Termination*—Removing or discontinuing the information asset from the organization's operating environment.

Defense

The **defense risk control strategy** attempts to prevent the exploitation of the vulnerability. This is the preferred approach and is accomplished by means of countering threats, removing vulnerabilities in assets, limiting access to assets, and adding protective safeguards. This approach is sometimes referred to as **avoidance**.

There are three common methods of risk defense:

- *Application of policy*—As discussed in Chapter 4, the application of policy allows all levels of management to mandate that certain procedures always be followed. For example, if the organization needs to control password use more tightly, it can implement a policy requiring passwords on all IT systems. But policy alone may not be enough. Effective management always couples changes in policy with the training and education of employees, or an application of technology, or both.
- *Application of training and education*—Communicating new or revised policy to employees may not be adequate to assure compliance. Awareness, training, and education are essential to creating a safer and more controlled organizational environment and to achieving the necessary changes in end-user behavior.
- *Implementation of technology*—In the everyday world of InfoSec, technical controls and safeguards are often required to reduce risk effectively. For example, systems administrators can configure systems to use passwords where policy requires them and where the administrators are both aware of the requirement and trained to implement it.

Risks can be avoided by countering the threats facing an asset or by eliminating the exposure of a particular asset. Eliminating the risk posed by a threat is virtually impossible, but it is possible to reduce the risk to an acceptable level.

Transferal

The **transferal risk control strategy** attempts to shift the risk to other assets, other processes, or other organizations. This goal may be accomplished by rethinking how services are offered, revising deployment models, outsourcing to other organizations, purchasing insurance, or implementing service contracts with providers.

In their best-selling book *In Search of Excellence*, management consultants Thomas Peters and Robert Waterman presented case studies of high-performing corporations. One of the eight characteristics of excellent organizations is that they "stick to their knitting," the authors wrote. "They stay reasonably close to the business they know."[1] What does this mean? It means that Nabisco focuses on the manufacture and distribution of foodstuffs, while General Motors focuses on the design and manufacture of cars and trucks. Neither company spends strategic energies on the technology for securing Web sites. They focus energy and resources on what they do best while relying on consultants or contractors for other types of expertise.

Organizations should consider this whenever they begin to expand their operations, including information and systems management, and even InfoSec. When an organization does not have adequate security management and administration experience, it should hire individuals or firms that provide expertise in those areas. For example, many organizations want Web services, including Web presences, domain name registration, and domain and Web hosting. Rather than implementing their own servers and hiring their own Webmasters, Web systems administrators, and even specialized security experts, savvy organizations hire Web consulting organizations. This approach allows them to transfer the risk associated with the management of these complex systems to other organizations with more experience in dealing with those risks. A side benefit of specific contract arrangements is that the provider is responsible for disaster recovery and, through service-level agreements, for guaranteeing server and Web site availability.

Of course, outsourcing is not without its own risks. It is up to the owner of the information asset, IT management, and the InfoSec team to ensure that the disaster recovery requirements of the outsourcing contract are sufficient and have been met before they are needed.

Mitigation

The **mitigation risk control strategy** is the control approach that attempts to reduce, by means of planning and preparation, the damage caused by a realized incident or disaster. This approach includes three types of plans, which you learned about in Chapter 3: the incident response (IR) plan, the disaster recovery (DR) plan, and the business continuity (BC) plan. Mitigation depends on the ability to detect and respond to an attack as quickly as possible. As was mentioned in Chapter 3, sometimes organizations use the term "business resumption" to describe a combined DR and BC plan.

Table 9-1 summarizes the three types of mitigation plans, including descriptions and examples of each.

Acceptance

As described earlier, mitigation is a control approach that attempts to reduce the effects of an exploited vulnerability by preparing to react if and when it occurs. In contrast, the

Plan	Description	Example	When Deployed	Time frame
Incident response (IR) plan	Actions an organization takes during incidents (attacks)	• List of steps to be taken during disaster • Intelligence gathering • Information analysis	As an incident or disaster unfolds	Immediate and real-time reaction
Disaster recovery (DR) plan	• Preparations for recovery should a disaster occur • Strategies to limit losses before and during a disaster • Step-by-step instructions to regain normalcy	• Procedures for the recovery of lost data • Procedures for the reestablishment of lost services • Shutdown procedures to protect systems and data	Immediately after the incident is labeled a disaster	Short-term recovery
Business continuity (BC) plan	Steps to ensure continuation of the overall business when the scale of a disaster exceeds the DRP's ability to quickly restore operations	• Preparation steps for activation of secondary data centers • Establishment of a hot site in a remote location	Immediately after the disaster is determined to affect the continued operations of the organization	Long-term organizational stability

Table 9-1 **Summary of mitigation plans**

Copyright © 2014 Cengage Learning®.

acceptance risk control strategy is the decision to do nothing to protect an information asset from risk, and to accept the outcome from any resulting exploitation. It may or may not be a conscious business decision. Unconscious acceptance of risk is not a valid approach to risk control. Acceptance is recognized as a valid strategy *only* when the organization has:

- Determined the level of risk posed to the information asset
- Assessed the probability of attack and the likelihood of a successful exploitation of a vulnerability
- Estimated the potential damage or loss that could result from attacks
- Evaluated potential controls using each appropriate type of feasibility
- Performed a thorough CBA
- Determined that the costs to control the risk to a particular function, service, collection of data, or information asset do not justify the cost of implementing and maintaining the controls

This strategy assumes that it can be a prudent business decision to examine the alternatives and conclude that the cost of protecting an asset does not justify the security expenditure. Suppose it would cost an organization $100,000 a year to protect a server. The security assessment determines that for $10,000 the organization could replace the information contained in the server, replace the server itself, and cover all associated recovery costs. Under those circumstances, management may be satisfied with taking its chances and saving the money that would otherwise be spent on protecting this particular asset.

An organization that decides on acceptance as a strategy for every identified risk of loss may in fact be unable to conduct proactive security activities and may have an apathetic approach to security in general. It is not acceptable for an organization to plead ignorance and thus abdicate its legal responsibility to protect employees' and customers' information. It is also unacceptable for management to hope that if they do not try to protect information, the opposition will imagine that little will be gained by an attack. The risks far outweigh the benefits of this approach, which usually ends in regret as the exploitation of the vulnerabilities causes a seemingly unending series of InfoSec lapses.

Termination

Like acceptance, the **termination risk control strategy** is based on the organization's need or choice *not* to protect an asset. Here, however, the organization does not wish the information asset to remain at risk and so removes it from the environment that represents risk.

Sometimes, the cost of protecting an asset outweighs its value. In other cases, it may be too difficult or expensive to protect an asset, compared to the value or advantage that asset offers the company. In either case, termination must be a conscious business decision, not simply the abandonment of an asset, which would technically qualify as acceptance.

Managing Risk

Risk appetite (also known as **risk tolerance**) is the quantity and nature of risk that organizations are willing to accept as they evaluate the trade-offs between perfect security and unlimited accessibility. For instance, a financial services company, regulated by government and conservative by nature, seeks to apply every reasonable control and even some invasive controls to protect its information assets. Other less closely regulated organizations may also be conservative and thus seek to avoid the negative publicity and perceived loss of integrity caused by the exploitation of a vulnerability. A firewall vendor might install a set of firewall rules that are far more stringent than necessary, simply because being hacked would jeopardize its market. Other organizations may take on dangerous risks because of ignorance. The reasoned approach to risk is one that balances the expense (in terms of finance and the usability of information assets) against the possible losses, if exploited.

James Anderson, Executive Consultant and Director at Emagined Security, formerly a senior executive with Inovant (the world's largest commercial processor of financial payment transactions), believes that InfoSec in today's enterprise should strive to be a "well-informed sense of assurance that the information risks and controls are in balance."[2] The key is for the organization to find balance in its decision-making processes and in its feasibility analyses, thereby assuring that its risk appetite is based on experience and facts, not on ignorance or wishful thinking.

When vulnerabilities have been controlled to the degree possible, there is often remaining risk that has not been completely removed, shifted, or planned for—in other words, residual risk. **Residual risk** is the amount of risk that remains after the organization has implemented policy, education and training, and technical controls and safeguards. Figure 9-1 illustrates how residual risk persists even after safeguards are implemented, reducing the levels of risk associated with threats, vulnerabilities, and information assets.

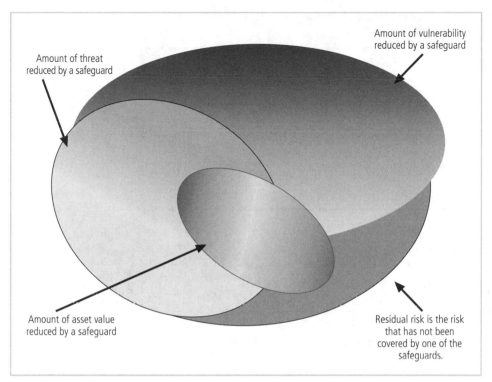

Figure 9-1 Residual risk

Copyright © 2014 Cengage Learning®.

Although it might seem counterintuitive, the goal of InfoSec is not to bring residual risk to zero; rather, it is to bring residual risk in line with an organization's risk appetite. If decision makers have been informed of uncontrolled risks and the proper authority groups within the communities of interest decide to leave residual risk in place, then the InfoSec program has accomplished its primary goal.

Figure 9-2 illustrates the process by which an organization chooses from among the risk control strategies. As shown in this diagram, after the information system is designed, you must determine whether the system has vulnerabilities that can be exploited. If a viable threat exists, determine what an attacker will gain from a successful attack. Then, estimate the expected loss the organization will incur if the vulnerability is successfully exploited. If this loss is within the range of losses the organization can absorb, or if the attacker's gain is less than the likely cost of executing the attack, the organization may choose to accept the risk. Otherwise, it must select one of the other control strategies.

Here are some rules of thumb for selecting a strategy (keeping in mind that the level of threat and the value of the asset should play major roles in strategy selection):

- *When a vulnerability (flaw or weakness) exists in an important asset*—Implement security controls to reduce the likelihood of a vulnerability being exploited.

- *When a vulnerability can be exploited*—Apply layered protections, architectural designs, and administrative controls to minimize the risk or prevent the occurrence of an attack.

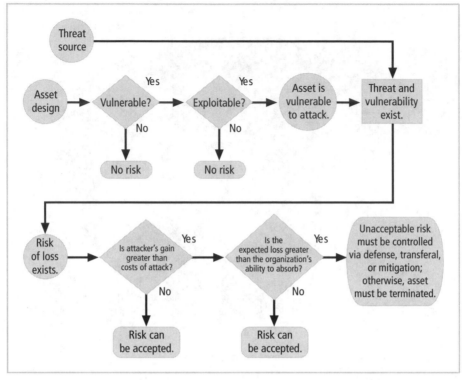

Figure 9-2 Risk-handling action points

Copyright © 2014 Cengage Learning®.

- *When the attacker's potential gain is greater than the costs of attack*—Apply protections to increase the attacker's cost or reduce the attacker's gain by using technical or managerial controls.

- *When the potential loss is substantial*—Apply design principles, architectural designs, and technical and nontechnical protections to limit the extent of the attack, thereby reducing the potential for loss.[3]

Once a control strategy has been selected and implemented, controls should be monitored and measured on an ongoing basis to determine their effectiveness and to maintain an ongoing estimate of the remaining risk. Figure 9-3 shows how this cyclical process ensures that risks are controlled.

At a minimum, each information asset–threat pair that was developed in the risk assessment created in Chapter 8 should have a documented control strategy that clearly identifies any residual risk that remains after the proposed strategy has been executed. This approach must articulate which of the fundamental risk-reducing strategies will be used and how multiple strategies might be combined. This process must justify the selection of the chosen strategies by referencing the feasibility studies. Organizations should document the outcome of the control strategy selection process for each information asset–threat pair in an action plan. This action plan includes concrete tasks, with accountability for each task being assigned to an organizational unit or to an individual. It may include hardware and software requirements, budget estimates, and detailed timelines.

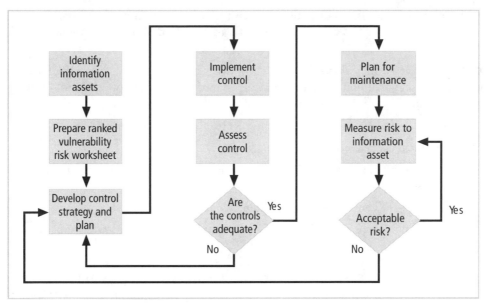

Figure 9-3 Risk control cycle

Copyright © 2014 Cengage Learning®.

Feasibility and Cost-Benefit Analysis

Before deciding on the strategy for a specific asset–vulnerability–threat combination, an organization must explore all readily accessible information about the economic and noneconomic consequences of an exploitation of the vulnerability, when the threat causes a loss to the asset. This exploration attempts to answer the question "What are the actual and perceived advantages of implementing a control as opposed to the actual and perceived disadvantages?"

While the advantages of a specific strategy can be identified in a number of ways, the primary way is to determine the value of the information assets it is designed to protect. There are also many ways to identify the disadvantages associated with specific risk controls. The following sections describe some of the more commonly used techniques for making these choices. Some of these techniques use dollar-denominated expenses and savings from economic cost avoidance, while others use noneconomic feasibility criteria. **Cost avoidance** is the money saved by using the defense strategy via the implementation of a control, thus eliminating the financial ramifications of an incident.

Cost-Benefit Analysis

The criterion most commonly used when evaluating a strategy to implement InfoSec controls and safeguards is economic feasibility. While any number of alternatives may solve a particular problem, some are more expensive than others. Most organizations can spend only a reasonable amount of time and money on InfoSec, although the definition of "reasonable" varies from organization to organization, even from manager to manager. Organizations can begin this type of economic feasibility analysis by valuing the information assets and determining the loss in value if those information assets became compromised. Common sense dictates that an organization should not spend more to protect an asset than it is worth. This decision-making process is called a **cost-benefit analysis (CBA)** or an economic feasibility study.

Cost Just as it is difficult to determine the value of information, it is difficult to determine the **cost** of safeguarding it. Among the items that affect the cost of a control or safeguard are the following:

- Cost of development or acquisition (hardware, software, and services)
- Training fees (cost to train personnel)
- Cost of implementation (installing, configuring, and testing hardware, software, and services)
- Service costs (vendor fees for maintenance and upgrades)
- Cost of maintenance (labor expense to verify and continually test, maintain, train, and update)

Benefit **Benefit** is the value to the organization of using controls to prevent losses associated with a specific vulnerability. It is usually determined by valuing the information asset or assets exposed by the vulnerability and then determining how much of that value is at risk and how much risk exists for the asset. This result is expressed as the annualized loss expectancy (ALE), which is defined later in this chapter.

Asset Valuation **Asset valuation** is the process of assigning financial value or worth to each information asset. As you learned in Chapter 8, the value of information differs within organizations and between organizations. Some argue that it is virtually impossible to accurately determine the true value of information and information-bearing assets, which is perhaps one reason why insurance underwriters currently have no definitive valuation tables for information assets. Asset valuation can draw on the assessment of information assets performed as part of the risk identification process you learned about in Chapter 8.

Asset valuation can involve the estimation of real or perceived costs. These costs can be selected from any or all of those associated with the design, development, installation, maintenance, protection, recovery, and defense against loss or litigation. Some costs are easily determined, such as the cost of replacing a network switch or the cost of the hardware needed for a specific class of server. Other costs are almost impossible to determine, such as the dollar value of the loss in market share if information on a firm's new product offerings is released prematurely and the company loses its competitive edge. A further complication is that over time some information assets acquire value that is beyond their **intrinsic value**—their essential worth. This higher **acquired value** is the more appropriate value in most cases.

Asset valuation is a complex process. While each organization must determine exactly how to value information assets, the approaches used include the following:

- *Value retained from the cost of creating the information asset*—Information is created or acquired at a cost, which can be calculated or estimated. For example, many organizations have developed extensive cost-accounting practices to capture the costs associated with collecting and processing data as well as the costs of developing and maintaining software. Software development costs include the efforts of the many people involved in the systems development life cycle for each application and system. Although this effort draws mainly on IT personnel, it also includes the user and general management community and sometimes the InfoSec staff. In today's marketplace, with high programmer salaries and even higher contractor expenses, the average cost to complete even a moderately sized application can quickly escalate. For example, multimedia-based training software that requires 350 hours of development for each hour of content will require the expenditure of as much as $10,000 per hour.

- *Value retained from past maintenance of the information asset*—It is estimated that for every dollar spent to develop an application or to acquire and process data, many more dollars are spent on maintenance over the useful life of the data or software. If actual costs have not been recorded, the cost can be estimated in terms of the human resources required to continually update, support, modify, and service the applications and systems.

- *Value implied by the cost of replacing the information*—The costs associated with replacing information should include the human and technical resources needed to reconstruct, restore, or regenerate the information from backups, independent transactions logs, or even hard copies of data sources. Most organizations rely on routine media backups to protect their information. When estimating recovery costs, keep in mind that you may have to hire contractors to carry out the regular workload that employees will be unable to perform during recovery efforts. Also, real-time information may not be recoverable from a tape backup unless the system has built-in journaling capabilities. To restore this information, the various information sources may have to be reconstructed, with the data reentered into the system and validated for accuracy. This restoration can take longer than it initially took to create the data.

- *Value from providing the information*—Separate from the cost of developing or maintaining the information is the cost of providing the information to those users who need it. Such costs include the values associated with the delivery of the information through databases, networks, and hardware and software systems. They also include the cost of the infrastructure necessary to provide access to and control of the information.

- *Value acquired from the cost of protecting the information*—The value of an asset is based in part on the cost of protecting it, and the amount of money spent to protect an asset is based in part on the value of the asset. While this is a seemingly unending circle, estimating the value of protecting an information asset can help you better understand the expense associated with its potential loss. The values listed previously are easy to calculate with some precision. This value and those that follow are likely to be estimates of cost.

- *Value to owners*—How much is your Social Security number worth to you? Or your telephone number? Placing a value on information can be quite a daunting task. A market researcher collects data from a company's sales figures and determines that a new product offering has a strong potential market appeal to members of a certain age group. While the cost of creating this new information may be small, how much is the new information actually worth? It could be worth millions if it successfully captures a new market share. Although it may be impossible to estimate the value of information to an organization or what portion of revenue is directly attributable to that information, it is vital to understand the overall cost that could be a consequence of its loss so as to better realize its value. Here again, estimating value may be the only method possible.

- *Value of intellectual property*—The value of a new product or service to a customer may ultimately be unknowable. How much would a cancer patient pay for a cure? How much would a shopper pay for a new flavor of cheese? What is the value of a logo or advertising slogan? Related but separate are intellectual properties known as trade secrets. Intellectual information assets are the primary assets of some organizations.

- *Value to adversaries*—How much is it worth to an organization to know what the competition is doing? Many organizations have established departments tasked with the assessment and estimation of the activities of their competition. Even organizations in traditionally nonprofit industries can benefit from knowing what is going on in political, business, and competitive organizations. Stories of industrial espionage abound, including the urban legend of Company A encouraging its employees to hire on as janitors at Company B. As custodial workers, the employees could snoop through open terminals, photograph and photocopy unsecured documents, and rifle through internal trash and recycling bins. Such legends support a widely accepted concept: Information can have extraordinary value to the right individuals. Similarly, stories are circulated of how disgruntled employees, soon to be terminated, steal information and present it to competitive organizations to curry favor and achieve new employment. Those who hire such applicants in an effort to gain from their larceny should consider whether benefiting from such a tactic is wise. After all, such thieves could presumably repeat their activities when they become disgruntled with their new employers.

- *Loss of productivity while the information assets are unavailable*—When a power failure occurs, effective use of uninterruptible power supply (UPS) equipment can prevent data loss, but users cannot create additional information. Although this is not an example of an attack that damages information, it is an instance in which a threat (deviations in quality of service from service providers) affects an organization's productivity. The hours of wasted employee time, the cost of using alternatives, and the general lack of productivity will incur costs and can severely set back a critical operation or process.

- *Loss of revenue while information assets are unavailable*—Have you ever been purchasing something at a retail store and your credit card would not scan? How many times did the salesperson rescan the card before entering the numbers manually? How long did it take to enter the numbers manually in contrast to the quick swipe? What if the credit card verification process was offline? Did the organization have a manual process to validate or process credit card payments in the absence of the familiar approval system? Many organizations have all but abandoned manual backups for automated processes. Sometimes, businesses may even have to turn away customers because their automated payments systems are inoperative. Most grocery stores no longer label each item with the price, because the UPC scanners and the related databases calculate the costs and inventory levels dynamically. Without these systems, could your grocery store sell goods? How much would the store lose if it could not? The Federal Emergency Management Agency estimates that 40 percent of businesses do not reopen after a disaster and another 25 percent fail within one year.[4] Imagine, instead of a grocery store, an online book retailer such as Amazon.com suffering a power outage. The entire operation is instantly closed. Even if Amazon's offering system were operational, what if the payment systems were offline? Customers could make selections but could not complete their purchases. While online businesses may be more susceptible to suffering a loss of revenue as a result of a loss of information, most organizations would be unable to conduct business if certain pieces of information were unavailable.

Once an organization has estimated the worth of various assets, it can begin to calculate the potential loss from the successful exploitation of vulnerability; this calculation yields an estimate of potential loss per risk. The questions that must be asked at this stage include the following:

- What damage could occur, and what financial impact would it have?
- What would it cost to recover from the attack, in addition to the financial impact of damage?
- What is the single loss expectancy for each risk?

A **single loss expectancy** (**SLE**) is the calculated value associated with the most likely loss from a single occurrence of a specific attack. It takes into account both the value of the asset and the expected percentage of loss that would occur from a particular attack. In other words:

$$\text{SLE} = \text{asset value (AV)} \times \text{exposure factor (EF)}$$

where

EF = the percentage loss that would occur from a given vulnerability being exploited

An example would be if a Web site had an estimated value of $1,000,000 (as determined by asset valuation) and a sabotage or vandalism (hacker defacement) scenario indicated that 10 percent of the Web site would be damaged or destroyed in such an attack (the EF). In this case, the SLE for the Web site would be $1,000,000 = 0.10 × $100,000. This estimate is then used to calculate another value, ALE, which is discussed later in this section.

As difficult as it is to estimate the value of information, estimating the probability of a threat occurrence or attack is even more difficult. There are not always tables, books, or records that indicate the frequency or probability of any given attack, although some sources are available for certain asset–threat pairs. For instance, the likelihood of a tornado or thunderstorm destroying a building of a specific type of construction within a specified region of the country is available to insurance underwriters. In most cases, however, an organization can rely only on its internal information to calculate the security of its information assets. Even if the network, systems, and security administrators have been actively and accurately tracking these threat occurrences, the organization's information will be sketchy at best. As a result, this information is usually estimated.

Usually, the probability of a threat occurring is depicted as a table that indicates how frequently an attack from each threat type is likely to occur within a given time frame (e.g., once every 10 years). This value is commonly referred to as the **annualized rate of occurrence** (**ARO**). ARO simply indicates how often you expect a specific type of attack to occur. For example, if a successful act of sabotage or vandalism occurs about once every two years, then the ARO would be 50 percent (0.5). A network attack that can occur multiple times per second might be successful once each month and would have an ARO of 12.

Once you determine the loss from a single attack and the likely frequency of successful attacks, you can calculate the overall loss potential per risk expressed as an **annualized loss expectancy (ALE)** using the values for the ARO and SLE from the previous sections.

$$ALE = SLE \times ARO$$

To use our previous example, if SLE = $100,000 and ARO = 0.5, then

$$ALE = \$100,000 \times 0.5$$
$$ALE = \$50,000$$

Thus, the organization could expect to lose $50,000 per year unless it increases its Web security. Now, armed with a figure to justify its expenditures for controls and safeguards, the InfoSec design team can deliver a budgeted value for planning purposes. Sometimes, noneconomic factors are considered in this process, so even when ALE amounts are not large, control budgets can be justified.

The CBA determines whether the benefit from a control alternative is worth the associated cost of implementing and maintaining the control. Such analyses may be performed before implementing a control or safeguard, or they can be performed after controls have been in place for a while. Observation over time adds precision to the evaluation of the benefits of the safeguard and the determination of whether the safeguard is functioning as intended. Although many CBA techniques exist, the easiest way to calculate it is by using the ALE from earlier assessments:

$$CBA = ALE(\text{precontrol}) - ALE(\text{postcontrol}) - ACS$$

where

$ALE(\text{precontrol})$ = ALE of the risk before the implementation of the control
$ALE(\text{postcontrol})$ = ALE examined after the control has been in place for a period of time
ACS = annual cost of the safeguard

Once the controls are implemented, it is crucial to examine their benefits continuously to determine when they must be upgraded, supplemented, or replaced. As Frederick Avolio states in his article "Best Practices in Network Security":

> *Security is an investment, not an expense. Investing in computer and network security measures that meet changing business requirements and risks makes it possible to satisfy changing business requirements without hurting the business's viability.*[5]

Other Methods of Establishing Feasibility

Earlier in this chapter, the concept of economic feasibility was employed to justify proposals for InfoSec controls. The next step in measuring how ready an organization is for the introduction of these controls is to determine the proposal's organizational, operational, technical, and political feasibility.

Organizational Feasibility Organizational feasibility analysis examines how well the proposed InfoSec alternatives will contribute to the efficiency, effectiveness, and overall operation of an organization. In other words, the proposed control approach must contribute to the organization's strategic objectives. Does the implementation align well with the strategic planning for the information systems, or does it require deviation from the planned expansion and management of the current systems? The organization should not invest in technology that changes its fundamental ability to explore certain avenues and opportunities. For example, suppose that a university decides to implement a new firewall. It takes a few months for the technology group to learn enough about the firewall to configure it completely. A few months after the implementation begins, it is discovered that the firewall as configured does not permit outgoing Web-streamed media. If one of the goals of the university is the pursuit of distance-learning opportunities, a firewall that prevents that type of communication has not met the organizational feasibility requirement and should be modified or replaced.

Operational Feasibility Operational feasibility refers to user acceptance and support, management acceptance and support, and the system's compatibility with the requirements of the organization's stakeholders. Operational feasibility is also known as **behavioral feasibility**. An important aspect of systems development is obtaining user buy-in on projects. If the users do not accept a new technology, policy, or program, it will inevitably fail. Users may not openly oppose a change, but if they do not support it, they will find ways to disable or otherwise circumvent it. One of the most common methods of obtaining user acceptance and support is via user engagement. User engagement and support can be achieved by means of three simple actions: communication, education, and involvement.

Organizations should *communicate* with system users, sharing timetables and implementation schedules, plus the dates, times, and locations of upcoming briefings and training. Affected parties must know the purpose of the proposed changes and how they will enable everyone to work more securely.

In addition, users should be *educated* and trained in how to work under the new constraints while avoiding any negative performance consequences. A major frustration for users is the implementation of a new program that prevents them from accomplishing their duties, with only a promise of eventual training.

Finally, those making changes should *involve* users by asking them what they want and what they will tolerate from the new systems. One way to do so this is to include representatives from the various constituencies in the development process.

Communication, education, and involvement can reduce *resistance* to change and can build *resilience* for change—that ethereal quality that allows workers to not only tolerate constant change but also understand that change is a necessary part of the job.

Technical Feasibility Unfortunately, many organizations rush to acquire new safeguards without thoroughly examining what is required to implement and use them effectively. Because the implementation of technological controls can be extremely complex, the project team must consider their **technical feasibility**—that is, determine whether the organization already has or can acquire the technology necessary to implement and support them. For example, does the organization have the hardware and software necessary to support a new firewall system? If not, can it be obtained?

Technical feasibility analysis also examines whether the organization has the technological expertise to manage the new technology. Does the staff include individuals who are qualified (and possibly certified) to install and manage a new firewall system? If not, can staff be spared from their current obligations to attend formal training and education programs to prepare them to administer the new systems, or must personnel be hired? In the current environment, how difficult is it to find qualified personnel?

Political Feasibility Politics has been defined as "the art of the possible."[6] **Political feasibility** analysis considers what can and cannot occur based on the consensus and relationships among the communities of interest. The limits imposed by the InfoSec controls must fit within the realm of the possible before they can be effectively implemented, and that realm includes the availability of staff resources.

In some organizations, the InfoSec community is assigned a budget, which they then allocate to activities and projects, making decisions about how to spend the money using their own judgment. In other organizations, resources are first allocated to the IT community of interest, and the InfoSec team must compete for these resources. Sometimes, the CBA and other forms of justification discussed in this chapter are used to make rational decisions about the relative merits of proposed activities and projects. Unfortunately, in other settings, these decisions are politically charged and do not focus on the pursuit of the greater organizational goals.

Another methodology for budget allocation requires the InfoSec team to propose and justify use of the resources for activities and projects in the context of the entire organization. This approach requires that arguments for InfoSec spending articulate the benefit of the expense for the whole organization, so that members of the organizational communities of interest can understand and perceive their value.

Alternatives to Feasibility Analysis

Rather than using CBA or some other feasibility reckoning to justify risk controls, an organization might look to alternative models. Many of these have been described in earlier chapters (especially in Chapter 5). A short list of alternatives is provided here:

- Benchmarking is the process of seeking out and studying the practices used in other organizations that produce the results you desire in your organization. When benchmarking, an organization typically uses either metrics-based or process-based measures.

- Due care and due diligence occur when an organization adopts a certain minimum level of security—that is, what any *prudent* organization would do in similar circumstances.

- Best business practices are considered those thought to be among the best in the industry, balancing the need to access information with adequate protection.

- The gold standard is for those ambitious organizations in which the best business practices are not sufficient. They aspire to set the standard for their industry and are thus said to be in pursuit of the gold standard.

- Government recommendations and best practices are useful for organizations that operate in industries regulated by governmental agencies. Government

View Point
The Intersection of Risk Management and Information Security

By Tim Callahan, an information technology, technology risk, and information security executive with more than 30 years' experience in the public and private sectors. Tim is currently the Senior Vice President, Business Continuity and Information Assurance, at SunTrust Bank in Atlanta, Georgia.

Many an InfoSec professional has wrestled with the topic of how risk management principles integrate with InfoSec practices. This generally rears its head when corporate is starting or refining an Enterprise Governance Risk and Compliance (EGRC) program. This article explores the complementary nature of the two programs.

For the purposes of this discussion, "information security" refers to the protection of the confidentiality, integrity, and availability of information, which includes systems, hardware, and networks that process, store, and transmit the information. As for "risk management," it involves understanding "risk" and applying the controls commensurate with the mission and goals of the organization.

At face value, we may see a paradox, or seeming contradiction, between these two concepts. One implies full protection, with less regard for cost or mission, while the other implies knowledge and judgment of the controls appropriate for the mission. A security purist might say we need to protect information at any cost, whereas someone with a risk management mindset would weigh the benefits, rewards, and practicality of controls against business objectives.

However, there is no contradiction. The InfoSec profession has matured significantly in the last decade; it has now grown beyond computer security and encompasses aspects of subdisciplines, including physical, personal, data, communications, and network security. The InfoSec professional sees these subdisciplines as interconnected, where a weakness in one affects the other. So the inclination is to ensure that all are "bolted down." This premise is correct; they are all interconnected and should be bolted down. However, over the last few years, cost and benefit discussions as well as a proliferation of security tools have influenced InfoSec practice. It is not practical to have every security tool that is available. This reality has brought about the merging of risk management practices with security practice.

As a result, one now sees job titles such as Information Risk Officer.

The majority of security professionals have embraced this concept; in fact, many would argue that the risk-based approach was always a part of the profession. There is truth to that; however, this merging has brought about a need for greater discipline in documenting risk practices. Solid risk management programs provide a formal process to understand risk, document risk, determine the organization's risk tolerance, and decide on the appropriate risk strategy.

Understanding risk begins with an "organizational" risk assessment. A good risk assessment will document the company profile: the company's purpose, its mission

(Continued)

and objectives, the risks found within the industry, the risks that are particular to the company (based on internal and external threat), and the company's tolerance for risk. As part of the assessment, risk should be considered in terms of the threat level, the regulatory environment, and the impacts to an organization's reputation. These should all be viewed from an industry-specific aspect. A bank, for instance, would have different concerns than a manufacturing company. Also, being secured in one aspect does not mean being secured in all aspects. Whereas an organization may have sound practices in addressing perceived threats, it may not be compliant with regard to its regulatory environment. Another organization may have sound practices to defend from threats and may meet all matters of regulatory compliance but still have a negative reputation with the public. All should be addressed.

Risk assessment should define controls that may be in place that reduce or mitigate the risk. The assessment should also document the strategy for risk management in terms of defense, transferal, mitigation, acceptance, or termination. Within InfoSec, there are places where the strategy should be one of termination. For instance, technology is sometimes employed that detects a threat and seeks to eliminate the threat. A simple example would be eliminating all malware. In other instances, there could be a strategy of risk acceptance if the risk is deemed low or if the protection cost far outweighs the penalty.

You may be wondering, "Why should I go to all this trouble? I just want to secure the environment!" Well, the goal of a formal risk management program is to employ a governance framework to achieve a known and consistent state—a state that can be measured, discussed, and continuously improved in an organized manner over time. Additionally, a formal program provides a way to ensure that corporate governance entities such as a corporate risk committee or the board of directors has sufficient awareness of risk and what the program is doing to address risk. One can then align the security program with the threat level, the regulatory environment, and the need to defend the organization's reputation. This will manage agreed-upon risk and help prioritize security initiatives. The program, in essence, provides a form of corporate agreement on what the security professional should be working toward. It is actually liberating in that sense.

In summary, the key to solid risk management is to understand your company's objectives, risk tolerance, and risk profile, and then make risk-based decisions that meet the company's mission and objective.

recommendations, which are, in effect, requirements, can also serve as excellent sources for information about what some organizations may be doing, or are required to do, to control InfoSec risks.

- A baseline is derived by comparing measured actual performance against established standards for the measured category.

Recommended Risk Control Practices

Assume that a risk assessment has determined it is necessary to protect a particular asset from a particular threat, at a cost of up to $50,000. Unfortunately most budget authorities focus on the "up to" and then try to cut a percentage off the total figure to save the organization money. This tendency underlines the importance of developing strong justifications for specific action plans and of providing concrete estimates in those plans.

Consider also that each control or safeguard affects more than one asset–threat pair. If a new $50,000 firewall is installed to protect the Internet connection infrastructure from hackers launching port-scanning attacks, the same firewall may also protect other information assets from other threats and attacks. The final choice may call for a balanced mixture of controls that provides the greatest value for as many asset–threat pairs as possible. This example reveals another facet of the problem: InfoSec professionals manage a dynamic matrix covering a broad range of threats, information assets, controls, and identified vulnerabilities. Each time a control is added to the matrix, it undoubtedly changes the ALE for the information asset vulnerability for which it has been designed, and it may also change the ALE for other information asset vulnerabilities. To put it more simply, if you put in one safeguard, you decrease the risk associated with all subsequent control evaluations. To make matters worse, the action of implementing a control may change the values assigned or calculated in a prior estimate.

Between the difficult task of valuing information assets and the dynamic nature of the ALE calculations, it is no wonder that organizations typically look for a more straightforward method of implementing controls. This preference has prompted an ongoing search for ways to design security architectures that go beyond the direct application of specific controls for specific information asset vulnerability. The following sections cover some of these alternatives.

Qualitative and Hybrid Measures

The steps described previously use actual values or estimates to create a quantitative assessment. In some cases, an organization might be unable to determine these values. Fortunately, risk assessment steps can be executed using estimates based on a qualitative assessment. For example, instead of placing a value of once every 10 years for the ARO, the organization might list all possible attacks on a particular set of information and rate each in terms of its probability of occurrence—high, medium, or low. The qualitative approach uses labels to assess value rather than numbers.

A more granular approach, the hybrid assessment, tries to improve upon the ambiguity of qualitative measures without resorting to the unsubstantiated estimation used for quantitative measures. Hybrid assessment uses scales rather than specific estimates. For example, a scale might range from 0, representing no chance of occurrence, to 10, representing almost certain occurrence. Organizations may, of course, prefer other scales: 0–10, 1–5, 0–20. These same scales can be used in any situation requiring a value, even in asset valuation. For example, instead of estimating that a particular piece of information is worth $1,000,000, you might value information on a scale of 1–20, where 1 indicates relatively worthless information and 20 indicates extremely critical information, such as a certain soda manufacturer's secret recipe or the 11 herbs and spices of a popular chicken vendor.

Delphi Technique

How do you calculate the values and scales used in qualitative and quantitative assessment? An individual can pull the information together based on personal experience, but, as the saying goes, "two heads are better than one"—and a team of heads is better than two. The **Delphi technique**, named for the oracle at Delphi, which predicted the future (in Greek mythology), is a process whereby a group rates or ranks a set of information. The individual responses are compiled and then returned to the group for another iteration. This process continues until the entire group is satisfied with the result. This technique can be applied to the development of scales, asset valuation, asset or threat ranking, or any scenario that can benefit from the input of more than one decision maker.

The OCTAVE Methods

Until now, this book has presented a general treatment of risk management, synthesizing information and methods from many sources to present the customary or usual approaches that organizations use to manage risk. This and the following sections present alternative approaches to risk management that come from a single source. One such source, the Operationally Critical Threat, Asset, and Vulnerability Evaluation (OCTAVE) Method, is an InfoSec risk evaluation methodology that allows organizations to balance the protection of critical information assets against the costs of providing protective and detection controls. This process can enable an organization to measure itself against known or accepted good security practices and then establish an organization-wide protection strategy and InfoSec risk mitigation plan. (For more detailed information about the OCTAVE Method, you can download its implementation guide from *www.cert.org/octave/omig.html*.)

Promoted by the Computer Emergency Response Team (CERT) Coordination Center (*www.cert.org*), the OCTAVE process can enable an organization to measure itself against known and accepted good security practices and then establish an organization-wide protection strategy and InfoSec risk mitigation plan. There are three variations of the OCTAVE Method:

- The original OCTAVE Method, which forms the basis for the OCTAVE body of knowledge and which was designed for large organizations (300 or more users)
- OCTAVE-S, for smaller organizations of about 100 users
- OCTAVE-Allegro, a streamlined approach for InfoSec assessment and assurance

For more information on these OCTAVE methods, see *www.cert.org/octave*.

Microsoft Risk Management Approach

Microsoft has recently updated its Security Risk Management Guide, which can be found at *http://technet.microsoft.com/en-us/library/cc163143.aspx*. The guide provides the company's approach to the risk management process. Because this version is comprehensive, easily scalable, and repeatable, it is summarized here and discussed in additional detail in the Appendix.[7]

Microsoft asserts that risk management is not a stand-alone subject and should be part of a general governance program to allow the organizational general-management community of interest to evaluate the organization's operations and make better, more informed decisions. The purpose of the risk management process is to prioritize and manage security risks. Microsoft presents four phases in its security risk management process:

1. Assessing risk
2. Conducting decision support
3. Implementing controls
4. Measuring program effectiveness

These four phases, which are described in detail in the Appendix, provide an overview of a program that is similar to the methods presented earlier in the text, including the OCTAVE Method. Microsoft, however, breaks the phases into fewer, more manageable pieces.

FAIR

Factor Analysis of Information Risk (FAIR), a risk management framework developed by Jack A. Jones, can help organizations understand, analyze, and measure information risk. The outcomes are more cost-effective information risk management, greater credibility for the InfoSec profession, and a foundation from which to develop a scientific approach to information risk management. The FAIR framework, as described on the host Web site (*http://fairwiki.riskmanagementinsight.com*), includes:

- A taxonomy for information risk
- Standard nomenclature for information risk terms
- A framework for establishing data collection criteria
- Measurement scales for risk factors
- A computational engine for calculating risk
- A modeling construct for analyzing complex risk scenarios

Basic FAIR analysis comprises 10 steps in four stages:

Stage 1—Identify Scenario Components

1. Identify the asset at risk.
2. Identify the threat community under consideration.

Stage 2—Evaluate Loss Event Frequency (LEF)

3. Estimate the probable Threat Event Frequency (TEF).
4. Estimate the Threat Capability (TCap).
5. Estimate Control Strength (CS).

6. Derive Vulnerability (Vuln).

7. Derive Loss Event Frequency (LEF).

Stage 3—Evaluate Probable Loss Magnitude (PLM)

8. Estimate worst-case loss.

9. Estimate probable loss.

Stage 4—Derive and Articulate Risk

10. Derive and articulate risk.

Unlike other risk management frameworks, FAIR relies on the qualitative assessment of many risk components, using scales with value ranges—for example, very high to very low. Figure 9-4 shows the basic structure of the FAIR method.

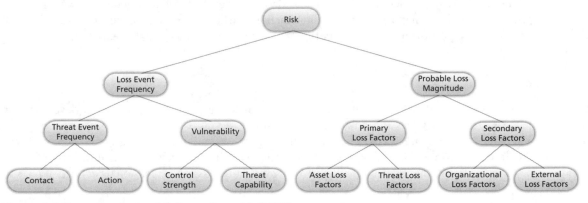

Figure 9-4 Factor analysis of information risk (FAIR)

Source: Copyright © 2014 Cengage Learning®. (Based on concepts from Jack A. Jones)[8]

ISO 27005 Standard for InfoSec Risk Management

The ISO 27000 series includes a standard for the performance of risk management: ISO 27005 (*www.27000.org/iso-27005.htm*), which includes a five-stage risk management methodology:

1. Risk assessment

2. Risk treatment

3. Risk acceptance

4. Risk communication

5. Risk monitoring and review

NIST Risk Management Model

As was briefly discussed in Chapter 8, the National Institute of Standards and Technology (NIST) has modified its fundamental approach to systems management and certification/ accreditation to one that follows the industry standard of effective risk management. As discussed in "Special Publication 800-39: Managing Information Security Risk: Organization, Mission, and Information System View" (*http://csrc.nist.gov/publications/nistpubs/800-39 /SP800-39-final.pdf*):

Risk management is a comprehensive process that requires organizations to: (i) frame risk (i.e., establish the context for risk-based decisions); (ii) assess risk; (iii) respond to risk once determined; and (iv) monitor risk on an ongoing basis using effective organizational communications and a feedback loop for continuous improvement in the risk-related activities of organizations. Risk management is carried out as a holistic, organization-wide activity that addresses risk from the strategic level to the tactical level, ensuring that risk-based decision making is integrated into every aspect of the organization.

The first component of risk management addresses how organizations frame risk or establish a risk context—that is, describing the environment in which risk-based decisions are made. The purpose of the risk framing component is to produce a risk management strategy that addresses how organizations intend to assess risk, respond to risk, and monitor risk—making explicit and transparent the risk perceptions that organizations routinely use in making both investment and operational decisions. The risk frame establishes a foundation for managing risk and delineates the boundaries for risk-based decisions within organizations. Establishing a realistic and credible risk frame requires that organizations identify: (i) risk assumptions (e.g., assumptions about the threats, vulnerabilities, consequences/impact, and likelihood of occurrence that affect how risk is assessed, responded to, and monitored over time); (ii) risk constraints (e.g., constraints on the risk assessment, response, and monitoring alternatives under consideration); (iii) risk tolerance (e.g., levels of risk, types of risk, and degree of risk uncertainty that are acceptable); and (iv) priorities and trade-offs (e.g., the relative importance of missions/business functions, trade-offs among different types of risk that organizations face, time frames in which organizations must address risk, and any factors of uncertainty that organizations consider in risk responses). The risk framing component and the associated risk management strategy also include any strategic-level decisions on how risk to organizational operations and assets, individuals, other organizations, and the Nation, is to be managed by senior leaders/executives. Integrated, enterprise-wide risk management includes, for example, consideration of: (i) the strategic goals/objectives of organizations; (ii) organizational missions/business functions prioritized as needed; (iii) mission/business processes; (iv) enterprise and InfoSec architectures; and (v) system development life cycle processes.

The second component of risk management addresses how organizations assess risk within the context of the organizational risk frame. The purpose of the risk assessment component is to identify: (i) threats to organizations (i.e., operations, assets, or individuals) or threats directed through organizations against other organizations or the Nation; (ii) vulnerabilities internal and external to organizations; (iii) the harm (i.e., consequences/impact) to organizations that may occur given the potential for threats exploiting vulnerabilities; and (iv) the likelihood that harm will occur. The end result is a determination of risk (i.e., the degree of harm and likelihood of harm occurring). To support the risk assessment component, organizations identify: (i) the tools, techniques, and methodologies that are used to assess risk; (ii) the assumptions related to risk assessments; (iii) the constraints that may affect risk assessments; (iv) roles and responsibilities; (v) how risk assessment information is collected, processed, and communicated throughout organizations; (vi) how risk assessments are conducted within organizations; (vii) the frequency of risk assessments; and (viii) how threat information is obtained (i.e., sources and methods).

The third component of risk management addresses how organizations respond to risk once that risk is determined based on the results of risk assessments. The purpose of the risk response component is to provide a consistent, organization-wide, response to risk in accordance with the organizational risk frame by: (i) developing alternative courses of action for responding to risk; (ii) evaluating the alternative courses of action; (iii) determining appropriate courses of action consistent with organizational risk tolerance; and (iv) implementing risk responses based on selected courses of action. To support the risk response component, organizations describe the types of risk responses that can be implemented (i.e., accepting, avoiding, mitigating, sharing, or transferring risk). Organizations also identify the tools, techniques, and methodologies used to develop courses of action for responding to risk, how courses of action are evaluated, and how risk responses are communicated across organizations and as appropriate, to external entities (e.g., external service providers, supply chain partners).

The fourth component of risk management addresses how organizations monitor risk over time. The purpose of the risk monitoring component is to: (i) verify that planned risk response measures are implemented and InfoSec requirements derived from/traceable to organizational missions/business functions, federal legislation, directives, regulations, policies, and standards, and guidelines, are satisfied; (ii) determine the ongoing effectiveness of risk response measures following implementation; and (iii) identify risk-impacting changes to organizational information systems and the environments in which the systems operate.

To support the risk monitoring component, organizations describe how compliance is verified and how the ongoing effectiveness of risk responses is determined (e.g., the types of tools, techniques, and methodologies used to determine the sufficiency/correctness of risk responses and if risk mitigation measures are implemented correctly, operating as intended, and producing the desired effect with regard to reducing risk). In addition, organizations describe how changes that may impact the ongoing effectiveness of risk responses are monitored.[9]

This approach is illustrated in Figure 9-5.

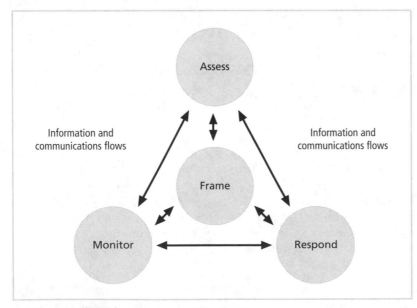

Figure 9-5 NIST risk management process

Source: NIST.[10]

Other Methods

The few methods described in this section are by no means all of the other available methods. In fact, there are two organizations that compare methods and provide recommendations for risk management tools that the public can use:

- *European Network and Information Security Agency (ENISA)*—This agency of the European Union ranks 12 tools using 22 different attributes. It also provides a utility on its Web site that enables users to compare risk management methods or tools (*www .enisa.europa.eu/activities/risk-management/current-risk/risk-management-inventory*). The primary risk management process promoted by ENISA is shown in Figure 9-6.

- *New Zealand's IsecT Ltd—An independent Governance, Risk Management and Compliance consultancy, IsecT maintains the ISO 27001 Security Web site at http:// iso27001security.com.* This Web site describes a large number of risk management methods (*www.iso27001security.com/html/risk_mgmt.html*).

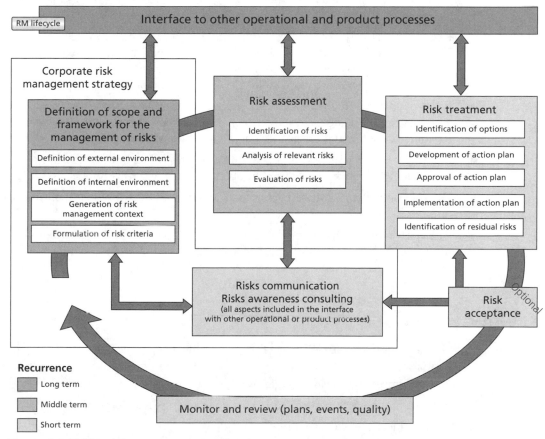

Figure 9-6 ENISA risk management process

Source: © 2005–2013 by the European Network and Information Security Agency (ENISA).[11]

Chapter Summary

- Once vulnerabilities are identified and ranked, a strategy to control the risks must be chosen. Five control strategies are: defense, transferal, mitigation, acceptance, and termination.

- Economic feasibility studies determine and compare costs and benefits from potential controls (often called a "cost-benefit analysis"). Other forms of feasibility analysis include analyses based on organizational, operational, technical, and political factors.

- An organization must be able to place a dollar value on each collection of information and the information assets it owns. There are several methods an organization can use to calculate these values.

- Single loss expectancy (SLE) is calculated from the value of the asset and the expected percentage of loss that would occur from a single successful attack. Annualized loss expectancy (ALE) represents the potential loss per year.

- Cost-benefit analysis (CBA) determines whether a control alternative is worth its associated cost. CBA calculations are based on costs before and after controls are implemented and the cost of the controls. Other feasibility analysis approaches can also be used.

- Organizations may choose alternatives to feasibility studies to justify applying InfoSec controls, including: benchmarking with either metrics-based measures or process-based measures; due care and/or due diligence; best security practices up to and including the near-mythic gold standard; and/or baselining.

- Risk appetite defines the quantity and nature of risk that organizations are willing to accept as they evaluate the trade-offs between perfect security and unlimited accessibility. Residual risk is the amount of risk unaccounted for after the application of controls.

- It is possible to repeat risk analysis using estimates based on a qualitative assessment. The Delphi technique can be used to obtain group consensus on risk assessment values.

- Once a control strategy has been implemented, the effectiveness of controls should be monitored and measured.

- Alternative approaches to risk management include the OCTAVE Method, the Microsoft risk management approach, ISO 27005, the NIST risk management approach, and FAIR.

Review Questions

1. What is competitive advantage? How has it changed in the years since the IT industry began?

2. What is competitive disadvantage? Why has it emerged as a factor?

3. What are the five risk control strategies presented in this chapter?

4. Describe the strategy of defense.

5. Describe the strategy of transferal.

6. Describe the strategy of mitigation.

7. Describe the strategy of acceptance.

8. Describe residual risk.

9. What four types of controls or applications can be used to avoid risk?

10. Describe how outsourcing can be used for risk transference.

11. What conditions must be met to ensure that risk acceptance has been used properly?

12. What is risk appetite? Explain why risk appetite varies from organization to organization.

13. What is a cost-benefit analysis?

14. What is the difference between intrinsic value and acquired value?

15. What is single loss expectancy? What is annual loss expectancy?

16. What is the difference between benchmarking and baselining?

17. What is the difference between organizational feasibility and operational feasibility?

18. What is the difference between qualitative measurement and quantitative measurement?

19. What is the OCTAVE Method? What does it provide to those who adopt it?

20. How does Microsoft define "risk management"? What phases are used in its approach?

Exercises

1. Using the following table, calculate the SLE, ARO, and ALE for each threat category listed.

XYZ Software Company (Asset value: $1,200,000 in projected revenues)		
Threat Category	**Cost per Incident**	**Frequency of Occurrence**
Programmer mistakes	$5,000	1 per week
Loss of intellectual property	$75,000	1 per year
Software piracy	$500	1 per week
Theft of information (hacker)	$2,500	1 per quarter
Theft of information (employee)	$5,000	1 per 6 months
Web defacement	$500	1 per month
Theft of equipment	$5,000	1 per year
Viruses, worms, Trojan horses	$1,500	1 per week
Denial-of-service attack	$2,500	1 per quarter
Earthquake	$250,000	1 per 20 years
Flood	$250,000	1 per 10 years
Fire	$500,000	1 per 10 years

Copyright © 2014 Cengage Learning®

2. How did the XYZ Software Company arrive at the values shown in the table that is included in Exercise 1? For each row in the table, describe the process of determining the cost per incident and the frequency of occurrence.

3. How could we determine EF if there is no percentage given? Which method is easier for determining the SLE: a percentage of value lost or cost per incident?

4. Assume a year has passed and XYZ has improved its security. Using the following table, calculate the SLE, ARO, and ALE for each threat category listed.

XYZ Software Company (Asset value: $1,200,000 in projected revenues)				
Threat Category	Cost per Incident	Frequency of Occurrence	Cost of Controls	Type of Control
Programmer mistakes	$5,000	1 per month	$20,000	Training
Loss of intellectual property	$75,000	1 per 2 years	$15,000	Firewall/IDS
Software piracy	$500	1 per month	$30,000	Firewall/IDS
Theft of information (hacker)	$2,500	1 per 6 months	$15,000	Firewall/IDS
Theft of information (employee)	$5,000	1 per year	$15,000	Physical security
Web defacement	$500	1 per quarter	$10,000	Firewall
Theft of equipment	$5,000	1 per 2 year	$15,000	Physical security
Viruses, worms, Trojan horses	$1,500	1 per month	$15,000	Antivirus
Denial-of-service attack	$2,500	1 per 6 months	$10,000	Firewall
Earthquake	$250,000	1 per 20 years	$5,000	Insurance/backups
Flood	$50,000	1 per 10 years	$10,000	Insurance/backups
Fire	$100,000	1 per 10 years	$10,000	Insurance/backups

Copyright © 2014 Cengage Learning®.

Why have some values changed in the following columns: Cost per Incident and Frequency of Occurrence? How could a control affect one but not the other?

5. Assume that the costs of controls presented in the table for Exercise 4 were unique costs directly associated with protecting against that threat. In other words, do not worry about overlapping costs between threats. Calculate the CBA for each control. Are they worth the costs listed?

6. Using the Web, research the costs associated with the following items when implemented by a firm with 1,000 employees and 100 servers:

   • Managed antivirus software (not open source) licenses for 500 workstations

   • Cisco firewall (other than residential models from LinkSys)

   • Tripwire host-based IDS for 10 servers

- Java programming continuing education training program for 10 employees
- Checkpoint Firewall solutions

Closing Case

Mike and Iris were reviewing the asset valuation worksheets that had been collected from all the company managers.

"Iris," Mike said after a few minutes, "the problem, as I see it, is that no two managers gave us answers that can be compared to each other's. Some gave only one value, and some didn't actually use a rank order for the last part. In fact, we don't know what criteria were used to assess the ranks or even where they got the cost or replacement values."

"I agree," Iris said, nodding. "These values and ranks are really inconsistent. This makes it a real challenge to make a useful comprehensive list of information assets. We're going to have to visit all the managers and figure out where they got their values and how the assets were ranked."

Discussion

1. If you could have spoken to Mike Edwards before he distributed the asset valuation worksheets, what advice would you have given him to make the consolidation process easier?

2. How would you advise Mike and Iris to proceed with the worksheets they already have in hand?

Ethical Decision Making

Suppose Mike and Iris make a decision to simply take the higher of each of the values without regard to how the values were determined by the person who made the initial assessment. Then, they determine their own rankings among all of the compiled assets. When the list is later included in the planning process, they represent it as being authoritative since it came from "all of the managers."

Is this method, even if it is faster and easier, an ethical way to do business? Why or why not?

Endnotes

1. Peters, Thomas, and Robert Waterman. *In Search of Excellence: Lessons from America's Best-Run Companies*. New York: Harper and Row, 2004.

2. Anderson, James. "Panel Comments at 2002 Garage Technology Venture's State of the Art Conference," 2002.

3. "Special Publication 800-30, Revision 1: Guide for Conducting Risk Assessments." *National Institute of Standards and Technology (NIST)*, September 2012.

4. "Ready Business Mentoring Guide Working with Small Businesses to Prepare for Emergencies" *FEMA*. Accessed December 17, 2012 @ *www.ready.gov/document/ready -business-mentoring-guide-working-small-businesses-prepare-emergencies*.

5. Avolio, Frederick. "Best Practices in Network Security." *Network Computing*, March 20, 2000. Accessed March 19, 2013 @ *www.networkcomputing.com/1105/1105f2.html.*

6. Mann, Thomas. "Politics Is Often Defined as the Art of the Possible." Speech in the Library of Congress, Washington, DC, May 29, 1945. Bismark, Otto Von. Interview (11 August 1867) with Friedrich Meyer von Waldeck of the St. Petersburgische Zeitung; reprinted in *Fürst Bismarck: neue Tischgespräche und Interviews*, Vol. 1, p. 248.

7. "Microsoft Security Risk Management Guide." *Microsoft.com*, March 15, 2006. Microsoft. Accessed June 13, 2013 @ *http://technet.microsoft.com/en-us/library/cc163143 .aspx.*

8. Jones, J. "An Introduction to Factor Analysis of Information Risk (FAIR): A Framework for Understanding, Analysing, and Measuring Information Risk." (2005). Accessed July 1, 2013 @ *www.riskmanagementinsight.com/media/documents/FAIR _Introduction.pdf.*

9. "SP 800-39: Managing Information Security Risk: Organization, Mission, and Information System View." *National Institute of Standards and Technology*, March 2011. Accessed December 17, 2012 @ *http://csrc.nist.gov/publications/nistpubs/800-39 /SP800-39-final.pdf.*

10. "SP 800-37, Rev. 1: Guide for Applying the Risk Management Framework to Federal Information Systems: A Security Life Cycle Approach." National Institute of Standards and Technology, February 2010. Accessed July 1, 2013 @ *http://csrc.nist.gov.*

11. ENISA. Accessed July 25, 2013 @ *www.enisa.europa.eu/activities/risk-management /current-risk/risk-management-inventory/rm-process.*

## chapter 10

Protection Mechanisms

*If you think technology can solve your security problems, then
you don't understand the problems and you don't understand
the technology.*

BRUCE SCHNEIER

One night toward the end of his shift, Drew Brown, a technician at Random Widget Works,
Inc. (RWW), received a call from his wife. One of their children was ill, and she wanted
Drew to pick up some medicine on his way home from work. He decided to leave a few min-
utes early.

Like all watch-standing employees in the operations center, Drew had a procedures manual,
which was organized sequentially. He used the checklists for everyday purposes and had an
index to look up anything else he needed. Only one unchecked box remained on the checklist
when Drew snapped the binder closed and hurriedly secured his workstation. That oversight
would cause the whole company grief in the next few hours.

Since he was the second-shift operator and RWW did not have a third shift in its data center,
Drew carefully reviewed the room shutdown checklist next to the door, making sure all the
room's environmental, safety, and physical security systems were set correctly. That activated
the burglar alarm, so Drew quickly exited the room and the building, and was soon on his
way to the drugstore.

At about the same time, a 10th-grader in San Diego was up late, sitting at her computer.
Her parents assumed she was listening to music while chatting with school friends online.

In fact, she had become bored with chatting and had discovered some new friends on the Internet—friends who shared her interest in programming. One of these new friends sent the girl a link to a new *warez* (illegally copied software) site.

The girl downloaded a kit called Blendo from the warez site. Blendo is a tool that helps novice hackers create attack programs that combine a mass e-mailer with a worm, a macro virus, and a network scanner. The girl clicked her way through the configuration options, clicked a button labeled "custom scripts," and pasted in a script that one of her new friends had e-mailed to her. This script was built to exploit a brand-new vulnerability (announced only a few hours before). Although she didn't know it, the anonymous high-schooler had created new malware that was soon to bring large segments of the Internet to a standstill.

She exported the attack script, attached it to an e-mail, and sent it to an anonymous remailer service to be forwarded to as many e-mail accounts as possible. The 10th-grader had naively set up a mailback option to an anonymous e-mail account so she could track the progress of her creation. Thirty minutes later, she checked that anonymous e-mail account and saw that she had more than 800,000 new messages; the only reason there were not even more messages was that her mailbox was full.

Back at RWW, the e-mail gateway was sorting and forwarding all the incoming e-mail. The mailbox for sales@rww.biz always received a lot of traffic, as did service@rww.biz. Tonight was no exception. Unfortunately for RWW, and for the second-shift operator who had failed to download and install the patch that fixed the new vulnerability, which had been announced by the vendor, the young hacker's attack code tricked the RWW mail server into running the program. The RWW mail server, with its high-performance processors, vast RAM storage, and high-bandwidth Internet connection, began to do three things at once: It sent an infected e-mail to everyone with whom RWW had ever traded e-mail; it infected every RWW server that the e-mail server could reach; and it started deleting files, randomly, from every folder on each infected server.

Within seconds, the network intrusion detection system had determined that something was afoot. By then, it was too late to stop the infection, but just before it sputtered into silence, the system sent a message to Iris's smartphone.

LEARNING OBJECTIVES

Upon completion of this material, you should be able to:

- Describe the various access control approaches, including authentication, authorization, and biometric access controls

- Identify the various types of firewalls and the common approaches to firewall implementation

- Enumerate and discuss the current issues in dial-up access and protection

- Identify and describe the types of intrusion detection systems and the strategies on which they are based

- Explain cryptography and the encryption process, and compare and contrast symmetric and asymmetric encryption

Introduction

You should know by now that technical controls alone cannot secure an information technology (IT) environment, but they are almost always an essential part of the information security (InfoSec) program. Managing the development and use of technical controls requires some knowledge and familiarity with the technology that enables them. In this chapter, you will learn about firewalls, intrusion detection systems, encryption systems, and some other widely used security technologies. The chapter is designed to help you evaluate and manage the technical controls used by InfoSec programs. If you are seeking expertise in the configuration and maintenance of technical control systems, you will need education and training beyond the overview presented here.

Technical controls can enable policy enforcement where human behavior is difficult to regulate. A password policy that specifies the strength of the password (its length and the types of characters it uses), regulates how often passwords must change, and prohibits the reuse of passwords would be impossible to enforce by asking each employee if he or she had complied. This type of requirement is best enforced by the implementation of a rule in the operating system.

Figure 10-1 illustrates how technical controls can be implemented at a number of points in a technical infrastructure. The technical controls that defend against threats from outside the organization are shown on the left side of the diagram. The controls that defend against threats from within the organization are shown on the right side of the diagram. Because individuals inside an organization often have direct access to the information, they can circumvent many of the most potent technical controls. Controls that can be applied to this human element are also shown on the right side of the diagram.

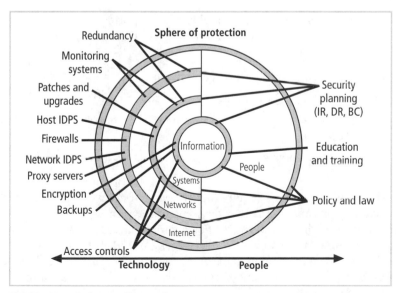

Figure 10-1 Sphere of security

Copyright © 2014 Cengage Learning®.

Access Controls

As explained in Chapter 6, **access controls** regulate the admission of users into trusted areas of the organization—both logical access to information systems and physical access to the organization's facilities. Access control is maintained by means of a collection of policies, programs to carry out those policies, and technologies that enforce policies. Access control approaches involve four processes: obtaining the identity of the entity requesting access to a logical or physical area (identification), confirming the identity of the entity seeking access to a logical or physical area (authentication), determining which actions that entity can perform in that logical or physical area (authorization), and documenting the activities of the authorized individual and systems (accountability). A successful access control approach—whether intended to control logical or physical access—always incorporates all four of these elements, known collectively as IAAA (I triple-A).

Identification

Identification is a mechanism that provides information about an unverified entity—called a **supplicant**—that wants to be granted access to a known entity. The label applied to the supplicant is called an identifier (ID). The ID must be a unique value that can be mapped to one and only one entity within the security domain being administered. Some organizations use composite IDs that concatenate elements—department codes, random numbers, or special characters—to make unique IDs within the security domain. Most organizations use a single piece of unique information, such as name or first initial with surname. These IDs are assigned to both those in the organization and those outside the organization who need access to the organization's secured systems and services.

Authentication

Authentication is the process of validating a supplicant's purported identity. It ensures that the entity requesting access is the entity it claims to be. There are four types of authentication mechanisms:

- Something you *know* (e.g., a password or passphrase)
- Something you *have* (e.g., a cryptographic token or smart card)
- Something you *are* (such as fingerprints, palm prints, hand topography, hand geometry, and retina and iris scans)
- Something you *produce* (such as a voice or signature that is analyzed using pattern recognition)

Certain critical logical or physical areas require higher levels of access controls and therefore use **strong authentication**—at minimum, two different authentication mechanisms (usually something you have and something you know). For example, access to a bank's automated teller machine (ATM) requires a banking card plus a personal identification number (PIN). Such systems are called two-factor or multifactor authentication because more than one separate mechanism is used. Strong authentication requires that one of the mechanisms be something other than what you know.

The following sections describe each of the four authentication mechanisms.

Something You Know This authentication mechanism verifies the user's identity by means of a password, passphrase, or some other unique authentication code, such as a PIN.

The technical infrastructure for something you know is commonly built into computer and network operating systems software and is in use unless it has been deliberately disabled. In some older client operating systems, such as Windows 95 and Windows 98, password systems are widely known to be insecure. Implementing other authentication mechanisms often requires separate supplemental physical devices. Some product vendors offer these hardware controls as built-in features; for example, some laptop vendors include thumbprint readers on certain models.

A **password** is a secret word or combination of characters that only the user should know. One of the biggest security debates focuses on password complexity. A password should be difficult to guess, which means it cannot be a word that is easily associated with the user, such as the name of a spouse, child, or pet. Nor should it be a series of numbers easily associated with the user, such as a phone number, Social Security number, or birth date. At the same time, the password must be something the user can easily remember, which means it should be short or have an association with the user that is not accessible to others.

A **passphrase** is a plain-language phrase, typically longer than a password, from which a **virtual password** is derived. For example, while a typical password might be 23skedoo, a passphrase could be May The Force Be With You Always, from which the virtual password MTFBWYA is derived. Another way to create a virtual password is to use a set of construction rules applied to facts you know very well, such as the first three letters of your last name, a hyphen, the first two letters of your first name, an underscore, the first two letters of your mother's maiden name, a hyphen, and the first four letters of the city in which you were born. This may sound complicated, but once memorized, the construction rules are easy to use. If you add another rule to substitute numeric digits for certain letters—1 for L or I, 0 for O, and 3 for E, and capitalize the first letter of each section, then you have a very powerful virtual password that you can easily reconstruct. Using the preceding rules would create a virtual password for Charlie Moody (born in Atlanta, mother's maiden name Meredith) of M00-Ch_M3-At1a, a very strong password.

Another method for creating strong passwords is to use a password memory support software application such as eWallet from Ilium Software (*www.iliumsoft.com/ewallet*), as is shown in Figure 10-2. This application, and other similar ones, provides an encrypted database to store the system name (or URL), username, and password for a large number of systems, as well as things like credit card numbers, frequent flyer numbers, and any portable data that needs protecting. Most systems like this use strong encryption, such as 256-bit AES, which is described later in this chapter.

How important is it to have a long, not-obvious password? As shown in Table 10-1, the longer the password, the lower the odds of it being guessed in a brute-force attack using random bit combinations (you will learn more about such attacks later in this chapter).

A good rule of thumb is to require that passwords be at least 10 characters long and contain at least one letter, one number, and one special character. If the system allows case-sensitive passwords (or requires them), then at least one uppercase and one lowercase letter should be used as well.

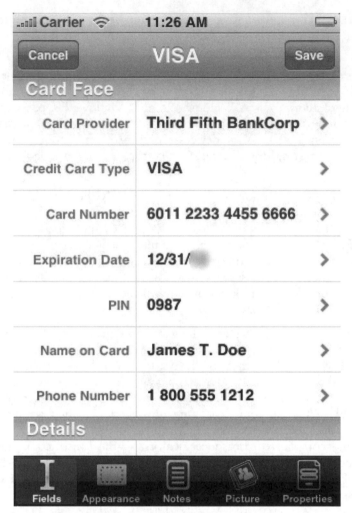

Figure 10-2 eWallet from Ilium Software

Source: Ilium Software.

Something You Have This authentication mechanism makes use of something (a card, key, or token) that the user or the system has. While there are many implementations of this mechanism, one example is a **dumb card,** a category that includes ID and ATM cards with magnetic strips containing the digital (and often encrypted) PIN against which user input is compared. A more capable object is the **smart card,** which contains a computer chip that can verify and validate information in addition to PINs. Another often-used device is the cryptographic token, a computer chip in a card that has a display. This device contains a built-in seed number that uses a formula or a clock to calculate a number that can be used to perform a remote login authentication.

Tokens may be synchronous or asynchronous. Once **synchronous tokens** are synchronized with a server, each device (server and token) uses the time to generate the authentication number that is entered during the user login. **Asynchronous tokens** use a challenge-response

Case Insensitive Passwords Using a Standard Alphabet Set (No Numbers or Special Characters)		
Password Length	**Odds of Cracking: 1 in (Based on Number of Characters ^ Password Length):**	**Estimated Time to Crack***
8	208,827,064,576	2.3 seconds
9	5,429,503,678,976	1.0 minutes
10	141,167,095,653,376	25.5 minutes
11	3,670,344,486,987,780	11.1 hours
12	95,428,956,661,682,200	12.0 days
13	2,481,152,873,203,740,000	311.8 days
14	64,509,974,703,297,200,000	22.2 years
15	1,677,259,342,285,730,000,000	577.5 years
16	43,608,742,899,428,900,000,000	15,014.4 years

Case-Sensitive Passwords Using a Standard Alphabet Set (With Numbers and 20 Special Characters)		
Password Length	**Odds of Cracking: 1 in (Based on Number of Characters ^ Password Length):**	**Estimated Time to Crack***
8	2,044,140,858,654,980	6.2 hours
9	167,619,550,409,708,000	21.1 days
10	13,744,803,133,596,100,000	4.7 years
11	1,127,073,856,954,880,000,000	388.0 years
12	92,420,056,270,299,900,000,000	31,820.0 years
13	7,578,444,614,164,590,000,000,000	2,609,238.9 years
14	621,432,458,361,496,000,000,000,000	213,957,589.4 years
15	50,957,461,585,642,700,000,000,000,000	17,544,522,333.3 years
16	4,178,511,850,022,700,000,000,000,000,000	1,438,650,831,334.6 years

Table 10-1   Password power

*Estimated Time to Crack is based on an average 2012-era Intel i7 PC (875K) chip performing 92,100 MIPS (million instructions per second) at 2.93 GHz.

Copyright © 2014 Cengage Learning®.

system in which the server challenges the user with a number. That is, the user enters the challenge number into the token, which in turn calculates a response number. The user then enters the response number into the system to gain access. Only a person who has the correct token can calculate the correct response number and thus log into the system.

Figure 10-3 Access control tokens
Copyright © 2014 Cengage Learning®.

This system does not require synchronization and does not suffer from mistiming issues. Figure 10-3 shows two examples of access control tokens from Google 2-Step and PayPal enhanced authentication.

Something You Are This authentication mechanism takes advantage of something inherent in the user that is evaluated using biometrics, which you will learn more about later in this chapter. Biometric authentication methods include the following:

- Fingerprints
- ID cards with face representations
- Facial recognition
- Hand geometry
- Retina scan
- Iris scan
- Voice recognition
- Palm vein authentication

Most of the technologies that scan human characteristics convert these images to obtain some form of minutiae—that is, unique points of reference that are digitized and stored. Some technologies encrypt the minutiae to make them more resistant to tampering. Each subsequent scan is also digitized and then compared with the encoded value to determine whether users are who they claim to be. One limitation of this technique is that some human characteristics can change over time, due to normal development, injury, or illness. Among the human characteristics currently employed for authentication purposes, only three are considered truly unique:

- Fingerprints
- Retina (blood vessel pattern)
- Iris (random pattern of features found in the iris, including freckles, pits, striations, vasculature, and coronas)

DNA or genetic authentication will be included in this category if it ever becomes a cost-effective and socially accepted technology.

Something You Produce This type of authentication makes use of something the user performs or produces—for example, a signature or voice pattern. (In some authentication methodologies, this type of authentication is placed within the "something you are" category, since it is sometimes difficult to differentiate biometric output from the biometric feature.) Signature recognition is commonplace. Many retail stores use signature recognition, or at least signature capture, for authentication during a purchase. Customers sign a special pad using a stylus; the signatures are then digitized and either compared to a database for validation or simply saved. Signature capture is much more widely accepted than signature comparison, because signatures can vary due to a number of factors, including age, fatigue, and the speed with which they are written.

Voice recognition for authentication captures the analog waveforms of a human's speech and compares these waveforms to a stored version. Voice recognition systems provide users with a phrase they must read—for example, "My voice is my password, please verify me. Thank you."

Another pattern-based approach is keystroke pattern recognition. This authentication method relies on the timing between key signals when a user types in a known sequence of keystrokes. When measured with sufficient precision, this pattern can provide a unique identification.

Figure 10-4 depicts some of these biometric and other human recognition characteristics.

Evaluating Biometrics Two of the four authentication mechanisms (something you are and something you produce) are biometric, which literally means life measurement. Biometric technologies are generally evaluated according to three basic criteria:

- *False reject rate*—The percentage of authorized users who are denied access
- *False accept rate*—The percentage of unauthorized users who are allowed access
- *Crossover error rate*—The point at which the number of false rejections equals the number of false acceptances

False Reject Rate The **false reject rate** is the rate at which authentic users are denied or prevented access to authorized areas as a result of a failure in the biometric device. This

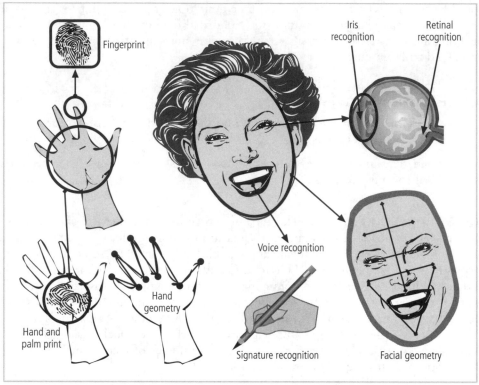

Figure 10-4 Recognition characteristics

Copyright © 2014 Cengage Learning®.

failure is also known as a "Type I error" or a "false negative." Rejection of an authorized individual represents not a threat to security but a hindrance to legitimate use. Consequently, it is often not seen as a serious problem until the rate increase is high enough to irritate users.

False Accept Rate The **false accept rate** is the rate at which fraudulent users or nonusers are allowed access to systems or areas as a result of a failure in the biometric device. This failure, known as a "Type II error" or a "false positive," represents a serious security breach. Often, multiple authentication measures must be used to back up a device whose failure would otherwise result in erroneous authorization.

Crossover Error Rate The **crossover error rate** (CER), also called the "equal error rate," is the point at which the rate of false rejections equals the rate of false acceptances. It is the optimal outcome for biometrics-based systems. CERs are used to compare various biometrics and may vary by manufacturer. A biometric device that provides a CER of 1 percent is considered superior to one with a CER of 5 percent, for example.

Acceptability of Biometrics A balance must be struck between the acceptability of a system to its users and the effectiveness of the same system. Many of the reliable, effective biometric systems are perceived as being somewhat intrusive by users. Organizations implementing biometrics must carefully balance a system's effectiveness against its perceived intrusiveness and acceptability to users. The rated effectiveness of a system is roughly inverse to its acceptability, as shown in Table 10-2. Since this study originally came out, iris scanning has experienced a rapid growth in popularity due mainly to its use of inexpensive camera equipment and the acceptability of the technology. Iris scanners only need a snapshot of the eye rather than an intrusive scan. As a result, iris scanning is ranked lower than retina scanning in terms of effectiveness (as iris scanning results in more false negatives), but it is believed to be the most accepted biometric, even compared to keystroke pattern recognition.

Effectiveness of Biometric Authentication Systems Ranking from Most Secure to Least Secure	Acceptance of Biometric Authentication Systems Ranking from Most Accepted to Least Accepted
• Retina pattern recognition	• Keystroke pattern recognition
• Fingerprint recognition	• Signature recognition
• Handprint recognition	• Voice pattern recognition
• Voice pattern recognition	• Handprint recognition
• Keystroke pattern recognition	• Fingerprint recognition
• Signature recognition	• Retina pattern recognition

Table 10-2   Orders of effectiveness and acceptance[1]

Source: Tipton and Krause, Information Security Management Handbook.

Authorization

The **authorization** process begins with an authenticated entity—a person or a virtual identity such as another computer program. In general, authorization can be handled in one of three ways:

- Authorization for each authenticated user, in which the system performs an authentication process to verify each entity and then grants access to resources to only that entity. This quickly becomes a complex and resource-intensive process in a computer system.

- Authorization for members of a group, in which the system matches authenticated entities to a list of group memberships and then grants access to resources based on the group's access rights. This is the most common authorization method.

- Authorization across multiple systems, in which a central authentication and authorization system verifies entity identity and grants a set of credentials to the verified entity. These credentials (sometimes called an "authorization ticket") are honored by all systems within the authentication domain. Sometimes called "single sign-on" (SSO) or "reduced sign-on," this approach is becoming more common and is frequently enabled using a shared directory structure such as the Lightweight Directory Access Protocol (LDAP).

Accountability

Accountability ensures that all actions on a system can be attributed to an authenticated identity. These actions could be ones that the entity is authorized for, such as looking up or modifying certain data, or they could include unauthorized attempts to escalate privileges or look at or modify data that is beyond its access level. Accountability is most often accomplished by implementing system logs and database journals and by auditing these records. **Systems logs** are records maintained by a particular system that has been configured to record specific information, such as failed access attempts and systems modifications. Logs have many uses, such as intrusion detection, determining the root cause of a system failure, or simply tracking the use of a particular resource. Table 10-3 lists some of the items that logs can track.

Category	Data Type
Network performance	• Total traffic load in and out over time (packet, byte, and connection counts) and by event (new product or service release) • Traffic load (percentage of packets, bytes, connections) in and out over time sorted by protocol, source address, destination address, other packet header data • Error counts on all network interfaces
Other network data	• Service initiation requests • Name of the user/host requesting the service • Network traffic (packet headers) • Successful connections and connection attempts (protocol, port, source, destination, time) • Connection duration • Connection flow (sequence of packets from initiation to termination) • States associated with network interfaces (up, down) • Network sockets currently open • Mode of network interface card (promiscuous or not) • Network probes and scans • Results of administrator probes
System performance	• Total resource use over time (CPU, memory [used, free], disk [used, free]) • Status and errors reported by systems and hardware devices • Changes in system status, including shutdowns and restarts • File system status (where mounted, free space by partition, open files, biggest file) over time and at specific times • File system warnings (low free space, too many open files, file exceeding allocated size) • Disk counters (input/output, queue lengths) over time and at specific times • Hardware availability (modems, network interface cards, memory)
Other system data	• Actions requiring special privileges • Successful and failed logins • Modem activities • Presence of new services and devices • Configuration of resources and devices

Table 10-3   Log data categories and types of data

Category	Data Type
Process performance	• Amount of resources used (CPU, memory, disk, time) by specific processes over time; top resource-consuming processes • System and user processes and services executing at any given time
Other process data	• User executing the process • Process start-up time, arguments, filenames • Process exit status, time, duration, resources consumed • Means by which each process is normally initiated (administrator, other users, other programs or processes) with what authorization and privileges • Devices used by specific processes • Files currently open by specific processes
Files and directories	• List of files, directories, attributes • Cryptographic checksums for all files and directories • Accesses (open, create, modify, execute, delete), time, date • Changes to sizes, contents, protections, types, locations • Changes to access control lists on system tools • Additions and deletions of files and directories • Results of virus scanners
Users	• Login/logout information (location, time): successful attempts, failed attempts, attempted logins to privileged accounts • Login/logout information on remote access servers that appears in modem logs • Changes in user identity • Changes in authentication status (such as enabling privileges) • Failed attempts to access restricted information (such as password files) • Keystroke monitoring logs • Violations of user quotas
Applications and services	• Application information (such as network traffic [packet content], mail logs, FTP logs, Web server logs, modem logs, firewall logs, SNMP logs, DNS logs, intrusion detection system logs, database management system logs) • FTP file transfers and connection statistics • Web connection statistics, including pages accessed, credentials of the requestor, user requests over time, most requested pages, and identities of requestors • Mail sender, receiver, size, and tracing information for mail requests • Mail server statistics, including number of messages over time and number of queued messages • DNS questions, answers, and zone transfers • File server transfers over time • Database server transactions over time

Table 10-3   Log data categories and types of data (continued)

Copyright © 2014 Cengage Learning®.

10

Some systems are configured to record a common set of data by default; other systems must be configured to be activated. To protect the log data, you must ensure that the servers that create and store the logs are secure. According to NIST, log management infrastructure involves two tiers, each with its own subtasks: (1) log generation and (2) log analysis and storage.[2]

Log Generation Log generation involves the configuration of systems to create logs as well as configuration changes needed to consolidate logs if this is desired. This typically requires activating logging on the various servers, and defining where to store logging data, locally (on the system that generated the logs) or otherwise (such as on a centralized log analysis system). Issues in log generation include:

- *Multiple log sources*—The diversity of systems that generate logs, with some servers generating multiple logs, such as Microsoft's application, system, security and setup logs, prevalent in most Windows OSs, can result in issues. Some logs consist of pieces of information collected from multiple sources, such as from network monitoring agents. The reintegration of the data collected from these logs can also cause complexity in the log consolidation process.

- *Inconsistent log content*—What gets stored in a log may be dependent on options chosen by the operating system developer or configuration options chosen by the systems administrator. Some systems allow the administrator to specify what gets logged, while others predefine what they believe should to be logged.

- *Inconsistent timestamps*—In addition to the fact that the dates and times in logs may be formatted differently, servers that are not associated with a central time server or service may result in different times recorded for events that are in fact simultaneous. If an incident hits a number of servers in a particular sequence but the timestamps on those machines are off by even a few seconds or even fractions of a second, it becomes much more difficult to analyze the incident.

- *Inconsistent log format*—Because many different systems create logs, the structure and content of those logs may differ dramatically. Even a simple data element such as a date can be stored in multiple different formats, such as the difference between the standard in the United States—Month, Day, Year (MMDDYYYY)—and the standard used in many European countries—Day, Month, Year (DDMMYYYY). Some systems store ports by number, others by name.

In order to interpret data from the Log Generation tier, the following functions must be addressed:

- *Log parsing*—Dividing data within logs into specific values, as some log data may consist of a solid stream of data.

- *Event filtering*—The separation of "items of interest" from the rest of the data that the log collects.

- *Event aggregation*—The consolidation of similar entries or related events within a log. Aggregation is critical for the organization to be able to handle the thousands of data points multiple servers will generate.[3]

Log Analysis and Storage Log analysis and storage is the transference of the log data to an analysis system, which may or may not be separate from the system that collects the log data. Collectively, systems of this type are known as **security event information management (SEIM) systems**. These systems are specifically tasked to collect log data from a number of servers or other network devices for the purpose of interpreting, filtering, correlating, analyzing, storing, and reporting the data.

Important management functions within log storage include:

- *Log rotation*—The file-level management of logs (e.g., when a single log file is closed and another started), usually done on a set schedule.
- *Log archival*—The backup and storage of logs based on policy or legal/regulatory requirements. This function includes log retention (the routine storage of all logs for a specified duration) and log preservation (the saving of logs of particular interest based on content).
- *Log compression*—The reduction in file size of logs to save drive space, using compression tools like Zip or Archive.
- *Log reduction*—The removal of unimportant or uneventful log entries to reduce the size of a log file, also known as "event reduction."
- *Log conversion*—The modification of the format or structure of a log file to allow it to be accessed by another application, such as an analysis tool.
- *Log normalization*—The standardization of log file structures and formats, using log conversion.
- *Log file integrity*—The determination as to whether the log files have been modified or not, usually through message digest or hashes.

Important management functions within log analysis include:

- *Event correlation*—The association of multiple log file entries according to a predefined event or activity.
- *Log viewing*—The display of log data in a form that is easily understandable by humans, usually involving adding field data.
- *Log reporting*—The display of the results of log analysis.

The final responsibility within this tier is the management of the logs once they no longer have value. Log disposal or log clearing is the specification of when logs may be deleted or overwritten within a system, whether you are referring to the system that generated the logs or the system that stores and analyzes them.[4]

General suggestions for managing logs include:

- Make sure that data stores can handle the amount of data generated by the configured logging activities. Some systems may generate multiple gigabytes of data for each hour of operation.
- Rotate logs when unlimited data storage is not possible. Some systems overwrite older log entries with newer entries to accommodate space limitations. Log rotation settings must be configured for your system, which may require modifying the default settings.

- Archive logs. Log systems can copy logs periodically to remote storage locations. Security administrators disagree about how long log files should be retained. Some argue that log files may be subpoenaed during legal proceedings and thus should be routinely destroyed to prevent unwanted disclosure. Others argue that the information gained from analyzing legacy and archival logs outweighs the risk. Still others propose aggregating the log information, then destroying the individual entries. Regardless of the method employed, some plan must be in place to handle these files or risk loss.

- Secure logs. Archived logs should be encrypted to prevent unwanted disclosure if the log data store is compromised. This should also protect the integrity of the log data, as many attackers will seek to delete or obfuscate log data to cover the tracks of the attack.

- Destroy logs. Once log data has outlived its usefulness, it should be securely destroyed.[5]

The process of reviewing the information collected in logs to detect misuse or attempted intrusion is part of a larger process called **auditing**. Logs are of no value to an organization if their contents are not reviewed periodically and included as part of the records trail used for auditing. Auditing can combine automated and manual mechanisms and can be done internally in an organization or as part of an external review that may or may not include financial auditing procedures.

Managing Access Controls

To appropriately manage access controls, an organization must have in place a formal **access control policy**, which specifies how access rights are granted to entities and groups. This policy must include provisions for periodically reviewing all access rights, granting access rights to new employees, changing access rights when job roles change, and revoking access rights as appropriate. Without an access control policy, system administrators may implement access controls in a way that is inconsistent with the organization's overall philosophy. Once a policy is in place, implementing access controls becomes a technical issue.

Firewalls

A physical firewall in a building is a concrete or masonry wall running from the basement through the roof to prevent fire from spreading. In the aircraft and automotive industries, a firewall is an insulated metal barrier that keeps the hot and dangerous moving parts of the motor separate from the interior, where the passengers sit. In InfoSec, a firewall is any device that prevents a specific type of information from moving between the outside world, known as the **untrusted network** (e.g., the Internet), and the inside world, known as the **trusted network**. The firewall may be a separate computer system, a service running on an existing router or server, or a separate network containing a number of supporting devices.

The Development of Firewalls

Firewalls have made significant advances since their earliest implementations. The first generation of firewalls, **packet filtering firewalls**, are simple networking devices that filter

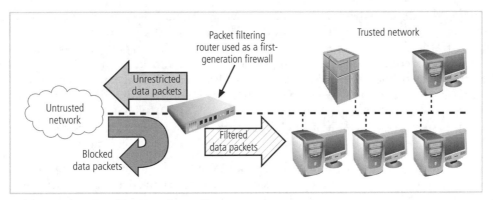

Figure 10-5 Packet filtering firewall

Copyright © 2014 Cengage Learning®.

packets by examining every incoming and outgoing packet header. They can selectively filter packets based on values in the packet header, accepting or rejecting packets as needed. These devices can be configured to filter based on IP address, type of packet, port request, and/or other elements present in the packet. The filtering process examines packets for compliance with or violation of rules configured into the firewall's database. The rules most commonly implemented in packet filtering firewalls are based on a combination of IP source and destination address, direction (inbound or outbound), and/or source and destination port requests. Figure 10-5 shows how such a firewall typically works.

The ability to restrict a specific service is now considered standard in most modern routers and is invisible to the user. Unfortunately, these systems are unable to detect whether packet headers have been modified, as occurs in IP spoofing attacks. Early firewall models only examined the packet's destination and source addresses. Table 10-4 presents a simplified example of a packet filtering rule set.

Source Address	Destination Address	Service Port	Action
10.10.x.x	Any	Any	Deny
192.168.x.x	10.10.x.x	Any	Deny
172.16.121.1	10.10.10.22	SFTP	Allow
Any	10.10.10.24	SMTP	Allow
Any	10.10.10.25	HTTP	Allow
Any	10.10.10.x	Any	Deny

Table 10-4   Example of a packet filtering rule set

Notes: These rules apply to a network at 10.10.x.x. This table uses special, nonroutable IP addresses in the rules for this example. An actual firewall that connects to a public network would use real address ranges.

Copyright © 2014 Cengage Learning®.

A network configured with the rules shown in Table 10-4 blocks inbound connection attempts by all computers or network devices in the 10.10.x.x address range. This first rule blocks traffic that is attempting to spoof an internal address and thus bypass the firewall filters. The second rule is an example of a specific block, perhaps on traffic from an objectionable location; the rule effectively blacklists that external network from connecting to this network. The third rule could be used to allow an off-site administrator to directly access an internal system by Secure File Transfer Protocol (SFTP). The next two rules would allow outside systems to access e-mail and Web servers, but only if using the appropriate protocols. The final rule enforces an exclusionary policy that blocks all access not specifically allowed.

Second-generation firewalls, known as **application-level firewalls**, often consist of dedicated computers kept separate from the first filtering router (called an edge router); they are commonly used in conjunction with a second or internal filtering router. This second router is often called a **proxy server** because it serves as a proxy for external service requests to internal services.

With this configuration, the proxy server, rather than the Web server, is exposed to the outside world from within a network segment called the **demilitarized zone (DMZ)**. The DMZ is an intermediate area between a trusted network and an untrusted network (see Figure 10-8, later in this chapter). Using this model, additional filtering routers are placed between the proxy server and internal systems, thereby restricting access to internal systems to the proxy server alone. If these servers store the most recently accessed pages in their internal caches, they may also be called **cache servers**.

Suppose an external user wanted to view a Web page from an organization's Web server. Rather than expose the Web server to direct traffic from the users and potential attackers, the organization can install a proxy server, configured with the registered domain's URL. This proxy server receives Web page requests, accesses the Web server on behalf of external clients, and then returns the requested pages to users.

The primary disadvantage of application-level firewalls is that they are designed for a specific protocol and cannot easily be reconfigured to work with other protocols.

Third-generation firewalls, **stateful inspection firewalls**, keep track of each network connection established between internal and external systems using a **state table**. State tables track the state and context of each exchanged packet by recording which station sent which packet and when. Like first-generation firewalls, stateful inspection firewalls perform packet filtering; whereas simple packet filtering firewalls merely allow or deny certain packets based on their addresses, though, a stateful inspection firewall can restrict incoming packets by restricting access to packets that constitute responses to internal requests. If the stateful inspection firewall receives an incoming packet that it cannot match in its state table, it defaults to its access control list (ACL) to determine whether to allow the packet to pass.

The primary disadvantage of this type of firewall is the additional processing requirements of managing and verifying packets against the state table, which can expose the system to a denial-of-service (DoS) attack. In such an attack, the firewall is subjected to a large number of external packets, slowing it down as it attempts to compare all of the incoming packets first to the state table and then to the ACL. On the positive side, these firewalls can track connectionless packet traffic such as User Datagram Protocol (UDP) and remote procedure call (RPC) traffic.

Whereas static filtering firewalls, such as those in the first and third generations, allow entire sets of one type of packet to enter in response to authorized requests, fourth-generation firewalls, called **dynamic packet filtering firewalls**, allow only a particular packet with a specific source, destination, and port address to pass through the firewall. It does so by understanding how the protocol functions and by opening and closing "doors" in the firewall based on the information contained in the packet header. Dynamic packet filters are an intermediate form between traditional static packet filters and application proxies.

The most recent generation of firewall isn't truly a new generation at all but a hybrid built from capabilities of modern networking equipment that can perform a variety of tasks according to the organization's needs. Known as **Unified Threat Management** (UTM), these devices are categorized by their ability to perform the work of a stateful inspection firewall, network intrusion detection and prevention system, content filter, and spam filter as well as a malware scanner and filter. UTM systems take advantage of increasing memory capacity and processor capability and can reduce the complexity associated with deploying, configuring, and integrating multiple networking devices. With the proper configuration, these devices are even able to "drill down" into the protocol layers and examine application-specific data, encrypted, compressed, and/or encoded data. The primary disadvantage of UTM systems is the creation of a single point of failure should the device experience technical issues.[6]

Firewall Architectures

Each of the firewall generations can be implemented in a number of architectural configurations. These configurations are sometimes mutually exclusive but sometimes can be combined. The configuration that works best for a particular organization depends on the uses of its network, the organization's ability to develop and implement the architectures, and the available budget. Although literally hundreds of variations exist, four architectural implementations of firewalls are especially common: packet filtering routers, screened-host firewalls, dual-homed host firewalls, and screened-subnet firewalls.

Packet Filtering Routers Most organizations with an Internet connection use some form of router between their internal networks and the external service provider. Many of these **packet filtering routers** can be configured to block packets that the organization does not allow into the network. This is a simple but effective means of lowering the organization's risk of external attack. Such an architecture lacks auditing and strong authentication, and the complexity of the ACLs used to filter the packets can grow and degrade network performance. Figure 10-5 showed an example of this type of architecture.

Screened-Host Firewall Systems Screened-host firewall systems combine the packet filtering router with a separate, dedicated firewall such as an application proxy server. This approach allows the router to screen packets to minimize the network traffic and load on the internal proxy. The application proxy examines an application layer protocol, such as HTTP, and performs the proxy services. This separate host, which is often referred to as a **bastion host**, represents a single, rich target for external attacks and should therefore, be very thoroughly secured. Because it stands as a sole defender on the network perimeter, it is also commonly referred to as the **sacrificial host**.

Even though the bastion host/application proxy contains only cached copies of the internal Web documents, it can present a promising target. An attacker that infiltrates the bastion host can discover the configuration of internal networks and possibly provide external sources with internal information. To its advantage, the proxy requires the external attack to compromise two separate systems before the attack can access internal data. As a

10

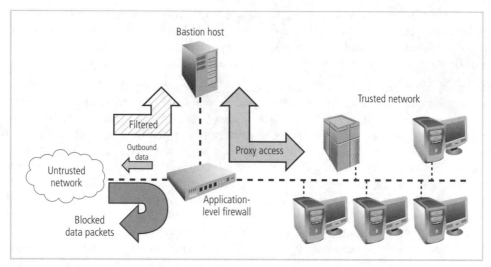

Figure 10-6 Screened-host firewall

Copyright © 2014 Cengage Learning®.

consequence, the bastion host protects the data more fully than the router alone. Figure 10-6 shows a typical configuration of a screened-host architectural approach.

Dual-Homed Host Firewalls
The next step up in firewall architectural complexity is the **dual-homed host**. In this configuration, the bastion host contains two network interfaces: one that is connected to the external network and one that is connected to the internal network. All traffic *must* go through the firewall to move between the internal and external networks.

A technology known as **network-address translation** (**NAT**) is often implemented with this architecture. NAT is a method of converting multiple real, routable external IP addresses to special ranges of internal IP addresses, usually on a one-to-one basis; that is, one external valid address directly maps to one assigned internal address. A related approach, called **port-address translation** (**PAT**), converts a single real, valid, external IP address to special ranges of internal IP addresses—that is, a one-to-many approach in which one address is mapped dynamically to a range of internal addresses by adding a unique port number when traffic leaves the private network and is placed on the public network. This unique number serves to identify which internal host is engaged in that specific network connection. The combination of the address and port (known as a **socket**) is then easily mapped to the internal address. Both of these approaches create a barrier to intrusion from outside the local network because the addresses used for the internal network cannot be routed over the public network. These special, nonroutable addresses have three possible ranges:

- Organizations that need very large numbers of local addresses can use the 10.x.x.x range, which has more than 16.5 million usable addresses.

- Organizations that need a moderate number of addresses can use the 192.168.x.x range, which has more than 65,500 addresses.

- Organizations with smaller needs can use the 172.16.0.0—172.16.15.0 range, which has approximately 4000 usable addresses.

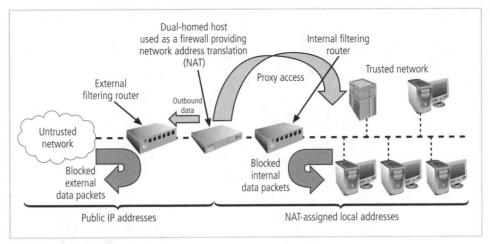

Figure 10-7 Dual-homed host firewall

Copyright © 2014 Cengage Learning®.

Taking advantage of NAT or PAT prevents external attacks from reaching internal machines with addresses in specified ranges. This type of translation works by dynamically assigning addresses to internal communications and tracking the conversations with sessions to determine which incoming message is a response to which outgoing traffic. Figure 10-7 shows a typical configuration of a dual-homed host firewall that uses NAT or PAT and proxy access to protect the internal network.

A dual-homed host is able to translate between the protocols of two different data link layers, such as Ethernet, Token Ring, Fiber Distributed Data Interface (FDDI), and asynchronous transfer method (ATM). However, this approach has two disadvantages: If the dual-homed host is compromised, it can take out the connection to the external network, and as traffic volume increases, the dual-homed host can become overloaded. Compared to more complex solutions, though, this architecture provides strong protection with minimal expense.

Screened-Subnet Firewalls (with DMZ)

Screened-Subnet Firewalls (with DMZ) The screened-subnet firewall consists of one or more internal bastion hosts located behind a packet filtering router, with each host protecting the trusted network. Many variants of the screened-subnet architecture exist. The first general model uses two filtering routers, with one or more dual-homed bastion hosts between them. In the second general model, as illustrated in Figure 10-8, the connections are routed as follows:

- Connections from the outside or untrusted network are routed through an external filtering router.
- Connections from the outside or untrusted network are routed into—and then out of—a routing firewall to the separate network segment known as the DMZ.
- Connections into the trusted internal network are allowed only from the DMZ bastion host servers.

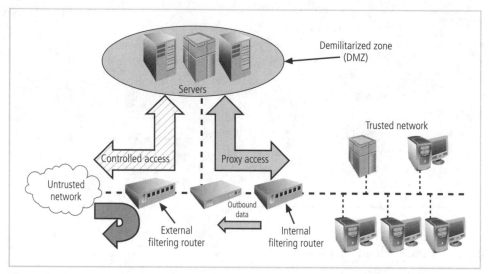

Figure 10-8 Screened subnet (DMZ)

Copyright © 2014 Cengage Learning®.

As depicted in Figure 10-8, the screened subnet is an entire network segment that performs two functions: It protects the DMZ systems and information from outside threats, and it protects the internal networks by limiting how external connections can gain access to internal systems. Though extremely secure, the screened subnet can be expensive to implement and complex to configure and manage; the value of the information it protects must justify the cost.

The screened-subnet firewall architecture provides an intermediate area—a DMZ—between the trusted network and the untrusted network. This DMZ can be a dedicated port on the firewall device linking a single bastion host, or it can be connected to a screened subnet or DMZ, as shown in Figure 10-8. Until recently, servers providing services via the untrusted network were commonly placed in the DMZ. Examples include Web servers, FTP servers, and certain database servers. More recent strategies utilizing proxy servers have provided much more secure solutions. UTM systems could be deployed in virtually any of these architectures, according to the needs of the organization.

Selecting the Right Firewall

When evaluating a firewall for your networks, ask the following questions:

1. What type of firewall technology offers the right balance between protection and cost for the needs of the organization?

2. What features are included in the base price? What features are available at extra cost? Are all cost factors known?

3. How easy is it to set up and configure the firewall? How accessible are the staff technicians who can competently configure the firewall?

4. Can the candidate firewall adapt to the growing network in the target organization?

Question 2 addresses another important issue: cost. A firewall's cost may put a certain make, model, or type out of reach for a particular security solution. As with all security decisions, the budgetary constraints stipulated by management must be taken into account. It is important to remember that the total cost of ownership for any piece of security technology, including firewalls, will almost always greatly exceed the initial purchase price. Costs associated with maintenance contracts, rule set acquisition or development, rule set validation, signature subscriptions (for vendor produced rules to filter current malware threats) as well as expenses for employee training all add to the total cost of ownership.

Managing Firewalls

Any firewall device—whether a packet filtering router, bastion host, or other firewall implementation—must have its own set of configuration rules that regulates its actions. With packet filtering firewalls, these rules may be simple statements regulating source and destination addresses, specific protocol or port usage requests, or decisions to allow or deny certain types of requests. In all cases, a policy regarding the use of a firewall should be articulated before it is made operable.

In practice, configuring firewall rule sets can be something of a nightmare. Logic errors in the preparation of the rules can cause unintended behavior, such as allowing access instead of denying it, specifying the wrong port or service type, or causing the network to misroute traffic. These and a myriad of other mistakes can turn a device designed to protect communications into a choke point. For example, a novice firewall administrator might improperly configure a virus-screening e-mail gateway (think of it as a type of e-mail firewall), resulting in the blocking of all incoming e-mail, instead of screening only e-mail that contains malicious code. Each firewall rule must be carefully crafted, placed into the list in the proper sequence, debugged, and tested. The proper rule sequence ensures that the most resource-intensive actions are performed after the most restrictive ones, thereby reducing the number of packets that undergo intense scrutiny.

The ever-present need to balance performance against restrictions imposed by security practices is very obvious in the use of firewalls. If users cannot work due to a security restriction, then the security administration will most likely be told by management to remove it. Organizations are much more willing to live with a potential risk than certain failure.

Using a computer to protect a computer is fraught with problems that must be managed by careful preparation and continuous evaluation. For the most part, automated control systems, including firewalls, cannot learn from mistakes, and they cannot adapt to changing situations. They are limited by the constraints of their programming and rule sets in the following ways:

- Firewalls are not creative and cannot make sense of human actions outside the range of their programmed responses.

- Firewalls deal strictly with defined patterns of measured observation. These patterns are known to possible attackers and can be used to their benefit in an attack.

- Firewalls are computers themselves and are thus prone to programming errors, flaws in rule sets, and inherent vulnerabilities.

- Firewalls are designed to function within limits of hardware capacity and thus can only respond to patterns of events that happen in an expected and reasonably simultaneous sequence.

- Firewalls are designed, implemented, configured, and operated by people and are subject to the expected series of mistakes from human error.[7]

There are also a number of administrative challenges to the operation of firewalls:

1. *Training*—Most managers think of a firewall as just another device, more or less similar to the computers already humming in the rack. If you get time to read manuals, you are lucky.

2. *Uniqueness*—You have mastered your firewall, and now every new configuration requirement is just a matter of a few clicks in the Telnet window; however, each brand of firewall is different, and the new e-commerce project just brought you a new firewall running on a different OS.

3. *Responsibility*—Since you are the firewall guy, suddenly everyone assumes that anything to do with computer security is your responsibility.

4. *Administration*—Being a firewall administrator for a medium or large organization should be a full-time job; however, that's hardly ever the case.[8]

Laura Taylor, Chief Technology Officer and founder of Relevant Technologies, recommends the following practices for firewall use:

- All traffic from the trusted network is allowed out. This way, members of the organization can access the services they need. Filtering and logging outbound traffic is possible when indicated by specific organizational policy goals.

- The firewall device is never accessible directly from the public network. Almost all access to the firewall device is denied to internal users as well. Only authorized firewall administrators access the device via secure authentication mechanisms, with preference for a method based on cryptographically strong authentication using two-factor access control techniques.

- Simple Mail Transport Protocol (SMTP) data is allowed to pass through the firewall, but all of it is routed to a well-configured SMTP gateway to filter and route messaging traffic securely.

- All Internet Control Message Protocol (ICMP) data is denied. Known as the ping service, this is a common method for hacker reconnaissance and should be turned off to prevent snooping.

- Telnet/terminal emulation access to all internal servers from the public networks is blocked. At the very least, Telnet access to the organization's Domain Name Service (DNS) server should be blocked to prevent illegal zone transfers and to prevent hackers from taking down the organization's entire network. If internal users need to reach an organization's network from outside the firewall, use a virtual private network (VPN) client or other secure authentication system to allow this kind of access.

- When Web services are offered outside the firewall, HTTP traffic is prevented from reaching your internal networks via the implementation of some form of proxy access or DMZ architecture. That way, if any employees are running Web servers for internal use on their desktops, the services will be invisible to the outside Internet. If your Web server is located behind the firewall, you need to allow HTTP or HTTPS (SHTTP) data through for the Internet at large to view it. The best solution is to place the Web servers containing critical data inside the network and to use proxy services from a DMZ (screened network segment). It is also advisable to restrict incoming HTTP traffic to internal network addresses such that the traffic must be responding to requests originating at internal addresses. This restriction can be accomplished through NAT or firewalls that can support stateful inspection or are directed at the proxy server itself. All other incoming HTTP traffic should be blocked. If the Web servers contain only advertising, they should be placed in the DMZ and rebuilt when (not if) they are compromised.[9]

Intrusion Detection and Prevention Systems

Intrusion detection and prevention systems (IDPSs) work like burglar alarms. When the system detects a violation—the IT equivalent of an opened or broken window—it activates the alarm. This alarm can be audible and visible (noise and lights), or it can be a silent alarm that sends a message to a monitoring company. With almost all IDPSs, administrators can choose the configuration and alarm levels. Many IDPSs can be configured to notify administrators via e-mail and numerical or text paging. The systems can also be configured to notify an external InfoSec service organization, just as burglar alarms do.

Systems that include intrusion prevention technology attempt to prevent the attack from succeeding by one of the following means:

- Stopping the attack by terminating the network connection or the attacker's user session

- Changing the security environment by reconfiguring network devices (firewalls, routers, and switches) to block access to the targeted system

- Changing the attack's content to make it benign—for example, by removing an infected file attachment from an e-mail before the e-mail reaches the recipient

Intrusion prevention technologies can include a mechanism that severs the communications circuit—an extreme measure that may be justified when the organization is hit with a massive *Distributed Denial of Service (DDoS)* or malware-laden attack.

All IDPSs require complex configurations to provide the appropriate level of detection and response. These systems are either network based to protect network information assets or they are host based to protect server or host information assets. IDPSs use one of two basic detection methods: signature based or statistical anomaly based. Figure 10-9 depicts two typical approaches to intrusion detection and prevention where IDPSs are used to monitor both network connection activity and current information states on host servers.

Host-Based IDPS

A **host-based IDPS (HIDPS)** works by configuring and classifying various categories of systems and data files. In many cases, IDPSs provide only a few general levels of alert notification. For example, an administrator might configure an IDPS to report changes to certain folders, such as system folders (such as C:\Windows), security-related applications (C:\Tripwire), or critical data folders; at the same time, the IDPS might be instructed to ignore changes to other files (such as C:\Program Files\Office). Administrators might configure the system to instantly page or e-mail them for high-priority alerts but to simply record other lower-priority activity. Most administrators are concerned only if unauthorized changes occur in sensitive areas. After all, applications frequently modify their internal files, such as dictionaries and configuration templates, and users constantly update their data files.

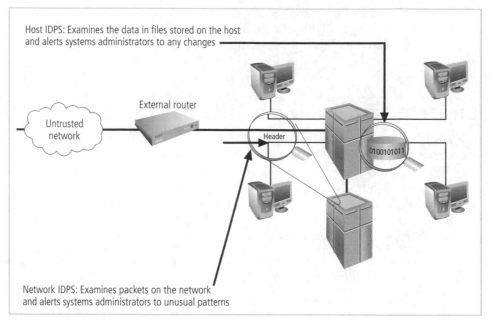

Host IDPS: Examines the data in files stored on the host and alerts systems administrators to any changes

External router

Untrusted network

Header

0100101011

Network IDPS: Examines packets on the network and alerts systems administrators to unusual patterns

Figure 10-9 Intrusion detection and prevention systems

Copyright © 2014 Cengage Learning®.

Unless the IDPS is precisely configured, these benign actions can generate a large volume of false alarms. Some organizations will use a variable degree of reporting and recording detail. During times of routine operation, the system will provide alerting for only a few urgent reasons and will provide recording only for exceptions. During periods of increased threat, however, it may send alerts on suspicious activity and record all activity for later analysis.

Host-based IDPSs can monitor multiple computers simultaneously. They do so by storing a client file on each monitored host and then making that host report back to the master console, which is usually located on the system administrator's computer. This master console monitors the information from the managed clients and notifies the administrator when predetermined attack conditions occur.

Network-Based IDPS

In contrast to host-based IDPSs, which reside on a host (or hosts) and monitor only activities on the host, **network-based IDPSs (NIDPSs)** monitor network traffic. When a predefined condition occurs, the network-based IDPS notifies the appropriate administrator. Whereas host-based IDPSs look for changes in file attributes (create, modify, delete), the network-based IDPS looks for patterns of network traffic, such as large collections of related traffic that can indicate a DoS attack or a series of related packets that could indicate a port scan in progress. Consequently, network IDPSs require a much more complex configuration and maintenance program than do host-based IDPSs. Network IDPSs must match known and unknown attack strategies against their knowledge base to determine whether an attack has occurred. These systems yield many more false-positive readings than do host-based IDPSs because they are attempting to read the network activity pattern to determine what is normal and what is not.

Most organizations that implement an IDPS solution install data collection sensors that are both host based and network based. A system of this type is called a hybrid-IDPS, and it also usually includes a provision to concentrate the event notifications from all sensors into a central repository for analysis. The analysis makes use of either signature-based or statistical anomaly–based detection techniques.

Signature-Based IDPS

IDPSs that use signature-based methods work like antivirus software. In fact, antivirus software can be classified as a form of signature-based IDPS. A **signature-based IDPS**, also known as a **knowledge-based IDPS**, examines data traffic for something that matches the signatures, which comprise preconfigured, predetermined attack patterns. The problem with this approach is that the signatures must be continually updated as new attack strategies emerge. Failure to stay current allows attacks using new strategies to succeed. Another weakness of this method is the time frame over which attacks occur. If attackers are slow and methodical, they may slip undetected through the IDPS, as their actions may not match a signature that includes factors based on duration of the events. The only way to resolve this dilemma is to collect and analyze data over longer periods of time, which requires substantially larger data storage ability and additional processing capacity.

Anomaly-Based IDPS

Another popular type of IDPS is the **anomaly-based IDPS** (formerly called a **statistical anomaly–based IDPS**), which is also known as a **behavior-based IDPS**. The anomaly-based IDPS first collects data from normal traffic and establishes a baseline. It then periodically samples network activity, using statistical methods, and compares the samples to the baseline. When the activity falls outside the baseline parameters (known as the **clipping level**), the IDPS notifies the administrator. The baseline variables can include a host's memory or CPU usage, network packet types, and packet quantities.

The advantage of this approach is that the system is able to detect new types of attacks because it looks for abnormal activity of any type. Unfortunately, these IDPSs require much more overhead and processing capacity than do signature-based versions because they must constantly attempt to pattern matched activity to the baseline. In addition, they may not detect minor changes to system variables and may generate many false-positive warnings. If the actions of the users or systems on the network vary widely, with unpredictable periods of low-level and high-level activity, this type of IDPS may not be suitable, as it will almost certainly generate false alarms. As a result, it is less commonly used than the signature-based approach.

Managing Intrusion Detection and Prevention Systems

Just as with any alarm system, if there is no response to an IDPS alert, it does no good. An IDPS does not remove or deny access to a system by default and, unless it is programmed to take an action, merely records the events that trigger it. IDPSs must be configured using technical knowledge and adequate business and security knowledge to differentiate between routine circumstances and low, moderate, or severe threats to the security of the organization's information assets.

A properly configured IDPS can translate a security alert into different types of notification— for example, log entries for low-level alerts, e-mails for moderate-level alerts, and text messages or paging for severe alerts. Some organizations may configure systems to automatically take action in response to IDPS alerts, although this technique should be carefully considered and undertaken only by organizations with experienced staff and well-constructed InfoSec procedures. A poorly configured IDPS may yield either information overload—causing the IDPS administrator to shut off the pager—or failure to detect an actual attack. When a system is configured to take unsupervised action without obtaining human approval, the organization must be prepared to take accountability for these IDPS actions.

The human response to false alarms can lead to behavior that can be exploited by attackers. For example, consider the following tactic—a car theft strategy that exploits humans' intolerance for technological glitches that cause false alarms. In the early morning hours—say, 2:00 a.m.—a thief deliberately sets off the target car's alarm and then retreats a safe distance. The owner comes out, resets the alarm, and goes back to bed. Twenty to thirty minutes later, the thief does it again, and then again. After the third or fourth time, the owner assumes that the alarm is faulty and turns it off, leaving the vehicle unprotected. The thief is then free to steal the car without having to deal with the now disabled alarm.

Most IDPSs monitor systems by means of agents. An **agent** (sometimes called a **sensor**) is a piece of software that resides on a system and reports back to a management server. If this piece of software is not properly configured and does not use a secure transmission channel to communicate with its manager, an attacker could compromise and subsequently exploit the agent or the information from the agent.

A valuable tool in managing an IDPS is the consolidated enterprise management service. This software allows the security professional to collect data from multiple host-based and network-based IDPSs and look for patterns across systems and subnetworks. An attacker might potentially probe one network segment or computer host and then move on to another target before the first system's IDPS has caught on. The consolidated management service not only collects responses from all IDPSs, thereby providing a central monitoring station, it can identify these cross-system probes and intrusions.

Remote Access Protection

Before the Internet emerged as a public network, organizations created private networks and allowed individuals and other organizations to connect to them using dial-up or leased-line connections. In the current networking environment, firewalls are used to safeguard the connection between an organization and its Internet (public network) connection. The equivalent level of protection is necessary to protect connections when using private networks that allow dial-up access. While large organizations have replaced much of their dial-up capacity with Internet-enabled VPN connectivity, the maintenance and protection of dial-up connections from users' homes and in small offices remains a concern for some organizations.

Unsecured dial-up access represents a substantial exposure to attack. An attacker who suspects that an organization has dial-up lines can use a device called a **war-dialer** to locate the connection points. A war-dialer is an automatic phone-dialing program that dials every number in a configured range (e.g., 555–1000 to 555–2000) and checks whether a person, answering machine, or modem picks up. If a modem answers, the war-dialer program makes a note of the number and then moves to the next target number. The attacker then attempts to hack into the network through the identified modem connection using a variety of techniques.

Dial-up connections are usually much simpler and less sophisticated than Internet connections. For the most part, simple user name and password schemes are the only means of authentication. Some newer technologies have improved this process, including Remote Authentication Dial-In User Service (RADIUS) systems, Challenge Handshake Authentication Protocol (CHAP) systems, and even systems that use strong encryption. The most prominent of these approaches are RADIUS and -TACACS, which are discussed in the following section.

RADIUS and TACACS

While broadband Internet access has widely replaced dial-up access in most of the modern world, there is a substantial number of users of dial-up access. With the lower cost and wider availability of dial-up connectivity, it remains important for organizations to retain familiarity with methods necessary to protect dial-up connections. RADIUS and TACACS are systems that authenticate the credentials of users who are trying to access an organization's network via a dial-up device or a secured network session. Typical remote access systems place the responsibility for the authentication of users on the system directly connected to the modems. If the dial-up system includes multiple points of entry, such an authentication scheme is difficult to manage. The **Remote Authentication Dial-In User Service (RADIUS)** system centralizes the management of user authentication by placing the responsibility for authenticating each user on a central RADIUS server. When a remote access server (RAS) receives a request for a network connection from a dial-up client, it passes the request along with the user's credentials to the RADIUS server. RADIUS then validates the credentials and passes the resulting decision (accept or deny) back to the accepting RAS. Figure 10-10 shows the typical configuration of a RAS system making use of RADIUS authentication.

Similar in function to the RADIUS system is the **Terminal Access Controller Access Control System (TACACS)**, commonly used in UNIX systems. This remote access authorization system is based on a client/server configuration. It makes use of a centralized data service, such as the one provided by a RADIUS server, and validates the user's credentials at the TACACS server.

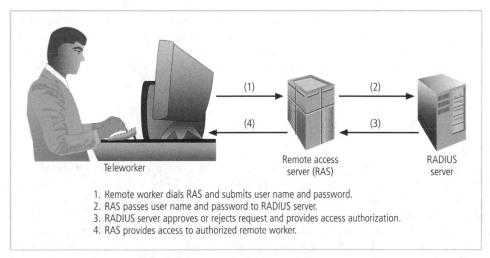

1. Remote worker dials RAS and submits user name and password.
2. RAS passes user name and password to RADIUS server.
3. RADIUS server approves or rejects request and provides access authorization.
4. RAS provides access to authorized remote worker.

Figure 10-10 RADIUS configuration

Copyright © 2014 Cengage Learning®.

Three versions of TACACS exist: TACACS, Extended TACACS, and TACACS+. The original version combines authentication and authorization services. The extended version authenticates and authorizes in two separate steps, and records the access attempt and the requestor's identity. The plus version uses dynamic passwords and incorporates two-factor authentication.[10]

Managing Dial-Up Connections

Many organizations that once operated large dial-up access pools are now reducing the number of telephone lines they support in favor of Internet access secured by VPNs. An organization that continues to offer dial-up remote access must do the following:

- *Determine how many dial-up connections it has*—Many organizations do not even realize they have dial-up access, or they leave telephone connections in place long after they have stopped fully using them. This creates two potential problems. One, the organization continues to pay for telecommunications circuits it is not using; two, an alternative, and frequently unauthorized, method of accessing organizational networks remains a potential vulnerability. For example, an employee may have installed a modem on an office computer to do a little telecommuting without management's knowledge. The organization should periodically scan its internal phone networks with special software to detect available connections. It should also integrate risk assessment and risk approval into the telephone service ordering process.

- *Control access to authorized modem numbers*—Only those authorized to use dial-up access should be allowed to use incoming connections. Furthermore, although there is no security in obscurity, the numbers should not be widely distributed and the dial-up numbers should be considered confidential.

- *Use call-back whenever possible*—Call-back requires an access requestor to be at a preconfigured location, which is essential for authorized telecommuting. Users call into the access computer, which disconnects and immediately calls the requestor back. If the caller is an authorized user at the preconfigured number, the caller can then connect. This solution is not so useful for traveling users, however.

- *Use token authentication if at all possible*—Users can be required to enter more than user names and passwords, which is essential when allowing dial-up access from laptops and other remote computers. In this scheme, the device accepts an input number, often provided by the computer from which access is requested, and provides a response based on an internal algorithm. The result is much stronger security.

Wireless Networking Protection

The use of wireless network technology is an area of concern for InfoSec professionals. Most organizations that make use of wireless networks use an implementation based on the IEEE 802.11 protocol. A wireless network provides a low-cost alternative to a wired network because it does not require the difficult and often expensive installation of cable in an existing structure. The downside is the management of the wireless network **footprint**—the geographic area within which there is sufficient signal strength to make a network connection. The size of the footprint depends on the amount of power the transmitter/receiver **wireless access points (WAPs)** emit. Sufficient power must exist to ensure quality connections within the intended area, but not so much as to allow those outside the footprint to receive them.

Just as war-dialers represent a threat to dial-up communications, so does war driving for wireless. **War driving** is moving through a geographic area or building, actively scanning for open or unsecured WAPs. In some cities, groups of war-drivers move through an urban area, marking locations with unsecured wireless access with chalk ("war-chalking"). A number of encryption protocols can be used to secure wireless networks. The most common is the Wi-Fi Protected Access (WPA) family of protocols. The predecessor of WPA, unfortunately still in use, is Wired Equivalent Privacy (WEP), considered by most to be insecure and easily breached.

Wired Equivalent Privacy (WEP)

Wired Equivalent Privacy (WEP) is part of the IEEE 802.11 wireless networking standard. WEP is designed to provide a basic level of security protection to these radio networks, to prevent unauthorized access or eavesdropping. However, WEP, like a traditional wired network, does not protect users from each other; it only protects the network from unauthorized users. In the early 2000s, cryptologists found several fundamental flaws in WEP, resulting in vulnerabilities that can be exploited to gain access. These vulnerabilities ultimately led to the replacement of WEP as the industry standard with WPA.

Wi-Fi Protected Access (WPA)

Created by the Wi-Fi Alliance, an industry group, **Wi-Fi Protected Access (WPA)** is a set of protocols used to secure wireless networks. The protocols were developed as an intermediate solution until the IEEE 802.11i standards were fully developed. IEEE 802.11i has been implemented in products such as WPA2. This is an amendment to the 802.11 standard published in June 2004, specifying security protocols for wireless networks. While WPA works with virtually all wireless network cards, it is not compatible with some older WAPs. WPA2, on the other hand, has compatibility issues with some older wireless network cards. Compared to WEP, WPA and WPA2 provide increased capabilities for authentication and encryption as well as increased throughput.

Unlike WEP, both WPA and WPA2 can use an IEEE 802.1X authentication server, similar to the RADIUS servers mentioned in the previous section. This type of authentication server can issue keys to users that have been authenticated by the local system. The alternative is to allow all users to share a key. Use of these preshared keys is quite convenient but is not secure compared to other authentication techniques. WPA also uses a Message Integrity Code (a type of message authentication code) to prevent certain types of attacks. WPA was the strongest possible mechanism that was backwardly compatible with the older systems. WPA2 introduced newer, more robust security protocols based on the Advanced Encryption Standard (discussed later in this chapter) to improve greatly the protection of wireless networks. The WPA2 standard is currently incorporated in virtually all Wi-Fi devices.

WiMAX

The next generation of wireless networking is WiMAX, also known as WirelessMAN; it is essentially an improvement on the technology developed for cellular telephones and modems. Developed as part of the IEEE 802.16 standard, WiMAX is a certification mark that stands for "Worldwide Interoperability for Microwave Access." As noted by the WiMAX Forum, an industry-sponsored organization that serves as an informal IEEE Standard 801.16 wireless standards evaluation group:

> *WiMAX is not a technology per se, but rather a certification mark, or "stamp of approval" given to equipment that meets certain conformity and interoperability tests for the IEEE 802.16 family of standards. A similar confusion surrounds the term Wi-Fi (Wireless Fidelity), which like WiMAX, is a certification mark for equipment based on a different set of IEEE standards from the 802.11 working group for wireless local area networks (WLAN). Neither WiMAX, nor Wi-Fi, is a technology but their names have been adopted in popular usage to denote the technologies behind them. This is likely due to the difficulty of using terms like "IEEE 802.16" in common speech and writing.*[11]

Bluetooth

Bluetooth is a de facto industry standard for short-range wireless communications between devices such as wireless telephones and headsets, between PDAs and desktop computers, and between laptops. The Bluetooth wireless communications link can be exploited by anyone within its approximately 30-foot range unless suitable security controls are implemented. It has been estimated that there will be almost a billion Bluetooth-enabled devices by the end of the decade. In discoverable mode—which allows other Bluetooth systems to detect and connect—devices can easily be accessed. Even in nondiscoverable mode, the device is susceptible to access by other devices that have connected with it in the past.

By default, Bluetooth does not authenticate connections; however, Bluetooth does implement some degree of security when devices access certain services, such as dial-up accounts and local area file transfers. Paired devices—usually a computer or a phone and a peripheral that a user plans to connect to it—require that the same passkey be entered on both devices. This key is used to generate a session key used for all future communications. The only way to secure Bluetooth-enabled devices is to incorporate a twofold approach: (1) Turn off Bluetooth when you do not intend to use it, and (2) do not accept an incoming communications pairing request unless you know who the requestor is.

Managing Wireless Connections

Users and organizations can use a number of measures to implement a secure wireless network. These safeguards include the wireless security protocols mentioned earlier, VPNs, and firewalls. It is also possible to restrict access to the network to a preapproved set of wireless network card MAC addresses. This is especially easy in small or personal networks where all possible users are known.

One of the first management requirements is to regulate the size of the wireless network footprint. The initial step is to determine the best locations for placement of the WAPs. In addition, by using radio-strength meters, network administrators can adjust the power of the broadcast antennae to provide sufficient but not excessive coverage. This is especially important in areas where public access is possible.

WEP used to be the first choice in network installation and is still available as an option on many technologies but generally should not be used. Even in a home or small office/home office (SOHO) setting, WPA is preferred; for most installations, WPA2 is preferred. The setups of wireless networks are also slightly different than what many users are familiar with.

Most smaller wireless networks require the use of a preshared key, which is a specific-length password. WEP networks require a 5-character or 13-character passphrase. In WPA and WPA2 settings, the passphrase can be any length, with longer being more secure. On some older equipment, the preshared key must be converted into a string of hexadecimal characters that is entered into both the configuration software used to set up the WAP and each associated wireless network access card. This can quickly turn into a labor-intensive process for all but the smallest of networks.

Scanning and Analysis Tools

In the previous section, wireless network controls were covered. Now, we return to the technology and tools that are useful in all compound (wired and wireless) networks. Although they are not always perceived as defensive tools, scanners, sniffers, and other analysis tools enable security administrators to see what an attacker sees. Scanner and analysis tools can find vulnerabilities in systems, holes in security components, and other unsecured points in the network. Unfortunately, they cannot detect the unpredictable behavior of people.

Some of these devices are extremely complex; others are very simple. Some are expensive commercial products; others are available for free from their creators. Conscientious administrators will have several hacking Web sites bookmarked and should frequently browse for discussions about new vulnerabilities, recent conquests, and favorite assault techniques. There is nothing wrong with security administrators using the tools used by hackers to examine their own defenses and search out areas of vulnerability. A word of caution: Many of these tools have distinct signatures, and some ISPs scan for these signatures. If the ISP discovers someone using hacker tools, it may choose to deny access to that customer and discontinue service. It is best to establish a working relationship with the ISP and notify it before using such tools.

Scanning tools collect the information that an attacker needs to succeed. Collecting information about a potential target is known as footprinting. **Footprinting** is the organized research of the Internet addresses owned or controlled by a target organization. Attackers may use public Internet data sources to perform keyword searches to identify the network addresses of the organization. They may also use the organization's Web page to find information that can be used in social engineering attacks. For example, the Reveal Source option on most popular Web browsers allows users to see the source code behind the graphics on a Web page. A number of clues can provide additional insight into the configuration of an internal network: the locations and directories for Common Gateway Interface (CGI) script bins, and the names and possibly addresses of computers and servers.

A scanner can be used to augment the data collected by a common browser. A Web site crawler program can scan entire Web sites for valuable information, such as server names and e-mail addresses. It can also do a number of other common information collection activities, such as sending multiple ICMP information requests (pings), attempting to retrieve multiple and cross-zoned DNS queries, and performing common network analysis queries—all powerful diagnostic and/or hacking activities.

The next phase of the preattack data gathering process, **fingerprinting**, entails the systematic examination of all the organization's Internet addresses (collected during the footprinting phase). By means of the tools described in the following section, fingerprinting yields a detailed network analysis that provides useful information about the targets of the planned attack. The tool discussions here are necessarily brief; to attain true expertise in the use and configuration of these tools, you will need more specific education and training.

Port Scanners

Port scanners are a group of utility software applications that can identify (or fingerprint) computers that are active on a network, as well as the active ports and services on those computers, the functions and roles fulfilled by the machines, and other useful information. These tools can scan for specific types of computers, protocols, or resources, or they can conduct generic scans. It is helpful to understand your network environment so that you can select the best tool for the job. The more specific the scanner is, the more detailed and useful the information it provides. However, you should keep a generic, broad-based scanner in your toolbox as well, to help locate and identify rogue nodes on the network that administrators may not be aware of.

A port is a network channel or connection point in a data communications system. Within the TCP/IP networking protocol, TCP and UDP port numbers differentiate among the multiple communication channels used to connect to network services that are offered on the same network device. Each service within the TCP/IP protocol suite has either a unique default port number or a user-selected port number. Table 10-5 shows some of the commonly used port numbers. In total, there are 65,536 port numbers in use. The well-known ports are those from 0 through 1023. The registered ports are those from 1024 through 49,151, and the dynamic and private ports are those from 49,152 through 65,535.

Port Numbers	Description
20 and 21	File Transfer Protocol (FTP)
25	Simple Mail Transfer Protocol (SMTP)
53	Domain Name Services (DNS)
67 and 68	Dynamic Host Configuration Protocol (DHCP)
80	Hypertext Transfer Protocol (HTTP)
110	Post Office Protocol v3 (POP3)
161	Simple Network Management Protocol (SNMP)
194	Internet Relay Chat (IRC) port (used for device sharing)
443	HTTP over SSL
8080	Proxy services

Table 10-5   Commonly used port numbers

Copyright © 2014 Cengage Learning®.

The first step in securing a system is to secure open ports. Why? Simply put, an open port can be used to send commands to a computer, gain access to a server, and exert control over a networking device. As a general rule, you should secure all ports and remove from service any ports not required for essential functions. For instance, if an organization does not host Web services, there is no need for port 80 to be available in its network or on its servers.

Vulnerability Scanners

Vulnerability scanners, which are variants of port scanners, are capable of scanning networks for very detailed information. As a class, they identify exposed user names and groups, show open network shares, and expose configuration problems and other server vulnerabilities. One vulnerability scanner is Nmap, a professional freeware utility available from *www.insecure.org/nmap*. Nmap identifies the systems available on a network, the services (ports) each system is offering, the operating system and operating system version they are running, the type of packet filters and firewalls in use, and dozens of other characteristics. Several commercial vulnerability scanners are available as well, including products from IBM's Internet Security Systems, and from Foundstone, a division of McAfee.

Packet Sniffers

A packet sniffer is a network tool that collects and analyzes copies of packets from the network. It can provide a network administrator with valuable information to help diagnose and resolve networking issues. In the wrong hands, it can be used to eavesdrop on network traffic. The commercially available and open-source sniffers include Sniffer (a commercial product), Snort (open-source software), and Wireshark (another open-source software). An excellent free network protocol analyzer is Wireshark (*www.wireshark.com*), which allows administrators to examine both live network traffic and previously captured data. This application offers a variety of features, including language filters and TCP session reconstruction utility.

Typically, to use a packet sniffer effectively, you must be connected directly to a local network from an internal location. Simply tapping into any public Internet connection will flood you with more data than you can process and technically constitutes a violation of wiretapping laws. To use a packet sniffer legally, you must satisfy the following criteria: (1) Be on a network that the organization owns, not leases, (2) be under the direct authorization of the network's owners, (3) have the knowledge and consent of the content creators (users), and (4) have a justifiable business reason for doing so. If all four conditions are met, you can selectively collect and analyze packets to identify and diagnose problems on the network. Conditions 1 and 2 are self-explanatory, and condition 3 is usually a stipulation for using the company network. Incidentally, these conditions are the same as for employee monitoring in general.

Content Filters

Another type of tool that effectively protects the organization's systems from misuse and unintentional DoS conditions is the content filter. Technically not a firewall, a **content filter** is a software program or a hardware/software appliance that allows administrators to restrict content that comes into a network. The most common application of a content filter is the restriction of access to Web sites with nonbusiness-related material, such as pornography or entertainment. Another application is the restriction of spam e-mail from outside sources. Content filters can consist of small add-on software for the home or office, such as Net Nanny or SurfControl, or major corporate applications, such as Novell's BorderManager and Microsoft's Forefront Security applications.

Content filters ensure that employees are not using network resources inappropriately. Unfortunately, these systems require extensive configuration and constant updating of the list of unacceptable destinations or incoming restricted e-mail source addresses. Some newer content filtering applications update the restricted database automatically, in the same way that some antivirus programs do. These applications match either a list of disapproved or approved Web sites, for example, or key content words, such as "nude" and "sex." Of course, content creators work to bypass such restrictions by avoiding these trip words, creating additional problems for networking and security professionals.

Trap and Trace

Trap and trace applications, another set of technologies, are growing in popularity. Trap function software entices individuals who are illegally perusing the internal areas of a network in order to determine who they are. While perusing, these individuals discover indicators of particularly rich content areas on the network, but these areas are set up to attract potential attackers. Better known as **honey pots**, these directories or servers distract the attacker while the software notifies the administrator of the intrusion.

The accompaniment to the trap is the trace. Similar in concept to telephone Caller ID service, the trace is a process by which the organization attempts to determine the identity of someone discovered in unauthorized areas of the network or systems.

Managing Scanning and Analysis Tools

It is vitally important that the security manager be able to see the organization's systems and networks from the viewpoint of potential attackers. Therefore, the security manager should develop a program, using in-house resources, contractors, or an outsourced service provider, to periodically scan the organization's systems and networks for vulnerabilities, using the same tools that a typical hacker might use.

There are a number of drawbacks to using scanners and analysis tools, content filters, and trap and trace tools:

- These tools are not human and thus cannot simulate the more creative behavior of a human attacker.

- Most tools function by pattern recognition, so only previously known issues can be detected. New approaches, modifications to well-known attack patterns, and the randomness of human behavior can cause them to misdiagnose the situation, thereby allowing vulnerabilities to go undetected or threats to go unchallenged.

- Most of these tools are computer-based software or hardware and so are prone to errors, flaws, and vulnerabilities of their own.

- All of these tools are designed, configured, and operated by humans and are subject to human errors.

- You get what you pay for. Use of hackerware may actually infect a system with a virus or open the system to outside attacks or other unintended consequences. Always view a hacker kit skeptically before using it and especially before connecting it to the Internet. Never put anything valuable on the computer that houses the hacker tools. Consider segregating it from other network segments, and disconnect it from the network when not in use.

- Specifically for content filters, some governments, agencies, institutions, and universities have established policies or laws that protect the individual user's right to access content, especially if it is necessary for the conduct of his or her job. There are also situations in which an entire class of content has been proscribed and mere possession of that content is a criminal act—for example, child pornography.

- Tool usage and configuration must comply with an explicitly articulated policy, and the policy must provide for valid exceptions. This mandate prevents administrators from becoming arbiters of morality as they create a filter rule set.[12]

Cryptography

Although it is not a specific application or security tool, cryptography represents a sophisticated element of control that is often included in other InfoSec controls. In fact, many security-related tools use embedded encryption technologies to protect sensitive information. The use of the proper cryptographic tools can ensure confidentiality by keeping private information concealed from those who do not need to see it. Other cryptographic methods can provide increased information integrity by providing a mechanism to guarantee that a message in transit has not been altered by using a process that creates a secure message digest, or hash. In e-commerce situations, some cryptographic tools can be used to assure that parties to the transaction are authentic, so that they cannot later deny having participated in a transaction—a feature often called **nonrepudiation**.

Encryption is the process of converting an original message into a form that cannot be used by unauthorized individuals. That way, anyone without the tools and knowledge to convert an encrypted message back to its original format will be unable to interpret it. The science of encryption, known as **cryptology**, actually encompasses two disciplines: cryptography and cryptanalysis. **Cryptography**—from the Greek words "kryptos," meaning "hidden," and "graphein," meaning "to write"—is the set of processes involved in encoding and decoding messages so that others cannot understand them. **Cryptanalysis**—from "analyein," meaning "to break up"—is the process of deciphering the original message (or **plaintext**) from an encrypted message (or **ciphertext**) without knowing the algorithms and keys used to perform the encryption.

Cryptography Definitions

You can better understand the tools and functions popular in encryption security solutions if you know some basic terminology:

- *Algorithm*—The mathematical formula or method used to convert an unencrypted message into an encrypted message

- *Cipher*—The transformation of the individual components (characters, bytes, or bits) of an unencrypted message into encrypted components or vice versa (see *decipher* and *encipher*)

- *Ciphertext or cryptogram*—The unintelligible encrypted or encoded message resulting from an encryption

- *Cryptosystem*—The set of transformations necessary to convert an unencrypted message into an encrypted message

- *Decipher*—To decrypt or convert ciphertext to plaintext

- *Encipher*—To encrypt or convert plaintext to ciphertext

- *Key*—The information used in conjunction with the algorithm to create the ciphertext from the plaintext; can be a series of bits used in a mathematical algorithm or the knowledge of how to manipulate the plaintext

- *Keyspace*—The entire range of values that can possibly be used to construct an individual key

- *Plaintext*—The original unencrypted message that is encrypted and that is the result of successful decryption

- *Steganography*—The process of hiding messages (e.g., when a messages is hidden within the digital encoding of a picture or graphic, so that it is almost impossible to detect that the hidden message even exists)

- *Work factor*—The amount of effort (usually expressed in units of time) required to perform cryptanalysis on an encoded message

Cryptology is a very complex field based on advanced mathematical concepts. The following sections provide a brief overview of the foundations of encryption and a short discussion of some of the related issues and tools in the field of InfoSec. You can find more information about cryptography in Bruce Schneier's book *Secrets and Lies: Digital Security in a Networked World*, which discusses many of the theoretical and practical considerations in the use of cryptographic systems.

Encryption Operations

Encryption is accomplished by using algorithms to manipulate the plaintext into the ciphertext for transmission. Some widely used encryption operations are explained in the sections that follow.

Common Ciphers In encryption, the most commonly used algorithms include the following three functions: substitution, transposition, and XOR. In a **substitution cipher**, you substitute one value for another. For example, using the lines labeled "input text" and "output text" that are shown here, you can replace each character in the plaintext with the character that is three values to the right of that character in the alphabet:

```
Input text:   ABCDEFGHIJKLMNOPQRSTUVWXYZ
Output text: DEFGHIJKLMNOPQRSTUVWXYZABC
```

Thus, a plaintext of BERLIN becomes EHUOLQ in ciphertext.

This is a simple method, but it becomes very powerful if combined with other operations. Our example was based on a **monoalphabetic substitution**, as it uses only one alphabet, but more advanced substitution ciphers use two or more alphabets and are called **polyalphabetic substitutions**. For example, consider the following block of text:

```
Input text:            ABCDEFGHIJKLMNOPQRSTUVWXYZ
Substitution cipher 1: DEFGHIJKLMNOPQRSTUVWXYZABC
Substitution cipher 2: GHIJKLMNOPQRSTUVWXYZABCDEF
Substitution cipher 3: JKLMNOPQRSTUVWXYZABCDEFGHI
Substitution cipher 4: MNOPQRSTUVWXYZABCDEFGHIJKL
```

Here, the plaintext is matched character by character to the input text row. The next four lines are four sets of substitution ciphers. In this example, you can encode the word TEXT as WKGF, as you select letters from the second row for the first letter, letters from the third row for the second letter, and so on. This type of encryption is substantially more difficult to decipher without the algorithm (rows of ciphers) and key (use of the second row for the first letter, the third row for the second letter, and so on). It is also easy to randomize the cipher rows completely to create more complex substitution operations.

Another simple example of the substitution cipher is the daily cryptogram in your local newspaper, or the well-known Little Orphan Annie decoder ring. Julius Caesar reportedly used a three-character shift to the right (using the Roman alphabet), in which A becomes D and so on, giving that particular substitution cipher his name—the Caesar cipher.

Like the substitution operation, transposition is simple to understand but can be complex to decipher if properly used. Unlike the substitution cipher, the **transposition cipher (or permutation cipher)** simply rearranges the values within a block to create the ciphertext. This can be done at the bit or byte (character) level. For an example of how a transposition cipher works, consider the following plaintext and key:

```
Plaintext: 001001010110101110010101010100
Key:       1 > 3, 2 > 6, 3 > 8, 4 > 1, 5 > 4, 6 > 7, 7 > 5, 8 > 2
```

10

The key works like this: Bit 1 moves to position 3, bit 2 moves to position 6, and so on, with bit position 1 being the *rightmost* bit and position 2 being just to the left of position 1.

Applying this key, here is the plaintext (broken into 8-bit blocks for ease of discussion) and the corresponding ciphertext:

```
Plaintext 8-bit blocks: 00100101 01101011 10010101 01010100
Ciphertext:             11000100 01110101 10001110 10011000
```

To make this easier to follow, consider the following example of character transposition (in which spaces count as characters and are transposed as well):

```
Plaintext: MY DOG HAS FLEAS
Key:       Same key but with characters transposed rather than bits
```

Here, then, is the plaintext and the corresponding ciphertext:

```
Plaintext in 8-character blocks: MY DOG HAS FLEAS
Ciphertext:                      G YDHMO E ASFSAL
```

Note that the key is repeated as needed to transpose all plaintext to ciphertext.

Transposition ciphers and substitution ciphers can be used together in multiple combinations to create a very secure encryption process. To make the encryption stronger (more difficult to cryptanalyze), the keys and block sizes can be made much larger (64-bit or 128-bit), resulting in substantially more complex substitutions or transpositions.

In the **XOR cipher** conversion, the bit stream is subjected to a Boolean XOR function against some other data stream, typically a key stream. The symbol commonly used to represent the XOR function is "^". XOR works as follows:

```
"0" XOR'ed with "0" results in a "0". (0 ^ 0 = 0)
"0" XOR'ed with "1" results in a "1". (0 ^ 1 = 1)
"1" XOR'ed with "0" results in a "1". (1 ^ 0 = 1)
"1" XOR'ed with "1" results in a "0". (1 ^ 1 = 0)
```

Simply put, if the two values are the same, you get "0"; if not, you get "1". Suppose you have a data stream in which the first byte is 01000001. If you have a key stream in which the first "byte" is 0101 1010, and you XOR them:

```
Plaintext:  0100 0001
Key stream: 0101 1010
Ciphertext: 0001 1011
```

This process is reversible. That is, if you XOR the ciphertext with the key stream, you get the plaintext.

Vernam Cipher Also known as the one-time pad, the **Vernam cipher** was developed at AT&T and uses a set of characters for encryption operations only one time and then discards it. The values from this one-time pad are added to the block of text, and the resulting sum is converted to text. When the two sets of values are added, if the resulting values exceed 26, 26 is subtracted from the total (a process called modulo 26). The corresponding results are then converted back to text. The following example demonstrates how the Vernam cipher works:

Plaintext	M	Y	D	O	G	H	A	S	B	L	E	A	S
Corresponding values	13	25	04	15	07	08	01	19	06	12	05	01	19
One-time pad	F	P	Q	R	N	S	B	I	E	H	T	Z	L
Pad corresponding values	06	16	17	18	14	19	02	09	05	08	20	26	12
Sum	19	41	21	33	21	27	03	28	11	20	25	27	31
Subtraction (modulo 26)		15		07		01		02					
Ciphertext	P	O	U	G	U	A	C	B	K	T	Y	A	E

Copyright © 2014 Cengage Learning®.

Book or Running Key Cipher Another method, one seen in the occasional spy movie, is the use of the **book or running key cipher** in which the words (or, in some cases, characters) found in a book act as the algorithm to decrypt a message. The key relies on two components: (1) knowing which book to refer to and (2) having a list of codes representing the page number, line number, and word number of the plaintext word. Dictionaries and thesauruses are the most popular sources, as they provide every needed word, although almost any book will suffice. For example, using a particular printing of a popular novel, one might send the following message: 67,3,1;145,9,4;375,7,4;394,17,3. If the receiver knows which book is used, he or she goes to page 67, line 3 and selects the first word from that line; then goes to page 145, line 9, and selects the fourth word; and so forth. The resulting message, cancel operation target compromised, can then be read. When using dictionaries, it is necessary to use only a page and word number. An even more sophisticated version of this cipher uses multiple books in a particular sequence, with a new book for each word or phrase.

Symmetric Encryption Each of the aforementioned encryption and decryption methods requires that the same algorithm and key—a **secret key**— be used to both encipher and decipher the message. This is known as **private key encryption**, or **symmetric encryption**. Symmetric encryption is efficient and easy to process as long as both the sender and the receiver possess the encryption key. Of course, if either copy of the key becomes compromised, the adversary can decrypt and read the messages. One challenge in symmetric key encryption is getting a copy of the key to the receiver, a process that must be conducted out-of-band (i.e., through a different channel or band than the one carrying the ciphertext) to avoid interception. Figure 10-11 illustrates the concept of symmetric encryption.

A number of popular symmetric cryptosystems are available. One of the most familiar is Data Encryption Standard (DES). DES was developed in 1977 by IBM and is based on the Data Encryption Algorithm (DEA), which uses a 64-bit block size and a 56-bit key. With a 56-bit key, the algorithm has 2^{56} (more than 72 quadrillion) possible keys.

DES was a federally approved standard for nonclassified data (see "Federal Information Processing Standards Publication 46-2" at *www.itl.nist.gov/fipspubs/fip46-2.htm*). It was

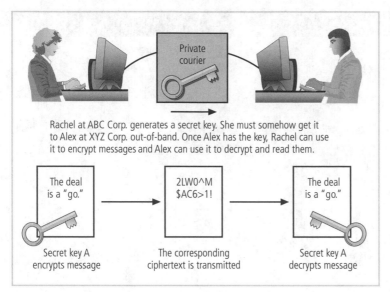

Rachel at ABC Corp. generates a secret key. She must somehow get it to Alex at XYZ Corp. out-of-band. Once Alex has the key, Rachel can use it to encrypt messages and Alex can use it to decrypt and read them.

Figure 10-11 Symmetric encryption

Copyright © 2014 Cengage Learning®.

cracked in 1997 when the developers of a competing algorithm called Rivest-Shamir-Aldeman (RSA) offered a $10,000 reward for the first person or team to do so. Fourteen thousand users collaborated over the Internet to break the encryption! Triple DES (3DES) was then developed as an improvement to DES. It uses as many as three keys in succession and is substantially more secure than DES, not only because it uses as many as three keys instead of one but because it performs three different encryption operations.

The successor to 3DES is the Advanced Encryption Standard (AES). It is based on the Rijndael Block Cipher, which features a variable block length and a key length of 128, 192, or 256 bits. In 1998, it took a special computer designed by the Electronic Freedom Frontier (*www.eff.org*) more than 56 hours to crack DES. It would take the same computer approximately 4,698,864 quintillion years (4,698,864,000,000,000,000,000) to crack AES.

Asymmetric Encryption Another encryption technique is **asymmetric encryption**, also known as public key encryption. Whereas symmetric encryption systems use a single key both to encrypt and decrypt a message, asymmetric encryption uses two different keys. Either key can be used to encrypt or decrypt the message. However, if Key A is used to encrypt the message, then only Key B can decrypt it; conversely, if Key B is used to encrypt a message, then only Key A can decrypt it. This technique is most valuable when one of the keys is private and the other is public. The public key is stored in a public location, where anyone can use it. The private key, as its name suggests, is a secret known only to the owner of the key pair.

Consider the following example, illustrated in Figure 10-12. Alex at XYZ Corp. wants to send an encrypted message to Rachel at ABC Corp. Alex goes to a public key registry and obtains Rachel's public key. Recall the foundation of asymmetric encryption: The same key cannot be used to both encrypt and decrypt the same message. Thus, when Rachel's public

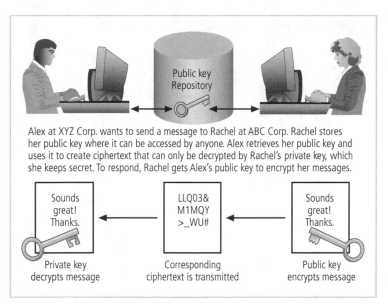

Figure 10-12 Asymmetric encryption
Copyright © 2014 Cengage Learning®.

key is used to encrypt the message, only her private key can be used to decrypt it—and that private key is held by Rachel alone. Similarly, if Rachel wants to respond to Alex's message, she goes to the registry where Alex's public key is held and uses it to encrypt her message, which of course can be read only by using Alex's private key to decrypt it.

The problem with asymmetric encryption is that it requires four keys to hold a single conversation between two parties. If four organizations want to exchange messages frequently, each must manage its private key and four public keys. It can be confusing to determine which public key is needed to encrypt a particular message. With more organizations in the loop, the problem grows geometrically. Also, asymmetric encryption is not as efficient in its use of CPU resources as symmetric encryptions when performing the extensive mathematical calculations. As a result, the hybrid system described in the section titled "Public Key Infrastructure" (later in this chapter) is more commonly used.

Digital Signatures When the asymmetric process is reversed—the private key is used to encrypt a (usually short) message, and the corresponding public key is used to decrypt it—the fact that the message was sent by the organization that owns the private key cannot be refuted. This nonrepudiation is the foundation of **digital signatures**. Digital signatures are encrypted messages whose authenticity can be independently verified by a central facility (registry) but that can also be used to prove certain characteristics of the message or file with which they are associated. They are often used in Internet software updates (see Figure 10-13). A pop-up window shows that the downloaded files did, in fact, come from the purported agency and thus can be trusted. **A digital certificate** is a block of data similar to a digital signature, attached to a file certifying that the file is from the organization it claims to be from and has not been modified from the original format. **A certificate authority (CA)** is an agency that manages the issuance of certificates and serves as the electronic notary public to verify their origin and integrity.

Properties

General

Amazon.com Checkout: Payment

Protocol: HyperText Transfer Protocol with Privacy

Type: Not Available

Connection: TLS 1.0, RC4 with 128 bit encryption (High); RSA
                with 1024 bit exchange

Address: https://www.amazon.com/gp/checkout/ship/select.
(URL)   html

Size: Not Available

Created: Not Available

Modified: Not Available

Certificates

OK   Cancel   Apply

Figure 10-13 Example digital signature

Source: Firefox.

RSA One of the most popular public key cryptosystems is a proprietary model called Rivest-Shamir-Aldeman (RSA), which is named after its developers. The first public key encryption algorithm developed for commercial use, RSA has been integrated into both Microsoft Internet Explorer and Netscape Navigator. (The window on the left side of Figure 10-13 includes a reference to the RSA algorithm in the "Connection" field.)

Public Key Infrastructure A **public key infrastructure** (**PKI**) is the entire set of hardware, software, and cryptosystems necessary to implement public key encryption. PKI systems are based on public key cryptosystems and include digital certificates and certificate authorities. Common implementations of PKI include:

- Systems that issue digital certificates to users and servers
- Systems with computer key values to be included in digital certificates
- Tools for managing user enrollment, key generation, and certificate issuance
- Verification and return of certificates
- Key revocation services
- Other services associated with PKI that vendors bundle into their products

The use of cryptographic tools is made more manageable when using PKI. An organization can increase its cryptographic capabilities in protecting its information assets by using PKI to provide the following services:

- *Authentication*—Digital certificates in a PKI system permit individuals, organizations, and Web servers to authenticate the identity of each of the parties in an Internet transaction.

- *Integrity*—Digital certificates assert that the content signed by the certificate has not been altered while in transit.

- *Confidentiality*—PKI keeps information confidential by ensuring that it is not intercepted during transmission over the Internet.

- *Authorization*—Digital certificates issued in a PKI environment can replace user IDs and passwords, enhance security, and reduce some of the overhead for authorization processes and controlling access privileges for specific transactions.

- *Nonrepudiation*—Digital certificates can validate actions, making it less likely that customers or partners can later repudiate a digitally signed transaction, such as an online purchase.

Hybrid Systems Purely asymmetric key encryption is not widely used except in the area of certificates. For other purposes, it is typically employed in conjunction with symmetric key encryption, creating a **hybrid encryption system**. The hybrid process in widespread use is based on the **Diffie-Hellman key exchange method**, which provides a way to exchange private keys without exposure to any third parties. In this method, asymmetric encryption is used to exchange symmetric keys so that two organizations can conduct quick, efficient, secure communications based on symmetric encryption. Diffie-Hellman is the foundation for subsequent developments in public key encryption.

The process, which is illustrated in Figure 10-14, works like this: Because symmetric encryption is more efficient than asymmetric encryption for sending messages, and because asymmetric encryption does not require out-of-band key exchange, asymmetric encryption can be used to transmit symmetric keys in a hybrid approach. Suppose Alex at XYZ Corp. wants to communicate with Rachel at ABC Corp. First, Alex creates a session key—a symmetric key for limited-use, temporary communications. Alex encrypts a message with the

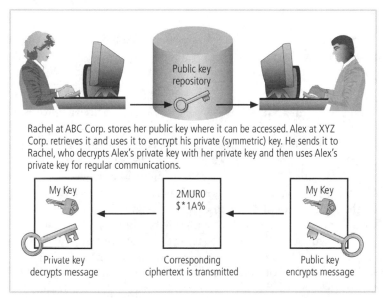

Rachel at ABC Corp. stores her public key where it can be accessed. Alex at XYZ Corp. retrieves it and uses it to encrypt his private (symmetric) key. He sends it to Rachel, who decrypts Alex's private key with her private key and then uses Alex's private key for regular communications.

| My Key | 2MUR0 $*1A% | My Key |

Private key decrypts message   Corresponding ciphertext is transmitted   Public key encrypts message

Figure 10-14 Hybrid encryption

Copyright © 2014 Cengage Learning®.

session key and then gets Rachel's public key. He uses her public key to encrypt both the session key and the message that is already encrypted. Alex transmits the entire package to Rachel, who uses her private key to decrypt the package containing the session key and the encrypted message, and then uses the session key to decrypt the message. Rachel can then continue the electronic conversation using only the more efficient symmetric session key.

Using Cryptographic Controls

Cryptographic controls are often misunderstood by those new to the area of InfoSec. While modem cryptosystems can certainly generate unbreakable ciphertext, it is possible only when the proper key management infrastructure has been constructed and when the cryptosystems are operated and managed correctly. As in many InfoSec endeavors, the technical control is valuable, as long as it is founded on sound policy and managed with an awareness of the fundamental objectives of the organization. Unfortunately, many cryptographic controls have been sold to organizations that were not able to deploy them to improve their security programs. This may have been due to poor project planning, errors in executing the implementation plans, or failures to put sound policies in place before acquiring the controls. Whatever the causes, many organizations have failed to make full use of their investment in cryptographic controls.

Organizations with the need and the ability to use cryptographic controls can use them to support several aspects of the business:

- Confidentiality and integrity of e-mail and its attachments
- Authentication, confidentiality, integrity, and nonrepudiation of e-commerce transactions
- Authentication and confidentiality of remote access through VPN connections
- A higher standard of authentication when used to supplement access control systems

E-Mail Security A number of cryptosystems have been adapted to help secure e-mail, a notoriously insecure method of communication. Some of the more popular adaptations include Secure Multipurpose Internet Mail Extensions, Privacy Enhanced Mail, and Pretty Good Privacy.

Secure Multipurpose Internet Mail Extensions (S/MIME) builds on the Multipurpose Internet Mail Extensions (MIME) encoding format by adding encryption and authentication via digital signatures based on public key cryptosystems. Privacy Enhanced Mail (PEM) has been proposed by the Internet Engineering Task Force (IETF) as a standard that will function with public key cryptosystems. PEM uses 3DES symmetric key encryption and RSA for key exchanges and digital signatures. Pretty Good Privacy (PGP) was developed by Phil Zimmerman and uses the International Data Encryption Algorithm (IDEA) cipher, a 128-bit symmetric key block encryption algorithm with 64-bit blocks for message encoding. Like PEM, it uses RSA for symmetric key exchange and to support digital signatures. PGP relies on a "web of trust" model to allow its users to share key information easily, albeit with some loss in the degree of control and trust in the key information. With PGP, if user A has established a trusting relationship with user B, and if user B has a trusting relationship with user C, then user A is presumed to have a trusting relationship with user C and can exchange encrypted information with that user.

Securing the Web Just as S/MIME, PEM, and PGP help secure e-mail operations, a number of cryptosystems help to secure Web activity, especially transactions between customers' browsers and the Web servers at e-commerce sites. Among the protocols used for this purpose are Secure Electronic Transactions, Secure Sockets Layer, Secure Hypertext Transfer Protocol, Secure Shell, and IP Security.

Secure Electronic Transactions (SET) was developed by MasterCard and VISA in 1997 to provide protection from electronic payment fraud. It works by encrypting the credit card transfers with DES for encryption and RSA for key exchange. SET provides the security for both Internet-based credit card transactions and the encryption of card swipe systems in retail stores.

Secure Sockets Layer (SSL) was developed by Netscape in 1994 to provide security for online e-commerce transactions. It uses a number of algorithms but mainly relies on RSA for key transfer and IDEA, DES, or 3DES for encrypted symmetric key-based data transfer. Figure 10-13 shows the certificate and SSL information that is displayed when you perform the check-out step on an e-commerce site. If the Web connection does not automatically display the certificate, you can right-click in the window and select Properties to view the connection encryption and certificate properties.

Secure Hypertext Transfer Protocol (SHTTP) is an encrypted solution to the unsecured version of HTTP. It provides an alternative to the aforementioned protocols and can provide secure e-commerce transactions as well as encrypted Web pages for secure data transfer over the Web using a number of different algorithms.

Secure Shell (SSH) is a popular extension to the TCP/IP protocol suite. Sponsored by the IETF, SSH provides security for remote access connections over public networks by creating a secure and persistent connection. It provides authentication services between a client and a server and is used to secure replacement tools for terminal emulation, remote management, and file transfer applications.

IP Security (IPSec) is the primary and now dominant cryptographic authentication and encryption product of the IETF's IP Protocol Security Working Group. It supports a variety of applications, just as SSH does. A framework for security development within the TCP/IP family of protocol standards, IPSec provides application support for all uses within TCP/IP, including VPNs. This protocol combines several different cryptosystems:

- Diffie-Hellman key exchange for deriving key material between peers on a public network
- Public key cryptography for signing the Diffie-Hellman exchanges to guarantee the identity of the two parties
- Bulk encryption algorithms, such as DES, for encrypting the data
- Digital certificates signed by a CA to act as digital ID cards

IPSec has two components: (1) the IP Security protocol itself, which specifies the information to be added to an IP packet and indicates how to encrypt packet data; and (2) the Internet Key Exchange (IKE), which uses asymmetric key exchange and negotiates the security associations.

IPSec works in two modes of operation: transport and tunnel. In **transport mode**, only the IP data is encrypted—not the IP headers themselves. This allows intermediate nodes to read the source and destination addresses. In **tunnel mode**, the entire IP packet is encrypted and inserted as the payload in another IP packet. This requires other systems at the beginning and end of the tunnel to act as proxies to send and receive the encrypted packets. These systems then transmit the decrypted packets to their true destinations.

IPSec and other cryptographic extensions to TCP/IP are often used to support a **virtual private network (VPN)**. A VPN is a private, secure network operated over a public and insecure network. It keeps the contents of the network messages hidden from observers who may have access to public traffic. Using the VPN tunneling approach described earlier, an individual or organization can set up a network connection on the Internet and send encrypted data back and forth, using the IP-packet-within-an-IP-packet method to deliver the data safely and securely. VPN support is built into most Microsoft Server software, including Windows Server 2003 and later versions, and client support for VPN services is included in most modern Windows clients (such as Windows 7 and Windows 8). While true private network services can cost hundreds of thousands of dollars to lease, configure, and maintain, a VPN can be established for much less.

Securing Authentication

Cryptosystems can also be used to provide enhanced and secure authentication. One approach to this issue is provided by **Kerberos**, named after the three-headed dog of Greek mythology (Cerberus in Latin) that guarded the gates to the underworld. Kerberos uses symmetric key encryption to validate an individual user's access to various network resources. It keeps a database containing the private keys of clients and servers that are in the authentication domain it supervises. Network services running on the servers in the shared authentication domain register with Kerberos, as do clients that want to use those services.[13]

The Kerberos system recognizes these private keys and can authenticate one network node (client or server) to another. For example, it can authenticate a client to a print service. To understand Kerberos, think of a typical multiscreen cinema. You acquire your ticket at the box office, and the ticket-taker then admits you to the proper screening room based on the contents of your ticket. Kerberos also generates temporary session keys—that is, private keys given to the two parties in a conversation. The session key is used to encrypt all communications between these two parties. Typically, a user logs into the network, is authenticated to the Kerberos system, and is then authenticated by the Kerberos system to other resources on the network.

Kerberos consists of three interacting services, all of which rely on a database library:

- *Authentication Server (AS)*—A Kerberos server that authenticates clients and servers.
- *Key Distribution Center (KDC)*—Generates and issues session keys.
- *Kerberos Ticket Granting Service (TGS)*—Provides tickets to clients who request services. An authorization ticket is an identification card for a particular client that verifies to the server that the client is requesting services and that the client is a valid member of the Kerberos system and, therefore, authorized to receive services. The ticket consists of the client's name and network address, a ticket validation starting and ending time, and the session key, all encrypted in the private key of the target server.

Kerberos operates according to the following principles:

- The KDC knows the secret keys of all clients and servers on the network.
- The KDC initially exchanges information with the client and server by using the secret keys.

- Kerberos authenticates a client to a requested service on a server through TGS and by issuing temporary session keys for communications between the client and the KDC, the server and the KDC, and the client and the server.

- Communications take place between the client and server using the temporary session keys.[14]

Kerberos may be obtained free of charge from MIT at *http://ist.mit.edu*. If you decide to use it, however, be aware of some concerns. If the Kerberos servers are subjected to DoS attacks, no client can request (or receive) any services. If the Kerberos servers, service providers, or clients' machines become compromised, their private key information may also be compromised.

Managing Cryptographic Controls

Cryptographic controls require close management attention. Some of the more important managerial issues are as follows:

- Don't lose your keys. Any key-based system is contingent upon the physical security of its keys. If the keys are compromised, so is all communication. If the keys are lost, any data encrypted with those keys may be lost as well. Unlike your car keys, which the dealer can replace, cryptographic keys are not known to the software vendors and are usually not recoverable. The purpose of the encryption algorithm is to prevent unauthorized entities from viewing the data. Unless your organization has made an investment in a key management solution that enables key recovery, if you lose your key, you may lose your data or the service being protected. Loss of unrecoverable keys will deny access to everyone. Given the current state of cryptographic technology, breaking the code is very likely impossible.

- Know who you are communicating with. One of the most popular encryption-based attacks is the man-in-the-middle attack in which the attacker pretends to be the second party in a conversation and relays the traffic to the actual second party. The attacker collects, decrypts, reads, possibly modifies, reencrypts, and transmits the information. This type of operation is possible only if the attacker is involved in the initial key exchange. Always verify the public keys in a public key exchange.

- It may be illegal to use a specific encryption technique when communicating to some nations. Federal export regulation still restricts the countries with which you can share strong encryption. Check the U.S. Department of Commerce's export frequently asked questions (FAQs) (*www.bis.doc.gov/Encryption/default.htm*) for more information.

- Every cryptosystem has weaknesses. Make sure you can live with the weaknesses of any system you choose. Research your selection before trusting any cryptosystem.

- Give access only to those users, systems, and servers with a business need, a principle known as "least privilege." Do not load cryptosystems on systems that can be easily compromised.

- When placing trust in a CA, ask the following question: *Quis custodiet ipsos custodes*? That is, who watches the watchers? CAs do not assume any liability for the accuracy of their information, which is strange given that their purpose is to validate the identity of a third party. However, if you read the fine print on the CA agreement, you will most likely find statements to that effect.

- There is no security in obscurity. Just because a system is secret does not mean it is safe. It is better to put your trust in a tried-and-true tested solution.

View Point
Leveraging Protection Mechanisms to Provide Defense in Depth
By Todd E. Tucker, CISSP, Research Director, Technology Business Management Council

Defense in depth is a protection strategy with a long history. It is characterized by layers of protection that, while not impenetrable, provide the advantage of increasing the time and resources necessary to penetrate through every layer of defense. Perhaps the best-known physical example of defense in depth comes from the archetypical fortress, built with high walls, manned by armed guards, and placed behind a protective moat. In information security, protection mechanisms are essential for providing defense in depth. Each mechanism, when considered alone, may provide little protection against today's sophisticated attacks. However, InfoSec architects build systems and networks by implementing layers of protection. For example, architects leverage a secured physical perimeter to protect media and hardware, implement firewalls to secure the internal networks from untrusted ones, install antivirus applications to detect and eradicate malicious code, implement intrusion detection and prevention systems to identify and inhibit attacks, and harden critical platforms to reduce vulnerabilities. These protection mechanisms become the walls, guards, and moats of today's electronic fortresses and effectively provide defense in depth.

Defense in depth provides several advantages to organizations. The obvious benefit is the added security that results from requiring an attacker to spend more time and resources to break in. Another benefit is the flexibility it provides in responding to specific threats. For example, consider a worm that exploits databases via a specific TCP port. The options for responding to the threat include shutting down the port the worm uses, hardening the database directly, or perhaps setting intrusion detection rules to spot and terminate an attack. Flexibility is important in production environments, where one action may adversely impact mission critical systems, requiring other actions to be considered.

Defense in depth provides a major disadvantage, too: complexity. Defense in depth increases the number of protection mechanisms implemented. It requires architects and administrators to consider the overall design of the network. Moreover, they must consider all the protection mechanisms to ensure they adequately protect against threats and do not conflict with one another.

As you learn about protection mechanisms, think not just about their technical aspects and the security they provide. Think about their ability to work with other mechanisms to provide defense in depth. How can they work together to increase the overall security of the system? Also, consider the management implications of each mechanism. Remember that these mechanisms are often implemented on a large scale and each one requires maintenance, administration, and monitoring. One of the greatest challenges in information security today is in managing the protection mechanisms on an enterprise-scale and effectively leveraging them to provide defense in depth.

Security protocols and the cryptosystems they use are subject to the same limitations as firewalls and IDPSs. They are all installed and configured by humans and are only as secure as their configuration allows. VPNs are particularly vulnerable to direct attacks; compromise of the remote client can directly result in compromise of the trusted system. Home-computing users frequently use the Windows "remember passwords" function, which could present a real problem if these systems are compromised. Don't let telecommuters use this option.

As with all other InfoSec program components, make sure that your organization's use of cryptography is based on well-constructed policy and supported with sound management procedures. The tools themselves may work exactly as advertised, but if they are not used correctly and managed diligently, your organization's secrets may soon be public knowledge.

Chapter Summary

- Identification is a mechanism that provides basic information about an unknown entity to the known entity that it wants to communicate with.

- Authentication is the validation of a user's identity. Authentication devices can depend on one or more of four factors: what you know, what you have, what you are, and what you produce.

- Authorization is the process of determining which actions an authenticated entity can perform in a particular physical or logical area.

- Accountability is the documentation of actions on a system and the tracing of those actions to a user, who can then be held responsible for those actions. Accountability is performed using system logs and auditing.

- To obtain strong authentication, a system must use two or more authentication methods.

- Biometric technologies are evaluated on three criteria: false reject rate, false accept rate, and crossover error rate.

- A firewall in an InfoSec program is any device that prevents a specific type of information from moving between the outside world (the untrusted network) and the inside world (the trusted network).

- Types of firewalls include packet filtering firewalls, application-level firewalls, stateful inspection firewalls, and dynamic packet filtering firewalls. There are four common architectural implementations of firewalls: packet filtering routers, screened-host firewalls, dual-homed firewalls, and screened-subnet firewalls.

- A host-based IDPS resides on a particular computer or server and monitors activity on that system. A network-based IDPS monitors network traffic; when a predefined condition occurs, it responds and notifies the appropriate administrator.

- A signature-based IDPS, also known as a knowledge-based IDPS, examines data traffic for activity that matches signatures, which are preconfigured, predetermined attack patterns. A statistical anomaly-based IDPS (also known as a behavior-based IDPS) collects data from normal traffic and establishes a baseline. When the activity is outside the baseline parameters (called the clipping level), the IDPS notifies the administrator.

- The science of encryption, known as cryptology, encompasses cryptography and cryptanalysis. Cryptanalysis is the process of obtaining the original message from an encrypted code without the use of the original algorithms and keys.

- In encryption, the most commonly used algorithms employ either substitution or transposition. A substitution cipher substitutes one value for another. A transposition cipher (or permutation cipher) rearranges the values within a block to create the ciphertext.

- Symmetric encryption uses the same key, also known as a secret key, to both encrypt and decrypt a message. Asymmetric encryption (public key encryption) uses two different keys for these purposes.

- A public key infrastructure (PKI) encompasses the entire set of hardware, software, and cryptosystems necessary to implement public key encryption.

- A digital certificate is a block of data, similar to a digital signature, attached to a file, certifying that the file is from the organization it claims to be from and has not been modified.

- A number of cryptosystems have been developed to make e-mail more secure. Examples include Pretty Good Privacy (PGP), Secure Multipurpose Internet Mail Extensions (S/MIME), and Privacy Enhanced Mail (PEM).

- A number of cryptosystems work to secure Web browsers, including Secure Electronic Transactions (SET), Secure Sockets Layer (SSL), Secure Hypertext Transfer Protocol (SHTTP), Secure Shell (SSH), and IP Security (IPSec).

Review Questions

1. What is the difference between authentication and authorization? Can a system permit authorization without authentication? Why or why not?

2. What is the most widely accepted biometric authorization technology? Why?

3. What is the most effective biometric authorization technology? Why?

4. What is the typical relationship between the untrusted network, the firewall, and the trusted network?

5. How is an application-layer firewall different from a packet filtering firewall? Why is an application-layer firewall sometimes called a proxy server?

6. What special function does a cache server perform? Why does this function have value for larger organizations?

7. How does screened-host firewall architecture differ from screened-subnet firewall architecture? Which offers more security for the information assets that remain on the trusted network?

8. What is a DMZ? Is this really a good name for the function that this type of subnet performs?

9. What is RADIUS? What advantage does it have over TACACS?

10. How does a network-based IDPS differ from a host-based IDPS?

11. What is network footprinting? What is network fingerprinting? How are they related?

12. Why do many organizations ban port scanning activities on their internal networks? Why would ISPs ban outbound port scanning by their customers?

13. Why is TCP port 80 always of critical importance when securing an organization's network?

14. What kind of data and information can be found using a packet sniffer?

15. What are the main components of cryptology?

16. Explain the relationship between plaintext and ciphertext.

17. Define asymmetric encryption. Why would it be of interest to information security professionals?

18. One tenet of cryptography is that increasing the work factor to break a code increases the security of that code. Why is that true?

19. Explain the key differences between symmetric and asymmetric encryption. Which can the computer process faster? Which lowers the costs associated with key management?

20. What is a VPN? Why are VPNs widely used?

Exercises

1. Create a spreadsheet that takes eight values that a user inputs into eight different cells. Then create a row that transposes the cells to simulate a transposition cipher, using the example transposition cipher from the text. Remember to work from right to left, with the pattern 1 > 3, 2 > 6, 3 > 8, 4 > 1, 5 > 4, 6 > 7, 7 > 5, 8 > 2 where 1 is the right-most of the eight cells. Input the text ABCDEFGH as single characters into the first row of cells. What is displayed?

2. Search the Internet for information about a technology called personal or home office firewalls. Examine the various alternatives, select three of the options, and compare their functionalities, cost, features, and types of protection.

3. Go to the Web site of VeriSign, one of the market leaders in digital certificates. Determine whether VeriSign serves as a registration authority, certificate authority, or both. Download its free guide to PKI and summarize VeriSign's services.

4. Go to *csrc.nist.gov* and locate "Federal Information Processing Standard (FIPS) 197." What encryption standard does this address use? Examine the contents of this publication and describe the algorithm discussed. How strong is it? How does it encrypt plaintext?

5. Search the Internet for vendors of biometric products. Find one vendor with a product designed to examine each characteristic mentioned in Figure 10-4. What is the crossover error rate (CER) associated with each product? Which would be more acceptable to users? Which would be preferred by security administrators?

Closing Case

Iris's smartphone beeped. Frowning, she glanced at the screen, expecting to see another junk e-mail.

"We've really got to do something about the spam!" she muttered to herself. She scanned the header of the message.

"Uh-oh!" Glancing at her watch and then looking at her incident response pocket card, Iris dialed the home number of the on-call systems administrator. When he answered, Iris asked "Seen the alert yet? What's up?"

"Wish I knew—some sort of virus," the SA replied. "A user must have opened an infected attachment."

Iris made a mental note to remind the awareness program manager to restart the refresher training program for virus control. Her users should know better, but some new employees had not been trained yet.

"Why didn't the firewall catch it?" Iris asked.

"It must be a new one," the SA replied. "It slipped by the pattern filters."

"What are we doing now?" Iris was growing more nervous by the minute.

"I'm ready to cut our Internet connection remotely, then drive down to the office and start our planned recovery operations—shut down infected systems, clean up any infected servers, recover data from backups, and notify our peers that they may receive this virus from us in our e-mail. I just need your go-ahead."

The admin sounded uneasy. This was not a trivial operation, and he was facing a long night of intense work.

"Do it," Iris said. "I'll activate the incident response plan and start working the notification call list to get some extra hands in to help." Iris knew this situation would be the main topic at the weekly CIO's meeting. She just hoped her team would be able to restore the systems to safe operation quickly. She looked at her watch: 12:35 a.m.

Discussion

1. What can be done to minimize the risk of this situation recurring? Can these types of situations be completely avoided?

2. If you were in Iris's position, once the timeline of events has been established, how would you approach your interaction with the second-shift operator?

3. How should RWW go about notifying its peers? What other procedures should Iris have the technician perform?

4. When would be the appropriate time to begin the forensic data collection process to analyze the root cause of this incident? Why?

Ethical Decision Making

Regarding the actions taken by the San Diego 10th-grader as described in this chapter's opening scenario, was this youngster acting illegally? (You may want to look ahead in the text to Chapter 12 regarding the applicable laws.) If, in fact, she did not break any laws, was the purposeful damage to another via malware infection an unethical action? If not, why not?

Regarding the actions taken by the second-shift operator, was his oversight in running the routine update of the malware pattern file a violation of law? Was it a violation of policy? Was the mistake an ethical lapse?

Endnotes

1. Tipton, Harold, and Micki Krause. *Information Security Management Handbook*, 6th ed. Boca Raton, FL: CRC Press, 2007.

2. Kent, K., and Souppaya, M. "Special Publication 800-92: Guide to Computer Security Log Management." *National Institute of Standards and Technology*, 2006. Accessed February 11, 2013 @ *http://csrc.nist.gov/publications/nistpubs/800-92/SP800-92.pdf*.

3. Ibid.

4. Ibid.

5. Ibid.

6. Cobb, M. "What Are Common (and Uncommon) Unified Threat Management Features?" *SearchMidmarketSecurity*. Accessed February 14, 2013 @ *http://searchmidmarketsecurity.techtarget.com/tip/What-are-common-and-uncommon-unified-threat-management-features*.

7. Day, Kevin. *Inside the Security Mind: Making the Tough Decisions*. Upper Saddle River, NJ: Prentice-Hall, 2003: 220.

8. Grigorof, Adrian. "Challenges in managing firewalls." Accessed February 13, 2013 @ *www.eventid.net/show.asp?DocId=18*.

9. Taylor, Laura. "Guidelines for Configuring Your Firewall Rule-Set." *ZDNet*, April 12, 2001. Accessed February 10, 2013 @ *www.zdnet.com/news/guidelines-for-configuring-your-firewall-rule-set/298790*.

10. Harris, Shon. *CISSP Certification All-in-One Exam Guide*, 6th ed. Berkeley, CA: Osborne McGraw-Hill, 2012.

11. "The Implications of WiMAX for Competition and Regulation." *OECD*. Accessed February 10, 2013 @ *www.oecd.org/dataoecd/32/7/36218739.pdf*.

12. Day, Kevin. *Inside the Security Mind: Making the Tough Decisions*. Upper Saddle River, NJ: Prentice-Hall, 2003: 225.

13. Steiner, Jennifer, Clifford Neuman, and Jeffrey Schiller. "An Authentication Service for Open Network Systems." Paper presented for Project Athena, March 30, 1988. Accessed February 14, 2013 @ *www.scs.stanford.edu/nyu/05sp/sched/readings/kerberos.pdf*.

14. Krutz, Ronald, and Russell Dean Vines. *The CISSP Prep Guide: Mastering the Ten Domains of Computer Security*. New York: John Wiley and Sons, 2001: 40.

10

## chapter 11

Personnel and Security

If an attacker can call one trusted person within the company, and that person complies, and if the attacker gets in, then all that money spent on technology is essentially wasted.

KEVIN MITNICK

Mike Edwards stuck his head into Iris's office and asked, "Iris, are you free for the next hour or so?"

Iris glanced at her calendar and said, "Sure. What's up?"

Mike was standing in the hall with Erik Paulson, the manager of Random Widget Works, Inc.'s (RWW's) help desk. Both men looked grave.

"Can you bring the human resources policy manual with you?" Mike asked.

Without asking any further questions, Iris pulled the manual from her bookshelf and joined the pair. As they walked down the hall, Mike filled her in on the developing situation.

In the meeting room that adjoined the Chief Executive Officer's (CEO's) office, three people were already seated. Mike and Paul took seats at the table, and Iris took a chair along the wall. Robin Gateere, RWW's CEO, cleared her throat and said, "Okay. Let's get started."

Jerry Martin from legal was facilitating the meeting. Also in the room was Gloria Simpson, senior vice president of human resources. Mike had asked Iris to join this upper-level management meeting because of her familiarity with human resources policy regarding information security.

Jerry spoke first.

"Recent events have caused us to revisit our hiring policies," he said. "Last week, one of our employees was arrested, and our company name was plastered all over the newspapers and on television. It turns out that the employee was on parole for sexual assault. He was hired into our IT department to work at the help desk. The police have discovered that he is running a pornography Web site. His parole was revoked, and he's now in state prison. What I want to know is how he came to be an employee of this company in the first place, and what do we do now?"

Robin took the floor. "As to the second question," she said, "we terminated his employment for cause since he did not report to work, because he is in jail. As to the first question...." She looked pointedly at Erik and said, "What do you know?"

Erik seemed uneasy. "This is the first time I became aware that Sam had trouble with the law," he said. "As a matter of fact, I was the hiring manager who recruited him, and all of this is news to me. Of course, we followed the required human resources procedures when we hired him, although I have always wondered why a hiring manager doesn't get to see the whole personnel file for new hires."

Gloria spoke up. "That practice does seem odd in light of this case," she said. "According to his file, Sam did write about his conviction and parole status on his application. In fact, we did an identity check and received a criminal background report that confirmed the conviction and his parole status. He didn't lie on his application, but it's beyond me how Erik was ever cleared to make him a job offer."

Erik lifted the folder he was holding. "Here's the whole hiring manager's packet on Sam," he said. "This is the actual file I received from HR. I happened to save it in the employee jacket in my files. As you can see, the standard clearance to extend an offer is right here." He slid the folder down the table to Gloria, who looked at the approval signature on the form.

Iris realized several things: Some of the archaic practices in human resources were about to change, somebody in human resources was in a lot of trouble, and it was time for her to revisit all of the company's personnel information security policies.

LEARNING OBJECTIVES

Upon completion of this material, you should be able to:

- Identify the skills and requirements for information security positions

- List the various information security professional certifications, and identify which skills are encompassed by each

- Discuss and implement information security constraints on the general hiring processes

- Explain the role of information security in employee terminations

- Describe the security practices used to control employee behavior and prevent misuse of information

Introduction

Maintaining a secure environment requires that the information security (InfoSec) department be carefully structured and staffed with appropriately skilled and screened personnel. It also requires that the proper procedures be integrated into all human resources activities, including hiring, training, promotion, and termination practices.

The first part of this chapter discusses InfoSec personnel hiring issues and practices, including information about the most sought-after professional certification credentials. Some aspects of managing InfoSec personnel—such as the placement of the InfoSec department within the organization—were covered in Chapter 5. This chapter provides more details about the proper staffing (or adjusting the staffing plan) of the InfoSec function. It also describes how to adjust IT job descriptions and documented practices to fulfill InfoSec requirements throughout the organization.

The second part of this chapter presents strategies for integrating InfoSec policies into an organization's general hiring practices. This effort requires collaboration between the general management community of interest and InfoSec professionals.

Staffing the Security Function

Selecting an effective mix of InfoSec personnel for your organization requires that you consider a number of criteria. Some of these criteria are within the control of the organization; others are not, such as the supply and demand of various skills and experience levels. In general, when the demand for any commodity—including personnel with critical InfoSec technical or managerial skills—rises quickly, the initial supply often fails to meet it. As demand becomes known, professionals entering the job market or refocusing their job skills seek to gain the required skills, experience, and credentials. Until this new supply can meet the demand, however, competition for the scarce resource will continue to drive up costs. Once the supply is level with or higher than demand, organizations can become more selective and no longer need to pay a premium for those skills.

This process swings back and forth like a clock pendulum, because the real economy, unlike an econometric model, is seldom in a state of equilibrium for long periods of time. For example, there was excess demand for experienced enterprise resource planning (ERP) professionals in the 1990s and for experienced Common Business-Oriented Language (COBOL) programmers at the turn of the 21st century, because of concerns about Y2K issues. At the time of this writing, the outlook is still good for experienced security professionals, and many new entrants to the field are able to find work. But funding priorities have precluded massive hiring to meet this predicted need for skilled InfoSec professionals. Many economic forecasters expect this deferred demand to become active as organizations seek to meet the perceived demand for InfoSec workers. The cold reality is that as long as there are hackers and other security "bad guys," there will be a need for competent InfoSec professionals. The "2012 (ISC)² Career Impact Survey" found less than 4 percent of the over 2250 survey respondents were unemployed, and half of those for reasons other than job availability. Some reported retiring, leaving the area, or pursuing higher education, for example. There is still high turnover in the field, with over 35 percent of respondents reporting changing jobs in 2012, but this was mostly due to advancement opportunity (53 percent) or personal preference (17 percent).[1]

Qualifications and Requirements

Due to the relatively recent emergence of InfoSec as a distinct discipline, many organizations are still not certain which qualifications competent InfoSec personnel should have. In many cases, the InfoSec staff lacks established roles and responsibilities. To move the InfoSec discipline forward, organizations should take the following steps:

- The general management community of interest should learn more about the requirements and qualifications for both InfoSec positions and relevant IT positions.

- Upper management should learn more about InfoSec budgetary and personnel needs.

- The IT and general management communities of interest should grant the InfoSec function—in particular, the chief information security officer (CISO)—an appropriate level of influence and prestige.

In most cases, organizations look for a technically qualified InfoSec generalist with a solid understanding of how organizations operate. In many other fields, the more specialized professionals become, the more marketable they are. In InfoSec, overspecialization can actually be a drawback.

When hiring InfoSec professionals at all levels, organizations frequently look for individuals who:

- Understand how organizations are structured and operated

- Recognize that InfoSec is a management task that cannot be handled with technology alone

- Work well with people in general, including users, and have strong written and verbal communication skills

- Acknowledge the role of policy in guiding security efforts

- Understand the essential role of InfoSec education and training, which helps make users part of the solution rather than part of the problem

- Perceive the threats facing an organization, understand how these threats can become transformed into attacks, and safeguard the organization from InfoSec attacks

- Understand how technical controls (including firewalls, intrusion detection systems [IDSs], and antivirus software) can be applied to solve specific InfoSec problems

- Demonstrate familiarity with the mainstream information technologies, including the most popular and newest Windows, Linux, and UNIX operating systems

- Understand IT and InfoSec terminology and concepts

Entering the Information Security Profession

Many InfoSec professionals enter the field after having prior careers in law enforcement or the military, or careers in other IT areas, such as networking, programming, database administration, or systems administration. Recently, college graduates who have tailored their degree programs to specialize in InfoSec have begun to enter the field in appreciable numbers. Figure 11-1 illustrates these possible career paths.

Many information technologists believe that InfoSec professionals must have an established track record in some other IT specialty. However, IT professionals who move into InfoSec tend to focus on technical problems and solutions to the exclusion of general InfoSec issues.

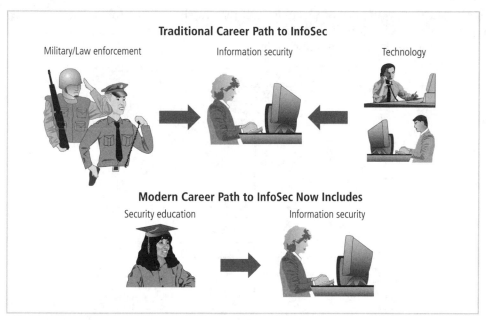

Figure 11-1 Information security career paths

Copyright © 2014 Cengage Learning®.

Organizations can foster greater professionalism in the InfoSec discipline by clearly defining their expectations and establishing explicit position descriptions.

Information Security Positions

Standardizing job descriptions can increase the degree of professionalism in the field of InfoSec, as well as improve the consistency of roles and responsibilities among organizations. Organizations can find complete InfoSec job descriptions in Charles Cresson Wood's book *Information Security Roles and Responsibilities Made Easy, Version 3*. Excerpts from this book are provided later in this chapter.[2]

As you learned in Chapter 5, Schwartz et al. classify InfoSec positions into one of three areas: those that *define*, those that *build*, and those that *administer*:

> *Definers provide the policies, guidelines, and standards.... They're the people who do the consulting and the risk assessment, who develop the product and technical architectures. These are senior people with a lot of broad knowledge, but often not a lot of depth. Then you have the builders. They're the real techies, who create and install security solutions.... Finally, you have the people who operate and [administer] the security tools, the security monitoring function, and the people who continuously improve the processes. This is where all the day-to-day, hard work is done. What I find is we often try to use the same people for all of these roles. We use builders all the time.... If you break your information security professionals into these three groups, you can recruit them more efficiently, with the policy people being the more senior people, the builders being more technical, and the operating people being those you can train to do a specific task.[3]*

One could find a number of position titles that fit these three roles. The following sections discuss some specific job titles that follow this model. Figure 11-2 shows typical InfoSec job positions and the departmental hierarchy.

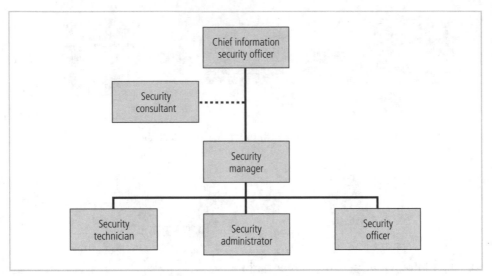

Figure 11-2 Possible information security positions and reporting relationships

Copyright © 2014 Cengage Learning®.

Chief Information Security Officer (CISO)
Though not usually an executive-level position, the **chief information security officer (CISO)** is often considered the top InfoSec officer in the organization. He or she frequently reports to the **chief information officer (CIO)**, unless the organization employs a **chief security officer (CSO)** who oversees both physical and InfoSec areas. Although CISOs are business managers first and technologists second, they must be conversant in all areas of InfoSec, including technology, planning, and policy. They are expected to draft or approve a range of InfoSec policies. They also work with their CIOs and other executive managers on strategic planning, they develop tactical plans, and they work with security managers on operational planning. Finally, they develop InfoSec budgets based on available funding, and they make decisions or recommendations about purchasing, project and technology implementation, and the recruiting, hiring, and firing of security staff. Ultimately, the CISO is the spokesperson for the security team and is responsible for the overall InfoSec program.

Qualifications and Position Requirements The most common qualifications for the CISO include the Certified Information Systems Security Professional (CISSP) and the Certified Information Security Manager (CISM), which are described later in this chapter. A graduate degree in business, technology, criminal justice, or another related field is usually required as well. A candidate for this position should have experience as a security manager as well as in planning, policy, and budgets. As mentioned earlier, some organizations prefer to hire individuals with law enforcement experience.

Charles Cresson Wood's *Information Security Roles and Responsibilities Made Easy, Version 3* defines and describes the CISO position, which he calls the information security department manager, as follows:

Information Security Department Manager

Job Title: Information Security Department Manager [Also known as Information Security Manager, Information Systems Security Officer (ISSO), Chief Information Security Officer (CISO), Chief Information Security Strategist, or Vice President of Information Security. Note that if the Chief Security Officer [...] does not exist at the organization in question, and is not appropriate at this point in time, then some of the CSO duties may instead be performed by the Information Security Department Manager.]

Department: Information Security

Reports To: Chief Information Officer (CIO) [Most common but least recommended option], Chief Operating Officer (COO), Chief Financial Officer (CFO), Chief Executive Officer (CEO) [The latter is the most desirable option ...], Chief Security Officer (CSO), or Chief Legal Counsel...

Dotted Line: Board of Directors Audit Committee

Summary: The Information Security Department Manager directs, coordinates, plans, and organizes InfoSec activities throughout Company X. He or she acts as the focal point for all communications related to InfoSec, both with internal staff and third parties. The Manager works with a wide variety of people from different internal organizational units, bringing them together to manifest controls that reflect workable compromises as well as proactive responses to current and future InfoSec risks.

Responsibilities and Duties: The Information Security Department Manager is responsible for envisioning and taking steps to implement the controls needed to protect both Company X information as well as information that have been entrusted to Company X by third parties. The position involves overall Company X responsibility for InfoSec regardless of the form that the information takes (paper, blueprint, CD-ROM, audio tape, embedded in products or processes, etc.), the information handling technology employed (portable computers, wireless devices, smart phones, fax machines, telephones, local area networks, file cabinets, etc.), or the people involved (contractors, consultants, employees, vendors, outsourcing firms, etc.).

- Threats to information and information systems addressed by the Information Security Department Manager and his or her staff include, but are not limited to: information unavailability, information corruption, unauthorized information destruction, unauthorized information modification, unauthorized information usage, and unauthorized information disclosure. These threats to information and information systems include consideration of physical security matters only if a certain level of physical security is necessary to achieve a certain level of InfoSec [*for example, as is necessary to prevent theft of portable computers*]

- Acts as the central point of contact within Company X when it comes to all communications dealing with InfoSec, including vulnerabilities, controls, technologies, human factors issues, and management issues

- Establishes and maintains strong working relationships with the Company X groups involved with InfoSec matters (Legal Department, Internal Audit Department, Physical Security Department, Information Technology Department, Information Security Management Committee, etc.) [*Note that the Information Security Department Manager is, in most cases, the chairperson of the Information Security Management Committee.*]

11

- Establishes, manages, and maintains organizational structures and communications channels with those responsible for InfoSec; these responsible parties include individuals within Company X departments (such as Local Information Security Coordinators) as well as Company X business partners (outsourcing firms, consulting firms, suppliers, etc.)

- Assists with the clarification of individual InfoSec responsibility and accountability so that necessary InfoSec activities are performed as needed, according to preestablished procedures, policies, and standards

- Coordinates the InfoSec efforts of all internal groups, to ensure that organization-wide InfoSec efforts are consistent across the organization, and that duplication of effort is minimized [*The Physical Security Department Manager does the same duty, but only for physical security efforts.*]

- Coordinates all multiapplication or multisystem InfoSec improvement projects at Company X [*A good example would be converting all operating system access control systems to enforce a standard minimum password length.*]

- Represents Company X and its InfoSec-related interests at industry standards committee meetings, professional association meetings, InfoSec technical conferences, industry specific Internet discussion groups, and similar public forums [*Smaller or less visible organizations will generally dispense with this duty. If the CSO role is going to be adopted in addition to the Information Security Department Manager role, then who represents the organization in what public forums will need to be clarified.*]

- Completes, obtains management concurrence on, and formally files government forms and questionnaires dealing with InfoSec [*Generally, this task this would appear in a job description only in those industries which are highly-regulated, such as financial institutions and health care providers.*]

- Investigates the ways that InfoSec-related technologies, requirements statements, internal processes, and organizational structures can be used to achieve the goals found in the Company X strategic plan [*This effort should include consideration of the long range information systems plan, which in turn should be an intermediate link between the business strategic plan and the InfoSec plan.*]

- Creates a strategic InfoSec plan with a vision for the future of InfoSec at Company X (utilizing evolving InfoSec technology, this vision meets a variety of objectives such as management's fiduciary and legal responsibilities, customer expectations for secure modern business practices, and the competitive requirements of the marketplace) [*If the CSO role is going to be adopted, then this InfoSec strategic plan can be a subsection of, and incorporated into, a five-year security plan prepared by the CSO.*]

- Understands the fundamental business activities performed by Company X, and based on this understanding, suggests appropriate InfoSec solutions that adequately protect these activities

- Develops action plans, schedules, budgets, status reports and other top management communications intended to improve the status of InfoSec at Company X

- Obtains top management approval and ongoing support for all major InfoSec initiatives at Company X (or advises and assists others in their efforts with these proceedings)

- Brings pressing InfoSec vulnerabilities to top management's attention so that immediate remedial action can be taken (this includes consideration of reputation risk and damage to Company X's brand image)

- Performs and/or oversees the performance of periodic Company X risk assessments that identify current and future security vulnerabilities, determines the level of risk that management has currently accepted, and identifies the best ways to reduce InfoSec risks [*In a general sense, the Information Security Department Manager performs InfoSec risk management or else establishes a management structure that has others (such as line managers) perform this function.*]

- Examines InfoSec from a cross-organizational viewpoint including Company X's participation in extranets, electronic data interchange (EDI) trading networks, ad hoc Internet commerce relationships, and other new business structures, and makes related recommendations to protect Company X information and information systems [*The prior paragraph discussing risk assessments deals with internal information systems, while this paragraph is advisable whenever new multiorganizational networks are contemplated or deployed.*]

- Identifies laws, regulations, and legal contracts which define InfoSec requirements to which Company X must comply, and maintains definitive evidence indicating whether or not Company X information systems are in compliance with these same requirements

- Directs the development of, or originates self-assessment questionnaires and other tools that assist user department managers and other members of the management team in their efforts to determine the degree of compliance with InfoSec requirements within their respective organizational units

- Periodically initiates quality measurement studies to determine whether the InfoSec function at Company X operates in a manner consistent with standard industry practices (these include customer satisfaction surveys, competitor benchmarking studies, industry baseline controls comparisons, peer review comparison efforts, and internal tests)

- Coordinates and directs the development, management approval, implementation, and promulgation of objectives, goals, policies, standards, guidelines, and other requirement statements needed to support InfoSec throughout Company X as well as within Company X business networks (such as extranets)

- Provides managerial guidance to user department staff on the development of local, system-specific, and application-specific InfoSec policies, guidelines, standards, procedures, and responsibility designations

- Assists with the establishment and refinement of procedures for the identification of Company X information assets as well as the classification of these information assets with respect to criticality, sensitivity, and value [*The availability of this asset inventory information allows appropriate controls to then be chosen by management; see the* Chapter 15 *for further details.*]

- Coordinates internal staff in their efforts to determine Company X InfoSec obligations according to external requirements (contractual, regulatory, legal, ethical, etc.)

- Closely monitors changes in society's InfoSec-related ethics, values, morals, and attitudes with an eye toward changes that Company X should make in response to these developments

- Designs and manages business processes for the detection, investigation, correction, disciplinary action, and/or prosecution related to InfoSec breaches, violations, and incidents [*These efforts would for example include an intrusion detection system, also known as an IDS.*]

- Manages internal Company X activities pertaining to the investigation, correction, prosecution, and disciplinary action needed for the resolution of InfoSec breaches, violations, and incidents (whether actual or alleged)

- Prepares postmortem analyses of InfoSec breaches, violations, and incidents to illuminate what happened and how this type of problem can be prevented in the future

- Directs the preparation of information systems contingency plans and manages worker groups, such as Computer Emergency Response Teams (CERTs), that respond to InfoSec-relevant events (hacker intrusions, virus infections, denial-of-service (DoS) attacks, etc.)

- Works with the Public Relations Department and top management to develop suitable public responses to InfoSec incidents, violations, and problems [*These responses should be scripted and ready-to-go, as well as decided upon in an ad hoc manner based on pre-established criteria.*]

- Acts as an external representative for Company X in the event of a hacker break-in or some other InfoSec-relevant event [*This may involve news media interviews, discussions with concerned customers, etc.*]

- Acts as an expert witness in InfoSec-related legal proceedings involving Company X

- Provides technical InfoSec consulting assistance for Company X staff disciplinary measures, civil suits, and criminal prosecutions, if and when needed

- Initiates and manages special projects related to InfoSec that may be needed to appropriately respond to ad hoc or unexpected InfoSec events

- Provides technical support consulting services on matters related to InfoSec such as the criteria to use when selecting InfoSec products

- Performs management and personnel administration functions associated with Company X's Information Security Department (coaches employees, hires and fires employees, disciplines employees, reviews employee performance, recommends salary increases and promotions, counsels employees, establishes employee task lists and schedules, trains staff, etc.)

- Acts as the primary liaison and decision-maker regarding the work of InfoSec consultants, contractors, temporaries, and outsourcing firms

- Stays informed about the latest developments in the InfoSec field, including new products and services, through online news services, technical magazines, professional association memberships, industry conferences, special training seminars, and other methods[4]

In addition to taking on these roles and responsibilities, CISOs should follow six key principles to shape their careers:

- *Business engagement*—It is important to build professional relationships with key stakeholders in the organization. These relationships become key to understanding the level of investment needed to support various areas of the organization that are outside the CISO's areas of expertise.

- *Focus initiatives on what is learned*—The knowledge gained from business engagement becomes a tool in developing and prioritizing efforts for the InfoSec department. Security initiatives and strategies will naturally follow the needs of the organization and increase support from those stakeholders.

- *Align, target, and time initiatives*—Once the priority of effort is developed, along with stakeholder buy-in, it is important to convey resource availability and constraints to the organization to maintain organizational support and confidence. This information, along with an understanding of the requirements of the department for both planned and unplanned security efforts, will help manage expectations.

- *Service delivery*—Maintaining a professional "sales and service" perspective for the organization will enhance the organization's opinion of the InfoSec department's value. The CISO should focus on communicating with the business stakeholders and executive management using appropriate nontechnical language, and emphasize the value-added, return-on-investment contribution of the InfoSec department.

- *Credibility*—Promoting the value of the InfoSec department, its skill, expertise and quality of efforts, is important for the CISO. The CISO should seek to elevate his or her visibility through internal involvement in the organization and external involvement within the field. This credibility will benefit not only the CISO (professionally) but the value of the department within the organization.

- *Relationship management*—Finally, the CISO should understand the decision makers in the organization and cultivate professional relationships with those decision makers. Having a relationship with other decision makers will enable the CISO to better understand how someone who evaluates alternatives and provides or recommends resource distribution is important.[5]

CISOs, like all security professionals, should consider their education as a continuous process, and they should expect to be constantly looking for sources of information on new security threats, methodologies, approaches, and technologies, regardless of whether such a process is required for a professional certification.

Security Manager A security manager is accountable for the day-to-day operation of all or part of the InfoSec program. They accomplish objectives identified by the CISO and resolve issues identified by the technicians. Security managers are often assigned specific managerial duties by the CISO, including policy development, risk assessment, contingency planning, and operational and tactical planning for the security function. They often liaise with managers from other departments and divisions in joint planning and development sections, such as security functions in human resources hiring and termination procedures, plant operations in environmental controls, and physical security design.

Management of technology requires an understanding of the technology that is administered but not necessarily proficiency in its configuration, operation, or fault resolution. Managing a technology is very different from administering it. For example, systems administrators are expected to be very technically proficient in the technology used by the systems under their control, and they are responsible for ensuring that systems are used in compliance with the organization's policies. They may have some management functions, but they are not held accountable, as managers are. Within the InfoSec community, security managers are those true managers who are given responsibility for specific tasks, assigned resources to control and apply to those tasks, and held responsible and accountable for the accomplishment of those tasks.

The following is a list of duties that organizations expect their security managers to be competent at:

- Providing the organization with InfoSec oversight:
  - Maintain current and appropriate body of knowledge necessary to perform the InfoSec management function.
  - Effectively apply InfoSec management knowledge to enhance the security of networks and associated systems and services.
  - Maintain working knowledge of applicable legislative and regulatory initiatives. Interpret and translate requirements for implementation.
  - Develop appropriate InfoSec policies, standards, guidelines, and procedures.
  - Work with other organization InfoSec personnel, committees, and executive management in the governance process.
  - Provide meaningful reports for higher management, prepare effective presentations, and communicate InfoSec objectives.
  - Participate in short-term and long-term planning.
  - Monitor the InfoSec program measurement process and evaluate compliance effectiveness.
  - Oversee and conduct InfoSec reviews and liaison with the broader organization.
  - Coordinate and perform reviews of contracts, projects, and proposals.
  - Assist information units with standards compliance.
  - Oversee the conduct of investigations of InfoSec violations and computer crimes and work with management and external law enforcement to resolve these issues.
  - Review instances of noncompliance and work tactfully to correct deficiencies.
- Managing the InfoSec office personnel:
  - Determine positions and personnel necessary to accomplish InfoSec goals. Request staffing positions, screen personnel, and take the lead in the interviewing and hiring process.
  - Develop meaningful job descriptions. Communicate expectations and actively coach personnel for success.
  - Prioritize and assign tasks. Review performed work. Challenge staff to better themselves and advance the level of service provided.
  - Provide meaningful feedback to staff on an ongoing basis and formally appraise performance annually.

Qualifications and Position Requirements As mentioned earlier, it is not uncommon for a security manager to have a CISSP or CISM. These individuals must have experience in traditional business activities, including budgeting, project management, personnel management, and hiring and firing, and they must be able to draft middle-level and lower-level policies as well as standards and guidelines. Experience with business continuity planning is usually considered a plus. There are several types of InfoSec managers, and the people who fill these roles tend to be much more specialized than CISOs. For instance, a risk manager performs a different role than a manager hired to administer the security education training and awareness (SETA) program. A careful reading of the job description can identify exactly what a particular employer is looking for.

Wood's job description for the InfoSec department manager (provided earlier in this chapter) assumes that a single management-level professional performs all the organization's InfoSec management functions. In such a case, the security manager and the CISO are the same person. However, larger organizations that require 24/7 management oversight generally have several positions that collaborate to fulfill the functions that Wood describes. For example, an InfoSec manager-of-managers—the CISO—may supervise managers who are accountable for specialized areas. These managers directly supervise the analysts, technicians, and support staff, and often have additional managerial responsibilities.

Security Technician
A **security technician** is a technically qualified individual who may configure firewalls and Intrusion Detection and Prevention Systems (IDPSs), implement security software, diagnose and troubleshoot problems, and coordinate with systems and network administrators to ensure that security technical controls are properly implemented. The role of security technician is the typical InfoSec entry-level position, albeit a technical one. One dilemma for those seeking employment in the field is that it does require a certain level of technical skill, which can be difficult to obtain without experience. As a result, security technicians are likely to be IT technicians who have adopted a different career path.

Like network technicians, security technicians tend to be specialized, focusing on one major security technology group (firewalls, IDPSs, servers, routers, and software) and then further specializing in a particular software or hardware package within the group (such as Check Point firewalls, Cisco advanced security appliances, or Tripwire IDPSs). These areas are sufficiently complex to warrant this level of specialization. Security technicians who want to move up in the corporate hierarchy must expand their technical knowledge horizontally and obtain an understanding of the general organizational side of InfoSec as well as all technical areas.

Qualifications and Position Requirements The technical qualifications and position requirements for a security technician vary. Organizations typically prefer expert, certified, proficient technicians. Job requirements usually include some level of experience with a particular hardware and software package. Sometimes, familiarity with a particular technology is enough to secure an applicant an interview; however, experience using the technology is usually required.

Wood's *Information Security Roles and Responsibilities Made Easy, Version 3* defines and describes the InfoSec Engineer position as follows:

Information Security Engineer

Job Title: Information Security Engineer

Department: Information Security

Reports To: Information Security Department Manager

Summary: An InfoSec Engineer provides technical assistance with the design, installation, operation, service and maintenance of a variety of multiuser InfoSec systems such as virtual private networks (VPNs) and cloud-based data replication systems. A hands-on technical specialist, an Engineer handles the complex and detailed technical work necessary to establish security systems such as firewalls and encryption-based digital signature software. An Engineer configures and sets-up InfoSec systems such as Intrusion Detection Systems, or else trains others such as Access Control System Administrators, Systems Administrators, Network Administrators, and/or Database Administrators to do these tasks themselves.

Responsibilities and Duties:

- Provides hands-on InfoSec technical consulting services to teams of technical specialists working on the integration of shared, centralized and/or networked systems [*Examples of such systems include an active data dictionary, a data warehouse, a data mart, and a storage area network (SAN).*]

- Provides technical assistance with the initial set up, secure deployment, and proper management of systems that support InfoSec including virus detection systems, spyware and adware detection systems, spam filtering systems, content control software systems, Web site blocking systems, intuition detection systems, intrusion prevention systems (IPSs), and software license management systems [*Other systems of this nature include single sign-on systems, centralized multiplatform access control databases, and enterprise security management systems.*]

- Offers technical InfoSec consulting services to distributed personnel who are responsible for one or more InfoSec systems; these people include Network Administrators, Systems Administrators, and Database Administrators

- Evaluates information system bug reports, security exploit reports, and other InfoSec notices issued by information system vendors, government agencies, universities, professional associations, and other organizations, and as needed, makes recommendations to internal management and technical staff to take precautionary steps [*An example of these notices involves the periodic reports issued by the CERT at Carnegie-Mellon University.*]

- Acts as the primary technical support liaison in charge of distributing and loading updates to antivirus systems, IDSs, firewalls, data loss prevention systems, and other deployed security systems within Company X

- Configures and tunes one or more IDSs and IPSs to ensure that only authorized personnel have access to Company X systems and networks, and that only authorized activity is taking place on Company X systems and networks [*The monitoring of an IDS could be done by computer operations staff, network operations staff, or a*

Monitoring System Specialist. Note that a Systems Administrator may manage a host-based IDS and IPS, while this Engineer, or a Monitoring Systems Specialist, or another technical staff person in the Information Security Department, may manage a network-based IDS and IPS.]

- Runs or works with others that periodically run vulnerability identification software packages and related tools to immediately highlight errors in systems configuration, the need for the update of software with fixes and patches, and other security-related changes [*To leave this task solely to Systems Administrators introduces a conflict of interest because the results of such software will often indicate that Systems Administrators need to perform additional work. Internal Audit should also check-up on the status of software updates, patches, fixes, etc., to make sure all is as it should be.*]

- Runs, or works with others who periodically run, fixed password guessing software, unauthorized wireless network access point detection software, unprotected dial-up modem identification software, and similar tools, and then informs those responsible about the need to change their systems to improve security [*The first clause in this task may not be necessary if the organization in question has gotten away from user-chosen fixed passwords (and user-chosen encryption keys), perhaps through the use of dynamic passwords along with digital certificates.*]

- With management authorization, collects, securely stores, and utilizes software that is able to decrypt encrypted files, automatically guess user passwords, copy software that has been copy-protected, or otherwise circumvents InfoSec measures [*These tools may be critical to off-site recovery efforts, successful security incident investigations, and other special-situation security-related tasks.*]

- Compiles, maintains, and documents a collection of software that is able to trace the source of and otherwise investigate attacks on Company X systems [*Forensic tools are an example of this software.*]

- Acts as a technical consultant on InfoSec incident investigations and forensic technical analyses [*An example of such a forensic analysis would be determining whether a certain user had been downloading pornography with Company X computers, and then deleting these files from his or her desktop computer.*]

- Conducts selected tests of InfoSec measures in accordance with specific instructions provided by the Information Security Department Manager [*This effort usually includes white hat penetration tests.*]

- Interprets InfoSec policies, standards, and other requirements as they relate to a specific internal information system, and assists with the implementation of these and other InfoSec requirements

- Redesigns and reengineers internal information handling processes so that information is appropriately protected from a wide variety of problems including unauthorized disclosure, unauthorized use, inappropriate modification, premature deletion, and unavailability

- Serves as an active member of the CERT and participates in security incident response efforts by, among other things, having an in-depth knowledge of common security exploits, vulnerabilities and countermeasures

- Develops technical documentation describing the deployment, configuration, and management of shared, networked, and multiuser InfoSec systems

- Regularly attends conferences, professional association meetings, and technical symposia to remain aware of the latest InfoSec technological developments [*An example would be digital rights management (DRM) systems.*][6]

Other Position Titles Organizations often find that many (if not all) non-InfoSec job descriptions should include InfoSec roles and responsibilities. The following list of positions with InfoSec elements, which is drawn from *Information Security Roles and Responsibilities Made Easy, Version 3*, shows the breadth of job titles that may be affected. The job description elements have been grouped according to the community of interest.

Information Security Community:

- Chief security officer
- InfoSec department manager
- Access control system administrator
- Internal InfoSec consultant
- InfoSec engineer
- Security monitoring systems specialist
- InfoSec documentation specialist
- InfoSys contingency planner
- Local InfoSec coordinator

IT Community:

- Chief information officer
- Chief technology officer
- InfoSys analyst/business analyst
- Systems programmer
- Business applications programmer
- Computer operations manager
- Computer operator
- Data librarian
- InfoSys quality assurance analyst
- Help desk specialist
- Archives manager/records manager

- Telecommunications manager
- Systems administrator/network administrator
- Web site administrator/commerce site administrator
- Database administrator
- Data administration manager

General Business Community:

- Physical security department manager
- Physical asset protection specialist
- Building and facilities guard
- Office maintenance worker
- Mail room clerk
- Internal audit department manager
- InfoSys auditor
- Internal intellectual property attorney
- Ethics officer
- Chief knowledge officer
- Chief compliance officer
- Chief legal officer
- Human resources department manager
- Human resources consultant
- Receptionist
- Outsourcing contract administrator
- In-house trainer
- Insurance and risk management department manager
- Insurance and risk management analyst
- Business contingency planner
- Public relations manager
- Chief financial officer
- Purchasing agent
- Chief executive officer[7]

Information Security Professional Credentials

Many organizations rely to some extent on professional certifications to ascertain the level of proficiency possessed by a given candidate. Because the certification programs are relatively new, their precise value is not fully understood by most hiring organizations. The certifying bodies work diligently to educate their constituent communities on the value and qualifications of their certificate recipients. Employers struggle to match certifications to position requirements, while potential InfoSec workers try to determine which certification programs will help them in the job market. This section identifies widely recognized InfoSec certification programs and describes their test contents and methodologies.

(ISC)^2 Certifications

The International Information Systems Security Certification Consortium ((ISC)^2; *www.isc2 .org*) offers security certifications, among them the Certified Information Systems Security Professional (CISSP), the Systems Security Certified Practitioner (SSCP), and the Certified Secure Software Lifecycle Professional (CSSLP).

CISSP The CISSP certification, considered to be the most prestigious certification for security managers and CISOs, recognizes mastery of an internationally identified common body of knowledge (CBK) in InfoSec. To sit for the CISSP exam, the candidate must have at least five years of direct, full-time security professional work experience in two or more of 10 domains or four years of direct security work experience in two or more domains and a four-year college degree.

The CISSP exam consists of 250 multiple-choice questions (with four choices each) and must be completed within six hours. It covers the following 10 domains of InfoSec knowledge:

- Access control
- Business continuity and disaster recovery planning
- Cryptography
- InfoSec governance and risk management
- Legal, regulations, investigations, and compliance
- Operations security
- Physical (environmental) security
- Security architecture and design
- Software development security
- Telecommunications and network security

CISSP certification requires both successful completion of the exam and, to ensure that the applicant meets the experience requirement, attestation to submitted information and responses to the following questions, which are included in the "CISSP Candidate Information Bulletin":

1. *Have you ever been convicted of a felony; a misdemeanor involving a computer crime, dishonesty, or repeat offenses; or a Court Martial in military service, or is there a felony charge, indictment, or information now pending against you?*

2. *Have you ever had a professional license, certification, membership or registration revoked, or have you ever been censured or disciplined by any professional organization or government agency?*

3. *Have you ever been involved, or publicly identified, with criminal hackers or hacking?*

4. *Have you ever been known by any other name, alias, or pseudonym?*[8]

The breadth and depth covered in each of the 10 domains makes CISSP certification one of the most challenging InfoSec certifications to obtain. Holders of the CISSP must earn a specific number of continuing education credits every three years to retain the certification.

Once candidates successfully complete the exam, they may be required to submit an endorsement by an actively credentialed CISSP or by their employer, who can serve as a reference for their professional experience.

CISSP Concentrations In addition to the major certifications that $(ISC)^2$ offers, a number of concentrations are available for CISSPs to demonstrate advanced knowledge beyond the CISSP CBK. Each concentration requires that the applicant be a CISSP in good standing, pass a separate examination, and maintain the certification in good standing through ongoing continuing professional education. These concentrations and their respective areas of knowledge are shown here as they are presented on the $(ISC)^2$ Web site:

ISSAP®: Information Systems Security Architecture Professional

- *Access control systems and methodology*
- *Communications and network security*
- *Cryptography*
- *Security architecture analysis*
- *Technology-related business continuity planning and disaster recovery planning*
- *Physical security considerations*

ISSEP®: Information Systems Security Engineering Professional

- *Systems security engineering*
- *Certification and accreditation/risk management framework*
- *Technical management*
- *U.S. government information assurance-related policies and issuances*

ISSMP®: Information Systems Security Management Professional Enterprise Security Management Practices

- *Business continuity planning and disaster recovery planning*
- *Security management practices*
- *System development security*
- *Law, investigations, forensics, and ethics*
- *Security compliance management*[9]

SSCP Because it is difficult to master all 10 domains covered on the CISSP exam, many security professionals seek other less-rigorous certifications, such as $(ISC)^2$'s SSCP certification. Like the CISSP, the SSCP certification is more applicable to the security manager than to the technician, as the bulk of its questions focus on the operational nature of InfoSec. The SSCP focuses on practices, roles, and responsibilities as defined by experts from major InfoSec industries.[10] Nevertheless, the InfoSec technician seeking advancement can benefit from this certification.

The SSCP exam consists of 125 multiple-choice questions and must be completed within three hours. It covers seven domains:

- Access controls
- Cryptography
- Malicious code and activity
- Monitoring and analysis
- Networks and telecommunications
- Risk, response, and recovery
- Security operations and administration

Many consider the SSCP to be a scaled-down version of the CISSP. The seven domains are not a subset of the CISSP domains; they contain slightly more technical content. Just as with the CISSP, SSCP holders must earn continuing education credits to retain the certification or else they must retake the exam.

CSSLP   The Certified Secure Software Lifecycle Professional (CSSLP)[11] is a new (ISC)^2 certification focused on the development of secure applications. In order to qualify for the CSSLP, you must have at least four years of recent experience with the software development life cycle and be defined as an expert in four of the seven experience assessment topics areas, which are:

- *Secure software concepts*—Security implications in software development
- *Secure software requirements*—Capturing security requirements in the requirements-gathering phase
- *Secure software design*—Translating security requirements into application design elements
- *Secure software implementation/coding*—Unit testing for security functionality and resiliency to attack, and developing secure code and exploit mitigation
- *Secure software testing*—Integrated QA testing for security functionality and resiliency to attack
- *Software acceptance*—Security implication in the software acceptance phase
- *Software deployment, operations, maintenance, and disposal*—Security issues around steady state operations and management of software

You must compose an essay in each of your four areas of expertise and submit it as your exam. This is radically different from the multiple-choice exams (ISC)^2 normally administers. Once your experience has been verified and you successfully complete the essay exam, you can be certified. If you lack the experience, you can qualify as an (ISC)^2 Associate (described in the following section) until you obtain the necessary experience.

Associate of (ISC)²

(ISC)² has an innovative approach to the experience requirement in its certification program. Its Associate of (ISC)² program is geared toward individuals who want to take the CISSP or SSCP exams before obtaining the requisite experience for certification. (ISC)² describes the program as follows:

> The Associate program has been defined by (ISC)² as a means to award recognition to these candidates who have demonstrated the ability to pass one of the (ISC) certification exams. Those exams include the Certified Information Systems Security Professional (CISSP®), the Certified Secure Software Lifecycle Professional (CSSLP®), the Certified Authorization Professional (CAP®), or the Systems Security Certified Practitioner (SSCP®). In recognition of the fact that these candidates do not have the needed number of years of professional experience to fully satisfy the needs of the (ISC)² certifications, such candidates are able to complete the experience requirement after having passed the examination.
>
> Those who have become Associates of (ISC)² gain access to the professional community sponsored by (ISC)² and are allowed to access the resources and services of (ISC)² to help them advance their careers.[12]

(ISC)² has recently begun providing certification examinations exclusively via electronic testing, which has greatly improved its exam-offering schedules and locations.

ISACA Certifications

Formerly known as the Information Systems Audit and Control Association (ISACA), it sponsors four certifications: Certified Information Security Manager (CISM), Certified Information Security Auditor (CISA), Certified in the Governance of IT (CGEIT), and Certified in Risk and Information Systems Control (CRISC).

CISM The CISM credential is geared toward experienced InfoSec managers and others who may have InfoSec management responsibilities. The CISM can assure executive management that a candidate has the required background knowledge needed for effective security management and consulting. This exam is offered annually. The CISM examination covers the following practice domains described in the certification's "2013 Bulletin of Information":

1. *Information Security Governance (24 percent)—Establish and maintain an information security governance framework and supporting processes to ensure that the information security strategy is aligned with organizational goals and objectives, information risk is managed appropriately and program resources are managed responsibly.*

2. *Information Risk Management and Compliance (33 percent)—Manage information risk to an acceptable level to meet the business and compliance requirements of the organization.*

3. *Information Security Program Development and Management (25 percent)—Establish and manage the information security program in alignment with the information security strategy.*

4. *Information Security Incident Management (18 percent)—Plan, establish and manage the capability to detect, investigate, respond to and recover from information security incidents to minimize business impact.*[13]

To be certified, the applicant must:

- Pass the examination
- Adhere to a code of ethics promulgated by ISACA
- Pursue continuing education as specified
- Document five years of InfoSec work experience with at least three years in InfoSec management in three of the four defined areas of practice

CISA The Certified Information Systems Auditor (CISA) certification, while not specifically a security certification, does include many InfoSec components. ISACA touts the certification as being appropriate for auditing, networking, and security professionals. CISA requirements are as follows:

- Successful completion of the CISA examination
- Experience as an InfoSec auditor, with a minimum of five years' professional experience in information systems auditing, control, or security
- Agreement to the Code of Professional Ethics
- Payment of maintenance fees, a minimum of 20 contact hours of continuing education annually, and a minimum of 120 contact hours during a fixed three-year period
- Adherence to the Information Systems Auditing Standards

The exam covers the following areas of information systems auditing as described in the certification's "2013 Bulletin of Information":

1. *The Process of Auditing Information Systems (14 percent)—Provide audit services in accordance with IT audit standards to assist the organization with protecting and controlling information systems.*

2. *Governance and Management of IT (14 percent)—Provide assurance that the necessary leadership and organizational structures and processes are in place to achieve objectives and to support the organization's strategy.*

3. *Information Systems Acquisition, Development and Implementation (19 percent)—Provide assurance that the practices for the acquisition, development, testing, and implementation of information systems meet the organization's strategies and objectives.*

4. *Information Systems Operations, Maintenance and Support (23 percent)— Provide assurance that the processes for information systems operations, maintenance and support meet the organization's strategies and objectives.*

5. *Protection of Information Assets (30 percent)—Provide assurance that the organization's security policies, standards, procedures and controls ensure the confidentiality, integrity and availability of information assets.*[14]

The CISA exam is offered only a few times each year, so planning is a must.

CGEIT Also available from ISACA is the Certified in the Governance of IT (CGEIT) certification. The exam is targeted at upper-level executives (including CISOs and CIOs, directors, and consultants with knowledge and experience in IT governance). The CGEIT areas of knowledge include risk management components, making it of interest to upper-level InfoSec managers. The exam covers the following areas as described in the certification's "2013 Bulletin of Information":

1. *Framework for the Governance of Enterprise IT (25 percent)—Ensure the definition, establishment, and management of a framework for the governance of enterprise IT in alignment with the mission, vision and values of the enterprise.*

2. *Strategic Management (20 percent)—Ensure that IT enables and supports the achievement of enterprise objectives through the integration and alignment of IT strategic plans with enterprise strategic plans.*

3. *Benefits Realization (16 percent)—Ensure that IT-enabled investments are managed to deliver optimized business benefits and that benefit realization outcome and performance measures are established, evaluated and progress is reported to key stakeholders.*

4. *Risk Optimization (24 percent)—Ensure that an IT risk management framework exists to identify, analyze, mitigate, manage, monitor, and communicate IT-related business risk, and that the framework for IT risk management is in alignment with the enterprise risk management (ERM) framework.*

5. *Resource Optimization (15 percent)—Ensure the optimization of IT resources including information, services, infrastructure and applications, and people, to support the achievement of enterprise objectives.*[15]

The certification requirements are similar to other ISACA certifications, with a minimum of one year of experience in IT governance and additional experience in at least two of the domains listed.

CRISC The newest ISACA certification is the CGEIT. The exam is targeted at upper-level executives (including CISOs and CIOs, directors, and consultants with knowledge and experience in IT governance). The CGEIT areas of knowledge include risk management components, making it of interest to upper-level InfoSec managers. The exam covers the following areas as described in the certification's "2013 Bulletin of Information":

1. *Risk Identification, Assessment, and Evaluation (31 percent)—Identify, assess, and evaluate risk factors to enable the execution of the enterprise risk management strategy.*

2. *Risk Response (17 percent)—Develop and implement risk responses to ensure that risk factors and events are addressed in a cost-effective manner and in line with business objectives.*

3. *Risk Monitoring (17 percent)—Monitor risk and communicate information to the relevant stakeholders to ensure the continued effectiveness of the enterprise's risk management strategy.*

4. *Information Systems Control Design and Implementation (17 percent)—Design and implement information systems controls in alignment with the organization's risk appetite and tolerance levels to support business objectives.*

5. *Information Systems Control Monitoring and Maintenance (18 percent)—
Monitor and maintain information systems controls to ensure that they function effectively and efficiently.*[16]

The certification requires the candidate to have a minimum of three years of experience in risk management and information systems control across at least three of the stated domains, although the candidate may elect to take the exam before having the experience. This practice is accepted and encouraged by ISACA, but the candidate will not receive the certification until the experience requirement is met.

SANS Certifications

In 1999, the SANS Institute, formerly known as the System Administration, Networking, and Security Institute (*www.sans.org*), developed a series of technical security certifications known as the Global Information Assurance Certification (GIAC; *www.giac.org*). GIAC certifications not only test for knowledge, they require candidates to demonstrate application of that knowledge. With the introduction of the GIAC Information Security Professional (GISP) and the GIAC Security Leadership Certification (GSLC), SANS now offers more than just technical certifications. The GIAC family of certifications can be pursued independently or combined to earn a comprehensive certification called GIAC Security Engineer (GSE). The GISP is an overview certification that combines basic technical knowledge with an understanding of threats, risks, and best practices, similar to the CISSP. Unlike other certifications, some GIAC certifications require the applicant to complete a written practical assignment that tests the applicant's ability to apply skills and knowledge. These assignments are submitted to the SANS Information Security Reading Room for review by security practitioners, potential certificate applicants, and others with an interest in InfoSec. Only when the practical assignment is complete is the candidate allowed to take the online exam. According to SANS:

> *GIAC now offers three types of certification: Silver, Gold, and Platinum. The requirements for Silver certification are the completion of exam(s). Full certifications require two exams; certificates require a single exam. After earning Silver certification, a candidate can apply for Gold certification, which requires a technical paper. The technical paper demonstrates real-world, hands-on mastery of security skills. Passing technical papers will be posted to the GIAC List of Certified Professionals pages and to the SANS Information Security Reading Room to share candidates' knowledge and research, and to further educate the security community.*
>
> *GIAC platinum certifications require a multiple-choice test, along with a day-long lab to test candidates' hands-on skill.*[17]

The GIAC Management Certificates and Certifications include:

- GIAC Information Security Professional (GISP)
- GIAC Security Leadership Certification (GSLC)
- GIAC Certified ISO-27000 Specialist (G2700)
- GIAC Certified Project Manager Certification (GCPM)

GIAC has also added a number of shorter programs known as Skills Test and Reports (S.T.A.R.s), which are "less involved but more focused" than standard GIAC certifications.

Most GIAC certifications are offered in conjunction with SANS training. For more information on the GIAC security-related certification requirements, visit *www.giac.org/certifications*.

EC-Council Certifications

A new competitor in the security management certification field, EC-Council now offers a Certified CISO (C|CISO) certification, which is designed to be a unique recognition for those at the peak of their professional careers The C|CISO tests not only security domain knowledge but also executive business management knowledge. The C|CISO domains include the following:

- *Domain 1: Governance (Policy, Legal, and Compliance)*—This domain focuses on the external regulatory and legal issues any CISO faces as well as the strategic InfoSec governance programs promoted in forward-thinking organizations. It also contains areas related to security compliance to ensure that the organization meets the laws and regulations applicable to it. And it includes areas of InfoSec standards such as Federal Information Processing Standards and ISO 27000. Finally, it incorporates areas in risk management.[18]

- *Domain 2: IS Management Controls and Auditing Management (Projects, Technology, and Operations)*—This domain includes knowledge areas associated with information systems controls and auditing, similar to those found in ISACA certifications. These include developing, implementing, and monitoring IS controls as well as reporting the findings to executive management. Auditing areas include planning, conducting, and evaluating audits in the organization.[19]

- *Domain 3: Management (Project and Operations)*—This domain contains basic managerial roles and responsibilities any security manager would be expected to have mastered. It includes the fundamentals of management covered in earlier chapters, including planning, organizing, staffing, directing, and controlling security resources.[20]

- *Domain 4: Information Security Core Competencies*—This domain covers the common body of InfoSec knowledge that any CISO would be expected to possess. The domain includes subdomains in the following areas:

  - Access Control
  - Social Engineering, Phishing Attacks, Identity Theft
  - Physical Security
  - Risk Management
  - Disaster Recovery and Business Continuity Planning
  - Firewall, IDS/IPS, and Network Defense Systems
  - Wireless Security
  - Virus, Trojans, and Malware Threats
  - Secure Coding Best Practices and Securing Web Applications
  - Hardening Operating Systems
  - Encryption Technologies
  - Vulnerability Assessment and Penetration Testing
  - Computer Forensics and Incident Response[21]

- *Domain 5: Strategic Planning and Finance*—This domain addresses those CISO tasks associated with conducting strategic planning and financial management of the security department. The domain includes performance measures, IT investments, internal and external analyses, and developing and implementing enterprise security architectures.[22]

CompTIA Certifications

From Computing Technology Industry Association (CompTIA) (*www.comptia.com*)—the organization that offered the first vendor-neutral professional IT certifications, the A+ series—comes another certification program: the Security+ certification.

The CompTIA Security+ certification tests for security knowledge mastery of an individual with two years of on-the-job networking experience, with an emphasis on security. The exam covers industry-wide topics, including communication security, infrastructure security, cryptography, access control, authentication, external attack, and operational and organization security. CompTIA Security+ curricula are being taught at colleges, universities, and commercial training centers around the globe. CompTIA Security+ is being used as an elective or prerequisite to advanced vendor-specific and vendor-neutral security certifications.[23]

The exam covers six domains, as shown in Table 11-1.

Domain	Percentage of Examination
1.0 Network security	21%
2.0 Compliance and operational security	18%
3.0 Threats and vulnerabilities	21%
4.0 Application, data, and host security	16%
5.0 Access control and identity Management	13%
6.0 Cryptography	11%

Table 11-1 **Domains covered in the CompTIA Security+ exam**

Source: CompTIA[24].

ISFCE Certifications

The International Society of Forensic Computer Examiners (ISFCE) offers two levels of its certification.

Certified Computer Examiner (CCE) Certified Computer Examiner (CCE)® is a computer forensics certification provided by the ISFCE (*www.isfce.com*). To complete the CCE certification process, the applicant must:

- Have no criminal record
- Meet minimum experience, training, or self-training requirements
- Abide by the certification's code of ethical standards
- Pass an online examination
- Successfully perform actual forensic examinations on three test media

The CCE certification process covers the following areas:

- Ethics in practice
- Key legislation in, and its impact on, digital forensics
- Software licensing and validation
- General computer hardware used in data collection
- Networking and its involvement in forensics and data collection
- Common computer operating and file systems organization and architecture
- Forensics data seizure procedures
- Casework and other forensics examination procedures
- Common computer media used as evidence, physical and logical storage media operations, and procedures for sterilization and use
- Use of forensic boot disks
- Forensic examination skills and procedures

This certification also has concentrations/endorsements corresponding to the various operations systems present in the current business environments. A CCE who earns three or more of these endorsements qualifies as a Master Certified Computer Examiner (MCCE).[25]

Certification Costs

Certifications cost money, and the more preferred certifications can be expensive. Individual certification exams can cost as much as $750, and certifications that require multiple exams can cost thousands of dollars. In addition, the cost for formal training to prepare for the certification exams can be significant. While you should not wholly rely on certification preparation courses as groundwork for a real-world position, they can help you round out your knowledge and fill in gaps. Some certification exams, such as the CISSP, are very broad; others, such as the components of the GIAC, are very technical. Given the nature of the knowledge needed to pass the examinations, most experienced professionals find it difficult to do well on them without at least some review. Many prospective certificate holders engage in individual or group study sessions, and purchase one of the many excellent exam review books on the subject.

Certifications are designed to recognize experts in their respective fields, and the cost of certification deters those who might otherwise take the exam just to see if they can pass. Most examinations require between two and three years of work experience, and they are often structured to reward candidates who have significant hands-on experience. Some certification programs require that candidates document certain minimum experience requirements before they are permitted to sit for the exams. Before attempting a certification exam, do your homework. Look into the exam's stated body of knowledge as well as its purpose and requirements to ensure that the time and energy spent pursuing the certification are well spent. Figure 11-3 shows several approaches to preparing for security certification.

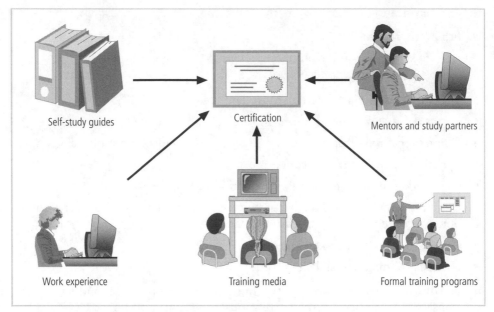

Figure 11-3 Preparing for security certification

Copyright © 2014 Cengage Learning®.

In regard to professional certification for InfoSec practitioners, Charles Cresson Wood reports the following:

> With résumé fraud on the rise, one of the sure-fire methods for employers to be sure that the people they hire are indeed familiar with the essentials of the field is to insist that they have certain certifications. The certifications can then be checked with the issuing organizations to make sure that they have indeed been conferred on the applicant for employment. [...] The key is to insist that they have certain certifications. The certifications can then be checked with the issuing organizations to make sure that they have indeed been conferred on the applicant for employment. The [...] professional certifications are relevant primarily to centralized information security positions. They are not generally relevant to staff working in decentralized information security positions, unless these individuals intend to become information security specialists. You may also look for these certifications on the résumés of consultants and contractors working in the information security field. You may wish to list these designations in help wanted advertisements, look for them on résumés, and ask about them during interviews. Automatic résumé scanning software can also be set up to search for these strings of characters.[26]

Employment Policies and Practices

The general management community of interest should integrate solid InfoSec concepts across all of the organization's employment policies and practices. The following sections examine important concepts associated with recruiting, hiring, firing, managing, and releasing human resources. Including InfoSec responsibilities in every employee's job description and subsequent performance reviews can make an entire organization take InfoSec more seriously.

View Point
The Hardest Part of the Job
By Alison Gunnels, Assistant Director at Ernst & Young

A career in InfoSec may seem like the best gig going. In a time of high unemployment throughout the United States, the security profession unemployment rate is almost nil. Both private and public industries are incorporating security as a prerequisite of new technology and business expansion. It's a seller's market for our experience, and our asking price is rising. We get peppered with questions about how to get started in security. Sanitized war stories generate a rapt audience, reminding us that the late nights and gray hairs are worthwhile.

There's a darker aspect of our profession, and it is not the Advanced Persistent Threat, anonymous hacker coalitions, dumpster divers, or any of the daily disasters we avert or triage. We have an unusual ability for non-law enforcement, nonmilitary personnel: We can directly harm other people in the course of doing our jobs.

Security professionals are involved in company personnel matters and in the court systems. We report violations of Rules of Behavior. We routinely scan and report on illicit activities performed during work hours, on work property, or using organizational equipment. We answer subpoenas, testify in court as expert witnesses, and explain to nontechnical personnel how evidence should be interpreted. We make recommendations about hiring, firing, suspension, and probation for other workers. It's no wonder our fellows regard us with distrust; our mistakes impact their finances and employment history. On occasion, we help send them to jail.

I have had the good fortune to make terrific mistakes in tolerant environments. I've recommended termination of someone who was brilliant at his work and became an asset to the company. I've lost evidence I was required to preserve. I've put someone in the position of firing his drinking buddy, and I've strained relationships with heavyweights in organization politics.

These mistakes—and all my others—are precious. Each reminds me to take my job seriously, because others certainly do! If you can, learn from my errors by doing the following:

- *Understand the relationships*—Managers invest in their employees, and they know more about those personnel than you likely do. Accept that your recommendation is not the only basis for action. Involve skip-level management if friendships may impede action. Realize that you do not know the entirety of most personnel situations.

- *Ask for a sanity-check*—Sometimes we see what we expect. Have a peer independently review your facts when dealing with a person you dislike. When your work is particularly stressful, write notes around the situation and submit them

(Continued)

to your supervisor in case details later get lost. Read and reread policies that seem to have been violated, and consider whether they are equally enforced.

- *Brace for impact*—Organizations handle personnel security issues according to unique needs. Some companies terminate for theft of intellectual property but shrug off the presence of pornography. Unauthorized port scanning can be cause for suspension or written off as an interest in technology. Report objectively, but remember that you did not cause the action or the consequence. You are responsible for impartial, accurate reporting, but you didn't cause the situation and shouldn't feel guilty.

Finally, have a life that is not just your job. InfoSec is enjoyable and meaningful work with significant stress. If you leave it at the office, you'll have a longer career and a better balance in life.

Hiring

From an InfoSec perspective, the hiring of employees is laden with potential security pitfalls. The CISO, in cooperation with the CIO and relevant InfoSec managers, should establish a dialogue with human resources personnel so that InfoSec considerations become part of the hiring process. Figure 11-4 highlights some of the hiring concerns.

Figure 11-4 Hiring issues

Copyright © 2014 Cengage Learning®.

Job Descriptions Integrating InfoSec into the hiring process begins with reviewing and updating job descriptions to include InfoSec responsibilities. Organizations that provide complete job descriptions when advertising open positions should omit the elements of the job description that describe access privileges.

Interviews Some interviews are conducted by members of the human resources staff; others include members of the department that the employee will eventually join. When a position within the InfoSec department opens up, the security manager can take the opportunity to educate human resources personnel on the various certifications, the specific experience each credential requires, and the qualifications of a good candidate. In general, the InfoSec department should advise human resources to limit the information provided to the candidates on the access rights of the position. When an interview includes a site visit, the tour should avoid secure and restricted sites because the visitor could observe enough information about the operations or InfoSec functions to represent a potential threat to the organization.

New Hire Orientation New employees should receive, as part of their orientation, an extensive InfoSec briefing. This orientation should cover policies, security procedures, access levels, and training on the secure use of information systems. By the time new employees are ready to report to their positions, they should be thoroughly briefed on the security component of their particular jobs as well as the rights and responsibilities of all personnel in the organization.

On-the-Job Security Training Organizations should conduct the periodic security awareness and training activities described in Chapter 5 to keep security at the forefront of employees' minds and minimize employee mistakes. Formal external and informal internal seminars also increase the level of security awareness for all employees, but especially for InfoSec employees.

Security Checks A background check should be conducted before the organization extends an offer to any candidate, regardless of job level. A background check can uncover past criminal behavior or other information that suggests a potential for future misconduct or a vulnerability that might render a candidate susceptible to coercion or blackmail. A number of regulations govern which areas organizations are permitted to investigate and how the information gathered can influence the hiring decision. The security and human resources managers should discuss these matters with legal counsel to determine which local and state regulations apply.

Background checks differ in their levels of detail and depth. In the military, background checks are used to help determine the individual's security clearance. In the business world, the thoroughness of a background check can vary with the level of trust required for the position being filled. Candidates for InfoSec positions should expect to undergo a reasonably detailed and thorough background check. Those applying for jobs in law enforcement or high-security positions may be required to submit to polygraph tests. Some of the common types of background checks are as follows:

- *Identity checks*—Personal identity validation
- *Education and credential checks*—Institutions attended, degrees and certifications earned, and certification status
- *Previous employment verification*—Where candidates worked, why they left, what they did, and for how long
- *Reference checks*—Validity of references and integrity of reference sources
- *Worker's compensation history*—Claims from worker's compensation

- *Motor vehicle records*—Driving records, suspensions, and other items noted in the applicant's public record

- *Drug history*—Drug screening and drug usage, past and present

- *Medical history*—Current and previous medical conditions, usually associated with physical capability to perform the work in the specified position

- *Credit history*—Credit problems, financial problems, and bankruptcy

- *Civil court history*—Involvement as the plaintiff or defendant in civil suits

- *Criminal court history*—Criminal background, arrests, convictions, and time served[27]

Organizations must comply with federal regulations regarding the use of personal information in employment practices. Among those regulations is the Fair Credit Reporting Act (FCRA), enacted in 1970, which governs the activities of consumer credit reporting agencies as well as the uses of the information procured from these agencies. Credit reports contain information on a job candidate's credit history, employment history, and other personal data.[28]

Among other things, FCRA prohibits employers from obtaining a credit report unless the candidate gives written permission for such a report to be released. This regulation also allows the candidate to request information on the nature and type of reporting used in making the employment decision, and to know the content of these reports and how they were used in making the hiring decision. FCRA restricts the time period that these reports can address. Unless the candidate earns more than $75,000 per year, they can contain only seven years of adverse information.[29]

Contracts and Employment

Once a candidate has accepted a job offer, the employment contract becomes an important security instrument. Many of the policies discussed in Chapter 6 require an employee to agree in writing to monitoring and nondisclosure agreements. It is important to have these contracts and agreements in place at the time of the hire because existing employees cannot necessarily be compelled to sign, nor can they be denied access to the systems that enable them to perform their duties. Job candidates, on the other hand, can be offered "employment contingent upon agreement," whereby they are not offered a position unless they agree to the binding organizational policies. While such a policy may seem harsh, it is a necessary component of the security process. Once a candidate signs the security agreements, the remainder of the employment contract may be executed.

Security as Part of Performance Evaluation

To heighten InfoSec awareness and change workplace behavior, organizations should incorporate InfoSec components into employee performance evaluations. Employees pay close attention to job performance evaluations, and including InfoSec tasks in them will motivate employees to take more care when performing these tasks.

Termination Issues

An organization can downsize, be bought out, be taken over, shut down, go out of business, or simply lay off, fire, or relocate its workforce. In any event, when an employee leaves an organization, a number of security-related concerns arise. Chief among these is the continuity of protection for all information to which the employee had access. When an employee leaves an organization, the following tasks must be performed:

- The former employee's access to the organization's systems must be disabled.
- The former employee must return all removable media.
- The former employee's hard drives must be secured.
- File cabinet locks must be changed.
- Office door locks must be changed.
- The former employee's keycard access must be revoked.
- The former employee's personal effects must be removed from the premises.
- The former employee should be escorted from the premises, once keys, keycards, and other business property have been turned over.

In addition to performing these tasks, many organizations conduct an exit interview to remind the employee of any contractual obligations, such as nondisclosure agreements, and to obtain feedback on the employee's tenure in the organization. At this time, the employee should be reminded that failure to comply with contractual obligations could lead to civil or criminal action.

Of course, most employees are allowed to clean out their own offices and collect their personal belongings, and are simply asked to return their keys. From a security standpoint, however, regardless of the level of trust in the employee or the level of cordiality in the office environment, voluntary or involuntary termination inevitably brings a risk of exposure of organizational information.

Some organizations adopt a policy of immediate severance for all employees, or for employees in certain positions or areas of trust. These organizations have examined the risks of the customary two-week notice model and instead opt to pay two weeks' severance while asking the employee to leave the facility immediately.

Two methods for handling employee outprocessing, depending on the employee's reasons for leaving, are as follows:

- *Hostile departure (usually involuntary), including termination, downsizing, lay-off, or quitting*—Security cuts off all logical and keycard access before the employee is terminated. As soon as the employee reports for work, he or she is escorted into the supervisor's office to receive the bad news. The individual is then escorted from the workplace and informed that his or her personal property will be forwarded, or is escorted to his or her office, cubicle, or personal area to collect personal effects under supervision. No organizational property is allowed to leave the premises, including disks, pens, papers, or books. Terminated employees can submit, in writing, a list of the property they want to retain, stating their reasons for doing so. Once personal property has been gathered, the employee is asked to surrender all keys, keycards, and other organizational identification and access devices, PDAs, pagers, cell phones, and all remaining company property, and is then escorted from the building.
- *Friendly departure (voluntary) for retirement, promotion, or relocation*—The employee may have tendered notice well in advance of the actual departure date, which can make it much more difficult for security to maintain positive control over the

employee's access and information usage. Employee accounts are usually allowed to continue, with a new expiration date. The employee can come and go at will and usually collects any belongings and leaves without escort. The employee is asked to drop off all organizational property before departing.

In either circumstance, the offices and information used by departing employees must be inventoried, their files stored or destroyed, and all property returned to organizational stores. It is possible in either situation that departing employees have collected organizational information and taken home files, reports, data from databases, and anything else that could be valuable in their future employment. This outcome may be impossible to prevent. Only by scrutinizing system logs during the transition period and after the employee has departed, and sorting out authorized actions from system misuse or information theft, can the organization determine whether a breach of policy or a loss of information has occurred. If information has been illegally copied or stolen, it should be treated as an incident and the appropriate policy followed.

Personnel Security Practices

There are various ways of monitoring and controlling employees to minimize their opportunities to misuse information. Separation of duties is used to make it difficult for an individual to violate InfoSec and breach the confidentiality, integrity, or availability of information. This control is particularly important in financial matters. For example, banks typically require that it take two employees to issue a cashier's check. The first is authorized to prepare the check, acquire the numbered financial document, and ready the check for signature. The second, usually a supervisor, is authorized to sign the check. If one person has the authority to do both tasks, then that person can prepare checks made out to co-conspirators, sign them, and steal large sums from the bank.

Separation of duties can also be applied to critical information and information systems. For example, one programmer might update the software in the systems, and a supervisor or coworker might then apply the tested update to the production system following the procedures of the change management process. Alternatively, one employee might be authorized to initiate backups to the system, while another mounts and dismounts the physical media. This checks-and-balances method requires two or more people to conspire to commit a theft or other misadventure, which is known as **collusion**. The odds that two people will be able to collaborate successfully to misuse the system are much lower than the odds of one person doing so. A practice similar to separation of duties, known as **two-person control**, requires that two individuals review and approve each other's work before the task is considered complete. Figure 11-5 illustrates separation of duties and two-person control.

Another control used to prevent personnel from misusing information assets is job rotation. **Job rotation** requires that every employee be able to perform the work of at least one other employee. If that approach is not feasible, an alternative is **task rotation**, in which all critical tasks can be performed by multiple individuals. Both job rotation and task rotation ensure that no one employee is performing actions that cannot be knowledgeably reviewed by another employee. In general, this overlap of knowledge is just good business sense. Among the many threats to an organization's information, a major concern is the inability to perform the tasks of an employee who is unable or unwilling to perform them. If everyone

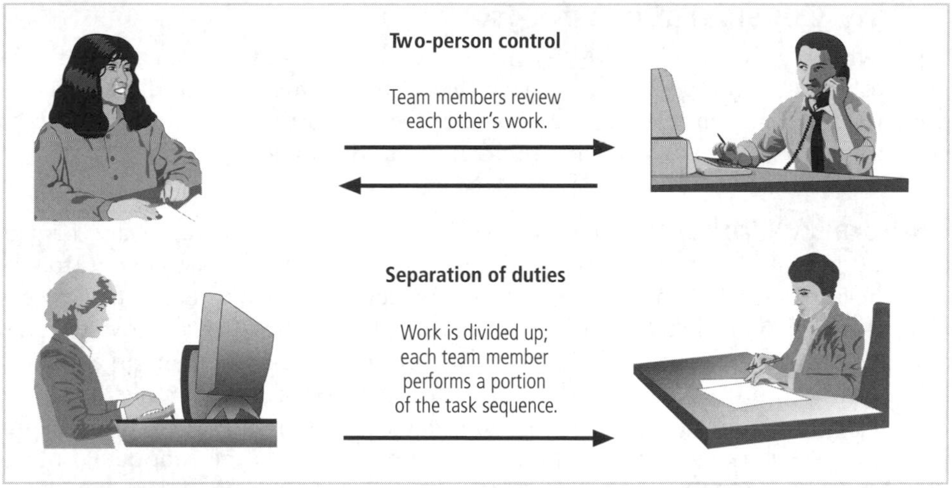

Figure 11-5 Personnel security needs

Copyright © 2014 Cengage Learning®.

knows at least part of another person's job (a human random array of independent disks [RAID] system), the organization can survive the loss of any single employee.

For similar reasons, many organizations implement a **mandatory vacation policy** that requires employees to take a vacation of at least one week per year. This policy gives the organization a chance to perform a detailed review of everyone's work and work area. Employees who are stealing from an organization or otherwise misusing information or systems are reluctant to take vacations for fear that their actions will be detected if they are not present to conceal them.

Finally, another important way to minimize opportunities for employee misuse of information is to limit access to information. That is, employees should be able to access only the information they need, and only for the period required to perform their tasks. This idea is referred to as the "principle of least privilege." Similar to the need-to-know concept, "least privilege" ensures that no unnecessary access to data occurs. If all employees can access all the organization's data all the time, it is almost certain that abuses—possibly leading to losses in confidentiality, integrity, and availability of information—will occur.

Security of Personnel and Personal Data

Organizations are required by law to protect sensitive or personal employee information, including personally identifying facts, such as employee addresses, phone numbers, Social Security numbers, medical conditions, and even names and addresses of family members. This responsibility also extends to customers, patients, and anyone with whom the organization has business relationships. While personnel data is, in principle, no different than other data that InfoSec is expected to protect, certainly more regulations cover its protection. As a result, InfoSec procedures should ensure that this data receives at least the same level of protection as the other important data in the organization. You will learn more about privacy and InfoSec in Chapter 12.

Security Considerations for Nonemployees

People who are not employees often have access to sensitive organizational information. Relationships with people in this category should be carefully managed to prevent threats to information assets from materializing. Some of the categories of nonemployees, and the security considerations specific to them, are discussed in the sections that follow.

Temporary Workers Temporary workers—often called temps—are brought in by organizations to fill positions temporarily or to supplement the existing workforce. In many cases, they are actually employees of a temp agency, a company that is paid to supply specially qualified individuals to an organization. Temps frequently provide secretarial or administrative support but can be used to fill almost any position in an organization, including executive positions. These workers are often exposed to a wide range of information as they perform their assigned duties. Because they are not employed by the organization for which they are working, however, they may not be subject to the contractual obligations or general policies that govern other employees. Therefore, if a temp violates a policy or causes a problem, the strongest action that the host organization can take is to terminate the relationship with the individual and request that he or she be censured. The employing agency is under no contractual obligation to do so but may want to accommodate a powerful or lucrative client. Unless specified in its contract with the organization, the temp agency may not be liable for losses caused by its workers.

From a security standpoint, temporary workers' access to information should be limited to what is necessary to perform their duties. The organization can attempt to have temps sign nondisclosure agreements and fair use policies, but the temp agency may refuse to go along, forcing the host organization to either dismiss the temp workers or allow them to work without such agreements. This can create an awkward—and potentially dangerous—situation. It may be impossible to limit a temp's access to information that is beyond the scope of his or her assigned tasks. The only way to combat this threat is to ensure that employees who are supervising temporary workers restrict their access to information, and to make sure that all workers—whether employees or temps—follow good security practices, especially clean desk policies and the securing of classified data. Temps can provide great benefits to organizations, but they should not be employed at the cost of sacrificing InfoSec.

Contract Employees Contract employees—often called contractors—are typically hired to perform specific services for the organization. In many cases, they are hired via a third-party organization. Typical contract employees include groundskeepers, maintenance services staff, electricians, mechanics, and other repair people, but they can also include professionals, such as attorneys, technical consultants, and IT specialists.

While professional contractors may require access to virtually all areas of the organization to do their jobs, service contractors usually need access only to specific facilities, and they should not be allowed to wander freely in and out of buildings. In a secure facility, all service contractors are escorted from room to room, and into and out of the facility. When these employees report for maintenance or repair services, someone must verify that services are actually scheduled or requested. As mentioned earlier in this book, attackers have been known to dress up as telephone repairers, maintenance technicians, or janitors to gain physical access to a building; therefore, direct oversight is a necessity. Any service agreements or

Offline
Social Engineering

The most nontechnical attack involves people. For this reason, this book dedicates a great deal of space to reinforcing the concept that security is a people problem, not a technology problem. Every day, thousands of systems are attacked successfully by individuals who take advantage of the natural gullibility of people. This gullibility is usually the result of a simple lack of computing knowledge and experience.

Social engineering (SE) uses persuasive techniques to gain the confidence of an individual in an effort to obtain information. Contrary to popular myth, most SE attacks don't come in as a phone call from "Joe in technology services" asking for your user name and password to fix your computer problem. Most attacks are subtle and involve the collection of small bits of seemingly innocuous information until a base of insider knowledge is built and then deployed to gain access to systems or information.

As the infamous superhacker Kevin Mitnick, who used SE as the primary means of gaining access to an organization's systems, once said: "I have never asked anyone for their password."[30] Now a security consultant, Mitnick once served five years for his crimes. How do you succeed at SE attacks, according to Mitnick? "You try to make an emotional connection with the person on the other side to create a sense of trust," Mitnick once told an interviewer. "That is the whole idea: to create a sense of trust and then exploit it."[31]

Some forms of SE attacks are so prevalent that there are formal warnings about them.

> *According to Computer Emergency Response Team Coordination Center (CERT/CC) users have reported social engineering attacks on users of Internet Relay Chat (IRC) and Instant Messaging (IM) services. In these situations, attackers trick users who are not paying attention into accepting and using software that does what the attacker wants. This may result in the attacker gaining the ability to use the victim's computer to attack other systems. These attacks might include using the computer to relay e-mail or become part of a distributed denial-of-service (DDoS) attack. It is reported that tens of thousands of systems are compromised using this form of attack along with other means used by these attackers.[32]*

Many people recognize these types of e-mails, IMs, and pop-ups for what they are. However, people with little computer experience may fail to discriminate between legitimate virus warnings and SE attacks.

A similar attack has been conducted recently to propagate viruses. An e-mail arrives, apparently from Microsoft (see Figure 11-6), insisting that the user immediately download a critical patch or upgrade to avoid leaving his or her system open

(Continued)

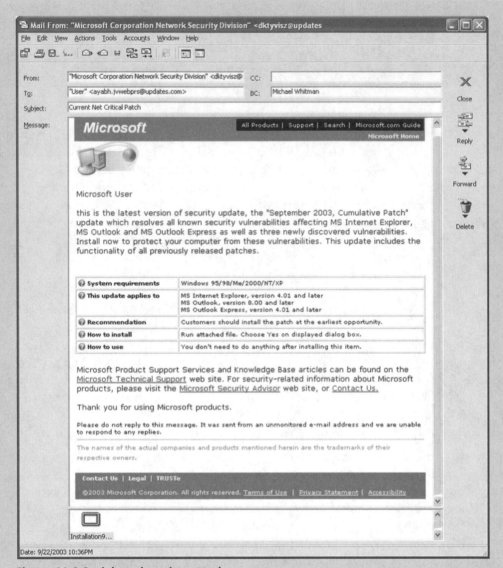

Figure 11-6 Social engineering attack

Source: Microsoft.

to attack. Because Microsoft does not e-mail individuals directly, experienced computer users simply delete the message. To the untrained eye, the message appears legitimate, however, and therefore it may be activated.

SE Attack Detection

It can be quite difficult to detect a SE attack. Indeed, attackers are becoming increasingly sophisticated. Sometimes they ask for seemingly innocuous information, such as

(Continued)

the name or telephone number of a coworker. Many employees may have given this information out routinely, without a second thought, allowing an attacker to begin building a story to get more information from the next person. To detect an SE attack, employees should be trained to detect anomalies in a conversation, e-mail, or pop-up window. According to an article by Susan Granger that was posted on the security software company Symantec's Web site, these anomalies include "refusal to give contact information, rushing, namedropping, intimidation, small mistakes (misspellings, misnomers, odd questions), and requesting forbidden information."

Granger adds: "Look for things that don't quite add up."[33]

SE Attack Prevention

The best method of preventing SE attacks is preparation. All employees must be trained and aware of the potential for these types of attacks. Security education, training, and awareness programs that focus on SE attacks can provide the organization with invaluable preparation and prevention techniques. Some additional prevention methods, along with the attacks they intend to thwart, include the following:

For the physical building:

- To avoid unauthorized physical access to the facility, ensure all employees have and use ID cards/name badges at all times, and when possible have physical security employees on site to monitor access.

- To prevent someone from digging through the dumpster, keep them in monitored and protected areas with regular inspections by physical security personnel.

For the office:

- To avoid shoulder surfing don't type in passwords with someone else there—or if you must, do so quickly.

- To eliminate individuals wandering through halls ensure all visitors are accompanied by an employee at all times.

- To prevent someone from stealing sensitive documents, ensure all documents are properly classified and labeled and locked when not actively in use.

- To prevent someone from stealing mail from the mailroom ensure the mailroom is locked at all times, preferably with keycard access.

For the phone:

- To prevent someone from impersonating an employee when speaking to the helpdesk, assign all employees a code (such as a PIN) to verify identity, or use employee numbers. Also train employees—including the help desk staff—to never give passwords or classified information over the phone.

(Continued)

- To prevent someone from stealing phone use, track all incoming and outgoing calls, and don't allow employees to transfer calls outside the organization.

For the networks and Internet connection:

- To prevent someone from tapping into the network, ensure the networking closet is locked and monitored, with a current inventory of equipment kept.
- To prevent someone from installing unauthorized software to capture internal traffic and passwords, monitor all system and network modifications and ensure all employees are trained on effective password policy and use.[34]

SE Attack Defense

The first thing an employee must do to defend against an SE attack is to tell someone. The organization should have an established procedure for reporting suspected SE attacks. If the organization uses some form of caller ID, the number of the suspected SE attacker should be documented and reported. The organization's incident response team should log these attacks and treat them no differently than any other form of attack.

A paper written by David Gragg and published by the SANS Institute overviews a multilayered defense against SE. Each layer offers some defense against an employee being compromised and, taken as a whole, offers the best defense. In his paper, Gragg defines the following layers of defense:

Security Policy Addressing Social Engineering—All organizations should have clearly stated objectives for strong security, as stated in an effective policy specifically addressing SE.

Security Awareness Training for All Users—Guidelines and motivation for all employees to understand data value, prevent information disclosure, and question inquisitive strangers and acquaintances.

Resistance Training for Key Personnel—Preparing employees to not only focus on InfoSec, but also to be resistant to threats and attacks.

Ongoing Reminders—Regular reminders of the need to be InfoSec conscientious.

Social Engineering Land Mines (SELM)—Traps set up to identify and expose an SE attack.

Incident Response—The need for a centralized and organized response to SE attacks when they occur.[35]

It is not difficult to protect against SE attacks, but employees must first know what they are and how they are conducted. Through these educational efforts, SE attacks can become your least dangerous threat rather than the most dangerous one.

contracts should contain the following regulations: The facility requires 24–48 hours' notice of a maintenance visit; the facility requires all on-site personnel to undergo background checks; and the facility requires advance notice for cancellation or rescheduling of a maintenance visit.

Consultants Organizations sometimes hire self-employed or agent contractors—typically called consultants—for specific tasks or projects. Consultants have their own security requirements and contractual obligations; their contracts should specify their rights of access to information and facilities. Security and technology consultants must be prescreened, escorted, and subjected to nondisclosure agreements to protect the organization from intentional or accidental breaches of confidentiality. Consultants tend to brag about the complexity of a particular job or an outstanding service provided to another client. If the organization does not want a consultant to make the relationship public or to disclose any detail, however small, about its particular system configuration, the organization must write these restrictions into the contract. Although these professionals typically request permission to include the business relationship on their résumés or promotional materials, the hiring organization is not obligated to grant this permission and can explicitly deny it.

Just because you pay security consultants, it does not mean that protecting your information is their number one priority. Always remember to apply the principle of least privilege when working with consultants.

Business Partners Businesses sometimes engage in strategic alliances with other organizations to exchange information, integrate systems, or enjoy some other mutual advantage. In these situations, a prior business agreement must specify the levels of exposure that both organizations are willing to tolerate. Sometimes, one division of an organization enters a strategic partnership with another organization that directly competes with one of its own divisions. If the strategic partnership evolves into an integration of the systems of both companies, competing groups may be provided with information that neither parent organization expected. For this reason, there must be a meticulous, deliberate process of determining what information is to be exchanged, in which format, and with whom. Nondisclosure agreements are an important part of any such collaborative effort. The level of security of both systems must be examined before any physical integration takes place, as system connection means that vulnerability on one system becomes vulnerability for all linked systems.

Chapter Summary

- The hiring of InfoSec personnel is affected by a number of factors, among them the law of supply and demand. In most cases, organizations look for a technically qualified InfoSec generalist, with a solid understanding of how the organization conducts its business, to serve as the chief information security officer.

- Many organizations rely on certifications to document the qualifications of current and/or prospective employees, recognizing that a professional association's assessment of skills and knowledge is a valid way of assessing the quality of these individuals.

- Many InfoSec professionals enter the field through one of two career paths: (1) as former members of law enforcement or the military, or (2) as IT professionals. A relatively new trend is the emergence of university-trained InfoSec specialists.

- During the hiring process, applying standard job descriptions can increase the degree of professionalism in the InfoSec field and improve the consistency of roles and responsibilities among organizations.

- Many organizations use recognizable certifications to identify the level of proficiency associated with the various security positions.

- Management should integrate InfoSec concepts and practices into the organization's employment activities.

- Organizations need the special services of nonemployees—temps, contractors, and consultants—and these relationships must be carefully managed to prevent InfoSec breaches.

- Separation of duties, two-person control, job and task rotation, mandatory vacations, and least privilege are among the practices and methods recommended to minimize employees' opportunities to misuse information.

- Government-mandated requirements for the privacy and security of personnel and personal data must be met by the organization's InfoSec program.

Review Questions

1. When an organization undertakes an InfoSec-driven review of job descriptions, which job descriptions must be reviewed? Which IT jobs not directly associated with information security should be reviewed?

2. List and describe the criteria for selecting InfoSec personnel.

3. What are some of the factors that influence an organization's hiring decisions?

4. What attributes do organizations seek in a candidate when hiring InfoSec professionals? Prioritize this list of attributes and justify your ranking.

5. What are the critical actions that management must consider taking when dismissing an employee? Do these issues change based on whether the departure is friendly or hostile?

6. How do the security considerations for temporary or contract workers differ from those for regular employees?

7. Which two career paths are the most commonly encountered as entrees into the InfoSec discipline? Are there other paths? If so, describe them.

8. Why is it important to have a body of standard job descriptions for hiring InfoSec professionals?

9. What functions does the CISO perform, and what are the key qualifications and requirements for the position?

10. What functions does the security manager perform, and what are the key qualifications and requirements for the position?

11. What functions does the security technician perform, and what are the key qualifications and requirements for the position?

12. What functions does the internal security consultant perform, and what are the key qualifications and requirements for the position?

13. What is the rationale for acquiring professional credentials?

14. List and describe the certification credentials available to InfoSec professionals.

15. In your opinion, who should pay for the expenses of certification? Under what circumstances would your answer be different? Why?

16. List and describe the standard personnel practices that are part of the InfoSec function. What happens to these practices when they are integrated with InfoSec concepts?

17. Why shouldn't you show a job candidate secure areas during interviews?

18. List and describe the types of nonemployee workers often used by organizations. What special security considerations apply to such workers, and why are they significant?

19. What is separation of duties? How can this method be used to improve an organization's InfoSec practices?

20. What is least privilege? Why is implementing least privilege important?

Exercises

1. Using the Internet, find at least five job postings for security administrators. What qualifications do the listings have in common? Did any of the listings include any qualifications that seemed unusual or different from what was expected?

2. Go to the (ISC)² Web site (*www.isc2.org*). Research the body of knowledge requirements for the CISSP and the SSCP. Which required areas are not covered in this text?

3. Using the Internet, search for three different employee hiring and termination policies. Review each and look carefully for inconsistencies. Does each have a section addressing the requirements for the security of information? What clauses should a termination policy contain to prevent disclosure of the organization's information? Create your own variant of either a hiring or a termination policy.

4. Using your local telephone directory, locate a service that offers background checks. Select one at random and call to determine the costs of conducting such checks. How much should an organization spend on conducting these checks if it interviews dozens of potential employees?

5. Using the descriptions given in this chapter, write a job description for Iris's new position, which is described in the following case scenario. What qualifications and responsibilities should be associated with this position?

Closing Case

Iris reviewed the scant stack of applications for the newly created security manager position and frowned. There should have been many more than just three applicants for the position.

After the human resources incident earlier in the month, she had been extremely careful in crafting the job description and was elated when Mike Edwards approved the creation of the position and the plan to hire. The new security manager was to assist in the drafting of security policies and plans, a need that had been highlighted by the recent HR problem.

Iris called Gloria in human resources. "I'm worried about the number of applicants we've had," she said. "I really thought there would be more than three, given the way the local economy is right now."

"Oh, there were dozens," Gloria said, "but I prescreened them for you."

"What do you mean?" Iris asked. "Prescreened how?"

"Well, we pass on only the most qualified applicants," Gloria replied. "According to our criteria, applicants for information security positions must have a CISA certification or some level of GIAD."

"Since I'm not aware of such a certification as a 'GIAD,' you must mean 'GIAC'?" Iris asked, her uneasiness building.

"No, the file says GIAD," Gloria replied confidently.

"Well, for this position we need a CISSP or CISM, not a GIAC or CISA," Iris said. "Those certifications don't match the job description I wrote, and I don't remember specifying any required certifications."

"You don't have to," Gloria said. "We've determined that the best people for the jobs are the ones who have the most certifications. We rewrote your position's screening criteria. We don't really look at anyone who isn't properly certified. Is there a problem?"

Discussion

1. If you were Iris, how would reply to Gloria's question?

2. What, if anything, is wrong with the human resources focus depicted here? Examine the relationship between certifications and experience. Do certifications alone identify the job candidates with the most appropriate expertise and work experience?

Ethical Decision Making

1. Looking back at the opening case scenario, did the HR staff that failed to report the candidate's conviction and parole on the "approval to hire" form commit an ethical lapse, or was it just a clerical error?

2. The company seems to prohibit the hiring of anyone with a felony conviction for any position. Do you think this is an ethically valid practice for this, or any, company to block hiring any felon, of should the nature of the crime for which they were convicted by part of the decision? Why or why not?

Endnotes

1. "(ISC)². 2012 Career Impact Survey." *(ISC)²*. Accessed January 12, 2013 @ *https:// www.isc2.org/uploadedfiles/2012careerimpactsurveyresults_final_020112.pdf*.

2. Wood, Charles Cresson. *Information Security Roles and Responsibilities Made Easy, Version 3*. Houston: InformationShield, 2012: 161–341.

3. Schwartz, Eddie, Dan Erwin, Vincent Weafer, and Andy Briney. "Roundtable: Infosec Staffing Help Wanted!" *Information Security Magazine Online*, April 2001. Accessed October 14, 2006 @ *www.infosecuritymag.com/articles/april01/features_roundtable.html*.

4. Wood, Charles Cresson. *Information Security Roles and Responsibilities Made Easy, Version 3*. Houston: InformationShield, 2012: 171.

5. Sehmbi, Avtar. "What Makes a CISO Employable?" *Information Security Magazine*. Accessed January 16, 2013 @ *www.infosecurity-magazine.com/view/11116/what-makes-a -ciso-employable*.

6. Wood, Charles Cresson. *Information Security Roles and Responsibilities Made Easy, Version 3*. Houston: InformationShield, 2012: 188.

7. Wood, Charles Cresson. *Information Security Roles and Responsibilities Made Easy, Version 3*. Houston: PentaSafe, 2012: Table of contents.

8. "CISSP Candidate Information Bulletin." *(ISC)*[2], January 1, 2012. Accessed January 13, 2013 @ *https://www.isc2.org/cib/default.aspx*.

9. "ISC2 Concentrations." *(ISC)*[2]. Accessed January 13, 2013 @ *https://www.isc2.org /concentrations/default.aspx*.

10. "About SSCP Certification." *ISC*[2]. Accessed January 13, 2013 @ *https://www.isc2.org /sscp/default.aspx*.

11. "CSSLP." *(ISC)*[2]. Accessed January 13, 2013 @ *https://www.isc2.org/uploadedFiles/(ISC)2 _Public_Content/Certification_Programs/CSSLP/CSSLP-Brochure.pdf*.

12. "(ISC)[2] Associate Program FAQs." *(ISC)*[2]. Accessed January 13, 2013 @ *https://www .isc2.org/uploadedFiles/Credentials_and_Certifcation/Associate_of_(ISC)2/Associate ProgramforCSSLPandCAPFAQs_FINAL.pdf*.

13. "Certified Information Security Manager 2013 Bulletin of Information." *ISACA*. Accessed January 13, 2013 @ *www.isaca.org/Certification/CISM-Certified-Information -Security-Manager/Register-for-the-Exam/Documents/CISM-BOI-June-2013-EN.pdf*.

14. "Certified Information Systems Auditor 2013 Bulletin of Information." *ISACA*. Accessed January 13, 2013 @ *www.isaca.org/Certification/CISA-Certified-Information -Systems-Auditor/Register-for-the-Exam/Documents/CISA-BOI-June-2013-EN.pdf*.

15. "Certified in the Governance of Enterprise IT (CGEIT) 2013 Bulletin of Information." *ISACA*. Accessed January 13, 2013 @ *www.isaca.org/Certification/CGEIT-Certified-in -the-Governance-of-Enterprise-IT/Register-for-the-Exam/Documents/June-2013-CGEIT -BOI.pdf*.

16. "Certified in Risk and Information Systems Controls (CRISC) 2013 Bulletin of Information." *ISACA*. Accessed January 13, 2013 @ *www.isaca.org/Certification/CRISC -Certified-in-Risk-and-Information-Systems-Control/Register-for-the-Exam/Documents /June-2013-CRISC-BOI.pdf*.

17. "GIAC Certifications." *GIAC*. Accessed January 16, 2013 @ *www.giac.org/certifications*.

18. "Governance." *EC-Council*. Accessed January 16, 2013 @ *https://www.eccouncil.org /ciso/dominion/governance*.

19. "Controls & Auditing." *EC-Council*. Accessed January 16, 2013 @ *https://www .eccouncil.org/ciso/dominion/controls-auditing*.

11

20. "Project and Operations." *EC-Council*. Accessed January 16, 2013 @ *https://www .eccouncil.org/ciso/dominion/projects-operations*.

21. "Core Competencies." *EC-Council*. Accessed January 16, 2013 @ *https://www.eccouncil .org/ciso/dominion/core-competencies*.

22. "Planning & Finance." *EC-Council*. Accessed January 16, 2013 @ *https://www .eccouncil.org/ciso/dominion/planning-finance*.

23. "CompTIA Security Certification." *CompTIA*. Accessed October 22, 2009 @ *www .comptia.org/certifications/listed/security.aspx*.

24. "CompTIA Security+ (2011 release) Certification Examination Objectives." Accessed February 19, 2013 @ *http://certification.comptia.org/Libraries/Exam_Objectives /CompTIA_Security_SY0-301.sflb.ashx*.

25. "CCE Certification Competencies." *ISFCE*. Accessed January 16, 2013 @ *www.isfce .com/policies/CCE%20Certification%20Competencies.pdf*.

26. Wood, Charles Cresson. *Information Security Roles and Responsibilities Made Easy, Version 3*. Houston: InformationShield, 2012: 577.

27. "Background Checks Are All We Do Since 1994." *Background Check International*. Accessed January 16, 2013 @ *www.bcint.com/services*.

28. "Fact Sheet 16b: Small Business Owner Background Check Guide." *Privacy Rights Clearinghouse*. Accessed January 16, 2013 @ *https://www.privacyrights.org/fs /fs16b-smallbus.htm*.

29. Ibid.

30. Lemos, Robert. "Mitnick Teaches 'Social Engineering.'" *Ziff-Davis News Net*, July 17, 2000. Accessed January 13, 2013 @ *www.infosecnews.org/hypermail/0007/2486.html*.

31. Ibid.

32. "Social Engineering Attacks via IRC and Instant Messaging." *CERT Incident Note IN-2002-03*, March 19, 2002. Accessed January 16, 2013 @ *www.cert.org/incident_notes /IN-2002-03.html*.

33. Granger, Sarah. "Social Engineering Fundamentals, Part II: Combat Strategies." *Symantec.com*, January 9, 2002. Accessed January 16, 2013 @ *www.symantec.com /connect/articles/social-engineering-fundamentals-part-ii-combat-strategies*.

34. Granger, Sarah. "Social Engineering Fundamentals, Part II: Combat Strategies." *Symantec.com*, January 9, 2002. Accessed January 16, 2013 @ *www.symantec.com /connect/articles/social-engineering-fundamentals-part-ii-combat-strategies*.

35. Gragg, David. "A Multi-Level Defense Against Social Engineering." *SANS Institute*, December 2002. Accessed January 16, 2013 @ *www.sans.org/reading_room/whitepapers /engineering/multi-level-defense-social-engineering_920*.

## chapter 12

Law and Ethics

*In law a man is guilty when he violates the rights of others. In ethics
he is guilty if he only thinks of doing so.*

IMMANUEL KANT *(1724–1804)*

Iris was just over halfway through her usual morning e-mail ritual when she came to a message that caught her attention. Just a few weeks before, Random Widget Works, Inc. (RWW) had set up a new Web server to facilitate open dialog and unrestricted feedback. This system would allow anyone, anywhere to send anonymous e-mail to the company's most senior executive. Apparently, someone had sent just such a message, and the CEO's executive assistant had relayed it to Iris. The e-mail read as follows:

To: Iris Majwabu
From: Cassandra Wilmington, Special Assistant to the CEO
Date: 2010-11-18 07:45 AM
Subject: FW: Anonymous Ethics Report – 2010-11-17 07:46 AM
Iris, you better look at this. The attached message came in on the anonymous
whistle-blower feed. I captured the text, encrypted it and have attached it
to this e-mail. The boss has already seen it and asked me to distribute
secure copies to you as well as Robin, Jerry, and Mike. He already has a
meeting with Mike set for this morning at 10:00. You and the others should
be there, too. A meeting invitation follows...

Iris opened her safe, retrieved and mounted her secure document drive, then exported the attachment file to it. She opened the decryption program, swiping her badge carrier and typing her personal identification number (PIN) to decrypt the message. The text appeared:

```
To: RWW Anonymous Ethics Mailbox
From: A Friend
Date: 2014-01-17 02:46 AM
Subject: HAL is for sale
You might want to look at the everythingz4zale.com auction site at www.
everythingz4zale.com/auctions/ref=19085769340
```

Iris opened her browser window and typed in the URL. She saw:

```
Item #19085769340
RWW, Inc. Customer and key accounts list
Starting bid: US $10,000.00
Time left: 1 day 22 hours 50 mins 3-day listing
History: 0 bids
Location: Cityville, WI
```

Iris picked up her phone and dialed RWW's legal affairs office. She knew it was going to be a busy morning—and a busy afternoon, too.

LEARNING OBJECTIVES

Upon completion of this material, you should be able to:

- Differentiate between law and ethics

- Describe the ethical foundations and approaches that underlie modern codes of ethics

- Identify major national and international laws that relate to the practice of InfoSec

- Describe the role of culture as it applies to ethics in InfoSec

- Discuss current laws, regulations, and relevant professional organizations

Introduction

This chapter covers relevant law and fundamental professional ethics related to information security (InfoSec). Although the two topics are intertwined, the first part of this chapter focuses on legislation and regulations concerning the management of information in an organization. The second part of this chapter discusses ethics and InfoSec, and offers a summary guide to professional organizations with established ethical codes. You can use this chapter both as a reference guide to the legal aspects of InfoSec and as an aid in planning your professional career.

As a future InfoSec professional, you will be required to understand the scope of an organization's legal and ethical responsibilities. The InfoSec professional should play an important role in an organization's approach to controlling liability for privacy and security risks. In the modern litigious societies of the world, sometimes laws are enforced in civil courts and plaintiffs are awarded large payments for damages or to punish defendants. To minimize these liabilities, the InfoSec practitioner must understand the current legal environment and keep apprised of new laws, regulations, and ethical issues as they emerge. By educating employees and management about their legal and ethical obligations and the proper use of information technology and information security, security professionals can keep their organizations focused on their primary objectives.

Law and Ethics in InfoSec

Within modern society, individuals elect to trade some aspects of personal freedom for social order. As Jean Jacques Rousseau explained in *The Social Contract, or Principles of Political Right*[1] (1762), the rules that members of a society create to balance an individual's right to self-determination with the needs of the whole are called laws. **Laws** are rules adopted and enforced by governments to codify expected behavior in modern society. They are largely drawn from the **ethics** of a culture, which define socially acceptable behaviors that conform to the widely held principles of the members of that society. The key difference between law and ethics is that law carries the sanction of a governing authority and ethics do not. Ethics, in turn, are based on **cultural mores**, which are the relatively fixed moral attitudes or customs of a societal group. Some ethics are thought to be universal. For example, murder, theft, and assault are actions that deviate from ethical and legal codes in most, if not all, of the world's cultures.

InfoSec and the Law

InfoSec professionals and managers involved in InfoSec must possess a rudimentary grasp of the legal framework within which their organizations operate. This legal environment can influence the organization to a greater or lesser extent, depending on the nature of the organization and the scale on which it operates.

Types of Law

There are a number of ways to categorize laws. **Civil law** embodies a wide variety of laws pertaining to relationships between and among individuals and organizations. **Criminal law** addresses violations harmful to society and is actively enforced and prosecuted by the state. **Tort law** is a subset of civil law that allows individuals to seek redress in the event of personal, physical, or financial injury. Tort law is pursued in civil court and is not prosecuted by the state.

Legislation that affects individuals in the workplace can be categorized as private law or public law. **Private law** regulates the relationships among individuals and among individuals and organizations; it encompasses family law, commercial law, and labor law. **Public law** regulates the structure and administration of government agencies and their relationships with citizens, employees, and other governments. Public law includes criminal, administrative, and constitutional law.

Relevant U.S. Laws

The United States has led the development and implementation of InfoSec legislation to prevent misuse and exploitation of information and information technology. The development of InfoSec legislation promotes the general welfare and creates a stable environment for a solid economy. In its capacity as a global leader, the United States has demonstrated a clear understanding of the problems facing the InfoSec field and has specified penalties for individuals and organizations that fail to follow the requirements set forth in the U.S. civil statutes. Table 12-1 summarizes the U.S. federal laws relevant to InfoSec. You can find more information about each of these laws by searching the Web.

Area	Act	Date	Description
Online commerce and information protection	Federal Trade Commission Act (FTCA) of 1914	1914	Recently used to challenge organizations with deceptive claims regarding the privacy and security of customers' personal information
Telecommunications	Communications Act of 1934 (47 USC 151 et seq.)	1934	Includes amendments found in the Telecommunications Deregulation and Competition Act of 1996. This law regulates interstate and foreign telecommunications (amended 1996 and 2001)
Freedom of information	Freedom of Information Act (FOIA)	1966	Allows for the disclosure of previously unreleased information and documents controlled by the U.S. government
Privacy	Federal Privacy Act of 1974	1974	Governs federal agency use of personal information
Privacy of student information	Family Educational Rights and Privacy Act (FERPA) (20 U.S.C. § 1232g; 34 CFR Part 99)	1974	Also known as the Buckley Amendment; protects the privacy of student education records
Copyright	Copyright Act of 1976 (update to U.S. Copyright Law [17 USC])	1976	Protects intellectual property, including publications and software
Cryptography	Electronic Communications Privacy Act (ECPA) of 1986 (update to 18 USC)	1986	Regulates interception and disclosure of electronic information; also referred to as the Federal Wiretapping Act
Access to stored communications	Unlawful Access to Stored Communications (18 USC 2701)	1986	Provides penalties for illegally accessing stored communications (such as e-mail and voicemail) stored by a service provider
Threats to computers	Computer Fraud and Abuse (CFA) Act (also known as Fraud and Related Activity in Connection with Computers) (18 USC 1030)	1986	Defines and formalizes laws to counter threats from computer-related acts and offenses (amended 1996, 2001, and 2006)
Federal agency information security	Computer Security Act (CSA) of 1987	1987	Requires all federal computer systems that contain classified information to have security plans in place, and requires periodic security training for all individuals who operate, design, or manage such systems
Trap and trace restrictions	General prohibition on pen register and trap and trace device use; exception (18 USC 3121 et seq.)	1993	Prohibits the use of electronic "pen registers" and trap and trace devices without a court order
Criminal intent	National Information Infrastructure Protection Act of 1996 (update to 18 USC 1030)	1996	Categorizes crimes based on defendant's authority to access a protected computer system and criminal intent
Trade secrets	Economic Espionage Act (EEA) of 1996	1996	Prevents abuse of information gained while employed elsewhere

Table 12-1   Key U.S. laws of interest to InfoSec professionals

Area	Act	Date	Description
Personal health information protection	Health Insurance Portability and Accountability Act (HIPAA) of 1996	1996	Requires medical practices to ensure the privacy of personal medical information
Encryption and digital signatures	Security and Freedom through Encryption Act of 1997	1997	Affirms the rights of persons in the United States to use and sell products that include encryption and to relax export controls on such products
Infrastructure protection	No Electronic Theft Act Amends 17 USC 506(a)—copyright infringement, and 18 USC 2319—criminal infringement of copyright (Public Law 105-147)	1997	These parts of the US Code amend copyright and criminal statutes to provide greater copyright protection and penalties for electronic copyright infringement
Copy protection	Digital Millennium Copyright Act (DMCA) (update to 17 USC 101)	1998	Provides specific penalties for removing copyright protection from media
Identity theft	Identity Theft and Assumption Deterrence Act of 1998 (18 USC 1028)	1998	Attempts to instigate specific penalties for identity theft by identifying the individual who loses their identity as the true victim, not just those commercial and financial credit entities who suffered losses
Banking	Gramm-Leach-Bliley (GLB) Act of 1999 (also known as the Financial Services Modernization Act)	1999	Repeals the restrictions on banks affiliating with insurance and securities firms; has significant impact on the privacy of personal information used by these industries
Terrorism	USA PATRIOT Act of 2001 (update to 18 USC 1030)	2001	Defines stiffer penalties for prosecution of terrorist crimes
Accountability	Sarbanes-Oxley (SOX) Act of 2002 (also known as the Public Company Accounting Reform and Investor Protection Act)	2002	Enforces accountability for executives at publicly traded companies; is having ripple effects throughout the accounting, IT, and related units of many organizations
General InfoSec	Federal Information Security Management Act of 2002 (44 USC § 3541, et seq.)	2002	Requires each federal agency to develop, document, and implement an agency-wide program to provide InfoSec for the information and information systems that support the operations and assets of the agency, including those provided or managed by another agency, contractor, or other source
Spam	Controlling the Assault of Non-Solicited Pornography and Marketing (CAN-SPAM) Act of 2003 (15 USC 7701 et seq.)	2003	Sets the first national standards for regulating the distribution of commercial e-mail, including mobile phone spam

12

Table 12-1   Key U.S. laws of interest to InfoSec professionals (continued)

Area	Act	Date	Description
Fraud with access devices	Fraud and Related Activity in Connection with Access Devices (18 USC 1029)	2004	Defines and formalizes law to counter threats from counterfeit access devices like ID cards, credit cards, telecom equipment, mobile or electronic serial numbers, and the equipment that creates them
Terrorism and extreme drug trafficking	USA PATRIOT Improvement Reauthorization Act of 2005 (update to 18 USC 1030)	2006	Renews critical sections of the USA PATRIOT Act
Privacy of PHI	American Recovery and Reinvestment Act (ARRA) of 2009	2009	In the privacy and security area, requires new reporting requirements and penalties for breach of Protected Health Information (PHI).
Privacy of PHI	Health Information Technology for Economic and Clinical Health (HITECH) Act (part of ARRA-2009)	2009	Addresses privacy and security concerns associated with the electronic transmission of PHI, in part, through several provisions that strengthen HIPAA rules for civil and criminal enforcement
Defense information protection	International Traffic in Arms Regulations (ITAR) Act of 2012	2012	Restricts the exportation of technology and information related to defense and military-related services and materiel, including research and development information

Table 12-1   Key U.S. laws of interest to InfoSec professionals (continued)

Copyright © 2014 Cengage Learning®.

General Computer Crime Laws

The Computer Fraud and Abuse (CFA) Act of 1986, presented in the adjoining Offline, is the cornerstone of many computer-related federal laws and enforcement efforts. It was amended in October 1996 by the National Information Infrastructure Protection Act of 1996, which modified several sections of the previous act and increased the penalties for selected crimes. Punishment for offenses prosecuted under this statute varies from fines to imprisonment for up to 20 years or can include both. The penalty depends on the value of the information obtained and whether the offense is judged to have been committed for one of the following reasons:

- For purposes of commercial advantage
- For private financial gain
- In furtherance of a criminal act

The CFA Act was further modified by the USA PATRIOT Act of 2001 (the abbreviated name for "Uniting and Strengthening America by Providing Appropriate Tools Required to Intercept and Obstruct Terrorism Act of 2001"), which was enacted in 2001 as a mechanism to provide the United States with a means to investigate and respond to the 9/11 attacks on the New York World Trade Center. The PATRIOT Act provides law enforcement agencies with broader latitude to combat terrorism-related activities. As presented in the discussion in the adjoining Offline, some of the laws modified by the PATRIOT Act are among the earliest laws created to deal with electronic technology.

Offline
Computer Fraud and Abuse Act of 1986
(Section 1030, Chapter 47, Title 18 USC)

Fraud and Related Activity in Connection with Computers

Whoever having knowingly accessed a computer without authorization or exceeding authorized access, and by means of such conduct having obtained information that has been determined by the United States Government … to require protection against unauthorized disclosure for reasons of national defense or foreign relations, or any restricted data … with reason to believe that such information so obtained could be used to the injury of the United States, or to the advantage of any foreign nation, willfully communicates, delivers, transmits, or causes to be communicated, delivered, or transmitted, or attempts to communicate, deliver, transmit or cause to be communicated, delivered, or transmitted the same to any person not entitled to receive it, or willfully retains the same and fails to deliver it to the officer or employee of the United States entitled to receive it; intentionally accesses a computer without authorization or exceeds authorized access, and thereby obtains information contained in a financial record of a financial institution, or of a card issuer …, or contained in a file of a consumer reporting agency on a consumer…; information from any department or agency of the United States; or information from any protected computer if the conduct involved an interstate or foreign communication; intentionally, without authorization to access any nonpublic computer of a department or agency of the United States, accesses such a computer of that department or agency that is exclusively for the use of the Government of the United States or, in the case of a computer not exclusively for such use, is used by or for the Government of the United States and such conduct affects that use by or for the Government of the United States; knowingly and with intent to defraud, accesses a protected computer without authorization, or exceeds authorized access, and by means of such conduct furthers the intended fraud and obtains anything of value, unless the object of the fraud and the thing obtained consists only of the use of the computer and the value of such use is not more than $5,000 in any 1-year period; knowingly causes the transmission of a program, information, code, or command, and as a result of such conduct, intentionally causes damage without authorization, to a protected computer; intentionally accesses a protected computer without authorization, and as a result of such conduct, recklessly causes damage; or intentionally accesses a protected computer without authorization, and as a result of such conduct, causes damage; knowingly and with intent to defraud traffics … in any password or similar information through which a computer may be accessed without authorization, if such trafficking affects interstate or foreign commerce; or such computer is used by or for the Government of the United States; with intent to extort from any person, firm, association, educational institution, financial institution, government entity, or other legal entity, any money or other thing of value, transmits in interstate or foreign commerce any communication containing any threat to cause damage to a protected computer.

12

Offline
USA PATRIOT Act of 2001 and the USA PATRIOT Improvement and Reauthorization Act of 2005

Authority to Intercept Voice Communications in Computer Hacking Investigations. Under previous law, investigators could not obtain a wiretap order to intercept wire voice communications for violations of the CFA Act. The PATRIOT Act identifies specific crimes under which investigators may obtain a wiretap order for wire communications by adding felony violations of the CFA Act to the list of offenses.

Obtaining Voice Mail and Other Stored Voice Communications. Previously, the Electronic Communications Privacy Act (ECPA) governed law enforcement access to stored electronic communications like e-mail, but not stored wire voice communications (voice mail). Instead, the wiretap act regulated these actions primarily because the definition of "wire communication" included stored voice communications; therefore, investigators were required to obtain a wiretap order from a judge to confiscate and review voice mail or answering machine messages. What was not envisioned when the original ECPA was developed was the creation of hybrid systems that stored voice communications as digital messages (digital voice mail). The PATRIOT Act alters the way that the wiretap statute and ECPA apply to stored voice communications. The amendments delete "electronic storage" of wire communications from the definition of "wire communication" and insert language to ensure that stored wire communications are covered under the same rules as stored electronic communications, allowing investigators to search these messages using standard search warrants, rather than wiretap orders.

Emergency Disclosures by Communications Providers. Previous law relating to voluntary disclosures by communication service providers (like ISPs) contained no special provision allowing providers to disclose customer records or communications in emergencies. If an ISP voluntarily provided account information or subscriber information to law enforcement officials, it risked being subject to civil suit, even if the information pointed to a potential crime or terrorist attack.

This PATRIOT Act permits, but does not require, ISPs to disclose customer information if it suspects an immediate risk of death or serious physical injury to any person. ISPs are also allowed to disclose such information to protect their property and rights.

Intercepting the Communications of Computer Trespassers. This law permits owners of computers and computer systems to monitor their systems to protect rights and property. However, it does not provide clear guidance as to what extent these owners can ask for assistance in this monitoring from the law enforcement community. The PATRIOT Act allows computer system owners to monitor trespassers on their systems and obtain support from law enforcement officials in conducting this monitoring. This provision also stipulates that *if* the owners or operators of the

(Continued)

system authorize law enforcement to monitor a suspected trespasser's traffic, *and* the individual intercepting the traffic is engaged in a lawful investigation, *and* the investigator has reason to suspect that the intercepted traffic is vital to the investigation, *and* only those communications conducted by the trespasser will be intercepted, *then* it is legal to intercept the wire or electronic communications of a computer trespasser—even if acting "under color of law" or as an agent of the law. A computer trespasser is defined as "any person who accesses a protected computer without authorization." The definition explicitly excludes individuals "known by the owner or operator of the protected computer to have an existing contractual relationship with the owner or operator for access to all or part of the computer."

Nationwide Search Warrants for E-mail. Current law requires the government to use a search warrant to compel a provider to disclose unopened e-mail less than six months old. Changes resulting from the PATRIOT Act allow investigators to obtain warrants for computer records outside their native jurisdiction, essentially permitting them to obtain records in other jurisdictions, such as other states or counties, which would normally require time-consuming inter-agency cooperation.

Deterrence and Prevention of Cyberterrorism. This section makes a number of changes to the CFA Act, increasing penalties for hackers from 10 to 20 years and clarifying the definition of "intent" to make explicit that a hacker need only intend damage. It creates new offenses for special types of computer crime, such as those targeting national security or the criminal justice system. It also allows aggregation of computer criminal offenses to meet some of the minimum requirements for stiffer penalties.

Development and Support of Cybersecurity Forensic Capabilities. This section requires the Attorney General to establish and fund a number of regional computer forensic laboratories as well as provide support for existing labs.

In 2005, with the signing of the USA PATRIOT Improvement and Reauthorization Act of 2005, several key sections were reauthorized and enhanced. Some of the provisions of this act were previously known by the following names:

- Combat Methamphetamine Epidemic Act of 2005
- Combating Terrorism Financing Act of 2005
- Reducing Crime and Terrorism at America's Seaports Act of 2005
- Secret Service Authorization and Technical Modification Act of 2005
- Terrorist Death Penalty Enhancement Act of 2005

Among its other provisions (as has been noted by Yeh and Doyle), it:

- Establishes 14 of the 16 primary elements of the USA PATRIOT Act sections that were initially planned to expire at the end of 2005
- Permits additional congressional and judicial oversight of section 215 of the Foreign Intelligence Surveillance Act (FISA), which covers business records, as well as section 206 FISA, which allows for roving wiretaps, enabling both sections until the end of 2009

(Continued)

- Allows broader law enforcement wiretap authority to cover more than 20 federal crimes

- Requires judicial review and enforcement procedures for national security letters

- Modifies provisions for federal criminal enforcement for enhanced seaport and maritime security

- Enables stronger federal money laundering and forfeiture authority, particularly in connection with terrorist offenses

- Enhances the ability of authorities to enforce federal regulation of foreign and domestic commerce in methamphetamine precursors

- Clarifies the technical aspects of federal capital punishment procedures

- Modifies how the Department of Justice and the Secret Service are to enforce the laws provisions[2]

The major sections of the act are as follows:
TITLE I—USA PATRIOT IMPROVEMENT AND REAUTHORIZATION ACT
TITLE II—TERRORIST DEATH PENALTY ENHANCEMENT
    Subtitle A—Terrorist Penalties Enhancement Act
    Subtitle B—Federal Death Penalty Procedures
TITLE III—REDUCING CRIME AND TERRORISM AT AMERICA'S SEAPORTS
TITLE IV—COMBATING TERRORISM FINANCING
TITLE V—MISCELLANEOUS PROVISIONS
TITLE VI—SECRET SERVICE
TITLE VII—COMBAT METHAMPHETAMINE EPIDEMIC ACT OF 2005
    Subtitle A—Domestic Regulation of Precursor Chemicals
    Subtitle B—International Regulation of Precursor Chemicals
    Subtitle C—Enhanced Criminal Penalties for Methamphetamine Production and Trafficking
    Subtitle D—Enhanced Environmental Regulation of Methamphetamine Byproducts
    Subtitle E—Additional Programs and Activities

Another law of critical importance to InfoSec professionals is the **Computer Security Act (CSA)** of 1987. This legislation was one of the first attempts to protect federal computer systems by establishing minimum acceptable security practices. The CSA charges the National Bureau of Standards, in cooperation with the National Security Agency (NSA), with the development of:

- Standards, guidelines, and associated methods and techniques for computer systems

- Uniform standards and guidelines for most federal computer systems

- Technical, management, physical, and administrative standards and guidelines for the cost-effective security and privacy of sensitive information in federal computer systems

- Guidelines for use by operators of federal computer systems that contain sensitive information in training their employees in security awareness and accepted security practice

- Validation procedures for, and evaluation of the effectiveness of, standards and guidelines through research and liaison with other government and private agencies[3]

The CSA also established a Computer System Security and Privacy Advisory Board within the Department of Commerce. This board identifies emerging managerial, technical, administrative, and physical safety issues relative to computer systems security and privacy, and it advises the Bureau of Standards and the Secretary of Commerce on security and privacy issues pertaining to federal computer systems. The board reports to the Secretary of Commerce, the Director of the Office of Management and Budget, the Director of the NSA, and the appropriate committees of Congress.

The CSA also amended the Federal Property and Administrative Services Act of 1949. The amendments require the National Bureau of Standards to distribute standards and guidelines pertaining to federal computer systems, making such standards compulsory and binding to the extent to which the secretary determines necessary to improve the efficiency of operation or security and privacy of federal computer systems. This act also permits the head of any federal agency to employ more stringent standards than those distributed.

Another provision of the CSA requires mandatory periodic training in computer security awareness and accepted computer security practice for all employees who are involved with the management, use, or operation of each federal computer system. This training for federal employees is intended to enhance their awareness of the threats to, and vulnerability of, computer systems and to encourage the use of good computer security practices. It also informs federal agencies as to who is responsible for computer systems security and privacy, requires the identification of systems that contain sensitive information, and outlines the requirements for formal security plans.

Privacy Laws   Many organizations collect, trade, and sell personal information as a commodity, and many people are becoming aware of these practices and are looking to governments to protect their privacy. In the past, it was not possible to create databases that contained personal information collected from multiple sources. Today, the aggregation of data from multiple sources permits unethical organizations to build databases with alarming quantities of personal information.

The number of statutes addressing individual privacy rights has grown. However, privacy in this context is not absolute freedom from observation; rather, it is defined as the "state of being free from unsanctioned intrusion."[4] It is possible to track this freedom from intrusion to the Fourth Amendment of the U.S. Constitution, which states the following:

> *The right of the people to be secure in their persons, houses, papers, and effects, against unreasonable searches and seizures, shall not be violated, and no Warrants shall issue, but upon probable cause, supported by Oath or affirmation, and particularly describing the place to be searched, and the persons or things to be seized.*[5]

The origins of this right can be traced to a 1772 document by Samuel Adams titled *The Rights of the Colonists and a List of Infringements and Violations of Rights*. This document in turn had its roots in a 1604 ruling by a British court that upheld the rights of a man to refuse entry to the king's men without royal warrant, or at least to restrict the search to items listed in a warrant.[6]

To better understand this rapidly evolving issue, some of the more relevant privacy laws and regulations are discussed in the following pages.

The Privacy of Customer Information in Section 222 of USC Title 47, Chapter 5, Subchapter II, Part I covering common carriers[7] (organizations that process or move data for hire) specifies that any proprietary information shall be used explicitly for providing services, and not for any marketing purposes. It also stipulates that carriers cannot disclose this information except when necessary to provide its services, or by customer request, and then the disclosure is restricted to that customer's information only.

The law does permit the use of aggregate information (which is created by combining non-private data elements) as long as the same information is provided to all common carriers and the carrier in question conducts business with fair competition. The use of aggregate information raises privacy concerns because an organization could assemble data from a variety of sources in ways that would allow correlation of seemingly innocuous information into something more intrusive. For example, the mapping of a government census database with telephone directory information, cross-indexed to bankruptcy court records, could be used to facilitate marketing efforts to people experiencing financial difficulties.

While this common carrier regulation controls public carriers' use of private data, the Federal Privacy Act of 1974 regulates the government's use of private information. The Federal Privacy Act was created to ensure that government agencies protect the privacy of individuals' and businesses' information, and it holds those agencies responsible if any portion of this information is released without permission. The act states the following: "No agency shall disclose any record which is contained in a system of records by any means of communication to any person, or to another agency, except pursuant to a written request by, or with the prior written consent of, the individual to whom the record pertains...."[8] The following entities are exempt from some of the regulations so that they can perform their duties:

- Bureau of the Census
- National Archives and Records Administration
- U.S. Congress
- Comptroller General
- Certain court orders
- Credit agencies

Also, individuals can access information controlled by others if they can demonstrate that it is necessary to protect their health or safety.

The **Electronic Communications Privacy Act (ECPA)** of 1986 is a collection of statutes that regulates the interception of wire, electronic, and oral communications. These statutes are frequently referred to as the Federal wiretapping acts. They address the following areas[9]:

- Interception and disclosure of wire, oral, or electronic communications
- Manufacture, distribution, possession, and advertising of wire, oral, or electronic communication intercepting devices
- Confiscation of wire, oral, or electronic communication intercepting devices
- Evidentiary use of intercepted wire or oral communications
- Authorization for interception of wire, oral, or electronic communications
- Authorization for disclosure and use of intercepted wire, oral, or electronic communications

- Procedure for interception of wire, oral, or electronic communications
- Reports concerning intercepted wire, oral, or electronic communications
- Injunction against illegal interception

The **Health Insurance Portability and Accountability Act (HIPAA)** of 1996, also known as the Kennedy-Kassebaum Act, attempts to protect the confidentiality and security of health care data by establishing and enforcing standards and by standardizing electronic data interchange. HIPAA affects all health care organizations, including small medical practices, health clinics, life insurers, and universities, as well as some organizations that have self-insured employee health programs. It provides for stiff penalties for organizations that fail to comply with the law, with up to $250,000 and/or 10 years imprisonment for knowingly misusing client information. Organizations were required to comply with the act as of April 14, 2003.[10] See *www.cms.gov* for specifics on compliance deadlines and components.

HIPAA affects the field of InfoSec in a number of ways. It requires organizations that retain health care information to use InfoSec mechanisms to protect this information, as well as policies and procedures to maintain them. This is known as the HIPAA Security Rule. The purpose of the law is summarized by the U.S. Department of Health and Human Services as follows:

> *The HIPAA Security Rule establishes national standards to protect individuals' electronic personal health information that is created, received, used, or maintained by a covered entity. The Security Rule, located at 45 CFR Part 160 and Subparts A and C of Part 164, requires appropriate administrative, physical and technical safeguards to ensure the confidentiality, integrity, and security of electronic PHI.[11]*

It also requires a comprehensive assessment of the organization's InfoSec systems, policies, and procedures. HIPAA provides guidelines for the use of electronic signatures based on security standards ensuring message integrity, user authentication, and nonrepudiation. There is no specification of particular security technologies for each of the security requirements, only that security must be implemented to ensure the privacy of the health care information.

The privacy standards of HIPAA severely restrict the dissemination and distribution of private health information without documented consent. This is known as the HIPAA Privacy Rule and is explained by the U.S. Department of Health and Human Services as follows:

> *The HIPAA Privacy Rule establishes national standards to protect individuals' medical records and other personal health information and applies to health plans, health care clearinghouses, and those health care providers that conduct certain health care transactions electronically. The Rule, located at 45 CFR Part 160 and Subparts A and E of Part 164, requires appropriate safeguards to protect the privacy of personal health information, and sets limits and conditions on the uses and disclosures that may be made of such information without patient authorization. The Rule also gives patients rights over their health information, including rights to examine and obtain a copy of their health records, and to request corrections.[12]*

The Privacy Rule also restricts the use of health information to the minimum required for the health care services required.

HIPAA has five fundamental privacy principles:

- Consumer control of medical information
- Boundaries on the use of medical information
- Accountability for the privacy of private information
- Balance of public responsibility for the use of medical information for the greater good measured against impact to the individual
- Security of health information

ARRA and HITECH Enacted in 2009, the American Recovery and Reinvestment Act (ARRA) was designed to provide a response to the economic crisis in the United States. The act was specifically focused on providing tax cuts and funding for programs, federal contracts, grants, and loans. While the base act is important, of particular interest to the InfoSec community was the inclusion of the Health Information Technology for Economic and Clinical Health (HITECH) Act, enacted as part of ARRA. The U.S. Department of Health and Human Services explains HITECH as follows:

> *The HITECH Act, which was enacted as part of the ARRA of 2009, modified the HHS Secretary's authority to impose civil money penalties for violations occurring after February 18, 2009. These HITECH Act revisions significantly increase the penalty amounts the Secretary may impose for violations of the HIPAA rules and encourage prompt corrective action.*
>
> *Prior to the HITECH Act, the Secretary could not impose a penalty of more than $100 for each violation or $25,000 for all identical violations of the same provision. A covered health care provider, health plan, or clearinghouse could also bar the Secretary's imposition of a civil money penalty by demonstrating that it did not know that it violated the HIPAA rules.[13]*

HIPAA and HITECH also require that covered entities notify information owners of breaches. The U.S. Department of Health and Human Services explains the Breach Notification Rule as:

> *Interim final breach notification regulations, issued in August 2009, implement section 13402 of the HITECH Act by requiring HIPAA covered entities and their business associates to provide notification following a breach of unsecured PHI. Similar breach notification provisions implemented and enforced by the Federal Trade Commission (FTC), apply to vendors of personal health records and their third party service providers, pursuant to section 13407 of the HITECH Act.[14]*

Gramm-Leach Bliley (GLB) Act of 1999 The Gramm-Leach-Bliley (GLB) Act (also known as the Financial Services Modernization Act of 1999) contains a number of provisions that affect banks, securities firms, and insurance companies. This act requires all financial institutions to disclose their privacy policies, describing how they share nonpublic personal information and how customers can request that their information not be shared with third parties. The act also ensures that the privacy policies in effect in an organization are fully disclosed when a customer initiates a business relationship and are distributed at least annually for the duration of the professional association.

Export and Espionage Laws The need to protect national security, trade secrets, and a variety of other state and private assets has led to several laws affecting what information and information management and security resources may be exported from the United States. These laws attempt to stem the theft of information by establishing strong penalties for related crimes.

To protect intellectual property and competitive advantage, Congress passed the Economic Espionage Act (EEA) in 1996. According to the U.S. Department of Justice, this law attempts to protect trade secrets "from the foreign government that uses its classic espionage apparatus to spy on a company, to the two American companies that are attempting to uncover each other's bid proposals, or to the disgruntled former employee who walks out of his former company with a computer diskette full of engineering schematics."[15]

The Security and Freedom through Encryption Act of 1997 provides guidance on the use of encryption and institutes measures of public protection from government intervention. Specifically, the act:

- Reinforces an individual's right to use or sell encryption algorithms without concern for the impact of other regulations requiring some form of key registration. Key registration is when a cryptographic key (or its text equivalent) is stored with another party to be used to break the encryption of the data under some circumstances. This is often called key escrow.

- Prohibits the federal government from requiring the use of encryption for contracts, grants, other official documents, and correspondence.

- States that the use of encryption is not probable cause to suspect criminal activity.

- Relaxes export restrictions by amending the Export Administration Act of 1979.

- Provides additional penalties for the use of encryption in the commission of a criminal act.

U.S. Copyright Law U.S. Copyright Law extends protection to intellectual property, which includes words published in electronic formats. The doctrine of fair use allows material to be quoted for the purpose of news reporting, teaching, scholarship, and a number of other related activities, so long as the purpose is educational and not for profit and the usage is not excessive. Proper acknowledgment must be provided to the author and/or copyright holder of such works, including a description of the location of source materials by using a recognized form of citation.

Freedom of Information Act (FOIA) of 1966 All federal agencies are required under the Freedom of Information Act (FOIA) to disclose records requested in writing by any person. However, agencies may withhold information pursuant to nine exemptions and three exclusions contained in the statute. FOIA applies only to federal agencies and does not create a right of access to records held by Congress, the courts, or by state or local government agencies. Each state has its own public access laws that should be consulted for access to state and local records.

Sarbanes-Oxley (SOX) Act of 2002 In the wake of the Enron and WorldCom financial scandals and the damage on financial markets from criminal violations of the federal securities laws, the U.S. Congress enacted the Sarbanes-Oxley (SOX) Act of 2002, which was designed to enforce accountability for the financial reporting and record-keeping at publicly traded corporations. While this law on its face would not seem to affect InfoSec or even general IT functions, in fact its effects are being felt throughout the organizations to which it applies.

The law requires that the Chief Executive Officer (CEO) and Chief Financial Officer (CFO) assume direct and personal accountability for the completeness and accuracy of a publicly traded organization's financial reporting and record-keeping systems. As these executives attempt to ensure that the reporting and recording systems are sound—often relying upon the expertise of chief information officers (CIOs) and chief information security officers (CISOs) to do so—they also must maintain the availability and confidentiality of information.

The provisions include:

- Creation of the Public Company Accounting Oversight Board (PCAOB)
- A requirement that public companies evaluate and disclose the effectiveness of their internal controls as they relate to financial reporting, and that independent auditors for such companies "attest to" (i.e., agree to or qualify) such disclosure
- Certification of financial reports by CEOs and CFOs
- Auditor independence, including outright bans on certain types of work for audit clients and precertification by the company's audit committee of all other nonaudit work
- A requirement that companies listed on stock exchanges have fully independent audit committees that oversee the relationship between the company and its auditor
- Ban on most personal loans to any executive officer or director
- Accelerated reporting of trades by insiders
- Prohibition on insider trades during pension fund blackout periods
- Additional disclosure
- Enhanced criminal and civil penalties for violations of securities law
- Significantly longer maximum jail sentences and larger fines for corporate executives who knowingly and willfully misstate financial statements, although maximum sentences are largely irrelevant because judges generally follow the Federal Sentencing Guidelines in setting actual sentences
- Employee protections allowing those corporate fraud whistleblowers who file complaints with OSHA within 90 days to win reinstatement, back pay and benefits, compensatory damages, abatement orders, and reasonable attorney fees and costs

CIOs are responsible for the security, accuracy, and reliability of the systems that manage and report the financial data. Therefore, the financial reporting process, along with other important processes, must be assessed for compliance with the SOX Act. Although the act signals a fundamental change in business operations and financial reporting and places responsibility in corporate financial reporting on the CEO and CFO, the CIO plays a significant role in the sign-off of financial statements.[16]

Payment Card Industry Data Security Standard (PCI DSS) Critical to any organization that handles online payments, the Payment Card Industry Data Security Standard (PCI DSS) is a set of industry standards that are mandated for any organization that handles credit, debit, and specialty payment cards. This standard was created by the Payment Card Industry Standards Council in an effort to reduce credit card fraud.

The current version of the standard is 2.0, October 2010. The standard is explained by the PCI Security Standards Council as focusing on three key steps:

- *Assess—Identifying cardholder data, taking an inventory of your IT assets and business processes for payment card processing, and analyzing them for vulnerabilities that could expose cardholder data*

- *Remediate—Fixing vulnerabilities and not storing cardholder data unless you need it*

- *Report—Compiling and submitting required remediation validation records (if applicable), and submitting compliance reports to the acquiring bank and card brands you do business with*[17]

According to Forrester Consulting's report on the state of PCI DSS compliance, over 81 percent of retail organizations store payment card information and over 57 percent store customer data from the card's magnetic stripe.[18] Furthermore, according to PrivacyRights.org, more than 606.8 million credit card records (with accompanying personal information) have been breached stemming from over 3500 successful attacks launched since January, 2005.[19] These issues have resulted in stiff regulations within the payment card industry. PCI DSS includes three sub-standards:

- *PCI Data Security Standard*—Focuses on general security standards for the processing of payment card

- *PIN Transaction Security Requirements*—Focuses on the protection of customer information related to transactions based on a PIN

- *Payment Application Data Security Standard*—Focuses on the protection of the information contained within customer applications for payment cards

The PCI Security Standards Council has identified the following six steps as representative of the requirements associated with PCI DSS:

- *Build and Maintain a Secure Network*
    1. *Install and maintain a firewall configuration to protect cardholder data.*
    2. *Do not use vendor-supplied defaults for system passwords and other security parameters.*
- *Protect Cardholder Data*
    3. *Protect stored cardholder data.*
    4. *Encrypt transmission of cardholder data across open, public networks.*
- *Maintain a Vulnerability Management Program*
    5. *Use and regularly update antivirus software or programs.*
    6. *Develop and maintain secure systems and applications.*
- *Implement Strong Access Control Measures*
    7. *Restrict access to cardholder data by business need to know.*
    8. *Assign a unique ID to each person with computer access.*
    9. *Restrict physical access to cardholder data.*

12

- *Regularly Monitor and Test Networks*
    10. *Track and monitor all access to network resources and cardholder data.*
    11. *Regularly test security systems and processes.*
- *Maintain an Information Security Policy*
    12. *Maintain a policy that addresses information security for all personnel.*[20]

Note that the requirements mirror generally accepted best security practices, as they were specifically designed to do. Organizations are expected to periodically review and validate their systems against these standards. Failure to do so can result in loss of ability to process payment information. Note that these standards apply to the organizations actually processing the credit card information, more so than the organizations allowing customers to use their cards in a retail setting.

The Future of U.S. Information Security Laws

Of particular interest is the number (and breadth) of bills that are fighting their way through the U.S. Congress on InfoSec-related topics. Several bills of note that almost had a substantial impact on public and private information protection and use, including the Data Security Act of 2010, the Data Security and Breach Notification Act of 2010, and the Cybersecurity Act of 2012, to name a few. Each of these acts was designed to protect consumers by requiring reasonable security policies and procedures to protect personal information. Many have provisions for various levels of notice in the event of a security breach. The Cybersecurity Act of 2012 was focused on enhancing the security of the critical infrastructure in the United States. While all these bills failed to pass, many dying in committee, it is expected that similar legislation will inevitably make its way through Congress, providing additional impact on the InfoSec landscape.

International Laws and Legal Bodies

IT professionals and InfoSec practitioners must realize that when their organizations do business on the Internet, they do business globally. Many domestic laws and customs do not apply to international trade, which is governed by international treaties and trade agreements. It may seem obvious, but it is often overlooked, that there are a variety of laws and ethical practices in place in other parts of the world. Different security bodies and laws are described in the following sections. Because of the political complexities of the relationships among nations and cultural differences, few international laws currently relate to privacy and InfoSec. Therefore, these international security bodies and regulations are sometimes limited in scope and enforceability.

European Council Cybercrime Convention

In 2001, the Council of Europe drafted the European Council Cybercrime Convention, which empowers an international task force to oversee a range of Internet security functions and to standardize technology laws across international borders. It also attempts to improve the effectiveness of international investigations into breaches of technology law. This convention is well received by advocates of intellectual property rights because it provides for copyright infringement prosecution.

As with any complex international legislation, the Cybercrime Convention lacks any realistic provisions for enforcement. The goal of the convention is to simplify the acquisition of information for law enforcement agents in certain types of international crimes as well as during the extradition process. The convention has more than its share of skeptics who see it as an attempt by the European community to exert undue influence to control a complex problem. Critics of the convention say that it could create more problems than it resolves. As the product of a number of governments, the convention tends to favor the interests of national agencies over the rights of businesses, organizations, and individuals.

Digital Millennium Copyright Act (DMCA) The Digital Millennium Copyright Act (DMCA) is the U.S.-based international effort to reduce the impact of copyright, trademark, and privacy infringement, especially via the removal of technological copyright protection measures. The European Union equivalents to the DMCA are Directive 95/46/EC of the European Parliament and the report from the European Council of 24 October 1995, which increase individual rights to process and freely move personal data. The United Kingdom has already implemented a version of this directive, called the Database Right.

Australian High Tech Crime High tech crimes are defined and prosecuted in Australia under its Commonwealth legislation Part 10.7—Computer Offences of the Criminal Code Act 1995. That law specifically includes:

- data system intrusions (such as hacking)
- unauthorized destruction or modification of data
- actions intended to deny service of computer systems to intended users, such as denial-of-service (DoS) attacks and distributed denial of service (DDoS) attacks using botnets
- the creation and distribution of malicious software (a.k.a malware)

Each state and territory in Australia also has implemented laws regarding computer-related offences that are similar to the national Commonwealth legislation.[21]

State and Local Regulations

Each state or locality may have a number of laws and regulations that affect the use of computer technology. It is the responsibility of InfoSec professionals to understand state laws and regulations and ensure that their organization's security policies and procedures comply with the laws and regulations. For a list of state security laws, see the Web site for the National Conference of State Legislatures at *www.ncsl.org*.

For example, the State of Georgia passed the Georgia Computer Systems Protection Act in 1991, which has various computer security provisions and establishes specific penalties for using IT to attack or exploit information systems in organizations. These laws do not affect people or entities outside the state unless they do business or have offices in the state. Key provisions of this law are presented in the Offline box.

The Georgia legislature also passed the Georgia Identity Theft Law in 1998 (Section 120 et seq., Chapter 9, Title 16, Official Code of Georgia Annotated). As explained by the State of Georgia, this law prohibits a business from discarding a record containing personal information unless it:

1. *Shreds the customer's record before discarding the record;*
2. *Erases the personal information contained in the customer's record before discarding the record;*

Offline
Georgia Computer Systems Protection Act (Section 90 et seq., Chapter 9, Title 16, Official Code of Georgia Annotated)

Computer Theft. Any person who uses a computer or computer network with knowledge that such use is without authority and with the intention of: Taking or appropriating any property of another, whether or not with the intention of depriving the owner of possession; Obtaining property by any deceitful means or artful practice; or Converting property to such person's use in violation of an agreement or other known legal obligation to make a specified application or disposition of such property shall be guilty of the crime of computer theft.

Computer Trespass. Any person who uses a computer or computer network with knowledge that such use is without authority and with the intention of; deleting or in any way removing, either temporarily or permanently, any computer program or data from a computer or computer network; obstructing, interrupting, or in any way interfering with the use of a computer program or data; or altering, damaging, or in any way causing the malfunction of a computer, computer network, or computer program, regardless of how long the alteration, damage, or malfunction persists shall be guilty of the crime of computer trespass.

Computer Invasion of Privacy. Any person who uses a computer or computer network with the intention of examining any employment, medical, salary, credit, or any other financial or personal data relating to any other person with knowledge that such examination is without authority shall be guilty of the crime of computer invasion of privacy.

Computer Forgery. Any person who creates, alters, or deletes any data contained in any computer or computer network, who, if such person had created, altered, or deleted a tangible document or instrument would have committed forgery under Article 1 of this chapter, shall be guilty of the crime of computer forgery. The absence of a tangible writing directly created or altered by the offender shall not be a defense to the crime of computer forgery if a creation, alteration, or deletion of data was involved in lieu of a tangible document or instrument.

Computer Password Disclosure. Any person who discloses a number, code, password, or other means of access to a computer or computer network knowing that such disclosure is without authority and which results in damages (including the fair market value of any services used and victim expenditure) to the owner of the computer or computer network in excess of $500.00 shall be guilty of the crime of computer password disclosure.

Penalties. Any person convicted of the crime of computer theft, computer trespass, computer invasion of privacy, or computer forgery shall be fined not more than $50,000.00 or imprisoned not more than 15 years, or both. Any person convicted of

(Continued)

computer password disclosure shall be fined not more than $5000.00 or incarcerated for a period not to exceed one year, or both.

Computer Trademark Infringement. It shall be unlawful for any person, any organization, or any representative of any organization knowingly to transmit any data through a computer network or over the transmission facilities or through the network facilities of a local telephone network for the purpose of setting up, maintaining, operating, or exchanging data with an electronic mailbox, home page, or any other electronic information storage bank or point of access to electronic information if such data uses any individual name, trade name, registered trademark, logo, legal or official seal, or copyrighted symbol to falsely identify the person, organization, or representative transmitting such data or which would falsely state or imply that such person, organization, or representative has permission or is legally authorized to use such trade name, registered trademark, logo, legal or official seal, or copyrighted symbol for such purpose when such permission or authorization has not been obtained; provided, however, that no telecommunications company or Internet access provider shall violate this Code section solely as a result of carrying or transmitting such data for its customers.[22]

3. *Modifies the customer's record to make the personal information unreadable before discarding the record; or*

4. *Takes actions that it reasonably believes will ensure that no unauthorized person will have access to the personal information contained in the customer's record for the period between the record's disposal and the record's destruction.*[23]

Personal information is defined as:

- *Personally identifiable data about a customer's medical condition, if the data are not generally considered to be public knowledge;*

- *Personally identifiable data that contain a customer's account or identification number, account balance, balance owing, credit balance, or credit limit, if the data relate to a customer's account or transaction with a business;*

- *Personally identifiable data provided by a customer to a business upon opening an account or applying for a loan or credit; or*

- *Personally identifiable data about a customer's federal, state, or local income tax return.*[24]

Failure to properly dispose of customer information can result in a fine of $500 per instance for up to a total of $10,000.

"Consumer victim" means any individual whose personal identifying information has been obtained, compromised, used, or recorded in any manner without the permission of that individual.

"Identifying information" includes, but is not limited to:

- Current or former names
- Social Security numbers

- Driver's license numbers
- Checking account numbers
- Savings account numbers
- Credit and other financial transaction card numbers
- Debit card numbers
- Personal identification numbers
- Electronic identification numbers
- Digital or electronic signatures
- Medical identification numbers
- Birth dates
- Mother's maiden name
- Selected personal identification numbers
- Tax identification numbers
- State identification card numbers
- Any numbers or information that can be used to access a person's or entity's resources

Policy versus Law

Most organizations develop and formalize descriptions of acceptable and unacceptable employee behavior, which are called policies (covered in detail in Chapter 4). Properly defined and enforced policies function in an organization the same way as laws, complete with penalties, judicial practices, and sanctions. Because policies function like laws, they must be crafted with the same care as laws to ensure that the policies are complete, appropriate, and fairly applied to everyone in the workplace. The key difference between policy and law is that ignorance of policy is a viable defense, and therefore policies must be:

- Distributed to all individuals who are expected to comply with them
- Readily available for employee reference
- Easily understood, with multilingual translations and translations for visually impaired or low-literacy employees
- Acknowledged by the employee, usually by means of a signed consent form
- Uniformly enforced for all employees

Only when all of these conditions are met does the organization have the reasonable expectation that policy violations can be appropriately penalized without fear of legal retribution.

Ethics in InfoSec

Some define ethics as the organized study of how humans ought to act. Others define it as a set of rules we should live by. The student of information security is not expected to study ethics in a vacuum, but within a larger framework. However, InfoSec professionals may be expected to be more informed about the topic than others in the organization, and they must often withstand a higher degree of scrutiny. The Ten Commandments of Computer Ethics (see the Offline box) are a useful guide to the field's ethical standards.

Offline
The Ten Commandments of Computer Ethics[25]

Although they've been around for over a decade, the Computer Ethics Institute's 10 Commandments of Computer Ethics—available from http://computerethicsinstitute.org/—are still of value in encouraging appropriate computer use. The commandments include (paraphrased):

1. Don't use computers to hurt others.

2. Don't interfere with other people's use of computers.

3. Don't view the contents of other people's computers without permission.

4. Don't steal using a computer.

5. Don't use a computer as a tool to fabricate information (as in bear false witness).

6. Don't illegally copy or use software.

7. Don't use a computer or computer-based resource without explicit permission or without paying for it.

8. Don't steal someone's intellectual property.

9. Don't remain ignorant or unconscious to the effect that computers have on society as a whole and on those individuals using them.

10. Don't devalue humanity by using computers in ways that disrespect others.

12

The foundations and frameworks of ethics include the following:

- *Normative ethics*—The study of what makes actions right or wrong, also known as moral theory—that is, how should people act?

- *Meta-ethics*—The study of the meaning of ethical judgments and properties—that is, what is right?

- *Descriptive ethics*—The study of the choices that have been made by individuals in the past—that is, what do others think is right?

- *Applied ethics*—An approach that applies moral codes to actions drawn from realistic situations; it seeks to define how we might use ethics in practice.

- *Deontological ethics*—The study of the rightness or wrongness of intentions and motives as opposed to the rightness or wrongness of the consequences; also known as duty-based or obligation-based ethics. This approach seeks to define a person's ethical duty.

From these fairly well-defined and agreed-upon ethical frameworks come a series of ethical standards as follows:

- *Utilitarian approach*—Emphasizes that an ethical action is one that results in the most good, or the least harm; this approach seeks to link consequences to choices.

View Point
Ethics in InfoSec
by Lee Imrey, Director of Information Protection, FINCA International, formerly Chair of the ISSA International Ethics Committee and Instructor of Computer Law and Ethics for (ISC)[2]

Competency is your ability to do something right; ethics is your willingness to do the right thing.

It is easy to configure a router to share routing table updates with peer devices. It is simple to configure file and directory permissions in a distributed file system. And with the right training, it is possible to test for, and conclusively demonstrate, the efficacy of each.

Ethical decisions are more complex. Ethics, in a general sense, is a common understanding of what constitutes appropriate behavior, or "doing the right thing." But as a common understanding, it lies somewhere between the belief of the individual and of the community. What constitutes right behavior varies with the values of each community. The community may be as small as a family unit, a social circle, or a village. This is why questions of ethical conduct may be brought to a parent, or village elders, in whom the ethical values of the community are vested. This can be seen in the U.S. legal system, as well as that of other countries, when people are judged by a jury of their peers. In other words, they are judged by members of the community with whom their ethics should be most aligned.

On the other hand, in some cases, the community defining ethical boundaries may be as large as a country or even larger. For instance, in cases of treason or crimes against humanity, people may be prosecuted for violation of laws that have been set up to codify ethical standards common across regional or national boundaries.

But these are the easy cases. The real challenge in determining ethical behavior is in determining the community whose ethical values should be applied. In today's world, we see members of different communities in conflict, individuals acting according to the ethical values of their communities:

- Pharmaceutical companies developing medicines for the sick
- Animal rights activists protesting animal testing
- Developed nations trying to impose strict emission controls on factories
- Third-world nations driving economic prosperity through the use of cheap fuel
- Intellectual property owners (i.e., copyright, patents, etc.) trying to profit from their investments
- Nations trying to reap the benefit of scientific and cultural progress without paying cost-prohibitive fees

In these examples, proponents of each side feel they are behaving ethically in the context of their own communities. The communities frame the ethical choices for their members.

(Continued)

Your ethical choices define who you are. If you want to be an activist, go be an activist. If your highest allegiance is to your country, or a political cause, then follow your dreams and enlist or sign up with the cause you believe in.

But if you want to be an InfoSec professional, you need to align your ethical values, your choices, and your behavior with the growing community of InfoSec professionals worldwide. Apply your efforts to building reliable information systems that businesses and consumers can trust, that function according to their design and minimize the opportunity for misuse. A professional engineer building a bridge or road is expected to hold public safety paramount in the performance of her duties. Follow this model, keeping the safety of the public and their information as your highest obligation, and you will gain credibility as an ethical InfoSec professional.

- *Rights approach*—Suggests that the ethical action is the one that best protects and respects the moral rights of those affected by that action; it begins with a belief that humans have an innate dignity based on their ability to make choices. The list of moral rights is usually thought to include the right to make one's own choices about what kind of life to lead, the right to be told the truth, the right not to be injured, and the right to a degree of privacy. (Some argue that nonhumans have rights as well.) These rights imply certain duties—specifically, the duty to respect the rights of others.

- *Fairness or justice approach*—Founded on the work of Aristotle and other Greek philosophers who contributed the idea that all persons who are equal should be treated equally; today, this approach defines ethical actions as those that have outcomes that regard all human beings equally, or that incorporate a degree of fairness based on some defensible standard. This is often described as a "level playing field."

- *Common good approach*—Based on the work of the Greek philosophers, a notion that life in community yields a positive outcome for the individual, and therefore each individual should contribute to that community. This approach argues that the complex relationships found in a society are the basis of a process founded on ethical reasoning that respects and has compassion for all others, most particularly the most vulnerable members of a society. This approach tends to focus on the common welfare.

- *Virtue approach*—A very ancient ethical model postulating that ethical actions ought to be consistent with so-called ideal virtues—that is, those virtues that all of humanity finds most worthy and that, when present, indicate a fully developed humanity. In most virtue-driven ethical frameworks, the virtues include honesty, courage, compassion, generosity, tolerance, love, fidelity, integrity, fairness, self-control, and prudence. Virtue ethics asks all persons to consider if the outcome of any specific decision will reflect well on their own and others' perceptions of them.

These ethical standards or approaches offer a set of tools for decision making in the era of computer technology. People remain responsible for the choices they make, whether a choice affects only themselves or many others as well.

Ethics and Education

Key studies reveal that the overriding factor in leveling the ethical perceptions within a small population is education. Employees must be trained and kept up to date on InfoSec topics, including the expected behaviors of an ethical employee. This is especially important in areas of information security, as many employees may not have the formal technical training to understand that their behavior is unethical or even illegal. One way to introduce employees and other stakeholders to thinking about ethics is to use scenarios based on practical situations where ethical choices have to be made in the world of work and school, as shown in the adjoining Offline box. Proper ethical and legal training is vital to creating an informed, well-prepared, and low-risk system user.

Offline
The Use of Scenarios in Computer Ethics Studies

The following vignettes can be used in an open and frank discussion of computer ethics. Review each scenario carefully and then choose from the following list the degree of ethical behavior you believe that person has displayed: *very ethical, ethical, neither ethical nor unethical, unethical, very unethical*. If you use these scenarios for class assignments, be sure to justify your responses.

Ethical Decision Evaluation

1. A scientist developed a theory that required proof through the construction of a computer model. She hired a computer programmer to build the model, and the theory was shown to be correct. The scientist won several awards for the development of the theory, but she never acknowledged the contribution of the computer programmer.

   The scientist's failure to acknowledge the computer programmer was _____.

2. The owner of a small business needed a computer-based accounting system. He identified the various inputs and outputs he felt were required to satisfy his needs, showed his design to a computer programmer, and asked the programmer if she could implement such a system. The programmer knew she could implement the system because she had developed much more sophisticated systems in the past. In fact, she felt this design was rather crude and would soon need several major revisions. But she didn't say anything about the design flaws because the business owner didn't ask her and she thought she might be the one hired to implement the needed revisions later.

   The programmer's decision not to point out the design flaws was _____.

3. A student suspected and found a loophole in her university's computer security system that allowed her access to other students' records. She told the system administrator about the loophole, but she continued to access other records until the problem was corrected two weeks later.

(Continued)

The student's action in searching for the loophole was _____.

The student's action in continuing to access others' records for two weeks was _____.

The system administrator's failure to correct the problem sooner was _____.

4. A computer user ordered a particular accounting system from a popular computer software vendor's Web site. When he received his order, he found that the store had accidentally sent him a very expensive word-processing program as well as the accounting package that he had ordered. The invoice listed only the accounting package. The user decided to keep the word-processing program.

   The user's decision to keep the word-processing program was _____.

5. A programmer at a bank realized that she had accidentally overdrawn her checking account. She made a small adjustment in the bank's accounting system so that her account would not have an additional service charge assessed. As soon as she deposited funds that made her balance positive again, she corrected the bank's accounting system.

   The programmer's modification of the accounting system was _____.

6. A computer programmer enjoyed building small computer systems (programs) to give to his friends. He would frequently go to his office on Saturday when no one was working and use his employer's computer to develop systems. He did not hide the fact that he was going into the building; he had to sign a register at a security desk each time he entered.

   The programmer's use of the company computer was _____.

   If the programmer sold the programs, his actions would have been _____.

7. A student enrolled in a computer class was also employed at a local business part time. Frequently, her homework in the class involved using popular word processing and spreadsheet packages. Occasionally, she worked on her homework on the office computer at her part-time job during her coffee or meal breaks.

   The student's use of the company computer was: _____.

   If the student had worked on her homework during "company time" (not during a break), her use of the company computer would have been _____.

8. A student at a university learned to use an expensive spreadsheet program in her accounting class. The student would go to the university computer lab and use the software to complete her assignment. Signs were posted in the lab indicating that copying software was forbidden. One day, she decided to copy the software anyway to complete her work assignments at home.

   If the student destroyed her copy of the software at the end of the term, her action in copying the software was _____.

   If the student forgot to destroy her copy of the software at the end of the term, her action in copying the software was _____.

   If the student never intended to destroy her copy of the software at the end of the term, her action in copying the software was _____.

(Continued)

9. A student at a university found out that a fellow student's personal Web site contained a "pirate" section (a section containing a collection of illegally copied software programs). He accessed the Web site and proceeded to download several games and professional programs, which he then distributed to several of his friends.

   The student's actions in downloading the games were _____.

   The student's actions in downloading the programs were _____.

   The student's actions in sharing the programs and games with his friends were _____.

Deterring Unethical and Illegal Behavior

It is the responsibility of InfoSec personnel to deter unethical and illegal acts, using policy, education and training, and technology as controls or safeguards to protect the information and systems. Many security professionals understand technological means of protection, but many underestimate the value of policy.

There are three general categories of unethical behavior that organizations and society should seek to eliminate:

- *Ignorance*—As you learned earlier, ignorance of the law is no excuse, but ignorance of policies and procedures is. The first method of deterrence is education. Organizations must design, publish, and disseminate organizational policies and relevant laws, and employees must explicitly agree to abide by them. Reminders and training and awareness programs support retention and, one hopes, compliance.

- *Accident*—Individuals with authorization and privileges to manage information within the organization have the greatest opportunity to cause harm or damage by accident. Careful placement of controls can help prevent accidental modification to systems and data.

- *Intent*—Criminal or unethical intent refers to the state of mind of the individual committing the infraction. A legal defense can be built on whether the accused acted out of ignorance, by accident, or with the intent to cause harm or damage. Deterring those with criminal intent is best done by means of litigation, prosecution, and technical controls. As you learned in Chapter 2, intent is only one of several factors to consider when determining whether a computer-related crime has occurred.

Deterrence is the best method for preventing an illegal or unethical activity. Laws, policies, and technical controls are all examples of deterrents. However, laws and policies and their associated penalties only deter if three conditions are present.

- *Fear of penalty*—Threats of informal reprimand or verbal warnings may not have the same impact as the threat of imprisonment or forfeiture of pay.

- *Probability of being caught*—There must be a strong possibility that perpetrators of illegal or unethical acts will be caught.

- *Probability of penalty being administered*—The organization must be willing and able to impose the penalty.

Professional Organizations and their Codes of Ethics

A number of professional organizations have established codes of conduct and/or codes of ethics that members are expected to follow. Codes of ethics can have a positive effect on an individual's judgment regarding computer use.[26] Unfortunately, many employers do not encourage their employees to join these professional organizations. The loss of accreditation or certification due to a violation of a code of conduct can be a deterrent, as it can dramatically reduce the individual's marketability and earning power.

In general, research has shown that some certifications have little impact on the long-term earning potential of practitioners, while other certifications, notably those in information security, have a lingering effect on the economic prospects of certificate holders.[27] The long-term value of an InfoSec certification adds leverage to the certification-granting authority to exert influence over its members, including influence in matters of ethical responsibility.

It remains the individual responsibility of security professionals to act ethically and according to the policies and procedures of their employers, their professional organizations, and the laws of society. It is likewise the organization's responsibility to develop, disseminate, and enforce its policies. The following sections describe several of the relevant professional associations.

Association for Computing Machinery (ACM)

The ACM (*www.acm.org*), a well-respected professional society, was established in 1947 as the world's first educational and scientific computing society. It is one of the few organizations that strongly promote education and provide discounted membership for students. The ACM's code of ethics requires members to perform their duties in a manner befitting an ethical computing professional. The code contains specific references to protecting the confidentiality of information, causing no harm (with specific references to viruses), protecting the privacy of others, and respecting the intellectual property and copyrights of others. The ACM also publishes a wide variety of professional computing publications, including the highly regarded *Communications of the ACM*.

International Information Systems Security Certification Consortium, Inc. (ISC)²

The (ISC)² (*www.isc2.org*) is not a professional association in the strictest sense, and it has no members or membership services. It is a nonprofit organization that focuses on the development and implementation of InfoSec certifications and credentials. The (ISC)² manages a body of knowledge on InfoSec and administers and evaluates examinations for InfoSec certifications. The code of ethics put forth by (ISC)² is primarily designed for InfoSec professionals who have earned one of their certifications.

This code includes four mandatory canons:

- Protect society, the commonwealth, and the infrastructure.
- Act honorably, honestly, justly, responsibly, and legally.
- Provide diligent and competent service to principals.
- Advance and protect the profession.[28]

12

Through this code, (ISC)^2 seeks to provide sound guidance that will enable reliance on the ethicality and trustworthiness of the InfoSec professional as the guardian of the information and systems.

SANS

Founded in 1989, SANS (*www.sans.org*), formerly known as the System Administration, Networking, and Security Institute, is a professional research and education cooperative organization. The organization, which enjoys a large professional membership, is dedicated to the protection of information and systems. Individuals who seek one of SANS's many Global Information Assurance Certification (GIAC) credentials must agree to comply with the organization's code of ethics, which opens with the following:

Respect for the Public

- *I will accept responsibility in making decisions with consideration for the security and welfare of the community.*
- *I will not engage in or be a party to unethical or unlawful acts that negatively affect the community, my professional reputation, or the InfoSec discipline.*

Respect for the Certification

- *I will not share, disseminate, or otherwise distribute confidential or proprietary information pertaining to the GIAC certification process.*
- *I will not use my certification, or objects or information associated with my certification (such as certificates or logos), to represent any individual or entity other than myself as being certified by GIAC.*

Respect for My Employer

- *I will deliver capable service that is consistent with the expectations of my certification and position.*
- *I will protect confidential and proprietary information with which I come into contact.*
- *I will minimize risks to the confidentiality, integrity, or availability of an information technology solution, consistent with risk management practice.*

Respect for Myself

- *I will avoid conflicts of interest.*
- *I will not misuse any information or privileges I am afforded as part of my responsibilities.*
- *I will not misrepresent my abilities or my work to the community, my employer, or my peers.*[29]

Information Systems Audit and Control Association (ISACA)

ISACA (*www.isaca.org*) is a professional association with a focus on auditing, control, and security. Its membership comprises both technical and managerial professionals. ISACA focuses on providing IT control practices and standards. The organization offers the Certified

Information Systems Auditor (CISA) certification, which does not focus exclusively on InfoSec but does contain many InfoSec components.

According to ISACA, its constituents must abide by the following code of ethics:

Members and ISACA certification holders shall:

1. *Support the implementation of, and encourage compliance with, appropriate standards, procedures and controls for information systems.*

2. *Perform their duties with objectivity, due diligence and professional care, in accordance with professional standards and best practices.*

3. *Serve in the interest of stakeholders in a lawful and honest manner, while maintaining high standards of conduct and character, and not engage in acts discreditable to the profession.*

4. *Maintain the privacy and confidentiality of information obtained in the course of their duties unless disclosure is required by legal authority. Such information shall not be used for personal benefit or released to inappropriate parties.*

5. *Maintain competency in their respective fields and agree to undertake only those activities that they can reasonably expect to complete with professional competence.*

6. *Inform appropriate parties of the results of work performed; revealing all significant facts known to them.*

7. *Support the professional education of stakeholders in enhancing their understanding of information systems security and control.*[30]

Source: © 2013 ISACA. All rights reserved. Used by permission.

Information Systems Security Association (ISSA)

The ISSA (*www.issa.org*) is a nonprofit society of InfoSec professionals. Its primary mission is to bring together qualified practitioners of InfoSec for information exchange and educational development. ISSA provides conferences, meetings, publications, and information resources to promote InfoSec awareness and education.[31] ISSA also supports a code of ethics, similar to those of (ISC)², ISACA, and the ACM, for "promoting management practices that will ensure the confidentiality, integrity, and availability of organizational information resources."[32] ISSA expects its members to follow the pledge as stated on their web site at http://www.issa.org/?page=CodeofEthics:

I have and will (paraphrased):

- *Promoted information security industry standards and best practices;*

- *Worked to the highest ethical standards and in compliance with all relevant laws;*

- *Worked to protect the confidentiality of sensitive and protected information entrusted to me;*

- *Done my job with honesty and diligence;*

- *Avoided any actions that may be construed as a conflict of interest or which could harm the reputation of my employers, my profession, or ISSA; and*

- *Acted in ways so that I have not maligned, harmed, slandered, nor libeled the actions or reputations of my peers, employers, or constituents.*[33]

Organizational Liability and the Need for Counsel

What if an organization does not support or even encourage strong ethical conduct on the part of its employees? What if an organization does not behave ethically? Even if there is no criminal conduct, there can be liability. **Liability**—an entity's legal obligation—can be applied to conduct even when no law or contract has been breached. Liability for a wrongful act includes the obligation to make payment or **restitution**—compensation for the wrong. If an employee, acting with or without authorization, performs an illegal or unethical act, causing some degree of harm, the organization can be held financially liable for that action. An organization increases its liability if it refuses to take measures—due care—to make sure that every employee knows what is acceptable and what is not, and the consequences of illegal or unethical actions. Due diligence requires that an organization make a valid and ongoing effort to protect others. Because of the Internet, it is possible that a person wronged by an organization's members could be anywhere, in any state, or any country, around the world. Under the U.S. legal system, any court can impose its authority over an individual or organization if it can establish **jurisdiction**—a court's right to hear a case if the act was committed in its territory or involving its citizenry. This is sometimes referred to as **long-arm jurisdiction**, as the long arm of the law reaches across the country or around the world to bring the accused into its court systems. Trying a case in the injured party's home area usually favors the injured party or parties, as it creates a home court advantage.[34]

Key Law Enforcement Agencies

Sometimes, organizations need assistance from law enforcement. While local law enforcement may be the first point of contact and is capable of handling physical security threats or employee problems, it is usually ill equipped to handle electronic crimes. Most states have law enforcement and investigation agencies. For example, the Georgia State Patrol and the Georgia Bureau of Investigation have separate structures and missions but do work together with local law enforcement to assist organizations and individuals.

In addition, a number of key federal agencies are charged with the protection of U.S. information resources and the investigation of threats to, or attacks on, these resources. Among them are the FBI InfraGard organization, Department of Homeland Security (DHS) National Protection and Programs Directorate, the NSA, and the U.S. Secret Service.

What was originally the Federal Bureau of Investigation's National Infrastructure Protection Center (NIPC) was established in 1998 and served as the U.S. government's focal point for threat assessment and the warning, investigation, and response to threats or attacks against critical U.S. infrastructures. The NIPC was folded into the DHS after the 2001 terrorist attacks to increase communications and focus the department's efforts in cyber defense. It is now a part of DHS's National Protection and Programs Directorate, which seeks to secure U.S. physical and information system infrastructures. DHS describes this role as follows:

The components of the National Protection and Programs Directorate include:

- *Federal Protective Service (FPS)—FPS is a federal law enforcement agency that provides integrated security and law enforcement services to federally owned and leased buildings, facilities, properties, and other assets.*

- *Office of Cybersecurity and Communications (CS&C)—CS&C has the mission of assuring the security, resiliency, and reliability of the nation's cyber and communications infrastructure.*

- *Office of Infrastructure Protection (IP)—IP leads the coordinated national effort to reduce risk to our critical infrastructure posed by acts of terrorism. In doing so, the department increases the nation's level of preparedness and the ability to respond and quickly recover in the event of an attack, natural disaster, or other emergency. [The FBI's NIPC was restructured under this department].*

- *US-VISIT—US-VISIT uses innovative biometrics-based technological solutions— digital fingerprints and photographs—to provide decision makers with accurate information when and where they need it.[35]*

Established in January 2001, **InfraGard** (https://*www.infragard.org*) began as a cooperative effort between the FBI's Cleveland field office and local technology professionals. The FBI sought assistance in establishing a more effective method of protecting critical national information resources. The resulting cooperative formed the first InfraGard chapter as a formal effort to combat both cyber and physical threats. Today, every FBI field office has established an InfraGard chapter and collaborates with public and private organizations and the academic community to share information about attacks, vulnerabilities, and threats. The National InfraGard Program serves its members using the following tools:

- Intrusion alert network using encrypted e-mail
- Secure Web site for communication about suspicious activity or intrusions
- Local chapter activities
- Help desk for questions

InfraGard's primary contribution is the free exchange of information to and from the private sector in the subject areas of threats and attacks on information resources.[36]

Another key federal agency is the National Security Agency (NSA). As the nation's cryptologic organization, the NSA coordinates, directs, and performs highly specialized activities to protect U.S. information systems and produce foreign intelligence information. It is also one of the government's most important centers of foreign language analysis and research.[37]

The NSA is responsible for the security of communications and information systems at many federal government agencies associated with national security. The NSA's Information Assurance Directorate (IAD) provides InfoSec "solutions including the technologies, specifications and criteria, products, product configurations, tools, standards, operational doctrine and support activities needed to implement the protect, detect and report, and respond elements of cyber defense."[38] The IAD also develops and promotes an Information Assurance Framework Forum in cooperation with commercial organizations and academic researchers. This framework provides strategic guidance as well as technical specifications for security solutions. IAD's Common Criteria is a set of standards designed to promote understanding of information security.

Prominent among the NSA's InfoSec efforts and activities are its InfoSec outreach programs. The NSA recognizes universities that offer InfoSec education opportunities and that integrate InfoSec philosophies and efforts into their internal operations. These recognized Centers of Excellence in Information Assurance Education (CAE/IAE) can display this recognition on their Web sites and in other materials, and are named on the NSA's Web site. Additionally, the NSA has an InfoSec curriculum certification program. The Information Assurance Courseware Evaluation process reviews an institution's InfoSec course offerings and gives three-year accreditation to those that meet its standards. Graduates of these programs receive certificates recognizing this accreditation. Coming in 2014, the Centers of Excellence program is evolving to a new initiative, the NSA/DHS Center of Academic Excellence in Information Assurance/Cyber Defense (IA/CD). This program moves the CAE/IAE program to match with new standards in InfoSec education and training, and program certifications such as the Accreditation Board for Engineering and Technology's Computer Accreditation Commission (ABET-CAC).

In addition to its well-known mission to protect key members of the U.S. government, the U.S. Secret Service is charged with the detection and arrest of any person committing a U.S. federal offense relating to computer fraud, as well as false identification crimes.[39] This is an extension of its original duty to protect U.S. currency. After all, the communications networks of the United States carry more funds, in the form of electronic data, than all the armored cars in the world combined. Protect the networks, protect the data, and you protect money, stocks, and other financial transactions.

The USA PATRIOT Act and subsequent PATRIOT Improvement and Reauthorization Act increased the Secret Service's role in investigating fraud and related activity in connection with computers. In addition, these acts authorized the director of the Secret Service to establish nationwide electronic crimes task forces to assist law enforcement, the private sector, and academia in detecting and suppressing computer-based crime. The acts increase the statutory penalties for the manufacturing, possession, dealing, and passing of counterfeit U.S. or foreign obligations; and they allow enforcement action to be taken to protect our financial payment systems while combating transnational financial crimes directed by terrorists or other criminals.

The Secret Service was transferred from the Department of the Treasury to the DHS effective March 1, 2003. Since that time, DHS has added to its critical infrastructure-defense strategies the protection of the nation's cyber infrastructures. To directly support the public, DHS promotes individual emergency preparedness through its READY Campaign and Citizen Corp (*www.ready.gov*). This site has content dedicated to cyber defense (see, for example, *www .ready.gov/cyber-attack*).

Managing Investigations in the Organization

When—not if—an organization finds itself having to deal with a suspected policy or law violation, it must appoint an individual to investigate it. How the internal investigation proceeds will dictate whether or not the organization has the ability to take action against the perpetrator if in fact evidence is found that substantiates the charge. In order to protect the organization and possibly to assist law enforcement in the conduct of an investigation, the investigator (whether the CISO, InfoSec manager, or other appointed individual) must document what happened and how. The investigation of what happened and how is called digital forensics.

Digital forensics is based on the field of traditional **forensics**, which is the coherent application of methodical investigatory techniques to present evidence of crimes in a court or court-like setting. Forensics allows investigators to determine what happened by examining the results of an event—criminal, natural, intentional, or accidental. It also allows them to determine how the event happened by examining activities, individual actions, physical evidence, and testimony related to the event. What it may never do is figure out the why.

Digital forensics involves the preservation, identification, extraction, documentation, and interpretation of computer media for evidentiary and/or root cause analysis. Like traditional forensics, it follows clear, well-defined methodologies but still tends to be as much art as science. This means the natural curiosity and personal skill of the investigator play a key role in discovering potential evidentiary material. **Evidentiary material (EM)**, also known as items of potential evidentiary value, is any information that could potentially support the organization's legal-based or policy-based case against a suspect. An item does not become evidence until it is formally admitted to evidence by a judge or other ruling official.

Related to the field of digital forensics is e-discovery. **E-discovery** is the identification and preservation of EM related to a specific legal action. Digital forensics and e-discovery are related in that digital forensics tools and methods may be deployed to conduct e-discovery or to extract information identified during e-discovery; however, e-discovery may simply focus on extensive e-mail and database searches to identify information related to specific key terms. Digital forensics used after litigation has begun falls under the umbrella of e-discovery. Digital forensics used prior to the initiation of legal proceedings falls under the umbrella of incident response (IR).

Based on this premise, digital forensics can be used for two key purposes:

- *To investigate allegations of digital malfeasance*—A crime against or using digital media, computer technology, or related components (computer as source or object of crime) is referred to as **digital malfeasance.** Investigating digital malfeasance is directly related to e-discovery if it is conducted after legal proceedings have begun.

- *To perform root cause analysis*—If an incident occurs and the organization suspects an attack was successful, digital forensics can be used to examine the path and methodology used to gain unauthorized access as well as to determine how pervasive and successful the attack was. Performing root cause analysis is directly related to IR. The IR team will use root cause analysis when examining their equipment after an incident.

Some investigations can be undertaken by organizational personnel, while others require immediate involvement of law enforcement. In general, whenever investigators discover evidence of the commission of a crime, they should immediately notify management and recommend contacting law enforcement. Failure to do so could result in unfavorable action against the investigator or organization.

The organization must choose one of two approaches when employing digital forensics:

- *Protect and forget*—This IR approach, also known as "patch and proceed," focuses on the defense of the data and the systems that house, use, and transmit it. An investigation that takes this approach focuses on the detection and analysis of events to determine how they happened and to prevent reoccurrence. Once the current event is over, who caused it and why is almost immaterial.

- *Apprehend and prosecute*—This approach, also known as "pursue and prosecute," focuses on the identification and apprehension of responsible individuals, with additional attention on the collection and preservation of potential EM that might support administrative or criminal prosecution. This approach requires much more attention to detail to prevent contamination of evidence that might hinder prosecution.

An organization might find it impossible to retain enough data to successfully handle even administrative penalties, but it should certainly adopt the latter approach if it wishes to pursue formal administrative penalties, especially if the employee is likely to challenge these penalties.

Digital Forensics Team

Most organization cannot sustain a permanent digital forensics team. In most organizations, such expertise is so rarely called upon that it may be better to collect the data and then out-source the analysis component to a regional expert. The organization can then maintain an arm's-length distance from the case and have additional expertise to call upon in the event the process ends in court. Even so, there should be people in the InfoSec group trained to understand and manage the forensics process. Should a report of suspected misuse from an internal or external individual arise, this person or group must be familiar with digital forensics procedures in order to avoid contaminating potential EM. This expertise can be obtained by sending staff members to a regional or national InfoSec conference with a digital forensics track, or to dedicated digital forensics training.

Affidavits and Search Warrants

Many investigations begin with an allegation or an indication of an incident. Whether via the help desk, the organization's sexual harassment reporting channels, or direct report, someone makes an allegation that another worker is performing actions explicitly prohibited by the organization or that make another worker uncomfortable in the workplace. The organization's forensics team must then request permission to examine digital media for potential EM. In law enforcement, the investigating agent would create an affidavit requesting a search warrant. An **affidavit** is sworn testimony that certain facts are in the possession of the investigating officer that the officer believes warrant the examination of specific items located at a specific place. The facts, the items, and the place must be specified in this document. When an approving authority signs the affidavit or creates a synopsis form based on this document, it becomes a **search warrant**—that is, permission to search for EM at the specified location and/or to seize items to return to the investigator's lab for examination. In corporate environments, the names of these documents may change and in many cases may be verbal in nature, but the process should be the same. Formal permission is obtained before an investigation occurs.

Digital Forensics Methodology

In digital forensics, all investigations follow the same basic methodology:

1. Identify relevant items of evidentiary value (EM).

2. Acquire (seize) the evidence without alteration or damage.

3. Take steps to assure that the evidence is at every stage verifiably authentic and is unchanged from the time it was seized.

4. Analyze the data without risking modification or unauthorized access.

5. Report the findings to the proper authority.

This process is illustrated in Figure 12-1.

To support the selection and implementation of a methodology, the organization may wish to seek legal advice or consult with local or state law enforcement. Other publications that should become part of the organization team's library include:

- "Electronic Crime Scene Investigation: A Guide for First Responders" (*www.ncjrs.gov /pdffiles1/nij/187736.pdf*)

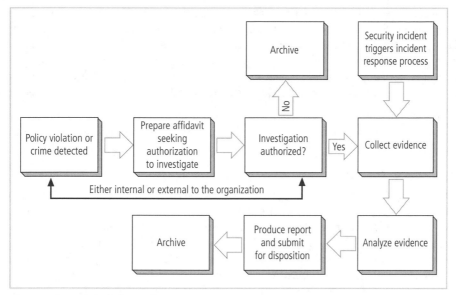

Figure 12-1 Digital forensics process

Copyright © 2014 Cengage Learning®.

- "First Responders Guide to Computer Forensics" (*www.cert.org/archive/pdf /FRGCF_v1.3.pdf*)
- "Searching and Seizing Computers and Obtaining Electronic Evidence in Criminal Investigations" (*www.justice.gov/criminal/cybercrime/docs/ssmanual2009.pdf*)

Identify Relevant Items A crucial aspect of any digital forensics investigation is identifying the potential EM and its probable location and then documenting that information in the search warrant or authorization document. Unless investigators have an idea of what to look for (such as evidence that the accused has been selling intellectual property related to future product offerings, or has been viewing objectionable or illegal content), they may never find it in the vast array of possible locations an individual user may have access to—such as flash drives, external storage drives, and Internet services.

Acquire the Evidence The principal responsibility of the response team is to acquire the information without altering it. Computers modify data constantly. Normal system file changes may be difficult to explain to a layperson (e.g., a jury member with little or no technical knowledge). A normal system consequence of the search for EM could be portrayed by a defense attorney as affecting the authenticity or integrity of the EM, which could lead a jury to suspect that the EM was planted or is otherwise suspect. The biggest challenge is to show that the person under investigation is the one who stored, used, and maintained the EM, or who conducted the unauthorized activity.

Other Potential Evidence Not all EM is on a suspect's computer hard drive. A technically savvy attacker is more likely to store incriminating evidence on other digital media, such as removable drives, CDs, DVDs, flash drives, memory chips or sticks, or on other computers accessed across the organization's networks or via the Internet. EM located outside the organization is particularly problematic, as the organization cannot legally search systems they don't own. However, the simple act of viewing EM on a system leaves clues about the location of the source material, and a skilled investigator can at least provide some assistance to law enforcement when conducting a preliminary investigation. Log files are another source of information about the access and location of EM, as well as about what happened when.

Some evidence isn't electronic or digital in nature. Many suspects have been further incriminated when the passwords to their digital media were discovered in the margins of user manuals, in calendars and day planners, and even on notes attached to their systems.

EM Handling Once the evidence is acquired, both the copy image and the original drive should be handled so as to avoid legal challenges based on authenticity and preservation of integrity. If the organization or law enforcement cannot demonstrate that no one had physical access to the evidence, they cannot provide strong assurances that it has not been altered. Once the evidence is in the possession of investigators, they must track its movement, storage, and access until the resolution of the event or case. This is typically accomplished by means of chain of evidence (also known as chain of custody) procedures. **Chain of evidence (a.k.a. chain of custody)** is defined as the detailed documentation of the collection, storage, transfer, and ownership of collected evidence from crime scene through its presentation in court. The evidence is then tracked wherever it is located. When the evidence changes hands or is stored, the documentation is updated. Not all evidence-handling requirements are met through the chain of custody process. Digital media must be stored in an environment designed for that purpose, one that can be secured to prevent unauthorized access. Individual items should be stored in electrostatic discharge (ESD) protective containers or bags, marked as sensitive to ESD and magnetic fields, and so forth.

Authenticate the Recovered Evidence A copy or image of the digital media containing the EM is typically transferred to the laboratory for the next stage of authentication. The team must be able to demonstrate that any analyzed copy or image is a true and accurate replica of the source EM. This is accomplished by the use of cryptographic hash tools. As you learned in Chapter 8, the hash tool takes a variable-length file and creates a single numerical value, usually represented in hexadecimal notation, rather like a digital fingerprint.

Analyze the Data The most complex part of an investigation is the analysis of the copy or image for potential EM. The first component of the analysis phase is indexing. During indexing, many investigatory tools create an index of all text found on the drive, allowing the investigator to quickly and easily search for a specific type of file.

Report the Findings As investigators examine the analyzed copies or images and identify potential EM, they can tag it and add it to their case files. Once they have found a suitable amount of information, they can summarize their findings as well as their investigatory procedures in a report and submit it to the appropriate authority. This authority could be law enforcement or management. The suitable amount of EM is a flexible determination made by the investigator. In certain cases, such as child pornography, one file is sufficient to warrant turning the entire investigation over to law enforcement. On the other hand, a dismissal on the grounds of the unauthorized sale of intellectual property may require a substantial amount of information to support the organization's assertion. Reporting methods and formats vary from organization to organization and should be specified in the digital forensics policy. The general guideline for the report is that it should be sufficiently detailed to allow a similarly trained person to repeat the analysis and achieve similar results.

Evidentiary Procedures

In information security, most operations focus on policies—those documents that provide managerial guidance for ongoing implementation and operations. In digital forensics, however, the focus is on procedures. When investigating digital malfeasance or performing root cause analysis, keep in mind that the results and methods of the investigation may end up in criminal or civil court. For example, during a routine systems update, a technician finds objectionable material on an employee's computer. The employee is fired and promptly sues the organization for wrongful termination, and so the investigation of that objectionable material will come under scrutiny by the plaintiff's attorney, who will attempt to cast doubt on the ability of the investigator. While technically not illegal, the presence of the material may have been a clear violation of policy, thus prompting the dismissal of the employee, but if an attorney can convince a jury or judge that someone else could have placed the material on the plaintiff's system, then the employee could win the case and potentially a large financial settlement.

When the scenario involves criminal issues, where an employee discovers evidence of a crime, the situation changes somewhat. The investigation, analysis, and report are typically performed by law enforcement personnel. However, if the defense attorney can cast reasonable doubt on whether organizational InfoSec professionals compromised the digital EM, the employee might win the case.

How do you avoid these legal pitfalls? Strong procedures for the handling of potential EM can minimize the probability of an organization's losing a legal challenge. Organizations should develop specific procedures, along with guidance on the use of these procedures. The policy document should specify:

- Who may conduct an investigation
- Who may authorize an investigation
- What affidavit-related documents are required
- What search warrant-related documents are required
- What digital media may be seized or taken offline
- What methodology should be followed
- What methods are required for chain of custody or chain of evidence
- What format the final report should take and to whom it should it be given

The policy document should be supported by a procedures manual based on the documents discussed earlier, along with guidance from law enforcement or consultants. By creating and using these policies and procedures, an organization can best protect itself from challenges by employees who have been subject to unfavorable action (administrative or legal) resulting from an investigation.

Chapter Summary

- Laws are formally adopted rules for acceptable behavior in modern society. Ethics are socially acceptable behaviors. The key difference between laws and ethics is that laws bear the sanction of a governing authority and ethics do not.

- Organizations formalize desired behaviors in documents called policies. Unlike laws, policies must be read and explicitly agreed to by employees before they are binding.

- Civil law encompasses a wide variety of laws that regulate relationships between and among individuals and organizations. Criminal law addresses violations that harm society and that are prosecuted by the state. Tort law is a subset of civil law that deals with lawsuits by individuals rather than criminal prosecution by the state.

- The desire to protect national security, trade secrets, and a variety of other state and private assets has led to several laws affecting what information and information management and security resources may be exported from the United States.

- U.S. copyright law extends intellectual property rights to the published word, including electronic publication.

- Deterrence can prevent an illegal or unethical activity from occurring. Successful deterrence requires the institution of severe penalties, the probability of apprehension, and an expectation that penalties will be enforced.

- As part of an effort to sponsor positive ethics, a number of professional organizations have established codes of conduct and/or codes of ethics that their members are expected to follow.

- A number of key U.S. federal agencies are charged with the protection of American information resources and the investigation of threats to, or attacks on, these resources.

- Digital forensics involves the preservation, identification, extraction, documentation, and interpretation of computer media for evidentiary and/or root cause analysis. E-discovery is the identification and preservation of evidentiary materials related to a specific legal action. Digital forensics and e-discovery are related in that digital forensics tools and methods may be deployed to conduct e-discovery or to extract information identified during e-discovery; however, e-discovery may simply focus on extensive e-mail and database searches to identify information related to specific key terms.

- Most organization cannot sustain a permanent digital forensics team. Even so, there should be people in the InfoSec group trained to understand and manage the forensics process.

- In digital forensics, all investigations follow the same basic methodology: identify relevant items of evidentiary value, acquire (seize) the evidence without alteration or damage, take steps to assure that the evidence is at every stage verifiably authentic and is unchanged from the time it was seized, analyze the data without risking modification or unauthorized access, and report the findings to the proper authority.

Review Questions

1. What is the difference between criminal law and civil law?

2. What is tort law and what does it permit an individual to do?

3. What are the three primary types of public law?

4. Which law amended the Computer Fraud and Abuse Act of 1986, and what did it change?

5. What is the USA PATRIOT Act? When was it initially established and when was it significantly modified?

6. What is privacy in the context of information security?

7. What is another name for the Kennedy-Kassebaum Act (1996), and why is it important to organizations that are not in the health care industry?

8. If you work for a financial service organization (such as a bank or credit union), which law from 1999 affects your use of customer data? What other effects does it have?

9. Which 1997 law provides guidance on the use of encryption?

10. What is intellectual property? Is it offered the same protection in every country? What laws currently protect intellectual property in the United States and Europe?

11. What is a policy? How does it differ from a law?

12. What are the three general categories of unethical and illegal behavior?

13. What is the best method for preventing illegal or unethical behavior?

14. Of the professional organizations discussed in this chapter, which has been in existence the longest time? When was it founded?

15. Of the professional organizations discussed in this chapter, which is focused on auditing and control?

16. What is the stated purpose of the SANS organization? In what ways is it involved in professional certification for InfoSec professionals?

17. Which U.S. federal agency sponsors the InfraGard program? Which agency has taken control of the overall National Infrastructure Protection mission?

18. What is due care? Why would an organization want to make sure it exercises due care in its usual course of operations?

19. What should an organization do to deter someone from violating policy or committing a crime?

20. How does due diligence differ from due care? Why are both important?

Exercises

1. The (ISC)^2 has several certifications. Use a Web browser connected to the Internet to read about the (ISC)^2 certifications. What does "CISSP" stand for? Using the Internet, find out which continuing education is required for the holder of a CISSP to remain current and in good standing.

2. Use a Web browser connected to the Internet to explore the career options in cybersecurity at the U.S. National Security Agency. For what kind of InfoSec jobs does the NSA recruit? What qualifications do the jobs you found call for?

3. Using the resources available in your library, find out what laws your state has passed to prosecute computer crime.

4. Using the Web, go to *www.eff.org*. What are the current top concerns of this organization?

5. Using the ethical scenarios presented in this chapter, consider each scenario and note your response. Bring your answers to class to compare them with those of your peers.

Closing Case

Iris was a little unsure of what to do next. She had just left the meeting with the other executives. At the meeting, they confirmed the need for action on the matter of the critical information offered for sale on a public auction site. That was the last point of agreement. This was a risk they had simply not planned for, and they were completely unprepared. Just before the meeting broke up, they had made assignments to various people in the meeting. Robin, the CEO, was going to contact the members of the board of directors to brief them so that if the story became public they would not be surprised. Jerry, the corporate counsel, was going to start an intensive effort to discover what peer companies had done in situations like this. Mike, the CIO, was assigned to contact the auction site to get the auction shut down and lay the groundwork for working with whatever authorities were brought in for the criminal aspects of the case.

Iris was assigned to investigate which law enforcement agency should be involved in the investigation. She already knew that the auction site was hosted on a server owned by a company that was not in the United States, where HAL was located. She reached for her business card box and began thumbing through the contacts she had.

Discussion

1. Do you think the response of the company so far indicates any flaws in company policy or practices that are revealed by the incident?

2. With which law enforcement agency do you think Iris should consult? On what factors do you base that recommendation?

3. What criminal acts might have occurred in this situation? Considering who the perpetrators might be, what do you think their relationship to RWW, Inc. might be?

Ethical Decision Making

Suppose that Cassandra, the CEO's executive assistant, had been involved in the criminal activity of selling company data. And suppose that when the anonymous tip came in, she deleted the message without bringing it to anyone else's attention. Cassandra's assignment is to delete any and all messages deemed to be "noise" or a nuisance and then bring the remaining messages to the attention of the CEO.

Had she been in on the caper, would Cassandra's act of deleting the message that prompted this response unethical? Would it have been illegal?

Endnotes

1. Noone, J. *Rousseau's Social Contract: A Conceptual Analysis.* University of Georgia Press, 1981.

2. Yeh, Brian and Charles Doyle. "USA PATRIOT Improvement and Reauthorization Act of 2005 (H.R. 3199): A Brief Look." Accessed April 26, 2013 @ *www.fas.org/sgp/crs /intel/RS22348.pdf.*

3. "Computer Security Act of 1987." *Epic*. Accessed April 26, 2013 @ *www.epic.org /crypto/csa/csa.html*.

4. *The American Heritage Dictionary of the English Language*, 4th ed., 2000.

5. "U.S. Constitution, Fourth Amendment." *Archives.gov*. Accessed April 26, 2013 @ *www .archives.gov/exhibits/charters/bill_of_rights_transcript.html*.

6. "Search and Seizure: History and Scope of the Amendment." *Findlaw*. Accessed April 26, 2013 @ *caselaw.lp.findlaw.com/data/constitution/amendment04/01.html#t2*.

7. "Title 47, Chapter 5, Subchapter II, Part I, § 222." *Cornell Law School*. Accessed April 26, 2013 @ *www4.law.cornell.edu/uscode/47/222.html*.

8. "The Privacy Act of 1974." *U.S. Department of Justice*. Accessed April 26, 2013 @ *www .usdoj.gov/opcl/privacyact1974.htm*.

9. "Title 18, Part I, Chapter 119." *Cornell Law School*. Accessed April 26, 2013 @ *www .law.cornell.edu/uscode/18/pIch119.html*.

10. "HIPAA Regulations." *HIPAA Advisory*. Accessed October 14, 2006 @ *www .hipaadvisory.com/regs*.

11. "The Security Rule." *U.S. Department of Health and Human Services*. Accessed February 20, 2013 @ *www.hhs.gov/ocr/privacy/hipaa/administrative/securityrule /index.html*.

12. "The Privacy Rule." *U.S. Department of Health and Human Services*. Accessed February 20, 2013 @ *www.hhs.gov/ocr/privacy/hipaa/administrative/privacyrule /index.html*.

13. "HHS Strengthens HIPAA Enforcement." *U.S. Department of Health and Human Services*, October 30, 2009. Accessed January 17, 2013 @ *www.hhs.gov/news/press /2009pres/10/20091030a.html*.

14. "The Breach Notification Rule." *U.S. Department of Health and Human Services*. Accessed February 20, 2013 @ *www.hhs.gov/ocr/privacy/hipaa/administrative /breachnotificationrule/index.html*.

15. "The Economic Espionage Act of 1996: An Overview." *U.S. Department of Justice*. Accessed October 14, 2006 @ *www.cybercrime.gov/usamay2001_6.htm*.

16. Wikipedia: The Free Encyclopedia. Information Technology and SOX. Accessed August 28, 2006 @ *en.wikipedia.org/wiki/Sarbanes-Oxley_Act#Information_technology_and_SOX _404*.

17. "PCI DSS Quick Reference Guide." *PCI Security Standards Council*, October, 2010. Accessed January 28, 2013 @ *https://www.pcisecuritystandards.org/documents/PCI %20SSC%20Quick%20Reference%20Guide.pdf*.

18. "The State of PCI Compliance." *Forrester Consulting*, September, 2007. Accessed January 29, 2013 @ *www.rsa.com/solutions/PCI/ar/RSA_AR_State_of_PCI_Compliance .pdf*.

19. "Chronology of Data Breaches: Security Breaches 2005–Present." *Privacy Rights Clearinghouse*. Accessed January 29, 2013 @ *https://www.privacyrights.org/data-breach*.

20. "Payment Card Industry (PCI) Data Security Standard: Navigating PCI DSS: Understanding the Intent of the Requirements, Version 2.0." *PCI Security Standards Council*,

October 2010. Accessed January 29, 2013 @ *https://www.pcisecuritystandards.org /documents/navigating_dss_v20.pdf*.

21. "High Tech Crime." *Australian Federal Police*. Accessed May 19, 2013 @ *www.afp .gov.au/policing/cybercrime/hightech-crime.aspx*.

22. Georgia Computer Systems Protection Act (O.C.G.A. §16-9-90 et seq).

23. "Official Code of Georgia Annotated (OCGA) §10-15-1. Definitions."

24. "Official Code of Georgia Annotated (OCGA) §10-15-2. Business Must Properly Dispose of Identifying Information."

25. "The Ten Commandments of Computer Ethics." *Computer Professionals for Social Responsibility*. Accessed May 19, 2013 @ *www.cpsr.org/issues/ethics/cei*.

26. Harrington, S. "The Effects of Codes of Ethics and Personal Denial of Responsibility on Computer Abuse Judgment and Intentions." *MIS Quarterly*, September 1996, 257–278.

27. Foote Partners, LLC. Press Release. August 18, 2003, New Canaan, CT.

28. "Code of Ethics." *(ISC)*². Accessed May 19, 2013 @ *www.isc2.org/ethics*.

29. "Code of Ethics." *GIAC*. Accessed May 19, 2013 @ *www.giac.org/overview/ethics .php*.

30. "Code of Ethics." *ISACA*. Accessed May 19, 2013 @ *www.isaca.org/Certification /Code-of-Professional-Ethics/Pages*.

31. "What Is ISSA?" *ISSA*. Accessed May 19, 2013 @ *www.issa.org/?page=AboutISSA*.

32. "Code of Ethics." *ISSA*. Accessed May 19, 2013 @ *www.issa.org/?page=CodeofEthics*.

33. Ibid.

34. Alberts, R. J., A. M. Townsend, and M. E.Whitman. "The Threat of Long-Arm Jurisdiction to Electronic Commerce." *Communications of the ACM*, December 1998, 41(12), 15–20.

35. "About the National Protection and Programs Directorate." *Department of Homeland Security*. Accessed May 19, 2013 @ *www.dhs.gov/about-national-protection-and -programs-directorate*.

36. "InfraGard: A Partnership That Works." *U.S. Federal Bureau of Investigation*. Accessed October 14, 2006 @ *www.fbi.gov/news/stories/2010/march/infragard _030810*.

37. "Introduction to NSA/CSS." *U.S. National Security Agency*. Accessed April 28, 2013 @ *www.nsa.gov/about*.

38. "Information Assurance." *U.S. National Security Agency*. Accessed April 28, 2013 @ *www.nsa.gov/ia*.

39. "Mission Statement." *U.S. Secret Service*. Accessed April 28, 2013 @ *www.secretservice .gov/mission.shtml*.

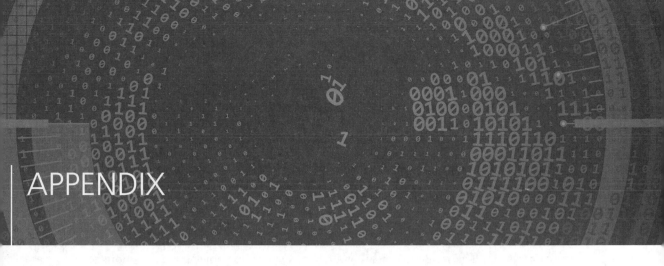

APPENDIX

NIST SP 800-26, Security Self-Assessment Guide for Information Technology Systems

The self-assessment questionnaire contains three sections: a cover sheet, questions, and notes. The cover sheet requires descriptive information about the major application, general support system, or group of interconnected systems being assessed.

The questions take a hierarchical approach to assessing a system by examining critical elements and subordinate questions. The critical element level is determined by the answers to the subordinate questions. The critical elements are derived primarily from OMB Circular A-130. The subordinate questions address the control objectives and techniques that can be implemented to satisfy the critical elements. Assessors will need to carefully review the levels of subordinate control objectives and techniques to determine which level has been reached for the related critical element. The control objectives were obtained from the list of source documents given in [the NIST SP 800-26] Appendix B. Note that there is some flexibility in implementing the control objectives and techniques. In some cases, not all control objectives and techniques may be needed to achieve the critical element.

The questionnaire section may be customized by the organization. An organization can add questions, require more descriptive information, and even pre-mark certain questions if applicable. For example, many agencies have personnel security procedures that apply to all systems within the agency. The level 1 and level 2 columns in the questionnaire can be pre-marked to reflect the standard personnel procedures in place. Additional columns may be added to reflect the status of the control (i.e., planned action date, not applicable, or location of documentation). The questionnaire should not have questions removed or questions modified to reduce the effectiveness of the control.

After each question, there is a comment field and an initial field. The comment field can be used to note the reference to supporting documentation that is attached to the questionnaire or is obtainable for that question. The initial field can be used when a risk-based decision is made not to implement a control or if the control does not apply to the system.

At the end of each set of questions, there is also an area provided for notes. This area may be used to denote where in a system security plan specific sections should be modified. It can be used to document why a particular control objective is not being implemented fully or why it is overly rigorous. The notes section may be a good place to mark where follow-up work is needed or where additional testing (e.g., penetration testing or product evaluations) should be initiated. Additionally, the section may reference supporting documentation on how the control objectives and techniques were tested and a summary of findings.

Utilizing the Completed Questionnaire

The questionnaire can be used for two purposes. First, agency managers who know their agency's systems and security controls can use it to quickly gain a general understanding of where security for a system, group of systems, or the entire agency needs improvement. Second, the questionnaire can serve as a guide for thoroughly evaluating the status of security for a system. The results of such comprehensive reviews provide a much more reliable measure of security effectiveness and may be used to fulfill reporting requirements, prepare for audits, and identify resource needs.

Questionnaire Analysis

Because this questionnaire is a self-assessment, ideally the individuals who are assessing the system will be the owners of the system or will be responsible for operating or administering it. The same individuals who completed the assessment can conduct the analysis of the completed questionnaire. Alternatively, a centralized group, such as an agency's Information System Security Program Office, can conduct the analysis as long as the supporting documentation is sufficient. The results of the analysis should be placed in an action plan, and the system security plan should be created or updated to reflect each control objective and technique decision.

Action Plans   How the critical element will be implemented—that is, specific procedures, equipment installed and tested, and personnel trained—should be documented in an action plan. This action plan must contain projected dates, an allocation of resources, and follow-up reviews to ensure that remedial actions have been effective. Routine reports should be submitted to senior management on weaknesses identified, status of the action plans, and resources still needed.

Management, Operational, and Technical Controls   The results from the completed questionnaires' 17 control topic areas can be used to summarize an agency's implementation of management, operational, and technical controls. For the report to give an accurate picture, these results must be summarized by system type, rather than being compiled into an overall agency grade level. As an example, suppose ten systems were assessed using the questionnaire. Five of the ten systems assessed were major applications; the other five were general support systems. The summary should then separate the systems into general support systems and major applications.

By further separating the systems and control objectives into groups according to criticality, the report stresses which ones require more attention based on their sensitivity and criticality. Not all systems require the same level of protection, of course; the report should reflect that diversity. The use of percentages for describing compliance (i.e., 50 percent of the major applications and 25 percent of the general support systems that are deemed high in criticality have complete system security plans that were developed within the past three years) can be used as long as a distinct division is made between the types of systems being reported.

All, or a sampling of, the completed questionnaires can be analyzed to determine which controls, if implemented, would affect the most systems. For example, if viruses frequently plague systems, then a stricter firewall policy that prohibits attached files in e-mail may be a solution. Also, systemic problems should be culled out. If an agency sees an influx of poor password management controls in the questionnaire results, then possibly password checkers should be used, awareness material issued, and password-aging software installed.

The report should conclude with a summary of planned IT security initiatives. This summary should include goals, actions needed to meet those goals, projected resources, and anticipated dates of completion.

Questionnaire Cover Sheet

The cover sheet provides instruction on completing the questionnaire, standardizing how the completed evaluation should be marked, indicating how systems are named, and labeling the criticality of the system.

All completed questionnaires should be marked, handled, and controlled at the level of sensitivity determined by organizational policy. Note that the information contained in a completed questionnaire could easily identify where the system or group of systems is most vulnerable.

The cover sheet of the questionnaire begins with the name and title of the system to be evaluated. As explained in NIST SP 800-18, each major application or general support system should be assigned a unique name/identifier. The purpose and objectives of the assessment should be identified as well. The names, titles, and sponsoring organizations of the individuals who will perform the assessment should also be listed, and the organization should customize the cover page accordingly. Finally, the start and completion dates of the evaluation should appear on the cover sheet.

Criticality of Information

The level of sensitivity of information as determined by the program official or system owner should be documented using the table on the questionnaire cover sheet. The premise behind formulating the level of sensitivity is that systems supporting higher-risk operations would be expected to have more stringent controls than those supporting lower-risk operations.

The questions are separated into three major control areas: management controls, operational controls, and technical controls. The division of control areas in this manner complements three other NIST Special Publications: NIST SP 800-12, *An Introduction to Computer Security: The NIST Handbook* (Handbook); NIST SP 800-14, *Generally Accepted Principles and Practices for Securing Information Technology Systems* (Principles and Practices); and NIST *SP 800-18, Rev. 1, Guide for Developing Plans for Federal Information Systems* (Planning Guide).

The method for answering the questions can be based primarily on an examination of relevant documentation and a rigorous examination and test of the controls. The five levels describing the state of the control objective provide a picture of each operational control; the determination of how well each one of these control objectives is met, however, is subjective. Criteria have been established for each of the five levels that should be applied when determining whether the control objective has fully reached one or more of these levels.

As stated previously, the critical elements are required to be implemented; the control objectives and techniques, however, tend to be more detailed and leave room for reasonable subjective decisions. If a particular control does not reasonably apply to the system, then "not applicable" or "NA" can be entered next to the question. Note that management controls focus on the management of the IT security system and the management of risk for a system; these techniques and concerns are normally addressed by management.

The Self-Assessment Guide Questions

To measure the progress of effectively implementing the needed security control, five levels of effectiveness are provided for each answer to the security control question:

- Level 1: control objective is documented in a security policy
- Level 2: security controls have been documented as procedures
- Level 3: procedures have been implemented
- Level 4: procedures and security controls are tested and reviewed
- Level 5: procedures and security controls are fully integrated into a comprehensive program

Each of the items shown in the following checklist is evaluated on this scale. Individuals using the guide will check the level that corresponds to their current readiness level.

Specific Control Objectives and Techniques	Level 1	Level 2	Level 3	Level 4	Level 5	Risk-Based Decision Made	Comments	Initials
Management Controls								
1. Risk Management								
1.1 Critical Element: Is risk periodically assessed?								
1.1.1 Is the current system configuration documented, including links to other systems?								
1.1.2 Are risk assessments performed and documented on a regular basis or whenever the system, facilities, or other conditions change?								
1.1.3 Has data sensitivity and integrity of the data been considered?								
1.1.4 Have threat sources, both natural and manmade, been identified?								
1.1.5 Has a list of known system vulnerabilities, system flaws, or weaknesses that could be exploited by the threat sources been developed and maintained current?								
1.1.6 Has an analysis been conducted that determines whether the security requirements in place adequately mitigate vulnerabilities?								
1.2 Critical Element: Do program officials understand the risk to systems under their control and determine the acceptable level of risk?								
1.2.1 Are final risk determinations and related management approvals documented and maintained on file?								
1.2.2 Has a mission/business impact analysis been conducted?								
1.2.3 Have additional controls been identified to sufficiently mitigate identified risks?								

Specific Control Objectives and Techniques	Level 1	Level 2	Level 3	Level 4	Level 5	Risk-Based Decision Made	Comments	Initials
2. Review of Security Controls								
2.1 Critical Element: Have the security controls of the system and interconnected systems been reviewed?								
2.1.1 Has the system and all network boundaries been subjected to periodic reviews?								
2.1.2 Has an independent review been performed when a significant change occurred?								
2.1.3 Are routine self-assessments conducted?								
2.1.4 Are tests and examinations of key controls routinely made, i.e., network scans, analyses of router and switch settings, penetration testing?								
2.1.5 Are security alerts and security incidents analyzed and remedial actions taken?								
2.2 Critical Element: Does management ensure that corrective actions are effectively implemented?								
2.2.1 Is there an effective and timely process for reporting significant weaknesses and ensuring effective remedial actions?								
3. Life Cycle								
3.1 Critical Element: Has a system development life-cycle methodology been developed?								
Initiation Phase								
3.1.1 Is the sensitivity of the system determined?								
3.1.2 Does the business case document the resources required for adequately securing the system?								

Specific Control Objectives and Techniques	Level 1	Level 2	Level 3	Level 4	Level 5	Risk-Based Decision Made	Comments	Initials
3.1.3 Does the Investment Review Board ensure any investment request includes the security resources needed?								
3.1.4 Are authorizations for software modifications documented and maintained?								
3.1.5 Does the budget request include the security resources required for the system?								
Development/Acquisition Phase								
3.1.6 During the system design, are security requirements identified?								
3.1.7 Was an initial risk assessment performed to determine security requirements?								
3.1.8 Is there a written agreement with program officials on the security controls employed and residual risk?								
3.1.9 Are security controls consistent with and an integral part of the IT architecture of the agency?								
3.1.10 Are the appropriate security controls with associated evaluation and test procedures developed before the procurement action?								
3.1.11 Do the solicitation documents (e.g., request for proposals) include security requirements and evaluation/test procedures?								
3.1.12 Do the requirements in the solicitation documents permit updating security controls as new threats/vulnerabilities are identified and as new technologies are implemented?								
Implementation Phase								
3.2 Critical Element: Are changes controlled as programs progress through testing to final approval?								

Specific Control Objectives and Techniques	Level 1	Level 2	Level 3	Level 4	Level 5	Risk-Based Decision Made	Comments	Initials
3.2.1 Are design reviews and system tests run prior to placing the system in production?								
3.2.2 Are the test results documented?								
3.2.3 Is certification testing of security controls conducted and documented?								
3.2.4 If security controls were added since development, has the system documentation been modified to include them?								
3.2.5 If security controls were added since development, have the security controls been tested and the system recertified?								
3.2.6 Has the application undergone a technical evaluation to ensure that it meets applicable federal laws, regulations, policies, guidelines, and standards?								
3.2.7 Does the system have written authorization to operate either on an interim basis with planned corrective action or full authorization?								
Operation/Maintenance Phase								
3.2.8 Has a system security plan been developed and approved?								
3.2.9 If the system connects to other systems, have controls been established and disseminated to the owners of the interconnected systems?								
3.2.10 Is the system security plan kept current?								
Disposal Phase								
3.2.11 Are official electronic records properly disposed/archived?								
3.2.12 Is information or media purged, overwritten, degaussed, or destroyed when disposed or used elsewhere?								

Specific Control Objectives and Techniques	Level 1	Level 2	Level 3	Level 4	Level 5	Risk-Based Decision Made	Comments	Initials
3.2.13 Is a record kept of who implemented the disposal actions and verified that the information or media was sanitized?								
4. Authorize Processing (Certification and Accreditation)								
4.1 Critical Element: Has the system been certified/recertified and authorized to process (accredited)?								
4.1.1 Has a technical and/or security evaluation been completed or conducted when a significant change occurred?								
4.1.2 Has a risk assessment been conducted when a significant change occurred?								
4.1.3 Have rules of behavior been established and signed by users?								
4.1.4 Has a contingency plan been developed and tested?								
4.1.5 Has a system security plan been developed, updated, and reviewed?								
4.1.6 Are in-place controls operating as intended?								
4.1.7 Are the planned and in-place controls consistent with the identified risks and the system and data sensitivity?								
4.1.8 Has management authorized interconnections to all systems (including systems owned and operated by another program, agency, organization, or contractor)?								
4.2 Critical Element: Is the system operating on an interim authority to process in accordance with specified agency procedures?								
4.2.1 Has management initiated prompt action to correct deficiencies?								

Specific Control Objectives and Techniques	Level 1	Level 2	Level 3	Level 4	Level 5	Risk-Based Decision Made	Comments	Initials
5. System Security Plan								
5.1 Critical Element: Is a system security plan documented for the system and all interconnected systems if the boundary controls are ineffective?								
5.1.1 Is the system security plan approved by key affected parties and management?								
5.1.2 Does the plan contain the topics prescribed in NIST Special Publication 800-18?								
5.1.3 Is a summary of the plan incorporated into the strategic IRM plan?								
5.2 Critical Element: Is the plan kept current?								
5.2.1 Is the plan reviewed periodically and adjusted to reflect current conditions and risks?								
Operational Controls								
6. Personnel Security								
6.1 Critical Element: Are duties separated to ensure least privilege and individual accountability?								
6.1.1 Are all positions reviewed for sensitivity level?								
6.1.2 Are there documented job descriptions that accurately reflect assigned duties and responsibilities and that segregate duties?								
6.1.3 Are sensitive functions divided among different individuals?								
6.1.4 Are distinct systems support functions performed by different individuals?								
6.1.5 Are mechanisms in place for holding users responsible for their actions?								
6.1.6 Are regularly scheduled vacations and periodic job/shift rotations required?								

Specific Control Objectives and Techniques	Level 1	Level 2	Level 3	Level 4	Level 5	Risk-Based Decision Made	Comments	Initials
6.1.7 Are hiring, transfer, and termination procedures established?								
6.1.8 Is there a process for requesting, establishing, issuing, and closing user accounts?								
6.2 Critical Element: Is appropriate background screening for assigned positions completed prior to granting access?								
6.2.1 Are individuals who are authorized to bypass significant technical and operational controls screened prior to access and periodically thereafter?								
6.2.2 Are confidentiality or security agreements required for employees assigned to work with sensitive information?								
6.2.3 When controls cannot adequately protect the information, are individuals screened prior to access?								
6.2.4 Are there conditions for allowing system access prior to completion of screening?								
7. Physical and Environmental Protection								
7.1 Critical Element: Have adequate physical security controls been implemented that are commensurate with the risks of physical damage or access?								
7.1.1 Is access to facilities controlled through the use of guards, identification badges, or entry devices such as key cards or biometrics?								
7.1.2 Does management regularly review the list of persons with physical access to sensitive facilities?								
7.1.3 Are deposits and withdrawals of tapes and other storage media from the library authorized and logged?								

Specific Control Objectives and Techniques	Level 1	Level 2	Level 3	Level 4	Level 5	Risk-Based Decision Made	Comments	Initials
7.1.4 Are keys or other access devices needed to enter the computer room and tape/media library?								
7.1.5 Are unused keys or other entry devices secured?								
7.1.6 Do emergency exit and reentry procedures ensure that only authorized personnel are allowed to reenter after fire drills, etc.?								
7.1.7 Are visitors to sensitive areas signed in and escorted?								
7.1.8 Are entry codes changed periodically?								
7.1.9 Are physical accesses monitored through audit trails and apparent security violations investigated and remedial action taken?								
7.1.10 Is suspicious access activity investigated and appropriate action taken?								
7.1.11 Are visitors, contractors, and maintenance personnel authenticated through the use of preplanned appointments and identification checks?								
Fire Safety Factors								
7.1.12 Are appropriate fire suppression and prevention devices installed and working?								
7.1.13 Are fire ignition sources, such as failures of electronic devices or wiring, improper storage materials, and the possibility of arson, reviewed periodically?								
Supporting Utilities								
7.1.14 Are heating and air-conditioning systems regularly maintained?								
7.1.15 Is there a redundant air-cooling system?								

Specific Control Objectives and Techniques	Level 1	Level 2	Level 3	Level 4	Level 5	Risk-Based Decision Made	Comments	Initials
7.1.16 Are electric power distribution, heating plants, water, sewage, and other utilities periodically reviewed for risk of failure?								
7.1.17 Are building plumbing lines known and do not endanger system?								
7.1.18 Has an uninterruptible power supply or backup generator been provided?								
7.1.19 Have controls been implemented to mitigate other disasters, such as floods, earthquakes, etc.?								
Interception of Data								
7.2 Critical Element: Is data protected from interception?								
7.2.1 Are computer monitors located to eliminate viewing by unauthorized persons?								
7.2.2 Is physical access to data transmission lines controlled?								
Mobile and Portable Systems								
7.3 Critical Element: Are mobile and portable systems protected?								
7.3.1 Are sensitive data files encrypted on all portable systems? (NIST SP 800-14)								
7.3.2 Are portable systems stored securely? (NIST SP 800-14)								
8. Production, Input/Output Controls								
8.1 Critical Element: Is there user support?								
8.1.1 Is there a help desk or group that offers advice?								
8.2 Critical Element: Are there media controls?								
8.2.1 Are there processes to ensure that unauthorized individuals cannot read, copy, alter, or steal printed or electronic information?								

Specific Control Objectives and Techniques	Level 1	Level 2	Level 3	Level 4	Level 5	Risk-Based Decision Made	Comments	Initials
8.2.2 Are there processes for ensuring that only authorized users pick up, receive, or deliver input and output information and media?								
8.2.3 Are audit trails used for receipt of sensitive inputs/outputs?								
8.2.4 Are controls in place for transporting or mailing media or printed output?								
8.2.5 Is there internal/external labeling for sensitivity?								
8.2.6 Is there external labeling with special handling instructions?								
8.2.7 Are audit trails kept for inventory management?								
8.2.8 Is media sanitized for reuse?								
8.2.9 Is damaged media stored and/or destroyed?								
8.2.10 Is hardcopy media shredded or destroyed when no longer needed?								
9. Contingency Planning								
9.1 Critical Element: Have the most critical and sensitive operations and their supporting computer resources been identified?								
9.1.1 Are critical data files and operations identified and the frequency of file backup documented?								
9.1.2 Are resources supporting critical operations identified?								
9.1.3 Have processing priorities been established and approved by management?								
9.2 Critical Element: Has a comprehensive contingency plan been developed and documented?								

Specific Control Objectives and Techniques	Level 1	Level 2	Level 3	Level 4	Level 5	Risk-Based Decision Made	Comments	Initials
9.2.1 Is the plan approved by key affected parties?								
9.2.2 Are responsibilities for recovery assigned?								
9.2.3 Are there detailed instructions for restoring operations?								
9.2.4 Is there an alternate processing site; if so, is there a contract or interagency agreement in place?								
9.2.5 Is the location of stored backups identified?								
9.2.6 Are backup files created on a prescribed basis and rotated off-site often enough to avoid disruption if current files are damaged?								
9.2.7 Is system and application documentation maintained at the off-site location?								
9.2.8 Are all system defaults reset after being restored from a backup?								
9.2.9 Are the backup storage site and alternate site geographically removed from the primary site and physically protected?								
9.2.10 Has the contingency plan been distributed to all appropriate personnel?								
9.3 Critical Element: Are tested contingency/disaster recovery plans in place?								
9.3.1 Is an up-to-date copy of the plan stored securely off-site?								
9.3.2 Are employees trained in their roles and responsibilities?								
9.3.3 Is the plan periodically tested and readjusted as appropriate?								
10. Hardware and System Software Maintenance								

Specific Control Objectives and Techniques	Level 1	Level 2	Level 3	Level 4	Level 5	Risk-Based Decision Made	Comments	Initials
10.1 Critical Element: Is access limited to system software and hardware?								
10.1.1 Are restrictions in place on who performs maintenance and repair activities?								
10.1.2 Is access to all program libraries restricted and controlled?								
10.1.3 Are there on-site and off-site maintenance procedures (e.g., escort of maintenance personnel, sanitization of devices removed from the site)?								
10.1.4 Is the operating system configured to prevent circumvention of the security software and application controls?								
10.1.5 Are up-to-date procedures in place for using and monitoring use of system utilities?								
10.2 Critical Element: Are all new and revised hardware and software authorized, tested, and approved before implementation?								
10.2.1 Is an impact analysis conducted to determine the effect of proposed changes on existing security controls, including the required training needed to implement the control?								
10.2.2 Are system components tested, documented, and approved (operating system, utility, applications) prior to promotion to production?								
10.2.3 Are software change request forms used to document requests and related approvals?								
10.2.4 Are there detailed system specifications prepared and reviewed by management?								
10.2.5 Is the type of test data to be used specified, i.e., live or made up?								
10.2.6 Are default settings of security features set to the most restrictive mode?								

Specific Control Objectives and Techniques	Level 1	Level 2	Level 3	Level 4	Level 5	Risk-Based Decision Made	Comments	Initials
10.2.7 Are there software distribution implementation orders including effective date provided to all locations?								
10.2.8 Is there version control?								
10.2.9 Are programs labeled and inventoried?								
10.2.10 Are the distribution and implementation of new or revised software documented and reviewed?								
10.2.11 Are emergency change procedures documented and approved by management, either prior to the change or after the fact?								
10.2.12 Are contingency plans and other associated documentation updated to reflect system changes?								
10.2.13 Is the use of copyrighted software or shareware and personally owned software/ equipment documented?								
10.3 Critical Element: Are systems managed to reduce vulnerabilities?								
10.3.1 Are systems periodically reviewed to identify and, when possible, eliminate unnecessary services (e.g., FTP, HTTP, mainframe supervisor calls)?								
10.3.2 Are systems periodically reviewed for known vulnerabilities and software patches promptly installed?								
11. Data Integrity								
11.1 Critical Element: Is virus detection and elimination software installed and activated?								
11.1.1 Are virus signature files routinely updated?								
11.1.2 Are virus scans automatic?								

Specific Control Objectives and Techniques	Level 1	Level 2	Level 3	Level 4	Level 5	Risk-Based Decision Made	Comments	Initials
11.2 Critical Element: Are data integrity and validation controls used to provide assurance that the information has not been altered and the system functions as intended?								
11.2.1 Are reconciliation routines used by applications, i.e., checksums, hash totals, record counts?								
11.2.2 Is inappropriate or unusual activity reported, investigated, and appropriate actions taken?								
11.2.3 Are procedures in place to determine compliance with password policies?								
11.2.4 Are integrity verification programs used by applications to look for evidence of data tampering, errors, and omissions?								
11.2.5 Are intrusion detection tools installed on the system?								
11.2.6 Are the intrusion detection reports routinely reviewed and suspected incidents handled accordingly?								
11.2.7 Is system performance monitoring used to analyze system performance logs in real time to look for availability problems, including active attacks?								
11.2.8 Is penetration testing performed on the system?								
11.2.9 Is message authentication used?								
12. Documentation								
12.1 Critical Element: Is there sufficient documentation that explains how software/hardware is to be used?								
12.1.1 Is there vendor-supplied documentation of purchased software?								
12.1.2 Is there vendor-supplied documentation of purchased hardware?								

Specific Control Objectives and Techniques	Level 1	Level 2	Level 3	Level 4	Level 5	Risk-Based Decision Made	Comments	Initials
12.1.3 Is there application documentation for in-house applications?								
12.1.4 Are there network diagrams and documentation on setups of routers and switches?								
12.1.5 Are there software and hardware testing procedures and results?								
12.1.6 Are there standard operating procedures for all the topic areas covered in this document?								
12.1.7 Are there user manuals?								
12.1.8 Are there emergency procedures?								
12.1.9 Are there backup procedures?								
12.2 Critical Element: Are there formal security and operational procedures documented?								
12.2.1 Is there a system security plan? FISCAM SP-2.1								
12.2.2 Is there a contingency plan?								
12.2.3 Are there written agreements regarding how data is shared between interconnected systems?								
12.2.4 Are there risk assessment reports?								
12.2.5 Are there certification and accreditation documents and a statement authorizing the system to process?								
13. Security Awareness, Training, and Education								
13.1 Critical Element: Have employees received adequate training to fulfill their security responsibilities?								

Specific Control Objectives and Techniques	Level 1	Level 2	Level 3	Level 4	Level 5	Risk-Based Decision Made	Comments	Initials
13.1.1 Have employees received a copy of the rules of behavior?								
13.1.2 Are employee training and professional development documented and monitored? FISCAM SP-4.2								
13.1.3 Is there mandatory annual refresher training?								
13.1.4 Are methods employed to make employees aware of security, i.e., posters, booklets?								
13.1.5 Have employees received a copy of or have easy access to agency security procedures and policies?								
14. Incident Response Capability								
14.1 Critical Element: Is there a capability to provide help to users when a security incident occurs in the system?								
14.1.1 Is a formal incident response capability available?								
14.1.2 Is there a process for reporting incidents?								
14.1.3 Are incidents monitored and tracked until resolved?								
14.1.4 Are personnel trained to recognize and handle incidents?								
14.1.5 Are alerts/advisories received and responded to?								
14.1.6 Is there a process to modify incident handling procedures and control techniques after an incident occurs?								
14.2 Critical Element: Is incident-related information shared with appropriate organizations?								

Specific Control Objectives and Techniques	Level 1	Level 2	Level 3	Level 4	Level 5	Risk-Based Decision Made	Comments	Initials
14.2.1 Is incident information and common vulnerabilities or threats shared with owners of interconnected systems?								
14.2.2 Is incident information shared with FedCIRC concerning incidents and common vulnerabilities and threats?								
14.2.3 Is incident information reported to FedCIRC, NIPC4, and local law enforcement when necessary?								
Technical Controls								
15. Identification and Authentication								
15.1 Critical Element: Are users individually authenticated via passwords, tokens, or other devices?								
15.1.1 Is a current list maintained and approved of authorized users and their access?								
15.1.2 Are digital signatures used and conform to FIPS 186-2?								
15.1.3 Are access scripts with embedded passwords prohibited?								
15.1.4 Is emergency and temporary access authorized?								
15.1.5 Are personnel files matched with user accounts to ensure that terminated or transferred individuals do not retain system access?								
15.1.6 Are passwords changed at least every 90 days or earlier if needed?								
15.1.7 Are passwords unique and difficult to guess (e.g., do passwords require alphanumeric, upper/lower case, and special characters)?								

Specific Control Objectives and Techniques	Level 1	Level 2	Level 3	Level 4	Level 5	Risk-Based Decision Made	Comments	Initials
15.1.8 Are inactive user identifications disabled after a specified period of time?								
15.1.9 Are passwords not displayed when entered?								
15.1.10 Are there procedures in place for handling lost and compromised passwords?								
15.1.11 Are passwords distributed securely and users informed not to reveal their passwords to anyone (social engineering)?								
15.1.12 Are passwords transmitted and stored using secure protocols/algorithms?								
15.1.13 Are vendor-supplied passwords replaced immediately?								
15.1.14 Is there a limit to the number of invalid access attempts that may occur for a given user?								
15.2 Critical Element: Are access controls enforcing segregation of duties?								
15.2.1 Does the system correlate actions to users?								
15.2.2 Do data owners periodically review access authorizations to determine whether they remain appropriate?								
16. Logical Access Controls								
16.1 Critical Element: Do the logical access controls restrict users to authorized transactions and functions?								
16.1.1 Can the security controls detect unauthorized access attempts?								
16.1.2 Is there access control software that prevents an individual from having all necessary authority or information access to allow fraudulent activity without collusion?								
16.1.3 Is access to security software restricted to security administrators?								

Specific Control Objectives and Techniques	Level 1	Level 2	Level 3	Level 4	Level 5	Risk-Based Decision Made	Comments	Initials
16.1.4 Do workstations disconnect or screen savers lock the system after a specific period of inactivity?								
16.1.5 Are inactive users' accounts monitored and removed when not needed?								
16.1.6 Are internal security labels (naming conventions) used to control access to specific information types or files?								
16.1.7 If encryption is used, does it meet federal standards?								
16.1.8 If encryption is used, are there procedures for key generation, distribution, storage, use, destruction, and archiving?								
16.1.9 Is access restricted to files at the logical view or field?								
16.1.10 Is access monitored to identify apparent security violations and are such events investigated?								
16.2 Critical Element: Are there logical controls over network access?								
16.2.1 Has communication software been implemented to restrict access through specific terminals?								
16.2.2 Are insecure protocols (e.g., UDP, FTP) disabled?								
16.2.3 Have all vendor-supplied default security parameters been reinitialized to more secure settings?								
16.2.4 Are there controls that restrict remote access to the system?								
16.2.5 Are network activity logs maintained and reviewed?								
16.2.6 Does the network connection automatically disconnect at the end of a session?								

Specific Control Objectives and Techniques	Level 1	Level 2	Level 3	Level 4	Level 5	Risk-Based Decision Made	Comments	Initials
16.2.7 Are trust relationships among hosts and external entities appropriately restricted?								
16.2.8 Is dial-in access monitored?								
16.2.9 Is access to telecommunications hardware or facilities restricted and monitored?								
16.2.10 Are firewalls or secure gateways installed?								
16.2.11 If firewalls are installed, do they comply with firewall policy and rules?								
16.2.12 Are guest and anonymous accounts authorized and monitored?								
16.2.13 Is an approved standardized logon banner displayed on the system warning unauthorized users that they have accessed a U.S. Government system and can be punished?								
16.2.14 Are sensitive data transmissions encrypted?								
16.2.15 Is access to tables defining network options, resources, and operator profiles restricted?								
16.3 Critical Element: If the public accesses the system, are there controls implemented to protect the integrity of the application and the confidence of the public?								
16.3.1 Is a privacy policy posted on the Web site?								
17. Audit Trails								
17.1 Critical Element: Is activity involving access to and modification of sensitive or critical files logged, monitored, and possible security violations investigated?								
17.1.1 Does the audit trail provide a trace of user actions?								

Specific Control Objectives and Techniques	Level 1	Level 2	Level 3	Level 4	Level 5	Risk-Based Decision Made	Comments	Initials
17.1.2 Can the audit trail support after-the-fact investigations of how, when, and why normal operations ceased?								
17.1.3 Is access to online audit logs strictly controlled?								
17.1.4 Are off-line storage of audit logs retained for a period of time, and, if so, is access to audit logs strictly controlled?								
17.1.5 Is there separation of duties between security personnel who administer the access control function and those who administer the audit trail?								
17.1.6 Are audit trails reviewed frequently?								
17.1.7 Are automated tools used to review audit records in real time or near real time?								
17.1.8 Is suspicious activity investigated and appropriate action taken?								
17.1.9 Is keystroke monitoring used? If so, are users notified?								

ISO 17799: 2005 Overview
ISO 17799: 2005 Scoring Methodology

This scoring methodology is designed to assess an organization's management practices using a framework based on ISO 17799 (now ISO 27001). The respondent is asked to assess the organization's implementation of security objectives for security standards across the domains of ISO 17799: 2005. For each objective, a respondent may choose one of the following degrees of compliance:

- Fully compliant: The standard objective has been fully implemented at the organization. Results in a score of 10 for the objective.

- Partially compliant: The standard objective has been partially implemented at the organization. Results in a score of 5 for the objective.

- Planned: The organization has made definite plans to implement the standard objective. Results in a score of 2 for the objective.

- Not compliant or planned: The standard objective has not been implemented (even partly) and there are no plans to implement it. Results in a score of 0 for the objective.

- Not applicable: The objective does not appear to apply to the organization. No score is given and the potential score of 10 is not incorporated in the calculation of the total score, as if the objective was not included in the index.

The scoring methodology is designed to illustrate a great benefit from implementing minimum and basic security standards, although implementation of all standards are required for a score of 100 percent. Individuals should review each low-level standard (i.e., 5.1.1) and assess their performance against a maximum score of 10 per item, as described above (1320 points max—if all low-level standards are applicable). Scores of 80 percent or higher indicate a strong performance against the standard. Scores of 60–79 percent indicate progress, but additional effort is required to become more compliant. Scores below 60 percent indicate that several areas are out of compliance and an overall strategic plan to improve general security management should be undertaken.

Praxiom's ISO/IEC 17799 2005 Information Security Standard in Plain English

From www.praxiom.com/iso-17799-2005.htm, reprinted here with permission.

5. Security Policy Management
    5.1   Establish a comprehensive information security policy
        5.1.1   Develop an information security policy document
        5.1.2   Review your information security policy

6. Corporate Security Management
    6.1   Establish an internal security organization
        6.1.1   Make an active commitment to information security
        6.1.2   Coordinate information security implementation
        6.1.3   Allocate information security responsibilities
        6.1.4   Establish an authorization process for new facilities

6.1.5   Use confidentiality agreements to protect information
6.1.6   Maintain relationships with other organizations
6.1.7   Maintain relationships with special interest groups
6.1.8   Perform independent information system reviews
6.2   Control external party use of your information
6.2.1   Identify risks related to the use of external parties
6.2.2   Address security before customers are given access
6.2.3   Address security using third-party agreements

7. Organizational Asset Management

7.1   Establish responsibility for your organization's assets
7.1.1   Compile an inventory of organizational assets
7.1.2   Select owners for your information and assets
7.1.3   Establish acceptable use rules for information and assets
7.2   Use an information classification system
7.2.1   Develop information classification guidelines
7.2.2   Use information handling and labeling procedures

8. Human Resource Security Management

8.1   Emphasize security prior to employment
8.1.1   Define your security roles and responsibilities
8.1.2   Verify the backgrounds of all new personnel
8.1.3   Use contracts to protect your organization's information
8.2   Emphasize security during employment
8.2.1   Expect your managers to emphasize security
8.2.2   Deliver information security training programs
8.2.3   Set up a disciplinary process for security breaches
8.3   Emphasize security at termination of employment
8.3.1   Assign responsibility for termination or reassignment
8.3.2   Make sure that assets are returned at termination
8.3.3   Remove information access rights at termination

9. Physical and Environmental Security Management

9.1   Use security areas to protect facilities
9.1.1   Use physical security perimeters to protect areas
9.1.2   Use physical entry controls to protect secure areas
9.1.3   Secure your organization's offices, rooms, and facilities
9.1.4   Protect your facilities from natural and human threats
9.1.5   Use work guidelines to protect secure areas
9.1.6   Isolate and control public access points
9.2   Protect your equipment
9.2.1   Use equipment siting and protection strategies
9.2.2   Make sure that supporting utilities are reliable
9.2.3   Secure power and telecommunications cables
9.2.4   Maintain your organization's equipment
9.2.5   Protect your organization's offsite equipment
9.2.6   Control equipment disposal and reuse
9.2.7   Control the use of assets offsite

10. Communications and Operations Management

10.1   Establish procedures and responsibilities

        10.1.1   Document your operating procedures

        10.1.2   Control changes to facilities and systems

        10.1.3   Segregate duties and responsibilities

        10.1.4   Separate development and operations

10.2   Control third-party service delivery

        10.2.1   Manage third-party service agreements

        10.2.2   Monitor third-party service delivery

        10.2.3   Control changes to third-party services

10.3   Carry out future system planning activities

        10.3.1   Monitor usage and carry out capacity planning

        10.3.2   Use acceptance criteria to test your systems

10.4   Protect against malicious and mobile code

        10.4.1   Establish controls to handle malicious code

        10.4.2   Control the use of mobile code

10.5   Establish backup procedures

        10.5.1   Back up your information and software

10.6   Protect computer networks

        10.6.1   Establish network security controls

        10.6.2   Control network service providers

10.7   Control how media are handled

        10.7.1   Manage your organization's removable media

        10.7.2   Manage the disposal of your organization's media

        10.7.3   Control information handling and storage

        10.7.3   Protect your system documentation

10.8   Protect exchange of information

        10.8.1   Establish information exchange policies and procedures

        10.8.2   Establish information and software exchange agreements

        10.8.3   Safeguard the transportation of physical media

        10.8.4   Protect electronic messaging and messages

        10.8.5   Protect interconnected business information systems

10.9   Protect electronic commerce services

        10.9.1   Protect information involved in ecommerce

        10.9.2   Protect online transaction information

        10.9.3   Protect information available on public systems

10.10 Monitor information processing facilities

        10.10.1 Establish and maintain audit logs

        10.10.2 Monitor information processing facilities

        10.10.3 Protect logging facilities and log information

        10.10.4 Log system administrator and operator activities

        10.10.5 Log information processing and communication faults

        10.10.6 Synchronize your system clocks

11. Information Access Control Management

11.1   Control access to information

        11.1.1   Develop a policy to control access to information

11.2 Manage user access rights
    11.2.1   Establish a user access control procedure
    11.2.2   Control the management of system privileges
    11.2.3   Establish a process to manage passwords
    11.2.4   Review user access rights and privileges
11.3 Encourage good access practices
    11.3.1   Expect users to protect their passwords
    11.3.2   Expect users to protect their equipment
    11.3.3   Establish a clear-desk and clear-screen policy
11.4 Control access to networked services
    11.4.1   Formulate a policy on the use of networks
    11.4.2   Authenticate remote user connections
    11.4.3   Use automatic equipment identification methods
    11.4.4   Control access to diagnostic and configuration ports
    11.4.5   Use segregation methods to protect your networks
    11.4.6   Restrict connection to shared networks
    11.4.7   Establish network routing controls
11.5 Control access to operating systems
    11.5.1   Establish secure logon procedures
    11.5.2   Identify and authenticate all users
    11.5.3   Establish a password management system
    11.5.4   Control the use of all system utilities
    11.5.5   Use session time-outs to protect information
    11.5.6   Restrict connection times in high-risk areas
11.6 Control access to applications and information
    11.6.1   Restrict access by users and support personnel
    11.6.2   Isolate sensitive application systems
11.7 Protect mobile and teleworking facilities
    11.7.1   Protect mobile computing and communications
    11.7.2   Protect and control teleworking activities

12. Information Systems Security Management

12.1 Identify information system security requirements
    12.1.1   Identify security controls and requirements
12.2 Make sure applications process information correctly
    12.2.1   Validate data input into your applications
    12.2.2   Use validation checks to control processing
    12.2.3   Protect message integrity and authenticity
    12.2.4   Validate your applications' output data
12.3 Use cryptographic controls to protect your information
    12.3.1   Implement a policy on the use of cryptographic controls
    12.3.2   Establish a secure key management system
12.4 Protect and control your organization's system files
    12.4.1   Control the installation of operational software
    12.4.2   Control the use of system data for testing
    12.4.3   Control access to program source code

Note: No organization should attempt a 17799 audit solely on the basis of this document. While the underlying methodology is sound, the level of detail is insufficient to successfully complete a meaningful assessment of the organization's information security management strategies. This information is presented for academic discussion and should only be used as such.

The OCTAVE Method of Risk Management

From Appendix D of OCTAVE Method Implementation Guide Version 2.0 *by C. Alberts and A. Dorofee, June 2001. Reprinted here with permission.*

The OCTAVE Method defines the essential components of a comprehensive, systematic, context-driven, self-directed information security risk evaluation. By following the OCTAVE Method, an organization can make information-protection decisions based on risks to the confidentiality, integrity, and availability of critical information technology assets. The operational or business units and the IT department work together to address the information security needs of the organization.

Using a three-phase approach, the OCTAVE Method examines organizational and technology issues to assemble a comprehensive picture of the information security needs of an organization. The phases are described below:

- Phase 1: Build Asset-Based Threat Profiles. This is an organizational evaluation. Key areas of expertise within the organization are examined to elicit important knowledge about information assets, the threats to those assets, the security requirements of the assets, what the organization is currently doing to protect its information assets (current protection strategy practices), and weaknesses in organizational policies and practice (organizational vulnerabilities).

- Phase 2: Identify Infrastructure Vulnerabilities. This is an evaluation of the information infrastructure. The key operational components of the information technology infrastructure are examined for weaknesses (technology vulnerabilities) that can lead to unauthorized action.

- Phase 3: Develop Security Strategy and Plans. Risks are analyzed in this phase. The information generated by the organizational and information infrastructure evaluations (Phases 1 and 2) is analyzed to identify risks to the organization and to evaluate the risks based on their impact to the organization's mission. In addition, an organization protection strategy and risk mitigation plans for the highest priority risks are developed.

Important Aspects of the OCTAVE Method

The OCTAVE Method is *self-directed*. A small, interdisciplinary team of the organization's personnel (called the analysis team) manages the process and analyzes all information. Thus, the organization's personnel are actively involved in the decision-making process. When organizations outsource risk assessments, they often detach from making decisions.

The OCTAVE Method requires an *analysis team* to conduct the evaluation and to analyze the information. The analysis team is an interdisciplinary team comprising representatives from both the mission-related and information technology areas of the organization. Typically, the analysis team will contain a core membership of about three to five people, depending on the size of the overall organization and the scope of the evaluation. The basic tasks of the analysis team are:

- To facilitate the knowledge elicitation workshops of Phase 1
- To gather any supporting data that are necessary
- To analyze threat and risk information

- To develop a protection strategy for the organization
- To develop mitigation plans to address the risks to the organization's critical assets

Thus, the analysis team must have knowledge of the organization and its business processes (including mission-related processes and information technology processes), facilitation skills, and good communications skills. It is also important to note that the analysis team is responsible for analyzing information and for making decisions. The core members of the analysis team may not have all of the knowledge and skills needed during the evaluation. At each point in the process, the analysis team members must decide if they need to augment their knowledge and skills for a specific task. They can do so by including others in the organization or by using external experts.

The OCTAVE Method uses a *workshop-based approach* for gathering information and making decisions. In Phase 1, key areas of expertise within the organization are examined in facilitated workshops (also called knowledge elicitation workshops). The analysis team facilitates these workshops. The result is the identification of important information assets, the threats to those assets, the security requirements of the assets, what the organization is currently doing to protect its information assets (current protection strategy), and weaknesses in organizational policies and practice (organizational vulnerabilities). The remainder of Phase 1, as well as Phases 2 and 3, include consolidation and analysis workshops to consolidate and analyze the information gathered during the Phase 1 knowledge elicitation workshops. The consolidation and analysis workshops yield information such as the key operational components of the information infrastructure, the risks to the organization, the protection strategy for the organization, and mitigation plans for addressing the risks to the critical assets.

The OCTAVE Method relies upon the following major *catalogs of information*:

- Catalog of practices: A collection of good strategic and operational security practices
- Threat profile: The range of major sources of threats that an organization needs to consider
- Catalog of vulnerabilities: A collection of vulnerabilities based on platform and application

An organization that is conducting the OCTAVE Method evaluates itself against the above catalogs of information. During Phase 1, the organization uses the catalog of practices as a measure of what it is currently doing well with respect to security (its current protection strategy practices) as well as what it is not doing well (its organizational vulnerabilities). The analysis team also uses the catalog of practices when it creates the protection strategy for the organization during Phase 3. After the analysis team selects the critical assets for the organization, they use the threat profile to create the range of threat scenarios that affect each critical asset. This occurs at the end of Phase 1. The analysis team uses software tools to examine their information technology infrastructure for weaknesses (technology vulnerabilities) in Phase 2.

Phases, Processes, and Activities

Each phase of the OCTAVE Method contains two or more processes. Each process is made of activities. The following list highlights the phases and processes of OCTAVE:

- Preparing for the OCTAVE Method

- Phase 1: Build Asset-Based Threat Profiles
  - Process 1: Identify Senior Management Knowledge
  - Process 2: Identify Operational Area Management Knowledge
  - Process 3: Identify Staff Knowledge
  - Process 4: Create Threat Profiles
- Phase 2: Identify Infrastructure Vulnerabilities
  - Process 5: Identify Key Components
  - Process 6: Evaluate Selected Components
- Phase 3: Develop Security Strategy and Plans
  - Process 7: Conduct Risk Analysis
  - Process 8: Develop Protection Strategy

Each of these is described in more detail in the following sections.

Preparing for the OCTAVE Method

Preparing for the OCTAVE Method creates the foundation for a successful or unsuccessful evaluation. Getting senior management sponsorship, the selection of the analysis team, scoping of the project, and the selection of the participants are all key to a successful evaluation. The preparation activities for the OCTAVE Method address the issues listed above. The following are the activities required when preparing to conduct the OCTAVE Method:

- Obtain senior management sponsorship of OCTAVE.
- Select analysis team members.
- Train analysis team.
- Select operational areas to participate in OCTAVE.
- Select participants.
- Coordinate logistics.
- Brief all participants.

Once the preparation is completed, the organization is ready to start the evaluation.

Phase 1: Build Asset-Based Threat Profiles

The OCTAVE Method enables decision makers to develop relative priorities based on what is important to the organization. This involves examining both organizational practices and the installed technology base to identify risks to the organization's important information assets. A comprehensive information security risk evaluation, like the OCTAVE Method, involves the entire organization, including personnel from the information technology department and the business lines of the organization.

The purpose of a risk evaluation is to help decision makers select cost-effective countermeasures by balancing the cost of addressing a risk with the benefit derived from avoiding a potential negative impact to the organization. The result of the evaluation is a mitigation plan for applying countermeasures designed to reduce the organization's risks.

In the OCTAVE Method, the analysis team conducts the evaluation. The analysis team is interdisciplinary in nature, including participants with various backgrounds and job roles. It is responsible for conducting workshops with the organization's staff, for analyzing the information that is elicited, and for ensuring that the evaluation process proceeds as scheduled.

During Phase 1, the analysis team facilitates workshop interviews with staff from multiple organizational levels. During these workshops, the participants identify important assets and discuss the impact on the organization if the assets are compromised. These knowledge elicitation workshops are held for the following organizational levels:

- Senior management
- Operational area management (middle management)
- Staff (including IT staff)

You should note that the organizational levels are not mixed during the workshops. In addition, the information technology staff normally participates in a separate workshop from the general staff members. The purpose of the knowledge elicitation workshops is to identify the following information from each organizational perspective:

- Important assets and their relative values
- Perceived threats to the assets
- Security requirements
- Current protection strategy practices
- Current organizational vulnerabilities

The OCTAVE Method requires workshop participants to examine the relative priority of assets based on the impact to the organization if the asset is lost. Participants are asked to examine threats to the highest-priority assets that they have identified. The participants create threat scenarios based on known sources of threat and typical threat outcomes (from the threat profile). Participants next examine security requirements. Security requirements outline the qualities of information assets that are important to an organization.

Process 1: Identify Senior Management Knowledge

The participants in this process are the organization's senior managers. The analysis team facilitates a knowledge elicitation activity with the managers in these activities:

- Identify assets and relative priorities.
- Identify areas of concern.
- Identify security requirements for the most important assets.
- Capture knowledge of protection strategy practices and organizational vulnerabilities.

Process 2: Identify Operational Area Management Knowledge

The participants in this process are the organization's operational area managers (middle managers). The analysis team facilitates a knowledge elicitation activity with the managers in these activities:

- Identify assets and relative priorities.
- Identify areas of concern.

- Identify security requirements for the most important assets.

- Capture knowledge of protection strategy practices and organizational vulnerabilities.

Process 3: Identify Staff Knowledge

The participants in this process are the organization's staff members. The analysis team facilitates a knowledge elicitation activity with them in these activities:

- Identify assets and relative priorities.

- Identify areas of concern.

- Identify security requirements for the most important assets.

- Capture knowledge of protection strategy practices and organizational vulnerabilities.

Process 4: Create Threat Profiles

The participants in this process are the analysis team members. During Process 4, the information elicited from the different organizational levels during the previous processes is grouped, critical assets are chosen, and a threat profile is created for each critical asset. The following are the activities of Process 4:

- Group assets, security requirements, and areas of concern by organizational level.

- Select critical assets.

- Refine security requirements for critical assets.

- Identify threats to critical assets.

After completion of the organization view, or Phase 1 of the OCTAVE Method, the organization is ready to move to the technological view. Phase 2 of the evaluation examines the organization's information technology infrastructure.

Phase 2: Identify Infrastructure Vulnerabilities

Each information technology system or component will have many specific technology vulnerabilities against which it can be benchmarked. The OCTAVE Method requires that technology be measured against a catalog of vulnerabilities. The Common Vulnerabilities and Exposures (CVE) is a list or dictionary that provides common names for publicly known vulnerabilities. It enables open and shared information without any distribution restrictions.

Technology vulnerability evaluations target weaknesses in the installed technology base of the organization, including network services, architecture, operating systems, and applications. The following basic activities are performed during a technology vulnerability evaluation:

- Identify key information technology systems and components.

- Examine systems and components for technology weaknesses.

The focus of a vulnerability evaluation of systems and components is to identify and evaluate the configuration and strength of devices on the organization network(s). The following list includes examples of tests performed during a technology vulnerability evaluation:

- Reviewing firewall configuration

- Checking the security of public Web servers

- Performing a comprehensive review of all operating systems
- Identifying services running and/or available on hosts and systems
- Listing all system user accounts
- Identifying known vulnerabilities in routers, switches, remote access servers, operating systems, and specific services and applications
- Identifying configuration errors
- Looking for existing signs of intrusion (Trojan horses, backdoor programs, integrity checks of critical system files, etc.)
- Checking file ownership and permissions
- Testing password usage and strength

Process 5: Identify Key Components

The participants in this process are the analysis team and selected members of the information technology (IT) staff. Prior to the workshop, the analysis team must ensure that documentation of the present state of the computing infrastructure is available. The network topology diagrams used by the organization's IT group to conduct its business are sufficient for this activity. The key is that the network topology information must be current. During Process 5, components to be evaluated for technology vulnerabilities are selected using these activities:

- Identify system of interest.
- Identify key classes of components.
- Identify infrastructure components to examine.

Process 6: Evaluate Selected Components

The participants in this process are the analysis team and selected members of the IT staff. A technology vulnerability evaluation supported by software tools is conducted prior to the workshop. The analysis team and IT staff review the results of the evaluation during the workshop in these activities:

- Run vulnerability evaluation tools on selected infrastructure components.
- Review technology vulnerabilities and summarize results.

After the organization completes the technology view, or Phase 2 of the evaluation, it is ready to develop a protection strategy and mitigation plans. During Phase 3 of the OCTAVE Method, the analysis team identifies the risks to its critical assets, develops a protection strategy for the organization, and develops mitigation plans for the risks to the critical assets.

Phase 3: Develop Security Strategy and Plans

Once the assets, threats, and vulnerabilities have been identified, an organization is positioned to analyze the information and to identify the information security risks. The analysis team leads the risk analysis effort. The goal is to determine how specific threats affect specific assets. A risk is essentially a threat plus the resulting impacts to the organization based on these outcomes:

- Disclosure of a critical asset (a violation of confidentiality)
- Modification of a critical asset (a violation of integrity)

- Loss or destruction of a critical asset (a violation of availability)
- Interruption of a critical asset (a violation of availability)

The analysis of risks in the OCTAVE Method is based on scenario planning. The analysis team constructs a range of risk scenarios, or a risk profile, for each critical asset. The risk profile for a critical asset comprises the threat profile for the critical asset and a narrative description of the resulting impact(s) to the organization. Because data on threat probability are limited for the scenarios, the risks are assumed to be equally likely. Thus, the analysis team establishes priorities based on the qualitative impact values assigned to the scenarios. After the risk analysis has been completed, the goal is to reduce risk through a combination of these actions:

- Implementing new security practices within the organization
- Taking the actions necessary to maintain the existing security practices
- Fixing identified vulnerabilities

Process 7: Conduct Risk Analysis

The participants in this process are the analysis team members. The goal of the process is to create a risk profile. The following are the activities of Process 7:

- Identify the impact of threats to critical assets.
- Create risk evaluation criteria.
- Evaluate the impact of threats to critical assets.

Process 8: Develop Protection Strategy

Process 8 consists of two workshops. The goal of Process 8 is to develop a protection strategy for the organization, mitigation plans for the risks to the critical assets, and an action list of near-term actions. The participants in the first workshop for Process 8 are the analysis team members and selected members of the organization. The following are the activities of the first workshop of Process 8:

- Consolidate protection strategy information.
- Create protection strategy.
- Create mitigation plans.
- Create an action list.

In the second workshop of Process 8, the analysis team presents the proposed protection strategy, mitigation plans, and action list to senior managers in the organization. The senior managers review and revise the strategy and plans as necessary and then decide how the organization will build on the results of the evaluation. The following are the activities of the second workshop of Process 8:

- Review risk information.
- Review and refine protection strategy, mitigation plans, and action list.
- Create next steps.

After the organization has developed the protection strategy and risk mitigation plans, it is ready to implement them. This completes the OCTAVE Method.

Microsoft Risk Management Approach

Microsoft has recently updated its Security Risk Management Guide, located at www.microsoft .com/technet/security/topics/complianceandpolicies/secrisk/srsgch03.mspx. The guide provides the company's approach to the risk management process. Since this version is comprehensive, easily scalable, and repeatable, it is summarized here with permission.

Microsoft asserts that risk management is not a stand-alone subject and should be part of a general governance program to allow the organizational general management community of interest to evaluate the organization's operations and make better, more informed decisions. The purpose of the risk management process is to prioritize and manage security risks. Microsoft presents four phases in its security risk management process:

- Assessing risk
- Conducting decision support
- Implementing controls
- Measuring program effectiveness

These four phases provide an overview of a program that is similar to the methods presented earlier in the text, including the OCTAVE Method. Microsoft, however, breaks the phases into fewer, more manageable pieces.

Assessing Risk

The first phase of the Microsoft Security Risk Management program is the same first step taken in both the OCTAVE Method and in Chapter 7: risk assessment—the identification and prioritization of the risks facing the organization.

- Plan data gathering. Discuss keys to success and preparation guidance.
- Gather risk data. Outline the data collection process and analysis.
- Prioritize risks. Outline prescriptive steps to qualify and quantify risks.

Conducting Decision Support

The second step is simply the identification and evaluation of controls available to the organization. Approaches used to evaluate the controls could include both the qualitative and quantitative methods discussed earlier, including cost-benefit analyses, which Microsoft stresses.

- Define functional requirements. Create the necessary requirements to mitigate risks.
- Select possible control solutions. Outline approach to identify mitigation solutions.
- Review solution. Evaluate proposed controls against functional requirements.
- Estimate risk reduction. Endeavor to understand reduced exposure or probability of risks.
- Estimate solution cost. Evaluate direct and indirect costs associated with mitigation solutions.
- Select mitigation strategy. Complete cost-benefit analysis to identify the most cost-effective mitigation solution.

Implementing Controls

The next step involves the deployments and operation of the controls selected from the cost-benefit analyses and other mitigating factors from the previous step.

- Seek holistic approach. Incorporate people, process, and technology in mitigation solution.
- Organize by defense-in-depth. Arrange mitigation solutions across the business.

Measuring Program Effectiveness

The last and first step in the rest of the program is the ongoing assessment of the effectiveness of the risk management program. As controls are used, and as the organization and its environment change and evolve, the process must be closely monitored to ensure the controls continue to provide the desired level of protection.

- Develop risk scorecard. Understand risk posture and progress.
- Measure program effectiveness. Evaluate the risk management program for opportunities to improve.

These steps are illustrated in Figure A-1.

Preliminary Tasks

Before beginning the risk management process, Microsoft suggests that the organization consider the level of effort involved, and the need to lay a good foundation. As shown in Figure A-2, while the amount of work involved in the early stages declines initially, as the organization enters the detailed risk analysis phase, the relative amount of work increases quickly, and could derail the program if the appropriate resources are not available.

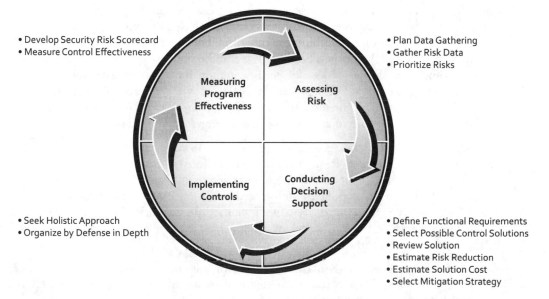

Figure A-1   Security risk management guide

Copyright © 2014 Cengage Learning®.

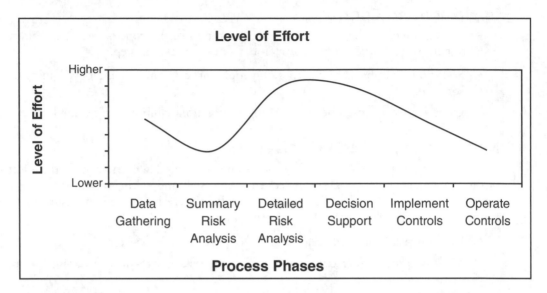

Figure A-2 Relative level of effort during the Microsoft security risk management process

Copyright © 2014 Cengage Learning®.

Laying a good foundation for risk management begins with ensuring that everyone involved knows the difference between risk management and risk assessment. This subject is discussed in Chapter 7 and earlier in this appendix. A good foundation also involves clearly communicating what risk is and what it represents to the organization. Next comes determining the organization's "risk management maturity." Microsoft uses the concept of the "well-formed risk statement" in its work, and, as illustrated in Figure A-3, this risk statement is based on both the probability and impact components of risk. While impact is based on the assets and threats facing those assets, probability in turn is based on vulnerabilities and any mitigation (or controls) the organization currently employs. From this we can derive the Microsoft definition of risk as "the probability of a vulnerability being exploited in the current environment, leading to a degree of loss of confidentiality, integrity, or availability, of an asset." Communicating the impact and probability of a risk can be accomplished using a complex metric; however, a simple method of using *high*, *moderate*, or *low* provides a more usable method. It is up to the organization's risk management team to define these.

The organization's risk management maturity level describes the experience the organization has with risk management. If an organization previously implemented a different risk management process, this points to a general understanding of risk and risk management, as well as to the existence of policies and procedures. One method the organization can use to gauge its maturity is to refer to the COBIT method described in Chapter 6. COBIT includes an IT Governance Maturity Model method, which can be used here. The COBIT model includes six levels, as shown in Table A-1.

To assess your organization's maturity, rate it on the issues presented in Table A-2, which are based on ISO 17799. Scoring each response on a scale of 0 to 5 with the COBIT levels as a guide provides a maximum score of 85.

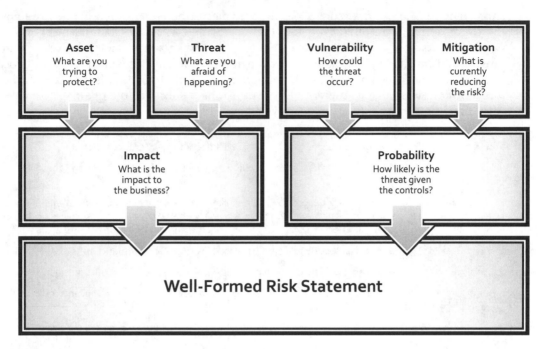

Figure A-3   The well-formed risk statement

Copyright © 2014 Cengage Learning®.

Level 0	A lack of recognizable process; no recognition that there is even an issue to be addressed exists.
Level 1 "Ad-Hoc"	Evidence that the organization has recognized issues to be addressed; no standardized processes; ad-hoc approaches are applied on an individual or case-by-case basis.
Level 2 "Repeatable"	Awareness of issues; performance indicators are being developed. Basic measurements have been identified, as have assessment methods and techniques.
Level 3 "Defined"	The need to act is understood and accepted. Procedures have been standardized, documented, and implemented. Balanced scorecard ideas are being adopted by the organization.
Level 4 "Managed"	Full understanding of issues on all levels; IT is fully aligned with the business strategy. Continuous improvement is addressed.
Level 5 "Optimized"	Continuous improvement; a forward-looking understanding of issues and solutions; processes have been refined to a level of external best practice based on the results of continuous improvement and maturity modeling with other organizations.

Table A-1   COBIT IT maturity levels

Source: Weymeir, 2004.

According to Microsoft, a score of 51 or better means the organization is ready to implement the Microsoft process. If the organization scores 34–51, it should implement the process gradually, possibly as a pilot. Below that level, an organization should be very cautious in how it implements the risk management program, but it can still benefit from the process by implementing it in a small area over a short time. SP 800-26 can also be used to help the organization determine its maturity level by creating a subset of the questions provided over the same areas as the ISO example provided in Table A-2.

Information security policies and procedures are clear, concise, well-documented, and complete.
All staff positions with job duties involving information security have been clearly articulated and their roles and responsibilities are well understood.
Policies and procedures for securing third-party access to business data are well documented. For example, remote vendors performing application development for an internal business tool have sufficient access to network resources to collaborate and complete their work effectively, but they have only the minimum amount of access that they need.
An inventory of IT assets such as hardware, software, and data repositories is accurate and up-to-date.
Suitable controls are in place to protect business data from unauthorized access by both outsiders and insiders.
Effective user awareness programs, such as training and newsletters regarding information security policies and practices, are in place.
Physical access to the computer network and other information technology assets is restricted through the use of effective controls.
New computer systems are provisioned following organizational security standards in a consistent manner using automated tools such as disk imaging or build scripts.
An effective patch management system is able to deliver software updates automatically from most vendors to the vast majority of the computer systems in the organization.
An incident response team has been created and has developed and documented effective processes for dealing with and tracking security incidents. All incidents are investigated until the root cause is identified and any problems are resolved.
The organization has a comprehensive antivirus program, including multiple layers of defense, user awareness training, and effective processes for responding to virus outbreaks.
User-provisioning processes are well documented and at least partially automated so that new employees, vendors, and partners can be granted an appropriate level of access to the organization's information systems in a timely manner. These processes should also support the timely disabling and deletion of user accounts that are no longer needed.
Computer and network access is controlled through user authentication and authorization, restrictive access control lists on data, and proactive monitoring for policy violations.
Application developers are provided with education and possess a clear awareness of security standards for software creation and quality assurance testing of code.
Business continuity and business continuity programs are clearly defined, well documented, and periodically tested through simulations and drills.
Programs have commenced and are effective for ensuring that all staff perform their work tasks in a manner compliant with legal requirements.
Third-party review and audits are used regularly to verify compliance with standard practices for security business assets.

Table A-2   Maturity level questions

Copyright © 2014 Cengage Learning®.

Roles and Responsibilities

Microsoft's next step is the definition and assignment of the roles and responsibilities of individuals who will participate in the risk management process. The primary roles that are involved include many of the same players described earlier, as shown in Table A-3.

The first step is to ensure that all participants know their roles and responsibilities in the risk management process. Even if some of these players were involved in previous efforts, the application of a different methodology requires a detailed discussion on what is expected.

To summarize, the Executive Sponsor is ultimately accountable for defining acceptable risk and provides guidance to the Security Risk Management Team in terms of ranking risks to the business. The Security Risk Management Team is responsible for assessing risk and

Title	Primary Responsibility
Executive Sponsor	Sponsors all activities associated with managing risk to the business; for example, development, funding, authority, and support for the Security Risk Management Team. This role, which is usually filled by an executive such as the chief security officer or chief information officer, also serves as the last escalation point to define acceptable risk to the business.
Business Owner	Responsible for tangible and intangible assets to the business. Business owners are also accountable for prioritizing business assets and defining levels of impact to assets. Business owners are usually accountable for defining acceptable risk levels; however, the Executive Sponsor owns the final decision, which incorporates feedback from the Information Security Group.
Information Security Group	Owns the larger risk management process, including the Assessing Risk and Measuring Program Effectiveness phases. Also defines functional security requirements and measures IT controls and the overall effectiveness of the security risk management program.
Information Technology Group	Includes IT architecture, engineering, and operations.
Security Risk Management Team	Responsible for driving the overall risk management program. Also responsible for the Assessing Risk phase and prioritizing risks to the business. At a minimum, the team is comprised of a facilitator and note taker.
Risk Assessment Facilitator	As lead role on the Security Risk Management Team, conducts the data-gathering discussions. This role may also lead the entire risk management process.
Risk Assessment Note Taker	Records detailed risk information during the data-gathering discussions.
Mitigation Owners	Responsible for implementing and sustaining control solutions to manage risk to an acceptable level. Includes the IT Group and, in some cases, Business Owners.
Security Steering Committee	Comprised of the Security Risk Management Team, representatives from the IT Group, and specific Business Owners. The Executive Sponsor usually chairs this committee. Responsible for selecting mitigation strategies and defining acceptable risk for the business.
Stakeholder	General term referring to direct and indirect participants in a given process or program; used throughout the Microsoft security risk management process. Stakeholders may also include groups outside IT, for example, finance, public relations, and human resources.

Table A-3 Primary roles and responsibilities in the Microsoft security risk management process

Copyright © 2014 Cengage Learning®.

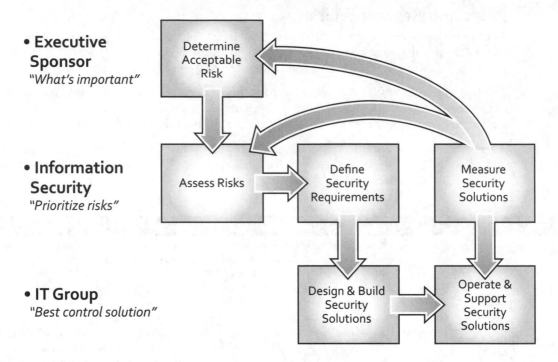

Figure A-4 Risk management roles and responsibilities

Copyright © 2014 Cengage Learning®.

defining functional requirements to mitigate risk to an acceptable level. The Security Risk Management Team then collaborates with the IT groups who own mitigation selection, implementation, and operations. The final relationship defined (in Figure A-4) is the Security Risk Management Team's oversight of measuring control effectiveness. This usually occurs in the form of audit reports, which are also communicated to the Executive Sponsor.

Figure A-4 illustrates the relationship between these individuals.

The Microsoft Risk Management process continues discussing the creation of the security risk management team and the assignment of the various roles and responsibilities. For additional information, refer to the complete document at www.microsoft.com/technet/security /topics/complianceandpolicies/secrisk/default.mspx.

Glossary

acceptance risk control strategy A conscious decision to do nothing to protect an information asset from risk, and to accept the outcome from any resulting exploitation.

access control lists (ACLs) Specifications of authorization that govern the rights and privileges of users to a particular information asset. Includes user access lists, matrices, and capability tables.

access control policy A security policy that specifies how access rights are granted to entities and groups.

access controls System components that regulate the admission of users into trusted areas of the organization, both logical access to information systems and physical access to the organization's facilities. Access control is maintained by means of a collection of policies, programs to carry out those policies, and technologies that enforce policies.

accountability The assurance that every activity undertaken can be attributed to a known entity, whether a named person or an automated process.

accreditation The authorization by an oversight authority of an IT system to process, store, or transmit information.

affidavit Sworn testimony that certain facts are in the possession of the investigating officer that the officer believes warrant the examination of specific items located at a specific place. The facts, the items, and the place must be specified in this document.

after-action review (AAR) A detailed examination by CSIRT team members and key players in the IR process of the events that occurred, from first detection to final recovery.

agent In IDPS, a piece of software that resides on a system and reports back to a management server.

alert message A scripted description of the incident that consists of just enough information so that each responder, CSIRT or otherwise, knows what portion of the IR plan to implement without impeding the notification process.

alert roster A document containing contact information on the individuals to be notified in the event of an actual incident.

Annualized Loss Expectancy (ALE) A comparative estimate of the losses from successful attacks on an asset over one year.

anomaly-based IDPS An IDPS method that first collects data from normal traffic and establishes a baseline, then periodically samples network activity, using statistical methods, compares the samples to the baseline, and notifies the administrator when the activity falls outside the clipping level.

application-level firewalls Firewalls that often consist of dedicated computers kept separate from the first filtering router (called an "edge router"); commonly used in conjunction with proxy servers.

asset valuation A process of assigning financial value or worth to each information asset.

asymmetric encryption An encryption method that uses two different keys, either of which can be used to encrypt or decrypt a message, but not both. Thus, if a private (secret) key is used to encrypt a message, only the public key can be used to decrypt it, and vice versa.

asynchronous tokens A category of access control tokens that use a challenge-response system in which the server challenges the user with a number, which the user enters into his or her token and then returns a generated value.

attack An act or event that exploits a vulnerability seeking to cause a loss to an information asset.

auditing The process of reviewing the information collected in and about systems in order to detect misuse or attempted intrusion; includes information collected in logs.

authentication The process of validating a supplicant's purported identity, thus ensuring that the entity requesting access is the entity it claims to be.

authorization A process that determines if a user (whether a person or a computer) has been specifically and explicitly authorized by the proper authority to perform a function, such as access, modify, or delete the contents of an information asset.

availability A state in which users have access to information in a usable format, without interference or obstruction.

avoidance *See* "defense risk control strategy."

baseline An assessment of the performance of some action or process measured against a prior assessment or an internal goal.

baselining A process of measuring some action or process against established internal values or standard.

bastion host In screened-host firewalls, a separate application proxy that examines an application-layer protocol, such as HTTP, and performs the proxy services, thus representing a single, rich target for external attacks and that should, therefore, be very thoroughly secured.

behavior-based IDPS *See* "anomaly-based IDPS."

Bell-LaPadula (BLP)confidentiality model A confidentiality model or "state machine reference model" that ensures the confidentiality of the modeled system by using MACs, data classification, and security clearances.

benchmarking Using the recommended or existing practices of a similar organization or using an industry-developed standard.

benefit The value to the organization of using controls to prevent losses associated with a specific vulnerability.

best security practices (BSPs) Those security efforts that are considered among the best in the industry.

Biba integrity model A confidentiality model or "state machine reference model" that is similar to BLP and based on the premise that higher levels of integrity are more worthy of trust than lower ones.

blueprint In information security, a specification of a model to be followed in the creation of the design, selection, and initial and ongoing implementation of all subsequent security controls, including InfoSec policies, security education and training programs, and technological controls.

book cipher An encryption method in which the words (or, in some cases, characters) found in a book act as the algorithm to decrypt a message. The key relies on two components: (1) knowing which book to refer to and (2) having a list of codes representing the page number, line number, and word number of the plaintext word.

bottom-up approach An implementation approach that uses grass-roots effort in which systems administrators attempt to improve the security of their systems.

business continuity plan (BC plan) A detailed set of processes and procedures that ensure that critical business functions can continue if a disaster occurs, usually by establishing operations at an alternate site.

business continuity planning (BCP) The actions taken to ensure that critical business functions can continue if a disaster occurs, usually by establishing operations at an alternate site.

business continuity team The team that manages and executes the BC plan by setting up and starting off-site operations in the event of an incident or disaster.

business impact analysis (BIA) The first phase of the CP process and a crucial component of the initial planning stages, the BIA serves as an investigation and assessment of the impact that various adverse events can have on the organization.

business process A task performed by an organization or organizational subunit in support of the overall organization's mission.

business resumption plan (BR plan) A set of plans and procedures combining the DR and BC functions, which is preferred by some organizations.

C.I.A. triangle A long-standing industry standard for computer security that focuses on three critical characteristics of information: confidentiality, integrity, and availability.

cache server A proxy server or application-level firewall that exists to store the most recently accessed Web content in its internal caches, minimizing the demand on proxy and internal servers.

capabilities table In a lattice-based access control, the row of attributes associated with a particular subject (such as a user).

certificate authority (CA) An agency that manages the issuance of certificates and serves as the electronic notary public to verify their origin and integrity.

certification A comprehensive assessment of both technical and nontechnical protection strategies for a particular system, as specified by a particular set of requirements.

chain of custody *See* "chain of evidence."

chain of evidence The detailed documentation of the collection, storage, transfer, and ownership of collected evidence from a crime scene through its presentation in court.

champion A member of the senior management of an organization who seeks to promote the successful outcome of a project or initiative by providing visibility, prestige, or resources.

chief information officer (CIO) The most senior manager or executive responsible for information technology and systems in an organization.

chief information security officer (CISO) The most senior manager or executive responsible for information security in an organization.

chief security officer (CSO) The most senior manager or executive responsible for physical and information security in an organization; sometimes misapplied to a functional CISO to follow industry trend.

ciphertext In cryptography, the result of encrypting plaintext.

civil law Laws pertaining to relationships between and among individuals and organizations.

cold site A facility used for BC operations that provides only rudimentary services and facilities, with no computer hardware or peripherals.

Common Criteria (CC) *See* "Common Criteria for Information Technology Security Evaluation."

Common Criteria for Information Technology Security Evaluation Also known as the "Common criteria" (CC), an international standard (ISO/IEC 15408) for computer security certification. It is widely considered the successor to both TCSEC and ITSEC in that it reconciles some of the differences between the various other standards.

communications security A specialized area of security that encompasses protecting the organization's communications media, technology, and content as well as its ability to use these tools to achieve the organization's objectives.

compartmentalization The use of specialty classification schemes, such as "Need-to-Know" and "Named Projects," to allow access to information only by individuals who need the information to perform their work; commonly used in federal agencies.

competitive disadvantage A state of falling behind the competition.

Computer Fraud and Abuse (CFA) Act The cornerstone of many computer-related federal laws and enforcement efforts, the CFA formally criminalizes "accessing a computer without authorization or exceeding authorized access" for systems containing information of national interest as determined by the U.S. federal government.

Computer Security Act (CSA) One of the first attempts to protect federal computer systems by establishing minimum acceptable security practices, the CSA is a U.S. federal Law that charges the National Bureau of Standards, now NIST, with the development of standards, guidelines, and associated methods and techniques for computer systems, among other responsibilities.

computer security incident response team (CSIRT) A subset of the IR team composed of technical and managerial IT and InfoSec professionals prepared to diagnose and respond to an incident.

confidentiality The characteristic of information whereby only those with sufficient privileges and a demonstrated need may access it.

content filter A software program or a hardware/software appliance that allows administrators to restrict content that comes into a network—for example, restricting access to Web sites with nonbusiness-related material, such as pornography or entertainment.

contingency planning (CP) The overall process of preparing for unexpected adverse events.

contingency planning management team (CPMT) The management team consisting of coordinating executive, representatives from major business and representatives from other teams that is responsible for collecting information about the organization and about the threats it faces, conducting the BIA, and coordinating the development of contingency plans.

controlling In project management, a process of monitoring progress toward completion and making necessary adjustments to achieve desired objectives.

controls Those means undertaken to reduce the risk that information assets face from attacks by threats. Also known as safeguards.

Cost Benefit Analysis (CBA) A form of feasibility study that compares the life-cycle cost of implementing a control mechanism against the estimated economic benefit that would accrue from the implementation of the control.

cost The resources needed to implement a control, whether money, time, fixed assets, or organizational focus.

covert channels Unauthorized or unintended methods of communications hidden inside a computer system.

criminal law Laws that address violations harmful to society, actively enforced and prosecuted by the state.

crisis management (CM) The steps taken during and after a disaster that affect the people inside and outside the organization.

crisis management team (CMT) The individuals from various functional areas of the organization who are tasked with the development and implementation of the CM plan.

Critical Path Method (CPM) A diagram-based planning process that focuses on the duration of the sequence of tasks, any of which, if delayed, will cause delay to the entire project.

critical path The sequence of events or activities that requires the longest duration to complete and that therefore cannot be delayed without delaying the entire project.

Crossover Error Rate (CER) Also called the "equal error rate," this is the point at which the rate of false rejections equals the rate of false acceptances.

cryptanalysis The process of deciphering the original message from an encrypted message without knowing the algorithms and keys used to perform the encryption.

cryptography The set of processes involved in encoding and decoding messages so that others cannot understand them.

cryptology The science of encryption and a very complex field based on advanced mathematical concepts.

data custodians Individuals who work directly with data owners and are responsible for the storage, maintenance, and protection of the information.

data owners Individuals who control (and are therefore responsible for) the security and use of a particular set of information. Data owners may rely on custodians for the practical aspects of protecting their information, specifying which users are authorized to access it, but they are ultimately responsible for it.

data users Systems users who work with the information to perform their daily jobs supporting the mission of the organization, everyone in the organization being responsible for the security of data (and thus playing an InfoSec role).

database shadowing The combination of electronic vaulting with remote journaling in which multiple copies of the database are written simultaneously to two separate locations.

decisional role A managerial role in which the manager must select from among alternative approaches and resolve conflicts, dilemmas, or challenges.

defense risk control strategy A mechanism to control risk by the prevention of an exploitation of a vulnerability.

demilitarized zone (DMZ) An intermediate area between a trusted network and an untrusted network, thereby restricting access to internal systems.

desk check The CP testing strategy in which copies of the appropriate plans are distributed to all individuals who will be assigned roles during an actual incident or disaster, with each individual reviewing the plan and creating a list of correct and incorrect components.

Diffie-Hellman key exchange method A methodology invented to enable the exchange of private keys over a non-secure channel without exposure to any third parties, using asymmetric encryption.

digital certificate A block of data, similar to a digital signature, that is attached to a file to certify that the file is from the organization it claims to be from and has not been modified from the original format.

digital forensics Investigations involving the preservation, identification, extraction, documentation, and interpretation of computer media for evidentiary and/or root cause analysis. Like traditional forensics, digital forensics follows clear, well-defined methodologies but still tends to be as much art as science.

digital malfeasance A crime against or using digital media, computer technology, or related components (computer as source or object of crime).

digital signature A process of using a reversed asymmetric encryption process in which a private key is used to encrypt a (usually short) message and the corresponding public key is used to decrypt it to provide nonrepudiation, thus creating encrypted messages whose authenticity can be independently verified by a central facility (registry).

disaster recovery plan (DR plan) A detailed set of processes and procedures that prepare for and help recover from the effects of disasters.

disaster recovery planning (DRP) The preparation for and recovery from a disaster, whether natural or human made.

disaster recovery team The team that manages and executes the DR plan by detecting, evaluating, and responding to disasters and by reestablishing operations at the primary business site.

discretionary access controls (DACs) Access controls implemented at the discretion or option of the data user.

dual-homed host A firewall configuration in which the bastion host contains two network interfaces: one that is connected to the external network and one that is connected to the internal network. All traffic must go through the firewall to move between the internal and external networks.

due care See "standard of due care."

due diligence See "standard of due diligence."

dumb card A category of access control token that includes ID and ATM cards with magnetic strips that contain the digital (and often encrypted) PIN against which user input is compared.

dumpster diving The retrieval of information from refuse or recycling bins.

dynamic packet filtering firewalls A class of firewalls that allow only a particular packet with a specific source, destination, and port address to pass through the firewall by understanding how the protocol functions and by opening and closing "doors" in the firewall based on the information contained in the packet header.

E-discovery The identification and preservation of evidentiary material related to a specific legal action.

Electronic Communications Privacy Act (ECPA) A collection of statutes that regulate the interception of wire, electronic, and oral communications. These statutes are frequently referred to as the "federal wiretapping acts."

electronic vaulting The bulk batch-transfer of data to an off-site facility, usually conducted via leased lines or secure Internet connections.

encryption The process of converting an original message into a form that cannot be used by unauthorized individuals.

enterprise information security policy (EISP) The high-level information security policy (also known as a "security program policy," "general security policy," "IT security policy," "high-level InfoSec policy," or simply "InfoSec policy") that sets the strategic direction, scope, and tone for all of an organization's security efforts.

ethical hackers See "white-hat hackers."

event-driven Refers to a corrective action that is in response to some event in the business community, inside the organization, or within the ranks of employees, customers, or other stakeholders.

evidentiary material (EM) Also known as "items of potential evidentiary value," any information that could potentially support the organization's legal-based or policy-based case against a suspect.

false accept rate The rate at which fraudulent users or nonusers are allowed access to systems or areas as a result of a failure in the biometric device. This failure is also known as a "Type II error" or a "false positive."

false reject rate The rate at which authentic users are denied or prevented access to authorized areas as a result of a failure in the biometric device. This failure is also known as a "Type I error" or a "false negative."

fingerprinting The next phase of the preattack data-gathering process that entails the systematic examination of all the organization's Internet addresses collected during the footprinting phase.

first-generation firewall *See* "packet filtering firewalls."

footprint In wireless networking, the geographic area within which there is sufficient signal strength to make a network connection.

footprinting The organized research of the Internet addresses owned or controlled by a target organization.

forensics The coherent application of methodical investigatory techniques to present evidence of crimes in a court or court-like setting. Forensics allows investigators to determine what happened by examining the results of an event—criminal, natural, intentional, or accidental.

fourth-generation firewall *See* "dynamic packet filtering firewalls."

framework In information security, the outline version of the more thorough blueprint.

full-interruption testing The CP testing strategy in which the individuals follow each and every IR/DR/BC procedure, including the interruption of service, restoration of data from backups, and notification of appropriate individuals.

general business community The community of interest within an organization that primarily seeks to articulate and communicate organizational policy and objectives and allocates resources to the other groups.

governance, risk management, and compliance (GRC) A process seeking to integrate the three, previously separate responsibilities into one holistic approach that can provide sound executive-level strategic planning and management of the InfoSec function.

guidelines Non-mandatory recommendations that the employee may use as a reference in complying with a policy. If the policy states "Use strong passwords, frequently changed," the guidelines should advise "We recommend you don't use family or pet names, parts of your Social Security number, your employee number, or your phone number in your password."

Health Insurance Portability and Accountability Act (HIPAA) Also known as the Kennedy-Kassebaum Act, this law attempts to protect the confidentiality and security of health care data by establishing and enforcing standards and by standardizing electronic data interchange.

honey pot *See* "trap and trace applications."

host-based IDPS (HIDPS) An IDPS that works by configuring and classifying various categories of systems and data files on predefined computer systems upon which it resides.

hot site A fully configured computer facility used for BC operations, with all services, communications links, and physical plant operations.

hybrid encryption system The use of asymmetric encryption to exchange symmetric keys so that two (or more) organizations can conduct quick, efficient, secure communications based on symmetric encryption.

identification A mechanism that provides information about a supplicant that wants to be granted access to a known entity.

incident candidate An adverse event that constitutes a possible incident.

incident classification The process of examining a possible incident or incident candidate and determining if it constitutes an actual incident.

incident response (IR) A set of procedures that commence when an incident is detected. IR must be carefully planned and coordinated because organizations heavily depend on the quick and efficient containment and resolution of incidents.

incident response plan (IR plan) A detailed set of processes and procedures that anticipate, detect, and mitigate the effects of an unexpected event that might compromise information resources and assets.

incident response planning (IRP) The preparation for an unexpected event that might compromise information resources and assets.

incident response team The team that manages and executes the IR plan by detecting, evaluating, and responding to incidents.

information security (InfoSec) The protection of information and its critical characteristics (confidentiality, integrity, and availability), including the systems and hardware that use, store, and transmit that information, through the application of policy, training and awareness programs, and technology.

information security community The community of interest within an organization that primarily seeks to protect the organization's information assets from the many threats they face.

information security policies Written instructions, provided by management, to inform employees and others in the workplace of the proper behavior regarding the use of information and information assets.

information security program An effort by an organization to contain the risks to its information assets.

information technology community The community of interest within an organization that primarily seeks to support the business objectives of the organization by supplying and supporting IT that is appropriate to the organization's needs.

Information Technology System Evaluation Criteria (ITSEC) An international set of criteria for evaluating computer systems, very similar to TCSEC.

informational role A managerial role in which the manager collects, processes, and uses information that can affect the completion of the objective.

InfoSec performance management A process of designing, implementing, and managing the use of specific measurements to determine the effectiveness of the overall security program.

InfraGard A U.S. group (sponsored by the FBI) made up of law enforcement and technology professionals that is working to establish a more effective method for protecting critical national information resources.

integrity A quality or state of being whole, complete, and uncorrupted.

interpersonal role A managerial role in which the manager interacts with superiors, subordinates, outside stakeholders, and other parties who influence or are influenced by the completion of a task.

intrusion detection and prevention system (IDPS) Specialized hardware and/or software that works like burglar alarms by detecting a violation, activating an alarm, and, under certain circumstances, reacting to the intrusion; combines features of an intrusion detection system and an intrusion prevention system.

IP Security (IPSec) The primary and now dominant cryptographic authentication and encryption product of the IETF's IP Protocol Security Working Group. A framework for security development within the TCP/IP family of protocol standards, IPSec provides application support for all uses within TCP/IP, including VPNs.

issue-specific security policy (ISSP) An organizational policy that provides detailed, targeted guidance to all members of the organization in the use of a resource, such as a process or a technology employed by the organization.

joint application design (JAD) A process in which designers, developers, and planners work with key end-users to formulate and/or assess design specifications for system implementation or improvement.

jurisdiction A court's right to hear a case. Under the U.S. legal system, any court can impose its authority if the act was committed in its territory or involve its citizenry.

Kerberos An authentication system based on encryption that uses symmetric key encryption to validate an individual user's access to various network resources by keeping a database containing the private keys of clients and servers that are in the authentication domain it supervises.

knowledge-based IDPS *See* "signature-based IDPS."

lattice-based access control A variation on the MAC form of access control that assigns users a matrix of authorizations for particular areas of access.

laws Rules that have been adopted and are enforced by a sovereign authority to codify expected behavior in modern society.

leadership A manager characteristic in which the manager encourages the implementation of the planning and organizing functions. It includes supervising employee behavior, performance, attendance, and attitude while ensuring completion of the assigned tasks, goals, and objectives.

least privilege The data access principle by which members of the organization can access the minimum amount of information for the minimum amount of time necessary to perform their required duties. Implies a need-to-know.

liability The obligation that may result from legal action.

likelihood The overall rating—a numerical value on a defined scale—of the probability that a specific vulnerability will be exploited.

long-arm jurisdiction Jurisdiction that enables the "long arm of the law" to reach across the country or around the world to bring the accused into its court systems.

management The process of achieving objectives using a given set of resources.

managerial controls Processes or tools that define, communicate, and enforce management's intent for the management of the security processes for information assets.

mandatory access control (MAC) A required structured data classification scheme that rates each collection of information as well as each user. These ratings are often referred to as sensitivity or classification levels.

mandatory vacation policy A common organizational policy that requires employees to take a vacation of at least one week per year to enable the organization to perform a detailed review of the employee's work and work area.

Maximum Tolerable Downtime (MTD) The total amount of time the system owner/authorizing official is willing to accept for a mission/business process outage or disruption and includes all impact considerations.

methodology A formal approach to solving a problem based on a structured sequence of procedures.

metrics *See* "performance measurements."

mitigation risk control strategy An approach to control risk by attempting to reduce the impact of the loss caused by a realized incident, disaster, or attack by means of planning and preparation.

monoalphabetic substitution A substitution cipher that uses only one alphabet.

mutual agreement A contract between two organizations in which each party agrees to assist the other in the event of a disaster by providing the necessary BC facilities, resources, and services until the receiving organization is able to recover from the disaster.

need-to-know The principle of limiting a user's access to the specific information required to perform the currently assigned task, not to the category of data required for a general work function.

network security A specialized area of security that encompasses protecting the organization's data networking devices, connections, and contents as well as protecting the ability to use that network to accomplish the organization's data communication functions.

network-address translation (NAT) A technology often implemented with dual-homed hosts in which multiple real, routable external IP addresses are converted to special ranges of internal IP addresses, usually on a one-to-one basis; that is, one external valid address directly maps to one assigned internal address.

network-based IDPS (NIDPS) An IDPS that monitors network traffic, looking for patterns of network traffic, such as large collections of related traffic that can indicate a DoS attack or a series of related packets that could indicate a port scan in progress.

nondiscretionary controls Access controls determined by a central authority in the organization that can be based on roles or tasks.

nonrepudiation The use of cryptographic tools to assure that parties to the transaction are authentic, so that they cannot later deny having participated in a transaction.

operational controls Processes or tools that deal with the operational functionality of security in the organization. They cover management functions and lower-level planning, such as disaster recovery and incident response planning.

operations security A specialized area of security that encompasses protecting the organization's ability to carry out its operational activities without interruption or compromise.

organizing The management function dedicated to the structuring of resources to support the accomplishment of objectives.

packet filtering firewalls Simple networking devices that filter packets by examining every incoming and outgoing packet header, accepting or rejecting packets as needed.

packet filtering routers A router that can be configured to block packets that the organization does not allow into the network, thus acting as a packet filtering firewall.

packet sniffer A network tool that collects and analyzes copies of packets from the network.

parallel testing The CP testing strategy in which individuals act as if an actual incident or disaster occurred and begin performing their required tasks and executing the necessary

procedures, without interfering with the normal operations of the business.

passphrase A plain-language phrase, typically longer than a password, from which a virtual password is derived.

password A secret word or combination of characters that only the user should know; used to authenticate the user.

penetration testing A process in which security personnel simulate or perform specific and controlled attacks to compromise or disrupt systems by exploiting documented vulnerabilities.

performance measurements Data or the trends in data that may indicate the effectiveness of security countermeasures or controls—technical and managerial—as implemented in the organization.

permutation cipher *See* "transposition cipher."

physical security A specialized area of security that encompasses protecting people, physical assets, and the workplace from various threats, including fire, unauthorized access, and natural disasters.

plaintext In cryptography, the original unencrypted message.

plan-driven Refers to a corrective action that is the result of a carefully developed planning strategy.

planning The process of developing, creating, and implementing strategies for the accomplishment of objectives.

polyalphabetic substitution A substitution cipher that uses more than one alphabet.

port scanners A group of utility software applications that can identify (or fingerprint) computers that are active on a network as well as the active ports and services on those computers, the functions and roles fulfilled by the machines, and other useful information.

port-address translation (PAT) A technology often implemented with dual-homed hosts in which multiple real, routable external IP addresses are converted to special ranges of internal IP addresses, usually on a one-to-many basis; that is, one external valid address is mapped dynamically to a range of internal addresses by adding a unique port number when traffic leaves the private network and is placed on the public network.

practices Example or sample actions illustrating compliance with policies. If the policy states "Use strong passwords, frequently changed," the practices would advise "According to X, most organizations require employees to change passwords at least semi-annually."

privacy A state in which information is used only in ways approved by the person who provided it.

private key encryption *See* "symmetric encryption."

private law Laws that regulate the relationships among individuals and among individuals and organizations; it encompasses family law, commercial law, and labor law.

procedures Step-by-step instructions designed to assist employees in following policies, standards, and guidelines. If the policy states "Use strong passwords, frequently changed," the procedures would advise "In order to change your passwords, first click on the Windows Start button, then…"

Program Evaluation and Review Technique (PERT) A project task-scheduling approach that was developed in the late 1950s to meet the needs of the rapidly expanding engineering projects associated with government acquisitions such as weapons systems. A PERT diagram depicts a number of events followed by key activities and their durations.

programs In information security, activities performed within the organization to improve security; they include security education, training, and awareness programs.

project management A process for identifying and controlling the resources applied to the project as well as measuring progress and adjusting the process as progress is made toward its goal.

proxy server A firewall or router that handles requests from external users made to internal services, thus preventing the internal server from being directly exposed to the outside network.

public key encryption *See* "asymmetric encryption."

public key infrastructure (PKI) The entire set of hardware, software, and cryptosystems necessary to implement public key encryption.

public law Laws that regulate the structure and administration of government agencies and their relationships with citizens, employees, and other governments. Public law includes criminal, administrative, and constitutional law.

qualitative risk assessment Risk assessment performed using categories instead of specific values to determine risk.

rapid-onset disasters Disasters that occur suddenly, with little warning, taking the lives of people and destroying the means of production. Examples include earthquakes, floods, storm winds, tornadoes, or mud flows.

recommended business practices Those security efforts that seek to provide a superior level of performance in the protection of information.

recovery point objective (RPO) The point in time, prior to a disruption or system outage, to which mission/business process data can be recovered (given the most recent backup copy of the data) after an outage.

recovery time objective (RTO) The maximum amount of time that a system resource can remain unavailable before there is an unacceptable impact on other system resources, supported mission/business processes, and the MTD.

red teams *See* "white-hat hackers."

reference monitor Within TCB, a conceptual piece of the system that manages access controls—in other words, it mediates all access to objects by subjects.

Remote Authentication Dial-In User Service (RADIUS) An authentication system that centralizes the management of user authentication by placing the responsibility for authenticating each user on a central RADIUS server.

remote journaling The transfer of live transactions to an off-site facility in which only transactions are transferred and the transfer takes place online and in real time or near real time.

residual risk The risk that remains even after the existing control has been applied.

restitution The legal obligation to make payment or compensation for a wrong.

risk analysis The identification and assessment of levels of risk in the organization; it is a major component of risk management.

risk appetite The quantity and nature of risk that organizations are willing to accept as they evaluate the trade-offs between perfect security and unlimited accessibility.

risk assessment A process that assigns a comparative risk rating or score to each specific information asset. This enables the organization to gauge the relative risk introduced by each vulnerable information asset and allows comparative ratings later in the risk control process.

risk assessment The determination of a relative risk rating or score for each vulnerability in the organization; a major component of risk management.

risk identification The process of discovering the risks to an organization's operations; a major component of risk management.

risk management A process that identifies vulnerabilities in an organization's information system and takes carefully reasoned steps to assure the confidentiality, integrity, and availability of all components in the organization's information system.

risk management The process of discovering and assessing the risks to an organization's operations and determining how those risks can be controlled or mitigated.

risk tolerance *See* risk appetite.

role-based access controls (RBACs) nondiscretionary controls assigned based on an individual's role or position in the organization. Assignment tends to be longer term than task-based controls.

rolling mobile site A specialized BC facility configured in the payload area of a tractor/trailer; or externally stored resources, such as a rental storage area containing duplicate or older equipment.

running key cipher *See* "book cipher."

sacrificial host *See* "bastion host."

safeguards *See* "controls."

scope creep A state that occurs when the quantity or quality of project deliverables is expanded from the original project plan.

screened-host firewall A firewall architectural model that combines the packet filtering router with a separate, dedicated firewall such as an application proxy server.

screened-subnet firewall A firewall architectural model that consists of one or more internal bastion hosts located behind a packet filtering router, with each host protecting the trusted network.

search warrant Permission to search for evidentiary material at a specified location and/or to seize items to return to the investigator's lab for examination. An affidavit becomes a search warrant when signed by an approving authority.

second-generation firewall *See* "application-level firewalls."

secret key In encryption, a set of encryption bits used to encrypt and/or decrypt a message, depending on the encryption process.

Secure Electronic Transactions (SET) A cryptographic method used to provide protection from electronic payment fraud. It works by encrypting the credit card transfers with DES for encryption and RSA for key exchange.

Secure Hypertext Transfer Protocol (SHTTP) An encrypted solution to the unsecured version of HTTP.

Secure Shell (SSH) A cryptographic method to provide security for remote access connections over public networks by creating a secure and persistent connection.

Secure Sockets Layer (SSL) A cryptographic method used to provide security for online e-commerce transactions. It uses a number of algorithms but mainly relies on RSA for key transfer and IDEA, DES, or 3DES for encrypted symmetric key-based data transfer.

security clearance The personnel security structure, in which each user of an information asset is assigned an authorization level that identifies the level of information classification he or she is "cleared" to access.

security education, training, and awareness (SETA) A program under the responsibility of the CISO that is designed to reduce the incidence of security breaches by communicating policy to employees, contractors, consultants, vendors, and business partners who come into contact with its information assets and keeping them continually alert to these policy requirements.

security event information management (SEIM) systems Log management systems specifically tasked to collect log data from a number of servers or other network devices for the purpose of interpreting, filtering, correlating, analyzing, storing, and reporting the data.

security manager A supervisory-level member of an organization accountable for some or all of the day-to-day operation of an InfoSec program.

security model A generic blueprint offered by a service organization.

security technician A technically qualified individual who may configure firewalls and IDPSs, implement security software, diagnose and troubleshoot problems, and coordinate with systems and network administrators to ensure that security technical controls are properly implemented.

sensor *See* "agent."

separation of duties The information security principle that requires significant tasks to be split up in such a way as to require more than one individual for completion.

service bureau A service agency that provides a BC facility as a service for a fee.

signature-based IDPS An IDPS method that examines data traffic for something that matches the signatures, which comprise preconfigured, predetermined attack patterns.

simulation The CP testing strategy in which each person works individually, rather than in a group setting, to simulate the performance of each task they would perform during a CP event.

single loss expectancy (SLE) The calculated value associated with the most likely loss from a single occurrence of a specific attack.

slack time The difference between the time needed to complete the critical path and the time needed to arrive at completion using any other path. Also, the amount of time allowed for task to be completed minus the time it would take to do the task.

slow-onset disasters Disasters that occur over time and gradually degrade the capacity of an organization to withstand their effects. Examples include droughts, famines, environmental degradation, desertification, deforestation, and pest infestation.

smart card A category of access control tokens containing a computer chip that can verify and validate information in addition to PINs.

socket In networking, the combination of a network address and application port number; also used in PAT.

stakeholder Those entities, whether people or organizations, that have a "stake" or vested interest in a particular aspect of the planning or operation of an organization.

standard of due care A means of assessing planned actions by considering what would be reasonable if done by another similar and prudent organization in similar circumstances.

standard of due diligence A requirement that implemented standards continue to be applied to provide the required level of protection.

standard A detailed statement of what must be done to comply with policy, sometimes viewed as the rules governing policy compliance. If the policy states "Use strong passwords, frequently changed," the standard would specify "There must be at least 8 characters, with at least one number, one letter, and one special character."

state table In third-generation firewalls, a table or function that tracks the state and context of each exchanged packet by recording which station sent which packet and when.

stateful inspection firewalls A type of firewall that keeps track of each network connection established between internal and external systems using a state table.

statistical anomaly-based IDPS *See* "anomaly-based IDPS."

storage channels A TCSEC-defined covert channel that communicates by modifying a stored object—for example, in steganography.

strategic planning A process to lay out the long-term direction to be taken by an organization to guide organizational efforts and focus resources toward specific, clearly defined goals in the midst of an ever-changing environment.

strong authentication The incorporation of at least two different authentication mechanisms (usually something you have and something you know).

structured review A process during which a project design team and its management-level reviewers decide whether a project should be continued, discontinued, outsourced, or postponed until additional expertise or organizational knowledge is acquired.

structured walk-through The CP testing strategy in which all involved individuals walk through and discuss the steps they would take during an actual CP event, either as an actual on-site walk-through or as more of a conference room talk-through or chalk talk.

substitution cipher An encryption operation in which one value is substituted or exchanged for another.

supplicant An unverified entity that wants to be granted access to a known entity by requesting identification.

symmetric encryption An encryption method in which the same algorithm and secret key is used to both encipher and decipher the message.

synchronous tokens A category of access control token that is synchronized with a server. Each device (server and token) uses that synchronized time to generate an authentication value that is entered by the user and then compared to the server's value to enable the user login.

system-specific security policies (SysSPs) Organizational policies that often function as standards or procedures to be used when configuring or maintaining systems. SysSPs can be separated into two general groups, managerial guidance and technical specifications, or they may be combined into a single unified SysSP document.

systems logs Records maintained by a particular system that has been configured to record specific information, such as failed access attempts and systems modifications.

task-based controls Nondiscretionary controls assigned based on an individual's task, assignment, or responsibility in the organization. Assignment tends to be shorter term than role-based controls.

technical controls Means by which technical approaches are used to implement security in the organization.

Terminal Access Controller Access Control System (TACACS) Commonly used in UNIX systems, a remote access authorization system based on a client/server configuration that makes use of a centralized data service in order to validate the user's credentials at the TACACS server.

termination risk control strategy A choice not to protect an asset and the removal of it from the environment that represents risk.

third-generation firewalls *See* "stateful inspection firewalls."

threat agent A specific instance of a threat.

threat An entity with the potential to damage or steal an organization's information or physical assets.

tiger teams *See* "white-hat hackers."

timeshare A facility that operates like a hot, warm, or cold site but is leased in conjunction with a business partner or sister organization, designed to allow the organization to provide a BC option while reducing its overall costs.

timing channels A TCSEC-defined covert channel that communicates by managing the relative timing of events—for example, in a system that places a long pause between packets to signify a 1 and a short pause between packets to signify a 0.

top-down approach A security approach in which upper-management directs actions and provides support and in which high-level managers provide resources; give direction; issue policies, procedures, and processes; dictate the goals and expected outcomes of the project; and determine who is accountable for each of the required actions.

tort law A subset of civil law that allows individuals to seek redress in the event of personal, physical, or financial injury. Tort law is pursued in civil court and is not prosecuted by the state.

transferal risk control strategy A mechanism to control risk by attempting to shift the risk to other assets, other processes, or other organizations.

transport mode In IPSec, an encryption method in which only a packet's IP data is encrypted, not the IP headers themselves, allowing intermediate nodes to read the source and destination addresses.

transposition cipher An encryption operation in which values within a predefined block are rearranged to create the ciphertext.

trap and trace applications Applications that entice individuals who are illegally perusing the internal areas of a network by providing simulated rich content areas but distract the attacker while the software notifies the administrator of the intrusion. Some are capable of tracking the attacker back through the network.

Trusted Computer System Evaluation Criteria (TCSEC) An older DoD system certification and accreditation standard that defines the criteria for assessing the access controls in a computer system; also known as the rainbow series due to the color coding of the individual documents that made up the criteria.

trusted computing base (TCB) Under TCSEC, the combination of all hardware, firmware, and software responsible for enforcing the security policy.

trusted network In networking, the network on the inside or internal connection of a firewall—for example, the organization's network.

tunnel mode In IPSec, an encryption method in which the entire IP packet is encrypted and inserted as the payload in another IP packet. This requires other systems at the beginning and end of the tunnel to act as proxies to send and receive the encrypted packets and then transmit the packets to their ultimate destination.

Unified Threat Management (UTM) Networking devices categorized by their ability to perform the work of a stateful inspection firewall, network intrusion detection and prevention system, content filter, and spam filter, as well as a malware scanner and filter.

untrusted network In networking, the network on the outside or external connection of a firewall—for example, the Internet.

Vernam cipher Developed at AT&T and also known as the "one-time pad," this cipher uses a set of characters for encryption operations only one time and then discards it.

virtual password The derivative of a passphrase. *See also* "passphrase."

virtual private network (VPN) A private, secure network operated over a public and insecure network, which keeps the contents of the network messages hidden from observers who may have access to public traffic.

vulnerability assessment A process of evaluating possible vulnerabilities in order to distinguish actual weaknesses from false reports.

vulnerability scanners Variants of port scanners, capable of scanning networks for very detailed information, including exposed user names and groups, showing open network shares, and revealing configuration problems and other server vulnerabilities.

vulnerability An identified weakness of a controlled information asset resulting from absent or inadequate controls.

war driving An attacker technique of moving through a geographic area or building, actively scanning for open or unsecured WAPs.

war-dialer An automatic phone-dialing program that dials every number in a configured range (e.g., 555–1000 to 555–2000) and checks whether a person, answering machine, or modem picks up.

warm site A facility used for BC operations that provides many of the same services and options as a hot site, but typically without installed and configured software applications.

white-hat hackers Persons given authority to engage in penetration testing in order to discover systems weakness that can be controlled to improve security. Also known as "ethical hackers," "tiger teams," or "red teams."

Wi-Fi Protected Access (WPA) A set of protocols used to secure wireless networks; created by the Wi-Fi Alliance. Includes WPA and WPA2.

Wired Equivalent Privacy (WEP) Part of the IEEE 802.11 wireless networking standard, a set of protocols designed to provide a basic level of security protection to wireless networks, to prevent unauthorized access or eavesdropping.

wireless access point (WAP) A device used to connect wireless networking users and their devices to the rest of the organization's network(s).

work breakdown structure (WBS) A straightforward planning process to develop a project plan in which larger and more complex tasks are decomposed into sequences of simpler tasks.

Work Recovery Time (WRT) The amount of effort (expressed as elapsed time) that is necessary to get the business function operational after the technology element is recovered (as identified with RTO).

XOR cipher conversion An encryption operation in which a bit stream is subjected to a Boolean XOR function against some other data stream, typically a key stream. The XOR function compares bits from each stream and replaces similar pairs with a "0" and dissimilar pairs with a "1."

Index